Eating
Shakespeare

GLOBAL SHAKESPEARE INVERTED

Global Shakespeare Inverted challenges any tendency to view Global Shakespeare from the perspective of 'centre' versus 'periphery'. Although the series may locate its critical starting point geographically, it calls into question the geographical bias that lurks within the very notion of the 'global'. It provides a timely, constructive criticism of the present state of the field and establishes new and alternative methodologies that invert the relation of Shakespeare to the supposed 'other'.

Series editors:

David Schalkwyk (Queen Mary, University of London, UK)
Silvia Bigliazzi (University of Verona, Italy)
Bi-qi Beatrice Lei (National Taiwan University, Taiwan)

Advisory board:

Douglas Lanier, University of New Hampshire, USA
Sonia Massai, King's College London, UK
Supriya Chaudhury, Jadavpur University, India
Ian Smith, Lafayette College, USA

Forthcoming titles

Shakespeare in the Global South: Stories of Oceans Crossed in Contemporary Adaptation
Sandra Young
Romeo and Juliet *in Diaspora: Shakespeare Among the Arts and in Translation*
Edited by Julia Reinhard Lupton and Ariane Helou
Migrating Shakespeare: First European Encounters, Routes and Networks
Edited by Janet Clare and Dominique Goy-Blanquet

Eating Shakespeare

Cultural Anthropophagy as Global Methodology

Edited by
Anne Sophie Refskou,
Marcel Alvaro de Amorim
and Vinicius Mariano
de Carvalho

THE ARDEN SHAKESPEARE
LONDON • NEW YORK • OXFORD • NEW DELHI • SYDNEY

THE ARDEN SHAKESPEARE
Bloomsbury Publishing Plc
50 Bedford Square, London, WC1B 3DP, UK
1385 Broadway, New York, NY 10018, USA

BLOOMSBURY, THE ARDEN SHAKESPEARE and the
Arden Shakespeare logo are trademarks of Bloomsbury Publishing Plc

First published in Great Britain 2019
Reprinted 2019

Cover design: Maria Rajka
Cover image: *Ofelia* © Cristine Borowski

A catalogue record for this book is available from the British Library.

Library of Congress Cataloging-in-Publication Data
Names: Refskou, Anne Sophie, editor. | Amorim, Marcel Alvaro de, editor. |
Carvalho, Vinicius Mariano de, editor.
Title: Eating Shakespeare : cultural anthropophagy as global methodology / edited
by Anne Sophie Refskou, Marcel Alvaro de Amorim and Vinicius Mariano de
Carvalho.
Description: London ; New York, NY : Bloomsbury Publishing, 2019. |
Series: Global Shakespeare inverted | Includes bibliographical references and index.
Identifiers: LCCN 2019015842| ISBN 9781350035706 (hb) |
ISBN 9781350035737 (epdf)
Subjects: LCSH: Shakespeare, William, 1564-1616–Criticism and interpretation. |
Shakespeare, William, 1564-1616–Adaptations–History and criticism. |
Shakespeare, William, 1564-1616–Translations–History and criticism.
Classification: LCC PR2880.A1 E33 2019 | DDC 822.3/3–dc23 LC record
available at https://lccn.loc.gov/2019015842

ISBN: HB: 978-1-350-03570-6
       ePDF: 978-1-350-03573-7
       eBook: 978-1-350-03571-3

Series: Global Shakespeare Inverted

Typeset by Integra Software Services Pvt. Ltd.
Printed and bound in Great Britain

To find out more about our authors and books visit www.bloomsbury.com
and sign up for our newsletters.

To all the indigenous peoples of Brazil,
who have been victims of discrimination and
extermination without regard for their humanity.

CONTENTS

FIGURES

CONTRIBUTORS

Marcel Alvaro de Amorim is Lecturer in English and Portuguese at the Federal Institute of Rio de Janeiro. He is also Associate Lecturer in Applied Linguistics at the Federal University of Rio de Janeiro. His research within the field of Global Shakespeare studies focuses on Brazilian and international film adaptation. He recently published the book *Shakespeare e Antropofagia: adaptações de Hamlet no cinema brasileiro*, based on his doctoral research on adapting *Hamlet* for Brazilian cinema from the perspective of Cultural Anthropophagy. Amorim has also published several essays in academic journals and contributed to books including *Shakespeare 450 anos*.

Cristiane Busato Smith is Lecturer in Shakespeare Studies at the Osher Institute (ASU) and a Research Scholar at the Arizona Center for Medieval and Renaissance Studies. She is Brazil Lead Editor for the MIT Global Shakespeares Digital Project. Her primary area of research is Brazilian appropriations of Shakespeare. She has published essays on Shakespeare in South America, North America, Asia and Europe. She is the author of *'What ceremony else?' Representations of Ophelia in Victorian England* (forthcoming).

Geraldo Carneiro has published nine books of poetry gathered in his *Collected Poems* (2010). In 1988, he received the Ana Cristina César Trophy for the best Brazilian poetry book of the year. He has published biographical books (*Vinicius de Moraes, A Fala da Paixão*, 1984), chronicles and translations (*O Discurso do Amor Rasgado, Poems, Scenes and Fragments by William Shakespeare*, 2013). He has written more than 200 original songs and a large number of TV series. In 2012, he received the Emmy International Prize for his series *O Astro*, co-written with Alcides Nogueira. In 2016, he was elected to the Brazilian Academy of Literature.

Koel Chatterjee teaches at Trinity Laban London and specializes in Academic English in Higher Education as well as in teaching Critical Thinking for Academia and Global Shakespeares. She was awarded her PhD in Shakespeare and Bollywood in 2018 from Royal Holloway, University of London (RHUL), and is currently working on a monograph on the history of Bollywood Shakespeares. Recent publications include 'Rediscovering Shakespeare through Exoticism: Examining the Mousetrap Sequence in *Haider*' in *Société Francaise Shakespeare Journal* (2018), and '*Qayamat Se Qayamat Tak* (1988): A Neglected Shakespeare Film' in *Shakespeare and Indian Cinemas* (2018). She has co-organized academic events including 'Indian Shakespeares on Screen', 2016 and 'India-Pakistan-UK: Intertwined Narratives', 2017 in collaboration with RHUL.

Aimara da Cunha Resende is a retired Full Professor of English Literature from the Catholic University of Minas Gerais and retired Associate Professor from the Federal University of Minas Gerais. She has published extensively on Shakespeare. Resende is translator of *Love's Labour's Lost* (2006); editor of *Foreign Accents: Brazilian Readings of Shakespeare* (2002); General Editor of the Brazilian CESh/Tessitura series on Shakespeare and his contemporaries; and Associate Editor of the *Cambridge Guide to the Worlds of Shakespeare* (2016). She is also co-founder and President of the Brazilian Shakespeare Studies Centre (CESh), and currently a consultant for various productions of Shakespeare's plays in Minas Gerais.

Diana Henderson is Professor of Literature and MacVicar Faculty Fellow at MIT, and the co-editor of the annual *Shakespeare Studies*. She is the author of *Collaborations with the Past: Reshaping Shakespeare across Time and Media* (2006) and the editor of Blackwell's *Concise Companion to*

Shakespeare on Screen (2007) and *Alternative Shakespeares 3* (2007). She has worked as a dramaturg, theatrical consultant and the PI for MIT's Global Shakespeares *Merchant* online module; her theatrical collaborators have included the Royal Shakespeare Company under Michael Boyd's leadership, Robert Lepage, the Potomac Theater Project and Karin Coonrod. Henderson was the 2014 President of the Shakespeare Association of America.

Paul Heritage is Professor of Drama and Performance at Queen Mary University of London and Director of People's Palace Projects. He has created arts-based prison projects in Britain and Brazil. From 2009 to 2012 he was funded by the AHRC to investigate knowledge transfer between Brazilian favela-based artists and youth and community groups in the UK. Heritage was also Executive Producer of 'Rio Occupation London', a project within the London 2012 Festival. He has been researching the development of projects focused on discussing the relation between creative economy, preservation and artistic exchange between artists and cultural agents in Brazil and the UK and indigenous communities based in Central Brazil.

Víctor Huertas Martín studied English Philology at the Universidad Autónoma of Madrid. He completed his PhD on the phenomenon of stage–screen hybridity in several Shakespeare television film productions recorded by the BBC and Illuminations Media between 2001 and 2012. He is researching metatheatricality in several Shakespeare TV-films, and Shakespearean appropriations in HBO and Netflix television series. He teaches Shakespeare and Popular Culture and Literature and Film at the Universidad Nacional de Educación a Distancia and Medieval, Renaissance and Baroque Literature at the Universidad Autónoma de Madrid. His recent publications include 'Theatrical Self-Reflexivity in Gregory Doran's *Hamlet* (2009)' (2016) and 'Rupert Goold's *Macbeth* (2010): Surveillance Society and Society of Control' (2017).

Vinicius Mariano de Carvalho is Senior Lecturer in Brazilian Studies at King's College London. He is also Honorary Associate Professor for Brazilian Studies at Aarhus University, Denmark. He holds a PhD from the University of Passau, Germany. His research within Brazilian Studies covers subjects such as literature, music, culture, arts and conflict studies. He is the Chief-Editor of *Brasiliana – Journal for Brazilian Studies* and Editor of the 'Anthem Brazilian Studies' series. Parallel to his academic career, he is a musician and currently conducts the King's Brazil Ensemble.

Alfredo Michel Modenessi is Professor of English Literature, Drama and Translation at the National University of Mexico (UNAM), as well as a stage translator and dramaturg. He has published and lectured on Shakespeare, drama, translation and film in the UK, Spain, France, Italy, Germany, Brazil and Mexico, among others. He is a member of the *International Shakespeare Conference*, and serves on advisory boards for MIT, Routledge and Cambridge University Press, among others. He has translated over forty-five plays, including Shakespeare, Marlowe and modern drama. He is currently writing a book on Shakespeare in Mexican film and editing a section for the *Shakespearean International Yearbook*.

Eleine Ng completed her PhD at the Shakespeare Institute, University of Birmingham. Ng's key research areas are in cross-cultural Shakespearean adaptation in theatre and new media, Shakespearean theatre history in non-anglophone cultures, and the implications of language and translation in intercultural Shakespeare performances. She is also an English Data Editor for the Asian Shakespeare Intercultural Archive (A|S|I|A), and her work on this digital platform has furthered her interests in how digital media and online archiving are impacting and reshaping the ways we approach cross-cultural Shakespeare production and our understanding of intercultural spectatorship.

Varsha Panjwani teaches at Boston University (London) and NYU (London). Panjwani's research focuses on the way Shakespeare is deployed in the service of diversity theatre and films. As well as publishing widely in leading international journals such as *Shakespeare Survey* and *Shakespeare,* in prestigious collections such as *Shakespeare and Indian Cinema* and *The Diverse Bard*, she has co-edited special issues of *Multicultural Shakespeare*. She has also won research grants from the Society of Theatre Research and Folger Shakespeare Library. She was one of the principal investigators of the multi-grant-winning project 'Indian Shakespeares on Screen', 2016. She is also an academic consultant for theatre and film companies.

Anne Sophie Refskou is a lecturer in Theatre and Performance at the University of Surrey, Guildford. Her research is focused on the ways Shakespearean performance addresses current challenges related to intercultural dialogue, diversity and otherness at global and local levels. She is currently preparing a study of contemporary Shakespearean performance, compassion and xenophobia. As part of her close collaboration with 'HamletScenen', she also looks at Shakespeare as a vehicle for cultural diplomacy and 'soft power'. Recent publications include 'Times out of Joint: A Glance at Hamlet in Elsinore 1816–2016' (*Peripeti* 2017) and 'Whose Castle Is It Anyway? Local/Global Negotiations of a Shakespearean Location' (*Multicultural Shakespeare* 2017).

Paulo da Silva Gregório is currently a teaching fellow in English at Universidade Potiguar (Brazil). He has recently completed his PhD in Shakespeare Studies at the Shakespeare Institute, investigating the influence of Samuel Beckett's theatre on modern adaptations of Shakespeare's plays in the theatre, cinema, television and literature. He has taught Portuguese language and Brazilian literature at the University of Essex (UK), and English as a foreign language (EFL) in Brazil. His current research interests are in the fields of Shakespearean adaptation, English language teaching, particularly in relation to EFL teacher education, and the role of literature and drama in the EFL classroom.

Mark Thornton Burnett is Professor of Renaissance Studies at Queen's University, Belfast. He is the author of *Masters and Servants in English Renaissance Drama and Culture: Authority and Obedience* (1997), *Constructing 'Monsters' in Shakespearean Drama and Early Modern Culture* (2002), *Filming Shakespeare in the Global Marketplace* (2007; 2nd edn 2012) and *Shakespeare and World Cinema* (2013), and co-author of *Great Shakespeareans: Welles, Kurosawa, Kozintsev, Zeffirelli* (2013). Currently he is writing a study of *Hamlet* and world cinema for Cambridge University Press.

FOREWORD

David Schalkwyk

That Shakespeare enjoys, and has for some time enjoyed, an unprecedented afterlife beyond what would in the past have been called his 'home' is now beyond doubt. Shakespeare is a world phenomenon. What is new is the growing interest in that afterlife by those who have previously imprisoned him in his home ground.

When did Shakespeare become 'global'? That's a difficult question. Some would say almost at once, with the movement of the English players on tours to the continent.[1] Others might mark his trajectory beyond the English-speaking world to the adoption of the Bard as the German national poet in the nineteenth century, as German Romanticism recognized in Shakespeare's 'mouldy tales' and 'rough magic' the overthrow of rule-bound Classicism, then exemplified by a French appropriation of Aristotle's *Poetics* in the service of tragic decorum and the unities of time, place and action. The belated French translations of Shakespeare, culminating in the nineteenth century in François-Victor Hugo's of 1865, was the basis of further translations of Shakespeare into languages as various as Arabic and Brazilian Portuguese. From the nineteenth century, then, three European languages, English, German and French – with their very different, often conflicting, cultural and political aspirations – provided the vehicles for Shakespeare's passage across the world.

But when did the idea of 'Global Shakespeare' as a serious pursuit within the academy and Shakespeare, literary and cultural studies, take hold?

Any answer would be arbitrary to some degree, but we could do worse than Dennis Kennedy's pathbreaking essay, 'Shakespeare without His Language', the introduction to *Foreign Shakespeare*.[2] Kennedy attacks the fetishization of 'Shakespeare's language' and the embalming of that language in performance. In other languages Shakespeare sounds like a Jericho horn, shattering a combination of complacent over-familiarity and historical strangeness. Reminding his readers that 'Shakespeare is foreign to all of us' (16), Kennedy puts paid to the idea that Shakespeare is at 'home' anywhere, even if, in 1993 (and, surprisingly, also in the second edition of 2008), his 'foreign' Shakespeare extended no further than post-war Germany and Eastern Europe and the occasional mention of Japan.

In 2010, Anston Bosman departs from the problematic concept of a 'foreign Shakespeare' in favour of 'Shakespeare and Globalization', and extends his home territories far beyond Europe and Japan, to Afghanistan, India, Taiwan, China, Brazil, the Islamic world, Canada, the USA, Germany and France – but also to the world of digital media virtually unknown to Kennedy in 1993.[3] Bosman is sensitive to theoretical issues that continue to dog Global Shakespeare, but which did not seem to trouble Kennedy overtly (although they are certainly implicit in his essay): the vexed (and now disavowed) idea of Shakespeare's universality; the relationship between the original and what is derived – bound up with the ideal of authenticity; the conflict between the local and the global (half resolved in the notion of the 'glocal'); the issue of whether Shakespeare is inevitably 'lost in translation'; and the vexed conceptual problems raised by concepts commonly used to describe the relationship involved in the production of different Shakespeares: production, translation, adaptation, appropriation. Each of these terms entails a notion of some kind of derivation: an original from which something else is produced, whether as an ideal to remain faithful to or as a freer variation. The problem lies in the concept of *relation*: Shakespeare, on the one hand, and what is done with or to him, on the other. In 2005, Sonia Massai turned to Bourdieu's notion of a 'field of forces' and struggle, 'stressing the fluidity of the field, its lack of any unilateral hierarchization and the permeability of its boundaries'.[4]

The *theatrical* event that encapsulated most completely Shakespeare's permeability was Shakespeare's Globe's 'World Shakespeare Festival 2012' that coincided with the London Olympic Games. The 'Globe-to-Globe' productions, which included thirty-seven Shakespeare plays in thirty-seven different languages,[5] have received most attention and commentary. There are many things to say about it, but I want to focus on two: first, its advertising slogan, 'Shakespeare's Coming Home', which may have had a local resonance for English theatre-goers with the 1996 European football championship theme song, but, in Paul Prescott's words, for others it 'positioned Shakespeare as an English invention whose popularity had since spread across the world but whose ultimate expression could only be realised on home soil'.[6] If this point indicates a certain ideological limitation, of at least The Globe's marketing department regarding the idea of global Shakespeare, the second is the very opposite: by ranging across the entire Shakespeare canon, the Globe-to-Globe festival extended the reach of Shakespeare in other languages and performance traditions beyond the 'usual suspects': that *handful* of the thirty-seven plays that are regularly thought of as being properly global.

The difficulty is in distinguishing among translations, adaptations, appropriations, invocations and mere allusions, and the fact that different Shakespeare plays appeal differently to different cultures, nations or in different languages. Shakespeare was not adopted to the same extent, at the same rate or at the same time in, say, Germany, where he has been considered properly German since at least the eighteenth century, and in Brazil, for example, where Shakespeare was mediated in the nineteenth century by French adaptations and translations of the complete works from English were completed as late as 1950.

The question is whether Shakespeare without his language refers to translations of the texts, as, for example, the classic

German Schlegel-Tieck version, or free adaptations, like the so-called 'Zulu-Macbeth', *Umabatha*, which contained none of Shakespeare's language and followed the plot of *Macbeth* only very loosely. The present artistic director of the Royal Shakespeare Company (RSC), Gregory Doran, has declared that *Umabatha* is 'the best production of the play [he] has ever seen'.[7] My *theoretical* question, then, is: in what sense can *Umabatha* be regarded as 'the play' (to use Doran's words) *Macbeth*?

On one interpretation of Kennedy's phrase, translated Shakespeare is *not* Shakespeare without his language – it's simply Shakespeare without English. I have argued elsewhere not only that a translation of Shakespeare might be considered *better* than the English original (as I believe is the case with the Afrikaans translation of *Twelfth Night* – Uys Krige's *Twaalfde Nag*), but also that few English-speakers who do not have access to Shakespeare translated into a different language can claim to understand him fully.[8]

Such a view holds that as much may be gained through translation as is commonly thought to be lost, but it is also informed by an assumption that translation maintains some kind of fidelity to the Shakespeare text (however that is finally determined or conceived). The very idea of fidelity or faithfulness to the Shakespeare text is currently anathema to those interested in Shakespeare's global afterlives. In a contribution to *Shakespeare and the Ethics of Appropriation*, Douglas Lanier states that 'we are now in an age of post-fidelity', and he offers a rhizomatic model of Shakespearean adaptation in contrast to the traditional root and branch model: 'within the Shakespearean rhizome, the Shakespearean text is an important element but not a determining one; it becomes less a root than a node that might be situated in relation to other adaptational rhizomes'.[9]

So let's ask: in an age of post-fidelity, in which faithfulness to the Shakespeare text is not an ethical value but rather a conservative, reactionary imposition, how do we give content to the concept of ethics? Especially, how does one formulate an ethics of appropriation, with its powerful sense of violent grasping, taking over, making one's own, obliterating otherness, and its specifically colonialist history? A Marxist should have no difficulty with the politics of appropriation, as Lanier concedes, but an ethics of appropriation is much more difficult to conceive. Alexa Huang and Elizabeth Rivlin defend their choice of appropriation (rather than the more neutral 'adaptation') by arguing, through Martin Buber and Immanuel Levinas, that appropriation need not be one-sided: that it may involve a dialogical or mutually respectful or engaged encounter between text and reader and that the roles of appropriator and appropriated may switch. I'm not sure that this deals with the problem of ethics as it has traditionally been understood in either deontological (post-Kantian) or consequentialist (Utilitarian) terms, in part because the projection of a relationship in which two people encounter each other is not transferable without difference to a relationship in which a person confronts a string of marks on a page. If Kant offers a categorical imperative to treat another person as an end and not a means, does this imperative transfer from person to text?

In a panel discussion at the 2015 Jaipur Literary Festival among the director, Vishal Bhardwaj, the screenwriter, Basharat Peer, Jerry Brotton of Queen Mary University of London, and Tim Supple of Dash-Arts (a London-based theatre company), about Bhardwaj's latest *Hamlet* film, *Haider*, Bhardwaj and Peer were asked why they adapted Shakespeare's play, over and above the now conventional remarks about the universality and timelessness of Shakespeare.[10] Peer indicated a fundamental congruence of *Hamlet* and the situation in Kashmir, remarking that Kashmir has been marked by the violent turning of brother against brother: 'The moment I looked at the play, I knew that Claudius came from that world.'

Supple, who has directed acclaimed multicultural and multilingual productions of *A Midsummer Night's Dream* and *1001 Nights*,[11] stated that he prefers to work from 'the text as written by Shakespeare' with his actors, without attempting to contextualize or concretize it. Supple's approach did not go down well: he was accused of trying to preserve Shakespeare's Englishness and of maintaining a narrow colonial hegemony over the Bard; at one point the film's director, Bhardwaj, seems to declare with some pride that he has not even read *Hamlet*. Never other than complimentary about the Indian film-makers' achievement and right to adopt their, dare we say it, appropriating approach, Supple insists on his desire to discover, communally with his actors from different cultural, linguistic and theatrical traditions, the *strangeness* of Shakespeare from within. In response to the chair, Subal Seth's, comment that 'you have to contemporize the text to make it relevant', he responds: 'That's fine; but it becomes *their Hamlet*. It's a film about Kashmir ... If you want to give people an experience of *Hamlet* you won't start with Kashmir. Then *Hamlet* would be much *stranger*. Somewhere deep in the human story you will *find* relevance.'

The ethics here are complex and uncertain: Peer and Bhardwaj surely have a right to use Shakespeare in whatever way they wish, especially when it results in as powerful a film as *Haider*. Supple harks back to a particular view of the ethics of reading that has its roots in a deontological ethics that, despite their differences, unites post-structuralists such as Paul de Man and J. Hillis Miller, and humanist critics like Wayne Booth and George Steiner. Both sets of critics desire, Buber and Levinas-like, to remain open to the imponderable, uncontrollable and unpredictable call of the text as something other and strange – not readily assimilable to an appropriating desire.

But Shakespeare is not a person, whose rights may be violated or whose body or soul may be subjected to torture, theft or repression and exploitation. Do we have business setting ourselves up as his guardians and protectors, and what are we protecting him from?

It may help to regard Shakespeare as a grammar or a language. If we treat what Derrida has called this 'thing' Shakespeare – as ghost or revenant – as a kind of language instead of an author or a text whose meaning defines its use, a number of the problems regarding authority, originality, faithfulness or ethics are attenuated. The Shakespeare language is an enabling, constitutive system – it can be mobilized by anyone, anywhere, anyhow. The accumulated resonances will sound in different ways in different places and contexts: the homecoming festival of any single resonance, as Bakhtin puts it, is always waiting in the wings – but it will always in some sense be strange, uncanny and *Unheimlich* – which, Freud teaches us, is also *Heimlich*. From this perspective, Shakespeare is less a black hole that swallows everything, as Gary Taylor has remarked, but rather an enormous, creative resource available to everyone who wants to use it.[12]

Global Shakespeare Inverted transforms the frame through which we try to fathom the paradoxically Western, neocapitalist order in which Shakespeare continues to operate as an abiding and growing 'cultural capital'. The title retains the extremely problematic notion of the 'Global' but seeks to turn that on its head, to invert it and subject both the notions of 'global' and 'Shakespeare' to critical pressure from a place other than their 'home'.

Eating Shakespeare, the first book in the series, moves the debate to a completely new space – literally – via the notion not of adapting or appropriating Shakespeare, but of *eating* him. It comes to theory, in the words of the South African writers John and Jean Comaroff, 'from the South', finding in the non-Western world the paths through which to make sense of Shakespeare's presence in that world.[13] This book opens up a Shakespeare cannibalized, subjected to the very terrors of the colonizing West as nutrition for what that direction has always considered as 'other', 'foreign', 'different'. It offers a complex story that combines antagonism with respect, of incorporating in terms of one's own needs, of symbolic violence that is also a form of renewal and growth. However harrowing that perspective may be, or refreshing or *wasteful*, it avoids the persistence of *relation*, with its preservation of difference, otherness, derivation. Shakespeare is always equally at home

and far away – for *everyone*. He is both infinitely nutritious
and intractably indigestible.

Notes

1   Anston Bosman, 'Shakespeare and Globalization', in *The New Cambridge Companion to Shakespeare*, ed. Margreta De Grazia, 2nd edn (New York: Cambridge University Press, 2010), 289–301.

2   Dennis Kennedy, *Foreign Shakespeare: Contemporary Performance*, rev. edn (Cambridge: Cambridge University Press, 2008).

3   The most successful and far-reaching project in this process is the MIT Shakespeare, whose myriad of worldly productions of Shakespeare on film is available at 'The Complete Works of William Shakespeare', http://shakespeare.mit.edu (accessed 10 October 2018).

4   Sonia Massai, 'Defining Local Shakespeares', in *World-Wide Shakespeares: Local Appropriations in Film and Performance*, ed. Sonia Massai (London: Routledge, 2005), 3–14.

5   See Colette Gordon, 'Shakespeare's African Nostos: Township Nostalgia & Performance at Sea', in *African Theatre 12: Shakespeare in & out of Africa*, ed. Jane Plaistow (Woodbridge: James Currey, 2012), 28–47.

6   Anthony Sher and Gregory Doran, *Woza Shakespeare: 'Titus Andronicus' in South Africa*, new edn (London: Methuen Drama, 2007), 238.

7   Ibid., 238.

8   David Schalkwyk, 'Shakespeare's Untranslatability', in *Transnational Mobilities in Early Modern Theater*, ed. Robert Henke and Eric Nicholson (Farnham: Ashgate, 2014), 229–244.

9   Alexa Huang and Elizabeth Rivlin, eds, *Shakespeare and the Ethics of Appropriation* (New York: Palgrave Macmillan, 2014), 21–40 (22 and 29).

10   Tom Holland, '#JLF 2015: The Father of History' [video], YouTube (uploaded 28 January 2015), www.youtube.com/watch?v=zwq5EATQKRg (accessed 10 October 2018).

11   See Dash Arts, 'About', www.dasharts.org.uk/about.html (accessed 10 October 2018).

12   Gary Taylor, *Reinventing Shakespeare: A Cultural History from the Restoration to the Present Day* (New York: Vintage, 1991).

13   Jean Comaroff and John L. Comaroff, *Theory from the South: Or, How Euro-America Is Evolving Toward Africa* (Boulder, CO: Routledge, 2011).

ACKNOWLEDGEMENTS

Words cannot express how much we appreciate the critical and open-minded engagement from our contributors. You have given us inspiration, insights and not least time, and without you this experiment would not have been possible. We are immensely grateful to David Schalkwyk for encouraging the idea of *Eating Shakespeare* at an early stage and for his continued guidance and support. Deepest thanks, too, to Lara Bateman, our patient and helpful editor, and the Arden Shakespeare team. To Cristine Borowski, who produced our anthropophagically stunning cover image, we hail and thank you. Sandra Young and Pompa Banerjee held a stimulating seminar on 'Shakespeare and the Global South' at the 2018 Shakespeare Association of America (SAA), which included a much welcome opportunity to present some of the ideas behind the book and receive valuable feedback from colleagues. We would also like to thank all our incredible students, in Brazil and the UK, for your enthusiasm, your questions and for everything you have taught us – we cannot wait to share this book with you.

Finally, but of course not least, our gratitude is due to dear friends and loved ones (you all know who you are) for patience and support, and especially to Søren Refskou, the best dad and most selfless reader.

Introduction

Anne Sophie Refskou, Vinicius Mariano de Carvalho and Marcel Alvaro de Amorim

Shakespeare's plays include a handful of references to the act of eating one's own species. Some are quite famous, like the banquet that accelerates the violence of *Titus Andronicus* to yet another level, or Othello's stories 'of the Cannibals that each other eat, the Anthropophagi' (*Oth* 1.3.144–145),[1] which are so captivating to Desdemona. And, of course, there is Caliban, whose name has historically been read as an anagram of 'cannibal', even if there is no definitive evidence or consensus on this.[2] Othello's stories (and Othello himself) and Caliban have come to represent complex encounters with a cultural, racial or colonized 'other', as many creatives and scholars continue to explore in the afterlives of the plays. In this sense, they are also present – sometimes directly and sometimes indirectly – in the essays and interviews in this collection, whose overarching engagement is with perceptions of otherness within the context of what has become widely referred to as 'Global Shakespeare'. This is a book that discusses and tries to understand how the world produces 'other' Shakespeares and how Shakespeare is perceived as 'other'. Although individual contributions vary in both form, themes and locations, they are unified by their attempt to undertake this dialogue through the very particular lens of Cultural Anthropophagy, a concept born out of Brazilian Modernism and a postcolonial search for identity, but, as this book demonstrates, widely applicable beyond its original context and highly relevant to current discourses and challenges of Global Shakespeare.

Another cannibalistic reference, more easily overlooked, occurs in *The Merry Wives of Windsor*, where 'Host', with wonderfully pompous and tongue-twisting éclat, warns 'Simple' – who has come to speak with Falstaff – that the latter will speak 'like an Anthropophaginian unto thee' (*MW* 5.4.7). Samuel Johnson set this down as a case of Shakespeare creating 'a ludicrous word' merely 'for the sake of a formidable sound' (1755: 138). Shakespeare, it seems, was for Johnson prioritizing effect over meaning and sense. Yet to many of our contributors, who examine how Shakespeare's *own* words are recreated, the playful handling of material to create 'formidable' effect is a meaningful act in and of itself and something to be celebrated rather than frowned upon. In other words, that aspect of Shakespearean creativity – his well-known transformations and re-creations of other material, sometimes in openly idiosyncratic or irreverent ways – is not so very alien to some of the creative principles of Cultural Anthropophagy, even if the two are worlds and centuries apart in other ways. The Brazilian poet and translator Geraldo Carneiro, interviewed in this volume, sees Shakespeare as a fellow cannibal; the implication is a perception of Shakespeare, not as origin and point of departure *fixe*, but as a link in a great chain of digestion and re-creation. Playfulness is seen, too, in this volume's cover image by Brazilian artist Cristine Borowski, who has recreated Millais's iconic image of Ophelia in a fishbowl: an act of simultaneous homage and subversive parody which, as we shall see, is at the heart of the anthropophagic tradition.

Carneiro's translation principles and Borowski's subtly ironic defamiliarization both inherit ideas of devouring Shakespeare (and other elements of European culture) famously set out by Brazilian modernist poet and polemicist Oswald de Andrade in 1928. Andrade's 'Manifesto Antropófago' (Cannibalist Manifesto) was first published in the newly established avant-garde journal *Revista de Antropofagia*, and in it Shakespeare makes a somewhat surprise appearance. Among Andrade's aphoristic lines, arranged in a manifesto-like manner, appears the following line in English: 'Tupy or not Tupy: *that* is the question' ([1928] 1991: 3). With 'Tupy', or 'Tupi', Andrade was referring to the Brazilian indigenous Tupi people, some of whom practised cannibalism, and although the Shakespearean connection might at first sight seem less than obvious, or there merely 'for the sake of a formidable sound', Andrade's transposition of Hamlet's iconic line has itself become iconic and synonymous with Cultural Anthropophagy. On a fundamental level the line incorporates the most cited ontological question in Western European literature into another and decidedly non-Western ontology: that of the cannibal.

Cannibalism is, as Peter Hulme has put it, 'the practice that, more than any other, is the mark of unregenerate savagery' (1986: 3). Despite some nuances, this has been the predominant view since Europeans first encountered the practice during colonial expansions in the fifteenth century. Shakespearean cannibals (or those referred to as cannibals, even if not literally so) also tend, not surprisingly, to be savage, violent and frightening, and in the aforementioned reference from *Merry Wives* the cannibal simply seems to stand for unintelligibility, another classic mark of perceived barbarism. In the first accounts of encounters with indigenous populations in the territory that now comprises Brazil, cannibalism is an object of extreme horrified fascination to the Europeans who wrote them, as Hulme's seminal book, *Colonial Encounters: Europe and the Native Caribbean, 1492–1797* (1986), also demonstrates. One of the most famous of these accounts, Hans Staden's *True Story and Description of a Country of Wild, Naked, Grim,*

Man-eating People in the New World, America (first published in 1557 and translated from the German *Warhaftige Historia und beschreibung eyner Landtschafft der Wilden Nacketen, Grimmigen Menschfresser-Leuthen in der Newenwelt America gelegen*), describes Staden's capture by a Tupinambá tribe, by whom he was held as a prisoner for a year. According to his own account, he narrowly escaped being killed and eaten. He did, however, also according to his own account, witness the eating of some captured enemies from other tribes, and he offers the reader a series of graphically detailed descriptions of the practice. A few decades later, the French Huguenot missionary, Jean de Léry, published an account of living with the Tupinambá in *History of a Voyage to the Land of Brazil, Also Called America* (translated from the French *Histoire d'un voyage fait en la terre de Brésil*, 1578). Léry, like Montaigne a few years later, used his descriptions of cannibalism in a cultural relativist manner to critique the violence of the European religious wars – claiming that Europeans were no less barbaric – and participated thus in creating the long-standing dichotomy between the 'noble savage' and the 'less-than-human primitive'. Yet whether idealized, condemned or mythologized, the cannibal remained (and remains) a representation of a distinct 'other' to the European mindset. As multiple scholars, including Hulme (1986, 1998), Gananath Obeyesekere (1992, 1998), William Arens (1998), Daniel Cottom (2001) and Gazi Islam (2011), point out, the encounter with the cannibal has allowed Europeans – and perhaps still allows the inheritors of a European Enlightenment world-view – to project internal uncertainties and anxieties onto that 'other'. Civilization inevitably, even if uneasily, defines itself *as civilization* against a perceived savage.

However, what is also important to note in the early accounts of Brazilian indigenous cannibalism, especially for the development of the concept of Cultural Anthropophagy, is the description of cannibalism as a ritual. What we can deduct from Staden and Léry's accounts is that among the Tupinambá, the practice was not a dietary condition, nor a form of religious sacrifice, nor, strictly speaking, an act of revenge. Instead it was a complex physical and metaphysical way of incorporating otherness. A captive from an enemy tribe would be eaten if he was deemed to have attributes worthy of acquisition – such as strength or bravery – and, importantly, he would be assimilated into the tribe before being eaten, often living over a year with his captors and receiving a wife as an additional form of integration. As Rogério Budasz explains, this process meant that ritual anthropophagy would function 'as a revitalizing force, [it] neutralized otherness and suppressed boundaries' (2005: 13). In other words, the cannibalist ritual demonstrates signs of being fundamentally inclusive rather than exclusive, even to the point of significantly blurring the distinction between 'self' and 'other'.

These understandings of cannibalism as enemy-incorporating ritual fuelled Oswald de Andrade's ideas in the late 1920s. Andrade was part of a movement within Brazilian intelligentsia and artistic circles wishing to end what they perceived as a continuous and mechanical imitation of European cultures, including that of their former Portuguese colonizers, which inevitably positioned Brazilian culture as derivative and inferior. It became imperative to Andrade, and fellow artists and members of the so-called 'Group of Five' Mário de Andrade, Anita Malfatti, Tarsila do Amaral and Menotti del Picchia, to negotiate a new cultural identity by celebrating the country's pre-colonial indigenous past of which the cannibal emerged as a newly heroic figure.[3] In the 'Cannibalist Manifesto', Andrade calls for 'the permanent transformation of the Taboo into a Totem' ([1928] 1991: 40), thus inverting the Freudian logic of totem and taboo in the development of civilization: cannibalism – perceived as the ultimate taboo – becomes totem and itself a source of logic. Significantly, however, European cultural elements and influences were not simply to be rejected but to be subsumed – 'eaten' – self-consciously and irreverently while mixed with native and contemporary elements. Andrade's cultural cannibal was to look at European culture in the same way as the Tupi people looked at the foreign invaders of their land: 'as a source of nutrients' (Budasz 2005: 2). The result of this process would be the creation of a whole new cultural product, combining the best of both worlds, and, importantly, which would have export potential for Brazil.

This unique approach in which the subaltern takes a self-empowering stance towards the hegemonic culture by selecting what he wants (and rejecting what is of no use to him) is a key feature of Andrade's vision – another line in the 'Manifesto' explicitly states the proud intent to appropriate: 'I am only concerned with what is not mine' ([1928] 1991: 38) – and it is an approach which is taken up and explored repeatedly throughout this book. However, Cultural Anthropophagy, by virtue of its celebration of intermixing, also offers self-empowerment by automatically liberating native cultural products from expectations to represent ethnographic authenticity or originality. In place of authenticity, it offers a product that is *authentically inauthentic*. For Andrade to construct a creative and ideological practice that subverts the divisive and hierarchical import – export chain in which Brazil is seen to *import* European culture and ideas, with itself 'just' *exporting* natural resources and raw materials, is thus extremely ingenious.

By drawing on European influences, yet creating a dense and intricate fabric in which they are thoroughly intermixed with Brazilian references, the 'Manifesto' explicitly practises what it preaches. It demonstrates links with European modernism and primitivism; Andrade had travelled in Europe and was fully aware of the avant-garde movements and the title plays on the surrealist manifestos by Yvan Goll and André Breton, published a few years earlier, as well as the 'Communist Manifesto' by Marx and Engels. What is important to reiterate is the fact that its Brazilian references unsettle and subvert European organizations of reality: at its core the 'Manifesto' insists on a defamiliarized ontology. Andrade's dating of his text, for example, offers an alternative perception of time by replacing 1928 with the 374th anniversary of the ritualistic eating by local tribes of the aptly named Portuguese Bishop

Sardinha, a sixteenth-century bishop of the Brazilian state of Bahia. An example that also encompasses the tendencies of Cultural Anthropophagy to utilize provocative wit and parody; as Gazi Islam explains, the anthropophagic method can function as 'a therapy for colonialism, acknowledging ironically and parodying colonialism in a carnavalesque fashion' (2011: 163).

In her recent book, *Antropofagia – Palimpsesto Selvagem*, Beatriz Azevedo meticulously reads the 'Manifesto' in an almost archaeological manner, demonstrating the layers of Andrade's thought: 'The "Manifesto" is a pluriform text, a blending of poetry and philosophy that incorporates rituality, violence and performance in a non-ending process' (Azevedo 2018: 210).[4] Highlighting the performative element of Cultural Anthropophagy is key here. Gazi Islam notes that indigenous anthropophagy may have acquired an element of self-conscious performance when encountering European colonizers: 'Aware of the salience of such practices for colonizers, natives assumed the role of barbarian in order to terrify, in an ambivalent act of both subordination and aggression' (2011: 163). This is reassumed by Cultural Anthropophagy, which carries the intent and ability to perform self-mockery even as it mocks the foreign and colonizing 'other'. As Islam continues, 'in addition to mimicking the colonizer, [the cultural anthropophagous] can self-mimic, self-positioning as an indigenous cannibal while simultaneously appropriating European cultural forms' (172). This is closely linked to the fact that Brazilian biological and cultural identity has been construed *through* colonization, not simply imposed by it (163). In other words, and as Aimara Resende also reminds us in her chapter in this volume, Brazilian identity cannot distil and separate its 'foreign blood'. Nor is Andrade himself at pains to hide his own European blood behind a native pose; on the contrary he revels in his mestizo identity. What this means is that, in the words of Islam, 'the deconstruction of colonial domination is simultaneously a self-reflexive and self-transformative act' (2011: 163).

In the 1960s, one of the most fruitful Brazilian artistic movements, the *Tropicalia* movement led by Gilberto Gil and Caetano Veloso – and including the director Zé Celso, whose seminal *Ham-let* production is also examined in this volume – demonstrated the continued influence of Cultural Anthropophagy on formations of Brazilian cultural identity, while the poet and critic Haroldo de Campos, during the following decades, developed an anthropophagical way of thinking as a hermeneutics that is not limited to a Brazilian context, but potentially present in other cultures formed and characterized by inclusivity. Campos resumes Andrade's anthropophagy to highlight the cultural cannibal as an aggressive and critical eater, a 'bad savage', rather than a 'noble savage who is insipid, resigned' (1986: 44). As Campos posits, Cultural Anthropophagy does not involve 'a submission (an indoctrination), but a transculturation, or, better, a "transvalorization"' (44), which dismantles essentialist perceptions.

However, one of the most complex and important tenets of Cultural Anthropophagy is found in the anthropologist Eduardo Viveiros de Castro's concept of Perspectivism. In his seminal study *From the Enemy's Point of View* (1986), Viveiros de Castro explores the meaning of cannibalism among the Amerindians in general and the Tupinambá specifically. What makes Viveiros de Castro's work so original is the fact that he is not describing the Amerindian perspective from the point of view of a Western ontology. Instead he analyses the survival of the metaphysical 'leftovers' of cannibalism, and their survival among Amerindian societies even after the literal act of cannibalism has been discontinued, in terms of the Amerindian cosmology itself.[5] Perspectivism develops the relation with otherness in Cultural Anthropophagy to destabilize the – to Europeans familiar – understanding of nature versus culture, as Viveiros de Castro moves towards replacing multiculturalism with what he calls 'multinaturalism'. The encounter with otherness in Amerindian cosmology, Viveiros de Castro posits, is not a question of encountering a different culture, but a different nature:

(Multi)cultural relativism supposes a diversity of subjective and partial representations each striving to grasp an external and unified nature, which remains perfectly indifferent to those representations. Amerindian thought proposes the opposite: a representational or phenomenological unity which is purely pronominal or deictic, indifferently applied to a radically objective diversity. One single 'culture', multiple 'natures' – perspectivism is multinaturalist for a perspective is not a representation. (1998: 478)

In other words, 'nature' is not seen as an essential, unchangeable and universal state – something that all humans share – while 'culture' is multiple and denotes certain 'exterior' habits, which can be changed rather like a set of clothes. This challenge of a deep-set binary presents a radical outlook that is highly helpful in understanding the mutual transformation effected by Cultural Anthropophagy at a deeper level as well as the deconstruction of essentialisms and universalisms. In Viveiros de Castro's Perspectivism the change in the 'self', effected by the encounter with otherness, is a 'transnaturalization': a change at the level of nature, not just a cultural 'change of habits'. Furthermore, the 'self' is not seen as impermeable but as open and in continuous transition: it is already becoming part of the 'other' and vice versa. Azevedo includes the following description of the anthropophagic process by Viveiros de Castro in the preface to *Antropofagia – Palimpsesto Selvagem*:

Eating the enemy is not a way of 'assimilating' him, making him the same as Me; or 'negating' him to affirm the identitarian substance of an I. Nor is it making myself the same as him, (an)other self by way of imitation. On the contrary, eating the enemy means self-transforming through him (or *by means* of him) to become a *self-Other*. It is a process of self-transfiguration with the aid of an opposite. It is not a question of seeing myself in the Other, but of seeing the Other in myself. Identity on the reverse, in short – the reverse of an identity.[6]

The act of eating to incorporate otherness is never unilateral in the Amerindian cosmology. As the Tupinambá ate their enemies, and kept them alive in their own bodies, they knew that they too would be eaten if captured by the enemy. The violation of their beings would ensure their survival, which helps Cultural Anthropophagy to formulate how one may deconstruct an(other) cultural sign – even violently so – but without negation. What this means to the negotiation of cultural signs is a syntagmatic rather than a paradigmatic relation: signs are not replaced but coexist in the creation of new meaning. The seed of this relation is again to be found in Andrade's eating of Shakespeare in the 'Cannibalist Manifesto'. It seems that Andrade's intent in appropriating 'To be, or not to be' in order to create 'Tupi or not Tupi' is not to replace one with the other. Instead he lets signs (and sounds) coexist in a radical new relationship, concomitantly transforming themselves and each other: Shakespeare and the Tupi become part of a mutually dependent and mutually empowering performative act. This relationship, first seeded by Andrade, is what is explored, expanded, challenged and recreated throughout this book in the attempt to outline and discuss ways in which Cultural Anthropophagy may represent an alternative point of view and methodology within contemporary studies of Global Shakespeare. From a variety of perspectives and dealing with a variety of cases and examples, contributors draw on the fundamental ideas of Cultural Anthropophagy, which, to summarize, underpin a creative *and* hermeneutic practice characterized by some or all the following principles:

- a self-empowering 'picking and mixing' of elements and influences from what might be seen as a hegemonic culture, and which means that rejection is no longer necessary because it has been replaced by ingestion;
- adaptation as co-creation with the emphasis on the potentials of the new creation, dismantling the notion of an original versus a derivative;

- a celebration of the *authentically inauthentic* cultural expression rather than the ethnographically verifiable one;
- self-conscious parody of 'native self' as well as 'foreign other' through performative 'double acts' that carry mutual transformation;
- a questioning and unfixing of preconditioned meanings, especially those that have been institutionalized or are asserted through institutional authority;
- an alternative to concepts founded on an essentialist perception of 'nature' versus relative 'culture(s)' (such as multiculturalism) via Viveiros de Castro's Perspectivism;
- and last, but not least, the engagement with an (to European thought) unfamiliar organization of reality and the acceptance of the cannibal discourse as unique and different in and of itself rather than as a convenient metaphor, which can be held up to – and explained through – a European or Western equivalent.

Global Shakespeare

While Shakespeare has had a global presence for centuries, 'Global Shakespeare' as a more distinct term and field has become an increasingly frequent reference within Shakespeare Studies in the last decade or so, but without stakeholders being quite able to reach a consensus about what it stands for. On a very basic, but clearly reductive, level, it seems to denote an interest in how 'others' do Shakespeare, and by 'others' are meant those representing non-anglophone cultures (which is in itself an untenable category). The danger of this producing simply a celebration of (a hegemonic) Shakespearean influence extending from Stratford-upon-Avon across the globe, trailing ghosts of colonialism in its wake, has been obvious to scholars for some time, including Sonia

Massai, who, in the introduction to her seminal collection of essays on Shakespeare's worldwide presence, flags the risk of ignoring or glossing over the uncomfortable aspects of that presence: 'Is the dream (or the threat) of a technologically linked, equalizing, world-wide culture for the global village and of a super-cultural, universally enjoyable and consumable Shakespeare imposing Western values over other cultural traditions and economies?' (2005: 4).

Some years after the publication of Massai's book, The World Shakespeare Festival, including the Globe-to-Globe festival at Shakespeare's Globe theatre in London, became instrumental in spurring renewed interest in this question. Almost paradoxically, some of the 'global' engagements with Shakespeare in 2012 revealed some ingrained perceptions of Britain (particularly Stratford-upon-Avon and London) as the first and ultimate authority on all things Shakespearean, combined at times with an (unwittingly) exotifying stance towards the rest of the world.[7] Thus, partly by being so closely connected with the inevitable celebrations of Britishness in the Olympic year of 2012, Global Shakespeare in its initial trajectories inherited many of the problems associated with placing Britain at the centre of a geographical and cultural world map. In the same vein, it has also inherited many of the problems and critique points associated with globalization itself. Whether globalization is understood to signify an expansion of worldwide consciousness – a coming together of peoples and cultures able to transcend material and immaterial borders in a freer fashion – or whether it 'simply' means a common marketplace for raw materials, goods and services to criss-cross the planet, it has at least become increasingly difficult to deny its downsides. Clearly globalization, rather than creating a fairer place to live for all, has on some level continued to generate winners and losers, economically, educationally and culturally, and with widespread disenfranchisement and discontent as tangible consequences. Global Shakespeare has inevitably been caught up in – and required to examine – its own relationship with global inequalities, sometimes rooted in colonial histories and sometimes caused by cultural politics that perpetuate an (Enlightenment) vision of Europe – or the West – as the centre and origin of knowledge and cultural development.

While events still take place that would seem to uncritically confirm the existence of 'a super-cultural, universally enjoyable and consumable Shakespeare', scholars have also continued to rigorously deconstruct that notion, as seen in the recently published *Oxford Handbook to Shakespeare in Performance* (2017), edited by James C. Bulman. The cover illustration, which shows black South African actor Atandwa Kani as Ariel struggling to escape an oversized white fist in a 2009 Royal Shakespeare Company (RSC) production of *The Tempest*, signals some of the cultural-political awareness and focus on diversity that has thankfully come to characterize many current Shakespearean approaches, both creatively and academically. One out of the four main parts of Bulman's volume is dedicated exclusively to 'Global Shakespeare', while other parts include contributions on race and feminist perspectives. Contributions in the Global Shakespeare section, such as those by Dennis Kennedy or Christie Carson, also illustrate an ever-more pervasive attention to personal responsibility in Global Shakespeare scholarship (including scholars' own biographies, linguistic ranges and cultural insider-knowledge) and the question of where scholars' voices are coming from – from a perceived economic and cultural centre, or from a deprived periphery; a question also addressed in the interview with Mark Thornton Burnett in this volume.

The centre – periphery issue can be further understood in terms of the relation between a 'Global North' and a 'Global South', helpfully introduced to Global Shakespeare studies by Sandra Young (2016).[8] The distinction describes the advantages – economic and social – of the nations situated in the Northern Hemisphere over those in the Southern Hemisphere, and, as Young argues, 'If Shakespeare studies, and early modern studies more generally, are to avoid complicity in perpetuating the global asymmetry between regions of the world – north and south – the field will have to take note of the lingering forms of disempowerment and continue to develop an incisive critical vocabulary' (2016: 135). The study of 'a global Shakespeare risks repeating earlier occlusions if it becomes simply an opportunity to affirm, uncritically, the extraordinary reach of Stratford's Shakespeare' (135). Young also refers to Jean and John Comaroff's seminal essay, 'Theory from the South: Or, How Euro-America is Evolving Toward Africa', and monograph of the same title, which use the north–south relation to address the relationship in which theory and insight are seen as stemming from cultures associated with the 'Global North' – going back to European Enlightenment thought – while cultures associated with the 'Global South' provide the unprocessed data (on which those theories can be tested). As Comaroff and Comaroff write, the 'Global South', as another term for what has previously been referred to as the 'Third World' or 'Developing World' (among others), represents 'other worlds' that 'are treated less as sources of refined knowledge than as reservoirs of raw fact: the minutiae from which Euromodernity might fashion its testable theories and transcendent truths' (2012: 114).[9]

This problem is clearly relevant to Global Shakespeare and its discontents, because despite the increasingly stronger emphasis on paying attention to Shakespeares from these 'other worlds', the fundamental theoretical paradigms of the field still rely predominantly on European thought. Sonia Massai discusses global and local Shakespeares from the perspective of Pierre Bourdieu's 'cultural field' (2005), and Alexa Alice Joubin's influential 'Global Shakespeare' methodology (Huang 2013) draws on Gilles Deleuze and Félix Guattari's 'rhizome'. The aforementioned *Oxford Handbook to Shakespeare in Performance*, even while extremely sensitive to diverse approaches, also lacks engagements with non-European theory, although the chapter by Alfredo Michel Modenessi (who has also provided the Afterword to this volume) differs, precisely by utilizing strands of Cultural Anthropophagy to underpin his analyses of Latin American case studies.[10] The point here is by no means to denigrate the importance of work that has brought the debate to its current fruition and already demonstrated its impact; only to argue that some of the next steps for Global Shakespeare could be to look closer at itself from unfamiliar perspectives and include 'other' Shakespeares, not just in terms of case studies from theatre, cinema or translation, but in terms of thought and theoretical models. Comaroff and Comaroff propose a simple thought experiment with potentially radical consequences. They ask: 'what if it is the so-called "Global South" that affords privileged insight into the workings of the world at large?' (2012: 114). *Eating Shakespeare* attempts to put that thought experiment into practice. Yet it does so without proposing a simple inversion that would ultimately only serve to reinforce binaries. In other words, it is not simply a question of substituting Andrade for Foucault, which would also contradict the dialectical nature of Cultural Anthropophagy itself. Instead, contributions in this volume have been encouraged to continue the dialogue initiated in the 'Cannibalist Manifesto', taking it as far and wide as possible. The result is a dialogue that, like Andrade's, is both experimental and self-reflexive. Some of the contributions take the form of actual conversations, both between scholars and creatives and between scholars and scholars, who all bring different cultural and linguistic backgrounds and perspectives to the table and who look for 'spaces in-between' to allow new positions to emerge. The presence of creative voices in the book represents partly the pertinent need for scholars and creatives to be able to exchange views on what Global Shakespeare(s) might mean, and partly reinforces the understanding of Cultural Anthropophagy itself as creative practice. Some of our contributions acknowledge the challenges that emerge in encounters between creatives and scholars, but they also demonstrate their value. Disagreements occur, both between individual chapters, and with some of the positions and definitions that we as editors propose. We have not wanted to impose a unilateral understanding of Cultural Anthropophagy as the be-all and end-all of the discussion, but welcomed questioning and the inclusion of other and affiliated terms, such as fusion or hybridity, for example. However, what we hope the book demonstrates is the potential of Cultural Anthropophagy – as an (inter)cultural concept, a creative practice, a hermeneutic model and a philosophical position – to offer alternative and illuminating perspectives on Global Shakespeare as a term and a field. Especially when the politics and histories of difference inherited by Global Shakespeare create an impasse which can inhibit both creative and critical inquiry. The fact that Cultural Anthropophagy is *inclusive* rather than exclusive – not in the name of sameness but through complex mechanisms of togetherness – can help Global Shakespeare both to face and, to some extent, overcome its own awkward relationships with otherness.

The structure of the book

The structure of *Eating Shakespeare* reflects our attempt to unshackle Cultural Anthropophagy from an exclusively Brazilian context and apply it to a wider set of global examples. It is well known that the concept has already been repeatedly applied to Shakespeare in Brazil and Latin America, by some of our contributors and other scholars, such as Anna Stegh Camati, Margarida Rauen, Fernanda Teixeira de Medeiros and José Roberto O'Shea, all of whom have amply demonstrated its value. In this sense Cultural Anthropophagy and Shakespeare are already old acquaintances (of which the 'Cannibalist Manifesto' itself is proof), but it is clear that this relationship – as well as the general potential of Cultural Anthropophagy as a postcolonial theory – has not been sufficiently noticed and recognized beyond Brazil and Latin America, which can be seen as another example of thought from the Global South travelling considerably slower towards the Global North than vice versa, as Cristiane Busato Smith also notes in her chapter.

In extending the geographical context of the book, and including examples from Britain, we have also wanted to avoid a regional or 'area studies' model, often seen in Global Shakespeare, which can sometimes reinforce an unnecessarily rigid organization and restrict the travelling potential of both creative and theoretical production. Thus, from the outset *Eating Shakespeare* was not a book about 'Shakespeare in Brazil', even if a substantial part of it deals with Brazilian case studies. Of course, we do not wish to water down the complexities of Cultural Anthropophagy, or imply that it is a 'one-size-fits-all' model; clearly Brazil's colonial history is very different from that of, say, the Indian subcontinent. Yet, many chapters demonstrate powerful intersections and affinities, both in locations already grappling with the potentialities and challenges of intercultural heritage and expression, as seen in Eleine Ng's analysis of Shakespeare on the Singaporean stage, or, perhaps slightly more surprising, in the immediate recognition of an anthropophagic creative identity by Spanish film director Miguel del Arco, in the chapter by Víctor Huertas Martín.

The first section (or, as we prefer, 'dialogue') is entitled 'Shakespeare and Cultural Anthropophagy in Practice' and explores both creative and hermeneutic approaches. It opens with a conversation between Vinicius Mariano de Carvalho and Geraldo Carneiro, Brazilian poet and Shakespeare translator. Carneiro describes and discusses a selection of examples from his Shakespearean translations into Portuguese and their contexts, which are then commented on by Carvalho in order to highlight the anthropophagic method employed by the translator. This conversation is followed by Víctor Huertas Martín's essay, which utilizes Cultural Anthropophagy, particularly theories by Eduardo Viveiros de Castro, to analyse the work of Spanish film and theatre director Miguel del Arco Herrera; particularly his 2016 film *Las Furias*, which creates a complex visual and textual framework drawing on Shakespearean and classical signifiers and, in the adaptation process, re-signifies them. Huertas Martín also refers to in-depth conversations with Del Arco as part of his methodology and relates some thought-provoking negotiations of meaning during these. In another exchange between a creative and a scholarly perspective, Paulo da Silva Gregório interviews Fernando Yamamoto, artistic director of the theatre company 'Clowns de Shakespeare' from north-east Brazil. Clowns de Shakespeare have gained widespread international recognition for their Shakespearean productions, such as *Sua Incelença, Ricardo III*, which adapts (or, as Gregório's introduction to the interview demonstrates, devours) *Richard III*, fusing Shakespearean signifiers with an eclectic framework of local and global references. Cristiane Busato Smith's essay deals with a seminal and highly anthropophagic Shakespeare production in Brazil: Zé Celso's *Ham-let* performed at the iconic Teatro Oficina in São Paulo in 1993 and revived in 2001. She analyses the production, however, focusing on its portrayal of Ophelia as a complex fusion of European visual references and the Afro-Brazilian deity *Oxum*, showing how the latter adds new layers of meaning as well as empowerment to the performance, and thus bringing a welcome feminist perspective to the anthropophagic discussion.

The second 'dialogue' uses Cultural Anthropophagy as a starting point or provocation for wider conversations about the challenges of Global Shakespeare as a field or discipline. First, Koel Chatterjee and Diana Henderson offer a rich, multifaceted and frank discussion of the shift in focus from anglophone to global Shakespeare, while responding to Cultural Anthropophagy as potentially taking part in this shift. Marcel Alvaro de Amorim's chapter provides a critical survey of current scholarly strands, methodologies and debates within the field of Global Shakespeare, fleshing out some of the problems also noted in this introduction. He then provides a detailed explanation of Cultural Anthropophagy and demonstrates how it might inform analyses of Shakespearean 'translocal' productions around the globe. In the third chapter of the section, Mark Thornton Burnett traces past and present trajectories of global Shakespeare(s) in conversation with Anne Sophie Refskou, sharing insights into his work on Shakespearean world cinema and exploring the potential of Cultural Anthropophagy as a methodology in relation to this.

The three chapters in the third 'dialogue' of the book all utilize Cultural Anthropophagy to unpack questions related to 'otherness' within so-called multicultural societies and to explore ways in which Shakespeare is performed in these societies. Varsha Panjwani and Anne Sophie Refskou both examine Shakespearean cultural production by and in relation to British minorities. Panjwani, through conversations with Samir Bhamra, Artistic Director of Phizzical, and with Tajpal Rathore and Samran Rathore, Artistic Directors of Tribe Arts, offers a richly detailed discussion of hybrid Shakespeare(s) by British-Asian artists (Panjwani's preferred term is 'Brasian', which, as she explains, 'connotes a more fused identity'). She proposes Cultural Anthropophagy as a productive way of understanding how these artists handle multiple cultural signifiers and shows how they have sometimes been misunderstood as 'inauthentic' for doing so, as if somehow required to 'detangle' their cultural identities. Importantly, she reveals that the criticism directed at some 'Brasian' Shakespeare productions for their supposed lack of clarity or cultural 'authenticity' shows a misinformed understanding of what is actually their strength and value. Similar problems are addressed by Refskou, whose chapter asks what Global Shakespeare has meant and might mean in Britain. Refskou argues that it is necessary to examine the ways that British Shakespeare constructs and negotiates its perception of internal and external 'otherness', and uses Cultural Anthropophagy to analyse two recent *Hamlet* productions, which might be classified as 'Global-British', but for very different reasons. In the final chapter of the section Eleine Ng re-situates Cultural Anthropophagy within the interculturalized context of Singaporean Shakespeare performances. She uses an anthropophagic perspective to explain how 'existing concepts of theatrical interculturalism can be inverted and reconstituted by modes of artistic and cultural creation that are intrinsically defined by hybridity', and finds an illuminating alignment between anthropophagic 'eating' and Singapore's own concept of *rojak*, a popular dish mixing different (cultural) ingredients.

The fourth and final 'dialogue' contains two engaging testimonies of witnessing the creatively and personally empowering effect of an 'anthropophagized' Shakespeare. Aimara da Cunha Resende's essay and personal account of her extraordinary project, *Shakespeare e as Crianças* (Shakespeare and the Children), which she has run for over ten years in the central state of Minas Gerais, in south-east Brazil, shows yet another aspect to the potential of Cultural Anthropophagy in relation to pedagogy. Resende uses an anthropophagic perspective to discuss the philosophy behind the project as well as its pedagogical methods, demonstrating an engagement with Shakespeare through subversive creativity. She makes the important point that simply studying the plays for meaning rarely offers opportunity to remove or de-centre Shakespeare from an anglophone sphere, while teaching methods that consciously subsume the plays into the students' own immediate reality and environment add empowerment to education. The final chapter sees Vinicius Mariano de Carvalho in another conversation, this time with British theatre director, scholar and founder of the arts organization People's Palace Projects, Paul Heritage. Through People's Palace Projects and other organizations, Heritage has worked between Brazil and the UK for more than twenty years, and he is in several ways the embodiment par excellence of an ongoing dynamic cultural exchange between the two countries. In the conversation with Carvalho he describes some of his first experiences in Brazil as anthropophagic encounters, and compares Brazilian and British understandings and performance traditions of Shakespeare, using the former to explain and critique the latter's sometimes counterproductive institutionalization of the Bard.

Finally, in the Afterword, Alfredo Michel Modenessi readdresses many of the questions and propositions raised in this introduction while taking a bird's-eye view of the history of Latin American Shakespearean criticism, elegantly teasing out both the links and the gaps between *Eating Shakespeare* and the seminal

Latin American Shakespeares, edited by Bernice W. Kliman in 2005. He reiterates both the problematic and the potentially productive interaction between the 'fat king' of the 'imported' culture and the 'lean beggar' of the 'host culture' in relation to Latin American Shakespeares, and expresses the hope that this interaction can now be better understood as well as transported beyond its sites of origin for the benefit of other 'others'.

Notes

1 All cited works of Shakespeare throughout the text refer to act, scene and line numbers. For example, *Oth* 1.3.144–145 is *Othello*, Act 1, Scene 3, Lines 144–145.

2 See Vaughan and Mason (1991: ch. 2) for an extensive examination of the etymology and history of Caliban's name.

3 Andrade also sets this out in his 'Manifesto of Pau-Brasil Poetry' ([1925] 1986) preceding the 'Cannibalist Manifesto'.

4 Azevedo (2018), translation by Anne Sophie Refskou and Vinicius Mariano de Carvalho.

5 As Viveiros de Castro explains: 'The initial stimulus for the present reflections were the numerous references in Amazonian ethnography to an indigenous theory according to which the way humans perceive animals and other subjectivities that inhabit the world – gods, spirits, the dead, inhabitants of other cosmic levels, meteorological phenomena, plants, occasionally even objects and artefacts – differs profoundly from the way in which these beings see humans and themselves' (1998: 470).

6 Viveiros de Castro (2018), translation by Anne Sophie Refskou and Vinicius Mariano de Carvalho.

7 In relation to the Globe-to-Globe festival there was talk of cultural imperialism (O'Toole 2012) and critique of the advertising rhetoric that emphasized The Globe's vision to bring Shakespeare 'home', as well as the ever-problematic notion of Shakespearean 'universality', although many critics also agreed that results of the project – the opportunity to see these productions, many of them experimental, surprising and

insightful – should be appreciated. For critique and nuanced reflections on the cultural politics of the 2012 World Shakespeare Festival and the Globe-to-Globe project see for example Sullivan (2013), Kennedy (2017) or Carson (2017).

8 Young's forthcoming volume in the Global Shakespeare Inverted series, *Shakespeare in the Global South: Stories of Oceans Crossed in Contemporary Adaptation*, also utilizes the 'the Global South' as a critical framework and continues this important discussion.

9 It is thought-provoking to compare this with Oswald de Andrade's challenge of the import – export relations between Europe and Brazil, and to be reminded that 1920s Cultural Anthropophagy, in many ways, already offered a way to reset this imbalance. The irony, of course, is the fact that Andrade's ideas have taken so long to be exported.

10 See Modenessi (2017).

References

Andrade, O. de ([1925] 1986), 'Manifesto of Pau-Brasil Poetry', trans. S. M. de Sá Rego, *Latin American Literary Review*, 14 (27): 184–187.

Andrade, O. de ([1928] 1991), 'Cannibalist Manifesto', trans. L. Bary, *Latin American Literary Review*, 19 (38): 35–47.

Arens, W. (1998), 'Rethinking Anthropophagy', in F. Barker, P. Hulme and M. Iversen (eds), *Cannibalism and the Colonial World*, 39–62, Cambridge: Cambridge University Press.

Azevedo, B. (2018), *Antropofagia – Palimpsesto Selvagem*, São Paulo: SESC-SP.

Budasz, R. (2005), 'Of Cannibals and the Recycling of Otherness', *Music and Letters*, 87 (1): 1–15.

Campos, H. (1986), 'The Rule of Anthropophagy: Europe under the Sign of Devoration', trans. M.T. Wolff, *Latin American Literary Review*, 14 (27): 42–60.

Carson, C. (2017), 'Performance, Presence and Personal Responsibility: Witnessing Global Theatre in and around the Globe', in J. C. Bulman (ed.), *The Oxford Handbook of Shakespeare and Performance*, 458–476, Oxford: Oxford University Press.

Comaroff, J. and J. L. Comaroff (2012), 'Theory from the South: Or, How Euro-America Is Evolving Toward Africa', *Anthropological Forum*, 22 (2): 113–131.

Cottom, D. (2001), *Cannibals and Philosophers: Bodies of Enlightenment*, Baltimore: Johns Hopkins University Press.

Huang, A. (2013), 'Global Shakespeares as Methodology', *Shakespeare*, 9 (3): 273–290.

Hulme, P. (1986), *Colonial Encounters: Europe and the Native Caribbean, 1492–1797*, London: Methuen.

Hulme, P. (1998), 'Introduction: The Cannibal Scene', in F. Barker, P. Hulme and M. Iversen (eds), *Cannibalism and the Colonial World*, 1–31, Cambridge: Cambridge University Press.

Islam, G. (2011), 'Can the Subaltern Eat? Anthropophagic Culture as a Brazilian Lens on Post-Colonial Theory', *Organization*, 19 (2): 159–180.

Johnson, S. (1755), *A Dictionary of the English Language*. Available online: http://johnsonsdictionaryonline.com/about-this-project/ (accessed 15 April 2018).

Kennedy, D. (2017), 'Global Shakespeare and Globalized Performance', in J. C. Bulman (ed.), *The Oxford Handbook of Shakespeare and Performance*, 441–457, Oxford: Oxford University Press.

Massai, S. (2005), 'Defining Local Shakespeares', in S. Massai (ed.), *Worldwide Shakespeares: Local Appropriations in Film and Performance*, 3–11, Abingdon: Routledge.

Modenessi, A. M. (2017), 'Victim of Improvisation: Shakespeare Out-sourced and In-taken', in J. C. Bulman (ed.), *The Oxford Handbook of Shakespeare and Performance*, 549–567, Oxford: Oxford University Press.

Obeyesekere, G. (1992), '"British Cannibals": Contemplation of an Event in the Death and Resurrection of James Cook, Explorer', *Critical Inquiry*, 18 (4): 630–654.

Obeyesekere, G. (1998), 'Cannibal Feasts in Nineteenth-century Fiji: Seamen's Yarns and the Ethnographic Imagination', in F. Barker, P. Hulme and M. Iversen (eds), *Cannibalism and the Colonial World*, 63–86, Cambridge: Cambridge University Press.

O'Toole, E. (2012), 'Shakespeare Universal? No, It's Cultural Imperialism', *The Guardian*, 21 May. Available online: www.theguardian.com/commentisfree/2012/may/21/shakespeare-universal-cultural-imperialism (accessed 20 January 2018).

Shakespeare, W. (1999), *The Merry Wives of Windsor*, ed. G. Melchiori, third series, London: Bloomsbury Arden Shakespeare.

Shakespeare, W. ([1997] 2016), *Othello*, ed. E. A. J. Honigmann, rev. edn with a new introduction by A. Thompson, third series, London: Bloomsbury Arden Shakespeare.

Sullivan, E. (2013), 'Olympic Performance in the Year of Shakespeare', in P. Edmondson, P. Prescott and E. Sullivan (eds), *A Year of Shakespeare: Re-living the World Shakespeare Festival*, 3–11, London: Bloomsbury.

Vaughn, A. T. and V. Mason (1991), *Shakespeare's Caliban: A Cultural History*, Cambridge: Cambridge University Press.

Viveiros de Castro, E. (1986), *From the Enemy's Point of View: Humanity and Divinity in an Amazonian Society*, trans. C. V. Howard, Chicago: University of Chicago Press.

Viveiros de Castro, E. (1998), 'Cosmological Deixis and Amerindian Perspectivism', *The Journal of the Royal Anthropological Institute*, 4 (3): 469–488.

Viveiros de Castro, E. (2018), 'Que temos nós com isso?', in B. Azevedo (ed.), *Antropofagia – Palimpsesto Selvagem*, 11–19, São Paulo: SESC-SP.

Young, S. (2016), 'Race and the Global South in Early Modern Studies', *Shakespeare Quarterly*, 67 (1): 125–135.

PART ONE

Dialogue I: Shakespeare and Cultural Anthropophagy in practice

1

We are all cannibals: reflections on translating Shakespeare

Geraldo Carneiro and Vinicius Mariano de Carvalho

The Brazilian poet Geraldo Carneiro talks about his translations and adaptations of Shakespeare into Portuguese with a commentary by Vinicius Mariano de Carvalho, highlighting Carneiro's anthropophagic method.

Geraldo Carneiro testimony

With the publication of the 'Manifesto Antropófago' (Cannibalist Manifesto) in 1928, the poet, novelist and playwright Oswald de Andrade made the expropriation of ideas and texts written by others one of the laws of his aesthetic: 'I am only concerned with what is not mine. Law of

Man. Law of the cannibal' (Andrade [1928] 1991: 36). Oswald de Andrade's literary anthropophagy was a conceptual novelty in Brazil. As we all know, however, literature has always fed off other literature. Literary cannibalism has existed since the dawn of time (or since the beginning of a written tradition), under the pretext of imitating the classics, or using the more recent alibi of intertextuality.

One of the biggest cannibals of literature is William Shakespeare himself. A play like *Romeo and Juliet*, according to Stephen Greenblatt, has among its various sources the play *The Tragical History of Romeus and Juliet* by Arthur Brooke, which in turn is derived from a French text, adapted from the Italian version written by Matteo Bandelo, which has as a source a tale by Luigi da Porto, which is in turn adapted from one by Masuccio Salernitano (Greenblatt 2016). As is widely known, Shakespeare rarely took the trouble to come up with his own plots – to use that odd metaphor that is common currency today, as if writers were gods able to create stories out of nothing. Shakespeare probably preferred to concentrate his efforts on rewriting them with better words – words cannibalized from everything that he saw and read. With this practice, he anticipates his disciple Molière, another cannibal of dramaturgy, who declared: 'Je prends mon bien où je le trouve.'

My first professional encounter with Shakespeare was in 1981, when I was commissioned to translate *The Tempest*. A group of young actors, called Pessoal do Despertar (People of Awakening), had looked at all the translations available in Portuguese. Having found these translations to be less poetic than their reading of the original had led them to expect, and having read some of my poems, they chose me to undertake a challenge that they considered almost impossible: producing a translation with the poetic qualities of the original. The first scene that I worked on from that play was a kind of trial by fire for everyone involved. It is Act 3 Scene 1, the love scene between Prince Ferdinand and Miranda, which I translated with a certain liberty:

Já amei mulheres diversas,
Por suas mais diversas qualidades;
Nenhuma assim, com toda a minha alma,
Pois sempre alguma sombra de defeito
Pairava sobre a graça mais perfeita
E desfazia o meu encantamento;
Mas você, ah, você é tão perfeita,
Parece feita da pequena parte
De perfeição que há em cada criatura. (Shakespeare 1992)

After working on this fragment, I imagined that it would be relatively easy to translate *The Tempest*. This turned out to be wishful thinking: the task took me four months. I felt overwhelmed in the face of so many beautiful images, and I confess that I was not fully satisfied with my translation, although my stage adaptation ran in Rio de Janeiro between 1982 and 1984. Among the characters in *The Tempest* the figure of Caliban particularly caught my attention. His name is interpreted by some people as an anagram of 'cannibal'. It is through him that the Europeans – among them his master, Prospero, the exiled Duke of Milan – transmit the image that they have painted of the savage of the New World. During the first decades in which the new territory was colonized, navigators thought that America might be an extension of Paradise. However, after their early difficulties there that image changed. Instead the newly arrived came to consider this place an extension of Hell (Souza 1987). Although Caliban is one of the villains of *The Tempest*, since he allies himself with the plotters who attempt to overthrow Prospero from his throne, Shakespeare does not shy away from giving a voice to this character: Caliban: 'O senhor me deu água com frutas e me ensinou o nome da luz maior, que ilumina o dia, e da luz menor, que ilumina a noite. [...] E eu, que sou seu único súdito, era antes o meu próprio rei' (Shakespeare 1992). In short, Caliban's speech seems to prefigure the anti-colonial attitude of the Cannibalist Manifesto published over 300 years later, and the perspective of all the peripheries of empires since time immemorial.

After *The Tempest*, I was called to translate and adapt *As You Like It*. This time, however, the group who commissioned the translation recommended that I did not confine myself to the original text but, rather, to take the liberty to adapt, create and remove scenes. I remember having followed the group's suggestions wholeheartedly. I added a series of quotations of dictums and verses of Brazilian poetry written by myself and others to the text. For example, when the old Adam is on the verge of exhaustion, at the end of a long walk through the forest, he asks his master Orlando stoically to abandon him, and blurts out: 'Esta é a parte que me cabe neste latifúndio' (This is my place in this latifundium). The reference to the line from João Cabral de Mello Neto, taken from his tragic poem *Morte e Vida Severina* (The Death and Life of a Severino), has a comic effect here. I added this as well as other fragments or anachronistic creations that were compatible within the context of the piece, extracted from erudite and popular sources. I also removed certain scenes in prose and added others in verse. I suggested to the audience and critics that they should try to work out which were the legitimate scenes and which were the illegitimate scenes; which were from the Bard and which were from the bastard – that is to say, mine. The director of montage, Aderbal Freire Filho, liked this game of mine and asked for more. As is widely known, the play ends with a famous epilogue spoken by Rosalind. Aderbal suggested to me that we write a new epilogue. I accepted his proposal, and so at the end of the play, Rosalind turns towards the audience and speaks as follows:

Não era hábito, no teatro elisabetano,
Uma mulher se incumbir de fechar o pano.
Aliás, naquela época não havia cortina,
Nem se permitia à classe feminina
A audácia de fazer teatro épico, lírico
                              /ou burlesco,
Na ilusão de certo parentesco
Entre a mulher e o diabo:
Uma questão de chifres e de rabo.

Mas vamos ao que interessa:
Eu estou aqui para dizer o epílogo da peça,
Essa ciranda de paixões, essa batalha
Em que a justiça farda, mas não talha,
Ou vice-versa.
E aproveitando o rumo da conversa,
Falando sério,
Eu quero esclarecer mais um mistério.
É a história de um tio meu, que é mago,
A que eu me referi de modo vago,
É rigorosamente confiável;
Ele inventou um artifício formidável
Pra conjurar as forças do acaso
E, conforme o caso,
Os humores inconstantes da plateia.
E eu vou lhes revelar qual é a ideia.
Vocês querem aprender?

The audience responds in chorus: 'We want to.' Then Rosalind speaks again:

Primeiro, erga a mão direita para o céu,
Até a altura do seu improvável chapéu.
Depois a esquerda, num movimento
                                    /semelhante,
Num gesto suplicante e singelo.
Agora alinhe as duas em paralelo,
Num arremedo de aceno.
Não tenha medo de parecer obsceno.
E enfim manifeste ruidosamente o seu agrado,
Caso contrário eu me sentirei arruinado.

During the performance the audience kindly responded when addressed during the false epilogue, the idea for which was stolen – or rather, cannibalized – from Shakespeare himself. At this point I had just published my translation of *The Tempest*. By coincidence, my friend the poet and translator,

Jorge Wanderley, had just been awarded funding to translate the totality of Shakespeare's 154 sonnets into Portuguese for the first time. Wanderley himself had already collaborated with me on the printed edition of *A Tempestade*, translating the verses for Ferdinand and Miranda's wedding scene. Knowing that a translation of a verbal repertoire as vast as Shakespeare's is a collective task for successive generations, I could not resist collaborating and started with Sonnet 18:

> Te comparar com um dia de verão?
> Tu és mais temperada e adorável;
> O vento em maio açoita a flor-botão
> É o império do verão não é durável.
> O sol às vezes brilha com rigor
> Ou sua tez dourada é mais escura;
> Toda beleza enfim perde o esplendor
> Por acaso ou descaso da Natura;
> Mas teu verão nunca se apagará,
> Perdendo a posse da beleza tua,
> Nem a morte rirá por te ofuscar,
> Se em versos imortais te perpetuas;
>   Enquanto alguém respire e veja e viva,
>   Viva este verso e nele sobrevivas.

I started to work with Shakespeare's sonnets regularly. For example, I translated Sonnet 76 as follows:

> Por que meu verso é sempre tão carente
> De mutações e variação de temas?
> Por que não olho as coisas do presente
> Atrás de outras receitas e sistemas?
> Por que só escrevo essa monotonia,
> Tão incapaz de produzir inventos,
> Que cada verso quase denuncia
> Meu nome e seu lugar de nascimento?
> Pois saiba, amor: só escrevo a seu respeito,
> E sobre o amor, são meus únicos temas;

E assim vou refazendo o que foi feito,
Reinventando as palavras do poema;
    Como o sol, novo e velho a cada dia,
    O meu amor rediz o que dizia.

For Sonnet 116 I tried to translate it keeping its baroque syntax:

Não tenha eu restrições ao casamento
De almas sinceras, pois não é amor
O amor que muda ao sabor do momento
E se move e remove em desamor.
Oh, não, o amor é marca mais constante,
Que enfrenta a tempestade e não balança;
É a estrela guia dos batéis errantes,
Cujo valor lá no alto não se alcança.
O amor não é o bufão do tempo, embora
Sua foice vá ceifando a face a fundo;
O amor não muda com o passar das horas,
Mas se sustenta até o final do mundo.
    Se é engano meu e assim provado for,
    Nunca escrevi, ninguém jamais amou.

After the sonnets, I was asked to translate *Love's Labour's Lost*, whose title itself is enough to intimidate a translator. The Portuguese translation is enshrined as *Trabalhos de Amor Perdidos*. A more fitting title would be 'In Search of Lost Alliterations'. However, my translation of *Love's Labour's Lost* is only a trial exercise. I was not capable of finding equivalents for the dozens of examples of word play that Shakespeare uses in the play. Some critics have spoken dismissively of the poet's passion for puns and all kinds of word play. In defence of Shakespeare, however, I would argue that those who do not like word play, in general, do not like it because they do not have an aptitude for it. Unlike the adaptation of *As You Like It*, in *Love's Labour's Lost* I tried to stay as close as possible to the original:

O sol de ouro não beija assim tão doce
O orvalho sobre a pétala da flor,
Como teu olhar que em raios derramou-se
E derramou meu pranto e me encantou.
Nem brilha cor de prata a luz da lua
Por entre as transparentes profundezas
Como brilha o esplendor da face tua
Entre as lágrimas minhas de tristeza.
Cada gota carrega-te em cortejo
Em teu triunfo sobre o meu amor.
Quanto mais lágrimas por ti despejo
Aumenta a tua glória e a minha dor.
Mas não te encantes por ti, eu te aconselho,
Nem faças minhas lágrimas de espelho.
Rainha das rainhas, tu ultrapassas
O que se pense ou diga de tuas graças.

After that, at the request of the director Paul Heritage and the actor Maria Padilha, I translated some key scenes from *Antony and Cleopatra*. The production was first staged in the favelas of Rio de Janeiro, as part of a project called *Amor em Tempos de Guerra* (Love in Time of War), and also ran in the theatres of Rio de Janeiro and São Paulo, directed by Paulo José. In one of the readings of the play, in a state school located between rival favelas, there were gunshots, with drug gangs exchanging tracer bullets, which leave marks in the sky. It was as if we were in the middle of a war between Mark Antony and his rival, the future emperor, Augustus. As many readers will appreciate, there is not space here to discuss all of the wonderful moments in the text. Here is just a small extract, Cleopatra's monologue when she is on the brink of committing suicide:

Me dá meu manto. Põe minha coroa.
Tenho desejos imortais em mim.
Depressa, Iras. Parece até que escuto
Antonio me chamando. Já o vejo
Se erguendo pra elogiar meu gesto nobre.

Ouço-o zombando da sorte de César.
Já vou, meu esposo. Que minha coragem
Comprove o meu direito a esse título.
Sou fogo e ar: meus outros elementos
Entrego à natureza mais vulgar.
Está tudo pronto? Então venham colher
O derradeiro ardor dos lábios meus.
Adeus, gentil Charmian. Iras, adeus.

My next commission was the translation of key scenes from *Romeo and Juliet*, directed by João Fonseca. After translating *Romeo and Juliet*, I selected some of Shakespeare's lyrical speeches and published them in a bilingual edition, with the title *O Discurso do Amor Rasgado* (Speeches of Torn Love) (Carneiro 2013). During the launch of the book in São Paulo, though, I was asked to translate *King Lear* for the stage by the actor Juca de Oliveira. I replied that there were already good translations in Portuguese, done by Millôr Fernandes, in prose, and by Jorge Wanderley, in verse. I thought *King Lear* to be too painful, too poetic, as well as requiring a big cast of high-level actors. I therefore suggested to Juca that we could write a monologue for Lear. Juca de Oliveira accepted the challenge. After this exchange, I had the experience and adventure of transforming *King Lear* into a narrative, without losing its best poetic lines. We toured the main cities in Brazil with this production. With the grace of the gods, we went back to being cannibals and devoured Shakespeare in our own way, as he had always done with his forebears.

Commentary by Vinicius Mariano de Carvalho

Geraldo Carneiro is perhaps one of the most highly esteemed contemporary translators of Shakespeare into

Brazilian Portuguese. Being also a poet, he incorporates an anthropophagic method into his translations. The reflections I am presenting here are designed to show how this cannibalistic method is mobilized in the translation process.

His text begins by referring to Oswald de Andrade's now well-known 'Cannibalist Manifesto'. Carneiro uses the word 'expropriation' to refer to what Andrade calls anthropophagy. This choice of term is interesting. To expropriate is to remove something from being the exclusive property of someone. As opposed to 'appropriate', an act involving someone taking possession of something that belonged to another, 'expropriate' suggests the removal of ownership from someone. This concept gives a good outline of what we can consider to be the paradigms of an anthropophagic translation: the removal, or taking away of property, and, by extension, of originality, of essentiality.

Carneiro goes on to highlight that although literary anthropophagy as proposed by Oswald de Andrade was a novelty in Brazil, practice preceded it, and it is, in a certain sense, common to all literature to the extent that it 'devours' the very notion of intertextuality, or in other words, the notion on intertextuality could be seen as a sort of 'cultural anthropophagy'. Therefore, literary texts are, for Carneiro, the result of anthropophagy and authors are naturally cannibals. According to Carneiro, Shakespeare is a literary anthropophagous.

This all sounds rather poetic but does not yet provide a methodological dimension of what an anthropophagic translation would be like. In order to explain how to translate anthropophagically, Carneiro provides comments on certain aspects of his translations. He begins with *The Tempest*. Act 3, Scene 1 is referred to by the translator as a key test. His translation, which he himself qualifies as having been carried out with a certain liberty, already gives us an indication of his anthropophagic method. Carneiro's translates the following part of Shakespeare's text:

> Full many a lady
> I have eyed with best regard, and many a time
> Th' harmony of their tongues hath into bondage
> Brought my too diligent ear. For several virtues
> Have I liked several women; never any
> With so full soul but some defect in her
> Did quarrel with the noblest grace she owed
> And put it to the foil. But you, O you,
> So perfect and so peerless, are created
> Of every creature's best.
>
> (*Tem* 3.1.39–48)

In the first lines Carneiro uses a reference to a popular song in Brazil, a samba by the composer and singer Martinho da Vila – 'Já tive mulheres de todas as cores' (I have been with women of all colours). By doing this, he makes Shakespeare's text familiar and incorporates it into Brazil's own literary-poetic tradition. 'Th' harmony of their tongues' and his 'too diligent ear' are lines that do not feed the translator-anthropophagous, and are discarded. Those body parts do not feed the complete image of Carneiro's Miranda. Carneiro shows that he is not satisfied by the translation that has been done; the translational-anthropophagic act is not complete, which provides another methodological lesson. The text to be devoured still retains some substance even as it is swallowed and transformed. The 'other' remains an 'other', even when it is incorporated into a new 'self'. The process of establishing relations of alterity in anthropophagic translations does not concern itself with definitive absolutes, but must keep the translated text 'alive' by reconfiguring it and breaking it up into pieces, discarding parts and sticking together the parts that interest the translator using references to other texts.

In his remarks on his celebrated translation of *The Tempest*, Carneiro underscores the postcolonial aspect of an anthropophagic translation, in that the anti-colonialism expressed in Caliban's lines already carries the essence of the 'Cannibalist Manifesto'. What Carneiro emphasizes is that by associating Prospero's island and the New World – an association that is made frequently in interpretations of the play – the resulting spatial dislocation also implies an ontological dislocation, which is demonstrated in the confrontation with this 'other', Caliban. Anthropophagic translations, in this sense, are voices from the global peripheries.

The commentary on the translation of *As You Like It* also provides other insights on anthropophagic translation. Carneiro mentions the fact that he was asked to adapt, create and remove scenes, and proceeds to reconfigure the body of the text violently. This process is only possible because an anthropophagic translation does not establish a hierarchical relationship between the original and the translation, between essence and existence. The anthropophagic translator is not concerned with preserving an essence, an ontological original. Here a question of fundamental otherness is established as being key to the understanding of Cultural Anthropophagy. In the words of Viveiros de Castro, 'the incorporation of the other required an exit from oneself' (2011: 46). This performative exercise also breaks with hierarchies of genre by its very nature. Comedy and tragedy are no longer absolutes, because they remain interdependent on one another in order to exist. The line included from the poem *Morte e Vida Severina* (The Death and Life of a Severino), by the Brazilian poet João Cabral de Mello Neto, has already been cannibalized by Carneiro's words. Carneiro makes it clear that this is a relationship of essential ontological incompleteness, since this same line is mentioned in Ozualdo Candeia's film *A Herança* (1971), which was itself an adaptation of *Hamlet*. That is to say, João Cabral de Mello Neto and Shakespeare are already blended together in the same poetic corpus. Legitimacies are a problem for audiences and critics who are preoccupied with hierarchies. Carneiro's anthropophagic translation tries to incorporate alterity, even that of the audience. The translation of the epilogue of the piece presented by Carneiro allows the audience to interact with Rosalind, in a way that is a performative act, incorporating the other and breaking the actor – character ontological boundary. In his translation, Carneiro continues Shakespeare's anthropophagic act, since Shakespeare says in the play: 'It is not the fashion to see the lady the epilogue' (*AYL* Epilogue 1–2). Furthermore, Rosalind incorporates other identities, other *ontos* in her epilogue, by involving the audience in the action, making them participate in this performative act, again breaking the assumed actor – audience hierarchy. Here Carneiro thus echoes an anthropophagic act present in Shakespeare's play.

The translations of Geraldo Carneiro's sonnets again show his concern with the musicality of the verse, revealing a fundamental preoccupation with the corporality of the text, which he calls the verbal repertoire. His translation of Sonnet 18 gains exuberant musical contours, and the two last lines in Portuguese are a long sequence of musical alliterations, potentializing the melody already present in English ('So long as men can breathe or eyes can see, / So long lives this, and this gives life to thee' [*Son* 18.13–14]). This continued presence of musicality is also striking in the translations of Sonnets 76 and 116 presented to us here by Carneiro. What the translator is doing is incorporating his translations into the model of the Brazilian musical tradition in such a way that when they are heard they are not immediately identifiable as translations of English, but instead have a sound that is reminiscent of the Portuguese musical-poetic tradition. In the translations, what we hear is an echo of the Galician-Portuguese troubadours, of popular Brazilian *modinha*, of the rhythm of song. Even when the anthropophagic translator says that he translated Sonnet 116 obeying its baroque syntax, the melody of this baroque syntax sounds like Góngora, so it comes from an Iberian tradition, not an Anglo-Saxon one. Prioritizing this Iberian tradition, the translator searches for an affinity based on correlations, instead of submitting the translation to an Anglo-Saxon syntax, substantially diverse from Brazilian Portuguese. The lesson here is that anthropophagic translation asserts a value found in a 'relational affinity' rather than a 'substantial affinity', to use Viveiros de Castro's terms (2011: 31).

When commenting on his translation of *Love's Labour's Lost*, Carneiro also points out how much the task of anthropophagic translation is process rather than product, performance rather than essence. By admitting his inability to devour Shakespeare's text anthropophagically, Carneiro humbly admits that this time it was he, the translator, who was swallowed. His affirmation that he 'tried to stay as close as possible to the original' is an interesting admission of the established ontological struggle, in which his 'enemy' – the original text – shows itself to be stronger. Viveiros de Castro remarks about the Amerindians: 'The Indians had no maniac desire to impose their identity on the other, nor did they reject the other in favor of their own ethnic excellence. Rather, they aimed, by producing a relationship with the other [...] to transform their own identity' (2011: 30). This anthropophagic translator, like the Amerindian, does not want to impose himself on the other, not completely turn into the other, but rather produce a translational relationship which mutually transforms their identities.

Carneiro's next remarks concern *Antony and Cleopatra*, which he was commissioned to translate by a project called *Amor em Tempos de Guerra* (Love in a Time of War). In 2004, this project brought a dramatized reading of this piece to a zone situated between the favelas of Vigário Geral and Parada de Lucas, in Rio de Janeiro. This is such a conflictive zone that it is known as the *Faixa de Gaza* (Gaza Strip). In this case, it is the performance context, rather than the text itself, which gives an anthropophagic dimension to the translation. Carneiro respects the classical verse, but the dialogues resonate as being totally Brazilian, since the immediate context of the favelas of Rio de Janeiro is incorporated into the context of the conflict presented in the play, the war between Mark Antony and Octavius. Thus, the performative context is also part of the process of anthropophagic translation. Here it is the atmosphere in which the play is staged, itself an integral part of the translation, which cannibalizes the context of the play.

Carneiro ends his testimony by referring to two other translations, *Romeo and Juliet* and *King Lear*. Regarding

Romeo and Juliet, he reveals that at the end of this he selected some of Shakespeare's lyrical speeches and published them as a volume, as if he and the playwright had become completely merged into one. In his own words, he had been colonized by the words of the Bard. This existential consubstantiation is exactly what allows him, as a translator, to also be the author in a dual form of originality, without the need for arguments about supremacy or imposition. Carneiro's verses are Shakespeare's, Shakespeare's verses are Carneiro's. Finally, in *King Lear*, Carneiro cannibalizes the form and method of poetic prose and prose poetry.

The object of these remarks on Geraldo Carneiro's testimony as an anthropophagic translator was, as this book proposes, to argue that Cultural Anthropophagy is more than a simple metaphor, but rather it constitutes ontologically a hermeneutic practice that is applicable to literary translation. The translations of Shakespeare by Geraldo Carneiro provide sustenance for this argument.

References

Andrade, O. ([1928] 1991), 'Cannibalist Manifesto', trans. L. Bary, *Latin American Literary Review*, 19 (38): 38–44.

Carneiro, G. (2013), *O discurso do amor rasgado: Poemas, Cenas e Fragmentos de William Shakespeare*, Rio de Janeiro: Editora Nova Fronteira.

Greenblatt, S. (2016), *The Norton Shakespeare*, New York: Norton & Company Inc.

Shakespeare, W. (1992), *A Tempestade*, trans. Geraldo Carneiro, Rio de Janeiro: Relume Dumará.

Shakespeare, W. (2011), *The Tempest*, ed. V. M. Vaughan and A. T. Vaughan, third series, London: Bloomsbury Arden Shakespeare.

Souza, L. (1987), *O Diabo e a Terra de Santa Cruz*, São Paulo: Companhia das Letras.

Viveiros de Castro, E. (2011), *The Inconstancy of the Indian Soul: The Encounter of Catholics and Cannibals in 16th Century Brazil*, Chicago: Paradigm Press.

2

Miguel Del Arco's *Las Furias* (2016): Cultural Anthropophagy as adaptation practice and as metafiction

Víctor Huertas Martín

Before its theatrical release, the poster publicizing *Las Furias* (2016) announced it as 'Miguel del Arco's first film' (see Figure 2.1) and exhibited the picture of the main characters: the Ponte Alegre family. The title suggested the film's indebtedness to its Graeco-Latin sources. The names printed in the poster anticipated the release of a prestige film featuring a dream-team of theatre, film and television stars: Jose Sacristán (Leo), Alberto San Juan (Aki), Carmen Machi (Casandra), Mercedes Sampietro (Marga), Barbara Lennie (Julia), Emma Suárez (Ana), Gonzalo de Castro (Héctor), Macarena Sanz (María). The director's and Machi's names might have

FIGURE 2.1 *Poster:* Las Furias *(2016), dir. Miguel del Arco, Aquí y Allí Films and Kamikaze Producciones.*

reminded the viewer of their recent collaborations in *Juicio a Una Zorra* (2013) and *Antígona* (2015), both of them written and adapted by Del Arco. In *Juicio*, Machi had played Helen of Troy's defence soliloquy for the blames historically laid on her. In *Antígona*, she played a re-gendered Creon intensely adamant in her upholding of the rule of law above all kinds of transgression.

As the poster shows, the family have been enjoying dinner under a canopy of branches covered with white and violet lilies. They turn their gazes towards some unexpected visitor – or visitors – approaching from the side of the picture's onlooker. Could these unexpected visitors be the fierce Aeschylean Erinyes? These tragic expectations are partly confirmed at the film's beginning, for in the first scene three actresses playing the Furies make a terrifying entrance in a performance of *Oedipus*. We know they are performers when, in the next shot, they are revealed as such in the artists' dressing room saying hello to María, the youngest of the family, who is recording this backstage event. In this flashback scene we are introduced to the Ponte Alegre family ten years before the get-together that the film poster represents. Leo, the great actor playing Oedipus and María's grandfather, has concluded his act and asks María to tell the myth of the Furies to the family. María recites what seems a paraphrased passage from Hesiod (2006: 154–207). Ten years after this event, Leo suffers from Alzheimer's and has almost forgotten everything. Nonetheless, he recalls fragments of Shakespeare's texts. In fact, Shakespearean references in the film are as abundant as Graeco-Latin ones.

Cultural Anthropophagy as an adaptation practice involves thinking of the adapter as an anthropophagus who eats someone else's texts (in the broader sense of the word). In *Furias*, Del Arco deploys Graeco-Latin and Shakespearean texts that serve to ultimately strengthen his authorial voice. This chapter uses the concept of anthropophagy to explore Del Arco's symbolic eating of Shakespearean inter-texts in *Furias*.[1] The Shakespearean and 'Shakespeare-inflected' (Harrison 2017) references I am identifying can be classified as citations, allusions and revisions.[2] After defining Del Arco's anthropophagic practice, I argue that the Shakespearean references in *Furias* are part of a process of adaptation projected in Del Arco's other dramaturgies. I compare the system of self-referentiality described in Eduardo Viveiros de Castro's *Cannibal Metaphysics* with the Shakespearean meta-theatricality Del Arco deploys. For Viveiros de Castro, taking Amerindian anthropology seriously involves thinking of cannibal philosophy as a self-referential system of production of concepts and symbols that represent themselves (2010: 210). Viveiros de Castro's lens helps demonstrate that a non-Western angle illuminates the alterations produced by Shakespearean inter-texts in this European work. The results of this research show that Del Arco's Shakespearean references do not simply stand as formalistic borrowings but are a crucial part of the author's dynamics of adaptation. Examining *Furias* in relation to Del Arco's previous Shakespearean and non-Shakespearean work does not only help us thinking of Shakespearean texts rhizomatically (see Lanier 2014) or thinking of Shakespeare's plays as 'salient signifiers of meaning and knowledge' (Burnett and Wray 2006: 1), but it illustrates how Shakespearean nutrients fuel the author's own works. Paying attention to the mythical discourse deployed in the film, following Viveiros de Castro's methodology, sheds light on the process by which Shakespearean references affect the reshaping of a pervasive tragic master narrative that, at first sight, determines the tone of the film.[3]

Defining Cultural Anthropophagy in Del Arco's work

An interview with the director helped me define his adaptation practice in light of 'Cultural Anthropophagy'. On 15 September 2017, I visited him at the Teatro Pavón Kamikaze in Calle Embajadores, a few yards away from the Madrilenian Puerta del Sol and Plaza Mayor, not far from the commercial theatres in Gran Vía and the alternative venues in La Latina and Lavapiés. The purpose of this meeting was to discuss the film as a possible example of textual anthropophagy. I explained to Del Arco that anthropophagy consisted of the acquisition of the strengths, qualities and virtues associated to the 'other'. Could we possibly refashion this concept to define his dramaturgic practice? To my pleasant surprise, Del Arco did not need much explanation to identify himself with anthropophagy as textual adaptation:

> Anthropophagy is the story of my life. The rewriting and subsequent staging of *La Función por Hacer* [The Performance in the Making], based on Luigi Pirandello's *Six Characters in Search of an Author* is nothing other than entering inside the play and devouring it [...] I try to own the texts in the same way an actor needs to own the words to embody a character. I devour the words. I phagocytise them. I enter inside them to eat them. And I do this to become part of them. So that they're inside me too. Thus, whatever I regurgitate will necessarily be mine and, yet, modified by what I have ingested. (Del Arco interview with author, Madrid, 15 September 2017)

Two types of anthropophagy may be discerned when studying *Furias*. One type helps explain Del Arco's adaptation strategies. The second type is embedded in the film's Graeco-Latin sources. Del Arco's definition of anthropophagy resembles Viveiros de Castro's explanations of the Amerindian cannibal ceremony, which involved the eating of the enemy by the tribe. The killer did not participate in the eating but retired to mourn for the victim (Viveiros de Castro 1992: 293). By the time the sacrifice victim had been killed, the initial rivalry between the two warriors had given way to a communion described by Viveiros de Castro as a zone of spiritual indiscernibility between both enemies (1992: 152). This spiritual interface was the basis of the killer's construction of identity, for though the killer had not ingested the victim's flesh, according to Amerindian beliefs, he had appropriated his enemy's qualities, strengths, names, symbolic resources and language (Viveiros de Castro 1992: 141, 152; 2010: 285). Before this acquisition would take place, the two enemies formed a temporal alliance. The future victim had been living as the tribe's prisoner for some time. He had married the killer's sister and had coexisted in invigilated freedom with the family. In exchange, he had provided children to them to guarantee their continuance (Viveiros de Castro 2010: 299–300). Similarly, Del Arco's works' frequent contacts with Shakespeare's texts create textual interfaces, provisional alliances involving textual and symbolic exchanges.

This productive anthropophagy differs from the destructive forms of cannibalism latent in Del Arco's Graeco-Latin sources. These sources show that the only purpose of parental cannibalism is to remove their offspring from existence (Sanz 2013: 114–133). At the backstage scene, we hear María's retelling of the origins of the Furies. They were born after the war Ghea and Crone held against the anthropophagous god Uranus. This battle echoes the Ponte Alegres' filial – parental conflicts. This metafictional configuration prepares the viewer for a tragic outcome, but such expectations are challenged.

This film reveals mythical obsessions that, at large, interrelate with other works by Del Arco. Since I am interested in the film both as part of an author's adaptation practice and as metafictional adaptation, I am taking into account the Oedipal and the Hesiodic narratives that seem to form the story's co-present foundational myths. For Viveiros de Castro, everything that human beings do either conforms to or challenges mythical expectations (2010: 189). Do Shakespearean references propel any movement forward beyond these mythical preconceptions as we find them in the film? For Del Arco, who accepts a common basis conformed by myths, tragedies and renaissance theatre, Shakespeare's emerges as a salient voice:

> It happens that all classical tragedy is so well-served in Shakespeare [...] Shakespeare is the great anthropophagus. He devours everything. And after this, he produced us. And

I'm much more interested in Shakespeare's use of words, which has more to do with what I pursue in drama. (Del Arco interview with author, Madrid, 15 September 2017)

This chapter's objective is not to dismiss or validate Del Arco's point on Shakespeare's demiurgic qualities but, rather, to use them as a point of departure for the transition that, I think, Shakespeare's texts facilitate in the film. A major point of departure that Amerindian philosophy takes from Graeco-Latin filial–parental relations is that the former refuses the acceptance of incestuous relationships. Rather than by incest, Amerindian peoples are ruled by principles of alliance. For Viveiros de Castro, alliance means the beginning of society and the end of myth (2010: 129). This effect parallels the transition we may observe in *Furias*. The film's characters transcend a mythical filial–parental entrapment and embrace a system of alliance. A major interest is the function played by Shakespeare in this transition.

Shakespearean references in *Furias* seem insignificant if we just examine them as citations. Rather, *Furias* is as determined by 'categories of the Shakespearean' – as Mark Thornton Burnett calls them (2017: 1) – as by Graeco-Latin sources. Following Burnett, non-anglophone manifestations of Shakespeare invite us to respond to:

> other verbal registers, to narrative strategies, and to emotional contours [which] recall the plays, but not with any precise equivalence, meaning that we concentrate not so much on issues of nomenclature as questions about how categories of the Shakespearean are mobilized. (2017: 1)

Viveiros de Castro's refusal to fully synthesize opposites (2010: 106) successfully parallels Burnett's distinction of 'categories of the Shakespearean' in non-anglophone films. These categories are visible traces of a complex process of textual anthropophagy that takes us to Del Arco's previous work, for the combined analyses of *Furias* and such precedents shed more light on the strength of the Shakespearean categories in this film than what may result from a reading of the film in isolation. If, as Viveiros de Castro says, the Amerindian construction of the self takes place in relation to the other (2010: 152), Del Arco's authorial self has been progressively strengthened in relation to the other's (including Shakespeare's) authorial self.

Shakespearean citations, allusions and revisions in *Las Furias*

Del Arco admits that the film's title leaves little room for interpretation (Del Arco interview with author, Madrid, 15 September 2017). The word 'Furias' conjures up cycles of murder between family members. Those to blame for such murders, following Aeschylus' *Eumenides*, arguably should be put to public trial and then, after the accused is exonerated or punished, a renewed pact should follow. Diana Mangas says that, while watching the film, the viewer slowly gets involved in the characters' 'peculiar traumas and fears and a feeling of unrest surfaces caused by a claustrophobic atmosphere which seems to offer no plausible alternative' (2016). If we accept that the film's para-texts predetermine the viewer's expectations in this way, the Shakespearean references indicate departures from such a template.

The film presents four unmistakable textual citations of Shakespeare's *Macbeth* (5.5.77–88), *Hamlet* (5.1.260, 263–268), *King Lear* (3.2.16–19) and *Twelfth Night* (5.1.382–385, 390–393). Such citations are uttered by Leo, who associates them to what happens in particular scenes. Apart from these citations, I identify nearly twenty allusions to Shakespearean works. The first shot features the Furies as threatening embodiments of evil visually resembling representations of the Witches in the opening scene of *Macbeth*. Ghost-like characters are frequent visitors at banquet scenes in *Furias*. The Ghost of Leo – dressed up as Oedipus – frightens María when the family dines at a time of extreme tension. Often, she also feels the presence of the Furies after heated family arguments have taken place over dinner. She has visions of the Furies on top of the cliffs in a shot paralleling Orson Welles's depiction of the Weird Sisters on top of a crag in *Macbeth* (1948). Aki's Oedipal obsession and his desire to find out the truth about his family through fictional devices approximates him to Hamlet. Though, contrarily to the Danish Prince, Aki's father Leo is alive, his Alzheimer's turns him into a ghost-like presence whose views on past events, contrarily to Old Hamlet's, cannot be heard.

Due to his artistic, personal and professional failures, Aki fancies himself an outcast and revels in that role. He calls himself 'the fish man' evoking how characters in *The Tempest* repeatedly refer to Caliban. And, like Prospero's slave, Aki is convinced that he is going to be deprived of his rightful inheritance. This suspicion is confirmed when he discovers Julia and Marga's relationship and by the fact that his mother plans to sell the family property, Casa Alegre, to travel around the world with Julia. The disgust he feels when he discovers his mother's romance parallels Hamlet's disgust at Gertrude's sexual relationship with Claudius.

María's psychotic stroke leads her to attempt suicide by drowning, recalling Ophelia's death. This scene's association with Shakespeare's play is strengthened with Leo's delivery of Hamlet's lines at Ophelia's grave while María is rescued:

> ¿Qué harías tú por ella? ¿Llorar? ¿Pelear? ¿Ayunar? ¿Despedazarte? ¿Beber vinagre? ¿Comerte un cocodrilo? Todo lo haré. ¿O has venido a lloriquear? ¿A hacerte el valiente saltando a su tumba? Si quieres enterrarte vivo con ella, yo también. (Del Arco 2016a: 97)[4]

While many viewers would have regarded María's death as too predictable an outcome, Del Arco's decision to let María survive was challenged by critics (Del Arco interview with author, Madrid, 15 September 2017). If these critics were expecting María's death, they might have thought of

Ophelia's drowning as a source for the scene. Aki previously refers to María and Leo as 'the mad king and his fool' (Del Arco 2016a: 41). In fact, during María's suicide attempt, comic absurdity surfaces when we perceive that neither of them handles the situation properly. Leo's Alzheimer's does not let him reason with his granddaughter to prevent her suicide. She cannot persuade Leo to leave her alone and her first attempts at drowning fail because the water flow repeatedly returns her to the surface. On the other hand, María and Leo's relationship reminds us of the intimate and affectionate love between Lear and Cordelia before the first and final scenes in Shakespeare's tragedy as much as of the complicity between Lear and the Fool. For this reason, considering Cordelia's fate, anyone familiar with both Shakespearean tragedies might have felt inclined to expect her death.

The film's conclusion, which tested some critics' tolerance to mixtures of genres, would not have been misplaced in Shakespearean romances, where forgiveness, sudden reconciliation and even apparent resurrections come when least expected. For all that, hints at reconciliation are shown long before the film's conclusion. Aki finds Leo shouting Lear's lines in the middle of the woods under the rain, a proper scenario for *Lear*. Unlike Lear, Leo has not been forsaken, but he lacks the authority he once had over his children and Marga. Father and son momentarily confront each other. With the citation from *Lear*, Leo unconsciously appeals to his son's filial love: 'Vuestro viejo padre, generoso, que os lo dio todo de corazón … *(Llora)* No me aman … No me aman' (Del Arco 2016a: 69).[5] Though Leo lacks the lucidity to verbalize his pain, we may discern his regret at Aki's harshness at him. Nevertheless, Aki, who has shown utter contempt for his father, now approaches him and helps him walk back home. Aki's surprising reaction proves that a narrative of forgiveness begins to counter-effect the film's tragic horizons.

Several other allusions emphasize the potentially traumatic experiences the family go through. While the Ponte Alegres ultimately engage in new dynamics of alliance transcending the state of division which has predominated, Héctor's rape of his fiancée Ana parallels the foundation of the Roman Republic after Tarquin's rape of an innocent woman in *The Rape of Lucrece*. Del Arco himself recognizes echoes of Lear's repudiation of Cordelia in Marga's rash decision to sell Casa Alegre, where the family has been meeting every summer for decades. In both *Lear* and *Furias*, not hearing what one wants to hear spurs family division. As Marga does not find her daughter's words comforting, she decides to forgo the only remaining space shared by them all (Del Arco interview with author, Madrid, 15 September 2017). Héctor's announcement of his upcoming death by cancer at his own wedding echoes the apparent time coincidence of Claudius and Gertrude's wedding and Old Hamlet's funeral.

The references also politically revise Shakespeare's source texts. In Shakespeare's comedies, the sexual attraction women feel for women disguised as men and the attraction men feel for women disguised as men are resolved by heterosexual standards; as Sebastian says to Olivia in *Twelfth Night*:

> So comes it, lady, you have been mistook;
> But nature to her bias drew in that.
> You would have been contracted to a maid,
> Nor are you therein, by my life, deceived.
>
> (*TN* 5.1.255–258)

As Keir Elam says, Sebastian absolves Olivia 'of the (well-founded) suspicion of homoerotic desire' (Shakespeare 2008: 342). In *Furias* the lesbian relationship between Marga and Julia is not hidden by cross-dressing. This union also seems to ironically respond to Orsino's prescription on the choosing of wives:

> Let still the woman take
> An elder than herself; so wears she to him,
> So sways she level in her husband's heart.
>
> (*TN* 2.4.29–31)

Contrarily to Shakespeare's text, in *Las Furias* it is an elder woman who bestows her hopes on a younger one. Prejudices based on age resonate with Hamlet's resentment at his mother's second marriage:

> You cannot call it love, for at your age
> The heyday in the blood is tame, it's humble
> And waits upon judgement
>
> (*Ham* 3.4.66–68)

When addressing Marga privately after his discovery, Aki pretends to be chilled at the image of the two women – Julia and Marga – together (Del Arco 2016a: 78).

Cultural Anthropophagy as adaptation process

Linda Hutcheon conceives adaptation as a process of creation and reception ([2006] 2013: 7–8). This allows us to think beyond the limits of a single work of art when tackling the author's decisions. In this light, Del Arco's ingestion of Shakespearean sources gives way to textual exchanges ultimately helping the author's delineation of recurrent themes in his dramaturgies.

Primarily, the author's interest in women's stories of struggle for emancipation and denunciation of abuse presents clear Shakespearean precedents. As a theatre director, Del Arco's first Shakespearean production was *La Violación de Lucrecia*, performed at the Teatro Español in 2010. In this meta-theatrical solo performance Nuria Espert played a rehearsal of Shakespeare's dramatic poem. After a few attempts at reciting the lines, Espert gets stuck at 'la *púdica* mujer de Colatino' (Espert's emphasis).[6] She breaks character unconvinced of the need to defend Lucrece's chastity: 'Esto a mí ya no me ... Eso ya no ...'.[7] So, she restarts the run-through rehearsal after politically implying that the play's stakes do not concern the loss of Lucrece's chastity but the denunciation of Tarquin's criminal act. Doubtless, underlining this idea addressed worries shared by Spanish audiences alarmed at the waves of gender violence of recent decades.

A similar concern is perceived in Del Arco's production of *Hamlet* (Teatro de la Comedia, Madrid, 2016), where Ophelia is openly sexually involved with the Prince. The actor playing Ophelia, Ángela Cremonte, capitalizes on Ophelia's sexual vivacity when she sings *reggaeton* in the madness scene. Yet, the political point Del Arco makes through Hamlet and Ophelia's relationship returns to the denunciation of gender violence. In Shakespeare's tragedy, Ophelia only retells her encounter with Hamlet to Polonius (*Ham* 2.1.84–93), but Del Arco stages the complete event as if Ophelia had omitted important details. In this version, after taking leave from the Ghost, Hamlet – played by Israel Elejalde – puts on a death mask and explains to the sleeping Ophelia the resolutions addressed to Horatio and Marcellus in Shakespeare's source:

Hay más cosas en la tierra y en el cielo
de las que sueña nuestra filosofía.[8] (*Silencio*)
A partir de ahora no será fácil entender mi conducta
pues en lo sucesivo tal vez deba vestirme de lunática actitud.
(Del Arco 2016b: 38)

Then he utters the last words Polonius will later read in the Prince's love letter:

Adiós, mi amor, tuyo por siempre
mientras esta máquina siga siendo mía.[9]
(Del Arco 2016b: 38)

After this, he tries to wipe away Ophelia's make-up with his shirt. She resists this, but he presses her face with a pillow for some seconds before she escapes (2016b: 38). Ophelia's omission of this attempt at smothering runs analogous to Ana's silence in *Furias*. This unpunished sexual abuse has been challenged by critics like Fon López, who claims that 'rape culture is still sheltered under cinema' (2016). Whatever we may think of this recurrent argument on the filmic representation of rape, Del Arco's characters' frequent anti-misogynist stances are noticeable in his works. In *Juicio* (2013) and *Refugio* (2017), the characters of Helen and Sima echo Hamlet's scornful evaluation of language ('Palabras, palabras, palabras').[10] The Ghost of Sima, a refugee drowned in the ocean with her child, accuses her surviving husband, Farid, of playing with words to excuse himself, for he abandoned them both to save his own life. Helen cites Hamlet to scorn men's historical fabrications through misogynist discourse: 'Palabras, palabras, palabras' (Del Arco 2017a: 22). Yet, the author's critiques of unsuccessful male – female cooperations are accompanied by alternatives of alliance. For Del Arco:

> Women have so often heard that there are things that they cannot do that they still think things through more than men before undertaking certain enterprises. It is necessary to achieve the boldness which considers the possibility of failure with less self-consciousness. (Del Arco interview with author, Madrid, 15 September 2017)

In his *Hamlet*, Gertrude (Ana Wagener) and Claudius (Daniel Freire) are visited by Rosencrantz and Guildenstern while they both enjoy themselves in bed. As the spectators see, the Queen – who, during sexual intercourse, cries '¡Viva Dinamarca!'[11] – disagrees with her son's prescriptions on age and sexuality. Marga also intends to enjoy a healthy sexual life with her much younger partner. Yet, like the Danish Queen, she finds herself pushed to a reckoning with Aki. The Prince of Denmark's taunts successfully provoke the Queen's remorse:

> O Hamlet, speak no more.
> Thou turn'st my very eyes into my soul
> And there I see such black and grieved spots
> As will leave there their tinct.
>
> (*Ham* 3.4.86–89)

Aki's reaction when he discovers Marga and Julia's relationship momentarily produces the same effect. Incapable of facing her son, Marga leaves the scene followed by Julia:

> **JULIA**   This had to happen sooner or later, Marga. It wasn't the best way, but now you've got the chance to …
> **MARGA**   I can't …
> **JULIA**   What's done is done!
> **MARGA**   I have seen myself in his eyes …
> **JULIA**   What, what have you seen? …
> **MARGA**   Myself. I …
> (Del Arco 2016a: 68)

Nevertheless, Marga's feeling of guilt is momentary and Aki's manipulative efforts backfire. Even Hamlet and Aki can see why their mothers' second relationships are just as natural as any other. If the Prince did not himself write the lines in which the Player King liberates his wife from any obligations of faithfulness in widowhood (*Ham* 3.2.180–209), he certainly allowed the players to keep that section in *The Murder of Gonzago*. As for Aki, once Julia publicly announces the relationship at Héctor's wedding, he appeals to the guests' knowledge of Shakespeare: 'There's still time for *a double wedding*!' (Del Arco 2016a: 83, emphasis mine). Under Aki's slightly homophobic joke lies the hidden recognition that Marga and Julia's relationship is legitimate, for he himself suggests the wedding. Double weddings, common in Shakespearean comedy and romance, are preceded by disturbing histories of jealousy, gender violence, slander, denigration, mistrust, remorse, separation and despair. They imply a new social pact leaving these disturbing, unsettling and violent past histories behind. What Aki has been describing as a tragic doom extending over their family, he now refashions as comedy or romance. After he knows of Julia and Marga's affair, he interrogates his own perception on the narrative embedding the family: 'Is this something you felt coming all your life or is it a recent discovery? It has made me rethink all our family history' (Del Arco 2016a: 78).

Aki's rethinking seems insufficient to effect any positive change in the environment, but his reasoning is prophetic, for the tragic narrative wherein he wants to entrap the family is consistently altered, among other things, by the arrival of a stranger. In this regard, the film's plot twists implicitly comment on the emotional, political and ideological crises that the Spanish nation has traversed in the last decades. At the film's première, a member of the jury for the 65th International Seminci Film Festival said that *Furias* reflected the current state of the nation like no other Spanish film had:

> The Ponte Alegres' internal division was seen as a metaphor of Spain: a bunch of people shouting at each other, never trying to pay attention to what the other has to say, never seeing that the other may have a reasonable point to defend … And, as a consequence, a great house is bound to fall down. (Del Arco interview with author, Madrid, 15 September 2017)

Marta Medina's review seems to rephrase this:

> Oh, the family! This distinctively Spanish 'neither-with-you-nor-without-you' obsession, a cross-section which turns Del Arco's *Las Furias* into this great set of contradictions, including the best and the worst qualities of human beings, and which could be the sketch of our contemporary Spain, filled with brothers and 'brothers-in-law',[12] a hen house where cackling prevails over 'please', 'thanks', or 'I apologise', so much so that sometimes they seem taboo. (2016)

As Del Arco suggests, Spanish media pundits and politicians rarely do much to disprove such diagnosis (Medina 2016; Del Arco interview with author, Madrid, 15 September 2017). Though he admits that he did not have such a metaphor in mind when making the film, his works reflect on this phenomenon. The downfall of the 'great house' resonates with Del Arco's reworking of Pyrrhus's speech in *Hamlet*. In his adaptation of the Danish play, he has the First Player recite Shakespeare's Sonnet 13 instead of Pyrrhus's speech. The speaker incites the reader to breed to prevent the father's great name and legacy from being lost:

> ¿Quién deja derrumbarse una casa tan imponente
> donde pueda preservarse todo este legado
> contra los duros días del invierno helado,
> contra el yermo y frío furor de la eterna muerte?
> (Del Arco 2016b: 45)[13]

The 'great house' in *Furias* resonates with the *casa imponente* in the sonnet, both of them arguably standing for the family seen as the nation in their respective contexts of performance. And, as far as Del Arco is concerned, the fall of the Spanish *casa imponente* has to do with the violent, intolerant, unreasonable, unreflective and rash ways in which language is perverted in the Spanish media by representatives and politicians of all affiliations (Del Arco interview with author, Madrid, 15 September 2017). It is not surprising that Hamlet's translated expression 'Palabras, palabras, palabras' iterates through Del Arco's work as words, as the author often affirms in many interviews, used as projectiles blocking social, political, educational, artistic and economic progress in Spain.

As suggested, a resource Del Arco frequently uses to destabilize established social dynamics is the inclusion of a stranger. In *Refugio*, the refugee Farid alters coexistence at the house of the socialist politician Suso Santisteban, who hosts him. This refugee dies in despair but the politician's strength is renewed through Farid's death, for he capitalizes on this incident by making use of a new discourse of compassion for campaign purposes. His theatrical-political speech is invigorated after the visitor's death. In *Hamlet*, the Argentinian

actor Daniel Freire plays Claudius, the Ghost and the First
Player. Freire belongs to the breed of actors from overseas
who have developed their careers in both the Spanish and
the Argentinian theatre and cinema. When Hamlet meets the
First Player, he asks him whether he is a good actor (Del Arco
2016b: 45). Polonius interjects: 'Buenísimo. ¡Es argentino!'[14]
This metafictional wink at the audience evokes the circulating
myths on the Argentinian obsessively psychological acting
method. For a while, Freire's Argentinian pedigree and the
strength the production gains thanks to his presence are
foregrounded. The Argentinian–Spanish coalition is intensified
when Elejalde as Hamlet interjects lines in English ('England?
Very good!') after Claudius announces to the Prince his
decision to send him away.[15] Having the most representative
character in English literature mockingly drop lines in English
might be read as the company's provocative reminder that
the Spanish language could be as natural to the Prince as the
English one. This Spanish–Argentinian alliance reappears in
Furias since Lennie, both Argentinian and Spanish, uses her
Latin American accent for Julia. It is her presence that, in
Aki's opinion, will alter the family's future (Del Arco 2016a:
81). After Aki proposes the 'double wedding', Héctor may
have picked up on the Shakespearean undertones, but he
does not find them funny and concludes his brother's farce
by announcing his own future death. A silent celebration
ensues in which it is difficult to distinguish where the wedding
ends and where the funeral begins, but some plot twists come
precipitately. Forgiveness, rescue and renewal of bonds of
love – between Marga and Julia, Gus and Casandra, Héctor
and Ana, Héctor and Aki – and the birth of a baby on the beach
transform the tragic burden of the film near its conclusion. The
help the united family lend to another stranger, Nekane, with
giving birth symbolizes their transcendence of myth and the
beginning of society, a process described by Viveiros de Castro
(2010: 129). By getting rid of the shackles of myth, the Ponte
Alegres seemingly embrace a new social order.

Cultural Anthropophagy as metafiction

Viveiros de Castro regards the philosophy of anthropophagy as a self-referential system of production of concepts (2010: 210). The cannibal ceremony involved highly theatricalized rituals consisting of the exchanges of symbols between warrior and victim. After the execution, the warrior exhibited the symbols he had acquired. Therefore, the construction of the warrior's identity had as much to do with the exchange as with its representation. If we accept Viveiros de Castro's thesis on the unity of spirit between peoples, we may draw parallels between the symbolic appeal of ancient anthropophagy and the pleasure the audiences must have felt, according to Jeremy Lopez (2003), at recognizing conventional theatrical and literary devices in the Renaissance theatre.

Examining the film's reflexivity in relation to Del Arco's previous works sheds light on the transition between myth and alliance I have traced as a key element in the plot. Del Arco's application of the *theatrum mundi* metaphor satirizes social and political hypocrisy, denounces artistic prostitution and creates analogies between fiction and the passage of time. In *Hamlet*, as he says, the hero

> is perfectly conscious of the strength of [a] theatrical machine … this noise one can hear all over the world. He feels himself part of this mechanism. He tries to play the game to profit from it, but he knows too well that this machine will crush him. (Del Arco interview with author, Madrid, 15 September 2017)

In Del Arco's *Hamlet*, curtains open and close inside the stage suggesting a performance offstage as well as in the playing area. When Rosencrantz and Guildenstern approach Hamlet, he shushes at them as a neurotic stage manager so they do not interrupt the farce taking place backstage.[16] *Furias* was written and shot before the rehearsals for *Hamlet* started. Nonetheless, in an interview, Del Arco suggests parallels between the mixture of tragedy and comedy in *Hamlet* and the repetition of this mixture in *Furias* (Ramón 2016). It does not seem implausible that Del Arco, directly or indirectly, drew on *Hamlet* when producing *Furias*. Also, *Furias* seems to anticipate how Del Arco capitalizes on metafiction in *Hamlet*. In *Furias*, the backstage scene is recorded and Aki uses the tape as a source for his book. In his editing room, he collects and patches up newspaper cuttings, photographs and other reminders of the past to reconstruct his family drama. Yet, Aki's book writing poses many questions for the viewers. For a start, we are not told whether it is intended as fiction or as family biography, for the Spanish word *historia* used by Aki can encompass both meanings. Despite Aki's apparent concern with telling the truth about the family (Del Arco 2016a: 40), we intuit that, like the Danish Prince, he takes several opportunities to rebuke his mother:

> **AKI**   Mum ... *(Silence)* I feel terrible for the things I said to you the other day on the phone.
> **MARGA**   And don't you feel terrible for the atrocities you wrote in the last pages you sent me?
> **AKI**   *(Smiling)* Are you asking me if I feel them terribly or if I feel terrible for having written them?
> (Del Arco 2016a: 35)

In this respect, Aki is his father's son. In the flashback scene, after María's retelling of the origins of the Furies, Leo stares at Marga – who, presumably, has recently divorced him or told him that she intends to do so – and declares:

> When somebody turns against the family, they [the Furies] inhabit this person's mind ... That's why we need to be careful with hurting our own people. It never goes unpunished. (Del Arco 2016a: 3)

Additionally, Aki does not miss a chance to imply parallels between the family's history and literary events, a tendency he champions though it is by no means only his. He takes for granted that everyone believes in the Furies' existence and, seriously or not, he seems to believe in them too. Also, the pleasure he feels at being trapped in his traumatic relationship with Leo and Marga smacks of Oedipal obsession. Likewise, judging from the allusion to 'the mad King and his fool', he shows an interest in his father's acting career, which fuels such obsessions. Interestingly, as we get to know, Aki has never pursued any career – drama or psychoanalysis – seriously. By contrast, Héctor, who, as far as we know, never wanted to become an artist, remembers lines from *Macbeth* when Leo delivers them in the park. His self-absorbed second repetition of the Scottish king's lines to himself evinces his knowledge that death is beckoning. The dangers of taking fiction too seriously are much more perceptible in María, who risks her life trying to kill a pig in order to appease the Furies.

As already explored, the film's reflexivity progressively leads us through the transition the family undertakes. The initial allusions to *Theogony*, *Oedipus* and *Macbeth* work as prolepses of tragedy. As already noted, Leo's recitation of Lear's fragment runs against the grain of the scene's resolution. Leo's recollection of Hamlet's lines seems entirely misplaced after María's rescue. When reconciliation, celebration and the new birth come together in Del Arco's finale, the Furies, whom María had seen rejoicing on top of the cliffs, have been banished and only the mountains, the sky, the sand and the sea water are visible. According to the script, 'María dances around [Leo] celebrating the Furies' appeasement. Leo follows her' (Del Arco 2016a: 99). In the film, Leo sings verses one and three of Feste's final song from *As You Like It* in Spanish. The first verse deals with the memory of childhood, when 'a foolish thing was but a toy' (*TN* 5.1.382–385). In Spanish, this line is translated with a more ambiguous meaning: 'Jugar era lo mismo que vivir.'[17] In the third verse, 'swaggering' is replaced with the more general concept of *juego*: 'El juego lleva siempre a perder.'[18] While the theatrical connotations of *playing* are more frequent in English than in Spanish, the use of the expression *juego teatral* is not infrequent in the latter. While the translation decontextualizes the song's cultural implications, it serves Del Arco's specific meta-theatrical purposes since the general allusion to life as a game where humans are bound to lose might point to Hamlet's negative vision of theatre in the director's adaptation. Yet, in *Furias*, pointing at 'playing' as a thing of the past may imply that the family moves beyond tragic obsessions. Alternatively, in this context where reconciliation and forgiveness have occurred with such dexterity, the author's suggestion may oppose the Prince's perception of theatre as a destructive machine. Rather, Del Arco's invitation may be read as a rethinking of Shakespeare's influence as a transitionary force towards alliance.

Conclusions

The abundance of references to Shakespearean sources in *Furias* reveals Shakespeare-inflected salient points in areas of indiscernibility between the Shakespearean literary materials and the adapter's words. Paying attention to such citations, allusions and revisitations allows us to define the adaptation process as a symbolic exchange of texts. Shakespearean references amount to no more than a collection of quotes if they are taken as isolated annotations. When seen in relation to Del Arco's previous work, they are indeed gear shifts in his ongoing authorial processes of textual anthropophagy. These Shakespearean references would have been less effective if they had not helped effect any transformation in the narrative.

Studying these references as part of the adaptation processes involves taking a retrospective look at Del Arco's dramaturgy, and drawing relations between *Furias* and his Shakespearean and non-Shakespearean works. This has permitted us to think – rhizomatically – of Del Arco's ingestion of Shakespeare's texts. The transformation those texts undergo while the author processes them delineates themes recurrent in his non-Shakespearean work. I have traced how Del Arco's interest in rape and gender violence narratives are partly the result of his Shakespearean feeding. While Shakespearean source materials are rethought in the process of adaptation, the works derived from processing these texts propel the author's own political statements in favour of social emancipation and dialogue.

Brazilian anthropophagy was a symbolic system of identity construction deeply ingrained in mythical beliefs. While this may sound alienating for members of non-Western and Western secular societies, these mythical narratives may be valuable if they run counter to self-destructive narratives. In *Furias*, uncritical attachment to Hesiodic and Oedipal myths seems to determine the tone of the story and, by extension, the viewers' expectations of it. I have pointed out the Shakespearean textual accidents that redirect the film's tragic horizons and, with these, the characters' horizons too. Therefore, while the meta-theatrical machinery in Del Arco's other works – such as *Hamlet* – may provoke sociopolitical anxiety, in *Furias*, reflexivity points at the replacement of past obsessions with alternative worldviews. In accordance with Viveiros de Castro's thesis, we may perceive the 'other' as the expression of a possible world for the self (2010: 211). Del Arco's film reformulates its own narrative to imagine a possible world in the other. Shakespearean references, as I have shown, run along this transition and often they drive it forward.

Notes

1   *Las Furias* tells the story of the Ponte Alegre family. The actor
    Leonardo Ponte and Margarita (Marga) Alegre, a practising
    psychologist, have christened their sons and daughter Héctor,
    Aquiles (Aki) and Casandra after Homer's characters. Héctor
    is a successful lawyer engaged to the healthcare worker
    Ana. Casandra works as a fortune-teller on a radio show.
    She is married to the unemployed musician Gus. After their

daughter María recovers from a psychotic episode, Gus discovers Casandra is having an affair with a colleague. In the meantime, Leo, affected by Alzheimer's, constantly recalls lines from Shakespeare's plays, which he occasionally delivers for imaginary audiences. Fully independent from Leo, Marga maintains a relationship with Julia, forty years her junior. Afraid of revealing her homosexuality, she decides to sell Casa Alegre, the family property, to eliminate all remaining bonds with her relatives. When he finds out about Marga's decision, Héctor suggests holding his wedding with Ana at the house for one last family gathering there. Aki is focused on writing the family history. During this intense re-encounter, grudges, aggravations and resentments set off huge arguments. When Aki discovers Marga and Julia's relationship, he threatens his mother with telling everyone unless she does not sell the house. The family soon discovers a secret harder to bear: Héctor announces that he will soon die of cancer. The film concludes with an accumulation of incidents that spontaneously solve themselves. Two family members attempt to commit suicide and another disappears into the sea. The two attempts are prevented and the lost person (Casandra) is found. Nekane, a friend of the family who has tried to help them, gives birth on the beach where everyone gathers.

2 Julie Sanders defines 'citation' as 'a passage cited or quoted, with the embedded legal sense of reference to works of authority'. For Sanders, allusions are 'indirect or passing' references. 'Revisions' involve a change in the politics embedded in a text (2006: 161, 163).

3 Acknowledgements are owed to Marta Cerezo Moreno, for her feedback and suggestions; to Miguel del Arco for partaking in an interview and for responding to many questions via email and telephone; to the Centro de Documentación Teatral (Spanish Ministry of Education, Culture and Sports) for facilitating access to the recordings of Del Arco's productions; to Kamikaze Producciones for answering several questions via email; to Pedro Hernández, Aitor Tejada and Kamikaze Producciones for granting permission to use the film poster.

4 See original text in *Hamlet* (5.1.260, 263–268).

5 See original text in *King Lear* (3.2.16–19).

6   Original text: 'Of Collatine's fair love, Lucrece the chaste' (7).
     In Katherine Duncan-Jones and H. R. Woudhuysen's edition of
     Shakespeare's Poems (Shakespeare 2007). Seen in *La Violación
     de Lucrecia* (Del Arco 2009). Recording by Instituto Nacional
     de las Artes Escénicas y de la Música (INAEM).

7   Translation to English: 'This doesn't [convince] me anymore…
     This doesn't, anymore… '. In *La Violación de Lucrecia* (Del
     Arco 2009).

8   Original text: 'There are more things in heaven and earth (…) /
     Than are dreamt of in your philosophy' (*Ham* 1.5.165–166).

9   Original text: 'Adieu. Thine evermore, most dear lady, whilst
     this machine is to him' (*Ham* 2.2.120–121).

10   Original text: 'Words, words, words' (*Ham* 2.2.189).

11   See recording of *Hamlet* (Del Arco 2016a). Recorded by INAEM.

12   In contemporary Spanish popular culture, the stereotype of the
     cuñado (brother-in-law) generally refers to the caricature of an
     opinionated male who constantly needs to prove his knowledge
     on any subject. While the term is colloquial, it is often used to
     refer to media pundits and politicians.

13   Original text: 'Who lets so fair a house fall to decay, / Which
     husbandry in honour might uphold / Against the stormy gusts
     of winter's day / And barren rage of death's eternal cold?'
     (9–12). See Katherine Duncan-Jones's edition of *Shakespeare's
     Sonnets* (Shakespeare 2004).

14   Translation to English: 'Very good! He's from Argentina!' See
     recording of Del Arco's *Hamlet*.

15   See recording of Del Arco's *Hamlet*.

16   Ibid.

17   Translation: 'Playing was the same thing as living.'

18   Translation: 'The game always makes us losers.'

References

Burnett, M. T. (2017), 'Adaptation, Shakespeare and World
     Cinema', *Literature/Film Quarterly*, 45 (2). Available online:

www.salisbury.edu/lfq/_issues/first/adaptation_shakespeare_and_world_cinema.html (accessed 27 February 2018).

Burnett, M. T. and R. Wray (2006), 'Introduction', in M. T. Burnett and R. Wray (eds), *Screening Shakespeare in the Twenty-First Century*, 1–12, Edinburgh: Edinburgh University Press.

Del Arco, M. (2016a), *Las Furias*, Madrid: Unpublished script.

Del Arco, M. (2016b), *Hamlet de William Shakespeare (Versión y Dirección de Miguel del Arco)*, Madrid: Ministerio de Educación, Cultura y Deporte, Secretaría de Estado de Cultura, INAEM – CNTC.

Del Arco, M. (2017a), *Juicio a una Zorra*, 3rd edition, Madrid: Ediciones Antígona.

Del Arco, M. (2017b), *Refugio*, Madrid: Centro Dramático Nacional, INAEM (Instituto Nacional de las Artes Escénicas y de la Música), Ministerio de Educación, Cultura y Deporte, Gobierno de España.

Hamlet (2016), [Film] Dir. Miguel del Arco, Madrid: Compañía Nacional de Teatro Clásico and Instituto Nacional de las Artes Escénicas y de la Música (INAEM).

Harrison, K. (2017), *Shakespeare, Bakhtin and Film (A Dialogic Lens)*, Nanaimo: Macmillan.

Hesiod (2006), *Theogony (Works and Days Testimonia)*, ed. and trans. Glenn W. Most, Cambridge, MA: Harvard University Press.

Hutcheon, L. ([2006] 2013), 'Beginning to Theorize Adaptation', in L. Hutcheon and S. O'Flynn (eds), *A Theory of Adaptation*, 2nd edition, 1–32, Abingdon: Routledge.

Lanier, D. (2014), 'Shakespearean Rhizomatics: Adaptation, Ethics, Value', in A. Huang and E. Rivlin (eds), *Shakespeare and the Ethics of Appropriation*, 21–40, New York: Palgrave Macmillan.

Las Furias (2016), [Film] Dir. Miguel del Arco, Spain: Aquí y Allí Films and Kamikaze Producciones.

La Violación de Lucrecia (2010), [Film] Dir. Miguel del Arco, Madrid: Teatro Español and Instituto Nacional de las Artes Escénicas y de la Música (INAEM).

Lopez, J. (2003), *Theatrical Convention and Audience Response in Early Modern Drama*, Cambridge: Cambridge University Press.

López, F. (2016), 'La Cultura de la Violación Sigue Amparada por el Cine', *El Palomitrón*, 8 November. Available online: http://elpalomitron.com/la-cultura-de-la-violacion-sigue-amparada-por-el-cine/ (accessed 17 September 2017).

Mangas, D. (2016), 'Crítica de Las Furias: Promesas de un Final
    Devastador', *Los Interrogantes*, 18 November. Available online:
    https://losinterrogantes.com/cine/criticas/pelicula-las-furias
    (accessed 1 October 2017).

Medina, M. (2016), '"Las Furias" de Miguel del Arco: España
    Como esa Familia Incapaz de Entenderse', *El Confidencial*,
    23 November. Available online: www.elconfidencial.com/
    cultura/2016-10-23/seminci-2016-61-edicion-valladolid-
    cine_1278072/ (accessed 30 July 2017).

Ramón, E. (2016), '"Las Furias", La Guerra de Troya Familia de
    Miguel del Arco', *RTVE*, 22 November. Available online: www.
    rtve.es/noticias/20161022/furias-guerra-troya-familiar-miguel-
    del-arco/1430381.shtml (accessed 17 September 2017).

Sanders, J. (2006), *Adaptation and Appropriation*, London:
    Routledge.

Sanz, D. F. (2013), 'El Fenómeno del Canibalismo en las Fuentes
    Literarias Grecorromanas: su Mención en la Mitología y la
    Filosofía Antigua', *Emérita, Revista de Lingüística y Filología
    Clásica*, 81 (1): 111–135.

Shakespeare, W. (1997), *King Lear*, ed. R. A. Foakes, third series,
    London: Bloomsbury Arden Shakespeare.

Shakespeare, W. (2004), *Shakespeare's Sonnets*, ed. Katherine
    Duncan-Jones, The Arden Shakespeare, third series, London:
    Thomson Learning.

Shakespeare, W. (2005), *Hamlet*, ed. A. Thompson and N. Taylor,
    third series, rev. edition, London: Bloomsbury Arden Shakespeare.

Shakespeare, W. (2007), 'The Rape of Lucrece', in Katherine
    Duncan-Jones and H. R. Woudhuysen (eds), *Shakespeare's Poems*,
    The Arden Shakespeare, third series, 10–81, London: Thomson
    Learning.

Shakespeare, W. (2008), *Twelfth Night*, ed. Keir Elam, The Arden
    Shakespeare, third series, London: Bloomsbury Publishing.

Shakespeare, W. (2015), *Macbeth*, ed. S. Clark and P. Mason, third
    series, London: Bloomsbury Arden Shakespeare.

Viveiros de Castro, E. (1992), *From the Enemy's Point of View
    (Humanity and Divinity in the Amazonian Society)*, trans.
    Catherine V. Howard, Chicago: University of Chicago Press.

Viveiros de Castro, E. (2010), *Metafísicas Caníbales (Líneas de
    Antropofagia Postestructural)*, trans. Stella Mastrangelo, Buenos
    Aires: Katz Editores.

3

Devouring Shakespeare in north-eastern Brazil: Clowns de Shakespeare director Fernando Yamamoto in conversation with Paulo da Silva Gregório

Clowns de Shakespeare's award-winning *Sua Incelença, Ricardo III* is emblematic of the company's adaptive approach to Shakespeare. In this production, the troupe establishes an intricate dialogue between Shakespeare's play, musical, literary and theatrical elements distinctive of Brazil's north-east region, Western theatrical conventions, Shakespearean criticism and English rock music. While set in the fifteenth century, in the aftermath of the Wars of the Roses, the enactment of Ricardo's bloodthirsty ascent to power and his subsequent reign of terror alludes to Brazilian politics and the violence that still afflicts the north-eastern countryside: Ricardo is both a villain and a clown, a member of the English monarchy and a power-hungry oligarch from the north-east of Brazil.

Clowns' adaptive approach to Shakespeare's *Richard III* shows that rather than being a determining force in the production, Shakespeare is made to serve the troupe's purpose to theatrically realize his play with a north-eastern accent. This method of manipulating Shakespeare and reconfiguring the central position he often holds in Shakespearean performance can be better understood in light of the principles of Cultural Anthropophagy according to which the colonized devours and ingests the qualities of the colonizer without being culturally destroyed (George 1985: 21). Widely disseminated among the Brazilian intelligentsia through Oswald de Andrade's 'Manifesto Antropófago' (1928), Anthropophagy encourages Brazilian artists to 'immerse themselves in the early native's thoughts, looking at the European as they would – as a source of nutrients. They should not mimic their food by emulating European modernists. Instead, they should devour what was useful in the civilization while maintaining their natural, "primitive" state' (Budasz 2005: 2). Clowns' anthropophagic engagement with Shakespeare is implied in Yamamoto's perception of Shakespeare as a source of themes and 'quality dramaturgy'. What the troupe sees as the attributes of his drama is 'digested' and assimilated into their distinct theatrical idiom, deeply rooted in – though not limited to – the traditions of the north-east's popular culture. 'Ingested' in the adaptive process employed by Clowns, Shakespeare becomes a useful tool by which the troupe accomplishes their dramatic purposes.

This re-modelling of Shakespeare also signals the troupe's affiliation with another Brazilian theatre company whose re-workings of canonical texts have influenced the way Shakespeare is reproduced in Brazil: Grupo Galpão. Clowns' debt to Galpão, acknowledged by director Fernando Yamamoto in the conversation that follows, urges us to consider the complex ways in which Galpão anthropophagically reimagined Shakespeare's most popular love story. Adapting *Romeo and*

Juliet through the lens of both local traditions and performance practices characteristic of Western theatre, the troupe negotiated Shakespearean performativity between a local and global sphere. Galpão have performed throughout Brazil – mainly as street theatre – and abroad, and their participation in theatre festivals like Globe-to-Globe in 2000 and 2012 illustrates how *Romeu e Julieta*'s intersection of local and foreign cultural references breaks away from 'the constrained sense of the local, the indigenous, and the popular used to market their Shakespeare at the Globe' (Worthen 2003: 162). In Galpão's production, Shakespeare is immersed in a complex articulation of intertwined components: music, folklore and literature representative of the Brazilian state of Minas Gerais; clowning, circus and *commedia dell'arte* conventions; and performance modes associated with the work of European directors such as Peter Brook. Engaging both with Shakespeare and a 'globalized network of theatrical practices', Galpão's *Romeu e Julieta* problematizes the partial understanding of a global Shakespearean performativity as being homogeneous and subservient to the capitalist interests of the United States and northern Europe (Worthen 2003: 123). Furthermore, the production's refusal to provide dramatic elements that could be immediately recognized as 'Brazilian' further complicated The Globe's attempt to frame foreign productions within a 'metonymic, Disneyfying rhetoric' (Worthen 2003: 161), which reduced them to stereotypical cultural products to be consumed by a global audience.

In the same vein, Clowns reject any facile labelling of their Shakespearean reproductions as either local or global. The dynamics and demands of street performance, for which *Sua Incelença* was initially designed, are instrumental in shaping the troupe's reconstruction of Shakespeare's *Richard III* through an elaborate intermingling of the Shakespearean play with regional and European models. The re-creation of Brazilian popular songs and British rock, for instance, replaces the adapted Shakespeare text at given moments, and functions as a transitional device between different scenes, giving rise to a fast-paced production that fosters a stronger audience engagement in street performances.[1]

Sua Incelença's acute musicality is, in fact, one of the main marks of Clowns' endeavour to devour Shakespeare and perform his play in Brazilian terms. Representative of the troupe's theatrical identity is its *solaridade* – a concept Yamamoto will explain further below – where music, especially Brazilian north-eastern music, is a key component. *Muito Barulho por Quase Nada* (Much Ado about Almost Nothing, 2003) was their first successful attempt at recreating the Shakespearean play by making it resonate with the idiom of Brazil's north-east region. Shakespeare's comic plot acquires a new significance when relocated to Natal, the capital of Rio Grande do Norte, and interwoven with linguistic and musical elements peculiar to this region. Wearing costumes that evoke folkloric traditions of the north-east, the characters' distinctive accent and use of certain expressions (e.g. *galado*)[2] delineated the production's regional features, which were further signalled through the articulation of *forró*[3] and musical instruments used in *forró* songs in the performance (e.g. accordion, triangle, tambourine and drums). Adapting *Much Ado* with Brazilian audiences in mind, Clowns offer them the richness of the Shakespearean (translated) text without subordinating the north-east traditions to the universality often claimed for Shakespeare's works. Despite Yamamoto's belief that the adaptability of Shakespeare lies in his universalizing power, Clowns' negotiation between 'Shakespeare' – both an 'English cultural icon' and a 'powerful global brand' (Rumbold 2011: 88) – and north-eastern traditions foregrounds, instead, the site-specificity of Shakespearean theatre. Dennis Kennedy notes that 'universality is a tricky concept: often what we believe to have comprehensive attraction turns out to be more local or more time-bound than we think' (2001: 252). Adding that Shakespeare's wide appeal over time and space 'may be the result of the indeterminacy of his work rather than its universality', he suggests that 'resilience to change based on an artefact's elasticity' is perhaps what universality means (252). The adaptive process Shakespeare's *Much Ado* underwent in Clowns' hands contests the supposed comprehensiveness of Shakespeare's works on the one hand, and endorses Kennedy's association between the playwright's enduring appeal and the indeterminate and elastic nature of his theatre, on the other. Clowns' cannibalistic appropriation of Shakespeare reaffirms both the adaptability of his plays – a desired attribute that is 'eaten' in the adaptation process – and the need to digest and recycle his theatre in order to make it theatrically appealing to the taste of the troupe's target audiences.

Yamamoto's seeming attempt at invoking Shakespeare's universality to authorize Clowns' irreverent manipulation of his plays reflects W. B. Worthen's understanding of how 'a theatrical practice that works to displace, disrupt, or disintegrate the Shakespearean text is sustained by a constant assertion of fidelity to the globby essence of "Shakespeare"' (1997: 63). This attitude seems, however, at odds with Clowns' anthropophagic methods of adaptation that go far beyond a simple realization of Shakespeare's 'universal' meanings onstage. Drawing a parallel between the term 'local Shakespeare' and the 'perceived universality' of Shakespearean works, Huang remarks that 'local appropriations and readings of Shakespeare are no longer perceived as straightforward mimicry of originals of a higher order [...], but as key sites that produce local banks of knowledge that, in turn, reshape the Shakespearean epistemology' (2007: 25). This creative appropriation of Shakespeare's works at specific performance sites problematizes the relationship between centre/margin, indigenous/foreign, in the development of distinctively local theatre language.

The processes by which Shakespeare was anthropophagically incorporated into an amalgam of elements of local and foreign cultures in *Muito Barulho* gained a new dimension in Clowns' *Sua Incelença, Ricardo III*, first performed in 2010 in the troupe's own acting space based in Natal, under the direction of Gabriel Villela (Grupo Galpão) and co-direction of Fernando Yamamoto. Villela's involvement with Clowns was instrumental in promoting their internationalization (Spinelli 2016: 112), and *Sua Incelença* marks their first effort to leap into the global marketplace and to achieve an international reputation. If Shakespeare's foreignness was mainly negotiated with Brazilian north-eastern cultural forms in *Muito Barulho*, this negotiation was further complicated through a creative engagement with both the local and other foreign dramatic sources in *Sua Incelença*. The production's costumes, sets and music were articulated to establish a dramatic connection between the cultural traditions of the north-east's *sertão*[4] and Elizabethan England. Giovana Villela's costume designs combined materials such as leather – evocative of the *cangaço*[5] movement – and fine fabrics like silk, with modern outfits inspired by international clothing brands. The mixture of stage props, such as a stylized circus arena, gypsy wagons, umbrellas and lanterns, is equally indicative of how regional and globalized elements are made to coexist in this anthropophagic performance, giving rise to an aesthetic that is at once circusy, Elizabethan and *sertaneja*. This intricate affiliation between discrete locations and historical periods is further devised through the interpolation of songs by famous British bands like Supertramp ('The Logical Song') and Queen ('Bohemian Rhapsody'), and by Brazilian songwriters such as Alceu Valença ('Ciranda da Rosa Vermelha') and Luiz Gonzaga ('Assum Preto, Sabiá'), whose songs are iconic of north-eastern culture. The anthropophagic assimilation of *commedia dell'arte* masks, clowning and circus conventions complicates the negotiation of 'Shakespeare' with local and foreign models to an even greater extent. Alongside the Shakespearean text, each one of the components constitutive of the production plays an active role in the dramatization of the Shakespearean play in an idiom that acquires both a regional and global resonance in the performance.

For Yamamoto, there is an intrinsic relationship between the acute violence and mournful tone that pervade Shakespeare's *Richard III* and the societal values that operate in the countryside of north-eastern Brazil. This connection is forged and delineated in several moments throughout the performance. The enactment of Ricardo's commissioning of Hastings, Rivers and the princes' deaths, and the executions that follow, for instance, alludes to both *cangaço* and *coronelism*, a system in which local oligarchs strive to concentrate the political power. The exchanges between Ricardo and his commissioned executioner Jararaca – a clear reference to a legendary *cangaceiro* – are delivered as a sung rhymed poem accompanied by the accordion played by Ricardo, an allusion to a distinctively north-eastern music form. Towards the end of the performance, the characters sing an *incelença* (*excelência* [excellency] in standard Portuguese) to express grief over Ricardo's death. *Incelença* is a music genre consisting of mournful songs, and provides a cultural reference to the practice of performing funerary rites in certain localities of the north-east region. Interwoven with a Shakespearean plot, these local traditions and references are thus re-signified and rediscovered. The connections established between these, Shakespeare's canonical text and other foreign sources not only problematize the apparent incompatibility between the erudite and the popular, but also encourage a new appreciation of the popular culture from the north-east of Brazil.

Yamamoto's view that adapting Shakespeare is a way of respecting his work urges us to rethink what fidelity means in Shakespearean adaptation. To him, 'respecting' Shakespeare means finding parallels between his plays and contemporary local culture. He clearly suggests that the often-sought correspondence between a Shakespeare theatrical adaptation should not be oriented by the Shakespeare-as-text paradigm on which critical judgements of Shakespearean adaptations are often based. While acknowledging that there should be some degree of fidelity in a Shakespeare adaptation for it to be considered as adaptation, Yamamoto denies the still pervasive assumption that adapters must engage primarily with the so-called original Shakespeare text. Instead, he approaches Shakespeare as a rhizome – to use Douglas Lanier's term borrowed from

Deleuze and Guattari – and situates the Shakespearean text in a network of other adaptations (e.g. Galpão's *Romeu e Julieta*) and dramatic sources.

The conversation that follows gives us a broader understanding of Clowns' relationship with Shakespeare, the relevance of reproducing Shakespeare's works in Brazil, the sources Clowns feed off, their experiences abroad, and the responses their Shakespearean productions evoke in local and foreign audiences.

Sua Incelença: Fernando Yamamoto interviewed by Paulo da Silva Gregório

PSG *Besides the well-known productions of* Muito Barulho por Quase Nada *and* Sua Incelença, *Clowns de Shakespeare has produced other Shakespearean plays such as* Twelfth Night, The Taming of the Shrew *and* Hamlet. *Could you talk about the company's relationship with Shakespeare's works and how it has developed over the years?*

FY The company was officially founded in 1993, but in 1992 we had a first experience which we call the prehistory of the company. It tells us about our genealogy before we got to Shakespeare. In 1992, Cesar Ferrario (another member of the company), I and several of our classmates in the final year of school had a very close relationship with our literature teacher at 'Objetivo School', in Natal. His name was Marco Aurélio Barbosa, and was a very nice character. Everyone was going to take the university entrance examination at the end of that year. He decided to gather some of the students to whom he was closer to mount a play about Brazil's literary movements as an extra support for the exam. He then invited me and another student, Jose Marcelo Rodrigues (a former member of Clowns), to be responsible for the direction and dramaturgy of the production. Neither of us had any experience with theatre, so it was super amateurish and empirical. We did a collage of different fragments from different literary movements, and there was a narrator leading the performance. We created scenes of meetings between literary figures that didn't exist; this was actually the core idea of the production. It was a very nice event which involved the entire school, and encouraged us to continue the following year. In 1993, we were invited to revive the production with the students from that year. Mr Barbosa suggested that this time the play should be performed at Alberto Maranhão Theatre (Natal's main theatre), rather than in the school's little auditorium. Influenced by all the fuss about a production of *A Midsummer Night's Dream* by Brazilian director Cacá Rosset, Mr Barbosa proposed that we mounted this play, and so we did. The production was a mockery of poor Shakespeare; we had no command of Shakespeare or theatre. Just before the opening night, we realized that we needed a name for our troupe. Obviously, we were not a theatre group, though we thought that the show had to be accredited to a particular name. We then recalled a poem by Manuel Bandeira called 'Poética'. It figured in our previous production about Brazilian literature, and talks about Shakespeare's clowns. We made a shallow and direct association between the poem and the fact that we were doing Shakespeare, and decided to call ourselves Shakespeare's Clowns without even knowing exactly what 'clowns' and 'Shakespeare' meant. Our *A Midsummer Night's Dream* was puerile, and I'd feel embarrassed if someone had access to it now. However, the approach taken was very good: instead of approaching Shakespeare according to the canon, we played a lot with him using our own references. This attitude allowed us to assimilate Shakespeare not as a playwright who is sometimes mistakenly considered dull. After this experience, I spent about a year in England with my mother, who went there to do a post-doc. While I was there I saw many things, studied a lot, and returned to Natal thinking that what we were doing with Shakespeare was completely wrong and that the best thing we could do was to invest in training. It was at this moment that the troupe, no longer affiliated to the school, started to acquire an understanding of theatre which was then still quite basic. I proposed that we mount *Twelfth Night*, a play I had read and seen performed while in England. While we had been too irresponsible in our first experience with Shakespeare, in the second we were excessively reverent to the Bard. In fact, in neither production had we enough knowledge or the relevant theatrical skills to put on a good show; and in this production we used the full text. Imagine Shakespeare's full text produced by actors and directors who were only beginners, using huge sets and long scene-change blackouts. Even though this production represented a first leap in the history of the troupe, it was boring and tedious. Professor Sávio Araújo, who now works at the Federal University of Rio Grande do Norte and was doing an MA in Education at that time, was one of the people who helped us after my return from England. We came across Sávio as we were looking for a theatre workshop, and established a very good relationship with him. He ended up using this experience with us as a case study for his MA research, while we benefitted from the opportunity to work with him. He saw our *Twelfth Night*, and after a few months we met again when we were trying to mount a non-Shakespeare play. Sávio then said we needed to do another Shakespeare, and joked about the stick-bending theory: our first Shakespeare had been too irresponsible, we had bent the stick in one direction; the second was excessively reverent, we had pulled the stick far too much in the other direction. It was now time to loosen the stick so that it could indicate a more balanced relationship with Shakespeare. We suggested that he should direct us, and he took up the challenge. We produced and rehearsed the play for over two years, and through this long process the company started to acquire a better understanding of theatre practices. Our work on our first 'trilogy' was instrumental in developing an enormous passion for Shakespeare's work, and in helping us understand its universality and how much he touches us and how much he has to say to those living in Brazil's north-east region in the twenty-first century. After those three productions, we carried on doing not only Shakespeare, though inevitably he's always present in our references, work and research. Our 2009 production of *O Capitão e a Sereira* (The Captain and the Mermaid), for example, opened with a quote from the first prologue in *Henry V*. Our bond with Shakespeare has since become tighter and tighter, and we have been constantly seeking this proximity.

PSG   *The idea of 'solaridade' is often pointed out by company members as an aesthetic element that defines the Clowns' identity. What does this 'solaridade' consist of? How does it manifest in productions such as* Muito Barulho *and* Sua Incelença?

FY   Eduardo Moreira, a member of Grupo Galpão who directed *Muito Barulho Por Quase Nada* and *O Casamento do Pequeno Burguês* with me, was the one who brought us this definition. *Solaridade* means a spark in the eyes, the joy of creating the *solaridade* of our musical elements and colours. In general, our work draws on this reference, conveys this joy. This concept started to become more clearly and effectively delineated during the process of mounting *Muito Barulho*, another big leap in our trajectory. It was a step up for the company, and a starting point in its professionalization. It was our first work that circulated and gave us an income, so that the company members started to envisage doing theatre for a living. We invited Eduardo, who kindly accepted our invitation to direct *Muito Barulho*, because of our great admiration for Grupo Galpão, whose work had been an inspiration to us since this company was founded. *Ricardo* was perhaps the consolidation of this passion for and proximity to Galpão. In fact, our relationship with Galpão stemmed from what we had heard about their *Romeu e Julieta*. Later, we met and worked with Gabriel Villela, who had directed Galpão's *Romeu e Julieta*. The *solaridade* we had previously noticed in Galpão's work was treated by Clowns in a different way. Our so*laridade* also relates to the culture, the climate, the coastline, the countryside – with its sunshine and hot weather – of Brazil's north-east region. Even though I wasn't born in the north-east, I see myself as a north-eastern artist. Clowns is essentially a north-eastern company: most of our members are from this region and enjoy doing theatre there. So, I think *solaridade* is also connected to the intense heat and sunlight of the north-east region, which are then transported to the stage. Our youth was an important element in the construction of our *solaridade* twenty-five years ago, and now it doesn't manifest in the same way: there's less enthusiasm and more thinking involved. Even though we've lost a bit of that spark in the eye mentioned earlier, it's something we've been trying to rescue.

PSG *The use of regional elements to reproduce Shakespeare's* Much Ado *and* Richard III *does indeed remind me of the stage methods employed by Grupo Galpão in their acclaimed* Romeu e Julieta. *Could you tell me more about the influence of Galpão's performance styles on the development of Clowns distinct aesthetics?*

FY Just to add to my previous response, our company was born under the influence of Galpão's *Romeu e Julieta*. In fact, we were more influenced by the aura, the echoes of this *Romeu e Julieta* rather than the production itself, since we only saw it performed at a later date. Galpão has, indeed, always influenced and inspired us. This influence became more direct after we started working with Eduardo Moreira in *Muito Barulho*, and was consolidated in *Ricardo III*. Some artists from Natal condescendingly used to call us a branch of Galpão. We've always laughed about it since we've never taken this as a criticism, but rather as a compliment. Although it's very clear to us that we've never attempted to plagiarize Galpão's work, and that each troupe has a very strong and distinct identity, there's a strong affiliation between the two troupes. Galpão members are not only idols who have inspired us; they are also our close friends. We are therefore connected to them both on an aesthetic, ethical and a personal level.

PSG *Galpão's incorporation of Brazilian literary, popular and musical traditions into Shakespeare's* Romeo and Juliet *has been analysed in the light of Oswald de Andrade's notion that foreign literary models should be devoured rather than copied.[6] Could Andrade's anthropophagic concept also be evoked to describe the methods of interweaving Shakespeare and cultural traditions mainly associated with Brazil's north-east region in productions like* Much Ado *and* Sua Incelença?

FY The notion of *north-easternness* has been present in our discussions since Clowns was founded. On the one hand, besides the fact that the company members are from different regions of Brazil, all of them were born and/or grew up in an urban environment. On the other hand, here in the north-east we have the privilege of being connected with the countryside, the *sertão*, and to a cultural universe whose representation has become our signature and raises people's expectations as to what characterizes a north-eastern theatre company. Notwithstanding our close relationship with what is understood as the essence of the north-eastern culture in Brazil, most of our references are either urban or littoral. The concept of anthropophagy could be then associated with the way in which we establish a link between regional and universal references, with no concern about being faithful to either of them. In fact, we try to encompass what makes sense to us within our imagination.

PSG *You've declared that Jan Kott's book* Shakespeare Our Contemporary *influenced the troupe's choice to produce* Ricardo III. *How do Kott's ideas on the contemporariness of Shakespeare's plays resonate in* Sua Incelença? *In what way does the critic's seminal reading of Shakespeare's* Richard III *relate to the intermingling of 'regional' and 'universal' sources in the production?*

FY   Kott's *Shakespeare Our Contemporary* is a great work, one of the greatest works ever written about Shakespeare. We turn to it whenever we feel like we need to feed off the universe of the Bard. We first encountered the book through Marco Aurélio during a workshop he delivered in São Paulo back in 2007. At that time, Natal was facing problems concerning the role of culture in public policies, and when we read Kott's essay on *Richard III* we immediately established associations between his ideas and what was happening in Natal. After a while we started working with Gabriel (Villela), and during his first visit to Natal it became clear to us that we were going to do Shakespeare, possibly in the street. We then decided to give a workshop based on *Richard III* and two other Shakespeare plays. Gabriel could immediately pick up on our latent desire to produce *Richard III*, and this was indeed the play we opted for. The way Kott unveils the structure of the 'Grand Mechanism' in Shakespeare's histories and, particularly, in *Richard*, really served as a foundation for our production. This assimilation of Kott's ideas stemmed from our collaborative work with a guest director, and it would have happened in a different way if I were the one directing the production. It is worth adding that the regionalism manifest in *Sua Incelença* relates to the presupposed universality of Shakespeare's works, another issue Kott touches upon in his book. Shakespeare is a playwright whose work can speak to all people, in all places, at all times; everyone is going to find in Shakespeare what interests and touches them. In this respect, Kott does endorse our choice for a certain type of adaptation.

PSG   *An adaptive approach to the Shakespearean text was adopted both in* Muito Barulho *and* Sua Incelença. *The addition of terms like 'Sua Incelença' and 'quase' to the titles of the productions, for example, subverts conventional translations of the plays' names into Portuguese. In addition, the play's plots were shortened, characters were added, and references to local dialects (e.g.* galado) *and tourist attractions (e.g.* Morro do Careca) *included. Despite these* *textual alterations, do you think the productions still retain the 'essence' of the plays which allows us to identify them as Shakespearean works?*

FY We have the habit of playing with the titles of works by renowned, classic writers: *Muito Barulho por Quase Nada* (*Much Ado About Almost Nothing*), *Sua Incelença, Ricardo III* (*His Excellency Richard III*), *Sonhos de uma Noite Só* (*A Single Night's Dream*), and even Brecht's *A Respectable Wedding* was retitled as just *O Casamento* (*The Wedding*). It's our way of expressing that it's *our* Shakespeare, *our* Brecht. Regarding theatrical adaptation, there are two aspects that need to be considered to justify our choices. The first one relates to an understanding of theatre's social role in England during the Elizabethan and Jacobean periods; the way in which theatrical productions were realized; the types of acting areas, like the open spaces. The main point, though, is our belief that the best way to respect Shakespeare is through adaptation, through the establishment of equivalences, like the use of *galado* in *Muito Barulho*. Borachio calls Dogberry an ass in the original play, and when we started reading and analysing it we wondered how Dogberry could be so infuriated for being called an ass. Today if you refer to someone as an ass in Portuguese it'll cause laughter, though we understand this is a double-meaning word in English. So, we decided to search for another term that could create an effect equivalent to the fury 'ass' provokes in Dogberry. Eduardo Moreira, who was directing the production with me, asked if there wouldn't be any north-eastern or *Potiguar*[7] word, and then we recalled *galado*. Like ass, it's double-meaning, and might sound rather strong and offensive. By incorporating this word, we believe that we brought the scene the closest it could be to what we imagine was initially intended by Shakespeare. Had we been 'respectful' towards Shakespeare's words, we would have, in fact, diminished their potency. When we take *Muito Barulho* on tour, whenever we can find a word characteristic of the place we are going to perform, we replace *galado* with the new word or expression. When we perform in places whose language variants are quite well known throughout the country – for example, Rio de Janeiro and São Paulo – *galado* evokes laughter and raises people's interest in the Potiguar prosody and idioms. This particular example illustrates our attitudes towards the Shakespearean text. We believe that attempting to find equivalences that allow for the full potency of Shakespeare's work to be released in a contemporary context is the best way to respect Shakespeare.

PSG   *Both* Sua Incelença *and* Muito Barulho *draw on popular traditions that are not considered mainstream in Brazil. Do you think that the intermingling of regional elements with canonical works such as Shakespeare's becomes a way of elevating those local traditions by showing their value to our current understanding of Shakespearean plays, often seen as highbrow?*

FY   It's quite complicated to talk about a dominant popular culture. However, I think north-east's popular culture is perhaps the most well known and widely disseminated across Brazil, especially if we think about the great number of people from the north-east scattered all over the country. But regardless of this, accessing popular culture means having a direct relationship with Shakespeare's work because he was a popular playwright. It's a mistake to take the term 'classic' as being synonymous with highbrow. The opposite of highbrow is the popular, not the classic. Shakespeare is both classic and popular; he is not highbrow. He was the son of a glove-maker who wrote plays to all people, some of whom would watch bear baiting one day, a public execution the next day and go to the theatre the day after; theatre was the most popular cultural manifestation at that time. Although Shakespeare's language is quite inaccessible today, even to those who have English as their mother tongue, it wasn't his intention to use an elaborate and a difficult language. On the contrary, Shakespeare is known as a neologist, and created over 1,000 words. So, when we talk about popular culture, inevitably we talk about Shakespeare; there is a link between the popular culture from two distinct periods and locations. When we mount Shakespeare in the north-east, we are in a place which is, essentially, the most closely associated with Shakespeare's work.

PSG *The production process of* Sua Incelença *included a period of open rehearsals in Acari, a small town in the Brazilian state of Rio Grande do Norte. How beneficial was this full immersion in the local culture to the rendering of Shakespeare's* Richard III *through the lens of north-east's distinctive cultural traditions?*

FY   Besides the fact that some members of the troupe who were cast in *Ricardo* are from the Seridó region,[8] we've always seen the Seridó as the cultural birthplace of Rio Grande do Norte, the heart of the Potiguar culture; one way or the other we're always feeding off this source. Gabriel wanted to reproduce the experience he'd had with Galpão, which presented a preview performance in Morro Vermelho, in Minas Gerais's countryside. The company spent a week or so interacting with the people in this town. As it had been such a remarkable experience for the production (*Romeu e Julieta*), Gabriel felt that it could be good for us too. What was different for us was that we only had four acts, and still needed to finish the last one. Initially, our idea was to mount the fifth act in Acari during a week, though it didn't happen in the end; we worked with what we already had, and 'tried' the performance on with the local audience. We were concerned that the idiom of the production might not reach the audience. There were no linguistic concessions (except for the third act for which we created the text). *Richard III* is a rather complicated play, and one of Shakespeare's plays with the largest cast list, so we had to cut and edit a great deal, also considering the fact that the audience's attention span is much shorter on the streets due to external interferences. Acari allowed us to, in the most radical way possible, try the production on with spectators who had never attended a theatrical performance before, as we did in the community of Gargalheiras. The relationship established with them from the very first day of rehearsal was very powerful: the performance reached them quite easily; they were very fascinated by it and followed the rehearsal process throughout the entire week. Chatting to them on the first day after we'd finished, the feedback they gave us revealed a very precise response to the whole performance. Then we started to understand the actual potency of the production. They would tell us that what we had shown them, the story about a guy who one day shakes your hand and the next day gives orders to kill you, was familiar to them, it was part of their history, something that they would see there. The potency of Shakespeare's universality then started to become clearer to us, since it speaks directly to the *coronelism* in the *sertão*, and establishes a relationship of equality with it. It was indeed a very remarkable and determining experience for the production.

PSG *In the same way that Shakespeare's* Richard III *was adapted through the incorporation of regional art forms, some of the latter were made to resonate with the Shakespearean play. The words 'Lady Ana', for example, were accommodated in the song 'Ciranda da Rosa Vermelha', and the verses taken from João Cabral de Melo Neto's poem* Morte e Vida Severina *were also slightly altered to fit well with the enactment of Richard's death at the end of the performance. Could you comment on how local traditions also had to be adapted in the process of reproducing* Richard III *and* Much Ado?

FY It's difficult to talk about a reappropriation of north-eastern elements because, in general terms, they are references that have been incorporated into our individual and collective life experience. Such references are invoked whenever the need arises during the production process, though not deliberately so; they don't fit into a concept. They are experimentations (e.g. Lady Ana) shamelessly carried out, though we understand that our attitude towards a work of such magnitude is overall respectful. In using the various references, we try not to treat the north-east culture as stagnant, something that ought to be kept under a glass dome like a museum piece. As much as we respect it we have the artistic and poetic freedom to do what we want with it. So, it's not about a conceptual presupposition – 'let's adopt this particular attitude towards our references'; there's much more freedom involved.

PSG *How would you describe the company's target audience? Could you comment further on the responses Clowns' re-workings of Shakespeare's plays evoke in the audience? Do the reactions to these productions normally correspond to what was initially intended by the actors and directors?*

FY We don't have a specific target audience. Owing mainly to our affiliation with popular theatre, our so-called grown-up productions are suitable for all audiences, even though not all of our productions fit into this idiom. Regarding reception, it's always surprising and never happens as expected. Our expectations towards the audience response are often shaped by the director's eye and coincides with what he/she expects. Obviously, such expectations are always subverted or expanded when we reach the spectators; it's only through the contact with them that the performance starts to materialize. Besides, it's hard to talk about an audience response when there are different audiences – both in Brazil and abroad – who respond differently to our productions. We start to notice, however, that there are certain standards that might lead to adjustments to the way the production is performed. These are not necessarily meant to please the audience and retain only what they might find enjoyable; rather, they are employed as an attempt to rework elements that may not reach the audience, enabling them to accomplish what we initially intended.

PSG *You've described Clowns de Shakespeare's 1995 production of* Twelfth Night *as being 'reverent' to Shakespeare, and attributed its failure to the traditionalism that characterized the production. Could you give more details about the* *approach used in this* Twelfth Night? *Do you think that staging Shakespeare in Brazil from a more traditional perspective makes his plays less appealing to a Brazilian audience?*

FY   *Noite de Reis* was very conventional – although it's tricky to talk about a conventional Shakespearean production – and it was produced when we were an incipient and completely inexperienced troupe, resulting in a very boring and tiresome performance. We were trying to put on a production we were unable to come to grips with. I was pretty much influenced by my experience of living in the UK for almost a year. As a novice who was starting to have access to theatre and reflect upon theatre and Shakespeare, I returned from the UK with a very museological and idolatrous attitude. I wouldn't say that it's not possible to mount Shakespeare properly in Brazil in a less anthropophagic way, though for us this would be meaningless; since *A Megera (DoNada)* we've tried to establish a meaningful connection between Shakespeare and us. As mentioned, we understand that the establishment of equivalences between the pulsating life of Shakespeare's work in the Elizabethan period and the present time is our way of respecting Shakespeare.

PSG   Sua Incelença *has been performed in countries like Spain, Uruguay and Chile. Could you comment on audiences' responses to the performances in these countries? Do you think* Sua Incelença *meets or subvert a foreign audience's expectations of what a Brazilian adaptation of a Shakespearean play should be?*

FY   The idiom of our *Richard* is very Brazilian, and seems rather unusual in comparison to the Shakespeare they are used to, so it always causes surprise. The director of the Chekhov Theatre Festival in Moscow paid a visit to us, saw a rehearsal of our production, and was fascinated by it. He even invited us to perform at the festival, though it didn't happen in the end due to financial issues. In general, spectators are surprised and fascinated by our production.

Except for Portugal, *Sua Incelenca* was performed in Spanish in the other countries, and this allowed for a more effective communication. The production is always very well received wherever it is staged, and this has to do with the wonder that our Shakespeare – performed in a very distinctive way – evokes.

PSG   *Besides* Richard III *and* Much Ado, *are there other Shakespeare plays that could be successfully staged through the assimilation of visual, literary and musical elements characteristic of a Brazilian region such as the north-east?*

FY   I have no doubt that any one of Shakespeare's plays can be successfully produced through the lens of Brazil's north-eastern traditions. I would risk saying that any play can be mounted in this way, though as I have more familiarity with Shakespeare's work I can say for sure that the universality of his texts establishes a relation with any epoch and place in the world. So, I think that any Shakespearean play can be easily staged according to this perspective.

PSG   *What is the value of using Shakespeare's influence as a global playwright to explore theatrical and cultural traditions that assert the cultural identity of local communities?*

FY   Using Shakespeare's works is a partnership, a twofold gain. On the one hand, Shakespeare gains force when he gets into contact with and becomes a part of the universe of a theatrical production staged in a specific time and place. On the other hand, I can mount my own play, my own theatrical creation, though if I use Shakespeare I have access to quality texts and dramaturgy that are beneficial to my production. Although I would be able to be much more literal and write whatever I wanted, the scenes I wanted, I find it 'easier' to search Shakespeare's work for themes I'd like to explore (establishing thus parallels within the production), than to take up the challenge of creating quality drama from scratch in order to talk about what I want.

Sua Incelença, Shakespeare

Watching a video recording of *Sua Incelença* with a non-local friend of mine unfamiliar with the Portuguese language and Brazilian theatre culture, she told me she was unable to see anything immediately recognizable as 'Brazilian' in the performance. Unable to pick up on the production's acute regional accent, and unaware of how the costumes and songs representative of the north-east region were being employed in the process of rendering Shakespeare north-eastern, she tried to make sense of the performance by focusing on dramatic elements she was more familiar with, namely the *Richard* plot, English songs, *commedia dell'arte* and circus. Since the production's Brazilianness is mainly conveyed through the language, the regional accent and the Brazilian songs, a non-Brazilian audience's inability to fully grasp the nuances of these theatrical elements might give rise to responses that either confirm pre-established views about Shakespeare and the play, or subvert the audience's expectations of what a Brazilian production should be like. Clowns' articulation of the Shakespeare text within a rhizomatic network of local and foreign sources fails to provide the exoticism that non-Brazilian audiences may expect from a Brazilian Shakespeare (one infused with carnivalesque spectacles and samba music, for instance). The troupe's anthropophagic approach to Shakespeare might be instrumental, therefore, in encouraging non-Brazilian spectators to rethink their understanding of foreign Shakespeare. On the other hand, Clowns' local spectators, most of whom have never been to the theatre and for whom Shakespeare is alien, are likewise invited into the performance through the recognition of the ways in which their own traditions are being recreated in the dramatization of a Shakespeare play. Devouring Shakespeare and other foreign sources, and even readjusting local cultural traditions (self-cannibalism) so that they can gain force *in* and *as* performance, Clowns' Shakespeare productions cater to both Brazilian and foreign audiences, who eat their Shakespeare in distinct ways. Their productions invite us to reconsider the binary relationship between the local and the global in Shakespearean performance.

Notes

1 Camati and Leão (2013: 99) note that Clowns' transient and unstable audience needs to be constantly seduced. The production's musical overtones, therefore, play an important role in capturing the attention of passersby.

2 A hilarious person. It also means 'contemptible' or 'detestable'.

3 *Forró* is a music genre originating in the north-east of Brazil, and despite having gained widespread popularity across the country, it remains closely associated with this region.

4 Term commonly used to refer to the semi-arid area in the north-east of Brazil.

5 A form of social banditry that permeated through the north-east of Brazil during the late nineteenth and early twentieth centuries.

6 See Alves and Noe (1999: 268).

7 Of or relating to the Brazilian state of Rio Grande do Norte.

8 Seridó is situated between the states of Rio Grande do Norte and Paraíba.

References

Alves, J. C. M. and M. Noe (1999), 'Life Is an Inverted Circus: Grupo Galpão's Romeu e Julieta Adapted from Pennafort's Translation of Shakespeare's', *Ilha do Desterro*, 36: 265–281.

Budasz, R. (2005), 'Of Cannibals and the Recycling of Otherness', *Music and Letters*, 87 (1): 1–15.

Camati, A. S. and L. C. Leão (2013), 'Um Shakespeare Brasileiro: A Música em Cena em Sua Incelença, *Ricardo III*', *Revista Cerrados*, 22 (35): 217–230.

George, D. (1985), *Teatro e Antropofagia*, trans. E. Brandão, São Paulo: Global.

Huang, A. C. Y. (2007), 'Site-specific Hamlets and Reconfigured Localities: Jiang'an, Singapore, Elsinore', in G. Bradshaw, T. Bishop and T. Kishi (eds), *The Shakespearean International Yearbook*, 22–48, 7th edition, Aldershot: Ashgate.

Kennedy, D. (2001), 'Shakespeare Worldwide', in M. de Grazia and S. Wells (eds), *The Cambridge Companion to Shakespeare*, 251–264, New York: Cambridge University Press.

Lanier, D. (2014), 'Shakespearean Rhizomatics: Adaptation, Ethics, Value', in A. Huang and E. J. Rivlin (eds), *Shakespeare and the Ethics of Appropriation*, 21–40, New York: Palgrave Macmillan.

Rumbold, K. (2011), 'Shakespeare Anthologized', in M. T. Burnett, A. Streete and R. Wray (eds), *The Edinburgh Companion to Shakespeare and the Arts*, 88–105, Edinburgh: Edinburgh University Press.

Spinelli, D. O. (2016), 'O Teatro de Grupo e a Relação com Encenadores Convidados na Formação, Profissionalização e Manutenção do Grupo de Teatro Clowns de Shakespeare', MA diss., Arts Institute, University of São Paulo, São Paulo.

Worthen, W. B. (1997), *Shakespeare and the Authority of Performance*, Cambridge: Cambridge University Press.

Worthen, W. B. (2003), *Shakespeare and the Force of Modern Performance*, Cambridge: Cambridge University Press.

4

Cannibalizing *Hamlet* in Brazil: Ophelia meets Oxum

Cristiane Busato Smith

The theme of Ophelia's death has captured the popular imagination for over two centuries. Seduced by the lyrical images that Gertrude employs to describe the heroine's watery death, painters and poets have promoted Ophelia to the status of an archetypal model as well as a cult heroine, suggesting a dynamic interplay that still thrives in contemporary culture. From Arthur Rimbaud's 'Blanche Ophélie' to Millais's iconic painting of the drowning siren, Ophelia's story has become indistinguishable from the story of her death. In these portrayals, Ophelia's beauty obliterates the horror of her death, a phenomenon observed by A. C. Bradley: 'the picture of her death, if our eyes grow dim in watching it, is still purely beautiful' (2000: 165). Nowadays, depictions of dead or drowning Ophelias proliferate across a whole host of twentieth-century media: on the stage, in books and paintings, on the screen and on the internet in blogs, amateur videos, mashups on YouTube, games and profile pictures. Ophelia's thriving afterlife in contemporary culture, whether or not rearticulated critically, has not only reflected cultural shifts but also generated interesting debates over the nature of art as a representational practice.

Since Elaine Showalter's groundbreaking essay 'Representing Ophelia: Women, Madness, and the Responsibilities of Feminist Criticism' (1985), Ophelia has also occupied a place of prominence in critical thought. While most scholarship devoted to the character traces her presence in British and American cultures, the subject has recently found its way to Brazil and helps chronicle how the Global South responds to and engages with the 'myth of Ophelia'. My aim in this chapter is thus to foment and expand the global and local critical discussions about Ophelia by analysing her death and burial scenes in the theatrical adaptation *Ham-let* (1993/2001) in light of the Brazilian aesthetics of Cultural Anthropophagy.[1]

Ham-let and the cannibal condition

Ham-let (1993/2001) is an exuberant theatrical production lasting more than five hours, directed by one of Brazil's most important theatre practitioners, José Celso Martinez Corrêa, better known as Zé Celso.[2] In this radical adaptation of Shakespeare's classic tragedy, *Hamlet* is re-signified through the tenets of Oswald de Andrade's 'Cannibalist Manifesto' ([1928] 1991), heralded by the refrain 'Tupi or not Tupi', which opens the play and reverberates throughout the show. Indeed, the concept of Cultural Anthropophagy is anchored on the idea that Brazil's strength lies in its talent to 'assimilate [rather than reject] the foreign experience into the Brazilian species, and to reinvent it on our own terms, with the ineluctable local qualities that will endow the resulting product with an autonomous character and confer on it, in principle, functionality as product for export' (Veloso 2002: 156).

Zé Celso's cannibalization of *Hamlet* involved a series of negotiations with the source text, which resulted in radical moves that poet and translator Haroldo de Campos would conceptualize as 'recreation' or 'transcreation' ([1963] 2010). The unconventional praxis of translation developed by Haroldo and his brother Augusto[3] does not exactly consist of 'writing back', if we are to understand it essentially as a subversive act that challenges the ideologies of the original. Instead, transcreation emphasizes the creative process and the potentials of the new text over the old one. In this respect, the Campos brothers reactivate the modernist paradigm of cannibalism formulated by Andrade, which expresses the idea that the colonized culture, rather than rejecting the hegemonic culture, should appropriate, digest and assimilate it in an anthropophagic fashion in order to be empowered rather than overpowered by it. Andrade's cannibal 'law' from the 'Cannibalist Manifesto', 'I am only interested in that which is not mine', highlights the self-empowering consumption of European culture – the cannibal eats his enemy to absorb his bravery and strength. In this logic, Shakespeare's 'To be, or not to be' becomes Andrade's 'Tupi or not Tupi' – the iconic slogan of Brazilian *Modernismo*. Alluding simultaneously to the indigenous Tupinambás, who allegedly practised cannibalism to incorporate the wisdom of the Europeans, and to Hamlet's famous line, 'Tupi or not Tupi' both embraces *and* rejects Shakespeare/European culture. It advocates cannibalism as a critical, aesthetic and political practice in order to assimilate whatever revitalizes and strengthens the Brazilian ethos. Artists have resourcefully adopted the anthropophagic practice to discover and reinvent meaning as well as establish fresh perspectives that reshape external influences. Adding to the critical debate, critic Silviano Santiago coined the term 'space in-between' in 1971 to refer to the Latin American cultural condition that legitimizes the incorporation of the hegemonic culture into Latin American art (see Santiago 2001). Displacing notions of source and influence, original and copy, Santiago reclaims the value of the model which, now clothed in different colours, not only gains the power to parody but also to operate a revision of the original.

Cannibalism, then, became a cornerstone concept to understand Brazilian aesthetics and has been rekindled in key moments of Brazil's history such as *Tropicalismo*, an artistic movement that redefined the culture of the 1970s. It was in the very nature of *Tropicalismo* to challenge the status quo and, in the process, it became a symbol of political resistance against the military dictatorship that ruled Brazil from 1964 to 1985. *Tropicalismo* applied Oswald de Andrade's legacy to create new hybridized forms of music, theatre and poetry used to contest and challenge the regime. One of the central members of the movement, Zé Celso, sees the rediscovery of Andrade's cannibal as a cultural revolution, 'a definitive moment when language, body and art were de-colonized' (Fioratti 2012).

While cultural cannibalism has been by and large associated with the Brazilian aesthetics of appropriation, it should also be regarded more broadly as a pioneer postcolonial epistemology. That Andrade's 1928 work was included in the postcolonial debate much later in history proves the extent to which the 'Global South' has been ignored by the 'Global North'. For instance, concepts such as hybridity and cultural translation have been completely assimilated into the postcolonial vocabulary since the 1980s and yet most theorists fail to trace them back to their Brazilian origins. More pointedly to Shakespeare Studies, Cultural Anthropophagy as a theory derived from the 'Global South' prompts us to reclaim the study of 'Global Shakespeare' as an example of what a genuine global project could be.

In true cannibalistic fashion, Zé Celso draws on Shakespeare but merges it unashamedly with *Candomblé*,[4] carnival, myth, ritual, eroticism, orgy, lyrical and indigenous songs, blues, bossa nova, samba and other stage practices to address issues concerning his theatre, Teatro Oficina, and contemporary Brazilian society. The phenomenal architectural space of Teatro Oficina – with its movable ceiling, its Elizabethan-style trap door and bleachers, its tree that integrates the indoor and outdoor spaces, and its glass wall, which reveals the neighbourhood of Bexiga in São Paulo – makes it the ideal stage for the production.[5]

Ophelia in performance

It is always worth recalling that Shakespeare was essentially interested in the performability of his scripts on the stage. In an uncut production, therefore, Ophelia would emerge as a complex, contradictory character, just as Shakespeare conceived her.[6] In the first part of the play, she would incorporate the stereotype of a beautiful, demure maiden, obedient to her father, gentle and servile to all. Her only soliloquy in Act 3 – a rare moment in which she articulates her feelings and subjectivity – would be preserved. The scene of her madness in Act 4 would, then, transform her radically: her physical appearance would be disturbing and her language denunciatory, disconnected and improper. As Ophelia changed, her sexuality would be accentuated, creating an image that ran counter to her initial depiction as a chaste maiden. In this ideal scenario, the two versions of her death would be present without any excessive glamorization of her suicide. For however much Gertrude may try to veil the truth with her poetic images, the fact is that the 'poor wretch' was pulled 'from her melodious lay to muddy death' (*Ham* 4.7.180–181). Finally, in the graveyard scene Ophelia's body would be present, as required by the stage direction in the Second Quarto version of the play, which calls for the entrance of the body ('corse'), and as expressed in the words of Laertes (maintained with due variations in Q1, Q2 and First Folio), who asks to 'Hold off the dirt awhile / Till I have caught her once more in my arms' while he leaps into the grave: 'Cast on the living and the dead / The earth' (*Ham* 5.1.247).

However, the history of *Hamlet* in performance reveals an Ophelia basically devoid of her original ambivalent and tragic contours. Playscripts from Victorian England, a period when Shakespearean characters were considered paragons of virtue, demonstrate how actor-managers effectively 'filtered' the role of Ophelia, removing everything that could be construed as improper or unseemly in her. A case in point is Henry Irving's playtext, the longest-running *Hamlet* on the nineteenth-century English stage, which in addition to heavily editing the character's lines also abridges other characters' references to her. The resulting Ophelia – who already has few lines in the original text – is moulded into a pathetic, infantile and considerably less complex character. The suppression of Ophelia's role continued to prevail throughout the twentieth and, to a lesser degree,[7] into the twenty-first century in both stage and screen productions. Suffice it to recall the major English film adaptations by Laurence Olivier (1948), Grigori Kosintsev (1964), Franco Zeffirelli (1990) and Michael Almereyda (2000), who, besides making several cuts to Ophelia's speeches, also edited out her only soliloquy. An exception is of course Kenneth Branagh's 1996 version, but while Ophelia's words (including her soliloquy) are preserved, she is still circumscribed to the same oppressive environment as her Victorian counterparts.[8] As Rutter (1998: 45) argues, the focus, particularly in the graveyard scene, is shifted away from Ophelia's death onto Hamlet's heroic return to Denmark, thus removing the farcical tone of the scene (Hamlet leaping into the grave and crying out that forty thousand brothers could not match his love) designed to destabilize the status of the tragic hero. While Hamlet's status as tragic hero is maintained at all costs, Ophelia remains 'a blank page to be rewritten over or on by the male imagination', as Showalter (1985: 108) points out. Granted, every performance involves a negotiation between page and stage, and this is especially conspicuous in such a lengthy play as *Hamlet*, which inevitably results in the suppression of scenes, lines and even characters. Yet it is also the job of performance criticism to raise questions about the choices directors make, because they inevitably affect the overall interpretation of the play. In any case, the widespread propensity to portray Ophelia as a foil character makes her less substantial. Thus, Hamlet's alleged madness is contrasted with Ophelia's 'real' folly, and the same is true of the question of the suicide in *Hamlet*. By the same token,

Hamlet's latent Oedipus complex is, in some productions, mirrored in Ophelia's relationship with her father, Polonius. As a general rule, directors opt to celebrate the heroic masculinity of Hamlet, the most famed protagonist of the Shakespearean canon. Laurence Olivier's words sum up the case: 'the story is seen through his eyes and, when he is not present, through his imagination. I saw the camera seeing most things through Hamlet's eyes' (Olivier 1986).

Zé Celso's carnivalesque and polysemic vision in *Ham-let* flies in the face of the monolithic stance taken by Laurence Olivier and other film and theatre directors. His protagonist, played by Marcelo Drummond, is a debauched, aggressive, irreverent Hamlet performed with more physical than intellectual or reflexive impetus, calling into question the prevailing view of the Prince of Denmark as a great humanist and scholar. But more significantly for the purposes of this chapter, his Ophelia is endowed with surprising contours that highlight and amplify her tragic decline.

As I will argue below, the director gives a literal take on Laertes' remark about Ophelia's death: 'too much of water hast thou, poor Ophelia' (*Ham* 4.6.183). Not only is the Shakespearean heroine (played by Tila Teixeira) submerged in water, but an unusual waterfall effect is created, which pours onto her body and into the 'brook', a swimming pool installed on the Teatro Oficina stage. Particularly after the scene of her death, the water – Ophelia's own element – overflows onto the stage, becoming one with the *mise-en-scène*. In another atypical scenic practice in the history of *Hamlet* in performance, Zé Celso takes Ophelia's dead body to the graveyard scene, reiterating his emphasis on ritual and bringing forth new potential analyses of Ophelia. Zé Celso's irreverent and provocative spectacle desacralizes the Shakespearean text in the light of anthropophagic aesthetics, and, while the highly dramatized nature of Ophelia's death scene preserves its mythical elements, a whole new layer of meaning is introduced when *Oxum*, the Afro-Brazilian *orixá* of the waters, is invoked in the reconfiguration of Ophelia.[9]

'Too much of water hast thou': Millais meets *Oxum*

There is a willow grows askant the brook
That shows his hoary leaves in the glassy stream.
Therewith fantastic garlands did she make
Of crowflowers, nettles, daisies and long purples,
That liberal shepherds give a grosser name
But our cold maids do dead men's fingers call them.
There on the pendent boughs her crownet weeds
Clambering to hang, an envious sliver broke,
When down her weedy trophies and herself
Fell in the weeping brook. Her clothes spread wide
And mermaid-like awhile they bore her up:
Which time she chanted snatches of old lauds;
As one incapable of her own distress,
Or like a creature native and endued
Unto that element: but long it could not be
Till that her garments, heavy with their drink,
Pulled the poor wretch from her melodious lay
To muddy death. (*Ham* 4.7.164–181)

I saw Mama Oxum at the waterfall
Sitting at the river shore,
Gathering lilies, lilies, aye
Gathering lilies, lilies, ah
Gathering lilies to decorate our altar.
(Umbanda song, unknown author)[10]

The description of Ophelia's death (quoted above) comes shortly after the scene in which Claudius and Laertes plot the duel to kill Hamlet and introduces a 'feminine' way of thinking about the theme of death in the play.[11] Ophelia's death is neither violent nor bloody; quite the contrary. Through her poetic words, Gertrude breaks the linearity of the revenge plot that structures Shakespeare's tragedy and opens up a singularly poetic space. Shakespeare delegates the account of the death to Gertrude, thereby uniting the play's only two female characters. Up to this point, both characters have been circumscribed to a masculine environment in which they have been seen as objects of desire or repulsion. Instead of describing the horror of the scene, Gertrude romanticizes the event and exalts its beauty. She emphasizes the beauty of the character with images that suggest sensuality, fluidity and madness. The images in her monologue portray a beautiful young woman who, crowned with flowers and clinging to fragile water lilies, is swallowed up by the cruel brook and led to muddy death.

In *Ham-let*, Ophelia's death is announced by the harrowing chanting of the furies (4:02:40).[12] This is a scene of great iconographic impact, starting with Gertrude, who walks down the stage as a sort of visual Ophelia *doppelgänger* – with wet hair and ivy twined around her neck – and announces to Laertes that his sister has drowned (4:02:52). A pregnant Ophelia enters the stage clad in the traditional diaphanous white dress of Victorian paintings and crowned with a garland of white lilies and ivy (4:02:55), with a disturbed and distracted expression, 'incapable of her own distress'. Dancing and carrying branches of green vegetation, she heads to the corner of the stage towards the brook/pool that will be her iconic deathbed. While Ophelia enters the water (4:03:33), Gertrude narrates her death with a mixture of fascination and emotion, moved by the uniqueness of the moment, which lives up to the poetic intensity of the Shakespearean text. The soft melody in the background and the noise of the water dripping into the brook/pool punctuate her monologue. The projection of the scene on the large screens installed along the traverse stage allows the audience to scrutinize the drama, alternating between the video displaying amplified images of Ophelia and the actual dramatization on stage. Ophelia floats in the water as if surrendering to the stream (Figure 4.1).

FIGURE   4.1 *Film   still: 'Ophelia   surrendering',   Ham-let (1993/2001), dir. Zé Celso, Teatro Oficina. Courtesy MIT Global Shakespeares Video & Performance Archive.*

The camera frames Ophelia 'in her own element' from different angles: from a bird-eye view, floating in the water (Figure 4.2); from straight on, allowing for the closest view of both the actress and the *mise-en-scène*; and from a low-angle shot. There is also a shot filmed from inside the brook/pool, which invites the viewers to 'immerse' themselves in the water with the actress. The scene unmistakably alludes to the influential painting *Ophelia* (1851–1852) by John Everett Millais. The visual references to the soaked dress as a second skin, the mouth half open as if still singing or catching a last breath, the hanging willow branches (seen from an overhead angle; 4:05:00) and the vegetation surrounding the actress's body should suffice to establish the visual legacy. However, the detail that jumps out most is the gesture of the actress's right hand, also captured in extreme close-up (4:05:35, Figure 4.3).

FIGURE 4.2 *Film still: 'Ophelia floating'*, Ham-let *(1993/2001), dir. Zé Celso, Teatro Oficina. Courtesy MIT Global Shakespeares Video & Performance Archive.*

FIGURE 4.3 *Film still: 'Ophelia's hand'*, Ham-let *(1993/2001), dir. Zé Celso, Teatro Oficina. Courtesy MIT Global Shakespeares Video & Performance Archive.*

Like the model Elizabeth Siddal, who posed for Millais, Zé Celso's Ophelia raises her hands to the heavens in a gesture of supplication and acceptance. From this perspective, Ophelia's suicide can be seen as a release from Denmark's patriarchy, Elsinore – representing civilization, rationality and the masculine – standing in stark contrast with Ophelia's province of nature, emotions and the feminine. Zé Celso makes a point of emphasizing martyrdom as another important dimension of Ophelia's death: an image of the drowning Ophelia floating in the brook is projected at the end of Fortinbras' speech to exemplify the 'collateral damage' (5:01:03) caused by the intrigue and corruption in the Danish court.[13]

Ophelia is taken out of the water (4:05:38–4:05:49) and carried off the stage by two men. The water from her soaked gown pours onto the stage and invades the vegetation scattered on the floor. The next scene, with the gravediggers (4:05:45), opens with a carnival song, providing the stark contrast between tragic and comic so typical of Shakespeare and highlighting the carnivalizing nature of Zé Celso's production. Ophelia's water continues to be part of the comedic scene as the gravediggers try to convince each other whether or not her death was suicide. At one point, one of the gravediggers picks out a member of the audience and pretends to throw a bucket of water over his head, but the water hits the other gravedigger. The benches where the audience are seated are very close to the stage, giving them a detailed view of the scene. Though Ophelia is not there, her presence is manifested both as the subject of the gravedigger's dialogue and the water on the stage.

That said, dare one ask – in such an iconoclastic and irreverent staging – whether Zé Celso makes concessions to his Ophelia at the time of her death? For one cannot deny that Ophelia's drowning scene interrupts the irreverent tone of the play and the exaggerated sexuality that permeates several scenes. The production here seems to pay reverence not so much to Shakespeare's text as to the whole history of Ophelia's representation. The impression it gives is that Zé Celso purposefully exposed the powerful and long-held obsession with the death of a beautiful woman only to challenge it.[14]

The overriding tone of the scene is pathos; it moves the audience rather than shocking them (unlike most of the other scenes). No longer is there an emphasis on the violence or despair of the scene of madness, another quintessential Ophelia moment. In *Ham-let*, Ophelia's madness and sexuality are contained in a straitjacket, and in a dramatic moment actress Tila Teixeira cuts off her long hair, foretelling the suicide of the Shakespearean character. From this angle, the scene of madness could be interpreted as a counter-narrative to the violence against the female body and the patriarchal system that existed in Shakespeare's time and still exists in similar forms nowadays. In any case, while in most of the scenes Zé Celso chooses to subvert the Shakespearean text, here he approaches it with clear respect. Admittedly, Ophelia is pregnant when she surrenders to death, but here the reference has none of the 'orgiastic' nature of the earlier scenes, particularly the scenes of masturbation, oral sex and rape by Hamlet, not to mention the suggestion of Laertes' incestuous desire. On the contrary, pregnancy fosters the idea of baptism and rebirth, while also constituting the kernel of the female universe and the unconscious undercurrents of the play. The symbolism of baptism is also implied in the green foliage surrounding Ophelia.

Yet, the obvious visual reference to Millais must be put into perspective when we consider another important reference in Zé Celso's conception of the Shakespearean character in view of his cannibalistic aesthetics: as a water goddess, Zé Celso's Ophelia alludes to *Oxum*,[15] the female *orixá* (deity) of 'watery flows' from Candomblé traditions. Such an approach makes sense in a theatre that Zé Celso fondly nicknames *terreiro eletrônico*: an electronic centre of worship where Afro-Brazilian traditions are carried out. There are several references to Afro-Brazilian religions and rituals in *Ham-let* and it would not be a stretch to say that most of them are recognizable to a Brazilian audience who are at home with such syncretic signs. Invoked by drum rhythms, Zé Celso, playing the ghost of the late King Hamlet, appears dressed in a costume that syncretizes Saint George and *Ogum*. Fittingly, Zé incarnates *Ogum*, the *orixá* of war and technology, 'the essence of divine justice and truth on Earth' (Karade 1994: 26), as well as Saint George, the patron saint of England.[16] Similarly to *Ogum, Oxum* is a fluid divinity that has suffered a transformation in Brazil to reach people from different ethnic roots and social levels. Whether worshipped orthodoxically in Yoruba tradition or in different forms, *Oxum's* power extends beyond *Candomblé*, her Catholic alter-image in Brazil being our Lady of Conception.

Oxum, whose name derives from the Osun River in Nigeria, bears many resemblances to the Shakespearean character, not least her profound connection with Ophelia's element: 'water is her [Oxum's] home and water is her sign' (Hale 2001: 213). *Oxum* is the female *orixá* of fresh waters, rivers and waterfalls and represents love, prosperity and beauty. Known for her grace, loveliness and femininity, she usually appears in a flowy golden dress, sometimes carrying or gathering flowers by the river side, as described by the lyrics of the popular Umbanda song quoted above. Sometimes tears run down *Oxum's* face to signify her compassion and her alliance with water. Akin to Ophelia's multifarious presence in popular culture, *Oxum* is found in different shapes and features in Brazilian music, painting, theatre, literature, folk shows and carnival parades. Her vibrant presence in Brazil's unique syncretic culture leads her many devotees to fondly call her '*Mãe Menininha*' (our Little Mother).

Beyond *Oxum's* and Ophelia's visceral affinity with water, *Oxum* is also known as the *orixá* of fertility in Brazilian society. Significantly, in another movement that brings *Oxum* closer to Ophelia, Zé Celso bequeaths the Shakespearean heroine with *Mother Oxum's* fertility at the end of *Ham-let*, 'giving life to all the players, recreating them for each new day's performance' (Pires 2005: 111), thus providing a restorative reading to Ophelia's tragic story.

What ceremony else?: Ophelia's burial

Enter KING, QUEEN, LAERTES, *and* [*other Lords, with a Priest after*] *the corpse*. (*Ham* 5.1)

HAMLET
  Who is this they follow,
  And with such maimed rites? This doth betoken
  The corpse they follow did with desperate hand
  Fordo its own life. (*Ham* 5.1.207–210)

In 1886, inspired by Romantic aesthetics, the French actress and sculptor Sarah Bernhardt (1844–1923), who, enchanted by Ophelia's death scene, had already produced two sculptures of the dead Shakespearean heroine, shocked audiences at a production of the play in Paris by being carried on stage in a coffin during the graveyard scene in Act 5. There is evidence to suggest that Bernhardt was responsible for ushering in a new trend of introducing Ophelia's dead body onto the stage during this scene, in line with the stage directions from Quarto 2 which has the 'corse' brought on stage.[17] This *coup de théâtre* caused such a furore in French theatregoing circles that it encouraged some directors to follow suit in their productions of *Hamlet* in the late nineteenth and early twentieth century. The impact of Sarah Bernhardt's innovations in the 1800s shows just how susceptible the theatre was to the visual representations of the Shakespearean heroine, and brings to the fore the morbid obsessive fascination with female sexuality at the heart of the cult of Ophelia.

Zé Celso reiterates his investment in the concept of ritual and ceremony and the presentation of the scene by following the Quarto 2 directions, contemporizing and building on the practice of bringing the dead Ophelia onto the stage during the graveyard scene. The scene follows the sequence of events in the source text. The audience joins Hamlet as he watches the funeral procession. The corpse is borne (4:19:32) on a simple stretcher and the cortege, including the main characters, follows behind with due pomp. The traverse stage of Teatro Oficina is perfect for the funeral rites, announced by the bells rung by the 'churlish priest'.[18] The body is placed alongside the grave (4:20:14). One of the furies, also with ivy around her neck and wearing a white dress – another Ophelia *doppelgänger* – enters the stage, casts earth on the body (4:21:35) and rubs her pregnant belly, while Laertes expresses the wish that 'from her fair and unpolluted flesh may violets spring'. Laertes sprinkles flowers over his sister's lifeless body, strokes her, kisses her on the lips and asks the priest 'what ceremony else?' and 'must there no more be done?'. A posy of flowers rests under Ophelia's immobile hands (Figure 4.4).

FIGURE 4.4 *Film still: 'A posy of flowers rests under Ophelia's immobile hands', Ham-let (1993/2001), dir. Zé Celso, Teatro Oficina. Courtesy MIT Global Shakespeares Video & Performance Archive.*

Her body is buried in a simple grave (4:22:02) in one of the traps in the middle of the stage, without the customary adornments, since her death was regarded with suspicion in the eyes of the church. The priest explains that 'if it weren't for a superior order that makes exceptions to the rule, she wouldn't be lodged in sacred grounds to wait for the last trumpets of doomsday' (5:20:52). Coloured petals rain down on her body. Gertrude, now clad in funereal black, casts more petals on Ophelia's body (4:22:26). Laertes throws himself into the trap/grave (4:23:12) and clasps the inanimate body 'so I may catch Ophelia once more in my arms' as she is immersed in a rain of petals. If in her death Ophelia merges with water, at her burial her body mingles with flowers. In a similar way to Shakespeare's text, the symbolism of the flowers associates Ophelia with her sexuality and the question of her deflowering, which in *Ham-let* occurs with the violence of rape,[19] making the association all the more pointed. The petals also allude to the wedding that could have taken place, as Gertrude reminds us. Laertes then calls out, 'now you can throw the earth upon the living and the dead', expressing his wish to be buried alongside her, and again clasps his sister's body. At this moment, Hamlet also leaps into the trap (4:23:55) in a bid to outdo her brother in his love for her: 'I loved Ophelia. The love of forty thousand brothers couldn't be compared to mine.' Laertes and Hamlet struggle over Ophelia's dead body, tugging her this way and that (4:24:22–4:25:25; Figure 4.5). Laertes is only persuaded to leave the grave at Claudius's behest.

If at the time of her death Ophelia's body is overexposed and laid out for the scrutiny of onlookers, now it is fought over, manhandled, clutched at and kissed, as if it still had the power to excite desire. Zé Celso's conception of the funeral scene in *Ham-let* retains the dramatic impact and original integrity of the source text.

In a staging that puts such emphasis on the visuality of Ophelia's death, allusions to the abundance of representations of the character are inevitable. While in the drowning scene there is a clear nod to Millais, at this point the first visual

FIGURE 4.5 *Film still: 'Hamlet and Laertes fighting over Ophelia's body', Ham-let (1993/2001), dir. Zé Celso, Teatro Oficina. Courtesy MIT Global Shakespeares Video & Performance Archive.*

reference that comes to mind is Cuban artist Ana Mendieta (1948–1985), who brands her body on nature in different ways in the photographic series *Silhouette*: on grassy ground, covered with grasses; on bare earth, surrounded by foliage or undergrowth; or even as a body floating in a murky stream.[20] Mendieta's images are disconcerting and therefore possess the power to desacralize Millais's *ars moriendi* aesthetic and cast into question the ideological underpinning of the whole iconographic history of Ophelia.[21]

The fact that Zé Celso gives us no hints whether or not he intended to make a reference to Mendieta should not prevent us from exploring the possibility. An essential feature of a polysemic theatrical production such as *Ham-let* is its potential to generate a wide range of cultural meanings, creating a network of allusions that sometimes transcends its original boundaries. This textuality is particularly manifest with Ophelia, a character whose citational quality operates in different art forms to reflect and/or challenge different constructions of femininity.

When we consider Mendieta's pictures as another reference, the representation of Ophelia in *Ham-let* acquires a more affirmative meaning, since the Cuban artist used her own body to create an Ophelia-like representation, challenging the prevailing discourse. Further, and more specifically to the anthropophagic exegesis applied to the Shakespearean character, the allusion to Mendieta's earth body art not only corroborates but also reinforces *Oxum's* fertile talents, celebrating Ophelia rather than mourning her. Both references associate women with nature and suggest their symbolic fertility, making them assimilated by their natural element. Ophelia-*Oxum* once more rises from the figure of a victim to one of a denouncer – a trait that is reprised at the end of the show, when an image of the drowned Ophelia is projected on the screens while Fortinbras utters his words of conciliation in reference to the 'collateral damage' caused by the intrigue and corruption in the Danish court.

Conclusion

Bucking the trend in stage and film productions of *Hamlet* to abridge the character of Ophelia, Zé Celso actually expands her role and includes her in scenes where the original stage directions do not put her. He draws inspiration from the visual arts both to echo the prevailing discourse and to challenge it. Meanwhile, he brings back the novel staging introduced by Sarah Bernhardt and effectively puts the dead Ophelia centre stage. Clearly, this decision has nothing to do with living up to the tastes of an audience moved by the morbid concerns of Romanticism, but is a politically motivated move that thrusts the 'collateral effects' of a corrupt society into the limelight. In *Ham-let*, the impact of the image and the way Ophelia's body is handled after her death compete on an equal footing with the iconic image of Hamlet holding Yorick's skull. Likewise, Zé Celso heightens the dramatization of the drowning of the female character in the brook in his fabulous theatre, even though he is not entirely able to sidestep the dominant discourse that has shaped the aestheticization of the character's death. After all, with its perennial appeal, this pervasive visual history of Ophelia has become an unavoidable reference for those who would embody the character on stage and screen.

True, Ophelia continues to reflect and produce new meanings of the feminine, mirroring 'where we are in history' (Coursen 2001: 61). It is this very same plasticity of the character that allows Zé Celso to take her in a different direction through the aesthetics of cannibalism, representing her as *Oxum*, the female *orixá* of the river, re-signifying the tradition of the lady of the lake that was so widespread in Victorian poetry and art, whose primary muse was Ophelia. As an *orixá* of the waters, Ophelia becomes a cornerstone of the play for her fertility, and her victimhood is moderated. In the closing scenes, Ophelia is resuscitated and thenceforth wanders around the stage in what constitutes one of the most important deviations from Shakespeare's text. Along with the audience, Ophelia watches Hamlet's duel with Laertes unfold, blurring the lines between theatre and life – one of Zé Celso's main goals in his stage work that he calls 'te-ato' (the-act), replacing the term *teatro* (theatre). In the final scene, the Ophelia – *Oxum* association reaches its climax by means of a ceremony that resembles trance rituals performed in Candomblés *terreiros* (centres of worship). Frantically shaking a rattle and moving her body in convulsions as if possessed by the spirit of *Oxum*, Ophelia confirms her fecundity and literally spreads her legs, straddling the trap in the middle of the stage, whence she 'gives forth' to all the characters to the sound of Afro-Brazilian drumming. At the very end, the actors dance in a circle and sing a song whose refrain is 'Tupi or not Tupi', crowning the extraordinary five-hour performance. While Zé Celso's cannibalistic boldness may reveal some traits of madness, its method cannot be denied.

Ham-let has left a unique mark on the history of Shakespearean theatre in Brazil for its bold experimental nature. So influential was it at the time that some young people started to wear 'Hamlet black' in homage to the prince of Denmark (Resende 2002: 27). Furthermore, in view of the extraordinary investment Zé Celso put into the visual and dramatic portrayal of Ophelia's death and burial scenes, I would hazard to suggest that *Ham-let* also influenced the sudden emergence of the new wave of depictions of Ophelia seen in Brazilian contemporary art (Smith 2016: 129–146), including the image that graces this volume's cover by artist Christine Borowski. Like countless other contemporary artworks, Borowski's *Ofélia* (2001) takes up Millais's painting as the point of departure but interrogates its realistic representational nature in the process. Ophelia's iconic deathbed is reinterpreted as a small aquarium whose water nevertheless overflows and takes over the canvas. This image would be yet another mournful symbol in Ophelia's long-lasting tragic trail were it not for its anthropophagic guise of irony and parody.

Notes

1 *Ham-let* was directed by Zé Celso in 1993 and revived in 2001. The production received the Shell awards for best costume and best direction and was nominated for lighting and music. At the Mambembe festival it received a special award for the opening of Teatro Oficina and was nominated for best actor. My analysis is based on the DVD of the 2001 production, available for viewing at the MIT Global Shakespeares Video & Performance Archive (http://globalshakespeares.mit.edu/). All the images reproduced here are film stills from the production film.

2 Throughout his over fifty-year theatre career, Zé Celso experimented with different theatre practices, from Stanislavskian representation, Brechtian epic theatre, the ideas of Artaud in 'teatro de agressão', street happenings to the establishment of cannibalistic-inspired theatre through re-readings of classic texts like *Hamlet* and *The Bacchae*. Zé Celso has developed his own

unique anthropophagic approach to theatre, which merges music, poetry readings, dance, performance, epic theatre, popular games, fiestas and carnival.

3 Haroldo (1929–2003) and Augusto de Campos (1931–) were extremely influential figures in Brazilian literature and arts. Together with Décio Pignatari, the Campos brothers founded the Concrete poetry movement in Brazil in the 1950s, which still resonates today.

4 Candomblé is a religion based on African beliefs, which is particularly popular along the north-east Brazilian coast.

5 Teatro Oficina was considered the best theatre in the world by *The Guardian* newspaper in 2015 (Moore 2015). Teatro Oficina was also a prize-winner at the Biennial of Experimental Architecture of Prague in 2011.

6 The Ophelia created by Shakespeare derives from two texts: the story of Amleth the Dane told in Latin by Saxo Grammaticus in *Historia Danica*, originally published in Paris (1514) and subsequently republished in *Histoires Tragiques* (*c.*1570) in translation by Belleforest. In both texts, Ophelia serves as a foil for an investigation of Hamlet. Belleforest's 'translation' gives Ophelia sensual overtones, suggesting a sexual relationship between her and Amleth. Shakespeare is also influenced by the story of Brutus and Lucretia, and combines the features of the young woman in Amleth the Dane with those of Lucretia, who takes her own life after being raped. Ophelia's complexity derives from this amalgam of prototypes by Shakespeare. For more details, see Vest (1989: 7–23) and Jenkins (1997: 82–103).

7 While some critics defend the view that Ophelia's role continues to be suppressed in the twenty-first century (Leonard, for instance, states that 'increasingly, we see Ophelia being treated by directors as an object only marginally necessary for the plot' [2012: 101]), it is true that interpretations of the character have evolved and reflect different attitudes towards women and madness according to different ideologies and political principles. It should be noted, however, that radical appropriations of Ophelia's story are not a novelty: in 1979, Melissa Murray's agitprop play *Ophelia* turns the Shakespearean character into a lesbian who runs off with a woman to join a guerrilla community. These challenging and rebellious Ophelias have the ability to foster more salutary interpretations of the character and re-signify what she stands for.

8   In Branagh's version, Ophelia's madness is treated as a female malady and the idea of erotomania is resurrected. While wide gold-framed mirrors capture Kate Winslet's Ophelia as a Pre-Raphaelite muse, Branagh reserves just a fleeting close-up image to her death. In her analysis of Ophelia in performance, Coursen (2001: 58) argues that Branagh's Ophelia is still 'a victim of a director who gives her nothing but her lines'.

9   I am adopting the Brazilian spelling of *Oxum* (*Oshun*) and *orixá* (*orisha*).

10 I take full responsibility for the English translations of Portuguese texts presented in this chapter.

11 Gertrude's description of Ophelia's death has inspired painters, sculptors, filmmakers, playwrights and poets. For more on the description of Ophelia's death, see: Dash (1997); Jenkins (1997); and Shakespeare (2006).

12 All citations to *Ham-let* are hours, minutes and seconds, for example, 4:02:40 is 4 hours, 2 minutes and 40 seconds into the play.

13 When *Ham-let* was first staged in 1993, it provided a fitting platform from which to reflect on the political scenario of the time that saw the scandalous political scenario of rampant corruption, spiralling inflation and escalating violence, which culminated with the impeachment of President Collor de Mello in 1992.

14 Indeed, the popularity of images of dead or subjugated women in the visual arts and poetry of the nineteenth century still pervades contemporary popular culture to a point where the subject has become normalized – confirming a perverse male obsession that makes death an ideal of female submission. See Dijkstra (1988) and Bronfen (1992).

15 See Murphy and Sanford (2001), particularly chapter 5, 'Nesta Cidade Todo Mundo é d'Oxum: In This City Everyone Is Oxum's' (68–83); chapter 6, 'Mãe Menininha' (84–86); and chapter 15, 'Mama Oxum: Reflections of Gender and Sexuality in Brazilian Umbanda' (213–229).

16 The Ogum-Saint George is another reference that associates Shakespeare with Afro-Brazilian traditions: Shakespeare's birthday is traditionally celebrated on Saint George's Day.

17 See Young (2013) and Rutter (1998).

18 For more on the history and architecture of Teatro Oficina, see Elito (1999).

19 As Griselda Pollock explains, 'floral symbolism was widespread in nineteenth-century art and literature and Rossetti and his circle made much use of the particular meanings associated with specific flowers. [...] Flowers have often been used as a metaphor for women's sexuality, or rather their genitals. [Flowers ...] function as a metaphor which simultaneously acknowledges and displaces those sexual connotations covering or masking the sexualized parts of the body which are traditionally erased' (2003: 186–187).

20 Ana Mendieta fell to her death from a window of the apartment where she lived with her husband, also an artist. Many believe her husband pushed her out, since the neighbours reported having heard a violent argument shortly before her death. As there was no conclusive evidence, her death was recorded as accidental or suicide. Another untimely death was that of Elizabeth Siddal, the wife of painter Gabriel Rossetti and the model for Millais's *Ophelia*. While Siddal sat for the Pre-Raphaelite painters, she was also a poet and painter in her own right. She died from an overdose of laudanum. Feminist critics like Griselda Pollock and Elizabeth Bronfen have analysed Siddal's and Mendieta's 'suicides' as being symptomatic of the oppression women artists experience in a male-dominated environment. The irony is that both embodied Ophelia in art and, tragically, in their death.

21 Mendieta's images also bring to mind the way Gertrude describes Ophelia's death: 'like a creature native and endued / unto that element' who was pulled 'to muddy death' (*Ham* 4.7.177–181).

References

Bronfen, E. (1992), *Over Her Dead Body: Death, Femininity and the Aesthetic*, Manchester: Manchester University Press.

Campos, H. (2010), 'Da tradução como criação e como crítica', in *Metalinguagem & outras metas: ensaios de teoria e crítica literária*, 31–48, São Paulo: Perspectiva.

Coursen, H. R. (2001), 'Ophelia in Performance in the Twentieth Century', in C. S. Kiefer (ed.), *The Myth and Madness of Ophelia*, 53–61, Amherst: Mead Art Museum.

Dash, I. (1997), 'Conflicting Loyalties: Hamlet', in *Women's Worlds in Shakespeare's Plays*, 111–153, Newark: University of Delaware Press.

De Andrade, O. ([1928] 1991), 'Cannibalist Manifesto', *Latin American Literary Review*, 19 (38): 38–47.

Dijkstra, B. (1988), *Idols of Perversity: Fantasies of Feminine Evil in Fin-de-siecle Culture*, Oxford: Oxford University Press.

Elito, E. (1999), *Teatre Oficina – 1980–1984*, Lisbon: Editora Blau, Instituto Lina Bo e P. M. Bardi. Available online: https://ayrtonbecalle.files.wordpress.com/2015/07/bo-bardi-lina-elito-edson-teatro-oficina.pdf (accessed 30 October 2017).

Fioratti, G. (2012), 'Cannibalism on Stage', *Revista Pesquisa Fapesp*, 11 September. Available online: http://revistapesquisa.fapesp.br/en/2012/09/11/cannibalism-on-stage/ (accessed 18 October 2018).

Hale, L. (2001), 'Mama Oxum: Reflections of Gender and Sexuality in Brazilian Umbanda', in J. M. Murphy and M. Sanford (eds), *Òsun Across the Waters: A Yoruba Goddess in Africa and the Americas*, 213–229, Bloomington: Indiana University Press.

Jenkins, H., ed. (1997), *Hamlet*, Walton-on-Thames: Methuen & Co. Ltd.

Karade, B. I. (1994), *The Handbook of Yoruba Religious Concepts*, York Beach: Red Wheel.

Leonard, K. P. (2012), 'The Lady Vanishes: Aurality and Agency in Cinematic Ophelias', in K. Peterson and D. Williams (eds), *The Afterlife of Ophelia*, 101–117, New York: Palgrave.

Moore, R. (2015), 'The 10 Best Theatres', *The Guardian*, 11 December. Available online: www.theguardian.com/artanddesign/2015/dec/11/the-10-best-theatres-architecture-epidaurus-radio-city-music-hall (accessed 10 August 2017).

Murphy, J. M. and M. Sanford, eds (2001), *Òsun Across the Waters: A Yoruba Goddess in Africa and the Americas*, Bloomington: Indiana University Press.

Olivier, L. (1986), *On Acting*, London: Weidenfeld and Nicolson.

Pires, E. (2005), *Zé Celso e a oficina-uzyna de corpos*, São Paulo: Annablume.

Pollock, G. (2003), *Vision and Difference*, London: Routledge.

Resende, A. (2002), 'Introduction: Brazilian Appropriations of Shakespeare', in A. Resende (ed.), *Foreign Accents, Brazilian Readings of Shakespeare*, 11–41, Newark: University of Delaware Press.

Rutter, C. C. (1998), 'Snatched Bodies: Ophelia in the Grave', *Shakespeare Quarterly*, 49 (3): 299–319.

Santiago, S. (2001), 'Latin American Discourse: The Space In-Between', in A. L. Gazzola (ed.), *The Space In-Between: Essays on Latin American Culture*, 25–38, Durham: Duke University Press.

Shakespeare, W. (1995), *Hamlet*, trans. A. A. Carneiro de Mendonça, Rio de Janeiro: Nova Fronteira.

Shakespeare, W. (2006), *Hamlet*, ed. A. Thompson and N. Taylor, third series, London: Bloomsbury Arden Shakespeare.

Showalter, E. (1985), 'Representing Ophelia: Women, Madness, and the Responsibilities of Feminist Criticism', in G. Hartman and P. Parker (eds), *Shakespeare and the Question of Theory*, 77–94, New York: Methuen.

Smith, C. B. (2016), '"What ceremony else?": Images of Ophelia in Brazil: the Politics of Subversion of the Female Artist', in T. Bishop and A. Huang (eds), *The Shakespearean International Yearbook* 16, 129–146, New York: Routledge.

Veloso, C. (2002), *Tropical Truth: A Story of Music & Revolution in Brazil*, São Paulo: Da Capo Press.

Vest, J. M. (1989), *The French Face of Ophelia from Belleforest to Baudelaire*, New York: University Press of America.

Young, A. (2013), 'Sarah Bernhardt's Ophelia', *Borrowers and Lenders*, 10 (2). Available online: www.borrowers.uga.edu/662/show (accessed 30 November 2017).

PART TWO

Dialogue II: global conversations and intricate intersections

5

De-centring Shakespeare, incorporating otherness: Diana Henderson in conversation with Koel Chatterjee

KC *To begin with, I was wondering what you think of Cultural Anthropophagy as a different way of examining global Shakespeares? Do you think it can be a useful tool for the study of global Shakespeare?*

DH One of the most fascinating aspects of Cultural Anthropophagy as a methodology is that it offers the alternative of viewing global Shakespeares from the perspective of a non-anglophone 'Other's' native tradition, with all the complexity that the articles make clear – which also means I, as an anglophone North American, should not be the person privileged to answer the second question. Such a tradition is hybrid and turning to pre-modern worlds for authenticity in the present has always been a complicated move. But this is not a return to origins in any simplistic way, and it *is* Brazilian. It is not a UK or US export of theory nor even an attempt to build on French theory, as has been true of much recent global Shakespeares thinking, perhaps most suggestively in Douglas Lanier's work. So, there is some irony in asking what I think, and the proof should be what people who are *not* me find valuable as a means of talking back against what are still perceived as centres of Global Shakespeares Studies. I will nonetheless add that, being a woman who is interested in modernist thinking and is struck by the fact that this is coming out of a modernist manifesto, I know how masculinist those manifesto movements tended to be. So, it is very interesting to see the development of a theory that at least initially had a lot in common with Dada, with Futurism, with other modernist movements, even with the UK's Wyndham Lewis. And many (though not all) of those male assertions were often linked with violence, right? Similarly, here is Cultural Anthropophagy going back to a violent act (especially if we are asked not to think of it predominantly as a metaphor); it is not going back to any form of –

KC *Yes, not going back to a gentle merging or assimilation. I have been preoccupied for a while with the vocabulary we use for analysing global Shakespeares. I am very uncomfortable with terms like adaptation, or remediation, or even translocations. I mean, with a term like remediation, it suggests a change of media. So, when a film maker interprets a Shakespeare text on film, that is a remediation, but is it Cultural Anthropophagy? When a series of words from the text are represented as a cinematic image, for instance, is it a form of cannibalization? One of the terms used in the introduction of this collection is 'incorporating Otherness', which I liked. Cannibalizing has the association of violence which I am not sure I am comfortable with. It is such an inherently negative word, just as appropriation has connotations of plagiarism.*

DH   I agree, and my feminist pacifist side objects a bit to using that particular term.

KC   *Yes, I am tempted to use a less aggressive term like absorbing or assimilating, though neither captures the sense*

*of anthropophagy quite as well as a metaphor, of course. But
they are gentler terms, more akin to collaboration, which is the
term you use quite a bit.*

DH   And you know warrior culture, where I feel sure it is
mainly men we are talking about ... I mean when we think of
the Tupi eating enemies and even one another: that seems to
me something difficult to celebrate, even if I understand the
value of such difficulty, the way it unravels dominant Western
philosophical assumptions and binaries.

KC   *But that's where the question of power comes in, doesn't
it? I mean the minute you talk of cannibalizing a culture there
is once again the power dynamic, that seeming imbalance of
power which a lot of postcolonial theory tries to address. You
are talking of trying to ingest another culture and absorb their
power and while you make something newer and stronger, it
also means the old body or old culture ceases to exist. So, I
wonder if that is the right term and whether we need to push
the vocabulary further. I am struggling with the term itself,
though I find the metaphor quite useful.*

DH   I am too, and that is why I think it is good to have a
conversation about it. I do not think I have the answer for
everyone, but as women, we may have a slightly different
perspective on the multiple ways that power functions and
the multiple valences of the concept. Which part do you
really want to push on? And I do not think finding the right
words is ever going to end, or the terminology be stable. I
mean, the fundamental problems of inequity and cultural
exchange are not going to be solved by a new word or even
a new methodology. But if it prompts new discussion, then
that is what we are hoping for. I have always liked the word
collaboration, obviously: I use that word for a reason, in part
because it shares with anthropophagy a focus on people, not
just on works. The notion of going back to what people do with
materials: I like that. I like the agency it makes visible, the power
relations it makes visible. I like that the conversation is not just

about property, which is a problem with 'appropriation'. I like that Cultural Anthropophagy is not progressivist in the sense that evolutionary narratives are, or that even 'adaptation', the term we so frequently use, is, at least implicitly. I like the human, visceral, embodied side of it. That is really great. At the same time, a lot of great postcolonial theory has not come from Europe exclusively, and it is worth considering: how does this new vocabulary supplement that important work? If we consider cultural critics such as Bhabha and Spivak, for example, originally from hybrid subcontinental traditions, and the ways they talk about mimicry and the subaltern respectively: what is different here in using Cultural Anthropophagy, and how is it different from rethinking a metaphor Bacon used in regard to reading books, or that Montaigne more directly cited and transposed to reflect on European conflicts – so, again going back to Europe, but rethinking it? I think there *are* differences, but I want to hear others thinking them through. One difference Cultural Anthropophagy has to offer is that it is not speaking from the position of the colonized Other but rather at a moment, historically, of contestation. So, the primary point is *not* that those originary Brazilian figures were being subordinated – and that fact in itself seems worth 'thinking with'.

KC   *Yes, because I was thinking of it in terms of when I teach Shakespeare, I find students these days respond better to, say a Bhardwaj film that has completely digested the text and reinterpreted it in a new way. I was giving a lecture a few weeks ago on* Othello *and we were discussing the position of women in society and Desdemona's motivations. When they saw some of the sequences from* Omkara *[2006, dir. Bhardwaj], a lot of them who weren't Indian or have never been to India and didn't recognize the social systems there related immediately and suddenly understood why Desdemona behaved the way she did much more easily than when they had approached Desdemona through the text. I think students these days are responding better to productions where Shakespeare has been* *internalized and then reproduced in new ways in which both sources have merged to create something stronger. So, I think anthropophagy might have some benefits from a pedagogical point of view. I would then ask you whether you think that Cultural Anthropophagy as a tool can take us beyond the existing paradigms of teaching Global Shakespeare?*

DH There are at least two ways of thinking about that question. One is to stress that Cultural Anthropophagy is coming out of one particular location, which itself contains multiple cultures and interactions, and to emphasize the ways its people later have gone back to their past, to a cannibal past and redeployed it in a radically creative new way. Another is that Cultural Anthropophagy can serve as a functional metaphor that speaks across cultures, translating the unfamiliar in a way similar to what Montaigne attempted when he was writing *Of Cannibals* using the Tupi example. By which I do not mean it is 'merely' a metaphor, but rather that it shows the dynamic, inevitable power of the metaphors and stories that fundamentally structure human thinking. So, Montaigne in talking about Brazilian cannibalism helped create a new myth of the Noble Savage, which of course would have its own problems, and Cultural Anthropophagy now is trying to get away from that – from the reinstantiation of a binary between self and other, even if their valuation is inverted. The further point, however, is that Montaigne was also using this example to expose reported cannibalism within the Civil War in France, arguably defying the binary itself. So, we might want to build upon our awareness that these inherited stories have been diversely, even contrarily reinterpreted to new ends when discussing specific examples of Shakespeare: perhaps this can help us break down simpler distinctions based on region or location, that a work is 'from' there or 'from' here. In a time of global circulation, no location can be static or definitive in itself – especially when discussing collaborative artworks. Yet a consciousness about location still matters. In a similar way I hope we can now agree that we are all living in the

Anthropocene age, and as a result there is no singular nature outside culture; that is another antiquated binary that Cultural Anthropophagy flips and re-numerates to make nature rather than culture plural. Even so, single versus plural is still binary thinking. It seems to me that, be it Bhardwaj or the RSC [Royal Shakespeare Company], there is no pure, singular culture that has not gone through versions of hybridity. And what this adds cannot always be allegorized as a symptom of hierarchical power differentials, within or between cultures. So, I think all that is interesting. Addressing that complexity is one dimension of what *Omkara* does so well too. Of course, we certainly get the infiltration of the West through the representation of Kesu and so forth, and that is not to be discounted. But, as you say, the material has been entirely digested, made its own thing – and maybe that also reminds us, whether we are in the anglophone tradition or not, that of course there is no pure, continuous heritage here, there or anywhere. Which makes visible that every production, every instance of Global Shakespeares, whether or not it is so labelled, is always being digested, has always already been digested.

KC *How does cultural cannibalism affect consumption of Shakespeare then? Even as recently as 2012, I felt that there was a certain amount of exoticization, of Othering, with productions such as the ones at The Globe. Do you think that has changed in any way in the last few years? I am thinking of the most recent RSC* Twelfth Night *where Viola and Sebastian are Indian royalty washed up on British shores, or Emma Rice's* Midsummer Night's Dream *at The Globe where brown people were representations of British society and not representations of an Other necessarily. There was a sense of integration there, an incorporation of otherness that was satisfying to someone like me. Do you think anthropophagy could be the kind of critical tool we need to consume Shakespeare or teach Shakespeare today?*

DH I would make a distinction between Global Shakespeares as a phenomenon of big institutions doing performances, or state-sponsored performances, and what we as scholars do or teachers do. It is crucial that we talk increasingly across those boundaries – that is the reason we are both where we are today, having this conversation in Stratford-upon-Avon at the 'Radical Mischief' conference co-sponsored by the Shakespeare Institute *and* the RSC. This weekend exemplifies an attempt to change and shows that people are trying to do a bit more talking across professional boundaries. It is a change that more scholars need to be involved in – in the sense of intervening, working with artistic companies in ways companies can hear, and being realistic about what that company has to do. Because the artistic companies do have a bottom line: they have to have people in seats (or standing!). 'Consumption' for them involves not just what they want to theorize about, what Shakespeare does but, rather, will people show up? And (usually) pay to watch? So, in that case, there are (at least) two kinds of consumption going on. I like the idea that the cannibalistic vision gives more power to whoever is consuming; maybe that takes us away from the Adorno–Horkheimer vision of the passive capitalist consumer (or at least the often overgeneralized description of their vision)[1] and allows a little more activity, even for consumers of mainstream commercial arts. Maybe we can draw on that to bring the worlds of what we actually do in Global Shakespeares as scholars closer together with those public performances. I have worked recently with a *Merchant of Venice* that began in Venice, in the Ghetto.[2] It was very actively trying to think about how 'we', as a multicultural performance group, may be sensitive to our location and not try to colonize it. Adjust to it. So 'digesting' the place, and time – perhaps that is another thing Cultural Anthropophagy might help us do, as artistic collaborators. I have since been filming that work in America because the same director, Karin Coonrod, has put on subsequent performances there – but she has made changes to fit the place. For example, she raises issues of race in America. Even if not in the Venetian Ghetto, Judaism is obviously still crucial because *Merchant* is still about Shylock; but having an

African American woman be the female Shylock howling in pain in the middle of the play happens because this is now a performance in America. It evokes different local histories and contexts and digests the play once again in specific ways. The more we as scholars likewise understand what is possible and what is not, and can listen with or to the performers, the more impact we will have.

KC *This Venetian production is of course quite well known now, but do you think that perhaps it is easier to find examples of anthropophagy when considering non-anglophone, or even non-UK- or non-US-centric Shakespeare productions? For instance, the Parsi theatre tradition in western India which assimilated Shakespeare quite irreverently along with other European, Sanskrit and indigenous sources. I like the idea, however, that it is not just non-anglophone productions that may be analysed through the metaphor of cannibalism.*

DH I don't think it is *just* non-anglophone, but it *is* non-anglophone. There is so much to be offered by looking at non-anglophone. I also think that there is a lot to learn from translation studies. That is another dimension of what we are talking about: who is consuming what. Making visible all the performers, all the collaborators, means including translators. Back in 2008 when I was editing *Alternative Shakespeares 3*, Rui Carvalho Homem from Portugal (perhaps that is ironic in the context of thinking about Brazil as a colonized power) was writing about a translator, and a Marxist translator at that, under Salazar, under a Portuguese tyrant. The translator, Álvaro Cunhal, was trying to use Shakespeare to challenge the politics of his time and place. So, attending to creative consumption can be helpful both in analysing geographically diverse cultures and in considering the translated text. But also, if we can stop dividing text from performance even in translation, if we can stop thinking about anglophone meaning only the text part, that would be incredibly helpful. When we were doing *Merchant*, it was framed with a bit of Ruzzante, in the Venetian local dialect, at the start, plus elements of the *commedia dell'arte* tradition – all before you got to Shakespeare. Which at the same time reminded us where Shakespeare's comic figure Lancelot Gobbo came from, so in a sense you are digesting it back. We were in Europe, but we could still start thinking in terms of colonialism: it was the Venetian Republic we were talking about. I am thinking too of the good work that people such as Yong Li Lan and Eleine Ng are doing through the A-S-I-A database, studying the mixture of theatrical traditions and also translating across languages – multiple languages – and not privileging any part of the production. That certainly has a lot to offer and resonates with Cultural Anthropophagy.

KC *That is a good precursor to the question I was going to ask you next. Do you think discussions on Global Shakespeares usually centre on how the East adapts the West? Do you think there is a cross-cannibalization happening now, as we have both noticed, where the West is now absorbing the East? How does that affect the studying or teaching of Global Shakespeare now that Global Shakespeares is a part of most Shakespeare courses?*

DH Well I would say two different things again. In terms of Cultural Anthropophagy, what I like is that it complicates East/West with North/South as well. It prompts us to think about what it means for this framework to come from Brazil, which has very rich theatrical traditions *and* Shakespeare traditions: among the best known, of course, being the theatre of the oppressed, of the worker, of the poor, in the practices of Augusto Boal and others. This tradition encourages us to think differently about aesthetics, to reconsider what roles theatre performs within the wider cultural surround. So, the North/South distinction as well as the East/West becomes very important for what Cultural Anthropophagy might add to much Global Shakespeares work. But the East/West dynamics at present absolutely matter too. Again, it is very hard to say where the boundaries are. I do not think there is any person now, no matter where or who you are, who has access to an uninterrupted chain from Shakespeare, his time and place. Making the complexities of inheritance more visible is crucial. Based on what I have seen working with those who create the MIT Global Shakespeares Video and Performance Archive, much of what gets shared is a direct result of which scholars and artistic companies we meet. Personal networks work. So do economic realities: where is the money, and where is the funding? Where are the traditions that are rich and where is there a cluster of people teaching or performing Shakespeare? Consumption follows from national or local structures. It follows the people who are moving across as well as within those spaces. So, for example, when you four [Koel Chatterjee, Varsha Panjwani, Preti Taneja, Thea Buckley] created an Indian Shakespeares on Screen event in London [2016, in collaboration with Asia House and the BFI], the impetus came from four people who straddle those two worlds. Are you East or West? Is the Brazilian who draws on modernist manifesto thinking and cannibalism to be located as North or South? Does it matter if he is the child of Italian immigrants? These networks of cosmopolitan transnational movement are overlaid on particular spaces and times. Acknowledging these realities can help us be more nuanced when discussing location. You know the debates in Asia, such as the attack on Ong Keng Sen for mixing different nations or languages or traditions, for mix-and-match kinds of hybridity. But you know too about the Parsi theatre's mixed traditions … it is not like doing traditional Kathakali, it is mixing. So how do we feel about that? You tell me what you think.

KC *Well that is the central question. I mean you go back to adaptation theory, don't you? People are still caught up in the question of fidelity, how faithful is this to the original. But there is no 'original' anymore.*

DH And never was, by the way – because theatre is a performance form. And we know that, every dimension of it, from publishing at that time to performance at that time, we just know that the process was dynamic and always changing.

KC *There is also an awareness now of how it's not the author. Of how he's not the only creator. There's the performers coming in to it, the editor coming in to it. So I think it is ... there's very distinct schools in India in terms of adaptation where people still are struggling with colonial reverence to the text so it's interesting that a Kathakali Shakespeare might cause quite a bit of reaction. But then again, Bhardwaj's Haider [2014] had quite a divisive reaction in India with two camps of people either strongly supported or strongly opposed the film.*

DH Though that was less about Shakespeare and more about how the film comments on Kashmir: the boldness of going into a contemporary minefield, quite literally.

KC *Yes, because it reminded me of the Thai Macbeth, Shakespeare Must Die [2012] by Ing Kanjanavanit, which was censored and banned in Thailand for the movie's anti-monarchy overtones. There is that space which is ... I wonder if cannibalizing Shakespeare is actually touching a chord in the way that Shakespeare perhaps meant it to, forcing people to get away from their elitist and anglo-centric way of thinking about Shakespeare. That's probably why, going back to my students, why they react so instinctively to the themes of the plays when they are presented a version which is not 'typical' Shakespeare, which has been cannibalized and reinterpreted in new and more familiar ways. Why perhaps Emma Rice's shows brought in packed houses at The Globe and attracted a demographic who usually stay away from theatres. They instinctively seem to relate to a Chinese or Japanese production in a way that promotes questioning and debate where they fail to react to more traditional productions.*

DH This also gets at the question, what are familiar genres for students now? More students are comfortable with film than with theatre. They have more experience of it. So, what feels more current or immediate and therefore gets their emotions involved are the conventions of film. Even if it is film from another culture in a different language. Film is still more familiar than going and watching people in live embodiment art forms. For most students. But you also brought up another aspect of the Cultural Anthropophagy vocabulary, which could be useful as a counter to the reintroduction of Shakespeare as the figure of the author, which has in the last fifteen years become oddly resurgent. Even among some people who were involved in new historicism and cultural materialism in the first place – which would seem to imply that you would not then go write in familiar Bardolatrous ways about the genius Shakespeare and how he foresaw everything that is happening now. But that genius-artist is a difficult romantic inheritance to let go of, for students as well as for 'consumers' in audience terms. It is very hard to resist … there is a self-interested reason for all of us to hold on to Shakespeare at a time when humanities and the arts are not generally given the prestige they once held. You talked about consumption, you talked about globalization. Given the economic realities in which we are living, I really do understand the strategic use of the author figure. But it is also good to fight against Shakespeare being the singular genius or invoking him as an author-figure unironically. So, I think 'Tupi or not Tupi' is a pretty funny one-liner for playing against all that, which could be useful.

KC *So where do you think Global Shakespeares as an academic discipline is going to go from here?*

DH Predictions are hard. I would hope it is going into new territories. I will say that Brazil is currently the most highly ranked nation in terms of the proportion of performance work included on the MIT open-access Global Shakespeares Video and Performance Archive. And, as mentioned earlier, that is not because the site aspires to be an accurate world map based on any form of scientific survey of productions worldwide. That result is based on networks, and local producers being interested and interesting enough to have captured attention from the local scholars who serve as regional editors, because the project is quite grassroots-orientated. To generalize from that: there needs to be more grassroots movement, there needs to be more bottom-up movement which involves both scholars and performers. In the MIT example, Brazil is a place that has done that, and therefore they have produced a high proportion of the collection. If I can speak on behalf of the MIT collaborators for a moment: we also intentionally have less anglophone work there for precisely the reason we do not want to replicate the hierarchies that events such as the Globe-to-Globe festival tend to reproduce; I am thinking about the marketing and language that surrounded the performances, that 'Coming home to the Globe' core/periphery inheritance, the ghosts (or perhaps zombies?) of colonialism. Especially but not only in Britain, English-language scholars and artists need to be conscious about the export mentality of our economy right now. Once again, trying to resist that dominant model is very hard, and it is also very hard to find people, enough people, who can record and do the labour of capturing alternatives. Cameras are getting cheaper, but it is still hard to get quality productions that can be explained by scholars so that others (students, general viewers) elsewhere can understand the performances in their local habitat with the subtleties that one needs. We are not trying just to say, 'I saw something, it was really exciting', or even to have students say, 'that was exciting!' and stop there. That is not enough in itself to warrant adding it to a scholarly archive or site. So, we need to get to know and hear from local scholars in order to enrich the picture. How do those scholars have the money to come to conferences, or how do we have the money to go and see them? These are complicated issues. As a result, for example, African countries are wildly under-represented – which sends us back to the issue of the global economy itself. As we talk about India, we are talking about the legacy of the Commonwealth still, even if subcontinental artists are doing their versions of Shakespeare in various languages and traditions that are not in English. When you talk about your students, Bhardwaj works very well, because *Bhardwaj* works very well. Because he is a good film maker with a good-sized budget. And so, if we post some low-budget filming of a low-budget performance, do we just reinscribe the inequities? Is it worse to have nothing? Is it worse to have tokenism? Is it worse to have something that the students will look at and say, 'I don't get that' and be put off? So, these are the concerns scholars, wherever they can, need to be thinking about, and listening. Listening is more important than me talking, telling others where the future is going. I want scholars from across the globe to come forward, to feel welcomed to tell us about what is going on where they are. Plus, as more people are used to a range of social media, we may be at a point when that big-budget or filmic bias is becoming less of a problem. Because really, all you need is a cell phone to record, if the work is sufficiently interesting in itself. There has to be more exchange, and that brings with it opportunities for younger generations – for our students too who are so at home online, for the first YouTube generation. I do think we have many more possibilities for sharing that diversity, so I hope that is at least one of the places Global Shakespeares is going.

Notes

1   See Adorno and Horkheimer ([1944] 1972).

2   The Compagnia de' Colombari production directed by Karin Coonrod was first performed as part of the 2016 commemorations of the 500th anniversary of its founding and the 400th anniversary of Shakespeare's death. Modified versions were subsequently performed in Montclair, New Jersey (2017) and at Yale University and Dartmouth College (2018), and Henderson has developed an online module and documentary incorporating some of the show's development and performance footage. Pertinent to what follows is that the show featured five different actors playing Shylock's scenes across each evening's performance, and included an extra-textual moment when all five gather in grief at his daughter Jessica's elopement; at that moment, the one female Shylock releases a loud, long howl.

References

Adorno, T. and M. Horkheimer ([1944] 1972) 'The Culture Industry: Enlightenment as Mass Deception', in M. Horkheimer and T.W. Adorno, *Dialectic of Enlightenment: Philosophical Fragments*, ed. Gunzelin Schmid Noerr, trans. Edmund Jephcott, 94–136, Stanford, CA: Stanford University Press.

Andrade, O. ([1928] 1991), 'Cannibalist Manifesto', trans. L. Bary, *Latin American Literary Review*, 19 (38): 38–44.

Budasz, R. (2005), 'Of Cannibals and the Recycling of Otherness', *Music and Letters*, 87 (1): 1–15.

Carvalho Homem, R. (2008), 'Memory, Ideology, Translation: *King Lear* Behind Bars and Before History', in D. E. Henderson (ed.), *Alternative Shakespeares 3*, 204–220, London: Routledge.

Islam, G. (2011), 'Can the Subaltern Eat? Anthropophagic Culture as a Brazilian Lens on Post-Colonial Theory', *Organization*, 19 (2): 159–180.

Johnson, R. (1987), 'Tupy or not Tupy: Cannibalism and Nationalism in Contemporary Brazilian Literature and Culture', in J. King (ed.), *Modern Latin American Fiction: A Survey*, 41–59, London: Faber & Faber.

Lestringant, F. (1997), *Cannibals: The Discovery and Representation of the Cannibal from Columbus to Jules Verne*, vol. 37, Berkeley: University of California Press.

Marchi, D. M. (1993), 'Montaigne and the New World: The Cannibalism of Cultural Production', *Modern Language Studies*, 23 (4): 35–54.

Simanowski, R. (2010), 'Digital Anthropophagy: Refashioning Words as Image, Sound and Action', *Leonardo*, 43 (2): 159–163.

6

Devouring Shakespeare translocally

Marcel Alvaro de Amorim

In this chapter, I discuss the ways in which the idea of Cultural Anthropophagy, explored in this volume, may enhance our understanding of how Shakespeare's texts are continuously re-signified across countless translocal settings – i.e. in permanent transit through a continuous array of de/recontextualizations taking place in various social and physical spaces (Blommaert 2005) – and from many different viewpoints. I shall try to answer the following questions: (1) What is the state-of-the-art in the field of investigation broadly known as 'Global Shakespeare'?; (2) Which theoretical-methodological approaches have been guiding researchers from this field in their analysis of Shakespearean performances, translations and adaptations produced around the world?; (3) How can the anthropophagic perspective be viewed as a means of conceiving Shakespeare as a translocal author, at once part and parcel of various natures? To achieve this, I interact with a number of circulating texts that construct the Bard as multiple and diversified across numerous social, political and geographical spaces. My contention is that it is impossible to posit a single *English* Shakespeare. Quite the contrary: I shall argue in favour of the existence of many different Shakespeares, each one apprehended through/by the various centres of intentionality that enact, translate and adapt the Bard by bringing their own uniqueness into the equation.

Between the months of March and April 2015, an enthralling musical named *Something Rotten*, directed and choreographed by Casey Nicholaw, premiered on Broadway. Its title makes a direct allusion to one of the most famous lines in *Hamlet*: 'Something is rotten in the state of Denmark' (1.4.90). Set in the 1590s, the playful musical tells the story of Nick and Nigel Bottom, two brothers who hopelessly attempt to write a blockbuster play at exactly the same time as a fictionalized Shakespeare consolidates his reputation as the superstar of the English Renaissance. Halfway through their journey, the Bottom brothers meet a clairvoyant, Nostradamus, who tells them that the theatre of the future will interweave singing, dancing and action. Intrigued by the prophecy and galvanized into action, Nick and Nigel go on to compose what will become the world's first musical.

As is the case in productions such as the much beloved and harshly criticized *Shakespeare in Love*, directed by John Madden in 1998, *Something Rotten* brings up Shakespeare, the most famous occidental writer, as a character. In the musical, Shakespeare is turned into a popstar of sorts. The character is described by the actor Adam Pascal, who played the role after the exit of Tony-winner Christian Borle, as 'a peacock-ish Frank-N-Furter, Freddie Mercury, David Lee Roth sort – guys who like to strut'.[1] Throughout the dialogue of the musical, allusions to the Shakespearean oeuvre abound, as do references to events of Renaissance England and to characters with whom Shakespeare himself allegedly met. And yet, there is little to claim to historical truthfulness, and all the Shakespeare-related facts are visibly distorted, made up and reconstructed in order to fit the new plot.

Douglas Lanier, in his 2007 essay 'Shakespeare™: Myth and Biographical Fiction', reminds us of Shakespeare's eminence in certain strands of the contemporary world's cultural realms. Lanier (2007: 93) maintains that, in the field of culture, Shakespeare's name and image evoke a number of qualities that can then be embedded into various texts and products, thereby re-signifying such objects. According to Lanier, Shakespeare's prominence is not limited to his name or to his plays, but extends even to his face: 'if, then, Shakespeare is the Coca-Cola of canonical culture, its most long-lived and widespread brand name, the face of Shakespeare, familiar from the Droeshout portrait that graces the First Folio, has become its trademark' (Lanier 2007: 93). In other words, as we associate Shakespeare's name or face with cultural products, according to Lanier (2007: 94), we are ascribing particular values to them – values that are, in turn, preserved, extended and transformed by means of the Shakespearean canon. This seems to be why spectacles and blockbuster productions, such as *Something Rotten* and *Shakespeare in Love*, display virtually no concern for historical faithfulness. Instead, they work by fabricating details of the Bard's biography; they emphasize worldly or otherwise questionable characteristics of Shakespeare's life 'in order to cut the mythic author down to size' (Lanier 2007: 101).

Something Rotten and *Shakespeare in Love* are but two among a range of examples attesting the current worldwide 'spread' of Shakespeare's image and work, which have travelled across social and cultural contexts for centuries with no clear points of departure or arrival.[2] As stated in Anston Bosman's essay 'Shakespeare and Globalization', the diffusion of Shakespeare's plays has generally been understood as constitutive of 'globalization', seen by Bosman as 'the compression of the world and the intensification of consciousness of the world as a whole' (2010: 185).[3] Bosman attempts to explain the dissemination of Shakespeare's work by shifting his attention to the author's own time and milieu – i.e. a moment of ever-increasing cultural exchange, not only among European nations but also towards the Atlantic and, to a lesser extent, the Pacific. Bosman also underscores the fact that Shakespearean works circulated not only in *Englishes* – emanating from the 'global centers of theatre (London) or film (Los Angeles)' (2010: 286) – but also in other languages. Shakespeare was diversely staged, translated and adapted, and at times even hailed as a fellow-countryman. It is worth recalling, as mentioned by Marlene Soares dos Santos (2010), 'our Shakespeare's trajectory to *unser* Shakespeare': in German Romanticism, writers, academics and theatre directors resorted to Shakespeare to invigorate their own nationalist ideals.

Despite Bosman's unquestionable insights, his text still seems to be subtly indebted to the ideas of *centre* and *margins* or *peripheries*. His debt becomes lexically visible in passages such as 'Shakespeare's worldwide *influence*' (2010: 292; emphasis mine), 'familiar *domesticating* strategy' (294; emphasis mine) and 'Shakespeare's global *dissemination*' (295; emphasis mine), and through his use of the concept of *Glocalization*, that is, the 'global flow of Shakespeare [...] *filtered* through *local* environments' (290; emphasis mine).[4] Thus, while certainly sophisticated, Bosman's reasoning seems slightly aligned with the Global Shakespeare imaginary constructed by the Massachusetts Institute of Technology's (MIT) Global Shakespeare project, and by the British Globe-to-Globe project. While the former seeks to passively apprehend 'the world-wide reception and production of Shakespeare's plays', the latter tries to set up an English play that then 'travels' around the globe.[5]

As regards Globe-to-Globe, Christy Desmet (2017: 17) argues that the enterprise's ambition is 'to take the Globe brand worldwide while simultaneously epitomizing the great globe itself within its traveling company'. A noteworthy success case would be Dominic Dromgoole's *Hamlet*, which travelled along a route of 197 countries between 2014 and 2016. Alexa Huang (2017) evokes a telling episode that took place during the tour's African leg: a sixteen-year-old girl, Annastacia, accompanied by a group of classmates, took a sixty-kilometre ride to the city where the play would be staged – Kasane, Botswana. According to Huang, the girl then reconstructed the play's meanings through the filter of her own experience, and allegedly said that 'in our culture when somebody marries his brother's wife this is dangerous because children end up doing mistakes in life' (Huang 2017: 425). From my point of view, Annastacia's testimony, while attesting the multiple perspectives that enrich the play's reception, has little to add to the idea of a truly Global Shakespeare, given that multiple perceptions are an inextricable part of any reading act.

In Brazil, I attended a performance of Dromgoole's *Hamlet* in the city of Rio de Janeiro, on 30 December 2014, in a city theatre called Cidade das Artes. While it was certainly interesting to witness an English-language Shakespearean performance in my own country, the feeling of being a Brazilian watching an English spectacle remained similar to what I felt in Shakespeare's Globe in London and in the Royal Shakespeare Company (RSC) theatres, located in Stratford-upon-Avon. It is also worth mentioning that the audience at the Rio performance was mostly composed of critics and members of academia, as well as upper-class citizens from Rio de Janeiro. The theatre itself is located in a well-off neighbourhood called Barra da Tijuca, locally nicknamed 'the Brazilian Miami' on account of how its structure, architecture and lifestyle supposedly reflect those found in Miami, in the United States. Furthermore, in an interview to *O Globo*, one of Brazil's most widely read newspapers,[6] Dominic Dromgoole states that the tour brought to life the Shakespearean view of the world as a stage. It begs the question: would the world be a special stage for English companies, like The Globe, to travel and transport Shakespeare from the *centre* to the *margins*?

This view of Shakespeare's oeuvre as a travelling product is also adopted, albeit more critically, in Andrew Dickson's 2015 book, *Worlds Elsewhere: Journeys Around Shakespeare's Globe*. Dickson's research highlights Shakespeare's curious mobility: while the author himself remained mostly in one place, his work is repeatedly adapted and adopted in a number of countries around the world. We are once again somehow introduced to the idea of a European/English author who, along his trajectory, is both aesthetically and socially appropriated by other countries and cultures. Dickson, however, relies on a more critical reading of Shakespeare's textual journey. One of his pieces for *The Guardian*, for instance, strongly criticizes the idea behind the Globe-to-Globe project. As it challenges the reasons motivating *Hamlet*'s worldwide circulation, the article asserts that the countries that hosted the play 'might not be so uncharted, that Shakespeare might already inhabit these places in a multiplicity of languages and forms'. Dickson goes on to argue that sending a British company to perform a canonical play around the world, with practically no dialogue with local forms of producing Shakespearean plays, may reveal a neocolonialist tone, especially if we consider that the play was being enacted in Renaissance English, often with no subtitles – all of which seems somehow at odds with the idea of constructing a truly 'global' Shakespeare (Dickson 2017).

As a methodology, the idea of a Global Shakespeare was systematized, among others, by Alexa Huang's (2013) important 'Global Shakespeare as Methodology' based on Deleuze and Guattari's *rhizome* concept. Huang establishes an interesting connection between so-called Global Shakespeare and business models; she also claims that the field tries to deal with 'political and aesthetic distances between cultures' (2013: 280). In that sense, Shakespeare is astutely viewed as an author of the globe, with a global structure, since 'Global Shakespeares seem to be all over the map' (280). Nonetheless, Huang still seems to subtly anchor her claims in the idea of a travelling Shakespeare. Stagings, translations and adaptations of Shakespearean drama, according to her, become global as they travel beyond their 'native' habitat by means of transnational financing and casting networks. Despite a valuable contribution to studies in the field, especially her claim that 'international artistic exchange is not always a rosy undertaking' – which opposes the passive idea of 'intercultural performance' – Huang's approach sometimes still seems to lexically hinge on a cordial understanding of the appropriation process: Global Shakespeares '*incorporated* the traditions' (282; emphasis mine), established themselves as '*hybrid* performances' (282; emphasis mine), and Shakespeare himself is an author with a 'global *reach*' (283; emphasis mine). In addition, Shakespeare is seen as an 'agent [...] to enable the subaltern to speak' (283), in a movement that could reify the centre–margin/periphery divide. Incidentally, such a divide is directly criticized in Gayatri Chakravorty Spivak's essay 'Can the Subaltern Speak?' (1988), here evoked by Huang.

In 'Global Shakespeare as Methodology', Huang also seems to posit the alleged lack of a Shakespearean tradition in countries such as South Africa, Brazil and India (2013: 285). And yet, to name but one example, in Brazil alone over ten films based on Shakespearean plays have been produced so far. The plays themselves have been recurrently staged in Brazil since the nineteenth century, from foreign companies visiting the country with their own cast to perform in Brazil's colonial capital to the more contemporary *Shakespeare 39* project, which aims to stage thirty-nine plays from the Shakespearean canon by 2020.[7]

In more recent articles, however, such as 'Global Shakespeare as a Tautological Myth' (2016) and 'Global Shakespeare Criticism Beyond the Nation State' (2017), Huang introduces the idea that 'Shakespeare and its global afterlife have formed a tautology: Shakespeare is believed to be universal, which is why the canon has gone global; on the other hand, global Shakespeare is seen as evidence of Shakespeare's universality' (2016: 3). She goes on to argue that Shakespearean performances have welcomed increasingly multinational and multilingual casts, embodying a multiplicity of culturally diverse accents (2017: 424). Huang sustains that this also happens in anglophone settings, where Shakespeare has been reshaped and hybridized by new accents, diverse styles, multinational casts and, oftentimes, international financing networks. In truth, engaging with intercultural repertoires would promote new levels of freedom in staging Shakespeare (Huang 2017: 424–425). Such ideas might be applied to the performance of *A Midsummer Night's Dream* directed by Emma Rice and broadcast worldwide via streaming services in September 2016. The play, part of the *Shakespeare Lives* project – a digital online festival co-held by the BBC and the British Council – established a close dialogue with the recording and adaptation styles adopted in Bollywood, India, which led the BBC to name it 'the Bollywood-infused *A Midsummer Night's Dream*'.[8]

The reverberations of Bollywoodian culture in Emma Rice's play stood out not only in the distribution of accents but also in the scenic composition, the use of music and actors' bodily performances. Rice, who had little first-hand experience with Shakespeare's plays – she had directed one performance of *Cymbeline* for the RSC – did not boast of any expertise, and risked dismaying members of a more purist audience by introducing potentially off-putting elements. The all-embracing Indian tone, the presence of a sign with the words 'Rock the Ground' hanging from the stage, and the introduction of Helena's outstanding transfiguration into Helenus, made the whole spectacle considerably more transnational, pop and queer. Soundtrack-wise, the Indian flavour was constructed through the ongoing sound of a zither and the use of bhangra dancing – all in dialogue with the voices of English poets and musicians such as George Formby, David Bowie and John Donne.

Despite the production's potential for devouring *Others* – an idea to which I shall return to in a minute – I harboured a major concern: it had to do with how Bollywoodian culture was incorporated into the performance. It seemed crucial to verify whether the translocal, potentially transformative elements were not merely added as exotic and secondary elements to the dramatic text. As argued by Nigerian writer Chimamanda Ngozi Adichie through one of the characters in *Purple Hibiscus*, whatever is seen as the *Other* is quite often used as an auxiliary tool in cultures of the so-called centre: 'Everyday our doctors [Nigerian doctors] go there [the United States] and end up washing plates for *oyinbo* because *oyinbo* does not think we study medicine right. Our lawyers go and drive taxis because *oyinbo* does not trust how we train them in law' (Adichie 2004: 244).

Huang believes that the action of 'borrowing' cultural factors – as done by Emma Rice – adds an element of novelty to Shakespeare's plays (Huang 2017: 245). The rationale behind the Global Shakespeare project is thereby re-signified: it ceases to pursue an international dissemination of Britishness and begins to focus on the possibility of dialogue between cultures. In Huang's words, '"Global Shakespeare" does not refer exclusively to non-Anglo-American performances made "elsewhere", away from the more familiar metropolitan centres of Shakespeare activities such as New York and London. Rather, a Shakespearean performance is global when it goes on an international tour or when it borrows themes or techniques across cultures' (Huang 2017: 427). Thus, Huang asserts that Global Shakespeare is a worldwide, widespread phenomenon lacking a source or a point of inception (2017: 431–432). Pinpointing it on a map does not seem to account for the transnational experience of cultural flux. Along these lines, the author also tries to deconstruct the idea of a so-called *country of origin*; she believes, instead, that the tracking of a Global Shakespeare should be grounded on the mobility of cultures and on translocality, rather than on the idea of a nation-state.

Paradoxically, despite her substantial contributions towards the deconstruction of oppositions such as country of origin/ country of staging, English Shakespeare/Global Shakespeare, etc., the author still seems to lexically reaffirm the local/global dichotomy in her more recent texts, not only by espousing the idea of *borrowing*, alluded to in the previous quotation, but through the use of binary oppositions: 'He may be *local* in England, but he is *universally* worshipped *elsewhere*' (Huang 2016: 5; emphasis mine) and 'These "*locally* grown" global Shakespeares' (7; emphasis mine). Equally worrisome is her repeated claim that Shakespeare could give voice to 'marginalized, oppressed, and disenfranchised cultural voices' (Huang 2017: 426), thereby becoming an instrument of empowerment: an agent for the promotion of what she calls 'multicultural good'. If not clearly understood, Huang's position could evoke a certain neocolonialist ideal according to which Shakespeare – a voice from the centre – would give voice to those in situations of oppression and marginalization – those on the margins of society.

In an attempt to dislodge the local/global binary and challenge the implications of a Global Shakespeare, Robert Sawyer and Varsha Panjwani, in the introduction to a special issue of *Multicultural Shakespeare: Translation, Appropriation and Performance*, opt for the term *cross-cultural*, largely because of the different meanings it evokes. According to the authors, the term may refer to the mere comparison and/or correlation between diverse cultures, but its meaning may also transcend what we regard as cultural differences. It may index an intersection, a cultural crossroads; or even allude to a clash between adversarial or irreconcilable cultures (Sawyer and Panjwani 2017: 9). The local/global distinction, seen by Christy Desmet (2017: 20) as intricate and oxymoronic, is averted. In fact, according to Desmet, even the word 'glocalization' is not exempt from criticism – as signalled in this chapter – as not only does it sustain the local/global opposition but it also seems to rely on the same egalitarian, pacifist objective proposed by the idea of an intercultural Shakespeare: 'like its cognate, intertextuality, interculturalism implies a relatively neutral, if imaginary space where two cultures meet, mingle, and converse' (21).

The approach favoured in this chapter – the use of Cultural Anthropophagy as a translocal methodology – may, in that sense, introduce a new dimension to Global Shakespeare studies by reconsidering Desmet's (2017: 18) contention that Shakespeare's plays are locally reconfigured via their interaction with local practices – which, as I have argued, does not decentre the local/global opposition. In fact, my understanding is that the texts of the Shakespearean canon belong to and are crossed by numerous viewpoints, each of which acts as a potential centre of intentionality, and each of which apprehends all the others from the perspective of its own potency and characteristics. The vision I defend stands apart from notions of multi/trans/interculturalism and draws closer to what Eduardo Viveiros de Castro (2015: 42), in his analysis of Amerindian Perspectivism, terms 'Multinaturalism': the idea that, in the anthropophagic movement, a meeting occurs not only between cultures but also between a number of natures constructed from different perspectives. Therefore, a Shakespearean staging, translation or adaptation brought about within specific geographical, social and political spaces may be understood as part of an ontology of multiple interchangeable natures.

To briefly consider the notion of anthropophagy in the field of Brazilian Social and Cultural Studies, let us remember that the notion initially refers to the act of eating parts of a human being – an abhorrent, transgressive and violent act condemned by virtually every single society, religion and culture, committed by so-called primitive, especially indigenous, peoples. The act, however, must be seen as more than a barbaric dietary habit: it is an exercise of 'devouring', in the sense that some of the peoples that practised it believed that, in doing so, they absorbed other people's – and tribes' – skills and strengths. For the Tupinambás indigenous people, for instance, more than an act of cannibalism linked to the notions of dietary habit and predatory behaviour, anthropophagy symbolized a movement of incorporation of, admiration for and revenge against the Other. Tellingly, in the Tupinambá cosmology, anthropophagy came to exist by means of powerful cannibal ceremonies akin to the ones described in Michel de Montaigne's essay 'On Cannibalism' (2002).

In the context of the Brazilian literary modernist movement, a well-known reference is Oswald de Andrade's 'Manifesto Antropofágico' (Cannibalist Manifesto), which establishes anthropophagy not only as an exercise of 'differentiation' between contexts but as a means for union and confluence. In the author's own words, 'ONLY ANTHROPOPHAGY UNITES US. Socially. Economically. Philosophically' (2011: 67).[9] The act of violently devouring a so-called foreigner, a stranger, turning them into part of us and vice versa, is seen as a cornerstone of the Brazilian cultural paradigm: 'We made Christ born in Bahia. Or in Belém do Pará' (Andrade 2011: 69). The construction of a precise definition of anthropophagy, however, is seen even by Andrade himself as a formidable task (2009: 65), because every possible definition may be seen as inherently flawed and incomplete. In an interview later published in *Os dentes do dragão* (The Dragon's Teeth), Andrade sketches a definition of the term:

Anthropophagy is the celebration of the New Land's instinctive aesthetics. Or perhaps: it is the decimation of imported idols, the ascension of racial totems. Or still: it is the land of America itself, the fruitful clay, as filtered by and expressed through the yielding temperaments of its artists. (2009: 65)

In other words: a violent movement of incorporating the Other, of integrating alterity, through a subconscious process of elaboration. A process that, according to Andrade, is devoid of hatred or bloodthirst: *we eat what we see as superior*. Andrade maintains that the movement of Cultural Anthropophagy seeks, in those possessing preternatural gifts, anything that could be devoured, for 'never has there been news of a man who swallowed that which disgusted him' (66).

Eduardo Viveiros de Castro revisits the notion of anthropophagy as a practice ascribed to Brazilian indigenous peoples in his essay 'O mármore e a murta: sobre a inconstância da alma selvagem' (The Inconstancy of the Indian Soul). In his understanding, the Tupinambás viewed, in their devoured enemies, facets of an alterity that attracted them and that they should attract in return. Their foes were potential figures of affinity. According to Viveiros de Castro, the inexistence of such forms of alterity would result in a bleak, indifference-ridden, paralytic world (2002: 207). 'The other', claims the Brazilian anthropologist, 'was not merely thinkable – it was indispensable' (195). Moreover, it was not a matter of randomly reproducing or imposing one identity over another; or, conversely, of resisting such a process. Rather, the act involved the creation a violent, yet dialogical, relationship with the Other with the ultimate goal of transforming one's own identity. Viveiros de Castro maintains that an aggressive and not always consensual 'exchange, rather than identity, was the central value being affirmed' (216). In fact, it is worth recalling that, according to him, the very idea of a 'relation can only exist between what differs and in so far as it differs' (2004: 20).

By taking the anthropophagic position as a way of challenging the idea of a Global Shakespeare, I shall see the tiresome distinction between global and local as a violent process of *transfertilization* (Moehn 2012); that is, of various criss-crossings and mutual transformations. It is my belief that any performance, translation or adaptation of Shakespeare's work, if understood through the lens of Cultural Anthropophagy, performs a radical existential deconstruction: the 'I' and the 'Other' become recognizable not as a third, ontologically definable element but as an ontology of multiple interchangeable natures. When we anthropophagically devour Shakespeare, we are in fact refusing the project of our own and the Other's autonomous existence; we are attempting to produce intelligibility about the point of intersection between the multiple natures that compose us.

The notion of anthropophagy may even help us to renegotiate the way texts are catalogued as canonical/non-canonical, or original/derivative; the diverse stagings, translations and adaptations of Shakespeare may be seen, instead, as an ongoing, dialogic and violent creative process that causes Shakespeare to be fully and happily incorporated under multiple worldviews. To take this one step further, understanding that process from the perspective of Cultural Anthropophagy means conceiving of a truly translocal Shakespeare: the bard becomes someone possessing such awe-inspiring qualities that it becomes necessary to capture and devour him – and, in doing so, pluralize him – and to comprehend him as the interaction of multiple natures. Shakespeare's qualities become an indistinguishable part of us, as we become parts of him.

Without a doubt, Shakespeare has been repeatedly devoured in many different settings, in a number of different stages, across the world. Akira Kurosawa's renowned *The Bad Sleep Well* (1960), for instance, retells the story of *Hamlet* in the context of the Japanese corporate world. The director positions the storyline in the twentieth century and integrates *Hamlet* to his story by means of fragments and allusions. Mark Thornton Burnett stresses that 'the film trades in partial parallels, breaks up and distributes Hamletian themes in a more wide-ranging fashion, and substitutes different characters for the Shakespearean "originals" at different points' (2013: 404). To achieve his purpose, Kurosawa embarks on the trajectory of *film noir* and of the then-popular Hollywood-style detective productions, reconstructing them in a context in which Japan, recently freed from the Allied Occupation, sought to build its own identity on the road to becoming a major political and economic power. The Japanese production cannot simplistically be seen as a by-product of a travelling Shakespeare, but must be taken as a translocal artistic product: a radical de/reconstruction of *Hamlet*. Its singularity is to be found even in its classification as *not quite a Shakesperean adaptation*.

A decade later, in Brazil, came Ozualdo Candeias's *A Herança* (The Heritage), another markedly anthropophagic production. Premiering in 1971 and set on a large farm in the São Paulo countryside, it adapts the story of the Danish prince whose father was murdered and whose mother married his uncle. Candeias not only shifts the narrative's chronological frame by recontextualizing the play's events in twentieth-century Brazil, but he also rereads the story's context and apprehends Shakespeare from a new perspective. In Candeias's words:

So I took Hamlet, this European, Middle Age monarch, and I put him in a farm in the São Paulo countryside in modern times. In Shakespeare, it's a king with a son. In my adaptation, it's a rich farmer with a son, Omeleto. (Candeias quoted in Reis 2010: 90)

The director's devouring movement is striking. He rereads, deconstructs and reconstructs the Elizabethan play in an attempt to produce a new, unique narrative that emerges from another point of view. In his reading of the *Hamlet*, the Brazilian director focuses on the social clash for the use of land – the Land Reform – as well as on issues related to ethnic discrimination. He thus engages with a series of social discourses that circulated throughout the 1960s and the 1970s both in Brazil and across the globe. Additionally, Candeias presents us with an aesthetically bold production that, through its near absence of dialogue, sparse use of subtitles and integration of a soundtrack filled with Brazilian countryside songs and animal sounds, brings into question not only the topics it addresses but the Shakespearean substance itself – the very nature of the Shakespearean canon: while most of the dialogue is muted, part of the 'To be, or not to be' soliloquy is included and is spoken in English, but in an ironical accent, which seems very relatable to the Cultural Anthropophagy perspective.

Finally, I must stress that the process of anthropophagically staging, translating or adapting Shakespeare does not come about automatically or intuitively: neither in political, geographical and social spaces within the so-called anglophone world, nor in spaces outside it. Anthropophagically devouring Shakespeare is part of a clear-cut project: it is an intentional endeavour on the part of those involved in the artistic creation of such works. Through the idea of Cultural Anthropophagy, I believe it is possible to view Shakespeare itself and the Shakespearean text, in this chapter's terms, as transnaturally constructed – as a series of textual/cultural faces constituted from various viewpoints that, far from erasing the Other's nature, incorporate it by devouring it: at once an awestruck act and a vengeful one.

Notes

1 This statement was given by Adam Pascal in an interview to *The Orange County Register* (Marchese 2017).

2 It is important to keep in mind, as argued by Bauman and Briggs (1990), that texts travel and produce so-called 'text trajectories' – i.e. they possess the ability to travel and circulate at high speeds, with no clear points of departure or arrival, while both embodying their historical characteristics and aggregating new meanings. In doing so, they promote individuals' socialization through myriad semiotic resources.

3 In a more in-depth discussion, B. Kumaravadivelu (2006: 130–131), based on Walter Mignolo's ideas, argues in favour of a three-phase model of globalization, namely: (1) 'the flags of Christiandom', referring to Spanish and Portuguese colonizing enterprises; (2) 'the civilizatory mission', concerning the industrializing wave led by Great Britain; and (3) 'development/ modernization', which refers to North American imperialism. The two latter stages, in particular, may add to our understanding of Shakespeare as a translocal phenomenon in the past three centuries.

4 Based on Burt's ideas, Desmet (2017: 20) reminds us that the concept of 'Glocal' stems from the field of Administration, meaning the collapse of 'global' within 'local'. The concept brings friction to the oppositions between 'centre' and 'margin', 'elite culture' and 'popular culture', 'authentic' and 'inauthentic', etc. While it is certainly a promising notion, it seems to leave untouched the distinction between opposing sides that, from my perspective, interweave and criss-cross. In this chapter, I espouse an understanding of the world and of culture as 'translocal'.

5 For more information on the Massachussetts Institute of Technology's Global Shakespeare project, see http:// globalshakespeares.mit.edu/. Information on the Globe-to-Globe project is available at http://globetoglobe.shakespearesglobe.com/ (accessed 23 January 2018).

6 See Reis (2014) for the complete news report focusing on the play's arrival in Brazil.

7   Marcia Martins (2008: 302) recalls that, at first, Shakespeare's
    plays arrived in Brazil on the occasion of foreign companies'
    trips to the country – French ones, in particular. Such companies
    brought their own stagings of some of the Bard's tragedies,
    including *Romeo and Juliet* and *Othello*. The performances
    were usually enacted in the companies' own language –
    French, usually, with the constant use of Jean-François
    Ducis's translations – or, occasionally, companies made use of
    Portuguese translations of the French versions. In the nineteenth
    century, Brazil had its own first great Shakespearean actor,
    João Caetano. In the twentieth century, a number of companies
    performed Shakespeare in Brazil, including the well-known
    Teatro do Estudante do Brasil (Brazil's Student Theater), the
    Grupo Galpão (Hangar Group) and the Grupo Nós do Morro
    (Us From the Hillside Group). While this chapter was being
    produced, in the first half of 2018, many Shakespearean or
    Shakespeare-based plays were being staged in Brazilian theatres,
    such as *Coriolanus*, in São Paulo, and *Romeo and Juliet*, in Rio
    de Janeiro.

8   For more information on Emma Rice's stagings and broadcast of
    A Midsummer Night's Dream, see BBC (2018).

9   I take full responsibility for the English translations of Portuguese
    texts presented in this chapter.

References

Adichie, C. N. (2004), *Purple Hibiscus*, London: 4th Estate.
Andrade, O. (2009), *Os Dentes do Dragão*, São Paulo: Globo.
Andrade, O. (2011), *A Utopia antropofágica*, São Paulo: Globo.
Bauman, R. and C. Briggs (1990), 'Poetics and Performance as
    Critical Perspectives on Language and Social Life', *Annual
    Review of Anthropology*, 19: 59–88.
BBC (2018), 'Shakespeare 2016 Lives'. Available online: www.
    bbc.co.uk/programmes/articles/h2vwgfPvGVLTZ95BWL6Yxf/
    riotous-and-celebratory-a-midsummer-night-s-dream-live-
    streamed-in-a-world-first (accessed 21 January 2018).
Blommaert, J. (2005), *Discourse*, Cambridge: Cambridge University
    Press.

Bosman, A. (2010), 'Shakespeare and Globalization', in M. De Grazia and S. Wells (eds), *The New Cambridge Companion to Shakespeare*, 285–301, Cambridge: Cambridge University Press.

Burnett, M. T. (2013), 'Re-reading Akira Kurosawa's "The Bad Sleep Well", a Japanese Film Adaptation of "Hamlet": Content, Genre and Context', *Shakespeare*, 9 (4): 404–417.

Desmet, C. (2017), 'Import/Export: Trafficking in Cross-Cultural Shakespearean Spaces', *Multicultural Shakespeare: Translation, Appropriation and Performance*, 15 (30): 15–26.

Dickson, A. (2015), *Worlds Elsewhere: Journeys Around Shakespeare's Globe*, London: The Bodley Head.

Dickson, A. (2017), 'Hamlet, Globe to Globe by Dominic Dromgoole Review – Neocolonial Folly?', *The Guardian*, 14 April. Available online: www.theguardian.com/books/2017/apr/14/hamlet-globe-to-globe-dominic-dromgoole-review-shakespeare (accessed 25 March 2018).

Huang, A. (2013), 'Global Shakespeare as Methodology', *Shakespeare*, 9 (3): 273–290.

Huang, A. (2016), 'Global Shakespeare as a Tautological Myth', *Scripta Uniandrade*, 14 (2): 1–7.

Huang, A. (2017), 'Global Shakespeare Criticism Beyond the Nation State', in J. C. Bulman (ed.), *The Oxford Handbook of Shakespeare and Performance*, 423–440, Oxford: Oxford University Press.

Kumaravadivelu, B. (2006), 'A Linguística Aplicada na era da globalização', in L. P. Da Moita Lopes (ed.), *Por uma linguística aplicada insdiciplinar*, 129–148, São Paulo: Parábola.

Lanier, D. (2007), 'Shakespeare™: Myth and Biographical Fiction', in R. Shaughnessy (ed.), *The Cambridge Companion to Shakespeare and Popular Culture*, 93–113, Cambridge: Cambridge University Press.

Marchese, E. (2017), 'Something Rotten Blasts Shakespeare with a Broadway Musical Sensibility', *The Orange County Register*, 3 November. Available online: www.ocregister.com/2017/11/03/something-rotten-blasts-shakespeare-with-a-broadway-musical-sensibility/ (accessed 23 January 2018).

Martins, M. A. P. (2008), 'Shakespeare em tradução no Brasil', in L. de C. Leão and M. S. Dos Santos (eds), *Shakespeare: sua época e sua obra*, 301–319, Curitiba: Editora Beatrice.

Moehn, F. (2012), *Contemporary Carioca: Technologies of Mixing in a Brazilian Music Scene*, Durham, NC: Duke University Press.

Montaigne, M. (2002), *Os Ensaios: Livro I*, São Paulo: Martins Fontes.

Reis, M. (2010), *Ozualdo Candeias: Pedras e Sonhos no Cineboca*, São Paulo: Imprensa Oficial.

Reis, L. F. (2014), 'Shakespeare's Globe Theatre traz seu 'Hamlet' para o Brasil', *O Globo*, 20 November. Avaiolable online: https://oglobo.globo.com/cultura/teatro/shakespeares-globe-theatre-traz-seu-hamlet-para-brasil-14608653 (accessed 28 January 2018) [in Portuguese].

Santos, M. S. (2010), 'Um discurso transcultural: our Shakespeare, unser Shakespeare, nosso Shakespeare', *Caderno de Letras (UFRJ)*, 26: 76–89.

Sawyer, R. and V. Panjwani (2017), 'Introduction: Shakespeare in Cross-Cultural Spaces', *Multicultural Shakespeare: Translation, Appropriation and Performance*, 15 (30): 9–14.

Shakespeare, W. (2016), *Hamlet*, ed. A. Thompson and N. Taylor, third series, rev. edition, London: Bloomsbury Arden Shakespeare.

Spivak, G. C. (1988), 'Can the Subaltern Speak?', in C. Nelson and L. Grossberg (eds), *Marxism and the Interpretation of Culture*, 271–313, London: Macmillan.

Viveiros de Castro, E. (2002), 'O mármore e a murta: sobre a inconstância da alma selvagem', in E. Viveiro de Castro, *A inconstância da alma selvagem*, 181–264, São Paulo: Cosac & Naify.

Viveiros de Castro, E. (2004), 'Perspectival Anthropology and the Method of Controlled Equivocation', *Journal of the Society for the Anthropology of Lowland South America*, 2 (1): 1–20.

Viveiros de Castro, E. (2015), *Metafísicas Canibais*, São Paulo: Ubu Editora.

7

Past and present trajectories for 'Global Shakespeare': Mark Thornton Burnett in conversation with Anne Sophie Refskou

ASR *I would like to begin by addressing that 'other word' in Global Shakespeare: 'global'. Although some scholars, such as Alexa Alice Joubin and yourself, have looked more closely at the implications of a 'global' rather than a 'world' or 'worldwide' Shakespeare, it seems worth re-evaluating the nomination of the discipline (if we can call Global Shakespeare a discipline) at this point in its life-cycle. This would, among other things, mean asking you to what extent you feel that Global Shakespeare has critically addressed globalization and globalization theories. Not least in terms of economics and capitalism.*

MTB To an extent I think scholarship related to 'Global Shakespeare' has addressed globalization in thinking about questions to do with economics, capitalism and the market, but there is much more work to be done on critically necessary issues here. It is very interesting how globalization impacts on culture because it can operate in so many different and sometimes contradictory ways. And I believe that sometimes there is an assumption that Shakespeare is a non-fluctuating barometer of cultural capital: that he works as a kind of constant. But if you drill down a little into the various examples, a much more diffuse picture emerges. As much as Shakespeare is seen as a passport to global visibility, he can also operate as box-office poison, as some critics and directors have claimed. To produce a global Shakespeare film, for example, does not necessarily mean guaranteeing yourself the limelight on the festival circuit or in cinemas and digital media. To give two different examples: Vishal Bhardwaj's films – the Shakespeare trilogy of *Maqbool* [2004], *Omkara* [2006] and *Haider* [2014] – now have their place assured in the Shakespearean film canon around the world. One needs to think about why that is. Is it to do with exposure? Is it to do with aesthetics and quality? Is it to do with Indian film industries and how these are plugged into other networks? And then there is such a film as *An Athens Summer Night's Dream* [dir. Dimitri Athanitis, 1999], which is a Greek adaptation of *A Midsummer Night's Dream* that seems to have vanished without a trace, at least as far as non-Greek circuits of communication are concerned. What this means is that whenever we are considering 'Global Shakespeare' we are dealing with an inevitably skewed and partial sample. And what that means in turn is that generalizations become difficult and complex: we always have to be careful and contextual, as a result. There are other questions, too. Who controls the circuits of visibility and invisibility, presence and non-presence, and why? All of this needs to be taken into account when we are thinking about the economic interstices of Shakespearean production.

That film – *An Athens Summer Night's Dream* – belongs to a different context and film culture, of course, but the point remains that globalization works multifariously and unpredictably in terms of Shakespeare's capital. There are the beginnings of very good scholarly work on this. Mariangela Tempera's chapter in the recent Routledge collection, *The Shakespearean World* [2017], for example, talks about European Shakespeare films as a neglected subject and addresses the issues to do with their market, but certainly there is room for new exploration using globalization theories such as those outlined by Michael Hardt and Antonio Negri in their book, *Empire* [2000]. I can think of a very useful project which would be some sort of a map of global Shakespearean activity in terms of infrastructures and the fluctuating monetary economy, potentially factoring in Brexit too. Such a map could be underpinned by globalization theories, and possibly political science and economics, and realized in collaboration with computer science. The 'Reviewing Shakespeare' project led by Paul Prescott and Paul Edmonson offers a wonderful model here and could be taken up elsewhere.

In other words, there are great opportunities here to think about Global Shakespeare and globalization side by side, and the 'big themes' in globalization theory – such as history, homogeneity, heterogeneity, bifurcated identities, the local and the global, national markets – are calling out to be extended to the increasing number of creative practices that we are now learning about.

ASR   *There are several points in that answer that I would like to return to, not least the notion of more interdisciplinary scholarly production in relation to Global Shakespeare, but firstly the notion of a different kind of map seems important to address. There has already been a strong focus on 'mapping' in relation to Global Shakespeare – in the form of archives, digital projects or books that collect examples from different locations (a methodology which this book also attempts to address in a critical manner) – as well as discussions as to how such maps should be constructed and perceived. What you suggest, however, seems to be less about locating Shakespearean cultural production in different parts of the world in order to describe*

and analyse it locally, and much more about highlighting
the economic and political links between locations. I would
expect there would be issues related to colonial histories (and
presents) to discuss too?

MTB   Yes, there certainly would, and any simulated map
of Shakespearean production would need, as I intimated
above, a historical dimension so that you could find out about
engagements with Shakespeare across time as well as place. One
of the fascinating things about global Shakespearean visibility is
how it taps into and illuminates the histories of the places with
which it is associated, and colonialism is certainly one historical
phenomenon that is very pertinent in such discussions, not
least in terms of education and performance. So, for example,
across Africa – although this is a very generalizing statement
– there is a very patchy record of Shakespeare and cinema,
which is due to infrastructural issues and the vacillations of
film industries within Africa, which are very much beholden
to former colonial practices. However, it is also due to an
education system where, at one point in history, Shakespeare
was the exemplar par excellence of high culture and seen as
a passport to certain cultural opportunity; I've interviewed
various Shakespearean practitioners from the 1960s who
were very much claiming this. Yet, at another moment in the
history of Africa, Shakespeare becomes anathema and the very
last thing that anybody wants to engage with because of the
reclamation of indigenous cultures. To instance some of the
critical thinking on Cultural Anthropophagy, namely the work
of Gazi Islam, 'anthropophagy marks moments of intercultural
contact' which point up 'desire for appropriation and an
aggressive process of deconstruction' [2011: 163]. So here is
certainly one instance where Shakespearean visibility on the
world stage and colonial histories are inseparable, but there
are all sorts of other examples where colonialism is inadequate
as a paradigm to explore Shakespeare through history, such as
in China or Japan which never had colonial relations with the
West but which do have very rich Shakespearean traditions.

So, there are several different paradigms which need to be brought into play here.

In terms of 'presents', one thinks of the multiple – and not always 'colonial' or 'postcolonial' – ways in which global engagements with Shakespeare signify. The recent glut of *Hamlet* film adaptations in China – including *The Banquet* [dir. Xiaogang Feng, 2006] and *Prince of the Himalayas* [dir. Sherwood Hu, 2006] – demonstrates, it could be argued, how China reflects, through Shakespeare, on its global rise, on, to adopt the phrase of Frank N. Pieke, the 'nation' as 'work in progress' [2016: 141]. China comes into its own through *The Banquet* and *Prince of the Himalayas*, making us aware of the sometimes continuous, sometimes contradictory, means whereby Shakespeare's franchise assists in the confrontation with emerging realities. A Thai film such as *Shakespeare Must Die* [dir. Ing Kanjanavanit, 2012] deals, again distinctively, with the implications of a repressive political system. Some contemporary Argentine Shakespearean productions and films, as Marianne Hewitt (a doctoral student at Queen's University) is discovering, are marked by their mediation of buried political pasts and a traumatic history. Equally powerfully, some contemporary film adaptations of *Romeo and Juliet* understand the play in relation to deterritorialization, demographic mobility and local realignments of race, emphasizing imperfectly acclimatized societies. In all of these 'present' instances, the 'colonial' or 'postcolonial' paradigm is not necessarily the first interpretive tool for analysis.

ASR *Might one of these alternative paradigms be 'Otherness', which is of course also strongly affiliated to postcolonial discourses, but not exclusively so, and certainly seems to be extremely relevant to discussions of how Global Shakespeare understands itself – both as a creative practice and as an academic discipline?*

MTB Yes. Firstly, I think it is important to resist any assumption that Global Shakespeare is an 'other'. We should be very careful about reifying global Shakespeares as a sort of perceived critical or academic treasure or discovery. I have written a little bit about this before, but I have become more self-conscious about it recently. There can be a tendency to fetishize and capitalize on what are perceived to be particular perspectives or interesting examples, and there is also a tendency to think that these examples represent progressive ideologies, which is not necessarily the case. And then there is the question of Global Shakespeare as 'other' at international film and cultural festivals, where it is almost de rigueur to have a fascinating example that serves certain cultural ends for the purposes of the festival logic. There is certainly more work to be done on appropriation of Shakespeare as 'other'.

ASR *Which brings me to the aims of this book and its use of Cultural Anthropophagy as a methodology which, among other things, allows us to do exactly that: interrogating the appropriation of Shakespeare's otherness in a global context. I am very interested in how you read Oswald de Andrade's 'Cannibalist Manifesto'? [Andrade (1928) 1991].*

MTB I see the 'Manifesto' as perfect for your purposes in this book because it is about Shakespeare as an outsider who somehow, through consumption and ingestion, becomes an insider, but not with the insider and outsider identifications being mutually distinct; instead, they are enwrapped and enveloped, which is very interesting indeed. However, I also think that a way of prioritizing the importance of the 'Manifesto' is to suggest that it is one of the earliest instances of an adaptation process producing something of value – or that recognizes that what adaptation produces is something of value. This is certainly a watchword in adaptation studies now, but Oswald de Andrade is saying it in 1928, so the 'Manifesto' reads as an *avant la lettre* understanding of adaptation. I also read the jokey appropriation of Shakespeare and *Hamlet* in 'Tupi or not Tupi, that is the question' as gesturing in multiple directions, both inwards and outwards, both locally and globally, both backwards in time and forwards in time, towards an indigenous language and a European language at the same time.

ASR   *Yes, and of course that phrase is the only one which Oswald de Andrade originally wrote in English.*

MTB   Exactly, and it is interesting, in that respect, to think of a Brazilian *Hamlet* adaptation from 1971, Ozualdo Candeia's *A Herança*, in which most of the dialogue is muted, but 'To be, or not to be' is included and is spoken in English, but in terms of acoustic distortion, which seems very relatable to what Andrade is exploring. And in another Brazilian *Hamlet* adaptation from the same year, *O Jogo da Vida e da Morte* [dir. Mario Kuperman, 1971], 'To be, or not to be' is included in terms of textual amputation: the words are seen on a printed advertisement, which is torn up and discarded on a rubbish heap – this also seems highly applicable to what Andrade is formulating.

ASR   *Absolutely. The image of the torn-up advertisement seems relatable to Andrade's thinking in the 'Manifesto' on so many levels. We could look at it both as a comment on the foreign consumerist cultures that Brazil discards in favour of its own more selective and self-conscious consumption: Andrade writes 'Down with all the importers of canned consciousness', doesn't he? But it might also demonstrate how Cultural Anthropophagy works in practice: the film, as an adaptation of* Hamlet, *has sucked the main nutrients out of the European source and, this done, has discarded the empty or torn-up packaging on the rubbish heap. It is a great image!*

MTB   It is striking how Global Shakespeare films return to rubbish as a site of value and as an instrument of commentary. *O Jogo da Vida e da Morte* is one example, but, at a different remove and in a different time period and locale, there is also a film such as the Serbian *Hamlet, Ciganski Princ* [dir. Aleksandar Rajković, 2007], which unfolds on a landfill site on the outskirts of Belgrade, makes a virtue of piles of *debris*, and, through a combination of Shakespeare and waste, represents the plight of the Roma peoples at a time of rapid political and social change. Staying with *Hamlet*, it is interesting that Andrade focuses in on that one line, 'To be, or not to be', because this represents a worldwide cultural mechanism for accessing and rewriting Shakespeare. Of all the plays, *Hamlet* tends to be cited most often and, of all the speeches, it tends to be 'To be, or not to be'. It is wonderful to see how 'To be, or not to be' is constantly being recast and rebranded – as fragment, translation, anecdote, first point of entry to Shakespeare. We come across it in so many forms and media. It also operates as a form of currency: once your identity is declared, it is the phrase most often on the lips of an embassy official when you're applying for a visa! So, because so well known around the world, 'To be, or not to be' lends itself to the distortion and amputation processes in which Andrade delights. Another thing which seems important to highlight in the 'Manifesto' is that the adaptation process is symbiotic. I really like that phrase, 'Without us Europe wouldn't even have its meager declaration of the rights of man.'

ASR *Symbiotic is another keyword, I think: Cultural Anthropophagy operates as a two-way process. We can think of this in terms of adaptation processes, where Andrade's thinking may help to destabilize the notion of an original versus a derivative. This in turn aligns with his challenging of 'Old World' versus 'New World' denominations and the notion that the cultures and knowledges of the old world are 'brought' to the new. Andrade writes: 'we already had Communism', 'we already had Surrealist language' and 'The Golden Age'. In other words, he displaces the sort of historical view that the New World was 'discovered' and has been trying to catch up ever since. Some of this also seems to haunt Global Shakespeare, perhaps in the form of distinctions between a 'centre' and a periphery', or 'the West' and 'the rest', which you have also addressed in your work. What are the challenges in trying to do so, and how far have we come in displacing such divisions, in your view?*

MTB   The divisions are certainly still there and the challenges are manifold. They are intra-national and intra-regional. For example, a common assumption is that Indian Shakespeare films are 'Bollywood'- or Mumbai-based. That's only part of the picture. As well as 'Bollywood', we need to be aware of 'Tollywood' and 'Mollywood' and the fact that Indian Shakespeare films exist and cross-fertilize across the range of Indian states and regions. As examples such as *Haider* [dir. Vishal Bhardwaj, 2014], *Hemanta* [dir. Anjan Dutt, 2016] and *Karmayogi* [dir. V. K. Prakash, 2011] indicate, *Hamlet* is a test-case for the variety and diversity of Indian engagements with Shakespeare, the play being taken on board in Bengali, Hindi and Malayalam contexts, suggesting north–south, as well as east–west, tensions and rivalries within the same landmass.

In general, divisions are apparent in languages, cultures, infrastructures, funding, attitude and technology. There are some great projects which address and amend these issues, such as the MIT Global Shakespeares, for example. I do think that any project attempting to address and bridge divisions needs to be on a large international scale with a large and diverse number of participants. On a positive note, I also think that British schools are increasingly trying to address Shakespeare from a more global and intercultural perspective, and many recent and current academic publications are certainly indicative of an awareness of this problem as well as a will to change it. We are also seeing some increasingly multifarious conference programmes, so there is undeniably progress, even if we are far from there yet.

ASR   *Absolutely, and I think Global Shakespeare as a kind of movement has been significant in these processes. I just wonder whether – although many of the projects we have seen so far have been gesturing towards inclusivity in very valuable ways – mapping Shakespearean activity in different and quite delimited areas of the world often still seems to set the tone, methodologically speaking. And that does not necessarily, or fundamentally, change a situation in which the west, or the* *anglophone Shakespeare, sits at the centre of the world map. Cultural Anthropophagy is inherently suspicious of essentially Western ways of mapping and organizing the world, and I think it is important to question systems, or at least to be more self-conscious about where and how they start and spread, but perhaps that is easier said than done? How do you think we can establish alternative methodologies?*

MTB I see what you mean. I think the methodological discussion is extremely important here and especially interdisciplinary methodologies. Unfortunately, there is a current tendency, despite the best intentions, for academic disciplines to segregate somewhat and work within our own areas. We have already talked about interdisciplinarity in the form of dialoging with globalization theories, which I have certainly found very helpful to an extent, but I have also found it useful to include world cinema theories in my work on Shakespearean films. So, for example, the recent *The Routledge Companion to World Cinema* [2018], edited by Rob Stone and others, offers what might be a terrific methodological template for global Shakespeare on film in that the content is organized according to two separate yet interconnected terms: 'longitude' and 'latitude'. These are understood quite generously: 'longitude' essentially corresponds to different parts of the world, whereas 'latitude' relates to content and theme, and this is very enabling. I know that you are interrogating the status of regional organization in this book and that Cultural Anthropophagy is a way of doing that, but, for me, in working on Shakespeare and film, the combination of 'longitude' and 'latitude' is helpful, because you can pay as much attention to place and location as you can to content and theme. So, in my current work on *Hamlet* and world cinema, for example, I am trying to draw on this as a methodology, but I am also overlaying it with the voices of creatives and practitioners, which I have done before and – hopefully – with due self-consciousness. I don't know if self-consciousness can be considered a methodology, so to speak, but it represents another narrative of engagement that involves the Shakespearean text and the particular local culture. These voices are not mechanisms for getting at some sort of mystery or truth, because they themselves are always mediated, and of course I am mediated too as a critic, which I have to be very up-front about, but I think they bring an important dimension, because they bridge that 'longitude' versus 'latitude' methodological procedure and mean that you are never doing the two separately: you are always trying to keep them balanced within the discussion. And if I can bring in my answer to your first question for a minute, in all of this, issues of history and context need to be kept in mind as methodology. That isn't too far a leap from uses of Cultural Anthropophagy in recent discourse. In his piece on 'Can the Subaltern Eat?', for example, Islam reflects on the usefulness of addressing anthropophagic culture from 'three and a half' different historical vantage-points, concluding that we need to treat 'anthropophagy as both historically situated and embedded in … reality' [2011: 175].

ASR *I certainly agree both with the need for Global Shakespeare as an academic discipline to be more determinedly interdisciplinary in its mind-set and with the self-conscious dialogue with creative voices, which we are also championing in this book. We have been having such dialogues for a long time in Shakespeare Studies, of course, but it seems to me that Global Shakespeare in particular needs them to feed its theories and methodologies. Indeed, Global Shakespeare can be said to have begun as a creative practice and perhaps it needs to continue looking at itself from a very practical perspective to develop further? There are challenges, though, in negotiating meanings and terms, as we are also seeing in this book?*

MTB Yes, just as with the manifold challenges in talking across different disciplines, there are also distinct challenges in the conversations between critics and creatives. Critics use language that creatives might find obscure, while creatives use language that critics want to unpack and interrogate. There is also the fact that creatives don't always say what the critic wants to hear – or what the critic is looking for – and vice versa! However, this is essentially positive, because it gives us the opportunity to renegotiate matters through dialogue. I also think that some fascinating and enriching conversations can occur when you bring a Shakespearean creative from one culture into another cultural audience or community. So, for example, we brought Sherwood Hu – the director of the *Hamlet* film adaptation, *The Prince of the Himalayas* – here to Belfast during the 'Being Human' festival a few years ago, and the reflections that he was able to make about Tibetan–Chinese relationships were very powerfully felt in a place – and for an audience – whose history has been associated with sectarianism and violence, at least for older generations. The fact that the film rewrites *Hamlet*, not so much as a revenge tragedy but as a parable of forgiveness had an additional weight in this context, because although the film does not articulate forgiveness in very specific terms, it deals with forms of reconciliation which tapped into a local experience in surprising ways.

ASR *So there is a great example of symbiosis occurring as part of one local cultural rewriting of Shakespeare in dialogue with another local cultural context; rather than the assumption that there is an original and authentic 'Shakespeare' who can be brought to bear on any given cultural or local issue. What you are describing sounds like a much more dynamic exchange, or indeed symbiosis. On another level this also brings me back to the initial interrogation of what 'global' means in Global Shakespeare. Is what you are describing a 'global' moment in which 'local' plus 'local' in some way equals 'global'? I also wanted to ask you about an issue which you may have come across in your work with creatives: the fact that the cultural production which academics might wish to include in the 'global pool' is not necessarily considered global by those who create it, or it may not occur to them that their work should be categorized in that way?*

MTB Yes, I think that is a moment when 'local' plus 'local' amounts to 'global'. Or, to use a more anthropophagic set of terms, this is a moment when, to cite Gazi Islam, there is 'cultural mixture … the hybrid co-production of ideas through intercultural encounters' [2011: 160]. Perhaps we might want to finesse this even more and talk about a mutual cannibalism of cultural elements that can lead to a uniquely creative product or experience. In answer to your second point about creatives, yes, the term 'global' can have limitations. A production – film or stage – is never considered sufficiently 'global' and yet it is always assumed that it is more than enough at the same time, because what is 'global' for one community is not 'global' for another. I think this links to the question of what Shakespeare signifies in different parts of the world. For example, in some Indian film industries Shakespeare is simply a means to an end – or indeed a plot to an end – and there is no necessity to advertise the Shakespearean borrowing or allusion. In several instances, I am sure that the borrowing or the allusion is not even conscious, and this is because, as Vishal Bhardwaj has said in several interviews, 'there is no copyright in Bollywood, only the right to copy', which also has a rather anthropophagic ring to it. Whereas in other situations, Shakespeare is more a signifier of cultural mobility and therefore the 'debt' to Shakespeare is more openly advertised and published in the form of on-screen credits. In other words, it is assumed he is going to be doing different work.

ASR *Self-consciousness seems important then for both creatives and scholars?*

MTB I think any methodology needs to be used self-consciously. You must be aware of your own context and your own location and history, because 'who is speaking for whom and why' is always the watchword. For Global Shakespeare particularly, there is an argument for saying that biography is caught up in our methodologies, or if it is not then it certainly needs to be. In my own case as an Englishman who has lived in Ireland for thirty years, this certainly applies. I got very self-conscious about teaching Shakespeare in an Irish context when I first came here given histories of colonialism, and I became very interested in how Shakespeare is made to signify in local contexts. Yet, almost paradoxically, this situation also pushed me elsewhere and further outwards. Perhaps I was inspired by being in a place which is so preoccupied with questions of its own identities and borders, with questions of belonging and not belonging. I think my living and working here inevitably made me more globally responsive.

ASR *Yes, I absolutely agree that biography seems to have been – and still is – incredibly important to Global Shakespeare. I'm certainly conscious of it myself in this book, although we are trying to create a more fluid and flexible way of writing inside, outside or between different cultural contexts. I think the self-consciousness and self-scrutiny that the attempt to think and speak globally has produced in scholars is very positive indeed, and it would perhaps be great to see this addressed more methodologically as you hinted earlier. Also, to avoid it becoming too inhibiting?*

MTB Absolutely. One can talk about the challenges of positioning oneself all day, but they should not be preventative, they should be enabling. If we get to a point where the challenges are such that the work stops, it would be a very sad state of affairs, because they should not be conditioned to prevent creativity – for scholars and practitioners alike – they should be conditioned to spark and spur discussions. In a way, this discussion is also interesting in relation to Cultural Anthropophagy as formulated by Oswald de Andrade. Because, although he draws extensively on indigenous Brazilian culture, he himself is not a 'Tupi Indian', is he? He is a Europhile incorporating all sorts of complex Europhile artistic elements while at the same time speaking for – and to some extent to – the indigenous, and he does this through so many different layers of history and cultural representation. All perspectives are always mediated.

ASR *Exactly. And Oswald de Andrade, instead of just problematizing this fact and allowing it to become inhibitive, embraces and celebrates it through Cultural Anthropophagy,* *which I think is greatly inspirational in the context of Global Shakespeare. We have tried to encourage contributors in this book to engage in a similar celebration and allow Cultural Anthropophagy as formulated by Andrade and other Brazilian thinkers to be mediated through their voices and contexts. In other words, we have encouraged a cannibalization of Cultural Anthropophagy in order to let the concept travel widely and make connections on the way: to free this way of thinking about Shakespeare from overly specific local constraints. Do you see Cultural Anthropophagy informing some of your most recent work?*

MTB There are only so many templates available – the sort of 'author template', a 'history template', a 'regional template' and, in the case of Shakespeare specifically, the 'play template'. But a 'theory template' provides multiple ways both for connections and for pushing the boundaries. I could certainly see how this template might offer ways of doing that, partly drawing on Andrade's mode of thinking and on aspects of Cultural Anthropophagy as outlined in Rogerio Budasz's more recent essay 'Of Cannibals and the Recycling of Otherness'. We have already mentioned the idea of the European source as a form of nutrient, which is explored and explained by Budasz, but he also talks about Cultural Anthropophagy as 'a cultural practice aimed at displacing frontiers' [2005: 2–3], which I find very productive. Recently, I have looked at the Argentine film director Matías Piñeiro's Shakespeare trilogy, *Rosalinda* [2010], *Viola* [2013] and *La Princesa de Francia* [2015] – actually it should perhaps be called a quartet, as he made another film. Piñeiro's films are in a sense already at the end process of cannibalization, I feel, because the nutrients that have been taken from Shakespeare have been completely transformed into something utterly different, brilliant and intriguing. It is sometimes hard to see where Shakespeare explicitly figures in Piñeiro's work, but suffice it to say that his films are based on the premise of a Shakespeare theatre production, yet not in the 'putting on a play' sort of genre; they are much more complicated than that. This is not least because the theatre production which is placed at the centre of the films is itself a mash-up, or to use the Rio de la Plata expression, a 'pasticcio'. So, to use the notions of consumption or ingestion from Cultural Anthropophagy, Piñeiro's Shakespeare is already consumed by the time we get to him in the film and that is one of the reasons why the films are so fascinating and, I believe, so successful. They really are work pushing at frontiers. Another example from my recent work is an *Othello* adaptation entitled *Jarum Halus* [2008] by Malaysian director, Mark Tan. Here the idea of the nutrient again becomes very relevant: we might ask what is nourishing about the play *Othello* for this director and this film? Interestingly, Tan has said that he has drawn on Shakespeare's *Othello* – in the process of confronting his own conflicted identity within a Malaysian system – as a way of reconfiguring ideas about race and equality in modern-day Kuala Lumpur, specifically the representation of relations between Malay and Chinese. In that sense, the film is also working towards displacing racial and national frontiers. The related example I wanted to mention again is the Thai film *Shakespeare Must Die* by Ing Kanjanavanit, which can certainly also be looked at in terms of an attempt to displace – inhibiting – frontiers of expression and speech. It revisits the political history of Thailand in order to make a statement about the chaos and confusion which characterize the present situation of the country, and it does so through the lens of *Macbeth*. The film was censored and not commercially released in Thailand, and this for me might represent another potential connection to Cultural Anthropophagy: we have talked about Global Shakespeare in terms of visibility and invisibility and the market, but not so much in terms of censorship, restrictions, permissions or consent, which is something I suspect the irreverent and subversive aspects of Cultural Anthropophagy might be connected to in highly interesting ways. Finally, in connection with irreverence, we shouldn't forget Cultural Anthropophagy's propensity for, and commitment to, parody. The anthropophagic project finds in Shakespeare fodder for – or nutrients towards – the parodic impulse. And parody, as we know from the case of *Hamlet* and films such as the Italian *Io, Amleto/I, Hamlet* [dir. Georgio Simonelli, 1952] and the Finnish *Hamlet liikemaailmassa/Hamlet Goes Business* [dir. Aki Kaurismäki, 1987], is a crucial instrument through which nation-states reflect on themselves, on their neighbours, on their pasts, present and futures. Through parody, the generic frontiers so often at stake in Cultural Anthropophagy are interrogated; to bring Andrade's original staging of his manifesto into the frame, the anthropophagic project always had a 'bawdy and ludic orientation' [Islam 2011: 165].

References

Andrade, O. ([1928] 1991), 'Cannibalist Manifesto', trans. L. Bary, *Latin American Literary Review*, 19 (38): 38–44.

Budasz, R. (2005), 'Of Cannibals and the Recycling of Otherness', *Music and Letters*, 87 (1): 1–15.

Hardt, M. and A. Negri (2000), *Empire*, Cambridge, MA: Harvard University Press.

Islam, G. (2011), 'Can the Subaltern Eat? Anthropophagic Culture as a Brazilian Lens on Post-Colonial Theory', *Organization*, 19 (2): 159–180.

Pieke, Frank N. (2016), *Knowing China: A Twenty-First Century Guide*, Cambridge: Cambridge University Press.

Stone, R., P. Cooke, S. Dennison and A. Marlow-Mann, eds (2018), *The Routledge Companion to World Cinema*, London: Routledge.

Tempera, M. (2017), 'Shakespeare on Film: Continental Europe', in J. L. Levenson and R. Ormsby (eds), *The Shakespearean World*, 190–206, Abingdon: Routledge.

PART THREE

Dialogue III: insiders and outsiders

8

'Tupi or not Tupi': conversations with Brasian Shakespeare directors

Varsha Panjwani

By asking, 'Tupi or not Tupi, that is the question', Brazilian theorist Oswald de Andrade (1991: 38) transforms 'Hamlet's classic formulation of identity struggle into a postcolonial struggle to make sense of one's historical identity' (Islam 2012: 166). Yoking Shakespeare's most memorable line with cannibalistic Brazilian Tupi tribes, Andrade indicates that to make sense of the cultural identity of Brazil, one must first embrace the quintessentially hybrid culture of Brazil. Two twenty-first-century companies, Phizzical and Tribe Arts, are engaged in a similar enterprise of making sense of cross-cultural intertwined histories of the South Asian diaspora in the United Kingdom.

'We wear our miniskirts but we also wear our head scarves and go to the temples. I hope I don't get chastised by religious leaders for saying that one could be eating *prasad* [food offering at a temple] with one hand and have a wine glass in the other!'[1] Thus, Samir Bhamra, artistic director of Phizzical, describes the ways in which we Brasians (my preferred term for British-Asians as it connotes identities that are not neatly separated with a gap but that bleed into each other) assimilate multiple cultural elements in our lives. I had arranged to meet Bhamra to talk about the two Shakespeare shows that he has directed: *Romeo + Laila* (2006) with a cast of young people from Leicester, and *Cymbeline* (2013), which employed adult actors of diverse backgrounds and played in Leicester before touring extensively. Kenyan-born, British Indian Bhamra is not the only Brasian director to find cultural expression in Shakespeare. Delia Jarrett-Macauley traces at least four stages of black and Asian Shakespeare in Britain. She places Bhamra's productions in the latest developmental phase characterized by a 'global ethos' and a 'cross-mingling' (2017: 3) of cultures. I include Samran Rathore and Tajpal Rathore's Tribe Arts in this category too.[2] In 2016, Tribe Arts produced *Darokhand*, a play combining six Shakespeare works: *Macbeth, Hamlet, Romeo and Juliet, Antony and Cleopatra, Othello* and *The Tempest*. The full-length play is still in production but I saw a taster where the company performed six scenes from the play. Samran Rathore reflects that the affinity between Shakespeare and Brasian productions might be because '[Shakespeare] was setting plays in Venice, in Verona, in remote islands but also infusing them with English subjects'.[3] According to Samran Rathore, Brasian Shakespeare productions can not only help to foster a nuanced understanding of intercultural Britain but can also illuminate elements of Shakespeare's own hybrid style. This is something that Global Shakespeare Studies have yet to appreciate.

Considering that Global Shakespeare has been *de rigueur* in Shakespeare scholarship and performance for several years, the lack of attention given to Shakespeare produced by visible minorities in Britain is inadmissible. Jarrett-Macauley rightly laments that, with the exception of *Othello*, 'scholars have been slow to include Black and Asian people in theatre histories in general and Shakespeare performance history in particular' (2017: 1). Her edited collection redresses this neglect by reproducing perspectives from black British and Brasian Shakespeare directors and actors. My chapter takes a cue from this pioneering work by providing extended, unpublished conversations with Bhamra and Samran and Tajpal Rathore.

Before delving into the conversations, however, it is worth pausing over one of the reasons why Brasian Shakespeare has been discussed inadequately. By cutting across borders and maps, which have hitherto been the organizing principle of Global Shakespeare marketing, consumption and critique, these productions have been discussed little and misunderstood often.[4] For instance, in 2012, Iqbal Khan (who is Brasian) directed a Royal Shakespeare Company (RSC) production of *Much Ado About Nothing* with a Brasian cast. A review on *Blogging Shakespeare*, a website set up specifically for addressing the Global performances of the 2012 World Shakespeare Festival in Britain, shows an unease with this Brasian production:

> judged in the hyper-global context of the World Shakespeare Festival, this *Much Ado* can come to seem pseudo-international, even inauthentic. The combination of the distinctive space of the Globe, the otherness of its foreign visitors, the absence of English language, and even the Globe's seeming proximity to Shakespeare, has evidently ascribed to participants in the 'Globe to Globe' festival in particular a new degree of 'authenticity.' (Rumbold 2012)

While the review acknowledges that 'one of the most positive outcomes of Khan's warm-hearted production might be to reopen debate about what constitutes "authenticity" in global Shakespeare performance', the discussion of what a higher degree of 'authenticity' would look like is worth noting. The review proposes that to qualify for authenticity, the production would need to mark its 'otherness' explicitly; it would have to indicate foreignness to the extent that even English language is absent from the stage as was the case in the Globe-to-Globe festival. The review seems to suggest that true internationalism (as opposed to pseudo internationalism) is somewhere outside of Britain and something to be brought to Britain by 'visitors' rather than something within Britain itself. Elsewhere, the same review proposes a different strategy for avoiding the charge of pseudo internationalism. It argues that 'Birmingham-born Khan's production is simplistic in its treatment of modern Indian life, and indeed, one could perhaps imagine a version in which the company's inevitable second-generation detachment from India is not ignored but ironised' (Rumbold 2012). So, according to the review, either the production should be from outside Britain (from India, in this case) or signal its 'inevitable second-generation detachment from India'. What is not given due credence is the extent to which Brasians are deeply attached to and draw upon *both* Asian and British cultures. In *Balti Britain*, a book on the Brasian experience, Ziauddin Sardar explains that for Brasians, 'being British does not mean you are going to ditch your heritage, abandon your family or jettison your memories. Untangling this nexus, reordering the fragments jumbled higgledy-piggledy by migration, is no straightforward matter. It is complex, convoluted, multiple and compound as the nature of Britishness itself' (2008: 48). Thus, Khan's production emphasizes the internationalism that characterizes Brasian life; as another Brasian director, Bhamra, puts it in the interview below, 'in the Brasian case, hybridity is authentic'.

To take another example of this unease with hybridity, sample the critique of Bhamra's own production of *Cymbeline*. In their review of the production, Sonja Kleij, Romano Mullin and Matt Williamson opine that:

> Whilst ambitious, the production is not without its problems. The sheer range of the references invoked results in a lack of clarity and consistency [...] there were times when the result seemed simply a grab-bag of Indian tropes without logic or consistency. (2013)

Here, even when they acknowledge that Shakespeare's play itself 'is a world away from the unity and structure of his earlier work' or that 'it is a mixture of tones and styles very like the diverse cultural references which the company has brought to bear on it', the reviewers still find it hard to engage with the hybrid ethos of the production which seems to them to be a 'grab-bag of Indian tropes' lacking in 'consistency' (2013). In the interview below, Bhamra describes how 'the sheer range of references' are informed not only by the environments he grew up in but the neighbourhoods in Britain, such as Leicester and Manchester, characterized by diverse religions and populations. Moreover, this style builds upon the work of director Jatinder Verma who developed a theatre practice called Binglish: a 'distinct contemporary theatre praxis [...] featuring Asian and black casts, produced by independent Asian or black theatre companies [...] to directly challenge or provoke the dominant conventions of the English stage' (Verma 1996: 194). One of the chief features of Binglish is the 'heaping together of fragments of diverse cultures' (Verma 1998: 131). The citing of multiple references, thus, is a Brasian theatre practice born out of living within several cultures.

These scholarly reviews of two different productions are indicative of the way in which critics find the hybridity of Brasian Shakespeare itself challenging rather than any one production's handling of its diverse cultural sources. The study of Brasian Shakespeare, therefore, requires a theoretical model that, instead of simplifying and distancing, allows for slipping between a palimpsest of cultural identities. Bearing affinities with Edward Said's theory of overlapping territories (1993) and Homi Bhabha's conceptualization of the third-space (Bhabha and Rutherford 2006) but going further than both in blurring boundaries, the Brazilian theory of Cultural Anthropophagy allows for a nuanced understanding of these productions.

In 'Manifesto of Pau-Brasil Poetry' (1986) and 'Cannibalist Manifesto' ([1928] 1991), Andrade reclaimed the figure of the indigenous Brazilian cannibal and advocated understanding Brazilian cultural products in anthropophagic terms. The cannibal does not wish to remain aloof and separated from the Other and instead strives to erase boundaries between self and the Other by devouring the Other. Thus, one of the advantages of this theoretical standpoint is that it allows for seeing modern cultures as based on encounters with each other rather than perceiving them as sealed off from one another. As Sergio Bellei explains, anthropophagy creates a 'world in which frontiers should be abolished or at least made unstable and vulnerable to trespassing' (1998: 95). Although Andrade applied this model to Brazilian culture, this framework is highly portable for understanding intercultural work generally. It is this world that the Brasian Shakespeare productions inhabit, conceptually going back and forth across the frontiers, which the ancestors of Brasians would have physically crossed in the past.

In the late sixteenth century, Bishop Pero Fernandes Sardinha was eaten by the Brazilian Tupi tribes. Rogerio Budasz teases out the irony of Sardinha ending up on the cannibalistic menu: 'Sardinha, the one who wished to prevent the Jesuits from incorporating elements of the Tupi culture, was himself incorporated – *in corpore* – into their stomachs' (2005: 11). Budasz elaborates that 'otherness was exactly what the cannibal wanted' (2005: 11) because they believed that this eating would have a metamorphic effect: the eater would now combine their own qualities with those of the Other. Cultural Anthropophagy allows opposition, dialectic, difference and multiplicity to exist within a single unified entity. Seen from within this framework, Brasian Shakespeare productions can finally be understood as unified entities despite their diverse seeding elements. The complexity allowed by this theoretical model is just the right context in which to discuss the work of Brasian Shakespeare companies.

Samir Bhamra, artistic director of Phizzical – interview with Varsha Panjwani, 6 July 2016

VP *What prompted you to kick-start Phizzical?*

SB I did not set out to form a theatre company; it just happened organically. In 1999, I was working for a media company in their creative design department and juggled this alongside performing with a dance company I had founded. In 2002, my mum was diagnosed with a terminal illness and I moved to Leicester to look after her. My dad was also disabled after two strokes and his mobility was very limited. I didn't want to be working nine-to-five and not have enough time to care for them. I wanted to be at home so I thought – what could I do that would allow me the time that I needed but keep me creatively engaged? That's how Phizzical was born.

VP *You hadn't thought about theatre as a career before then?*

SB I loved dance but I wanted to grow and to push myself. I also loved design, mobile telecommunications and internet technologies. For me, these were all ways of communication. Theatre allowed me to incorporate all these things to communicate with people at all levels.

VP *Indeed!*

SB Once the company was created, I had to decide what kind of show we would like to make. The go-to man really is Shakespeare for me. The only things I've known all my life are Bollywood cinema, the [Hindu] scriptures and Shakespeare so I knew that whatever I created was going to be a mash-up of all three.

VP *Tell me more about the Shakespeare productions or Shakespeare-inspired shows that you've directed.*

SB The first Shakespeare show I directed was *Romeo + Laila*. In 2006, I was working with young people, helping them to learn about Shakespeare, but I thought that it would be great if, while doing so, I could also show them the similarities between a Western text and an Eastern text. Since the Persian text, *Laila-Majnu* by Hashmet Shah, has parallels with *Romeo and Juliet*, it just seemed natural to marry the two. So, I collaborated with an emerging writer, Omar Khan, and our version was very different to either story because our play sometimes followed *Laila-Majnu* and at other times adapted *Romeo and Juliet*, and then there were moments when the show was borrowing elements from both and was becoming an amalgam of the two.

VP *As far as the plots are concerned, I can see how the two stories fit together, but how did you weave the contexts together?*

SB I was adamant that I wanted to set Shakespeare in a context that would be relevant to the young people I was working with so I began by looking around me. I observed Leicester and took inspiration from cities I'd resided in since I moved to the UK. I had lived in Manchester for a while and it has a significant Muslim population. When I moved to Leicester, I encountered a large South Asian population with myriad religions and there's also the most beautiful cathedral in the city. This context not only made sense to me but made sense to the young people in Leicester who inhabited this environment. So, I became interested in exploring the relationship between a Catholic Romeo and a Muslim Laila.

VP *So, you were not only fusing the two texts but also setting the production in the very particular context of Leicester, where the tensions between the different religious groups could potentially erupt into 'new mutiny'.*

SB Yes, but the conflict between the two religions was amplified by class war. Laila's side of the family were more prominent in the marketplace, because they did some dangerous drug dealing on the side. If you think about the time in which *Laila-Majnu* is written, that period was filled with opium and drugs …

VP   *… so is Shakespeare's text – from Friar's potions to the apothecary's poison.*

SB   Precisely! So, the drugs connection was true to both texts as well. In contrast, Romeo's family were from a more impoverished background. There's an area in Leicester, Braunstone, which has a disproportionate amount of poverty. In fact, people always speak about minority poverty in Leicester, but we rarely speak enough about white poverty that exists in this city.

VP   *In wrapping the class conflict around drugs, you were tying present-day Leicester's context with …*

SB   … the settings of the texts? Yes. In our production, the two families were dangerous in their own ways. One had guns and the other had knives. There is a tribal-ness that exists in *Laila-Majnu* and *Romeo and Juliet* and I was trying to bring that into *Romeo + Laila*.

VP   *With all these changes, would you say that you have an irreverent approach to Shakespeare?*

SB   I want to make Shakespeare incredibly accessible and I want to make it as fun as possible. We mixed everything from Shakespeare's text to *Star Wars* – there was a big lightsaber fight with Mercutio and Romeo! We were just trying to have fun with the text. We wanted to keep the audience engaged and give them a sense of who these kids were. I still remember the surprised gasp, cheer and applause when the show opened with an incredible dance to the song 'Lady Marmalade'!

VP   *For this production you used Shakespeare's words sparingly, is that right?*

SB   Yes, Shakespeare's language is magnificent and it paints such vivid pictures, but I needed to do Shakespeare outside of that before I could work with the language. That is my journey from *Romeo + Laila* to *Cymbeline*. By the time I directed *Cymbeline*, I was working with Shakespeare's language, and making my own connections with his literary pictures.

VP *Tell me about the process behind* Cymbeline. *Didn't the RSC support this production?*

SB I was selected to work at the RSC during the World Shakespeare Festival [WSF]. There, the WSF artistic director Deborah Shaw created an opportunity to shadow Gregory Doran (who was an associate director at that time), and what I found most interesting was the way in which he nurtures and trains the actors to be able to create a vision for the show and become part of that vision. The RSC also lent us Nia Lynn to help the actors and myself to get a real sense of the text because the iambic pentameter isn't natural to me at all. I struggle with the iambic pentameter and who better than someone from the RSC to support me with that. Nia was the best teacher – absolutely fantastic! The support of the RSC was critical in another way too because it introduced the RSC to actors from diverse backgrounds, who weren't on their books, who weren't even on their radar. Sophie Khan Levy, who played Innogen (Innojaan in our production), fresh out of university from Guildhall, was subsequently cast by the RSC in their season.

VP *Sounds like a mutually beneficial exchange. The RSC helped to train your actors but also ended up learning about talented actors from a range of backgrounds.*

SB *Cymbeline* was a steep learning curve in many respects. I had several conversations with the twenty-two venues we toured and each wanted us to cater to their specific audience. Moreover, the costumes of the show were meant to be designed by Bhanu Athaiya, the first Indian woman to win an Academy Award (for *Gandhi*). I spent some time workshopping with her but she was unwell and couldn't do the costuming. So, I ended up doing it. It was unfortunate that she was ill, but that learning, the process, was incredible. I discovered that I really enjoyed designing costumes because I could control how I wanted the show to look. I understand Asian fabrics and Asian cuts well because my mum, who was a seamstress, taught me. The experience with Bhanu enhanced that and reshaped my thinking as a director-designer.

VP *Even with your IT work, you were saying that you were interested in how aesthetic and design can enhance communication. Perhaps costume design is part of that?*

SB I hope so! When you're watching my shows, I want you to feel something. When the lead actor is sweeping the heroine off her feet, I want you to feel that you're being swept off your feet too and the fabric of her dress, which swooshes off the stage, should help you in feeling that way.

VP *Sometimes people talk about style and substance as if they were two separate things but in your shows they're interlinked; there is no substance without style and there's no style without substance. I think that came through in* Cymbeline.

SB When I read the play, the thing that I kept thinking was that this is like a Manmohan Desai film. It's like, say, *Naseeb* from the 1970s, with separation, people lost and found, love lost, the tragedy, the parental disapproval. It was like a Bollywood film and I thought that I really need to set this in Bollywood. I didn't adopt a Bollywood style for the production, but I set the play in the Bollywood industry and the kind of people that exist in that industry. The play became about the family of a film studio owner. His daughter is a princess, because film studio owners' daughters tend to be treated like royalty. She happens to marry the manager, much to her father's and her stepmother's disapproval. I set the play in 1990s Bollywood and in Bombay, because there was a film called *Bombay* that was released during that time. It really spoke to me because in the film there was this Muslim woman getting married to a Hindu man so that their children were both Muslim and Hindu. That's me in a way because my parents are of different religious backgrounds. So, I wanted to recast the parental disapproval in religious terms – a theme I had explored in *Romeo + Laila* and seem to keep returning to.

VP *You did use a lot of religious symbolism in the show.*

SB Shakespeare's works use religious iconography and language so when you set your show in the vast and diverse cultural landscape of India, then you must pay attention to the religious aspects of that landscape. It's lucky that those visuals automatically placed themselves in my mind. The scene where Iachimo steals the bracelet [*Cym* 2.2] ... I could have used a bracelet but I wanted it to be a little bit more significant. It was to be the symbol of marriage itself. In Asian culture, a mother-in-law-to-be would give the bride-to-be bangles as a *shagun* [an auspicious gift] when a marriage is fixed. Or, on the wedding night, the husband could offer bangles before he can unveil his bride. However, the ultimate symbol of marriage is the *mangalsutra* [a traditional necklace of black and gold beads worn by married Hindu women and only taken off when the husband dies]. Moreover, I wanted to convey that she's a Hindu girl and her husband is a Muslim man and he's given her a *mangalsutra*, which means he's accepting her as she is without trying to change her religion. I wanted to challenge the Islamophobic narrative that if you fall in love with someone who's Muslim, they will insist that you convert.

VP *I also liked how you battled another persistent fiction that if a Brasian girl is independent or opting for a love marriage then she will forgo all her Indian traditions and become thoroughly westernized. I find that narrative racist, so I loved how Innojaan was a fierce, independent woman who knew her own mind but wore the 'mangalsutra' and 'saris', and worshipped at a temple.[5]*

SB ... because we do. We wear our miniskirts but we also wear our head scarves and go to the temples. I hope I don't get chastised by religious leaders for saying that one could be eating *prasad* with one hand and have a wine glass in the other!

VP *Now that we are talking about religious rituals, I found the correspondence between the Hindu goddess, Sita, and Innogen in your production very illuminating too. Sita is subjected to multiple chastity tests and Innogen's purity, too, is questioned even though both these women are devoted to the men they love. Indian religious mythology inspires you a lot?*

SB I think because I am steeped in Indian mythology, it was natural for me to draw the comparison. I didn't deliberately think about it. I was reading the text and it just made sense to me. It was as if Shakespeare wrote that just for me. I often wonder if a copy of the *Ramayana* and the *Mahabharata* landed in his hands when Britain began trading with India in the 1600s.

VP *What you're describing is something that other Brasian directors have told me too. They say that people keep referring to their shows as fusions and mash-ups, but it's not something that the directors are doing deliberately. As they inhabit an environment where they are in touch with both Asian and British cultures, this method of thinking interculturally is organic to them. In other words, they're not trying to forcibly fuse things and signifiers; they are simply representing the way they think and this way of thinking, in turn, illuminates parallels between texts across cultures and countries.*[6]

SB In this context, it's interesting to observe the reviews of my latest show, *Bring on the Bollywood*, which has elements of Oliver Goldsmith's *She Stoops to Conquer*, Shakespeare and Bollywood. It was warmly received by audiences but a section of the press simply did not understand what we're trying to do. Reading these reviews, it feels like a show can only be at one of the two extremes – this is a British show, this is an Indian show – whereas we're trying to bring together multiple art forms, stories, cultures and aesthetics. I think that a generation of reviewers don't get that because they have not grown up with layered identities. They have grown up thinking I'm white,

I'm Irish and so on. On the other hand, I've had to grow up being Kenyan, Indian, British Muslim, Sikh, Hindu, Christian, enjoying the indie Brit Pop scene, with Bollywood and *Friends*.

VP   *... and suddenly, if you try and aim for some kind of pure 'authenticity', it becomes a farce, because it's not there.*

SB   It's not there and we're not those people anymore, if we ever were. In the Brasian case, hybridity is authentic.

VP   *These layered identities which we are talking about are very much present in Bollywood as well, aren't they?*

SB   Bollywood is one of the most secular and hybrid industries I've ever known which is one of the reasons for setting *Cymbeline* within the Bollywood industry. Moreover, there is another type of layering between Shakespeare and Indian culture in Bollywood.

VP   *Yes, the ideas for the first Bollywood films came from either Shakespeare or Indian mythology and sometimes a mixture of the two!*

SB   That's right and the reason that this is possible is because Shakespeare does create characters on a truly global scale. His characters speak to humanity. Yet, if we look at politics in the world right now, we're moving back from being global to being national.

VP   *Sadly, I agree.*

SB   That's the story worldwide; some people are trying to hold on to the idea of being global, but we're becoming ...

VP   *... more parochial?*

SB   We're trying to build walls.

VP   *Literally!*

SB   Literally trying to build walls in a world where our communications are instant and you don't have to travel 8,000 miles to work on a show. You can do it over Skype. We shouldn't be building walls. In fact, we need to be listening to each other and communicating more.

Tajpal Rathore and Samran Rathore, artistic directors of Tribe Arts – interview with Varsha Panjwani, 26 May 2016

VP *Tribe Arts is an interesting name; how did you settle on it?*

TR In 2014, we were thinking about our identity as a company. We considered a lot of names but we chose 'Tribe' because it has connotations of family, togetherness, roots ... going back to the first humans ... we were all tribal first. It is aggressive too, evoking a fierce world with warriors. The combination of community and combativeness in the word fascinates us.

VP *You also call yourselves 'radical, revolutionary, political'. How exactly do you plan to realize these aims?*

TR We're not the kind of political company where we will have placards on stage in a bid to ignite some kind of revolution, but there's actually two things we aim to do: we're trying to challenge the creative industry and the way that theatre is made in this country and we want to change the perception of British-Asians[7] because it's still very stereotypical.

VP *With regards to changing the perception of Brasians, your programme says that you want to 'amplify the stories and voices of the current Black and Asian generation'. How are you doing that through Shakespeare?*

TR Shakespeare's plays contain a lot of subjects that are of interest to us as British-Asians. In our play, we wanted to talk about family, about power, about marginalization, about the occult and black magic, so we thought why not combine characters from different Shakespeare plays in a fictional space and let them have debates on these issues.

VP *And who better to dissect the nature of power than Zohra Begum [based on Lady Macbeth] and Cassandra [based on Cleopatra] in one of the scenes which you presented yesterday!*

TR The full script has even more of these discussions; I think it runs for about two-and-a-half hours. The one relationship that didn't come through in the taster yesterday was the relationship between Cassandra and Princess Kumari [based on Juliet], which shows solidarity between women in Shakespeare, especially in Cleopatra's court.

VP *In the last scene, titled 'Kazimir and the Army of Death', I found it thought-provoking that Kazimir [based on Prospero] feels justified in exacting revenge upon Haider [based on Hamlet] because the former was banished from the court. On one level, this added to our understanding of the connections between Shakespeare's plays because both* Hamlet *and* The Tempest *are about brotherly bonds being broken for political power. On another level, however, the questions this scene raised – who gets banished from their own home and denied their rights? What is ethically justified in this scenario? Is family more important than power? – would have resonated with the Brasians in the audience.*

SR I think the interesting thing with Shakespeare is that his plays devote time to such reflection and give space to philosophical discussions. It was the relationship between characters across plays and the multiple viewpoints they offered upon the same topics that attracted us. For instance, Othello and Romeo both get married in secret and to women whom it would be dangerous to marry from a sociopolitical perspective, so we combined the two in General Khyber. To take another example, Prospero uses magic to fight his betrayal while Iago uses manipulation to avenge the fact that he has been overlooked in favour of Cassio, so we wanted to see the clash of ideologies between the two in our play.

VP *So, you chose Shakespeare because the subjects that you wanted to engage with resonated with the discussions in Shakespeare's plays? It was not because you wanted to tap into a mainstream Shakespeare audience?*

TR No, we did not think about Shakespeare as a crowd puller. When we make our shows, Sam [Samran Rathore] and I never say, 'what's gonna get the biggest audience?' Our use of Shakespeare is as much about his intrinsic style as it is about his cultural capital. In this country, Shakespeare's considered the benchmark for actors and directors but it's taught in a reverential and rigid way – the iambic pentameter, the exact way to say your lines, all this kind of stuff. We just wanted to break through that and say, 'right, this is Shakespeare. We don't want anyone to tell us how to do it. We're gonna read it and we want to perform in a way that feels natural to us as British-Asians. We are artists and Shakespeare is our legacy as much as anyone else's.'

SR Well, he was also very 'Tribe' in his sensibilities. We should remember that a layering of cultures and stories not only works for us in terms of British-Asian self-representation but it is also a good fit for Shakespeare's plays. He was setting plays in Venice, in Verona, in remote islands but also infusing them with English subjects. So, in that sense he was …

TR … he was doing the same thing that we're doing – just in different times. So, we are following a very Shakespearean style.

VP *I was fascinated by the Gothic-meets-Mughal aesthetic of your show. Given that the Mughal Empire was flourishing in India at the time Shakespeare was writing his plays in England, it is surprising that more productions have not combined the two.*[8]

TR Yes, Sam and I are interested in the rich Indian history of the Mughal period.

VP   *The Mughal period was a mix of cultures and languages too, was it not? I have a problem with movies set in the Mughal period which show everyone wearing the same style of clothes, following Islamic rituals, and speaking in pitch-perfect Urdu. It can't have been like that, especially since it is commonly believed that Jodhabai [a Hindu princess] was one of the influential wives of the Mughal and Islamic emperor, Akbar.*

TR   You are right. When I was researching the show, I read a book about the politics of the Mughal Court and it was arguing exactly what you just mentioned. It details how the Mughal emperors followed a sustained policy of incorporating Hindu classical texts in their court. They employed Mughal architects and poets to work with Hindu artists to integrate the Hindu culture into the court. A synthesis of cultures that we keep talking about was already going on in India at the time.

VP   *That is a great reason for setting your show in the Mughal context, isn't it?*

TR   Yes, but instead of just tacking on a Mughal setting we wanted to create something new out of it so we combined it with the Gothic because both these styles are quite regal and work well together. Around the time we were planning this show, we watched …

SR   … *Crimson Peak*.

TR   Yes, *Crimson Peak* by Guillermo del Toro. We straightaway knew that this is what we needed to fuse the Mughal world with!

SR   We then discovered that Gothic and Mughal styles have been combined before, but in architecture. In fact, the style was popular around the time of the British rule and was called Indo-Saracenic.[9]

TR   We wanted this style for our show and we contacted Chris [Dudgeon], who became our set and costume designer. He comes from a background of opera with grandiose styles so we knew that he would be right for us. At first, he was a bit apprehensive because he had never done anything to do with India. In the initial drawings, we weren't sure that the concept was working but then he designed the costume for one character, Zohra Begum, and we were instantly hooked!

VP *With Gothic makeup and jewellery and Mughal clothing which had a plaid border, her costume was Gothic-Mughal-Scottish all rolled into one.*

SR I think that we should not leave out Bollywood as part of our aesthetic because it has had a big influence on us and it is Bollywood that is a crowd puller for a British-Asian audience rather than Shakespeare. We do not want to limit our audience to British-Asians, but we do want a large population of British-Asians to come and see our shows and feel represented.

TR Yeah, exactly. A lot of my friends were apprehensive about seeing the show because they felt, 'Hmm, Shakespeare's not really my cup of tea.' I only persuaded them by mentioning that we were mixing Bollywood with Shakespeare.

VP *I hope that some day Brasians won't feel that Shakespeare is not for them because of companies like yours, which are changing the way it is done. So, when somebody thinks of Shakespeare, they won't think that Shakespeare is all received pronunciation accents and Renaissance costumes. Rather, they would be prepared for diversity in Shakespeare productions. But, let us talk about Bollywood and whose work in the industry inspires you.*

TR A lot of my inspiration comes from Sanjay Leela Bhansali's films; I really admire the way in which he mixes theatre and film. You can pause his films at any moment and the scene looks like a very sophisticated theatre set.

VP *That's interesting because the charge often levelled at Bhansali and one that can potentially be levelled at your work is that it is style or form over substance but, in fact, for both Bhansali and you, the form and style itself is political?*[10]

TR Yes, when you try and change a conventional form, you are disturbing what is considered the norm. When you start challenging accepted forms, you start disrupting the status quo. We're not playing with form just for the sake of doing something different. It's not like, 'Oh! Tara Arts are doing it this way. Shall we try to do it that way?' We do it a certain way because we feel it is the best way for our production. For instance, if that screen was not there on our stage, we wouldn't be able to tell that story. Each element of the show is integral to the production.

VP *It is worth registering that your company is fusing different media in exciting ways. Can the show we saw be classified as theatre? Is it film? Is it a multisensory, multimedia experience? By raising these questions, I think that the show pushed the boundaries of form. So, not only the content and the aesthetics but the form itself became an amalgam.*

TR Theatre, film and let us not forget music, which plays a big part too, especially in the *mujra* [an evening entertainment of song and dance performed by courtesans to entertain their clients] scene which was perhaps the most heavily influenced by Bollywood.

VP *Speaking of that scene, what is your take on language? I ask because it came up a lot in the post-show discussion yesterday. Some people were arguing that the song should have been in English or that there should have been surtitles whilst others were happy with it being in Urdu.*

SR And the interesting thing was that the white people in the audience were overwhelmingly in favour of the lyrics being left untranslated!

VP *I was of the opposite persuasion. I felt that it would be a shame if the audience and critics failed to appreciate the ways in which the song was linked to the storyline and playing with language in a Shakespearean manner. For example, the line, 'Khuda jaane kyun duniya mein Ishq ka mool nahin* *hai / Zamaane ko humara Bhi ishq qubool nahin hai' [God knows why the world devalues love / The society denies our love], foreshadowed the tragedy of the love affair between Princess Kumari and General Khyber who were members of the aristocratic party assembled on the stage, just as the Chorus of* Romeo and Juliet *foretells the doomed love of the titular protagonists. Elsewhere I appreciated the connection drawn between the alliterative sounds of 'ashq' [tears] and 'ishq' [love] that were used in the song for underscoring love's sweet sorrow; the song captures the poetry and punning of Shakespeare's language. So, the people who do not understand the lyrics just wouldn't get the nuances of language in this scene.*

TR   I understand your viewpoint but I still stand by our decision to have the song in Urdu. We're not gonna compromise on things that feel natural. It feels very unnatural to us to hear a *mujra* sung in English. While British-Asians speak in English, they do not translate Hindi/Urdu songs into English while singing and dancing to these. I think the people who do understand it will appreciate the deeper meaning of the song. As for the people who don't understand it, let them be intrigued. That's the whole point. I am a huge fan of *Game of Thrones*. If I don't understand something, I will do everything that I can to try and work it out and that is what makes a fan out of somebody.

SR   Me too. I was at the theatre recently and heard a Swahili song. I didn't know much about it but there was a colleague of mine who did and she told me about the language. So, I researched it and I found the song on YouTube, and I still felt connected to it, even though I couldn't fully understand what was being said. I think that there are a lot of people like me who will go away and do their own exploration and learn about the culture in this way.

TR   We use multiple languages in our dialogues too. Although the script is in English, we do use words like *huzoor* [sir] that also point to our cultural coordinates. We want to let people know that this generation of British-Asians [the second and third generation] speaks multiple languages and is a mix of both cultures – Asian and British. People are calling our show a fusion, as if it's something that's done intentionally. In fact, it's just something that's happening!

SR We have been calling it fusion too, but the word has also become a marketing ploy nowadays; people pay lip service to it as if it is something that you can put together artificially to prove a point. I suppose you can do fusion superficially but to us it is natural because we grew up with multiple influences that seeped into each other. We always say that we're creating what is us; we're not only doing something intercultural – we are intercultural.

Tupi or not Tupi, aye there's the point

HORATIO
    O day and night, but this is wondrous strange.
HAMLET
    And therefore as a stranger give it welcome.
(Ham 1.5.163–164)

It can be argued that Cultural Anthropophagy taps into such a 'wild and whirling' *(Ham* 1.5.132) moment of encountering strangers because it is based on the act of devouring, which is welcoming and inclusive at the same time as being fiercely violent. This chapter began with Andrade asking, 'Tupi or not Tupi, that is the question', but there is no question that Tribe Arts (with its name itself connoting both 'community and combativeness') and Phizzical exemplify the cultural Tupi stance in practice. In their case, to adapt Andrade and *Hamlet* Q1, it is more accurate to state that Tupi or not Tupi, aye there's the *point*. As is evident from the interviews, both companies adopt a cannibalistic attitude towards Shakespeare that simultaneously 'acknowledges an appetitive desire for appropriation and an aggressive process of deconstruction' (Islam 2012: 163). Tribe Arts' Tajpal Rathore asserts that although they chose Shakespeare because it resonated with them, their posture remains combative: 'we don't want anyone to tell us how to do it. We're gonna read it and we want to perform in a way that feels natural to us as British-Asians.' Similarly, Phizzical's Bhamra says that 'the go-to man really is Shakespeare for me' but he too is adamant that Shakespeare needs to accommodate to his productions, which will be a 'mash-up' of Shakespeare with 'Bollywood cinema' and 'the [Hindu] scriptures' in a bid to make 'Shakespeare incredibly accessible' and 'as fun as possible'. The emphasis on an aggressive appropriation in the cultural anthropophagic model makes it apt for studying Braisian Shakespeare productions because it recognizes that these directors are not succumbing to the status quo by borrowing elements from the mainstream dominant culture. Rather, their act of eating Shakespeare allows them 'to appropriate cultural tools without positioning oneself as subordinate to the other culture' (Islam 2012: 163).

Eating Shakespeare aggressively also allows these directors to rejuvenate both Shakespeare and Brasian culture. Weslei Roberto Candido and Nelci Alves Coelho Silvestre write that 'anthropophagy expresses devouring, deglutination, digestion of our European cultural heritage as a possible solution for Brazilian cultural stalemates' (2016: 245), thereby pointing out how a culture can be refreshed by assimilating multiple elements. Moreover, they stress that 'deglutination is also a metaphor for the creative process of a literature that appropriates the culture of the Other, or rather, it does not delete it, but places it within a creative relationship with an already canonical literature through a deliberate lack of respect for its privileged laws and place, considered untouchable by Eurocentric literary critique' (245). Due to their flouting of the established production conventions

in Britain, these directors place canonical Shakespeare
in a creative relationship with language, theatrical forms
and literatures from around the world and can invigorate
the practice and study of Global Shakespeare. When these
productions that are 'phizzing' with intercultural frissons
seem strange within the confines of a Eurocentric literary
critique, then we should give them welcome and employ
frameworks such as Cultural Anthropophagy to understand
them if we want to advance beyond the existing frontiers of
Global Shakespeare studies.

Notes

1 See interview below.

2 As the artistic directors have the same surname, I am using their
   full names throughout the chapter.

3 See interview below.

4 Alexa Huang similarly argues that 'diasporic and minority
   Shakespeares' and artists 'who work with more than one
   language or situate their performances in the diaspora' are 'less
   frequently studied' (2013: 283) because 'critics are ill-equipped to
   analyze works that do not fit neatly in geopolitical maps' (281).

5 For a fuller account of this narrative and how Bhamra's
   production dislodges it, see 'Much Ado About Knotting:
   Arranged Marriages in British-Asian Shakespeare Productions'
   (Panjwani 2017a: 96–109).

6 See Samran Rathore and Tajpal Rathore's interview below.

7 This company prefers being called British-Asian instead of
   Brasian because the term 'British-Asian', they feel, clearly
   emphasizes and gives due weight to both strands of their cultural
   heritage.

8 The Mughal dynasty ruled most of northern India from the early
   sixteenth century for over two centuries.

9 For Indo-Saracenic style, see *An Imperial Vision: Indian
   Architecture and Britain's Raj* (Metcalf 1989).

10   For a discussion of Bhansali's style, see 'Sanjay Leela Bhansali: In the Realm of Innovative Cinematic Experiences' (Panjwani 2017b: 110–128).

References

Andrade, O. ([1928] 1991), 'Cannibalist Manifesto', trans. L. Bary, *Latin American Literary Review*, 19 (38): 38–44.

Andrade, O. (1986), 'Manifesto of Pau-Brasil Poetry', trans. S. M. de Sá Rego, *Latin American Literary Review*, 14 (27): 184–187.

Bellei, S. L. P. (1998), 'Brazilian Anthropophagy Revisited', in F. Barker, P. Hulme and M. Iversen (eds), *Cannibalism and the Colonial World*, 87–109, Cambridge: Cambridge University Press.

Bhabha, H. K. and J. Rutherford (2006), 'Third Space', *Multitudes*, 26 (3): 95–107.

Bring on the Bollywood (2016), Dir. Samir Bhamra, Phizzical. 6 July, Arts Depot, London.

Budasz, R. (2005), 'Of Cannibals and the Recycling of Otherness', *Music and Letters*, 87 (1): 1–15.

Candido, W. R. and N. A. C. Silvestre (2016), 'The Discourse of Cannibalism as a Strategy of Building Brazilian Cultural Identity', *Acta Scientiarum. Language and Culture*, 38 (3): 243–252.

Cymbeline (2013), Dir. Samir Bhamra, Phizzical. The Curve, Leicester, 16 November.

Darokhand (2016), Dir. Samran Rathore and Tajpal Rathore, Tribe Arts. Mind The Gap, Bradford, 25 May.

Huang, A. (2013), 'Global Shakespeares as Methodology', *Shakespeare*, 9 (3): 273–290.

Islam, G. (2012), 'Can the Subaltern Eat? Anthropophagic Culture as a Brazilian Lens on Post-colonial Theory', *Organization*, 19 (2): 159–180.

Jarrett-Macauley, D. (2017), 'Introduction', in D. Jarrett-Macauley (ed.), *Shakespeare, Race and Performance: The Diverse Bard*, 1–20, London: Routledge.

Kleij, S., R. Mullin and M. Williamson (2013), '*Cymbeline* (Phizzical) @ Grand Opera House, Belfast, 2013', *Reviewing Shakespeare*, 29 October. Available online: http://

bloggingshakespeare.com/reviewing-shakespeare/cymbeline-phizzical-grand-opera-house-belfast-2013 (accessed 1 July 2015).

Metcalf, T. R. (1989), *An Imperial Vision: Indian Architecture and Britain's Raj*, London: Faber.

Panjwani, V. (2017a), 'Much Ado About Knotting: Arranged Marriages in British-Asian Shakespeare Productions', in D. Jarrett-Macauley (ed.), *Shakespeare, Race and Performance: The Diverse Bard*, 96–109, London: Routledge.

Panjwani, V. (2017b), 'Sanjay Leela Bhansali: In the Realm of Innovative Cinematic Experiences', in A. Viswamohan and V. Mohan (eds), *Behind the Scenes: Contemporary Bollywood Directors and Their Cinema*, 110–128, India: Sage.

Rathore, T. and S. Rathore (2016), 'Director's Note', in programme for *Darokhand*.

Romeo + Laila (2006), Dir. Samir Bhamra, Phizzical. Leicester.

Rumbold, K. (2012), '*Much Ado About Nothing*, dir. Iqbal Khan, Royal Shakespeare Company, 8 August 2012 at the Courtyard Theatre, Stratford-upon-Avon', *Blogging Shakespeare*, 10 August. Available online: http://bloggingshakespeare. com/year-of-shakespeare-much-ado-about-nothing-at-the-rsc#comment-617241970 (accessed 1 July 2015).

Said, E. (1993), *Culture and Imperialism*, New York: Vintage Books.

Sardar, Z. (2008), *Balti Britain: A Journey Through the British Asian Experience*, London: Granta.

Shakespeare, W. (2006), *Hamlet*, ed. A. Thompson and N. Taylor, third series, London: Bloomsbury Arden Shakespeare.

Shakespeare, W. (2012), *Romeo and Juliet*, ed. R. Weis, third series, London: Bloomsbury Arden Shakespeare.

Shakespeare, W. (2017), *Cymbeline*, ed. V. Wayne, third series, London: Bloomsbury Arden Shakespeare.

Verma, J. (1996), 'The Challenge of Binglish: Analysing Multi-cultural Productions', in P. Campbell (ed.), *Analysing Performance: A Critical Reader*, 193–202, Manchester: Manchester University Press.

Verma, J. (1998), 'Binglishing the Stage: A Generation of Asian Theatre in England', in J. Plastow and R. Boon (eds), *Theatre Matters: Performance and Culture on the World Stage*, 126–134, Cambridge: Cambridge University Press.

9

'Not where he eats, but where he is eaten': rethinking otherness in (British) Global Shakespeare

Anne Sophie Refskou

What does 'Global Shakespeare' mean in Britain? To begin where a number of recent scholarly discussions have also begun, the Globe-to-Globe festival of 2012, it seems that one initial understanding of Global Shakespeare in Britain was in fact not as a phenomenon *in* Britain at all, but something that was happening in the world *outside*. If one wanted to sample it, it was necessary to either invite it in, or to go out in search of it. Thus, thirty-seven (mostly) nationally and geographically foreign Shakespearean theatre productions were invited into Britain to perform at Shakespeare's Globe, and, later, The Globe's own *Hamlet* production went out in search of new performance places and spaces in other countries; nearly two hundred of them to be precise, as if the accumulation of borders crossed further and further away from Britain was a key criterion for making the venture 'global'.[1] In both cases, the notion that a global consciousness could exist or be produced internally without setting up international encounters involving the use of passports did not seem to be part of what Global Shakespeare was about.[2]

Both the Globe-to-Globe festival and the World Shakespeare Festival have been the subject of several critical and nuanced analyses (Sullivan 2013; Bennett 2016; Kennedy 2017; and Carson 2017, among others) that have contributed to marking them out – for better and for worse – as milestone events in the development of Global Shakespeare as an academic field or discipline. The purpose of this chapter is not to repeat what has already been problematized but to examine a somewhat overlooked question these events are uneasily linked to, and which still complicates cultural politics informing both creative and scholarly projects linked to Global Shakespeare in Britain: the question of how to deal with internal 'otherness'. As Varsha Panjwani also points out in her contribution to this volume – referring to Delia Jarrett-Macauley's important recent collection, *The Diverse Bard* – culturally and racially hybrid British Shakespeares have not yet received sufficient attention from scholarship operating under the banner of Global Shakespeare, despite the numerous performances being produced by and with British minority groups. Arguably part of the reason for this is that global Shakespeares were predominantly perceived as coming from the outside, as the term began to take stronger hold within British and anglophone Shakespeare Studies following the events of 2012. The slightly more uneasy part is whether some of the engagements with what were perceived as global Shakespeares in 2012 also became a conduit for projecting internal anxieties onto an external and seemingly more distinct 'other'?

As Tabish Khair points out, the construction of a 'stranger' as either someone from without, or someone living next door, is exactly that: a construction (2016: 12–14). It is a construction based on formulating a set of differences attributed to the stranger, or, in other words, deciding what makes the stranger different to oneself. As Khair writes, 'the strangeness of the stranger is always a definition of our own normality; without it the stranger ceases to come into being qua stranger' (13). Yet the difference of a stranger from without – what Khair also calls a 'pure stranger' – can be considerably simpler to construct than that of the stranger within, who may elude or defy facile categorizations. And this is, not surprisingly, a particularly complex issue within the messy cultural mosaic of societies such as Britain. When 'strangers' from within (who may be perceived as such because they differ, racially, culturally or religiously, from the hegemonic culture of a nation) are projected onto 'strangers' from the outside, it may be because such a projection (whether deliberate or subliminal) offers an anodyne for anxieties caused by the imbrication with the world and a consequent decentring of one's sense of identity. Shakespeare, of course, has played no small part in British identity and its relationship with the world, being deployed both as an emissary of empire and as a device for 'writing back'. Yet, the question of Shakespeare and internal otherness is on some level even more complicated than the questions raised by these routes, for how does one 'write back' from within?

Granted, much has happened to the British Shakespeare scene since 2012, with Shakespeare's Globe – under the direction of Emma Rice and now Michelle Terry – and the Royal Shakespeare Company (RSC) both embracing a decidedly more positive approach to diversity, especially regarding casting. However, even as these leading institutions seem more and more conscious of changing their politics and image to represent – and speak to – multicultural Britain, other aspects of British society and politics are dealing less well with internal xenophobia. The 'Windrush scandal', unfolding at the moment of writing, is a stark reminder of the country's still troubled perception of what constitutes a 'stranger'.[3] Jarrett-Macauley also points out that changing the environment and opportunities for British minorities working with Shakespeare does not happen overnight and cannot be taken for granted as permanent, especially since it depends on several independent factors: 'An artistic director's multicultural ethos is not necessarily understood and appreciated by venue managers, marketers or critics as anything other than "novelty Shakespeare"' (2017: 17).

What is clear is that the meaning of Global Shakespeare in Britain needs to encompass internal issues: some scholarship at least needs to 'begin at home' and address perceptions of internal otherness in a sustained manner, reiterating that intercultural encounters do not always involve national border crossings or passports. This would also help to dissolve the false distinction between British and Global Shakespeare with the latter representing the rest of the world – and sometimes with the implication of trying to follow a British lead. Because the institutionalization of Global Shakespeare as an academic field is inevitably – and somewhat ironically – dominated by British and anglophone scholarship, looking inwards as well as outwards is even more important.

Cultural Anthropophagy, the theoretical framework for this volume, offers a clarifying and productive perspective on what British-Global Shakespeare might mean – particularly concerning the question of internal otherness – and helps unpack the cultural politics of relevant theatre productions. This is partly thanks to Cultural Anthropophagy's fundamentally inclusive standpoint, and partly thanks to its subversion of notions of cultural authenticity; both of which are linked to an attempt to utilize culturally intermixed identities as fuel for intellectual and creative production. As discussed in the introduction to this volume, it also offers an alternative to the concept of multiculturalism, which has often been rightly criticized for ultimately furthering segregation and which, when applied to British Shakespeare, might (almost ironically) constitute a route towards marginalization. In what follows, I will revisit the Globe-to-Globe festival of 2012 as a starting point for analysing two contemporary *Hamlet* productions characterized by their different engagements with British-Global culture.

Audiences attending the visiting shows and staying for The Globe's own production of *Henry V* at the end of the Globe-to-Globe festival, might have been slightly confused by some of its casting and directorial choices. *Henry V*, with its – at the time – familiar Globe dramaturgy and predominantly white cast seemed to represent a version of Britishness almost untouched by the centuries of immigration to the island.[4] Rather than providing an answer to why it was necessary to invite a multinational, multicultural, multiracial plethora of artists to Britain and London particularly, when, in so many ways, they were already there and had been for centuries, the festival's finale seemed to reinforce its contradictory aspects. In a blog post for *Blogging Shakespeare*, Stephen Purcell looks at some of these contradictions, relating a statement by festival director Tom Bird in which Bird explains how the festival programming began by identifying minority languages spoken in London, and then invited companies speaking those languages to perform at the festival in a gesture to include 'part of London's own periphery' (2012). This was undoubtedly a productive idea and, judging by reviews, many performances and their audiences clearly created moments of intense collectivity underwritten by shared cultural memories and trajectories.[5] But as Purcell also argues, ultimately 'a celebration of the periphery serves to consolidate the centre' – in this case The Globe and its particular patent on Shakespearean English and 'Englishness' – and other aspects of the festival undermined inclusivity, not least the *Henry V* production, which Purcell describes as 'traditional and patriotic [...] separated from the rest of the festival by a gap of three days, and subject to none of the constraints imposed on the other festival productions' (2012).

One of these constraints, and perhaps the most controversial, was the requirement for visiting productions to stay within their 'own' language box and refrain from the use of English vocabulary on stage. Even if unwittingly, this seemed to imply a false sense of linguistic purity and a policing of intermixing, which felt blind to the past (including colonial) and present of the English language; as well as oddly un-Shakespearean, when so many of the plays themselves relish in interlinguistic mix-ups and puns, including, of course, *Henry V*. Given that the festival represented an opportunity that, for many of the companies, was felt as a blue-stamp, the power-structures to impose such restraints were quite firmly in place, yet it was interesting to observe that when productions, such as *Pericles* by the National Theatre of Greece, improvised some deliberately broken English expressions, it caused audience laughter and seemed to have potential for a subversive effect within the overall festival set-up.

Another potentially subversive element was London-based company Two Gents' revival of their production of *Two Gentlemen of Verona/Vakomana Vaviri ve Zimbabwe*, as also noted by Purcell and excellently analysed by Sonia Massai (2017). The company then consisted of Zimbabwean-born actors Denton Chikura and Tonderai Munyevu, and German-born director Arne Pohlmeier with links to Cameroon, the United States and South Africa. It was founded in 2008, which also saw the first performance of *The Two Gentlemen of Verona/Vakomana Vaviri ve Zimbabwe* at the Ovalhouse theatre in South London. Exploring their own cultural hybridity through and with Shakespeare – including mixing English and Shona as performance languages – is central to the company's identity, so the revival of *The Two Gentlemen of Verona/Vakomana Vaviri ve Zimbabwe* for the Globe-to-Globe festival with the premise of performing it exclusively in Shona was, as Massai demonstrates, problematic. Yet, as Massai also argues, the constraints of the festival only seemed to highlight the intercultural nature of the production, which ultimately destabilized the supposedly 'African' category imposed on it (2017: 484–490). Despite a relatively small body of work to date, Two Gents have attracted substantial scholarly attention, including from Gordon (2011), Woods (2013, 2014), Pearce (2017) as well as Massai (2017), with scholars mainly focusing on their explicit engagements with hybrid identities and diaspora.

This also means that their work lends itself exceptionally well to analysis informed by Cultural Anthropophagy. The ways in which Two Gents explicitly incorporate – and through incorporation rewrite – the Shakespearean text go beyond adaptation and appropriation, but feel very close to the anthropophagic attitude; not only because their relationship with Shakespeare is in every way playful and irreverent, but also because their relationship with their *own* hybrid cultural identity is self-referential and self-mimicking in ways that are both complex and entertaining. As explained in the introduction to this volume and by Gazi Islam, the performative strategies of Cultural Anthropophagy 'can be self-conscious and culturally affirmative, and in addition to mimicking the colonizer, can self-mimic, self-positioning as an indigenous cannibal while simultaneously appropriating European cultural forms' (Islam 2011: 172). This feature of Cultural Anthropophagy, inspired by the notion of indigenous 'performances' of cannibalism designed to frighten colonial invaders, and linked to Brazil's relationship with its biologically and culturally intermixed identity, means the freedom to perform from a position outside of a reductive and divisive definition of cultural selves (and others). There is a link here to be made to Homi K. Bhabha's crucial point that no culture can in fact be understood as essential – or 'pure' – because the very acts by which it signifies itself as culture show it to be a self-referential construction. As Bhabha states, 'we are very resistant to thinking how the act of signification, the act of producing the icons and symbols, the myths and metaphors through which we live culture, must always – by virtue of the fact that they *are* forms of representation – have within them a kind of self-alienating limit' (1990: 210). Cultural Anthropophagy, however, not only accepts the self-referential aspect of culture as formulated by Bhabha but explicitly performs it, displaying it as a philosophical and creative strength.

In terms of determining the cultural position of artists like Two Gents, the only answer is liminality: they seem able to perform 'inside' and 'outside' of Britain and Africa simultaneously, and, importantly, are able to effect mutual transformation of cultural signifiers in the process, as I will explore in more detail further on. This also makes audience expectations of any signs of cultural authenticity untenable and ultimately superfluous. As also demonstrated in the chapters by Varsha Panjwani and Eleine Ng in this volume, artists who are already deeply (self-)conscious of cultural intermixing can lead the way in celebrating the culturally *inauthentic* Shakespearean production. This also produces an alternative vision to the ethnographically oriented categorization of foreign Shakespeares, which can feel characteristic of events such as the Globe-to-Globe festival.[6] I will argue that Two Gents have found a way to hold up notions of cultural authenticity only to dismantle them and, consequently, perceptions of what is 'self' and what is 'other' – or what is local, original, foreign or imported – in their work are deliberately confused and put into dynamic play.

Apart from their performance at Shakespeare's Globe (which perhaps somewhat ironically contributed to their visibility), their shows have mostly appeared in what might be considered peripheral (both geographically and economically) venues in London and the UK. Yet the themes that characterize their work have arguably eaten their way in towards the 'centre', as recently seen in the 2016 RSC *Hamlet* (touring the UK and USA in 2018), which starred Paapa Essiedu as an African prince educated at 'Wittenberg University, Ohio', who returns home to find his grief and existential crises supposedly reinforced by a diasporic sense of displacement. There are no explicit links between Two Gents' Zimbabwean-set *Kupenga Kwa Hamlet* (The Madness of Hamlet), performed at the Harare International Festival of the Arts and Ovalhouse in London, and the RSC *Hamlet*, but comparing the very different ways in which the two productions deal with similar content is highly relevant to the discussion of this chapter.

A game of skulls

It would be unfair to say that Simon Godwin's 2016 *Hamlet* production for the RSC, set in an undefined African location and featuring an (almost) entirely black cast, was guilty of simplistic exoticism. Probably acutely aware of the possibility of such an accusation, the production handled its signifiers carefully and introduced elements that allowed for some engaging commentary on contemporary cultural (mis)understandings. It also made space for strong performances by the cast, not least by Paapa Essiedu, who handled the central role to widespread critical acclaim. In many ways, the production felt like a determined gesture to engage with diversity by the RSC; something that also seemed to be reflected in the choice of tour venues, notably the Hackney Empire as the London venue, rather than the Barbican, and with a broader range of ticket prices.

And yet the production gave rise to a number of questions about its Britishness, its 'Africanness' and its place in a globalized narrative. As with the questions regarding internal and external otherness discussed in the beginning of this chapter, it was unclear why the production needed an external setting – transporting itself to a distinct 'outside' of Britain – especially when the actors were British (and trained at such quintessentially British institutions as Central School of Speech and Drama, Guildhall School of Music and Drama or Bristol Old Vic). The diaspora-inspired trope of having Hamlet return to Africa from a Western education provides one answer to this question, and it is easy to see why the character's sense of conflict might be heightened by a cultural disconnect between Wittenberg and Elsinore. However, diaspora does not necessarily describe what happens in the confrontation between 'home' and 'away', especially not if these terms are essentialized and situated as opposites. Following Bhabha, it is rather connected to negotiating identity in a liminal space – Bhabha uses architectural images such as a pathway or a stair case (1994: 5). In other words, what is important is not the contrast, but the interstice or the gap.

Godwin's production, however, did begin by narrating diaspora in terms of contrast: a series of tableaus in the beginning showed Hamlet graduating at the 'University of Wittenberg, Ohio' with a sudden cut – marked by the sound of a gunshot and a blackout – to the procession of his father's coffin, presided over by his mother and uncle from a balcony, and with the visual and aural trappings of what one might associate with some present-day West African states. The opening scene reinforced those signifiers with the guards dressed in camouflaged uniforms, berets, carrying heavy machine guns and speaking in equally heavy accents, which sounded somewhat explicit in comparison with the predominance of received pronunciation (RP) in the rest of the show. Accents only came back in the gravedigger scene; this time in the form of slightly out-of-place Calypso or Caribbean-inflected intonation. On the one hand, it made sense to avoid the pan-African accent adopted by Gregory Doran's 2012 RSC production of *Julius Caesar* – also featuring an all-black British cast and set in an undefined African country – which might inadvertently send signals of clichéd 'Africanness'. On the other hand, the use of pseudo localized accents for characters of lower social status, while RP was reserved for those with a higher status, was not ideal either. Such a choice presents a problem within any given Shakespeare production, but here it was in danger of implying RP as the preferred *lingua franca* adopted by those materially able to live in a modern (Western-influenced) world. Of course, there is no ultimate or correct answer to many of these dilemmas, and my purpose here is not to assume a position from which it is deceptively easy to critique but mainly to examine how signifiers can be treacherously double-edged.

In addition to the contrast between the briefly sketched-out Western Wittenberg and the African Elsinore, there was also an implied contrast between two different 'Africas'. One was highly Westernized, employing Western designer clothes in its ostentatious display of power, while the other supplied traditional drums, robes and masks. The contrast between these two Africas was mostly handled with nuance, in the sense that the inhabitants of the court of Elsinore seemed more than able to command a mix-and-match attitude to local and imported signifiers in tune with notes of contemporary globalized consumerism. The problems mainly appeared when the contrast became at odds with contrasts within the play itself. As Stephen Purcell also notes in his review of the production for the *Shakespeare Survey*, the fact that the Ghost wore traditional robes in contrast to the outfits of the rest of the cast could be seen as one such problematic moment. The Ghost remained invisible to the audience in the opening scene and did not physically appear until its revelations to Hamlet in Act 1, Scene 5. Here it was 'invoked' with a drumming session reminiscent of traditional Yoruba ceremonies in which drums function as a form of communication with deities. Hamlet himself engaged briefly in a trance-like dance also potentially to be associated with ceremonial Yoruba incorporation of deities. As Purcell writes:

> Clearly this sequence was asking us to associate the Ghost's call to revenge with the eruption of a more traditional mode of 'Africanness'. While the moment was thrillingly effective, I was uncomfortable that once again, as in Doran's *Julius Caesar*, 'Africa' was being used to signify the mythic, the violent and the vengeful, and set in contrast with the rational, the intellectual and the 'civilized' as represented by the European Wittenberg. (2017: 302)

A counterbalance to such moments was provided by Rosencrantz and Guildenstern played as white and wide-eyed British tourists. Upon arrival, the pair were visibly excited to be in what was clearly the simplified, exoticized 'Africa' of their limited imaginations. Their costumes (which slyly began to appropriate some of the styles of the court), complete with cameras and Fjallraven bags, marked them out as both complacent and naïve, while their out-of-place London souvenir gifts to the king and queen were perhaps slightly overstating the point, but made for a comic moment. More subtle was the added complexity by this to Hamlet's confronting Guildenstern in Act 3 with 'you would pluck out the heart of my mystery' (3.2.357–358). That moment also felt like the culmination of the pair slowly realizing that they had no cultural compass with which to navigate their surroundings, while Hamlet's much more sophisticated intercultural experience allowed him to see straight through them. Using Rosencrantz and Guildenstern as examples of stereotypical Western cluelessness allowed the production to distance itself from what they were made to represent, and this seemed like an astute, manoeuvre. Yet, at the same time, it did polarize the cultural positions invoked and might ultimately – even if no doubt unintentionally – signify 'Britishness' as white and 'Africanness' as black.

However, the element that perhaps most strongly undermined the production's attempts at staging a discourse of cultural hybridity was the supreme rule of the Shakespearean text itself. All other signifiers, however they might be classified, were ultimately there to serve the text, which meant that they were slowly, but securely, emptied of autonomous meaning. This should not be surprising given the RSC's usual, masterful ability to turn any of Shakespeare's sometimes difficult and disjointed texts into clear, comprehensible, linear narratives. Their productions are superbly able to amend textual and dramaturgical eccentricities, and the words are spoken with such a degree of specificity that meaning feels as if carved out with surgical precision. But the problem with the RSC trademark of clarity is that it is inevitably at odds with hybrid – and certainly anthropophagic – discourses, because these actually thrive on the disjointed and the multifarious.

Curiously, this also undermined the otherwise important reference in the production design to the work of iconic African American graffiti artist and painter Jean-Michel Basquiat. Hamlet's costume featured explicitly Basquiat-inspired designs to denote his 'antic disposition', and he surrounded himself with multicoloured canvasses echoing Basquiat's style, while also assuming a rebellious attitude associated with the artist in order to undermine the power displays by his uncle and mother. Favoured motifs by Basquiat, such as the skull or the crown, featured prominently and seemed to create perfect links to the world of the play. Yet the production's inevitable loyalty to a highly institutionalized Shakespearean text blunted the subversive streak provided by the reference to Basquiat's work. Importantly his work might itself in some ways echo an anthropophagic attitude when mixing, for example, Picasso with hip-hop. His paintings are full of words, shooting across his images, which was also referenced in the production, but, whereas Basquiat's writing is about deconstructing words, dismantling and subverting meanings, the writing on Hamlet's clothes and canvasses mainly seemed to *quote* Shakespeare. Thus, the production's negotiation of otherness became secondary to its upholding of the Shakespearean text as a fixed point of reference, and Basquiat's skull began to look simply like an illustration of Shakespeare's (or Yorick's). In other words, the production felt underwritten by a game of looking for equivalents – such as an 'African Elsinore' – always presupposing the existence of an original. In terms of creating a Global-British *Hamlet* such a game is in danger of becoming unilateral and therefore also unable to fully represent the plurality of British cultural identity. Instead it is perhaps bound to participate in externalizing what might be perceived as 'other' within that identity, and transporting it to what it perceives to be a more distinctly different cultural location.

Madness in the method:
Kupenga Kwa Hamlet

One of only two props in Two Gents' *Kupenga Kwa Hamlet* was a large rush mat, which was perhaps an ironic nod to Peter Brook's carpet used for performing in African villages, when the director and his company toured the continent in the

1970s. Ironic, one suspects, because Two Gents' performance felt very far away from Brook's famous 'culture of links', so often criticized for its universalist premise.[7] Instead, actors Denton Chikura and Tonderai Munyevu, and director Arne Pohlmeier offered a complex set of cultural 'disjoints', unfettered by essentialist conceptions of any of the signifiers employed in the performance, as I will continue to explore in the following.[8]

The unique style of *Kupenga Kwa Hamlet* mixed South-African-inspired township theatre with oral storytelling devices, *commedia dell'arte*, physical stylization, improvisation, with Chikura and Munyevu switching from English to Shona at opportune moments, and always keeping a key focus of the performance on the audience, as Gordon also notes (2011: 66).[9] The actors broke off at several points to ask the audience questions such as 'do you know what we're talking about?' or 'are you still with us?', which was both comic and inclusive without feeling condescending. The premise seemed to be that both the performance space and the performed location were understood as liminal and in continuous negotiation with the audience. The two actors also used audience members to stand in for characters during the performance of 'The Mousetrap', playing deftly on the already highly meta-theatrical aspect of this scene, while also simply getting more bodies on stage, leaving themselves freer to move around. Otherwise Munyevu and Chikura managed to cover all roles between them, using distinctive physical gestures to denote each character, which were introduced to the audience at the beginning of the show. These gestures also enabled the actors to share roles, whenever necessary, further highlighting the sense of continuous and easy transformation characterizing the performance.

The production used the 1603 First Quarto version of *Hamlet*, also known derogatively as the 'Bad Quarto'. This provided a shorter and more action-driven narrative and, even more importantly, offered the advantage of an already de-familiarized version of the text, as both Gordon and Massai also note (Gordon 2011: 65; Massai 2017: 482).[10] Rather than 'bad', Q1's disjointed nature suited the performance perfectly and helped to desacralize the Shakespearean text, reminding the audience of the plural existences of the plays. During the introduction of the characters and when arriving at 'Corambis, otherwise known as Polonius', the audience was told that 'we are using the First Quarto of *Hamlet*, you see, which you might find confusing, but don't worry, we know our lines'.

The playful and irreverent situating of Shakespeare as a cultural 'other' in the performance was combined with an equally playful situating of the cultural 'self'. Neither Shakespeare nor Africa were held up as sacred but appeared to undergo mutual transformation, emerging as dynamically de-familiarized. As Gordon writes: 'The show cheerfully disappoints expectations of seeing *Hamlet* comfortably "set" in Zimbabwe, making the country and its history available for modern dress reinterpretations, or offering "authentically" infused spectacle' (2011: 64). The representation of Africa by Two Gents is also described by Denton Chikura: 'we presented an image of Africa that was unusual: clever, witty, sophisticated – which mocked us!' (pers. comm. quoted in Pearce 2017: 76).

This combination of 'mockery' – both of Shakespeare and self-referential – is, as already stated, a key reason why Cultural Anthropophagy provides such a suitable model for understanding the complexity of how this performance negotiated otherness – and why it was so different to the RSC *Hamlet* in this respect. Terms such as intercultural or cross-cultural have been used to describe the work by Two Gents and *Kupenga Kwa Hamlet*, but Cultural Anthropophagy avoids the baggage associated with the more Eurocentric perspectives and usages of these terms, and, I would argue, is more to the point when trying to explain the astounding cultural flexibility demonstrated by the company. This flexibility also builds on what in Cultural Anthropophagy would be a syntagmatic relation between signifiers, as explained in the introduction to this volume, using Oswald de Andrade's famous anthropophagic rendering of 'To be or not to be' as 'Tupi or not Tupi' (Andrade [1928] 1991) as an example of how signifiers can coexist and infuse each other with meaning without overwriting or negating 'self' or 'other'. In *Kupenga Kwa Hamlet* this was perhaps most powerfully demonstrated in the performance of the Player King's Hecuba speech from Scene 7 (of Q1) by Munyevu entirely in Shona. The words 'Hecuba', 'Priam' or 'Aeneas' repeated at certain points could be recognized by non-Shona speakers, but following the narrative of the 'Mobled Queen' to the letter was clearly not the point here. The speech was spoken at a fast pace and overlaid with highly stylized emotion, which did not only produce a very comical and engaging effect but created a multilayered dialogue with the stylized manner of the speech in the text.[11] Usually when the speech is subjected to naturalistic styles of performance, as in many mainstream performances, it becomes, at best, mildly tedious, but here it received an almost ecstatic applause. In anthropophagic terms, this moment showed not a paradigmatic translation of meaning from English into Shona nor an overwriting of Shakespeare's words, but a dialectical relation in which signifiers were mutually revitalized. By comparison, the same speech in the RSC *Hamlet* was performed naturalistically with actors holding up African masks to give physical substance to Pyrrhus and Hecuba. The problem here, as already described in relation to other aspects of that production, was that the masks were made to serve the text as illustrations of the action, which ultimately emptied them of meaning, keeping them fixed as pure objects. Another moment that is interesting to compare with the RSC equivalent was the Ghost's appearance to Hamlet. Like the RSC production, Two Gents also summoned their Ghost with a dance and song ritual, here performed in Shona, but, in a bold move, the Ghost was then incorporated by – or 'took place in' – Horatio (played by Munyevu while Chikura played Hamlet). This put the culturally specific elements of ritualistic incorporation of spirits into play with an explicit layering of multiple characters (while also pointing to the actor's own presence), recalling dramatic conventions implied by the Shakespearean text. The result was another mutual revitalization of these signifiers, making them coexist rather than overwrite each other. Thus, different to the RSC's staging of the same moment as a mildly exoticized ritual importing otherness into a framework predetermined by the higher authority of the Shakespearean text, Two Gents seemed able to create a new and unique performance framework through deconstructing, and then reconstructing, both 'Shakespeare' and 'Africa'.[12] Furthermore, the moment was again handled in an easy, self-consciously ironic manner, subtly mocking any implication of ethnographic authenticity.

Importantly, the self-mocking attitude employed by Two Gents is not to be misunderstood as self-deprecatory. Like many forms of mimicry, it has a subtle but sharp political edge. In the version of the show performed in Harare, Chikura and Munyevu wore identical khaki uniforms with shorts and bare feet, which created unmistakable and uncomfortable associations to Nelson Mandela and other black political prisoners on Robben Island being forced to wear shorts as an additional form of humiliation (in other and later versions Chikura and Munyevu wore equally politically conscious orange boiler suits). Thus, Two Gents do not shy away from deeply serious references, but these are included into the performance framework without idealization or victimization.

Nor is Two Gents' 'mockery' of Shakespeare to be understood as subversive for the sake of subversion only. It is inclusive: his cultural otherness is not held up to be rejected, it appears, but to be incorporated when it has the desired 'nutrients', to borrow from the language of Cultural Anthropophagy. In sum, Two Gents' anthropophagic method can be understood as one of self-conscious 'madness', which subverts other methods tending towards simplistic categorizations of cultural difference. Perhaps most importantly, they show that distinctions between external and internal otherness can be problematized and ultimately discarded in Global-British Shakespeare. Not in the name of sameness but by operating in a liminal space between cultural signifiers without polarizing them in the process.

Concluding remarks

To reiterate the question asked in the beginning of this chapter: what does Global Shakespeare mean in Britain? Does it describe the import of supposed authentic otherness as seen in the 2012 Globe-to-Globe festival, or the ultimately pastiche-like othering of internal cultural elements, such as in the 2016 RSC *Hamlet*? Or would it be suitable as a term describing the (inter)culturally flexible work by artists such as Two Gents? In the beginning of the chapter, I also noted that much has changed on the British Shakespeare scene since 2012, with diverse casting hopefully beginning to look more like the norm than a novelty. Yet diverse casting in itself is not enough. If a particular, and still fundamentally monocultural, understanding of Shakespeare remains fixed at the high point of hierarchies in leading institutions, diverse casting paradoxically only reinforces sameness under a Shakespearean banner. Cultural Anthropophagy, on the other hand, does not attempt to negate otherness or overwrite differences, imposing the kind of sameness that some societies confuse with integration, but helps to understand and embrace the processes that effect mutual change. As Jeroen Dewulf proposes,

> Instead of calling up, time after time, the spirit of cultural uniformity, and instead of slipping back into linguistic anti-Semitism, anthropophagy may nevertheless be seen as a significant attitude towards globalization. It stands for absorbing foreign influences, knowing and accepting, that afterwards one will never be the same again. (2007: 93)

It offers the possibility to perform 'culture' in a self-referential manner that can confront uneasy essentialist dilemmas head-on and humorously. The self-referential aspect of the anthropophagical attitude also means that externalizing otherness becomes impossible, because anthropophagy does not just include otherness into its cultural mix, it understands and accepts it as already there; as already internal. Ultimately this means an opportunity for British Shakespeare to participate in the processes that take place 'not where [Shakespeare] eats, but where he is eaten', celebrating global identity from within.

Notes

1 In his review of former Globe artistic director Dominic Dromgoole's book describing the trajectory of the Globe-to-Globe *Hamlet* tour, Andrew Dixon asks the critical 'why' of this (ad)venture:

> Why *are* his actors visiting all these countries? As with so many questions in *Hamlet,* this one doesn't really find an answer. 'Why not?' is a reply proffered near the end of the book, but Dromgoole's next suggestion, that the Globe was engaging in its own 'nuttily' aggrandising version of the 60s space programme, seems more telling – figuring these 'actor-astronauts' as heroic voyagers into deep, uncharted territory (2017).

As Dixon also acknowledges in the same review, the critical attitude from many academics towards this and other of Dromgoole's and Shakespeare's Globe's 'global' engagements might be felt as exasperating or downright dismissible at the receiving end, which is testimony to the sometimes awkward, even antagonistic, atmosphere between academics and creatives within Global Shakespeare debates. Some of my arguments in this chapter might derive from a similar position of academic scepticism, or rather an academic need to problematize matters, and I am aware of and sympathetic towards any irritation this might cause. Undoubtedly it is easy for academics to criticize without taking into account the enormous investment and difficulties – creative, economic, organizational – behind ventures such as the Globe-to-Globe festival or Globe-to-Globe *Hamlet* tour. Yet there are also ample examples of perfectly productive dialogue between academics and creatives to mutual benefit and, given the highly sensitive politics of Global Shakespeare, such dialogues are clearly necessary.

2 The fact that tickets to the Globe-to-Globe festival were in fact issued as so-called 'passports' seems slightly ironic. See also Bennett (2016) on the notion of tickets as passports.

3   The 'Windrush scandal' unfolded as it was revealed that members
     of the so-called Windrush generation (Windrush referring to the
     name of the *HTM Empire Windrush*, which brought nearly 500
     Caribbean immigrants to the UK in 1984) had been deported in
     error, or threatened with deportation, as well as being victims of
     other discriminatory treatment in the UK.

4   The Dauphin of France was played by black British actor Kurt
     Egyiawan, but, given the 'othering' of the French versus the
     English in the play itself, this might have had a slightly adverse
     effect; another example of the difficulty of absolutely 'colour-
     blind' or 'gender-blind' casting, when, in effect, there is no such
     thing as an entirely neutral signifier on the stage.

5   For reviews of the Globe-to-Globe productions see
     Edmondson, Prescott and Sullivan (2013).

6   The question of the *authentically inauthentic* cultural product
     is also discussed in the introduction to this volume.

7   See Brook (1996). Brook was most famously and vociferously
     criticized by Rustom Bharucha in *Theatre and the World*
     (1990). For an analysis of his essentialism, see also Gilbert and
     Lo (2002: 47).

8   The version of *Kupenga Kwa Hamlet* I refer to in this chapter
     was performed at the Harare International Festival of the Arts
     in 2010. I am extremely grateful to Arne Pohlmeier for lending
     me a DVD recording of the performance.

9   For a detailed discussion of Two Gents' performance styles, see
     also Pearce (2017).

10   As Massai writes, 'their decision to use Q1 proved particularly
     productive because it allowed them to present both the
     dialogue sung and spoken in Shona and the dialogue drawn
     from Q1 as "other" when compared to what English audiences
     are used to hearing in mainstream productions of *Hamlet*'
     (2017: 482).

11   In a personal conversation, Arne Pohlmeier explained to me
     that the purpose for him and the actors was not so much to
     narrate the Hecuba story, but exactly to create something that
     would spur the next moment: Hamlet's reaction to the player's
     emotion. The moment is also analysed in some detail by
     Gordon, who explains how Munyevu drew on oral traditions

of Shona storytelling. Impressed with the effect, she writes that 'this was the first time I cared about Hecuba' (2011: 68).

12   As Gordon also notes: 'Social practices of ritual, music, song, celebration, mourning and storytelling are so thoroughly woven into the production that they constitute both its represented world *and* a large part of its theatrical language. This is very different from ethnological display in performance' (2011: 65).

References

Andrade, O. ([1928] 1991), 'Cannibalist Manifesto', trans. L. Bary, *Latin American Literary Review*, 19 (38): 35–47.

Bennett, S. (2016), 'Shakespeare on Site: Here, There and Everywhere', in T. Bishop, A. Huang and S. Bennett (eds), *The Shakespearean International Yearbook, 16: Special Section, Shakespeare on Site*, 1–10, Abingdon: Routledge.

Bhabha, H. K. (1994), *The Location of Culture*, London: Routledge.

Bhabha, H. K. and J. Rutherford (1990), 'The Third Space: Interview with Homi Bhabha', in J. Rutherford (ed.), *Identity: Community, Culture, Difference*, 207–221, London: Lawrence & Wishart.

Brook, P. (1996), 'The Culture of Links', in P. Pavis (ed.), *The Intercultural Performance Reader*, 63–66, New York: Routledge.

Carson, C. (2017), 'Performance, Presence and Personal Responsibility: Witnessing Global Theatre in and around the Globe', in J. C. Bulman (ed.), *The Oxford Handbook of Shakespeare and Performance*, 458–476, Oxford: Oxford University Press.

Dewulf, J. (2007), 'As a Tupi-Indian, Playing the Lute: Hybridity as Anthropophagy', in J. Kuortti and J. Nyman (eds), *Reconstructing Hybridity: Post-Colonial Studies in Transition*, 81–97, Amsterdam: Rodopi.

Dixon, A. (2017), 'Hamlet, Globe to Globe by Dominic Dromgoole Review – Neocolonial Folly?', *The Guardian*, 14 April. Available online: www.theguardian.com/books/2017/apr/14/hamlet-globe-to-globe-dominic-dromgoole-review-shakespeare (accessed 2 March 2017).

Edmondson, P., P. Prescott and E. Sullivan, eds (2013), *A Year of Shakespeare: Re-living the World Shakespeare Festival*, London: Bloomsbury.

Gilbert, H. and J. Lo (2002), 'Toward a Topography of Cross-Cultural Theatre Praxis', *TDR: The Drama Review*, 46 (3): 31–53.

Gordon, C. (2011), 'Hamlet in England, Hamlet in Exile: What's Hecuba to Him, or Kupenga to Them?', *Shakespeare in Southern Africa*, 23: 64–69.

Islam, G. (2011), 'Can the Subaltern Eat? Anthropophagic Culture as a Brazilian Lens on Post Colonial Theory', *Organization*, 19 (2): 159–180.

Jarrett-Macauley, D. (2017), 'Introduction', in D. Jarrett-Macauley (ed.), *Shakespeare, Race and Performance: The Diverse Bard*, 1–20, Abingdon: Routledge.

Kennedy, D. (2017), 'Global Shakespeare and Globalized Performance', in J. C. Bulman (ed.), *The Oxford Handbook of Shakespeare and Performance*, 441–457, Oxford: Oxford University Press.

Khair, T. (2016), *The New Xenophobia*, Oxford: Oxford University Press.

Massai, S. (2017), 'Shakespeare With and Without Its Language', in J. C. Bulman (ed.), *The Oxford Handbook of Shakespeare and Performance*, 475–494, Oxford: Oxford University Press.

Pearce, M. (2017), '"Why then the World's Mine Oyster/Which I with Sword will Open", Africa, Diaspora, Shakespeare: Cross-cultural Encounters on the Global Stage', in D. Jarrett-Macauley (ed.), *Shakespeare, Race and Performance: The Diverse Bard*, 65–79, Abingdon: Routledge.

Purcell, S. (2012), 'Circles, Centres and the Globe to Globe Festival', *Blogging Shakespeare*. Available online: http://bloggingshakespeare.com/year-of-shakespeare-circles-centres-and-the-globe-to-globe-festival (accessed 28 March 2018).

Purcell, S. (2017), 'Shakespeare Performances in England, 2016', in P. Holland (ed.), *Shakespeare Survey 70: Creating Shakespeare*, 287–325, Cambridge: Cambridge University Press.

Shakespeare, W. (2016), *Hamlet*, ed. A. Thompson and N. Taylor, third series, rev. edition, London: Bloomsbury Arden Shakespeare.

Sullivan, E. (2013), 'Olympic Performance in the Year of Shakespeare', in P. Edmondson, P. Prescott and E. Sullivan (eds),

A Year of Shakespeare: Re-living the World Shakespeare Festival, 3–11, London: Bloomsbury.

Woods, P. (2013), 'The Two Gentlemen of Zimbabwe & Their Diaspora Audience at Shakespeare's Globe', in J. Plastow (ed.), *African Theatre 12: Shakespeare in and out of Africa*, 13–27, Woodbridge: James Currey.

Woods, P. (2014), 'Shakespeare/Two Gents Productions: Denton Chikura, Tonderai Munyevu and Arne Pohlmeier of Two Gents Productions in Conversations with Penelope Woods', in M. Laera (ed.), *Theatre and Adaptation: Return, Rewrite, Repeat*, 151–164, London: Bloomsbury.

10

Rojak Shakespeare: devouring the self and digesting otherness on the Singapore stage

Eleine Ng

Written almost ninety years ago, critic and poet Oswald de Andrade's provocative and polemical declaration of cultural 'cannibalism' in his now famous 'Manifesto Antropófago'[1] has become an important methodology for understanding how (post)colonial identities can be simultaneously formed through the indigenous and the cosmopolitan.[2] This rich paradigm is easily transposed beyond its Brazilian provenance to contextualize the global reproduction of Shakespeare and his work on the Singapore stage. Andrade's Cultural Anthropophagy articulates a process of recreation that springs from an incorporation and mediation of otherness that is already familiar to Singapore's diasporic, postcolonial and interculturalized context. Singapore and its people, as noted Singapore theatre practitioner Kuo Pao Kun remarks, 'have the mentality of cultural orphans' – at once alienated by and optimistic about 'the search for self' (2002: 113). To Kuo, Singapore's diasporic condition necessitates the Singaporean people to 'accept a few more lines of parentage so as to counter the cultural impurities already infused in [their] blood'. Rather than induce despair, the interstitial space a 'cultural orphan' occupies engenders potential, as cultural rootlessness leads to the possible reinvention of new identities based on intercultural plurality. In this sense, adapting Shakespeare to and for the Singapore stage involves ingesting the colonial 'other' and the patrimonial 'othered' selves; and digesting Shakespeare in Singapore inescapably places those that produce and receive in a position that transverses and resides both outside and within particularized cultural and theatrical localities.

My engagements with Andrade's cannibalistic paradigm of culture production are not rooted in validating the similarities of theatre-making between the postcolonial communities of Brazil and Singapore. Instead, anthropophagy is used as a discursive and critical framework to examine how existing concepts of theatrical interculturalism can be inverted and reconstituted by modes of artistic and cultural creation that are intrinsically defined by hybridity. The carnal desire of the cultural cannibalist to ingest his other, as Andrade proposes, can become 'elective, and creates friendship', 'when it is affective, it creates love' and 'when it is speculative, it creates science' (1928: 43). This cannibalizing instinct 'takes detours and moves around', and reacts to and renews both the eater and the eaten. Thus, anthropophagy does not 'operate by hiding its appropriation of the foreign' (Islam 2011: 169); it is a lens through which we can reconsider interculturalism and hybridization as processes that are able to point up the slippages between the borders that segregate Subject/Object and Us/Them, and not wholly as practices that consume otherness to expunge contradictions.

Singaporean director Mohammed Najib Soiman, studied in this chapter, acknowledges the impact of Kuo's ideology and praxis on his approaches to producing theatre in Singapore. As we will see, this adaptation of Shakespeare's *Much Ado About Nothing*, now playfully retitled *Ma' Ma Yong – About Nothing Much To Do* (2008),[3] resounds with echoes of both Kuo's ideas on cultural borrowing and Andrade's identity transformation, as Shakespeare is reinterpreted without inhibition and imbued with diverse local meanings. To Soiman (2014), 'Singapore is rojak' and Shakespeare is simply one of the many ingredients he used to create his *Ma' Ma Yong* production. The use of 'rojak', a local food metaphor expressing the eclectic mixture of things and people (we will return to this metaphorical appetizer later in this chapter), succinctly describes Singapore's authentically 'inauthentic' national culture, which encompasses the identities and traditions of the four main ethnic groups in Singapore, namely Chinese, Malay, Indian and Eurasian.

As a national site, Singapore is situated at the intersecting cultural crossroads of the East and West, and in-between the shifting boundaries of New Asia (a concept that espouses transcultural Asian identity, cultural diversity and Western models of social and economic development).[4] This simultaneously all-embracing and de-centredness of Singaporean identity is likewise revealed in Soiman's tongue-in-cheek reworking of Shakespeare's comedy.

Soiman's new multilingual script reset *Much Ado About Nothing* in a mental institution, and a play-within-a-play framework formed the crux of the dramatic structure of this anthropophagical reproduction. Shaped by this performative paradigm, *Ma' Ma Yong* was conspicuously marked as an adaptation, expressly since Shakespeare's play was consumed and now reframed as a performance re-enacted by a group of patients as a form of drama therapy. The most noticeable change to the Shakespearean plot in Soiman's localized adaptation was the inclusion of a new character, literature teacher Fatimah, a patient believed to be enchanted by the spirit of a *mak yong* (musical drama) performer. Actress Aidli 'Alin' Mosbit, who played Fatimah, was also cast as the production's title character, Ma'ma Yong, a key figure within the play-within-a-play dramatic device, as she became the narrator of the patients' Shakespeare performance. The *inauthenticity* of Singapore's national culture is best reflected in the anthropophagous interplay between local and regional languages and performance forms, and popular culture representations in *Ma' Ma Yong*. Different Asian vernaculars like Bahasa Melayu, English, Mandarin, Bahasa Kelantan, Cantonese and Hokkien were used throughout the performance; and contemporary hip-hop dance and music were likewise intermixed with traditional performance forms, for instance, Indonesian *wayang kulit* (shadow puppet drama), Kelantanese *mak yong* (musical drama) and *bangsawan* acting (Malay theatre, with musical accompaniment), in the presentation of this Shakespearean adaptation.

The director's use of diverse Asian performance traditions and languages, and the multiracial casting in this Shakespeare performance challenge the notion that local Shakespeares automatically grant native audiences and practitioners complete access to and knowledge of the polychromatic cultural and aesthetic threads that run through an intercultural performance. As such, Singaporean Shakespeare productions, like Soiman's *Ma' Ma Yong*, which emerge from cosmopolitanized sociocultural and theatrical environments, blur the supposedly distinguishable lines localized performances set up between what is deemed as native and alien. Interactions with Shakespeare that are characterized by hybridized creative approaches also prompt us to study the politics of cultural cannibalism by foregrounding and complicating the interconnected processes of consumption, digestion and possible rejection of what is being eaten in and served up as productions of globalized Shakespeare.

Ma' Ma Yong, written and directed by Soiman, was the inaugural production of the newly established local theatre company, Panggung Arts. Rather than view Singapore as a cultural wasteland devoid of rich theatre traditions, Soiman, like Kuo, believes that this cultural predicament actually facilitates transcultural exchange and encourages local practitioners to adopt and reanimate aesthetic cultures from outside of

Singapore. This non-touring production, which was funded by local government institutions,[5] was devised mainly with a local student audience in mind. When asked why he decided to stage a Shakespearean play as the company's first production, the director intimated that a Shakespearean comedy could attract sizable school audiences, since Shakespeare was still a literature staple in Singapore's secondary school curriculum (Soiman 2014). Nonetheless, this use of Shakespeare's inherited popularity to drive publicity was not as straightforward when staging Shakespeare for the company's target Singaporean youth spectatorship. To Soiman, 'Shakespeare's language' posed a challenge for 'Singaporean youngsters', and in order to 'bring [Shakespeare] closer to them', his work had to be presented in 'a new form, or a new genre, or a new style' to countervail his foreignness. Adapting Shakespeare, in Singapore, through different performance traditions, practices and vernaculars is not only an instinctive choice but also a necessary consequence. The director's candid remark about his appropriation of Shakespeare to suit his Singaporean stage draws our attention to the fluid duality an anthropophagist propagates when eating. On one hand, incorporation that is salient to the notion of cannibalism, as Maggie Kilgour evinces, 'depends upon and enforces an absolute division between inside and outside' (1990: 4). On the other hand, the methodological practice of cultural cannibalism also diffuses this dichotomous divide by dissolving 'the structure it appears to produce'. Soiman's intercultural reimagining of *Much Ado About Nothing* and different types of theatre traditions from around the region thus not only involved migrating Shakespeare, traditional performance practices and languages into a new aesthetic system that was extrinsic to themselves, but concomitantly readjusted the definition of what 'inside' means when watching a Singaporean Shakespeare performance constituted by elements from outside its localization.

Soiman turns this Singaporean Shakespeare production inside out by playing with the audience's expectations of 'Shakespeare' and his play, and their understanding of vernacular languages and identification. The use of Singapore's diverse local languages and different English registers was likewise emphasized as a distinctive feature of this multilingual Shakespeare adaptation, and can be seen as a critical response to Shakespeare's history in Singapore. The performance began with a doctor, Dr Lim, describing the mental condition of the patients in the psychiatric ward in a Standard Singapore English (SSE) register. As he exited the performance space, Fatimah, one of his patients, entered holding a book, which is later disclosed to be a copy of Shakespeare's *Much Ado About Nothing*. Dressed in a traditional *mak yong* costume, Mosbit's Fatimah danced onstage as musicians using traditional (*mak yong*) and modern instruments played live music. Her entrance was accompanied by a voice-over in Bahasa Melayu, and the audience was made privy to Fatimah's mystical healing abilities (a nod, perhaps, to *mak yong*'s ritualistic performance heritage). Unlike Fatimah who spoke in formal English, the character Ma'ma Yong sang and delivered her lines in Bahasa Melayu. Playing both Fatimah and Ma'ma Yong, Mosbit's dual character not only acted as a bridge between the production's two dramatic narratives and main linguistic modes, but was also a metatheatrical symbol that embodied the inside/outside state of the cultural cannibal. This pluralized figure accentuates how Cultural Anthropophagy in the Singaporean context bespeaks the happy ingestion of multiple kinds of otherness that are endemic and external to local frames of identification. This intercultural reworking of *Much Ado About Nothing*, rather than simply expressing cultural exchange, signals an interstitial cultural hybridity that is formed through mutal mediation and not friction.

As actress Mosbit's two characters were independent of the original Shakespearean play and the Shakespearean text was adapted loosely through non-English languages, it seemed somewhat unclear as to how Shakespeare figured into this new production. It was only in the second half of the performance that Shakespeare's *role* in *Ma' Ma Yong* became apparent. Playing Fatimah, Mosbit read Benedick's 'I will live a bachelor'

(*MA* 1.1.230) lines directly from the Shakespearean text to another patient-character in a mock classroom scene, and it became clear that Fatimah was a former English literature teacher.[6] Fatimah's composed SSE register contrasted comically with the patient-character's brash Singlish (a hybrid colloquial language that mixes vernacular localisms and dialects with Standard English) response: 'He's gay right?'[7] The explicit reference to Shakespeare's original text in a scene with two forms of English had a threefold function. In this instance, 'intercultural' does not just signify the interaction between diverse cultures but actually emphasizes the *intra*-historical actions that occur within a local culture across time. The use of Singapore's Englishes in this scene, and throughout the performance, alluded to Shakespeare's function as an instrument of 'Britishness' in Singapore's colonial history, the reverse appropriation of English in postcolonial Singapore in the form of Singlish, and likewise underscored how this reimagining of *Much Ado About Nothing* deviated considerably from the original source play through the use of local vernaculars and accents. Although the prose and poetry of Shakespeare's text were not retained in this production, the Shakespearean textual references, and the parallels between this new narrative and Shakespeare's play in terms of plot and character (with Shakespeare's character names being comically echoed in revised Malay role names), nevertheless denoted this reinterpretation as Shakespearean. *Ma' Ma Yong* was still recognisably a Shakespearean performance due to its anthropophagical composition, as this Singaporean production had to be understood through the disappearance and traces of the original play, and also through the adaptation's new performative context that in turn reshaped existing perceptions of how a Shakespearean play could be staged. Audiences are encouraged to identify the intercultural tracks that form loops through the original sources (both Shakespearean and non-Shakespearean) and the reinvented work when reading an anthropophagized performance. Cultural cannibalism, when used to frame an interculturalized creative process, thus avoids the erasure of foreignness but, instead, requires the cognizance of multiple Others in a single Self. In short, this mode of cannibalistic reconfiguration creates a *We* composed of hyphenated identities and diverse origins.

The naturalization of Shakespeare's play through local languages and Soiman's assimilative approach to adopting diverse Asian art forms was signposted in the scene that followed Fatimah's initial entrance. A narrator, played by Soiman himself, articulated the following verse in an exaggerated rhythmic modulation in both Singlish and Bahasa Melayu. This scene also prompted the start of the play-within-a-play storyline and cheekily announced the creative orientation of this Shakespearean reproduction:

> This tale is for everyone
> Regardless of your seniority
> Got the idea from William Shakespeare
> An English tale made to a blunder
> We *rojak* it into all sorts of genre
> We name ourselves the proud owner
> Much Ado About Nothing
> Is the original story we telling
> About Nothing Much To Do is what we showing
> Hope all enjoying looking how we playing
> …
> Panggung Arts presents, Ma' Ma Yong,
> About Nothing Much to Do![8]

The beginning of this speech was delivered in Bahasa Melayu and underscored issues regarding Shakespeare's canonical status and the cultural ownership of Shakespeare's works and that of other theatre traditions. Here, the interculturality of Singaporean theatre was being asserted and the ebullient act of cultural cannibalism championed. A reminder that localizing Shakespeare in Singapore relied on the absorption of the global. The inclusiveness and accessibility of this adaptation, as the opening lines suggest ('This tale is for everyone / Regardless of your seniority'), are not, however, the upshot of Shakespeare's often cited universality but are only made possible because 'William Shakespeare' and his play have been cannibalized and recontextualized in the making of *Ma' Ma Yong*. The use of a non-English language to express the subject matter of Shakespearean adaptation confronts the authority of Shakespearean textuality head-on, and advances this original intercultural performance as concurrently Shakespearean and non-Shakespeare. The latter half of this speech adopted a typical Singlish syntax, and the verbal particularities of Singlish again positioned this as a localized Shakespeare production. As this speech and its delivery illustrate, the interculturalizing of Shakespeare in/for Singapore splinters the essentialist dichotomies of an original and its derivative, since *Ma' Ma Yong* is an original performance of local Shakespeare contingent on alterity and unfamiliarity. An anthropophagic encounter is therefore not an aggressive acquisition of what one does not possess; quite the opposite, anthropophagy revels in 'its transformative potential as an agent of cultural hybridization', especially since it can 'engage in cultural appropriation without taking on a subaltern position' (Islam 2011: 169). The creative eating of texts, languages and diverse forms in this production furthermore emphasizes, metatheatrically, how cultural identity in Singapore is based on differences and absences, and, in this way, inherently 'inauthentic' in nature. Soiman's declaration to '*rojak*' Shakespeare's play 'into all sorts of genre' resonates with Andrade's playful but subversive anthropophagic mission, which sees non-native source materials as open access 'primary cultural products to [be] borrowed, assimilated, or recycled' (Budasz 2005: 3). The adaptation of Shakespeare in this irreverent and 'rojak' manner seemed to be an effect of the production's comic mode as opposed to a purposeful political statement about staging Shakespeare in postcolonial Singapore. Similarly, Soiman's use of traditional performance forms and contemporary pop culture references like Vanilla Ice's 'Ice Ice Baby', martial arts routines and the episodic style of television commercials was often re-dramatized with a farcical and comic treatment. In *Ma' Ma Yong*, both the adapted source text and adopted theatre traditions were co-opted by comedy to tell Soiman's new Shakespearean story, now conspicuously set as part of a Singaporean imaginary.

Soiman's unapologetic devouring and reconstruction of Shakespeare and other performance traditions, bring us back to the director's concept of 'rojak'. As observed in the above-mentioned verse, 'rojak' is used as a verb to describe how cultural and creative ownership over an 'English tale' can be asserted by the agency of intercultural adaptation. Using a food metaphor to express the consumption of Shakespeare in Singapore, is particularly apropos to our discussion of Cultural Anthropophagy, as there is value both in being eaten and in doing the eating (see also Nunes 2008: 166–174). This action of ingestion not only denotes a mediative and legitimatizing process that occurs in and through adaptation, but similarly reminds us that foreignness must first be desired before it can be edible (see Andrade 2009: 66). The term 'rojak' is both a word that means *mixture* in Malay, and also the name of a popular local dish in Singapore that is made from an assortment of vegetables and fruits. Food is culturally determining; and in a Singaporean context, food is a strong marker of the city-state's cultural lineages and modern multiculturalism. Soiman's use of this particular cuisine to explain his praxis is equally telling of his own artistic methodology and attitude towards cross-cultural theatrical adaptation, since *rojak* is a dish that is commonly found in Malaysia, Indonesia and Singapore. Moreover, within Singapore there are two different variations of *rojak* – an Indian version, which is slightly spicier, and another that is adapted from Chinese and Malay cuisine. Analogously, 'rojak', acting both as a verb and a noun, correlates with the anthropophagous activity of incorporating, altering and mixing the foreign with the familiar to create a heterogeneous process and object. As a modus operandi, 'rojak' recreates through integration and synthesis. Applying this notion of 'rojak' to the linguistically and aesthetically mixed *Ma' Ma Yong*, where Shakespeare and other Asian performance forms are commingled 'into all sorts of genres', then becomes a way for a culturally orphaned Singapore to lay claim to Shakespeare and the other adapted theatre traditions in the creation of an 'original story' that can be self-authenticating. When seen through the critical discourse of Cultural Anthropophagy, this concept of 'rojak' describes how cannibalistic desire is not just about eating otherness but is a craving that relies equally on how the other is processed before it can be eaten.

While Soiman borrowed from a myriad of Asian performance forms belonging to Singapore's neighbouring countries, like Indonesia and Malaysia, the most recognizable theatre tradition used in *Ma' Ma Yong*, as the performance title also hints at, is *mak yong*. Mosbit's dual character likewise referenced the *mak yong* performance mode, due to the style of her dance sequences, her traditional costume and her 'Ma'ma Yong' name. *Mak yong* is a female dance-theatre form that was made popular in Kota Bharu, the state capital of Kelantan state in Malaysia, in the early twentieth century (Brandon 1993: 198–199).[9] Traditional *mak yong* plays (there are twelve in the repertoire) typically begin with opening rituals called *buka panggung*, which are followed by a song segment for the lead actress and this segment concludes with the first dance ('Honouring the Rebab'). This presentation precedes the first scene of *mak yong* plays. The major roles found in the traditional repertoire include *mak yong* (queen), *mak yong muda* (princess), *pak yong* (king) and the *pak yong muda* (prince). A ceremonial dance presentation akin to traditional *mak yong* performance is likewise adopted in Soiman's *Ma' Ma Yong*. This dance sequence, however, dissimilar from the *buka panggung*, does not open the production but is interposed between Soiman's initial verse narration and the start of the play-within-a-play Shakespearean storyline.

Soiman (2014) emphasized that his adaptation of *mak yong* as a performative mode to re-narrativize a Shakespearean story was not an attempt to revive a dying art form, but a way to preserve performance traditions meaningful to contemporary theatre culture. Following this, Soiman's approach to Asian theatre cultures resembles that of other Singaporean practitioners like Ong Keng Sen,[10] who adapt Asian performance forms as a means to rediscover and connect with other cultural and aesthetic traditions in Asia. One of the obvious ways traditional *mak yong* conventions were recontextualized and modernized in this production was through the adaptation of a Western canonical text and the use of a multilingual script. Apart from this, Soiman's adaptation assigned male actors in principal roles, which breaks from the traditional *mak yong* practice of casting female actors as leads. The production also mixed *mak yong* costumes with 'home-made' outfits and contained traditional *mak yong* tunes and pop songs in its live music set. As *Ma' Ma Yong* consisted of many adapted forms of non-native theatre traditions and styles, performance forms like *dikir barat* (group singing, originally in Malay), which are familiar to Singapore's cultural landscape, were incorporated into the production to help bridge the gap between foreignness and sameness. The intermingling of contemporary presentational styles and cultural references with traditional performance modes from *other* theatre cultures was thus an effective method for drawing in its young audience. Within the framework of staging a Shakespeare production that is primarily for a local audience, this creative decision emphasizes how intercultural praxis is reliant on creative and spectatorial intervention, as the efficacious incorporation of diverse aesthetic and cultural elements in such performances is dependent on a spectatorship that, on some level, needs to be willing to identify some form of congruity in difference.

Comedy undoubtedly helped further connect the disparate aesthetic and linguistic modes in the production, and likewise played an essential role in creating a theatrical event that could appeal to a wide range of audiences. For example, the reimagining of the traditional art form, *wayang kulit*, in a way that consciously ran counter to its conventionality led to hugely comical moments that were productive for audience engagement. One such scene featured Borachio, a contemporary cartoon puppet, and Margaret, a traditional *wayang kulit* puppet, simulating intercourse through shadow play behind a screen. Another shadow puppetry scene showed the same cartoon puppet violently hitting Dono Jono (Don John), whose character was represented through a traditional *wayang kulit* puppet. Though these were risibly entertaining scenes, the fact remains that in a kaleidoscopic intercultural production that mobilizes a multitude of performance traditions outside of Singapore's theatre culture, the Shakespearean plot and characterization still seem to be dramatic references that are readily identifiable. Additionally, since characters names were translated into Malay role names that did not have obvious phonetic links with their Shakespearean equivalent, and because the actors played multiple parts, this fast-paced multilingual production was particularly hard to follow. Shakespeare's original play therefore offered, at least to an audience familiar with his text, a stable source of signification. The heightened interculturality of this performance calls for audiences to be fairly educated in diverse (Asian) theatre cultures and languages, and in the absence of that Shakespeare's textuality can inevitably be reasserted. The politics of cultural cannibalism, due to the often uneven terrain of intercultural exchange and reception, is therefore not a straightforward process. The extent of an audience's (inter)cultural knowledge then determines the scale and significance of Shakespeare's textual and cultural authority in productions of Shakespeare in a global context, regardless of the initial aims of the anthropophagous exercise.

The interculturality that is shaped by and informs the processes of Cultural Anthropophagy can also expose ideological gaps when this theory of eating otherness in the construction of a plurivocal self is put into practice. Put in another way, what is created through the cannibalistic means of absorbing and incorporating two or more disparate source materials when devising an intercultural performance, may contradict with how the final theatrical event is defined by its producers and, as aforementioned, received by its audiences. Although it is easy to classify Soiman's praxis as an anthropophagic engagement with foreignness and *Ma' Ma Yong* as an intercultural reproduction of Shakespeare that is expressly Singaporean, the director was hesitant to label this production as an intercultural one (see Soiman 2014). To Soiman, theatrical interculturalism is contingent on participating performers having ownership of the theatre culture(s) they adapt and remodel. This description of appropriating and adopting art forms and performance styles outside of one's cultural domain deviates from the principles of Andrade's anthropophagy, which regards cannibalism as a mediative action unfettered by one's origin or lack of (inherited) cultural authority (see Bary 1991; Islam 2011; Budasz 2005). Instead of regarding Soiman's views in direct conflict with the tenets of Andrade's original manifesto, Soiman's sense of cultural appropriation is perhaps useful in foregrounding how Cultural Anthropophagy, as process, is different from theatrical interculturalism, as product, though both are supported by similar notions of hybridity and cultural integration.

Soiman does consider his creative approaches of cultural and artistic mixing as a highly collaborative practice, which is able to facilitate local and international partnerships in the production of hybridized performances with a 'soul in common'. This is perhaps where Cultural Anthropophagy intersects more markedly with this Shakespearean adaptation. Unlike the cultural flattening that is suggested in Peter Brook's 'culture of links' (1996: 66), the hybridizing constitution of what Soiman calls a 'soul in common' does not try to locate unifiying relationships between (theatre) cultures in performance. The commonality Soiman refers to in his explanation of hybridized performances resists connecting divergences through universalities, and by contrast celebrates the fragmentations between cultures through the sharing of differences. The cannibalization of cultures can thus animate 'a type of communion' whereby 'both the killed and the killer become a little like their opposites' (Budasz 2005: 13). This ravenous act of incorporating and rewriting the Other, rather than efface the boundary of the insider/outsider binary, playfully twists and turns the borderline between what separates and affiliates Them from Us.

It is not surprising that Singlish and other local vernaculars were used to reconfigure Shakespeare's play within a Singaporean context. Singlish was also the perfect linguistic medium for a 'fast-paced comedy', due to its 'streetwise-snappiness and informality' (Diamond 2012: 168). But more than this, Singlish, to Soiman (2014), 'is original'. If intercultural exchange requires ownership and authority, Singlish then presents itself as the perfect expressive mode to translate Shakespeare for a local spectatorship. The amalgamation of the multifarious localisms found in Singlish, as Soiman notes, 'really belongs to us', and, correspondingly, connotes an inimitable Singaporean cultural uniqueness. Besides being mobilized as a performative shorthand for 'Singaporean-ness' in *Ma' Ma Yong*, Singlish further operated on a meta-theatrical level. The incorporation of Singlish coupled with extensive code-switching in the performance, while signalling Singapore's cultural plurality, also worked to challenge the taken-for-granted notion that national identification in intercultural theatre invariably falls within an unequivocal insider/outsider dichotomy. The performative use of different native languages and dialects in this production, however, encapsulates Una Chaudhuri's proposition that the heterological discourse of interculturalism 'dramatizes and enacts – ambiguously but unmistakably – the world(s) of difference' (1991: 195). Being a Chinese spectator/researcher who speaks English and Mandarin (with a limited knowledge of Hokkien and Cantonese dialects) and watching this as a live performance in Singapore with a Malay friend who speaks Bahasa Melayu and English, made for a distinctive and at times disruptive theatrical experience. Though English surtitles of the fully translated adapted script were projected throughout the performance, it was apparent that some comedic moments were inevitably lost in translation as there were instances where my responses to the onstage action differed from those of my Malay friend. When asked why certain scenes were comical to him, my friend replied that it was not what was being said but the manner in which it was being delivered in Bahasa Melayu that made the scene funny. These theatrical moments that confront the dialectical nature of Singapore's cultural syncretism, not only emphasize the production's diverse cast but also focus attention on the heterogeneous make-up of a Singaporean audience, as one is granted access to the production's comedy through interlingual fluency. The multilingual and multicultural Singaporean condition inherently places the insider anthropophagist within a complex oscillatory familiar/foreign position that is culturally porous. The unquestioned (and often overly celebrated) diversity that underlies the notion of Shakespeare as 'global', therefore, should not be seen as merely being constituted by myriads of neatly demarcated localizations but likewise account for localities that are composed of interlacing internal variations formed and configured by intraculturality.

Audiences of Asian intercultural Shakespeare productions, as Yong Li Lan posits, are often required to manoeuvre the 'unstable interstice' that exists between Shakespeare's original and Asian theatre traditions (Yong n.d.). Depending on one's familiarity with the various adopted source materials, audiences of intercultural performances are constantly engaged in the process of alternating 'between seeing each from the other side'. I would argue that the position of the intercultural spectator is further complicated in the Singaporean context, as seen in the case of *Ma' Ma Yong*. Bilingual native audiences of this multilingual production not only have to navigate between the complex connections of the adapted Shakespearean play and the various Asian performance forms, but also negotiate the shifting demarcations of a mono-/multilingual understanding of the playtext and an intercultural reading of the new Shakespeare performance. Furthermore, this production's multilingual script inevitably called for the necessary addition of English surtitles. While English surtitles act as a bridge for

different audiences to access the onstage action, the inclusion
of English surtitles also tacitly codifies this intercultural
performance as a monolingual event, since English is made to
fill the various linguistic cracks that stem from the coalescence
of a multilingual Shakespeare (Yong 2009: 185). Paradoxically,
Shakespeare productions like *Ma' Ma Yong*, because of
their linguistic and aesthetic diversity, require monolingual
translations (in this case, English) to enable audiences to mediate
foreignness in performance. The culturally anthropophagous
anatomy of *Ma' Ma Yong* reminds us that the reception of
such productions does not necessarily initiate spectatorship
that is equally formed from interculturalized point of views.
That being so, the anthropophagic methods that create
polycultural and polygottal local Shakespeares may, especially
when travelling through overseas routes, give rise to models of
interpretation that are still monocultural in nature.

Although non-anglophone Shakespeare productions
can maintain and reiterate neocolonialist perspectives
about Shakespearean authority and authenticity, the
reproduction and consumption of Shakespeare in *other*(ed)
cultures concomitantly expounds the dramatic potential of
Shakespeare's play and his continued relevance. But more
than this, the enactment of Shakespeare's text through
theatre traditions expressed through codified gestures and
embodied presentations can in fact extend the legibility of such
performance forms for non-native audiences. Put differently,
adapting Shakespeare's text through unscripted theatrical
modes like *mak yong* (*mak yong* texts typically exist in the
oral tradition), which consists of music, stylized acting and
dance, formalized and improvised dialogues and monologues,
can enable a stable textualization of such forms and afford
audiences an alternative (and conventionalized) way of
accessing these types of intercultural performances through
textual interpretation. Although it is commonly understood
that the translation of Shakespeare through different theatre
cultures transfigures our understanding of and approaches to
both the adapted performance traditions and Shakespeare's

original text, it is worth reiterating that such non-anglophone theatre cultures that practise embodied expressivity are not just reinterpreting and performing Shakespeare in their own humble way. The availability of these new playtexts and their translations, both in English and in non-English language(s), also means that foreign performance modes can start to be understood in a way that is not completely exoticized and decontextualized (especially in the absence of language and in the presence of Shakespeare). The value of a Shakespeare that is global is therefore not the combinative accumulation of multiple local Shakespeares as a field of study; instead, its significance lies in the potentiality of 'Global Shakespeares' to assimilate the local into international circuits of spectatorship, and, in so doing, help the Shakespearean foodie develop a more refined palate.

This case study of *Ma' Ma Yong* expands the ways in which we consider certain prevailing production-reception paradigms that assumedly accompany local intercultural productions. *Ma' Ma Yong* reveals the difficulties of classifying local Shakespeare productions, which are determined by anthropophagic practices that digest and reconstitute non-indigenous languages and performance traditions from diverse theatre cultures in Asia. The cultural authenticity of 'Local Shakespeare' performances is often understood in terms of exclusivity, ownership and an unadulterated ideal of indigenous classical theatre and cultural traditions.[11] This attitude towards authenticity is a recurring criterion to evaluate 'authentic' cultural representation in non-anglophone Shakespeare productions, and does not fully consider how native performance traditions and practices do evolve both through intracultural and intercultural revision (particularly when used in performances outside of the classical repertoire). While theatre traditions can help audiences (and critics) orient themselves in a performance, this principle of identification in the case of Singapore's amplified inter-theatrical and multicultural context is incongruous to the formation of a stable production-reception framework that readily demarcates the local from the foreign, and the authentic from the inauthentic. Contemporary Shakespeare performances in Asia, which adopt and reinvent diverse aesthetic styles, languages and approaches to adapt Shakespeare plays, urge us to continue to push the boundaries of how we expound the different and intersecting levels of the local, the national and the global when discussing Shakespeare adaptation.

Due to Singapore's colonial past, the young nation's migrant history and its current global city status, Singaporean Shakespeare performances like *Ma' Ma Yong* bring to the fore the intricate cultural and artistic activities that characterize cross-cultural performances produced in already interculturalized creative and national communities. *Ma' Ma Yong* underscores a type of intercultural performativity that is anthropophagical and underpinned by a plexus of polycultural, intracultural and inter-Asian adaptation. As such, this production seems to have 'nothing much to do' with Shakespeare but works towards accentuating the processes involved in making local Shakespeares in a global context. Localized Shakespeare adaptations that culturally cannibalize other theatre cultures disrupt the dichotomous Self/Other, Us/Them binaries to become productive and projective sites of intercultural theatre praxis and broaden our understanding of Global Shakespeares. These new locations of Shakespeare reproduction, through alternative mechanisms for cultural exchange, interrogate, negotiate and re-envision the significance of Cultural Anthropophagy as an adaptive method and ideology to reconsider theatrical interculturalism, and explore the limits of theory in practice.

Notes

1 Oswald de Andrade's 'Manifesto Antropófago' was first published in Alcântara Machado and Raul Bopp's *Revista de Antropofagia*, in 1928.

2 For more information, see Leslie Bary's 'Oswald de Andrade's "Cannibalist Manifesto"' (1991).

3 *Ma' Ma Yong – About Nothing Much To Do* was restaged
in 2015; however, my analysis of *Ma' Ma Yong – About
Nothing Much To Do* is based on my viewing of the live 2008
performance and the video-recording of the same production in
the Asian Shakespeare Intercultural Archive (A|S|I|A 2015).

4 The Singapore Tourism Board (STB) coined the term 'New
Asia-Singapore' in 1996. It describes Asian nation-states
that are deeply rooted in Asian values and at the same time
artistically, culturally, economically and socially dynamic
and advanced (a benchmark often measured against Western
models).

5 The production was supported by the National Arts Council,
Singapore, and the Singapore Arts Fund.

6 Quotes from *Much Ado About Nothing* are taken from the
Arden Shakespeare edition (2016).

7 The quoted script is taken from the A|S|I|A website. The
English language *Ma' Ma Yong – About Nothing Much To Do*
production script is translated by Mohd Zulfadi Mohd Rashid.

8 Emphasis added. For the production's full script and
translation, see A|S|I|A (2015).

9 Also see Ghulam-Sarwar Yousof's article, 'The Mak Yong
Dance Theatre as Spiritual Heritage: Some Insights' (2017),
for more information on *mak yong*. While Yousof details *mak
yong* performances from Patani, Thailand, this chapter focuses
specifically on Soiman's adaptation of Kelantanese *mak yong*.

10 Ong Keng Sen's high-profile Shakespeare trilogy and his
latest Shakespeare production, *Lear Dreaming* (2012), are
characterized by Ong's signature use of diverse theatre cultures
from Asia and the inclusion of an inter-Asian and international
mix of cast, production crew and creative team.

11 James R. Brandon, for example, describes Asian Shakespeare
adaptations as belonging to three broad categories, namely,
canonical Shakespeare, indigenous Shakespeare and
intercultural Shakespeare. Indigenous Shakespeare, as Brandon
posits, 'draws authority from local vernacular theatrical
traditions' and is 'rooted in the experience of national and
regional audiences' (2010: 26). Under this classification,
Shakespeare's plays are absorbed into indigenous theatre genres

to an extent where the original source material disappears and its foreignness is concealed. As Brandon puts it, in performance 'the play's local authenticity is reinforced by expression through indigenous theatrical techniques' (30). In this case, the claim to authenticity is heavily predicated upon the ownership of indigenous practices and traditions.

References

Andrade, O. ([1928] 1991), 'Cannibalist Manifesto', trans. L. Bary, *Latin American Literary Review*, 19 (38): 38–44.

Andrade, O. (2009), *Os dentes do dragão*, São Paulo: Globo.

Asian Shakespeare Intercultural Archive (A|S|I|A) (2015), *Asian Shakespeare Intercultural Archive*. Available online: http://a-s-i-a-web.org/ (accessed 31 December 2017).

Bary, L. (1991), 'Oswald de Andrade's "Cannibalist Manifesto"', *Latin American Literary Review*, 19 (38): 35–47.

Brandon, J. R., ed. (1993), *The Cambridge Guide to Asian Theatre*, Cambridge: Cambridge University Press.

Brandon, J. R. (2010), 'Other Shakespeares in Asia: An Overview', in P. Trivedi and R. Minami (eds), *Re-playing Shakespeare in Asia*, 21–40, New York: Routledge.

Brook, P. (1996), 'The Culture of Links', in P. Pavis (ed.), *The Intercultural Performance Reader*, 63–66, New York: Routledge.

Budasz, R. (2005), 'Of Cannibals and the Recycling of Otherness', *Music and Letters*, 87 (1): 1–15.

Chaudhuri, U. (1991), 'The Future of the Hyphen: Interculturalism, Textuality, and the Difference Within', in B. Marranca and G. Dasgupta (eds), *Interculturalism and Performance*, 192–207, New York: PAJ Publications.

Diamond, C. (2012), *Communities of Imagination: Contemporary Southeast Asian Theatres*, Honolulu: University of Hawaii Press.

Islam, G. (2011), 'Can the Subaltern Eat? Anthropophagic Culture as a Brazilian Lens on Post-colonial Theory', *Organization*, 19 (2): 159–180.

Kilgour, M. (1990), *From Communion to Cannibalism: An Anatomy of Metaphors of Incorporation*, Princeton, NJ: Princeton University Press.

Kuo, P. K. (2002), *Kuo Pao Kun: And Love the Wind and Rain*, trans. Teo Han Wue, Singapore: Cruxible Pte Ltd.

Nunes, Z. (2008), *Cannibal Democracy: Race and Representation in the Literature of the Americas*, Minneapolis: University of Minnesota Press.

Shakespeare, W. (2016), *Much Ado About Nothing*, ed. C. McEachern, third series, rev. edition, London: Bloomsbury Arden Shakespeare.

Soiman, M. N. (2014), 'Multilingual Shakespeare in Singapore', personal interview by Eleine Ng.

Yong, L. L. (2009), 'After Translation', in P. Holland (ed.), *Shakespeare Survey* 62, 283–295, Cambridge: Cambridge University Press.

Yong, L. L. (n.d.), 'Shakespeare, Asian Actors and Intercultural Spectatorship', *Shakespeare Performance in Asia*. Available online: http://web.mit.edu/shakespeare/asia/essays/LiLanYong.html (accessed 31 December 2017).

Yousof, G. S. (2017), 'The Mak Yong Dance Theatre as Spiritual Heritage: Some Insights', *SPAFA Journal*, 1 (1): 1–9.

PART FOUR

Dialogue IV: re-cultivating and re-disseminating Shakespeare beyond the institution

11

Engrafting him new: educating for citizenship via Shakespeare in a rural area in Brazil

Aimara da Cunha Resende

And all in war with time for love of you
As he takes from you, I engraft you new
WILLIAM SHAKESPEARE, SONNET 15 (LINES 13–14)

'Aimara, look what I found in the school library.' The young boy's eyes shone as he proudly showed me the book he had found: a translation of Shakespeare's *Romeo and Juliet*. 'The project is my life', said Vitoria, a twelve-year-old girl, during a discussion session of the project *Shakespeare e as Crianças* (Shakespeare and the Children). 'Alípio will die if he misses even one session of the Shakespeare', declared the mother of a twelve-year-old boy in a conversation on the street with the coordinator of the project. These and other remarks show the impact of the social, educational and cultural work we have been developing for fourteen years now in the central state of Minas Gerais, in south-eastern Brazil.

I devised this project when, retired from academic life, I moved with my husband to a small farm in the rural area of São Francisco de Paula, a town in Minas Gerais. The town, with 7,000 inhabitants, lives off the cultivation of coffee. Most of its inhabitants have guaranteed work for about four months a year during the harvest. When we moved here there was virtually no cultural event, except for the *Festa do Café* (Coffee Fiesta), during a weekend in August after the harvest, the only attractions of which were country music and gallons of beer. Born, brought up and educated in the capital, having taught English and comparative literatures at both Catholic and Federal universities of Minas Gerais, I never imagined that such cultural standards as those I found here existed. There was only one kind of cultural production to attract the local people, in the few events: country music. I will say nothing against country music, which in itself is not of poor quality. The notion of quality I am putting forward, however, consists of more elaborate productions, with the same principles as those guiding the Shakespeare project, whose objective is to expose children and adolescents to a variety of artistic performances and through group discussions help them to become aware of more creative productions that do not necessarily have to have their origins in big cities. There is no intention of favouring socially hierarchical performances or cultural productions, but to open these young people to new forms of art and cultural experience so that they may be encouraged to express their preferences more consciously.

Now living in a rural area, I became acquainted with the human needs of families and especially children in such an environment, where many fathers bought the staple rice and beans for their families and spent the remaining money on drink. The mothers either worked as maids in the houses of the few well-off people, trying to earn some money to take care of their family needs, or just let things go, taking medicine to feel calmer. The children were left to their own devices, with no creative leisure and no future to dream of except work in the fields. The luckier ones, after adolescence, might get one of the few jobs available in shops. There was one state school for those aged between eleven and eighteen, and two or three municipal ones for the younger students. Compared to other public schools in the country, these were not bad, but teaching methods were rather old-fashioned.[1]

I felt I had to do something to show my gratitude for the warm reception my husband and I had received in this small, quiet, lovely town. Having worked on Shakespeare for years as a university teacher and researcher, I thought his plays might be my way of giving back, so I devised the project *Shakespeare e as Crianças*, not aiming to teach the 'Bard's' work, but to use the plays as a means towards education for citizenship, cultural expansion and social role-playing. Confronted with the widespread belief, even if contested by scholars and specialists, in the myth of the great writer belonging to the colonizers of England/Europe, subversion had to be the way towards a desired outcome. Was there any sense in teaching Shakespeare's work to children who had probably never heard of even our own major authors, in a town where the great majority of the people, young and old, had never seen a play performed, or attended a concert of erudite music, or even enjoyed a show of regional folklore? Why not use Guimarães Rosa or Carlos Drummond de Andrade, both born in Minas Gerais, or other major Brazilian writers such as Machado de Assis, Jorge Amado or Manuel Bandeira? The answer may be in the conjunction of two facts: Shakespeare is my field of specialization, and his dramatic work encompasses multiple human predicaments. Besides, as put by Claude Lévi-Strauss,

Diversity is what must be saved, not the historic content given to it by each time and which no time would be able to perpetuate beyond itself. It is thus necessary to encourage secret potentialities, to waken all vocations for the communal life that history has kept in store; it is also necessary to face without surprise, without repugnance and without revolt what these new forms of social expression may offer of what has been unused. (Lévi-Strauss 1996: 66)[2]

Augusto Boal's words at the opening of *A Tempestade* (1979), an ironically 'anthropophagic' reconstruction of Shakespeare's *The Tempest*, ought nevertheless to be the core of my work: 'Let it be clear, very clear, that we are beautiful because we are ourselves, and no culture imposed on us is more beautiful than ours. It must needs be clear that we are Calibans' (7). I would use Boal's and Paulo Freire's theories as the basis of my new construct, as will be discussed below. The idea that we are Calibans or, at least, that we can admit the native blood in our veins, meant that Shakespeare had to be, as it were, swallowed, digested and then brought to life. In his well-known 'Manifesto Antropófago' Oswald de Andrade declared what he believed should be the case with respect to canonical foreign literature when it comes in contact with native artistic production: 'The job of the futurist generation was cyclopic. To put right the empire-watch of national literature. This job done, there is another task. To be regional and pure in one's time [...] The counterpart of native originality is to render useless the academic adherence' (1973: 207).

In the wake of the Brazilian modernist movement, Andrade and other writers and artists began, in 1928, to publish the journal *Revista de Antropofagia* to propagate the ideas of those artists who were attempting to set aside canonical European art then prevalent in Brazil in order to establish new native trends. The *Revista de Antropofagia* would thereafter serve as a guide for new Brazilian production, eliminating weaker aspects in the art that previous writers and artists had been imitating. Diversified, anarchically critical, its first edition encompassed what its creators intended; indeed, the edition was called 'first dentition'. Its first pages featured the 'Manifesto Antropófago' and an illustration of the modernist painter Tarsila do Amaral's *Abaporu*.[3] This painting, a present by Tarsila to her husband Oswald de Andrade, is said to have inspired his ideas of Cultural Anthropophagy. As I have written elsewhere:

For him [Oswald de Andrade], it is necessary to be aware of the irreversible situation, the presence of foreign blood in us, the unquestionable reality of the European mind that has grown among our intelligentsia and given rise to works of art now extant and established within the ranks of our artistic and intellectual tradition. Therefore, what has to be done is to devour the foreigner and then digest his parts, making the old non-native element become one with the truly national, the regional, the autochthonous, giving birth to a half-breed that will ostensibly show his marks of Brazilianity. Macunaíma![4] (Resende 2002: 16–17)

In 1928 Andrade stated: 'We had justice codifying vengeance. Science codifying magic. Anthropophagy. The permanent transformation of taboo into totem' (1973: 228).[5] 'Before the Portuguese discovered Brazil, Brazil had discovered happiness [...] Against the Indian carrying tapers. The Indian son of Mary, God-son to Catherine of Medici and son-in-law of Don Antonio de Mariz [...] Against memory source of custom. Personal experience renewed' (231).

This position, echoed in Retamar's *Caliban* of 1971, that we must deal with the miscegenation brought about by colonization but react against colonial intentions of exploitation and oppression, paves the way for a new Brazilian literature. Caliban may speak the language of the centre, but he will do it for his own purposes, to affirm his unique being in opposition to the destructive, plundering European invader. Andrade's ideas were first absorbed by artists and then gradually by professionals in other fields, the most important of which was education. Despite its continental size and diverse customs, Brazil has encompassed this diversity to a degree of conformity that has given it its somewhat indefinite national identity made up of mixed racial groups, who experience interchangeable dreams, expectations and mores, along with an incredibly joyful creativity. But there remains the task of turning these traits into positive behaviour to meet contemporary global tendencies without uncritically yielding to the demands of the capitalist ethos. This must be left to education, and it is at this point that the project *Shakespeare e as Crianças* enters the scene.

The task I saw before me was to render useless *my* academic adherence and start a *mestizo*[6] production aimed at offering the children, and, by extension, their families and the community, contact with new forms of leisure and showing them opportunities to expand their life-views. And not to forget that they and myself are Calibans, and that the project *Shakespeare e as Crianças* must be 'pure in its own time' and region. Shakespeare, icon of Western literature, must be metaphorically devoured and transformed into a hybrid construct to help establish identity and self-respect as well as respect for others. A hybrid to be offered to a group of children and adolescents in a country, Brazil, which is itself trying to find its place within the global system, and in a town apart from various current cultural trends followed around the world. Devoured and digested, this new Shakespeare would become part of the community, promoting, as its forerunner has been doing for centuries, situations of discomfort leading to investigation, discussion, and experimentation towards an awareness of the surrounding reality and the desired creativity, to produce new perspectives and improve life.

In Shakespeare's time, those 'hearing' his plays must have realized the need to face the hardships of their reality. In the present global world, similar situations apply and we, men and women of contemporary technological capitalist countries, experiencing similar problems, must also confront them. Of course, our world has changed, and our values are formulated in the production of capital by diversified groups that maintain division to keep power in their firmly circumscribed circles, but the desire for power is similar in both Shakespeare's world and ours. As difference is an important means to maintain division, it is ensured irrespective of its untrustworthy basis and inculcated into those groups that do not belong to the sphere of power. Mental and emotional borders are continuously reinforced. These borders must be transformed, if we want to achieve a more just world for all, whatever their origins, creeds and ethnicity. If one is to have a truly global world, it should be global in every sense, geographically, culturally, ethnically, not just in ways that prolong control of a minority over the oppressed. As Frederick Buell (1994: 340) has put it, 'under the influence of globalization, considerable work has been done culturally, not to erase, but to reformulate borders to allow new patterns of circulation to emerge'. Buell further explains:

> Still, the exploration of global interactiveness provides cultural workers with a viable, even urgent, ethical project for our altered world, however limited it may be. And such exploration is a fascinating, and occasionally startling, means of revising our picture of the past – our received picture of things as they supposedly were, but decidedly were not. (343)

Brazil has been undergoing different processes to establish both national identity and economic development, and yet so far, like most countries, especially those colonized by 'civilized' Europeans, it has not been able to construct a national identity in a definitive way. A unified nationality cannot be achieved owing to its continental size, which is partly responsible for huge social differences and for regional traditions independent of one another, with varied folklore and rituals, located in diverse geographical areas. In addition to geographical constraints, there is a political and economic system serving a hierarchical society in which school education helps to maintain an unjust social stratification. The poor are left with a sense of their inability to acquire more developed ways of communicating and thriving within the dominant system. Made to believe that the wealthy are superior, the poor often do not contest this view, with the result that there is wealth and excessive consumerism among certain groups and parts of the country, while in others there is hunger, illness, lack of schools and inadequate medical assistance. Brazil, this *mulato inzoneiro,*[7] needs better education to establish its position in the global world.

These circumstances can be found in most rural towns and villages in the country. And I had to face this fact when devising my project. I believed that Shakespeare's views were extensive enough to cover a great variety of possible human predicaments, both in how subtly he pinpoints crucial social problems, and in how attractive his characters are to the extent of luring spectators into aspiring to live in his dream worlds, and yet how the reality of these worlds can probe deeply into the human psyche. I had no doubt that his plays could be used to sustain the structure of the work I was to propose, but I was also sure that there was no reason at all to 'teach' Shakespeare in such a place and to such children, nor even to adolescents in big cities, where he has never been the culturally worshipped icon as he has been in anglophone countries. As Brazil was not colonized by the English, Shakespeare is taught only in drama schools and, at universities, only in the School of Letters (the Brazilian nomenclature for part of the English Humanities Department). In other words, he is not the quintessential representative of the 'best' kind of literature in Brazil. Consequently, he is never taught in elementary schools. If I were to teach literature to the children in São Francisco de Paula, I would teach Cecília Meirelles, Machado de Assis, Guimarães Rosa, Carlos Drummond de Andrade, even Nelson Rodrigues, not Shakespeare. But my intention was not to teach literature; I wished to help in the formation of better citizens, aware of their rights and their responsibilities.

I therefore realized that the way to make my intentions come true would be *via* Shakespeare, not through the study of his plays. And to achieve success, the work had to spring from the children's world, with its frailties as well as its strong possibilities. Education for social development would only be possible if based on creativity and understanding of the problems and advantages inherent in their environment. 'Sustainable development is possible only if the creative abilities of the society are involved in the development process', writes Mervyn Claxton, and 'Creative imagination is inseparable from the cultural surroundings that may stimulate as well as block creativity' (2000: 35). Being aware of the importance of personal conditioning resulting from the environmental and emotional reality, I felt that Paulo Freire's theories on education in the economically less developed countries should be my guideline. Freire insists on the use of people's everyday lives in their own environment for the formation of conscious behaviour aiming at freedom from acquired hierarchical notions of inferiority. Using their environment and its limitations, as well as the possibilities it affords, will open their minds and encourage creative attitudes towards self-esteem and prosperity.

In a small rural town where the children, taking after their older relatives, felt socially inferior because they thought they were culturally incapable, one of the main tasks would be to take a path that might lead them to understand that theirs was not an inferior culture; that they could, as much as the youth from higher social classes, be creative enough to change the status quo. It would be paramount not to follow the school system, which is not only weak but also helps to sustain the dominant groups.

In her work on language teaching, student failure and school withdrawal in Brazil, Magda Soares (1999) discusses how the concept of culture is wrongly adopted to serve the dominant group:

> There is no social group which lacks *culture,* since this term, in its anthropological sense, precisely signifies the way a group identifies itself as group, through behaviour, values, customs, traditions, which are both common and shared. Denying the existence of culture within a given group is denying the existence of the group itself. [...] What must be recognized is the fact that there is a *diversity* of 'cultures', *different* one from another, but all of them equally structured, coherent, complex. Any hierarchization of cultures would be scientifically incorrect. (4; italics in original)

Furthermore, 'as a consequence, the culture and the language of the dominated groups suffer a depreciation process and the acquisition and mastering of the cultural and linguistic capital become a demand from the market of symbolic assets' (60). Soares also states that 'thus pedagogical communication becomes an action of inculcation of "legitimate" culture, or of *cultural capital*, and simultaneously of the imposition, in an indirect way, of "legitimate" language, or of *linguistic capital*' (61). As I agree with Soares, I was concerned to ensure the necessary distance between the lives of the children in the school environment and the experiences in the project so that this undesired 'inculcation' might be avoided. One of the main staples of the project was the creation of situations that would lead to their self-confidence based on critical discussion and analysis of their social predicament. Using Freire's pedagogical method, as well as Augusto Boal's techniques for the construction of conscious self-appraisal in his *Teatro do Oprimido* (Theatre of the Oppressed), I hoped to attain my objective.

Both Boal and Freire share the idea that education for freedom and self-confidence must be based on the exchange between the individual and his environment, and that there is no superior culture. In addition, these thinkers make it clear that the belief in the existence of inferior and superior groups is the result of conditioning of the dominated cultures by the dominant ones, through which a hierarchy would be maintained and the oppressed would keep serving the oppressors, because they accept the notions of servitude springing from the acquired misconception of their own lack of capability. In the introduction to his book, Boal says:

> Those who intend to separate theatre from politics intend to lead us towards a mistake – and this is a political attitude. In this book I also intend to offer some proofs of the fact that theatre is a weapon. A very efficient weapon. That is why it is necessary to fight for it. That is why the domineering groups permanently try to get hold of theatre and use it as an instrument of domination. As they do so, they modify the

very concept of what theatre is. But theatre may, in the same way, be a weapon for liberation. To be that it is necessary to create the corresponding dramatic forms. It is necessary to transform. (2011b: 11)

And the project began ... It would be transforming Shakespeare, a writer from the past, into an anthropophagically created tool – not a subject for study – to modify and enrich the lives of children and future adult citizens in our rural environment. Britain, a country associated with the cultural 'centre', would now become one with 'peripheral' Brazil. No hierarchical difference between these two cultures would be found in the creative process leading to individual and group self-assertion and cultural expansion. The positive aspects of both, intermixed, would give rise to a new construct that does not necessarily have to belong to either. A third, new culture, as it were, would result from the exchange taking place at the 'crossroads of cultures', as imagined by Patrice Pavis (1991). Shakespeare's and these young people's cultures would act together to transform the latter's reality: 'Thus, there is not in the dialogical theory of action, a subject who dominates through some conquest and a dominated object. Replacing this duality, there are subjects who meet to "pronounce" the world, to transform it' (Freire 2016: 257).

The project has theatre study and practice at the centre of its activities. 'Theatre is transformation, movement, not simple performance of what exists. It is *to become*, not *to be*', says Boal (2011b: 66; emphasis in original), continuing: 'I think that all drama groups truly revolutionary must transfer to the people the *means of theatre production*, so that the people themselves may use them *in their own way* and *towards their own ends*' (2011b: 182; emphasis in original). Conscientious and transformative citizenship is to be created. An awareness of the need to offer the participants opportunities to confront their everyday lives and environment is paramount in the work, as is the care to help them to face what they have been witnessing within their homes, school, church and society.

They must be conscious of the responsibilities resulting from their own choices and of the right that they have to live well, in accordance with the ethos permeating their attitudes from now on. As Freire (2012) says, 'citizenship does not come at random. It is a sort of construction which, never complete, requires one's fighting for it. It requires commitment, political clarity, coherence, decision. It is for this very reason that democratic education cannot take place separate from education of, and for, citizenship' (195).

The project began with a small group of thirteen children from the poorest part of town. I counted on the support of the town mayor, Mr Altair Júnior da Silva, who has always believed in the values of the project and has never failed to be a great help, even after leaving the town's administration. As the work moved forward, I realized that I had to be much more aware of the circumstances of the children's lives. The project is devised to last from twenty-four to thirty months, depending on the evolution of each group. It is open to any child from the economically less favoured families in the community, by means of a call for enrolment posted in communal places such as supermarkets and schools, the customary way to announce events in the town. After the enrolment of up to thirty children, the first discussion meeting takes place. Our preliminary move at these first, preparatory meetings is to make the children realize that any choice has consequences and that one must be aware of one's responsibility for whatever one chooses. The idea is to focus on the children's reality through the consideration of how those who answer for the well-being and development of the town, the state and the country are chosen. As they are usually unaware of such a choice – made by the adults – the discussion of this issue takes more than just one meeting, generally two or three. After we feel that they are prepared to take on the responsibility for their own choices, we start preparing the field for the election of the Shakespeare play they would like to be used in the project. The monitors then choose three plays, the stories of which they tell the children, who will have to vote for the one they liked best and want to prepare for a final performance. Ready to vote, they use their right to choose. In the meeting after the election, we ask them to let us and their fellow participants know why they have chosen the play; they will tell us their reasons even if the play they have voted for was not the one chosen. This is an important step, as it allows them to scrutinize their likes and dislikes, beginning to relate the contents in the play to their individual and group lives; and as we ask them questions, they will also see the story in the play vis-à-vis their reality.

After warming up through techniques devised (many of them coming from Boal's *Jogos Para Atores e Não-Atores* [Games for Actors and Non-Actors], 2011a) as simultaneous liberation and involvement of the children in their own reality, the meetings for the study of the chosen play text will follow. I translate and adapt each chosen play and prepare the topics to be discussed at every meeting, with questions to be asked by the monitors. These questions arise scene by scene, sometimes stopping to clarify difficult verbal language and symbolism. Care is taken to highlight topics in the play text that bring to the fore situations typical of those the participants encounter in their daily lives.

As an example, from Act 1, Scene 1 of *A Midsummer Night's Dream,* we discuss the fact that Hermia's father decides to force her to marry Demetrius, even knowing that she loves Lysander and is loved by him. We investigate the issue of freedom to choose one's husband or wife and that of patriarchal authority and its validity. Depending on the children's reactions to these points, we continue the discussion, now focusing on the question of the sometimes excessively free contemporary love relationships and the possible consequences of such freedom. Again, from *A Midsummer Night's Dream*, after reading Act 4, Scene 1, when Bottom, now turned into a man with the head of an ass, talks to the small fairies serving the enamoured Titania, and declares that he prefers oats and hay to honey, we introduce the topic of nutrition, discuss its importance to people's health and then invite a nutritionist to talk to them about the importance of vegetables in one's diet, and the easy way to cultivate them in one's own orchard. The talk is followed by a lunch prepared with vegetables found in local gardens, inviting the children's parents for the preparation and tasting of the lunch. After one of these lunches, the mother of a girl from the project told me that since we had discussed how to clean vegetables to be prepared as salads, her daughter had been making a point of washing and cleaning the vegetables herself. Our work was already showing its results in reaching not only the children but also their families.

The Comedy of Errors serves as a stimulus to the consideration and discussion of marital relationships, work relations, the treatment of employees by their employers and the rights and duties of both, the issue of law enforcement, and the question of appearance versus reality. *Twelfth Night*, one of the favourite plays among different groups, served once as motivation for the whole group to write a new short play together using Shakespeare's characters. In it, a Christmas party is being prepared at Olivia's house. During the preparation, the characters from the source text are presented with their qualities and frailties, which showed that our young authors had clearly understood the various nuances present in Shakespeare's construction of his characters.

These are a few examples of how Shakespeare's texts may be 'devoured', 'digested' and become an important part of the children's transformation into more responsible, socially conscious future citizens. Every play may be thus used, since Shakespeare's work offers a myriad of human situations replete with current issues and problems. The assumption guiding the recreation of these texts from the past is the same as that guiding Freire's theories that there is neither superior nor inferior culture, and that any revolutionary transformation must consider the geographical and social environment of the 'inferiorized', dominated group. And theatre, with its potent communicative appeal, is a strong way to problematize issues that have been dormant. Shakespeare's drama becomes one with performative action towards revolutionary creativity.

Equally relevant are Eugenio Barba's words on the strength of mixed cultures, of past and present anthropophagically brought together through the theatre: 'Age made me realize that if theatre is discovery, this is based on a resurrection of the past, thanks to the unique individual temperature of each of us. But this past was not encrusted in a culture or a nation. It was the simultaneous and contiguous presence of all pasts' (2009: 237). Barba's position, focusing on theatre practice, encounters Oswald de Andrade's Cultural Anthropophagy, especially intended to transform literary canons, as can be seen in Barba's statement:

> It is through exchange, rather than in isolation, that a culture can develop, that is, transform itself organically. The same prowess applies to individuals and theatre performers. Therefore, in professional exchange one's historical-biographic identity is fundamental when confronted with its opposite pole, the meeting with otherness, with what is difficult. Not to impose one's own horizon or way of seeing, but rather to provoke a displacement which makes it possible to discover a territory beyond his known universe. (219)

Prior to the discussion meetings, the monitors study the questions I have prepared and try to organize their work, thinking of pervading issues in the children's life-views. The aim here is to follow Freire's theory of problematizing education and the role of dialogue between educators and educated, aiming at the transformation of the world of the educated, liberating them from the situation of oppression they have so far been living. As far as problematizing education 'serves liberation', says Freire, 'it is based on creativity and stimulates men's true careful consideration of – and action over – reality, responds to their vocation as beings who are not able to authenticate themselves beyond creative search and transformation' (2016: 126). 'There is no true word that is not praxis. Thus, speaking the true word is transforming the world' (127).

In the process of training the children to perform their chosen play, a process undertaken by a professional theatre director and drama teacher, other short plays or skits come to life (most of them written by me) to be performed as part of events offered by the Municipal Secretariats of Education and Culture, of Health, and of Social Assistance that usually want the project to participate in their meetings, aiming at the education of adults, adolescents and children.[8] So, our children have performed short plays on subjects such as precaution against *dengue*, an illness that is common where there is stagnant water; the care of old people (for this event, the play was written by Vitória, the girl who said 'the project is my life'); hygiene and health; parental care for the health of their kids; nutrition; Christmas celebrations; and others.

Over these fourteen years, with the children coming into contact with various kinds of cultural production, the project has brought both dramatic and musical groups of high quality to perform and play for the whole community. These productions, intended to broaden the children's and adolescents' cultural horizon, had as an important benefit free performances for the townspeople, regardless of their relation to the participants of the project. In addition, to help broaden the horizons of the participants, the project has created new possibilities of leisure and culture for the town inhabitants who, prior to its existence, had never seen artistic productions other than country music and displays of the students' work in educational 'cultural fairs'. These are events organized by the state school in the town to present the results of activities during the year. Some cultural presentations independent of the school curriculum are also offered and it is within this nucleus that the project appears.

Now, after fourteen years of experience – and experiments – with the project *Shakespeare e as Crianças,* I can say that it has been worth doing. We have faced great difficulties, the most pressing being lack of financial support. It has been hard work, but when I see how self-assured the children become, when I notice the gleam of happiness on their faces when they perform or play in public, I realize that not everything is lost in our large country after all, and that there may still be hope for a better future. As I moved forward with the project, I came to sense the possibility of using Shakespeare's plays also in school subjects other than language and literature (both English and Portuguese). Why not use some of his plays to teach geo-economics, for instance? Would not Act 3, Scene 2 in *The Comedy of Errors,* when Dromio of Syracuse describes the woman who insists that she is his wife, be much more interesting for the students to have a first contact with old and new countries, and their different landscapes and productivity? Could not his comical description, comparing her features with nations, do a better job? Appalled at the woman's insistence that they are husband and wife, he describes her to his master:

ANTIPHOLUS OF SYRACUSE   Then she bears some breadth?

DROMIO OF SYRACUSE   No longer from head to foot than from hip to hip: she is spherical, like a globe. I could find out countries in her.

ANTIPHOLUS OF SYRACUSE   In what part of her body stands Ireland?

DROMIO OF SYRACUSE   Merry, sir, in her buttocks; I found it out by the bogs.

ANTIPHOLUS OF SYRACUSE   Where Scotland?

DROMIO OF SYRACUSE   I found it by the bareness, hard in the palm of her hand.

ANTIPHOLUS OF SYRACUSE   Where France?

DROMIO OF SYRACUSE   In her forehead, armed and reverted, making war against her hair.

ANTIPHOLUS OF SYRACUSE   Where England?

DROMIO OF SYRACUSE   I looked for the chalky cliffs, but I could find no whiteness in them. But I guess it stood in her chin, by the salt rheum that ran between France and it.

ANTIPHOLUS OF SYRACUSE   Where Spain?
DROMIO OF SYRACUSE   Faith, I saw it not, but I felt it hot
 in her breath.
ANTIPHOLOUS OF SYRACUSE   Where America, the Indies?
DROMIO OF SYRACUSE   O, sir, upon her nose, all o'er
  embellished with rubies, carbuncles, saphires,
  declining their rich aspect to the hot breath of Spain,
  who sent whole armadas of carracks to be ballast at
  her nose.
ANTIPHOLUS OF SYRACUSE   Where stood Belgia, the
 Netherlands?
DROMIO OF SYRACUSE   O, sir, I did not look so low.
           (CE 3.2.113–144)

Though the feeling of superiority for being English, expressed by Dromio, in this passage may sound as going against the notions developed in the project of neither superior nor inferior cultures and countries, it may nevertheless be used as motivation for discussion of this issue, while the natural production suggested in it may also lead to students' easier assimilation of economic development of the countries in question. An expansion of this text may also be applied to history, in his mocking of the political relation between England and France, with the possibility of interrelated subjects for a school research project. And there is also the possibility of its use to motivate feminist discussion in the classroom.

Rediscovering Shakespeare's plays as motivating texts, I decided to try their reach and formed an experimental group with teachers from Belo Horizonte. We then explored the educational possibilities of some plays. We used, for instance, *Antony and Cleopatra* to teach both history and art, as we moved from the text to the analysis of pictures of two very different sculptures of the Roman soldier and the Egyptian queen to illustrate the marked ideologies they showed as a consequence of time and place, both in Shakespeare's play and in either sculpture. That was followed by the discussion of the film version starring Elizabeth Taylor and Richard Burton. We interrelated maths and *The Merchant of Venice*, using the meeting between Launcelot Gobbo and his father, in Act 2, Scene 2, to teach direction to young children. These and other passages were applied to different subjects. And it worked. 'The Shakespeare' successfully moved to the core of pedagogy and seems to be able to bring good results in the much-needed search for educational transformation.

My experience with the project *Shakespeare e as Crianças* suggests that similar projects might be applied abroad, if there is sufficient interest in helping children in less developed countries as well as in the more developed ones. Anthropophagically assimilated, Shakespeare has proved to be good material for renewal and new creations. His concerns with politics, power and, above all, human beings can be appropriated, digested and newly created for improved educational practices. I had the opportunity to follow the wonderful work done by Shakespeare's Globe in London, when I sat as an observer at workshops with students from different schools. Children from upper and lower social classes attended the workshops on different days and were brilliantly introduced to Shakespeare's plays. The pedagogical impact of such an introduction cannot be denied. But notwithstanding its power, there remains the fact that it is intended for the study of Shakespeare, the iconic playwright in anglophone countries. Anthropophagically transformed Shakespeare is not there. As far as I have been able to find, all that has been developed – and well developed – in countries over the world is the study of his work, mainly the plays. Boal spent some time at the Royal Shakespeare Company, using his method in workshops for the actors aiming, I believe, at the training of techniques to develop their own workshops with teachers. But their splendid work is intended as a tool towards the appreciation of the plays. Shakespeare has not yet been devoured, assimilated and reborn in a mixed form.

What there remains to be deepened is the exploration of new trends opened by anthropophagically transformed Shakespeare in the now unstoppable globalization of cultures. Though there is the claim that Shakespeare has become a globally owned signifier, no longer exclusive of British culture, his work is still seen as the quintessential literary and dramatic production – taboo, because of its canonical status. But if culture 'requires engagement, political clarity, coherence, decision', as Freire (2012: 195) sees it, and if, globalized, we are 'not to impose one's own horizon or way of seeing, but rather to provoke a displacement which makes it possible to discover a territory beyond our [his] known universe', as Barba (2009: 219) asserts, should not Shakespeare's comprehensive work, the literary and dramatic taboo, being displaced, become totem? Echoing Oswald de Andrade, we may say that now it is time for this signifier to be devoured, digested and recreated as totem for the benefit of a global community.

Notes

1 By old-fashioned I mean schools where teachers are poorly prepared for their tasks, with no systematic updating, where pedagogic devices are not found, only the old blackboard and chalk facing often malnourished students.

2 My translation into English. Hereafter all translations from Portuguese into English are mine.

3 The painting shows a man with huge feet and hands, indicative of hard work, characteristic of the modus operandi of most Brazilians at that time. On the other hand, his head is absurdly small, which might transmit the notion of lack of critical thinking, possibly suggesting the painter's criticism of the badly educated society. He is sitting by a cactus plant and has the sun shining behind him. The name *Abaporu* comes from the tupi-guarani language and means 'man who devours people'. See a copy of the painting in the link to *Revista de Antropofagia* (1975).

4   Macunaíma is the hero in the homonymous book by modernist
    Mário de Andrade (1975). An ironical literary portrait of the
    Brazilian people, Macunaíma, the 'hero with no character', is
    lazy, sly, selfish and always ready to have sexual intercourse,
    which he calls 'games'. He also represents the miscegenation of
    the Brazilian people, as he is an Indian at first, then transmuted
    into a Negro, and later on into a white man.

5   Oswald de Andrade uses Freud's ideas in *Totem and Taboo*
    (1913), where the psychoanalyst identifies the birth of social
    customs with the interdiction imposed on his sons by the
    patriarchal father in some primitive tribes. The father could
    have all the women of his clan, while they were interdicted to
    the sons whom he either killed or banished when they reached
    sexual maturity. So, desiring the prohibited women became a
    taboo. At a certain moment in history, the sons got together
    and rebelled, killing and eating the father to acquire his positive
    traits. This act brought about a sense of guilt which, to appease,
    after the 'totemic banquet', the sons decided to settle rules
    against having sexual intercourse with the women of their
    clan thus reinforcing exogamy. The totem, originated in the
    primeval social structure, was constituted as a substitute for
    the dead father, and became a tool for the organization of the
    clan, ritually respected and simultaneously protected by the very
    taboo from which it grew.

6   *Mestizo*, or *mestiço* in Portuguese, is a term used to indicate
    mixed native (Latin American Indian) and European (generally
    Spanish or Portuguese) ancestry.

7   This expression comes from the song 'Aquarela do Brasil',
    by Ari Barroso, considered by many as the second Brazilian
    national anthem. The word *inzoneiro* means subtly artful, skilful,
    ingenious and nice.

8   In the town there are events either commemorating a date or
    aiming at the general education of the community. They are
    normally promoted by one of the municipal secretariats. 'The
    Shakespeare', as Tiago's mother and other people in the town call
    the project, has become so effective in forming public opinion in
    the locality that its drama and music groups were invited in three
    consecutive years (the latest presentation was in March 2018) by
    a peripheral district association to perform at a *Leisure Sunday*,

during which educational and cultural activities are offered. The dramatic and musical groups of the project have successfully performed in Belo Horizonte and other cities, and at national and state festivals.

References

Andrade, M. (1975), *Macunaíma, o herói sem nenhum caráter*, 11th edition, São Paulo: Livraria Martins Editora.

Andrade, O. (1973), 'Manifesto Antropófago', in G. M. Teles (ed.), *Vanguarda Européia e Modernismo Brasileiro*, 2nd edition, 226–232, Petrópolis: Vozes.

Barba, E. (2009), 'Anthropological Theatre: A Document Presented to the Participants at the *Bahía Blanca Third Theatre Gathering*', trans. S. Epstein, in I. Watson et al. (eds), *Negotiating Cultures: Eugenio Barba and the Intercultural Debate*, 218–220, Manchester: Manchester University Press.

Boal, A. (1979), *A Tempestade* e *As Mulheres de Atenas*, Lisbon: Plátano.

Boal, A. (2011a), *Jogos Para Atores e Não-Atores*, 14th edition, Rio de Janeiro: Civilização Brasileira.

Boal, A. (2011b), *Teatro do Oprimido: e outras poéticas políticas*, 11th edition, Rio de Janeiro: Civilização Brasileira.

Buell, F. (1994), *National Culture and the New Global System*, Baltimore: Johns Hopkins University Press.

Claxton, M. (2000), 'Cultura, Desenvolvimento e o Papel do Teatro', in P. Heritage (ed.), *Mudança de Cena*, 29–42, Rio de Janeiro: The British Council.

Freire, P. (2012), *Professora, Sim; Tia, Não: cartas a quem ousa ensinar*, Rio de Janeiro: Civilização Brasileira.

Freire, P. (2016), *Pedagogia do Oprimido*, 60th edition, Rio de Janeiro: Paz e Terra.

Freud, S. (1913), *Totem and Taboo*, trans. A. Brill and J. Strachey, Boston, MA: Beacon Press.

Lévi-Strauss, C. (1996), *Raça e História*, 66, trans. Inácio Canelas, 5th edition, Lisbon: Editorial Presença.

Pavis, P. (1991), *Theatre at the Crossroads of Cultures*, London: Routledge.

Resende, A. (2002), 'Introduction: Brazilian Appropriations of Shakespeare', in A. Resende (ed.), *Foreign Accents: Brazilian Readings of Shakespeare*, 11–41, Newark: University of Delaware Press; London: Associated University Press.

Retamar, R. F. ([1971] 1989), *Caliban and Other Essays*, trans. E. Baker, Minneapolis: University of Minnesota Press.

Revista de Antropofagia (1975), April. Available online: https://joaocamillopenna.files.wordpress.com/2014/02/andrade-oswald-de-revista-deantropofagia.pdf (accessed 25 January 2018).

Shakespeare, W. (1997), *Shakespeare's Sonnets*, ed. K. Duncan-Jones, third series, London: Bloomsbury Arden Shakespeare.

Shakespeare, W. (2006), *As You Like It*, ed. J. Dusinberre, third series, London: Bloomsbury Arden Shakespeare.

Shakespeare, W. (2016), *Hamlet*, ed. A. Thompson and N. Taylor, third series, rev. edition, London: Bloomsbury Arden Shakespeare.

Shakespeare, W. (2017), *Comedy of Errors*, ed. K. Cartwright, third series, rev. edition, London: Bloomsbury Arden Shakespeare.

Soares, M. (1999), *Linguagem e Escola: uma perspectiva social*, São Paulo: Ática.

12

Cultural Anthropophagy and the deinstitutionalization of Shakespeare: Paul Heritage in conversation with Vinicius Mariano de Carvalho

For more than two decades, Paul Heritage has been one of the most active figures in the artistic exchange between Brazil and the UK. He has created several art-based projects in British and Brazilian prisons, working with thousands of prisoners, guards and their families, including award-winning HIV/AIDs education and human rights work. As a producer, Heritage has worked with major UK arts institutions to bring leading Brazilian companies to British audiences, including Grupo Galpão (Shakespeare's Globe Theatre), Grupo Piolin (Barbican), AfroReggae (Barbican) and Nós do Morro (RSC and Barbican). He also leads the ongoing practice-based research project 'Shakespeare Forum', which took place in Rio de Janeiro in 2011, in Salvador in 2013, toured four Brazilian cities in 2014 and in 2016 delivered three Portuguese-language productions by UK directors in three Brazilian cities. In the following conversation with Vinicius Mariano de Carvalho, Heritage discusses his understanding of Cultural Anthropophagy and its impact on Shakespearean creative practices and theory.

VMC *One of the key concepts in this collected volume of essays and interviews is that Cultural Anthropophagy should not be seen just as a metaphor for Brazilian culture, but as a creative and analytical method with wider applicability and, in this sense, a useful reinterpretation of the idea of a 'Global Shakespeare'. You have long-standing experience with theatrical practice in Brazil and the original context of Cultural Anthropophagy. Do you remember when you first encountered the concept and how you understood it?*

PH We are talking about the first time I arrived in Brazil in 1991. I was there to lecture on Shakespeare's comedies, and I was touring with the Cheek by Jowl production of *As You Like It*, giving a lecture the night before each performance. I arrived on 1 August, and the next night, I was standing in front of an audience in Teatro Villa Lobos[1] with Bárbara Heliodora[2] translating, as I did not speak Portuguese then. Bárbara was an amazing figure, and had an extraordinary knowledge of both Brazilian and Shakespearean history. But Bárbara did not just translate my talk; she commented on what I was saying: 'eating' my words. From that night onwards, I saw that there was nothing simple about translating these topics, something else was involved. My arrival was only two years after the return of direct elections of the president in Brazil.[3] As part of the tour we went to the city of Recife, which at that time looked so beautifully run-down to my European eyes; it was far from the new and very modern Recife that we see today. We performed at the Teatro do Parque, an outdoor theatre, which was built in 1915 in *belle époque* style with an open structure. So, there we were staging Shakespeare's fictional Forest of Arden, surrounded by a very real tropical forest. It was hard to imagine two forests more different; it was as if the tropical forest – the sounds and smells – was about to absorb the theatre. Three hours of Shakespeare in English to this audience in the state of Pernambuco – and without subtitles. Moreover, we had an all-male cast. While this seemed to be readily accepted by the audience, what shocked them was the fact that Rosalind was played by Adrian Lester, a black actor. As the cast presented themselves, they gradually created a free space around Adrian, who must have been twenty or twenty-three at the time and was left standing centre-stage. With a shift of his hips he was Rosalind, and the audience went berserk: 'is this black man playing Rosalind?' They suddenly realized that Adrian was actually antropophagically becoming a female character they thought of as 'white-skinned'. I will never forget that moment. Cast and audience participated in a powerful reminder of the fact that everything in performance is exchange – an act of becoming other – which is of course fundamental in anthropophagy.

VMC *So, you lived through a moment of Cultural Anthropophagical experience then? Is this when your fascination with Brazil began?*

PH There are so many moments to look back on and say that this was the reason I became so interested in Brazil, and that was certainly one of them. Following the 1991 tour, I returned to Brazil the following year, directing *Measure for Measure* in the federal capital of Brasília and making theatre with prisoners in the penitentiary complex known as Papuda. In 1994, on a visit to Rio de Janeiro, I went to see Nós do Morro, a theatre company based in the favela of Vidigal.[4] They were performing 'Machadianas', three short stories by Machado de Assis which they had adapted for the stage.[5] This favela-based company doing classical work was exquisite. I had never seen community theatre in the UK doing such highly accomplished classical work. I brought Bárbara

Heliodora – the theatre critic who had translated my first lecture – up to the favela to see the performance and she was completely enchanted and wrote about it in her column in the Brazilian newspaper *O Globo*. As a result, I thought: 'this is a company which would embrace working with Shakespearean work'. I invited Cicely Berry, director of voice from the Royal Shakespeare Company [RSC], to Rio and to Vidigal where she began doing Shakespeare workshops with the group. This resulted in a twelve-year collaboration between the RSC and Nós do Morro, culminating with the Brazilian company performing *The Two Gentlemen of Verona* at the Royal Shakespeare Theatre (RST) in Stratford-upon-Avon. To me the word anthropophagy signifies acts of exchange and sharing. I watched what happened to Shakespeare in that moment in Recife. I watched what happened to Shakespeare, and with Shakespeare, when Nós do Morro started to find a new and different voice in his works, creating new meanings. *The Two Gentlemen of Verona* is such a difficult play – it is a very early one – and it contains a very nasty sexual assault – a rape – at its centre, yet it is a comedy. It is so hard to a British sensibility to make that play mean something today. It all depends on everyone's emotions being able to shift and turn very rapidly, which is not what theatre today usually demands. Nós do Morro, however, found a way of doing exactly that. They conveyed adolescent emotions and still found the darkness of the play, through the emotional turmoil of the relationships they know. They also found within Shakespeare the celebratory ritual of theatre. This is very important. In Britain, so much of the interpretation of Shakespeare is heavily text-centred, but I believe that the interpretation of the actor–theatre relation should precede that. I found this so much easier in Brazil than in Britain, where things are often contained by a predetermined, formalistic ritual of theatre. What Brazilian theatre companies do so fantastically is break with such formalism. Grupo Galpão also excels in this in Belo Horizonte[6] but perhaps the master of them all is Zé Celso at Teatro Oficina in São Paulo.[7] In his *Ham-let* production of 1993 Zé Celso did not just reinterpret

Hamlet in a highly anthropophagic way, he also gave an anthropophagical interpretation of theatre itself. In Zé Celso's Teatro Oficina, the actor–theatre relation precedes the text, precedes the formal ritual of theatre, while in Britain the ritual of theatre always comes first as the determining factor of the audience's experience, and this kills any attempt to reinvent. When I was privileged enough to see his *Ham-let*, Zé Celso had been doing this for over fifty-six years and as with Nós do Morro or Grupo Galpão, he challenged what I knew, not just about Shakespeare but about theatre itself.

VMC   *Do you believe that Cultural Anthropophagy might help to deconstruct notions of essentiality in the Global Shakespeare discourse? Holding on to any notions of predetermined meaning in the text seems almost impossible from the perspective of an anthropophagical engagement. It also seems less a question of bringing 'Shakespeare' to the world; instead I hear you saying the world understood as theatre is being brought to Shakespeare in productions like Zé Celso's?*

PH   Absolutely. Sometimes it is hard to remember that Shakespeare and his companies were a part of an era that was inventing theatre. To understand this, we might compare the emergence of the internet and the digital age and how it has radically changed our perception and capacity to recreate the world. There are young artists out there on YouTube, rethinking and reinventing everything. Shakespearean theatre was a bit like that. The first commercial theatre in London was in 1576 – it was called 'The Theatre' – and Shakespeare was part of a moment in which theatre became an identifiable form, separate to the church or street entertainment. It became something you could close off in spatial terms and charge money for seeing. You could make money performing or writing for the theatre. But it is difficult to repossess this moment, to find it again, when everything about how/where/why we go to theatre has now been fixed and decided. In so many of our theatre-going experiences, we think not so much about theatre itself, as about what it presents to us. What is so fantastic about Nós do Morro, Grupo Galpão, Zé Celso and Teatro Oficina and so many other groups, like Clowns de Shakespeare from Natal,[8] is that they do not start from the assumption that theatre already exists – or that Shakespeare and his plays already exist, for that matter – they insist that the very essence of making theatre must be reinvented every time. The Brazilian Shakespeare productions that I most admire – the ones that I enjoyed the most and learned from – are those that took me back to the very reason of why we make theatre.

When Grupo Galpão came to perform their *Romeu e Julieta* at Shakespeare's Globe in 2000, you saw the Brazilian flag flying above the theatre. That to me was an amazing and anthropophagic moment. But it was also a reminder of why the flag above the theatre flies: to tell you that the play was on. When you arrived as an audience member, the performance was already happening outside the theatre, because the roots of Galpão as a company are their years of performing in the street. Even before the prologue was spoken they were already interacting with the public as they gathered for the play, blurring distinctions between audience and performance spaces. In fact, it was hard to tell if the play had already started. That seems to me to be where the learning is happening, rather than in a directorial interpretation of the play. The text of *Romeo and Juliet* used by Grupo Galpão was never entirely Shakespeare. There were interpolations from Guimarães Rosa[9] and from popular culture. Did it matter? No, of course not. Reviews and audiences were saying things like: 'this company has taken us back to something more Shakespearian than perhaps we have ever achieved'.

VMC *There is one moment in that performance which breaks – in an anthropophagic way – with our preconceptions of tragedy. Juliet's line to Romeo, 'O churl, drunk all, and left no friendly drop. To help me after!' is played with a hint of real annoyance and blame, which is both very funny and very touching. Exploring what you said, it sounds like you are saying Cultural Anthropophagy deinstitutionalizes Shakespeare and theatre. It calls for what we might call an indiscipline of performance. Is that correct?*

PH Yes indeed. Shakespeare is constructed by so many different institutions, not just the theatre but also universities, schools and in the common constructions of everyday life in the English-speaking world. He appears in news stories like the fall of Dominique Strauss-Kahn, the former director of the International Monetary Fund. Newspapers insistently describe it as a Shakespearean tragedy. Everyone uses Shakespeare. He is absorbed by British culture in a very institutionalized way and serves several purposes and a variety of agendas, many of them reductive in the way in which they understand and interpret the original Shakespearean text. We should be careful about thinking of Shakespeare in fixed terms which we have ourselves invented. Shakespeare *only* exists through multiple reinterpretations. What Brazilian Shakespeare has offered via an anthropophagical approach is the possibility to deinstitutionalize. I see this as the possibility to offer a fuller view of the complexity and uncertainty in Shakespeare. I prefer the anthropophagical lens as an approach because it is more plural and this can only be a good thing, especially in our world today.

Returning to your comment about Galpão's *Romeu e Julieta*, I think what is so important about that company is their ability to insert – and play with – a distance between the character and the actor. This is as important in relation to the stage-craft of Shakespeare's own time as it is to the possibilities it opens to our own. Galpão works with theatrical conventions that come from a time before the gap was closed between actor and character. Eduardo, the actor from Grupo Galpão who performed Romeu, was about forty-five, and when he came to perform at Shakespeare's Globe had been playing the role for twenty-five years. I can imagine Richard Burbage from Shakespeare's company doing the same because the cinematic romantic notion where the actor and the character are so closely absorbed that you cannot see the difference between them had not taken hold of our imagination. That is why the moment Adrian Lester stood on stage at the start of *As You Like It* in Recife seemed so profoundly anthropophagic, because we could see Rosalind in the movement of his hips, in the way he lifted a scarf, but we could also see Adrian, a black man from England.

VMC *This reminds me of the concept of Perspectivism by Viveiros de Castro,*[10] *where he maintains that the Amerindian ontology goes beyond the nature versus culture dichotomy. Again, this is a decided move away from essentialism, or the notion that nature is something essential, while culture is plural. In the anthropophagical performances of Shakespeare, what we see is a sort of 'multinatural' relation, where characters and actors play together.*

PH That idea from de Castro is one that makes my head spin every time I try to understand it. I think this is probably part of what most motivates me when working in Brazil. During the almost three decades that I have been working in Brazil – whether it is with the Kuikuro people in the Xingu[11] or in prisons in São Paulo – I have found these many natures. Brazil has always fuelled my interest in what art *does*. Brazilian performances of Shakespeare that excited me have been those that have brought to the foreground the act of art, rather than insisting on the discussion of the different languages of art. I would also add that making Shakespeare in prisons, or the work done by Dr Vitor Pordeus at the Instituto Nise da Silveira, performing Shakespeare with psychiatric patients, demonstrates not only the deinstitutionalization of Shakespeare, but also the capacity of Shakespeare to deinstitutionalize. I think this is partly my motive for doing Shakespeare in prisons. When juvenile offenders or prisoners perform Shakespeare, something happens because of that one culture that unites us and insists that the young man or woman, whom we *want* to see as a prisoner or offender, can take themselves and us somewhere else. You can describe that as anthropophagy or not, but it certainly demonstrates a multiple perspective. It goes against the grain of the reductive ways in which institutions operate.

Notes

1   Teatro Villa Lobos is located in Rio de Janeiro. It was built in 1978 and destroyed by a fire during refurbishment works in 2010.

2   Bárbara Heliodora (1923–2015) was a Brazilian theatre critic, writer and translator, specializing in Shakespeare. She was a highly influential figure in Brazilian theatre.

3   Brazil lived under a military regime from 1964 to 1985. In 1995, a civilian president was elected in an indirect election, but by the parliament. Direct elections were not held until 1989 when Fernando Collor de Mello was the first president directly elected since 1960. His government was disastrous and drove Brazil into hyperinflation and economic turmoil. He was involved in several corruption scandals and finally impeached in 1992.

4   Nós do Morro is a theatre company founded in 1986 in Morro do Vidigal, a favela in the southern part of Rio de Janeiro. The company, directed by Guti Fraga, aims to promote theatre at community level, training and preparing actors from the neighbourhood. In 1995, the group extended its engagement to cinema and began producing documentaries. Their first performance outside the favela was in 1996, when the company performed *Hamlet* at Centro Cultural do Banco do Brasil, in downtown Rio, under the supervision of Dominic Barter and Cicely Berry, from the RSC. In 2006, they performed *Two Gentlemen of Verona* at the International Festival in Stratford-upon-Avon.

5   Joaquim Maria Machado de Assis (1839–1908) was a Brazilian novelist, poet, playwright and short story writer and widely regarded as one of the greatest figures of Brazilian literature.

6   Grupo Galpão is a street theatre company founded in Belo Horizonte, Brazil, in 1982, by Teuda Bara, Eduardo Moreira, Wanda Fernandes and Antônio Edson. They became internationally famous in 1992 with their production of 'Romeu and Julieta'. In 2000, they brought the production to Shakespeare's Globe in London and returned for the Globe-to-Globe festival in 2012.

7   José Celso Martinez Corrêa (1937–), known as Zé Celso, is a Brazilian stage actor, director and playwright. He was one of the founders of Teatro Oficina, a politically engaged and innovative theatre company from the 1960s in Brazil. His adaptation of Oswald de Andrade's play *O rei da Vela*, in 1967, was a revolution in Brazilian theatre, revisiting Cultural Anthropophagy. In 1993, his anthropophagical *Ham-let* was celebrated for its originality and carnivalesque elements.

8   Formed in 1993 in Natal, Rio Grande do Norte, Clowns de Shakespeare has become another internally renowned Brazilian theatre group, drawing their main inspiration from the reworking of Shakespearean plays. Their practice combines physicality, musical elements and local popular cultures.

9   João Guimarães Rosa (1908–1967) was a Brazilian novelist, short story writer and diplomat. His most famous work, *Grande Sertão Veredas* (translated into English as *The Devil to Pay in the Backlands*), is a revolutionary text, inventing a particular language, often compared to James Joyce's *Ulysses*. Together with Machado de Assis, Guimarães Rosa is considered a great master of Brazilian literature.

10 Eduardo Viveiros de Castro (1951–) is a Brazilian anthropologist whose research on the Brazilian Tupinambas in Brazil resulted in the construction of the concept of Amerindian Perspectivism, fundamental for the understanding of Cultural Anthropophagy as also explained in the introduction to this collection. Seminal works include *From the Enemy's Point of View: Humanity and Divinity in an Amazonian Society* (1986) and *The Inconstancy of the Indian Soul* (2011).

11 The Kuikuro are an indigenous people from the Mato Grosso region in Brazil, with a population of about 592. They live in the Xingu Indigenous Territories. For further details see www. peoplespalaceprojects.org.uk (accessed 7 December 2018).

Afterword: fat king, lean beggar?

Alfredo Michel Modenessi

I was aware of *Eating Shakespeare* virtually from its inception, and as my own work shows, I gladly share its critical paradigms (see Modenessi 2017). After enjoying its final shape, crucial statements from equally crucial essays by two of the sharpest Latin American minds of our day immediately suggested themselves as suitable meeting points and touchstones for all its contents and positions, howsoever diverse, or even here and there at odds with the editors' fundamental tenets. The first is by Walter Mignolo: 'In essence [...] the geopolitics of knowledge is organized around the diversification, through history, of the colonial and the imperial differences' (2002: 59); the second, by Roberto Schwarz: 'The inevitability of cultural imitation is bound up with a specific set of historical imperatives over which abstract philosophical critiques can exercise no power' (1988: 82).

These quotes merely betoken the kind of incisive provocations constantly flowing from the pools of Latin American thinking and creativity. Unfortunately, save for collections like this and sundry sparse texts, they seldom find their way into discussions on Shakespeare, especially in their current, fashionably 'global' strain. The main reason is, of course, that the scarcity of translations into English articulates with the still staunchly monolingual and hence often culturally unidirectional, fatally 'global', character of international academic business and publishing. One of the merits of *Eating Shakespeare* should already shine through this, then, inasmuch as its editors made the decidedly non-conformist (and rare) choice of compiling, for a mainstream series, a collection of essays with a common, yet sufficiently uneven, platform of 'peripheral' thought (see Dussel 1995: esp. 9–11). It must be noted, as well, that at the same time, this initiative performs a major task of urgent divulgation.

On top of my personal affinities with its creative agents and their principles, the sheer chance to elaborate freely on the basis of statements like the ones above reminds of why I would have loved to play a different role in this stimulating collection. Sadly, 'time and the hour' would not have it so. However, almost twenty years ago I did contribute a chapter to a forerunner: the collection *Latin American Shakespeares*, which the much missed Bernice W. Kliman envisioned and started to compile near the end of the twentieth century. She eventually edited it in 2005, together with Rick J. Santos, making it the first book from an anglophone publishing house expressly dedicated to the presence of Shakespeare in Latin America. Although that is not exactly the subject of *Eating Shakespeare*, roughly 70 per cent of its pages have to do with a single Latin American culture, and with one of its particular contributions to critical discourse; more pointedly, with a theory that originated in Brazil to address its own pressing issues of cultural identity, belonging and diversity – a theory that, at the same time, can serve similar purposes in kindred cultures. The links between the two volumes are clear and may be profitably borne out.

Some crucial connections come in the shape of radical differences. The older book started as the idea of a brilliant and generous American scholar with a keen interest but little expertise in the subject, who, exercising her usual wisdom, sought help from a colleague with greater knowledge and personal nearness to the matter of her project. Instead, the present endeavour is the work of three scholars from outside the Anglo-American Shakespeare ranks (two Brazilians and a Dane with a Brazilian soul) who display their firm grasp on their fundamental paradigms, cases and contexts throughout, as well as on the 'foreign' language in which all that jazz is naturally encoded. Likewise, considering that the interest in 'international' Shakespeare among Anglo-American academics was well on its way from the early 1990s, and also that Shakespeare had been a frequent guest in Latin America from the early nineteenth century onwards, the release of *Latin American Shakespeares* seemed somewhat belated. In the light of that, *Eating Shakespeare* also looks a bit overdue. The gap has proven more worthwhile than disappointing, however.

The decade-and-a-half between these books has been both encouraging and frustrating. Encouraging, because the interest, the demand, the number of engaged scholars and the textual output on Shakespeare in Latin America have significantly increased since the publication of Kliman's collection, and one must hope that her initiative had much do with it – although, of course, her book and the ensuing interest also occurred inside a comparatively empty frame. Within that relative void, *Latin American Shakespeares* observed, documented and expounded instances of its general subject mostly from conventionally 'mainstream' vantage points and variegated theoretical premises, creating a then perhaps necessary bridge between the expressly local works and events under scrutiny and the predominantly Anglo-American minds that the collection would reach. Hence, an additional, and maybe greater, source of encouragement is that *Eating Shakespeare*, unlike its predecessor, addresses overtly political, and specifically geo-political, ways to do things with Shakespeare belonging in likewise avowedly local spaces and circumstances by means of an equally special way to examine and theorize such things from within their own sites of production and signification.

In other words, *Eating Shakespeare* rests on native, especially apt, premises that correlate with their objects in a manner that *Latin American Shakespeares* did not, and probably could not.

Then again, the time gap between these books has also been frustrating because the aforementioned rising interest in the Latin American Shakespeare scene must have also responded, and considerably so, to the development of so-called 'Global Shakespeare' studies in the twenty-first century. Moreover, it has been likewise frustrating not only because Kliman's volume was conspicuously flawed in its coverage of the Spanish-speaking areas of Latin America – i.e. the largest and most diverse portion of its geopolitical scope – but also because that weakness is still far from disappearing: witness the scarce contribution of scholars from Spanish-speaking Latin America to the international Shakespeare scene. To wit: of the sixteen chapters in *Latin American Shakespeares*, seven dealt with Shakespeare in Brazil, four involved Mexico, two Chile, one Cuba, one explored Jorge Luis Borge's texts on Shakespeare and one was a bibliographical survey. (Notoriously, there was nothing on Shakespeare in francophone Latin America.) Thus, like *Eating Shakespeare*, a sizable percentage of Kliman's book addressed the history and practice of Shakespeare in one single Latin American country – albeit the largest and best furnished with dedicated scholars, as well as the only one whose native language is Portuguese. More significantly, however, eight chapters of *Latin American Shakespeares* were written by Brazilians: five working in Brazil, and three teaching in the USA; another four were authored by English-speaking scholars: two from the USA, one a Canadian and the other a British professor; while of the four contributions by native Spanish-speakers, three were written by Spaniards and *only one* by a Spanish-speaking Latin American residing and working in the area.

Sadly, that situation has not changed much. Even though the number of items specifically concerning Shakespeare and Spanish-speaking Latin America within the world of Shakespeare studies has notably grown in recent years, only a handful of them have come from local scholars and from the area itself. Conversely, the contributions about Brazil, the sole, formidable, Portuguese-speaking culture of Latin America, come far more often from native minds and, more important, pointedly local and locally relevant perspectives, as this collection testifies. This is relevant because it contrasts with the notorious want of native or local theoretical paradigms in many items dealing with works or events originating in Spanish-speaking Latin America. Worse still, this happens in spite of the fact that Spanish-speaking Latin America is connected more than just geographically to Brazil, the source of Cultural Anthropophagy, the core paradigm of *Eating Shakespeare* and a concept that, if anywhere outside of Brazil, applies really well to the rest of our continent. Hopefully, this flaw will vanish in time.

Be that as it may, in the brief afterword to her volume, Kliman pointed out several things of particular relevance to this new and equally transcendent collection. A first, and obvious, fact to notice is that she was – albeit tentatively, tangentially and here and there downright inaccurately – aware of the significance of several notions that converge more fruitfully in *Eating Shakespeare*. Here, a revealing passage:

> To see yet again what Shakespeare can accomplish for stage, page, and screen, students of Shakespeare outside of Latin America might well look into the iconoclastic ways of Latin Americans and their mestizo Shakespeare. In Latin America, as everywhere, Shakespeare can be a god to be worshipped or overcome. But in Latin America, Shakespeare's works can also be a rich provider of material to be subsumed (cannibalized) by native traditions. For Latin American artists, the Shakespearean legacy is available for co-optation not only through parody, adaptation, and both reverent and irreverent (re)creation; they can also incorporate Shakespeare into unique indigenous genres. (Kliman 2005: 327)

Apart from the presence of anthropophagy under the troubling cover of 'cannibalization', Kliman manages to identify three crucial aspects of the Latin American experience of Shakespeare that *Eating Shakespeare* brings into sharper focus.

One is the paradigmatic potential of anthropophagy for cultures with similar histories and circumstances. Another is the vital and subversive role of irreverence, of a sense of humour, in the productive interaction between the 'fat king' of the 'higher' culture and the 'lean beggar' of the host culture. Finally, she hints at the transformative and revitalizing power of that interaction. In more than one way, Kliman suggested that, at present, Shakespeare makes better sense and spectacle, and brings greater pleasure, through multiple transformations and re-informations than by diversely disguised reiterations. Concomitantly, if at a distance, *Eating Shakespeare* illustrates how the anthropophagous approach and ritual produce valuable manifestations of creative freedom. It is worth noting that Kliman pointed all this out despite the awkward use of elements, like the qualifier 'mestizo', that smack of honest exoticism, perhaps due to the endemic lack of access in the Anglo-American milieu to more, and more elaborate, critical literature stemming from the region itself – often because of linguistic limitations. Moreover, she also pointed these things out despite her perceptible, but simply natural, detachment from the very agents and products that she wished, and managed, to bring carefully together in her groundbreaking volume.

Thus, what Kliman and her collection were patently wanting was a more appropriate, solid and profitable toolkit to handle with greater ease the often puzzling, Falstaffian body of Shakespeare-related Latin American artistic endeavours. She wanted, as it were, a more accurate grammar, syntax and vocabulary to speak more precisely and critically about *our* Shakespeares or, better still, with less stale, and often baffled, inflections. *Eating Shakespeare* happily outlines and elaborates on that language from its very roots in Brazilian culture and extends it to other areas, hopefully for the benefit of many readers and practitioners inside and outside its original site. Many questions are answered here, but better yet, many more can now be more decidedly asked.

References

Dussel, E. (1995), *The Invention of the Americas: Eclipse of 'the Other' and the Myth of Modernity*, trans. Michael D. Barber, New York: Continuum.

Kliman, B. W. (2005), 'Afterword', in B. W. Kliman and R. J. Santos (eds), *Latin American Shakespeares*, 327–328, Madison-Teaneck, NJ: Fairleigh Dickinson University Press.

Mignolo, W. (2002), 'The Geopolitics of Knowledge and the Colonial Difference', *The South Atlantic Quarterly*, 101 (1): 57–96.

Modenessi, A. M. (2017), '"Victim of Improvisation" in Latin America: Shakespeare Out-sourced and In-taken', in J. C. Bulman (ed.), *The Oxford Handbook of Shakespeare and Performance*, 549–467, Oxford: Oxford University Press.

Schwarz, R. (1988), 'Brazilian Culture: Nationalism by Elimination', *New Left Review*, 1 (167): 77–90.

INDEX

AN ODD UNDERTAKING

Enjoy!
Best Wishes
Bill.

BILL WOOD

The Book Guild Ltd

First published in Great Britain in 2022 by
The Book Guild Ltd
Unit E2 Airfield Business Park,
Harrison Road, Market Harborough,
Leicestershire. LE16 7UL
Tel: 0116 2792299
www.bookguild.co.uk
Email: info@bookguild.co.uk
Twitter: @bookguild

Typeset in 11pt Minion Pro

Printed and bound in Great Britain by CMP UK

ISBN 978 1915352 255

British Library Cataloguing in Publication Data.
A catalogue record for this book is available from the British Library.

For my family, past, present and future. With all my love.

STACKS OF TROUBLE

It was just after 2 a.m., and I was out for the count, desperately trying to make up the missed sleep from the previous night's call-outs followed by a demanding ten-hour day shift. Prematurely disturbed from my deep sleep, it took some time to realise the cause of my rude awakening. My slow response to the rather harsh rendition of Mozart's 40th symphony (the ringtone of my work mobile) had caused an adverse reaction from the other side of the bed and a sharp nudge in the ribs to increase my motivation to answer it was more than effective. Fumbling for my phone on the bedside table in the mottled darkness, once located I put it to my ear.

"Wakey wakey!" said an overly cheerful voice for that time in the morning. It was the duty manager from head office, Roger Dickinson. "There's a coroner's call-out in Finchley. Can you make your way into the yard as soon as possible?"

"Be there in twenty," I slurred, returning the phone to the bedside table and covering myself once again with the duvet.

"Get up, before you go back to sleep," a drowsy, disgruntled voice urged, turning over and getting all cosy to do exactly what I wanted to do.

Dragging myself out of bed, I got up and threw on the clothes strategically placed on the exercise-bike-cum-clothes-horse in the corner of the bedroom, grabbed the car keys and my jacket, and headed into work. Driving through Camden Town, the revellers were going strong, enjoying the warmth of the summer season. It didn't take me long to get to the yard; even so, when I arrived, Oliver and

Eddie, the other two thirds of the removal team, were already suited and booted and getting the van ready.

"Here we go again," said Oliver, loading a wheelie stretcher into the van.

"Hopefully it won't be as mad as last night," said Eddie. "I need to catch up on my beauty sleep."

"It's going to take more than a few hours of sleep to iron out those wrinkles!" chortled Oliver.

"Cheeky sod," Eddie retorted.

Once I'd got changed into my undertaker's attire, we headed off to Finchley in the van. Oliver driving, and Eddie and I forcibly huddled up on the inadequately sized and completely incorrectly described two-seater passenger seat.

Every now and again something in life happens that simply stops you in your tracks and challenges you to re-evaluate your thoughts on humanity and the world in which you live. The removal in Finchley, in the wee small hours that Friday morning, was one such occasion. The information given to us by the coroner had in no way prepared us for the events that were to unfold in the following hours.

As usual, for a coroner's removal, the police were on scene. Pulling up in front of the house and peering through the downstairs bay window, the most bizarre scene met our eyes. Two men in blue overalls were standing on a mountain of newspapers and magazines that was level with the height of the windowsill and that completely filled the room from wall to wall. This turned out to be the bedroom where the two bodies, an elderly man and woman, were located. The fact that there were two bodies was information we were previously unaware of, but luckily we always had more than one stretcher on board the van just in case we received a call-out while already attending another. The men in overalls who were from the local council were slowly removing the papers and magazines in order to reach the bodies that lay beneath. The shelving that the vast amount of papers and magazines was usually stacked upon, had evidently collapsed under the weight of its colossal load, creating an avalanche that had engulfed the couple while they lay in their bed.

At that point in my career as an undertaker, I'd been in a great many homes that were exceptionally cluttered and full to the brim of all sorts of accumulated miscellaneous matter, but this was totally beyond belief. How the elderly couple went about their daily lives was a complete mystery. Most of the rooms on the ground floor including the hallway, kitchen and toilet, were barely accessible. Books, newspapers and magazines of every type were piled from floor to ceiling taking up any vacant floor space. Hundreds, if not thousands, of those personal massage cards that you used to find plastered all over telephone boxes, placed there by women, or men I suppose, of dubious reputation, advertising their services (not that I'd ever really noticed them myself) were stacked along the hallway like a forest of the straightest pine. Empty cereal boxes by the ton were neatly collapsed and tied into bundles. Shelf upon shelf of Marmite jars, minus the labels, were full of various objects including buttons, marbles, and oddest of all, an exorbitant amount of broken Polo mints. And although their marbles were clearly safely stored, it was starting to look like the old couple had definitely lost a few of the more important ones along the way. Manuals for every electrical appliance you could think of, which I'm fairly sure they didn't possess, were piled high in alphabetical order. Boxes, jars, tins, pamphlets and brochures filled any available space for storage. You name it, they probably had a stockpile of it somewhere in the house, pointing skywards. And I can only assume that the rooms upstairs of the quite upmarket three-bedroom semi were in a similar state, because access to the first floor via the stairs due to them now being used for storage, was impossible.

Assisting the council workers and the police to shift the mountainous paper landscape, we too got stuck in with the big dig. After several hours of digging, the two bodies were revealed. Sadly, it was evident that the elderly man and woman had not died instantly under the weight of the paper avalanche. Lying side by side, hand in hand, they lay half on the bed and half on the floor as though, with all their effort, they had been trying to make their escape towards the bedroom door. During the burrowing process to reach the couple, Eddie found an old black and white photo in a frame. The glass was cracked, possibly from the weight of the paper mountain. It was of a young man in a naval officer's uniform and his beautiful young bride in a rather plain but pretty wedding dress. A wartime photo, presumably. They both looked so happy. Looking around us, we wondered what state of mind the couple had been in to hoard things to such an extent. Was it just one of them with the obsession, or both? It was a very sad ending indeed, to what seemed a long, and hopefully, happy life together. At least they were together to the end.

As we headed back to the yard after delivering our two passengers to the coroner's mortuary in Finchley, the darkness of the night was gradually surrendering to the brightness of a new day. Radiant yellows, flaming pinks and electric blues merged indiscriminately. The buildings and trees were silhouetted against the backdrop of a pearlescent sky.

Back at the yard, greeted by the early-morning birdsong, with only an hour to the start of our working day, it was pointless any of us returning home. Sleep had eluded us once more.

"Get the kettle on, Ed," called Oliver from the office.

"Already on it," Eddie replied, clattering around the tearoom.

"What time does Ron's café open?" I asked.

"They should be open now," said Oliver.

"Anyone fancy anything? My treat."

"Go on then, I'll have a bacon butty with brown sauce," replied Oliver, keenly.

I poked my head around the tearoom door.

"How about you, Eddie?"

"Sounds good. I'll have the same, but with ketchup on please, mate."

"Right you are, back in a mo."

It had been a strange old night. Quite surreal. It was a night that I will never forget as long as I live – dementia permitting, of course – given the genetic ancestral legacy that appears to be patiently lurking on the not too distant horizon.

IN THE VERY BEGINNING

Of course, I wasn't always an undertaker; there was life before dealing with death. A life that started twenty-nine years earlier in the idyllic rural county of Gloucestershire.

It was the swinging sixties. A time of radical social and cultural change. A time of revolution. The Dave Clark Five were singing about being glad all over. Cilla Black was glad for anyone who had a heart and The Beatles were taking the world by storm, usually being pursued by masses of screaming girls in skirts that were getting shorter by the minute. In Great Britain, presumably everything was great, as it said so in the title. The Great Train Robbers, sticking to the theme, were on trial. Although, that doesn't seem so great for them and they couldn't have been all that great if they were on trial, could they? The average weekly wage in the country at the time was £16, so I can see why the train robbery might have seemed like a great idea at the time.

In an ever-changing world some things were changing and others were being revamped. In 1964, the House of Commons was debating the abolition of the death penalty, which Parliament passed in 1965, the last two executions in Great Britain being in the August of '64. Not such great timing for some. Flower power, love and peace, seemed to be the message of the day. Although, the Mods and Rockers fighting on the beaches during the bank holidays obviously hadn't quite got the message. The *Sun* newspaper first came into publication in '64. And where would this great nation be without the good old *Sun* newspaper? We certainly wouldn't be the breast experts that we are today, that's for sure.

Television was revolting, joining in the revolution, that is. *Top of the Pops* aired for the first time adding a whole new dimension to our nation's musical entertainment. A third television channel was also introduced – BBC2. How on earth would the great British public cope with so much choice at their fingertips? Mind you, we didn't have remote controls in those days so you were much less likely to get up and change the channel unless you really had to.

Hello World

It was 4.30 p.m. on a warm, sunny Monday afternoon, 1 June 1964, when Mum's waters broke as she was getting off the bus in Cheltenham town centre in the glorious county of Gloucestershire. The Dave Clark Five could be heard faintly from an open doorway in a nearby shop singing about being glad all over. Not in person, but from a radio inside the shop. Mum, with bulbous belly and beehive hairdo, was swiftly transported to St Paul's Maternity Hospital, just a stone's throw away from the wet patch on the pavement where her body, despite my squatter's rights, had decided it was time to start the process of my eviction from the premises. Five hours later, she gave birth to a bouncing baby boy. Me! (It goes without saying, that it would have been extremely irresponsible to throw even the smallest of stones in such a built-up area to test the theory of how close the hospital was from where Mum was standing. And to be honest, I'm sure she was far too preoccupied at the time for it to have even crossed her mind to do so.)

I'm not entirely convinced that describing a newborn baby as bouncing is the most appropriate choice of words. In fact, I'm fairly certain, at a subtle 5lb 2oz, I wasn't up to much bouncing at all at that stage in my development. Perhaps it would be better to use another word to describe a newborn. Wriggling, for example. It might take a while for people to get used to, but it does seem far more suitable and much less likely to lead to any confusion or unfortunate incidents.

As far as Monday's child being fair of face goes, I think mine had rather more of a blueish tint to it and was pretty wrinkly, but not in a pretty sort of way. I'm led to believe that's fairly common among newborn babies, and not surprising considering the environment they've been inhabiting for the last nine months. Look how wrinkly your fingertips get when you've been in the bath or swimming pool for just a short time.

The Queen of our great nation, 'God bless her', had also given birth to a wriggling baby boy, in the March of '64, her fourth child, Prince Edward. (You see, it works. Wriggling is definitely a far more suitable verb to use when describing a newborn baby and much less likely to cause any unnecessary confusion.) An interesting snippet of royal trivia thrown in there. Obviously there's nothing trivial about a prince being born, or any other baby come to that, as I'm sure any woman having gone through the experience of giving birth would strongly agree.

Follow the Yellow Brick Road

Mum had a rather difficult time after I was born and suffered severely from post-natal depression. Trying to cope with a newborn baby couldn't have helped matters. Especially when they're not feeding well and you're being told they're underweight for their age. Determined to pack a few more pounds onto my somewhat lacking physique, Mum would create bodybuilding cocktails, adding selected high-calorie ingredients to the already nutrient-packed formula drink that I was being fed. The most difficult thing, so I was told, was keeping me awake long enough to drink it, as usually after only a few sips I was so worn out that I would fall asleep.

Whatever my bodybuilding concoctions contained they certainly had the desired effect, as photographic evidence will corroborate. I soon became a rather chubby little toddler with a physique resembling that of a Munchkin on steroids. (One of the little folk from that all-time classic and compulsory Christmas-viewing film, *The Wizard of Oz*.) My curly blonde hair, complete with kiss curl, finished off the Munchkin look perfectly.

Mum struggled during those first eighteen months. Depression eventually getting the better of her, over a period of several months, on and off, Mum received treatment at various local hospitals. Lesley, my sister, who was thirteen when I was born, had to help a great deal with my care during that difficult time. Other relatives would take it in turns to look after me in order for Lesley to try and keep up with her school work. Dad obviously had to keep the money coming in and would help out as much as he could, whenever he could.

The Fall Guy

My speech development, like many of my generation, was greatly influenced by children's television programmes of the day, classics such as *Bill and Ben*, *The Wooden Tops*, and *The Clangers* to name but a few. Which probably explains a great deal about my generation's skills of communication. On the other hand, at least we would be able to converse with confidence, if the need was ever to arise, with potted plants who spoke gibberish or little whistling creatures from outer space who shared a planet with a dragon that made soup. Looking at the way space exploration was going at the time, that need appeared to be creeping ever closer by the day!

I only have two clear memories of nursery school. The first involves me playing the leading role of the character Humpty Dumpty in a class re-enactment of a very tragic event. Like Steve McQueen, I was keen to do all my own stunts. At least I am led to believe he did – I know for certain that I did. Finding a suitable stunt double for myself wouldn't have been the easiest of tasks. Probably involving a trip to the Land of Oz to kidnap a Munchkin (as in, *The Wizard of Oz*, not Australia). Although, not having any ruby red slippers handy for the return journey, it wouldn't really have been a feasible option.

The simulated fall off the table that represented the wall Mr Dumpty was sat upon before the fateful event, was not intended to have been quite as dramatic as it turned out. However, I'm told the rest of my nursery companions were tremendously impressed, and I was given the rest of the day off for my Oscar-winning performance. Not because my monumental portrayal of Mr Dumpty was so convincing, but to recover from the mild concussion I had suffered.

The second and only other memory stored in the old grey matter of my time at nursery, is of a royal visit to our humble little pre-school educational facility. Actually, it was more of a royal drive-by really, involving a large black car and a majestically waving hand. Sitting on the wall outside the nursery, my fellow pre-schoolers and I vigorously waved back at the passing hand as instructed by the supervising adults. We were happy to be guided by their obvious superior knowledge of social protocol, and it seemed the most appropriate response. Despite great temptation, I fought back the urge to recreate my Oscar-winning performance of Humpty Dumpty for the passing royal. After weighing up the pros and cons and the possible consequences, I thought better of it. Even with my limited intellect, life's experiences were obviously teaching me something. Besides, I didn't want to steal the show from our royal passer-by, did I? I have no idea which royal it was that had graced us with their version of Sooty in the nude that day. It could have been the royal corgi-walker for all we saw of them. Whoever it was, we enjoyed the excitement and at least it got us out of the classroom for a bit of fresh air and some aerobic arm exercise.

Primary Thoughts

At the age of five, as was the norm, the next six years of my educational development were handed over to a local primary school. I remember my first day like it was yesterday. The more ample proportions of my physique gained from Mum's bodybuilding cocktails had now been worked off during my energetic toddler years. My skinny, little pale legs dangling out from my rather long grey shorts resembled two bits of string.

Mum convincingly assured me that I would grow into my spacious new school cap which donned my precious little head, eventually! As I would the rest of my new school attire. All garments and school-related items were extensively labelled in case anything was to somehow become separated from me long enough to be classified as lost. Sadly, the shiny new shoes of which I was so proud that completed my ensemble were not destined to remain in their immaculate state for long.

One of the last to arrive, Mum ushered my new clothing and I towards a group of assembled infants mingling in one of the classrooms. A smiling woman in the centre of the clearly confused and noisy gathering acknowledged my arrival with outstretched arms. The teacher, I presume. Nervously I clutched my drawstring gym bag for dear life which contained my black elasticated plimsolls. It was all we required to perform our physical education programme in those days, as it was carried out in our underwear. I'm not sure if that's still the case today, but it's probably not a good idea to go around asking such questions. Even for research purposes. I looked back at Mum, and after a final wave, she turned the corner and was gone. Not forever, naturally, just until later that afternoon. Although, I think a few of us did have some concerns involving parental abandonment.

It would be fair to say that I struggled with my work at primary school. It was not all fun and games and stunt work like nursery had been. Not once did I ever get the opportunity to show off or develop my newfound acting abilities, not even in the Christmas nativity play. I'm sure I would have made an excellent inn keeper – assertively informing Joseph and Mary there was no room at the inn but that they were welcome to stay in the barn – and then falling dramatically from the window. Oh well, their loss.

During the period of my primary education, I tried to memorise my times tables, repeating them mind-numbingly over and over again with the rest of the class. I tried to get as many of my spellings right on the spelling tests after spending an eternity reading through them and copying them over and over again the night before. It just didn't seem to be happening for me academically. My brain didn't seem at all interested in retaining the information that was being crammed into it at a rate of knots. If it was, it certainly wasn't allowing me to access it when I was required to do so.

My school reports reflected my struggles and would always insist that I needed to pay more attention, try harder, and that I was too easily distracted. All of which was true, I suppose. My teachers seemed to be obsessed with the capabilities of the elastic in my socks more than anything. Spending an exorbitant amount of time and energy telling me to pull them up. If only Mum had purchased the ones with the better quality elastic or shorter ones that didn't look like they'd fallen down even if they had. At least I wouldn't have had that problem to deal with on top of everything else. It was, of course, many years on that I learnt it was not actually the socks I was wearing that they were so concerned about, but a clever use of words in the form of an idiom referring to my attitude and lack of effort towards my education.

Interestingly, later on in life (much later), it was discovered that I have hearing problems. Problems which I may apparently have suffered with all my life. I'm not trying to make excuses, though it does make me wonder if that might have had something to do with my attention span, or rather the lack of it. I'll never know for sure, but it is a thought.

When I first started primary school there were a couple of unsavoury characters in the year above me, who for some reason had decided I was to be their next bullying project. I'd obviously passed the interview for the position without even applying for it, my slightly smaller stature probably being a large contributory factor to my new appointment, knowing bullies. Which at the time I didn't, but I do now. The bullying problem was eventually dealt with by giving the biggest one of my irksome tormentors a bloody nose with a wooden skipping-rope handle that came to hand at an opportune moment during one particular run-in. It probably wasn't the most politically correct move on my part, but in those days we were told it was okay to defend yourself against bullies and we were generally encouraged to do so whether we wanted to or not. My retaliation caused quite a commotion in the playground, but it certainly achieved the desired effect where dialogue had failed. Particularly, as most of my vocabulary at that point in my life had evolved from fictional television characters in the form of two flowerpot men and some whistling alien creatures.

I believe governments describe such actions of violence as peace through superior fire power, when they apply the same strategy to various volatile situations around the world. The nicely finished wooden skipping-rope handle was certainly far superior to anything those two intimidating scallywags had available at the time.

You can only push a person's buttons the wrong way for so long before they snap, and they had definitely pushed mine, too far, for far too long. My button's fastening capabilities hindered beyond repair, they, like me, were at the end of their tether. However, peace was achieved and a valuable lesson learned by all. Not the same lesson mind you, but valuable none the less.

I'm a great believer that no matter who you are you will get what's coming to you in the end – one way or another. It's the cause-and-effect principle. Reaping what one sews. What goes around comes around. Karma, etc., etc. Or whatever you might like to call it.

What's in a Name?

Throughout primary school the headmistress, Miss Redman, took it upon herself to inform me and the rest of the world, that Billy was a silly little boy's name. Sorry, I forgot to mention, that's my name. Albeit, not according to Miss Redman. Whilst at her school I was to be addressed by my proper name – the one I had been christened with – which was William.

I was, to say the least, slightly confused by this new revelation. I had always been called Billy by my family and friends up to that point. My dad's name was also Billy and he was not a silly little boy. In actual fact, he was quite sensible most of the time and most definitely not a little boy. I had noticed some people even called him Bill. After what Miss Redman had said, I became quite concerned that maybe people got sillier the shorter their name became. I would obviously have to keep a close eye on Dad in future and his level of silliness. I wonder if Miss Redman thought up the saying 'Silly Billy'. I bet she wouldn't have told Wild West Outlaw Billy the Kid that he had a silly little boy's name. Thinking about it, she probably would have done – then got a slug right between the eyes from his Colt 45 for her audacity. (A bullet, that is, not the squidgy garden pest variety.) Although, to call something a pest just because it's trying to survive, like the rest of us, seems a little unfair to me.

I was unfamiliar with my new name and for a while had problems with its spelling. I tended to leave the second 'i' out making it Willam instead of William. Much to the amusement of various teachers who seemed to take great pleasure in mocking my mistake and then sharing it with the rest of my classmates. I wish I'd come up with the idea of calling myself 'Will I Am'. How cool is that! Mind you, in those days, most people would definitely have thought you had a couple of screws loose just for suggesting such a ludicrous idea.

I wasn't very keen on Miss Redman. In truth, I found her quite terrifying, as did most of the other children. She was a small, stout woman, usually dressed in red outfits of a similar design to those that the Queen wears. Her very presence would strike fear into the heart of even the most rebellious child, and in all probability contributed to many an over-stimulated bladder. Miss Redman, that is, not the Queen. It's probably quite nerve racking being in the presence of the Queen, but in a nice way. I would put being in the presence of Miss Redman on an emotional par with being in the same room as the Child Catcher from the 1968 musical *Chitty Chitty Bang Bang*. As he, too, was an extremely scary character who without a doubt was the star of many a child's nightmare.

A firm believer in strict discipline, Miss Redman possessed a stick. A bamboo cane, to be more precise. Which probably wouldn't have caused any great concern to you if you were a panda, mountain gorilla, lemur, or bamboo rat. Indeed, you would no doubt be quite pleased and get very excited with the prospect of this edible treat being waved in front of you. It was, however, rather unnerving to us tender-skinned young children, bearing in mind the use we knew it to have.

I didn't ever experience the wrath of Miss Redman and her pain-inflicting companion personally. After all, I wasn't bad, I was just a silly little boy with the wrong name who couldn't spell, remember his times tables, and whose socks weren't quite up to the job they were designed for. I did, however, hear from a number of very reliable sources who were unable to sit down comfortably for many days after a disciplinary encounter with Miss Redman and her sturdy accomplice, that it was rather a painful experience and one that they would all do their very best to avoid repeating in future. A statement that may suggest to some that corporal punishment works. But like many, I tend to prefer the withdrawal of privileges as a method of disciplinary action. Admittedly, I had resorted to violence myself to deal with the bullies. However, I believe violence as an act of self-defence far more justified and more to do with survival, than violence as a form of discipline, which often does little more than gratify the desires of sadists.

Apparently, bamboo has a higher comprehensive strength than wood, brick, or concrete, and a tensile strength that rivals steel. Ouch! And double ouch! I'd like to think, as it was more the way of things back then, that when dishing out punishments to her extended family – rather than to satisfy any sadistic tendencies – Miss Redman only had our best interests at heart and a desire to see us all grow into thoughtful, well-adjusted adults with a healthy respect for authority. Especially, if that authority has a big stick. She was probably a real softy at heart.

Beam Me Up, Scotty

My best memories of primary school were definitely out of the classroom rather than in it. My favourites being P.E. and games. I wasn't very good at football, which was a shame because that was generally what we did in games. It was still better than doing classwork though. I can't remember what the girls did in games, apart from the fact that there always seemed to be a great deal of bean bags flying around. Not the large ones you sit on. That would certainly have been an entertaining games lesson! These were small ones about the size of a slice of bread.

My hankering for a Wolverhampton Wanderers football kit was admittedly less from a supporter's perspective, and more for the fact that it was gold with black edging around the neck and sleeves. The design and colour of the top closely resembled the uniform sported by Captain Kirk and his crew on the Starship Enterprise. A pure gem for any young boy's dressing-up box back in the seventies. Before I upset any Trekkies, I know they wore a selection of other colours as well, but it was the gold and black that really did it for me. For reasons unbeknown to myself I ended up with a Crystal Palace kit. A team I hadn't even heard of prior to walking into the shop, not being much of a football fan. The Crystal Palace kit, to be honest (and this is no disrespect to Crystal Palace Football Club or its fans), even though quite striking in artistic design, would just not have looked right 'boldly going where no man had gone before'. It just wouldn't. It would have given all alien life forms encountered a totally confusing first impression about our species' dress sense. The plain but smart gold and black of the Wolverhampton Wanderers kit was by far the better choice for intergalactic exploration, without a doubt.

The playing field for our games lessons was about a ten-minute walk from the school. Double that for the stragglers (not stranglers as my spell check is telling me). I think that might have held us up for slightly longer and involved a rather lengthy police investigation, no doubt leading to games being cancelled. Add another five minutes onto the journey because we were made to walk to the playing fields along the pavements in our studded football boots, which although making an impressive amount of noise like an army on the march, delighting our little male ears, was extremely difficult. Traction was rather haphazard to say the least, with more injuries being incurred during the journey there and back than we ever sustained on the field.

I live in hope that the karma effect is a real phenomenon and the person or persons responsible for making us undertake that perilous journey every week, are now reaping what they sowed and are having to negotiate slippery laminated flooring when venturing around their nursing homes wearing inappropriate footwear. A wicked thought, I know, but definitely justified. Unfortunately, merely having such negative thoughts, I may now in turn suffer from the same karma effect myself. Oh well, it'll be worth it!

Generally, I would say I had a fairly normal and happy childhood. Getting up to the usual things that children should and sometimes shouldn't get up to. There were minimal trips to the local A & E department. Once when I knocked myself out after running into a tree head on, I was kept in overnight for observation. Luckily, they didn't observe anything untoward and I was promptly discharged the next day without the need for any further treatment. They obviously weren't observing very closely! Then there was the time I ran into a barbed-wire fence and cut my face requiring several stitches, got a nail stuck in my hand, and was bitten on the arm by an Alsatian dog. I should add that these were all on separate occasions and not on one particularly disastrous day.

A Little Imagination Goes a Long Way

Like most children, I enjoyed television immensely and there was an abundance of captivating viewing on in the seventies. At least we thought so at the time. I've always loved the old classic slapstick stuff like Charlie Chaplin, Laurel and Hardy, and Abbott and Costello. You just can't beat a good laugh. It really is the best tonic and therapy for all ages. The list of programmes over the years that enthralled my generation would take absolutely forever to go through. Favourite comedy sitcoms, game shows, variety shows, and non-stop action. In the sci-fi genre, Dr Who and his universe-conquering, planet-destroying adversaries were generally watched at a safe distance from behind the sofa. And I doubt I was the only one observing it from that vantage point. The Robinson family were lost in space with the moaning and extremely sneaky Dr Zachary Smith and Robby the Robot, while Captain Kirk, in his Wolverhampton Wanderers football kit, was on the Starship Enterprise, constantly having problems with Klingons, despite advice from Doc McCoy, aka Bones, to eat more roughage. Scotty, the Starship's engineer always seemed to be having difficulty maintaining full thrust, but the less said about that the better. There was always a logical explanation for everything, according to Mr Spock.

Westerns like *The Virginian, Bonanza, The High Chaparral* and *Alias Smith and Jones*, were watched in suitable cowboy attire whilst sat astride the arm of an armchair representing my trusty steed. Various costumes required for role-play activities were designed and made by the very talented and resident costume artist – Mum. My cowboy outfit which also doubled as a Native American Indian outfit, depending on accompanying props, e.g., feather headdress and tomahawk or cowboy hat and gun with holster, looked fantastic. The only problem was that the imitation-leather material Mum had used for the trousers, complete with fringes down the sides, was a touch too thick and didn't allow my legs to bend at the knees very well. This limited my mobility somewhat during play and prompted sympathetic looks from the neighbours who I think thought I had some sort of disability. At least I looked the part when stationary.

Mum really excelled herself when she had to come up with the goods for my Jacques Cousteau marine biologist and explorer-of-the-deep costume. This required a little more imagination from the wardrobe department, but as always Mum came up trumps. Pink Marigold washing-up gloves on my feet for flippers, an empty washing-up liquid bottle strapped to my back with string for the oxygen bottle, and my blue woollen balaclava completing the intrepid diver's ensemble perfectly. I'm not sure Mr Cousteau would have worn inflatable armbands, but I wasn't taking any unnecessary risks in the murky, cat-infested waters of our living room.

Simon Templar, aka *The Saint*, played by Roger Moore, was one of my heroes. When Mum cut my hair, which was always an emotional experience for me, the only way I would allow her to do it was if she promised to make me look like the Saint. With a knowing, yet slightly nervous smile, she would always do her best. And while my hair was wet it was quite a close representation of my hero's own hairstyle. Unfortunately, as soon as it dried it would revert back to its natural, very curly state, which was far from Mr Templar's suave look and more like one of the Jackson Five.

Thank Heavens for the Weekends

The anticipation of Saturday-morning television was without a doubt what got me through the drudgery of a saggy-socked, distracted and unmemorable school week. In 1974, the greatest ever children's programme was born, changing the lives of millions forever. I don't think I'm mistaken either, by saying that a great many adults looked forward to it just as much as the younger generation. Its rather long title, *Today is Saturday, Watch and Smile*, was shortened to *TISWAS*, and it was the start of a revolution in children's entertainment as we knew it. It was organised chaos, madness and mayhem, with lashings of slapstick and hilarious ad-libbing at its very best.

The various presenters over the years included Chris Tarrant, John Asher, and the lovely Sally James. From what I gather, Miss James developed quite a following with the dads and the armed forces viewers. I suspect it may have had something to do with her regular appearances in her black thigh-length boots, which I can only presume were part of her pantomime attire. A very young Lenny Henry was a regular on the programme, doing impressions of various celebrities such as newsreader Trevor McDonald (the *TISWAS* character, comically known as Trevor McDoughnut), and botanist David Bellamy in Compost Corner. Bob Carolgees with his cunningly orchestrated puppet Spit the Dog which sat on an imitation arm, if nothing else, added copious amounts of spraying saliva to the show. As if they needed any more fluid-based humour.

TISWAS gave birth to such greats as the Phantom Flan Flinger, with custard pies and flans flying in all directions. No one was safe and no mercy shown, however famous you might have been. Buckets of gunge and water were never in short supply, especially in the direction of the cage which usually held various parents of young viewers, and invariably a few celebrity guests. The Four Bucketeers sang the 'Bucket of Water Song', and the 'Dance of the Dying Fly' caused sprains and muscle pulls nationwide among the less fit and flexible. It was absolutely brilliant!

If I had a time machine, I think my first stop would definitely have to be back to the time of *TISWAS*, to meet the characters as they were then, and to experience some of that fabulous, unbridled mayhem myself. Once I'd tried to help with as many important global issues as I could, of course.

My memories of the music scene in the early seventies are dominated by glam rock and bands like Slade, Mud, Sweet, Wizard,

T-Rex, Queen, and of course Mr Bowie. If nothing else, as well as a period of rather over-the-top and extremely glittery outfits, humongous shoulder pads and dodgy platform boots – and that was just the public – glam rock has at least left us with some great classic Christmas songs which traditionally alert us of the approaching festive season. And they will probably continue to do so for many generations to come. Whether they like it or not!

Trouble at t'Mill

It was in the mid-seventies that I realised things were not all they should have been at home between Mum and Dad. I would spend what seemed like an eternity sitting on the stairs listening to the verbal tennis match of articulated abuse. It became even more unpleasant when they wouldn't even be in the same room as each other. Having said that, there were obvious benefits to that arrangement. The dining room was allocated as Dad's living space, as well as him being redeployed to the small single bedroom. Mum retained use of the original front room as her space and remained in the larger double bedroom. The toilet and bathroom were fairly straightforward locations, only causing a few choice words from the other party wanting to use it if it was occupied. As it does in any household. The kitchen was probably the most problematic area.

Not wanting to upset either one of my parents by being in the other one's allocated section of the house and seemingly displaying any favouritism, I would retreat to neutral ground and take up my position on the stairs. It seemed the safest bet. It certainly wasn't the nicest of times in my family's history, that's for sure.

An Invitation to the White House

In 1974, my last year of primary school, instead of moving up to Class 1, which would normally have been the natural progression from Class 2, a small group of us – all boys – yours truly being one of them, did not. We were instead exiled, for want of a better word, into the little white house located next to the school, and called Class 2b. 2b or not 2b, that was the question. The answer is still not entirely clear to me to this day. Miss Redman's office was also located in the little white house, directly above our classroom. Weren't we the lucky ones!

The school secretary occupied the school office which was the room next to ours on the ground floor. Listening to her tapping away endlessly the whole day, every day, on her clattery typewriter that dinged every time she got to the end of a line, it soon became clear to us in Class 2b why Quasimodo was always so agitated. And no, he wasn't one of Class 1's rejects like the rest of us; I am of course referring to the character from *The Hunchback of Notre Dame*, written by Victor Hugo in 1831. There were also a few film adaptations, even a Disney animation. Like Quasimodo, we had also become outcasts plagued by the sound of the bells.

So, there we were, seven or eight of us if I remember correctly, and Mr Wise our teacher in his corduroy jacket with leather elbow pads and his pudding-basin haircut. Nice and cosy in our little classroom that was obviously once someone's cosy little living room, in the little white house next door to the school. Between you, me and the school gatepost, I'm not convinced our segregation was for our benefit. I'm inclined to believe it was more to do with getting us out of the way in order not to hinder the progress of our peers, rather than improve our prospects in life in any way. I certainly don't recall any particular effort being made to help us with our academic shortfalls. If anything, exactly the opposite seemed to be the case. Lessons became remarkably easy and even less memorable. At the time I suppose we all just thought we weren't as good as those that moved up to Class 1, because that's exactly how we were made to feel. Do I care? Am I bitter? Not really. More saddened. After all, we weren't bad or unruly – just not as clever – allegedly – and we deserved better.

My seat in Class 2b was positioned next to the window and provided me with an endless supply of distractions from the outside world for my already limited attention span. Even worse, it provided me with a perfect view of the pottery room just across the hallway of the little white house. At that point in my life one of my greatest ambitions, apart from appearing on *TISWAS* of course, was to experience the joy of creating a masterpiece on a potter's wheel. To mould a shapeless lump of clay into a work of art, have it fired in the kiln, paint it, glaze it, and then take it home and present it proudly to my parents. Although, I would probably have to make them one each to go in their allocated living space.

Heroes at Heart

Little did we know back then in Class 2b, that in our midst was a future hero of our great nation. A rather quiet and unassuming blonde-haired boy, in his NHS glasses complete with misty glass and a plaster holding one arm on (the arm of his glasses, not his limb). His name was Michael Edwards, otherwise known as Eddie, and in 1988, he represented Great Britain in the Winter Olympics in Canada in the ski jumping, earning himself the nickname 'Eddie the Eagle'. It was the same year the Jamaicans entered the bobsleigh event. Like Eddie, they won the hearts of the watching world who always love to see the underdog do well. Or at least, giving it all they've got. Admittedly, Eddie and the Jamaicans didn't win, but they were definitely the real heroes of the games for many that year.

It just goes to show, if you want something, you've got to go for it, and give it your best shot.

It's better to fail trying than not to try at all, as they say. Something I would tend to agree with, even if I don't always apply it to my own life. Mainly through lack of self-confidence. It's never pleasant to fail at anything, but the regret of never having tried will stay with you for a very long time.

I too, was fairly sporty, particularly in the sprinting department. I didn't quite reach the same speeds as the Jamaican bobsleigh team or the heights as Eddie, but I did win a few colourful ribbons for my speedy exploits. In my last year at primary school, I won the 100-metre sprint and the hurdles, and was thus presented the coveted 'Drinkwater Low Challenge Cup' as overall winner. I did a lap of honour around the track, but by then most of the other children and their parents had already left. I suppose they weren't really interested in someone else's child's achievements. I didn't care – I was on a high and Dad was there as usual to cheer me on as he always was, and that's what really mattered. I even made it into the local newspaper, the *Gloucestershire Echo*. Not quite front page, but it was in big bold letters. '**WILLIAM MAKES IT A DOUBLE**'... Damn you, Miss Redman!

Unfortunately, my last year at primary school in Class 2b was not the most productive academically. Most disappointingly, I never did get to grapple, spin, or shape the tiniest smidgen of clay into anything I could proudly present to my parents that might have taken pride of place in a location of their choosing. I was destined only to witness the joy of others where the art of pottery was concerned, from my perfectly positioned vantage point in Class 2b. If this was a film, a violin would surely be playing a sorrowful tune in the background at this point. I did however leave on a high, victorious on the sports field and my name in print. So, it wasn't all doom and gloom.

Secondary Thoughts

In 1975, a new chapter in my life began when I started secondary school. To be honest, my parents and I were surprised I was accepted by the one that I was. I'm inclined to believe my successful application may have been due more to my sporting success, rather than my academic achievements. If that outcome was at all possible. They seemed very keen on winning – as the trophy cabinet opposite the headmaster's office clearly indicated. Perhaps they thought I might be able to contribute in some way in adding a few more trophies to their collection. I'm not complaining. It enabled me to attend a decent secondary school and discover a multitude of new sports which I enjoyed and was quite good at. My speculation involving my acceptance may of course be completely wrong and more than a little arrogant on my part. I was the only one from my primary school to attend that particular secondary school, which I did think a bit odd at the time. I'm fairly sure it wasn't due to any conspiracy by my peers or their parents to avoid me. At least, I hoped not.

No longer did there seem to be any confusion about my name. We were addressed by our surnames. I was Wood or Woody to the teachers, and Billy once again, without shame, to my schoolmates. I continued to struggle in the classroom whatever I was called, preferring as I did at primary school to be on the running track or playing field. Rugby was part of my new sporting curriculum and I loved every minute of the gladiatorial contact. My geography teacher Mr Evans, who was Welsh, was a fanatical rugby fan and probably in a local choir with his bellowing baritone voice. Not that I'm being stereotypical in any way. So concerned was Mr Evans for my position on the rugby team, that he abolished the burden of my geography homework so it didn't interfere with practice sessions. During lesson time, to build up my fitness and speed, he would send me on errands around the school and time me. I thought it was brilliant at the time. Authorised to run around the school! Even 007 doesn't have a licence to do that. Unfortunately, my knowledge of all things related to geography suffered greatly and leaves a great deal to be desired to this day.

Then tragedy struck. I developed severe pains in my knees and hips. Just going up or down stairs the pain would be so excruciating that it would bring tears to my eyes. In an attempt to find out what might be causing me such pain, I attended various specialist hospitals, two of which were in London. Yet the experts were unable to shed any light on the problem. Growing pains seemed to be the most popular opinion suggested by various perplexed consultants staring intently at my legs while stroking their chins. The medical advice given to me was to stop doing sports and to hope things eventually got better. Which is exactly what I did!

Life became a great deal less energetic, in and out of school, and suddenly I had to try and catch up with all the geography I had missed out on. Not something I was relishing. I was no longer Mr Evans's star pupil. My privileges and celebrity-like status had now been withdrawn, and I had an exam to pass. My life changed quite dramatically. But little did I know that an even more dramatic change in my life was looming on the not too distant horizon.

The Looming Horizon

The atmosphere at home had become much worse and divorce proceedings between Mum and Dad ensued. For me, the custody battles for yours truly became bum-numbing, spending hours on end sitting on hard wooden benches in cold draughty corridors, within various legal buildings in Cheltenham and Gloucester.

Visits to my sister, Lesley, who now lived in Hampstead, London, as a live-in nanny, became a regular weekend occurrence. Dad would put me on the coach in Cheltenham on the Friday afternoon and Lesley would meet me at Victoria coach station in London, despatching me from Victoria on the Sunday evening for the return journey. My trips to London were a welcome distraction from the emotional battlefields of Cheltenham and I looked forward to them immensely. The journey itself was not so keenly anticipated. Suffering as I did from travel sickness, I usually arrived in London clutching a squidgy bag of sick, my poor travelling companions having had to endure the zesty fragrance of the ejected matter from my stomach, for most of the two-and-a-half-hour journey.

Once recovered from the trauma of the journey, I loved my weekend breaks with my sister, her dog, Max (who was half beagle and half something else), and the two little girls that she looked after, Bibi aged three and Ninka aged two. Over time, with the frequency of my visits and the amount of time the girls and I spent together, they became more like little sisters to me. Lesley and the girls and I would take Max for walks over Hampstead Heath and then go to the '31'-flavour ice-cream parlour. There were flavours I'd never even heard of and you could have hot fudge poured over your crushed nuts. Which was a whole new experience for me, I can tell you.

Mum eventually won the war of custody battles and moved out of the family home, taking me with her. It wasn't that I didn't want to be with Dad, and I did feel sorry for him. It just seemed that being with Mum was how it should be. Which evidently, was also the court's conclusion.

Mum and I wandered the streets of Cheltenham, suitcases in hand, and ended up staying with some friends of hers. The makeshift sleeping arrangements of cushions on the floor for Mum and an extremely uncomfortable and smelly army surplus camp bed for me didn't exactly promote restful sleep, but we really weren't in a position to complain. As kind and understanding as Mum's friends were, it wasn't long before we had clearly outstayed our welcome and it was time to find alternative accommodation, so we moved into a local bedsit. The room we shared in the terraced property advertised as central to local amenities, was bleak and basic and would have made Harry Potter's under-the-stairs living quarters seem positively spacious. Having said that, the sleeping arrangements were slightly more conducive to actually getting some sleep, and there are probably many experiences in life that are far worse than having to share a bunk bed with your mother. On the other hand, it's hardly a barrel of laughs either and not particularly something you would want broadcasted to the world. Whoops! Too late.

Viva Espana

In the summer of '77, I was invited to go to Spain for the whole of the six-week summer holiday, with Lesley, Bibi and Ninka, and their parents, Barbara and Henri (pronounced 'Onri'). It was my first trip abroad, and on an aeroplane. When we arrived in Spain, I was amazed at how hot it was. I'd never experienced heat like it. Even in the great heatwave of '76, when we were allowed to take our shirts off at school in break time. Only the boys, unfortunately! It seems absurd really when you think about it. We should have been protecting ourselves against the sun's harsh rays, not exposing our young lily-white bodies to them. It was a gentler type of heat in Spain. Even though it was more intense it seemed to caress and relax you rather than make you uncomfortable and sweaty.

We ate paella that was cooked on the beach in an enormous dish by a man called Manuel. Or was it Pepe? Actually, it was Miguel, Pepe was the taxi driver – or was that Pedro? I also got tipsy for the second time in my life, at one of the restaurants on the beach. Sangria is a very deceptively safe and healthy looking drink with all that fruit bobbing about. Deceptive being the operative word. The first time I was affected by the age-old art of the fermentation process, was when I was eleven and a half and drank Pomagne at a girl's birthday party who was in my class at school. The less said about that, the better.

While we were in Spain, Lesley and I had Spanish lessons from Jim. Jim was an Englishman but spoke the lingo like a native, having apparently lived there for a number of years. Jim was almost always inebriated, but he was a good teacher and made it lots of fun. Perhaps, because he was inebriated. Lesley and I became quite accomplished at a basic level. At least slightly more advanced than the please and thank you stage. Not that there's anything wrong with just being able to say please and thank you. I'm sure any nation appreciates please and thank you from its foreign visitors. That little bit of extra effort, mind you, can be quite rewarding and achieve a little more favour among the locals for your endeavours.

I would check my tan line daily in the bathroom mirror. My whiter than white bottom a clear indicator against the ever-darkening line above my shorts as to its progress. I also learnt the hard way not to wear cut-off jeans in the sea. When they dry in the sun they stiffen until they have the texture of a course grade sandpaper. That was one of the longest and most excruciating treks back from the beach, ever. I developed a rather interesting walking technique in order to try and avoid my testicles making contact with the very course denim material intent on altering my gender status. It looked like I was riding an invisible donkey. By the time we got back to the house my poor testicles were red raw and glowing like a pair of Christmas-tree baubles.

Bibi and Ninka's parents, Barbara and Henri, took me to a bull fight. It was the cruellest thing I had ever witnessed and made me deeply ashamed of my species, and for being there to watch the barbaric spectacle myself. During the more leisurely periods of the holiday, I also read the first book I'd ever read without any coercing or adult intimidation. Unfortunately, it was *Jaws*. Not the best choice of reading material on a holiday by the sea. The rest of the holiday was filled with frantic moments of pure panic as I repeatedly exited the water at speeds not often witnessed or exhibited by our species in the medium of H_2O, every time I saw a shadow or something move in the sea beneath me. My fellow beach revellers must have thought I was in training for a new Olympic swimming event, or completely mad.

I purchased the compulsory gifts for family back home: the miniature straw donkey with hat, a miniature flamenco guitar, a pair of decorative wooden maracas, and a very elegant fan with a picture of a lady flamenco dancer on it. Oh, I nearly forgot, Elvis Presley died while we were there and Lesley got very upset in the Spanish newsagents. It was brilliant. Not Elvis dying, of course, or Lesley getting upset – I mean, the holiday in general. Apart from the testicle episode, that is. Another valuable lesson learnt the hard way.

A Whole New World

On our return to England, I was surprised to find Mum at Lesley's flat in London. It was then that I was informed we would not be returning to Cheltenham, but staying in London. Seemingly, it had been agreed between Lesley and Mum, and Barbara and Henri, prior to the holiday, that Mum and I would stay with Lesley on our return until we could find accommodation of our own.

Mum wanted a fresh start and to be nearer to Lesley. I don't remember having any objections at the time to the arrangement, or living in London. It would be nice to see more of my sister, and I still had quite a few more flavours to try at the '31'-flavour ice-cream parlour. Except pistachio, because I didn't have a clue what it was but didn't want to appear stupid by asking and broadcasting my ignorance on the matter.

It was strange to be starting a new life in London. I hadn't said goodbye to any of my friends back in Cheltenham, sorted out any of my belongings, or officially left my old school. Nevertheless, in only two days I would be attending a completely new school in London I knew absolutely nothing about.

In the following weeks, Mum attempted to find a job which would include accommodation, such as a nanny or housekeeper, but unfortunately those types of jobs don't usually cater for a single mum and her offspring. Eventually, after quite a few interviews and feeling a bit disheartened but desperately needing to find work, she accepted a job as a nanny without accommodation, in the hope that something else might come along in the near future.

We'd only been staying with Lesley a few months when she told us she was thinking of moving on to pastures new. Bibi and Ninka seemed to like Mum, and she got on well with Barbara and Henri. Mum already helped out a lot with the children and other duties around the house, so the solution to Barbara and Henri's problem of replacing Lesley, and Mum's search for employment with accommodation for her and me, seemed obvious. And so it was.

The transition, when it came, couldn't have been simpler. Everyone was happy and finally I had a room of my own instead of having to sleep in the girls' old bunk bed in Lesley's hallway. Which was now our hallway. Result.

Yankee Doodle Dandy

My secondary school in London was worlds apart from what I'd been accustomed to back in Cheltenham. I'd been used to a very strict uniform dress code and almost regimental discipline. In my new school the discipline was a great deal less noticeable. Punk rockers, Teddy boys, skinheads, and ethnic-based gangs menacingly roamed the corridors and school grounds, in whatever dress code they were required to wear to fit into that particular group. Admittedly, it wasn't quite the Bronx, but it was quite a radical culture shock from what I'd been used to. I'd only known one black person in my secondary school back in Cheltenham. Although, using the word 'known' might be a bit misleading and a slight overstatement. I'd seen him on several occasions around school, and competed a number of times against him on the running track. I knew very little about other cultures, especially if it was something that had been taught in one of Mr Evans's geography lessons. In my new school in London, every colour, nationality, and religion on the planet seemed to be represented.

Break times consisted of a mass exodus to the local corner shop to purchase cigarettes from the considerate Asian proprietor who very kindly sold them individually to suit our adolescent, financial limitations. My new schoolmates were convinced I was American, mistaking my Gloucestershire twang for an American accent. And who was I to correct them and spoil their illusion? I liked being a bit more interesting. I think the brown and cream striped flares I used to wear that Mum had acquired from the charity shop, may have helped to complete my transatlantic impersonation somewhat. A bargain not to be missed, according to Mum. In comparison to the drainpipes and straight-cut trousers worn by my peers, they definitely set me apart from the crowd.

It wasn't that we were hard up when I was younger. At least not when Mum and Dad were together. Even so, Mum would acquire an abundance of our clothes and other items from various charity outlets. For her it was more about the hunt for that elusive bargain, the thrill of the chase, and then in for the kill. Some of the clothes were even quite fashionable. Only not usually in the year I was wearing them! It didn't matter so much when I was younger; fashion was but a far distant burden yet to be weighed on my, so far, rather narrow shoulders. It wasn't really until my move to London that such things began to concern me and I started to get more influenced by those around me and the society I was growing up in, coinciding with my own identity and self-awareness stage of development, presumably.

Apart from my unfashionable and slightly eccentric attire, I also used to wear a wild boar's tooth around my neck which I'd purchased on my Spanish adventure. One of my classmates convinced of its origin, told everyone it was a shark's tooth. Not wanting to belittle him in front of the rest of the class, I kept quiet. I was getting more exotic by the minute.

Like primary school, football was the only activity that seemed to be on offer during games lessons. Only it was played on the school's tarmac playground instead of a nice green field. I managed to score three goals in the first match I played in. Unfortunately, they were all own goals. In one crushing blow, my popularity plummeted and my newly gained exotic image crumbled into dust. The teachers didn't seem to care very much if you turned up for games or not, and as I was still getting the so-called growing pains in my legs, one letter from Mum excused me from games for the rest of my time at secondary school without any further questions or investigations.

Students actually turning up to lessons and leaving without anything untoward happening between the entry and exit point, was definitely the main objective of most of the teachers. Anything learnt during the lesson, even by accident, was probably considered a bonus and cause for boastful celebration in the staff room.

As with my time in Class 2b at primary school, copious amounts of the day seemed to be spent staring out of classroom windows. Of which there were many, within the mountainous concrete, multistorey, educational complex. I yearned to be a passenger in one of the endless streams of passing vehicles which I watched so intently, heading anywhere but where I was at that particular moment in time. The demand for views of the outside world was far less of a necessity during engineering, woodwork or science lessons. Not so much due to them being more interesting, even if they were, or the desire for educational advancement. It was generally advisable to pay more attention in order to avoid serious injury caused either by the lack of concentration, or a fellow classmate.

Although living in London was a very different experience from my weekend visits to London, the same couldn't be said of the coach journey to visit Dad in Cheltenham. The journey in reverse did nothing to alleviate the sickness I experienced whilst travelling, and most of the time I would arrive at my destination with more bags than I left with, my additional baggage containing the ejected fragrant matter from my stomach, fastidiously contained over the duration of the journey. On the plus side, my parents living such a distance apart helped me to experience a more positive relationship with them both, and as a result (all vomiting aside) these visits were something I would look forward to.

INTO THE BIG, BAD WORLD

School in London certainly was an education, but not so much in the academic sense of the word. Nevertheless, I managed to survive relatively unscathed. At least physically. And looking back on it, which I do on occasions, it was probably more of a positive life experience than a negative one. On reflection, I do wish I'd paid more attention, tried harder, and not been so easily distracted. If I learnt anything important during my school years, it was the advantages of wearing long trousers. Not only are they much warmer in winter and give more protection when falling over, people have no way of knowing whether your socks are up or down, rendering them unable to comment on whether you may need to pull them up or not.

In 1980, I left school and was unleashed into the slow lane of the rat race. I had decided to accept the offer of full-time employment at the garage where I was already working part-time after school as a trainee mechanic. It seemed to make sense and I enjoyed the work. Also, it didn't rely on my academic achievements on leaving school. Which was just as well, because they weren't very impressive.

With the pressure off to do well in my exams, when I arrived at my engineering exam to hand in representative pieces of my year's work only to discover they had locked together and could not be prized apart, instead of panicking which would have normally been my immediate response in such a situation – as it would for any examinee, I'm sure – I did not. In fact, I was unnaturally calm. It was quite a liberating experience. Without any hint of shame or embarrassment, I calmly handed over the toast rack and spiked receipt holder that were now locked together in what appeared to be a rather permanent embrace, as one piece of modern art. The teacher was not amused and the expression on his face, which will forever be imprinted on my mind, was priceless. Well worth any negative aspects in the marking process that was inevitably to follow due to my devil-may-care attitude. 'I cared not a jot', as Mr Billy Connolly, grandmaster and connoisseur of observational humour would say.

At seventeen I purchased my first motorcycle. A Yamaha DT 250. Which was the start of a long and mostly happy love of the two-wheeled motorised variety of transportation. One summer during my holiday break from the garage, I worked as a motorcycle courier to earn a bit of extra cash. It wasn't easy work but I enjoyed it and was getting paid for what I loved doing most. Well, next to the other obvious thing a red-blooded nineteen-year-old male loves doing, that is. But I don't think I was well enough equipped to do that for a living.

Doing the courier work got me thinking. To be honest, I was getting fed up with smelling of oil and having permanently filthy oil-engrained hands and fingernails, lying on cold, dirty, wet floors, getting rust in my eyes, and scraping the skin off my knuckles. So, it wasn't the hardest of decisions to make the career change, and off I rode into the sunset, leaving the oil and rust behind me.

Britain's Most Wanted

In 1982, Mum decided, for whatever reason, that it was time for a change for herself, and she applied for the position of manager at a branch of a local funeral directors, not far from where we were living in Hampstead. The position included accommodation, which, of course, if she left the employment of Barbara and Henri, she and I would require, as I was still living with her at the time. Mum was successful in her endeavours and was offered the post of manager of the Temple Fortune branch of Mortimer and Sons Funeral Directors. We were sad to be leaving the family. Barbara and Henri had been extremely kind to us, and we would miss Bibi and Ninka terribly. They really were more like family, and would always have a special place in our hearts no matter where we were.

The day of the big move came. One of Mum's friends, a stocky Jewish market purveyor of fruit and veg, with a broken nose, had kindly offered us the use of his transit van to move our belongings to our new home above the undertakers. Lesley drove the van, as I only had my motorcycle licence at the time, and she brought a man friend called Ben along to help with the heavy lifting. 'Bill and Ben Removals'. Very apt!

Everything was going fine until the final drop-off. We'd just taken the last few boxes up to the new flat and returned to the van, which was parked directly outside, when all of a sudden we were set upon by a considerable number of Her Majesty's constabulary and bundled into the back of a rather uncomfortable van decorated with particularly flamboyant go-faster stripes on the sides and blue lights on top. Lesley, Ben and I, were promptly taken to the local police station and put into a cell like we were Britain's most wanted. Three hours later a certain fruit and veg purveyor with a broken nose turned up at the police station, the police curious to hear his explanation of why the tax disc displayed on the windscreen of the van he had lent us was not for that vehicle. Three hours in a cell for that. Words fail me. Actually, they didn't.

Ordeal over, but still in disbelief of the whole incident and having run out of derogatory names to describe Mum's friend between the three of us, we joined Mum back at the flat above the undertakers in need of a good, stiff drink. If you'll pardon the expression.

Things That Go Bump in the Night

Call me naive if you will, and most of you probably will. When Mum got the job at the undertakers, I envisaged her duties would entail sitting in a cosy little office arranging funerals. It didn't occur to me that there would actually be any of the dearly departed residing on the premises.

The first night in my new room, I had a ghoulish nightmare. Zombie-like arms were crashing through the plaster of the walls, ceiling and floor, frenziedly trying to grab me. I awoke startled, in a cold sweat, my heart pounding, my brain probably having arranged the overnight entertainment due to over-active thoughts of dead bodies the previous day.

I didn't ever really feel that comfortable with our motionless guests in their coffins downstairs. In reality, I found it quite unnerving and rather creepy, as most people would, I'm sure. Mum didn't seem fazed at all by the bodies, which was just as well considering how much contact with them she actually had. She always used to say, 'It's the living you have to watch out for, Billy, not the dead'. I knew what she meant, but I wasn't totally convinced about the dead's lack of interest in us from the other side of life's veil.

Being close to a dead person is a very strange experience. They look like they're just sleeping, but obviously they're not. The essence of life is noticeably missing. There is a clear sense that something that was once there, is now very absent. When people I met discovered where I lived, most were intrigued and quite curious. They would want to know all about the bodies. 'Is it true that they can sit up and groan?' 'Had I ever seen a ghost?' That morbid fascination for death and the unknown. A few people were quite freaked out by it and would never be seen again. Particularly disappointing if they were a prospective girlfriend being wooed.

My motorcycle lived in the backyard of the undertakers, and to get to it I had to go past the chapels of rest which often had open coffins visible through the gaps in the curtains. More often than not, I would choose to go the long way around the front of the buildings to avoid our sleep-imitating guests. Especially, if it was late at night. I often felt like I was being watched. It was quite eerie. Cold chills would make the hairs on the back of my neck stand on end. Perhaps it was just my over-imaginative mind. Perhaps not. The atmospheric lighting and dancing shadows from the flickering candles surrounding the lifeless forms certainly didn't do much to subdue my lively imagination.

I used to get the same feelings when we visited my nan in Bristol (on Mum's side of the family), when I was a young boy. Not that Nan was eerie in any way – it was the spooky old building she lived at the top of that gave me the creeps. I used to feel like I was being watched there, too, and I would run up the several flights of stairs that led to

Nan's flat as fast as my pale, skinny legs would carry me. That really didn't help though, because then I felt like I was being chased, which scared the human waste product out of me. It wasn't until many years later that I found out Nan's flat was above a spiritualist church and that she was the live-in caretaker and cleaner. Makes you wonder!

Life's Lost Loves

I'd had a few romantic encounters as a young adult, though I would obviously have been much luckier at cards, because lucky in love, I was not. They say, 'It's better to have loved and lost, than never to have loved at all'. Personally, I'm not convinced, having experienced the pain of lost love on numerous occasions, and seriously question the composer of the famous saying's experience of love and the torment of having had it and then lost it. (Tennyson, I believe.)

In 1983, I met Emma. Part of the same group of friends, during the laughter and occasionally a few tears that are inevitable as we share the lives of others, Emma and I grew closer. She was beautiful, angelic, thoughtful, funny and kind, and it wasn't long before she had completely captured my heart. Certain that she was my soul mate and the one for me, I asked her to marry me at a flower festival in Liverpool. I was a motorcycle courier for a firm of solicitors at the time and it was the company's summer outing for the employees, plus one guest each. Who says the art of romance is dead? I was twenty, she was nineteen, and her parents were far from pleased about the idea of our marital union. After diplomatic negotiations in support of young love, during a meal at Emma's home with her parents, silver-tongued Mum was able to talk them around to the idea and paved the way for the event to proceed.

And so it was, that in the December of '84, after a rather short and simple ceremony at Burnt Oak Registry Office in the London Borough of Barnet, declaring our love and commitment to each other's wellbeing and happiness, the registrar was, apparently, very pleased to pronounce me and Emma, husband and wife. As we rode off into the drizzle of that cold December afternoon on our motorcycle and sidecar, I have a vague idea as to what the thoughts of those that watched us may have been and their concern as to what the future may have held for us – but we were young and in love, and happy to be starting a new chapter in our lives, together.

Not the most ideal beginning to our marriage, Emma and I lived above the undertakers with Mum for a while, but a wife and a mother under the same roof was never going to be a recipe for wedded bliss. For the sake of everyone's sanity and before tensions reached a point beyond repair, Emma and I moved out and rented our first home together, a rather compact ground-floor flat in a converted semi in Finchley Central.

Over the next few years, I ventured into various forms of employment, none of which really seemed to be filling me with much fulfilment, or that paid that well. Most involved driving a vehicle of some description with a significant amount of urgency, under a great deal of stress. Obtaining my car licence had opened up a whole new world of possible employment, passing my test in '85, with the help of Trevor, a BSM driving instructor. Trevor was a budding musician who was only doing the driving instructing part-time until his musical talents were discovered in one of the various venues he regularly played in. Whether he ever did make it or not, I don't know, I've not seen or heard of him since – which might indicate he didn't, unless it was within the realms of one of the less contemporary styles of music you don't get to hear about so much unless you're actually involved in its production or listen to.

At the age of twenty-two I applied to join the London Fire Brigade. After an extremely lengthy selection process involving an exceedingly difficult written exam that I was immensely surprised to have passed, and after completing a rigorous medical and strength test which involved running about with one of the other candidates over my shoulders, disappointedly, at the final interview several months later, I was deemed unsuitable. Disheartened, I decided to try and get involved in a career incorporating one of my passions – weight training. Eagerly, I embarked on a home study course to gain the qualifications that would hopefully enable me to find work in the world of fitness. With the studying, on top of my existing knowledge and experience, after a couple of trips up to Bolton to sit the exams, my ambition soon became a reality when I was offered a part-time position as a gym instructor in a North London gymnasium.

To survive financially, I worked in the gym in the evenings and cooked meals in a pub in the earlier part of the day. The landlady prepared the main meals – the most complicated meal on the menu I was permitted to cook was omelette and chips. Personally, I was amazed I was given that much responsibility with my limited experience in culinary preparation and cooking. I can't think why I ever thought I would be suitable for the job in the first place, or why I even applied for it. When I was actually offered the job, I assumed I must have been the only applicant and they were desperate. If ever I had a natural talent for anything, it certainly wasn't cooking. On the other hand, I loved being a gym instructor, and even if I do say so myself, I think I was a damn good one. I was soon asked to join the team at the gym full-time and dropped the lunchtime job in the pub. Which was probably for the best, and I imagine quite a relief to most of the pub's regular patrons.

As a gym instructor, helping people to achieve their goals and feel better about themselves was exceptionally rewarding. I worked with and met some wonderful people and made some lifelong friends. Among them were some rather eccentric characters, not to mention a few celebrities. Well, maybe I'll mention a few.

Sean Bean, on the verge of stardom, wanted a workout that would give him the body of a 1920's boxer for a role he had been offered. A genuinely nice and very down-to-earth bloke, despite numerous theatrical roles on and off screen I don't think it was really until Sean's portrayal of Richard Sharpe, the maverick Napoleonic Wars' rifleman in the series *Sharpe*, that he became the household name that he is today. I also had the pleasure of training the lovely Melanie Hill who was married to Sean for several years. Now a very renowned actress, early in her career, Melanie played Hazel in *Auf Wiedersehen, Pet* and Avaline in the hit comedy *Bread*. Since then, she has had many other well-known and varied roles and is a very talented and accomplished actress.

Hugh Laurie, actor, author, comedian, director, musician and singer, was as entertaining off screen as he was on it. Another genuinely nice bloke, Hugh was also a fan of the two-wheeled mode of transportation like myself. His professional partner in crime at the time, Mr Steven Fry, actor, broadcaster, comedian, director and writer, seemed a much more private person and for whatever reason was much less regular in his attendance at the gym than Hugh.

One of the most eccentric characters of all, was a chap called Dave Lea. Martial arts expert, bodyguard to the famous, and actor, Dave became Michael Keaton's Batman stunt double in the new *Batman* films in the late eighties. Following his *Batman* success, he moved to Hollywood to work on a film with Sylvester Stallone. Still there to this day, fight choreographer and stunt co-ordinator to the stars, he's making a pretty good living, by all accounts.

The icing on the cake for me, however, has to be when the guys from the band Madness joined the gym; one of my favourite bands at the time. The icing on top of the icing on the cake, was getting to know Lee Thompson, the saxophonist, and nuttiest by far of the nutty boys and enjoying a tasty pint around Camden Town in the nutty fella's company. Who'd have believed it?

It was around that time, in my early twenties, that various people in certain circles started to call me Bill. I can't remember exactly when or why this transition was first initiated, but it certainly wasn't at my request. Perhaps Billy is just too much effort for some people, or they think it's a little boy's name. It may be that being called Bill is an indication of reaching a particular position of maturity. My family still called me Billy, and also people who knew me as Billy from my youth. I was also called William on the odd occasion and on various official documentation.

Unfortunately, as the years went by and the pressures and stresses of everyday mundane life took their toll, Emma and I seemed to grow apart. It appeared we wanted different things out of life, and what she wanted didn't include me. Although, apparently, 'It's better to have loved and lost, blah de blah de blah'.

'*C'est la vie*', as the French say. But what do they know? They don't even drive on the right side of the road. Well, they do, but it's the wrong side, isn't it!

DEJA VOUS

In 1993, Emma and I parted company and after a short spell in a rather dingy bedsit I felt the need for a change of scenery. I decided to return to my roots and head back to the idyllic rural county of Gloucestershire. I know the grass isn't always greener on the other side, but there was definitely much more of it there, that's for sure. So, with high hopes and minimal luggage – mainly due to the extremely limited carrying capacity of the bike – engine rattling and exhaust rumbling, I eagerly set off homeward bound.

I hadn't been travelling for long and was happily plodding along through Hampstead when an idiot in a white Porsche 911 decided to pull out from a side road at Whitestone Pond and abruptly terminated my journey a little earlier than I had planned. As I was trying to extract the twisted wreckage of my motorcycle from under the Porsche, Mr Porsche and another motorist, Jag man (who had pulled up to give his twopenny worth), were making absurd accusations about how the accident was completely my fault. They were both accusing me of riding much too fast – which I promise you, I wasn't. Things were looking decidedly grim. After all, who would believe me? A lowly biker against the respectable Mr Porsche and his new 'bosom buddy' Jag man. At that point in time, I had pretty much resigned myself to the fact that the situation was not going to go my way and was probably going to get much worse. Ever the pessimist!

Just in case you were concerned, I was fine and managed to come out of the accident relatively unscathed. A few minor rips and tears added some personality to my jeans which, thanks to George Michael and various other denim-clad celebrities at the time, were only going to make me more fashionable. Which was a first for me!

As Mr Porsche and Jag man continued their accusatory exchange, I became aware that two men, who were in the car behind the Porsche when it had pulled out into my path, had got out of their car and were now walking towards our little gathering in the middle of the road. I must admit, my immediate thoughts were not positive ones: more wise guys with an opinion on my wanton disregard for speed limits and reckless devil-may-care attitude on the Queen's highway. It was at that point that I suddenly found myself demoted to the part of bystander in a situation where only moments earlier I had been the main character with a decidedly bleak outlook.

In my newly cast role, I watched in disbelief as the two men now entering the arena of my life declared themselves to be CID officers and said they had witnessed everything from their viewpoint behind Mr Porsche and that in their opinion the accident was entirely his fault. To my utter amazement and total relief, the officers calmly took complete control of the whole situation. Interestingly, after the rather timely introduction of the two new characters to our dramatic production, Mr Porsche and Jag man relinquished their speaking roles and all of a sudden had very little to say on the matter previously up for debate. The CID officers, now in their starring roles, swiftly dealt with the two 'bosom buddies' and sent them on their un-merry way with their tails clasped securely between their legs.

Although it was a somewhat happier ending than I was expecting to the unfolding tragedy I was cast in, as the final scenes rolled, I was still left with a motorcycle that would not be transporting me anywhere in the near future. It's fair to say, both the bike and I were in dire need of a little more than some TLC. On the plus side, to this day, I have never had an insurance claim go through so quickly and as unhindered as this one did. I think I only spoke to my insurance company twice throughout the whole period of the claim, which is pretty mind-blowing in itself, as I'm sure anyone who has ever had to undergo the performance of such proceedings will agree. Who says there's never a policeman around when you need one?

With plans of returning to the Shire thwarted, it seemed obvious I was not destined to leave London at that particular juncture of my life. Having moved out of the bedsit and with no fixed abode, Mum suggested I move back into my old room above the undertakers until I'd sorted myself out and decided what I wanted to do. She said it would be nice to have someone to cook for again and to have the company of someone with a bit more life in them than her usual guests downstairs. Although I questioned her wording of only 'a bit more life', I happily accepted her gracious offer – the thought of Mum's delicious home cooking definitely clinching the deal.

Lying on my bed back in my old room above the undertakers, my wounded bike dripping its watery thin and well-used black oil over the very same spot in the backyard where its mechanical fourth cousin twice removed once had, it was as though my absence had been merely an illusion. As though everything that had happened over the past eight and a half years had all been just a vivid dream.

Ding Ding

After moving back to Mum's, I returned to the occupation that I had been engaged in before my decision to re-relocate to Gloucestershire. This involved the timetabled transportation of the public to various destinations of their choice; unless of course, they didn't know where they were going! Or to put it in simpler terms – I was a bus driver. A change in career from being a gym instructor, which came about due to a period of confusion as to where my life was going and feeling the need for a job with more security. The bus company was happy to reclaim my services as they were always short of drivers, and then of course there was the added bonus that I didn't require any training at all.

I'd been living back above the undertakers for a few months but was feeling very unsettled and unsatisfied with life in general. Staring up at the familiar old cracks in the ceiling of my bedroom one night, listening to the music playing through my headphones, I found myself contemplating life. Mine in particular! It was during my reflective interlude that I experienced a Eureka! moment, and it suddenly hit me. No, it wasn't the unsavoury aroma of one of the bodies downstairs permeating through the floorboards, but rather a flash of inspiration. An extremely rare occurrence for me admittedly. Even so, it did occur. What I needed was a new challenge career-wise. Something completely different from anything I'd ever done before. The constant ringing of the bells on the buses day in and day out was driving me certifiable. Especially on that damn hail-and-ride hopper bus. It was like driving the local campanologist group around all day during bell-ringing practice. Class 2b and the Quasimodo syndrome all over again!

One of the most memorable moments of my bus-driving career, was when I was driving through Piccadilly one afternoon and had just stopped at some pedestrian lights. Hugh Laurie, from his vantage point across the road, had recognised me and headed over to the bus. Nonchalantly, as though leaning over his garden fence casually talking to a neighbour, he rested his folded arms on the bonnet of the bright red Routemaster and started chatting to me. The passengers, who by now were falling over each other to get a better view of the celebrity leaning on the bonnet of the bus, were in complete disarray. It was a classic Hugh moment, and I felt like a celebrity myself the way all the passengers were looking at me.

Returning to my Eureka! moment. My flash of inspiration. Perhaps I could be an undertaker? How much more different can you get?

Dairy Free

The following morning when I asked Mum about the possibility of there being any vacancies at the undertakers, she laughed. It wasn't quite the response I was after, or the confidence boost I required. Mum justified her laughter by reminding me of an incident that happened when I was a small boy, that I will describe as the cow incident. It was a story she used to tell people, sometimes even complete strangers, in order to embarrass me – which it did extremely effectively. To be precise, it was actually a multiple cow incident – possibly even a whole herd. Depending on how many cows dictate when it's classified as a herd that is. During my investigations into the numerical requirements in the classification of a herd, disappointingly, a clear-cut answer was not apparent.

Moooving on! Mum and little Billy, approximate age five or six, were visiting some friends of Mum's who lived on a new housing estate. All the access roads and pathways onto the new estate were still very much under construction. The quickest and least muddy route to reach our destination was going to be through a field occupied by 'numerous cows'. Truth be known, I wasn't that bothered by the presence of the bovine creatures as they were all at the far end of the field and appeared intensely focused on their lunchtime grazing duties. Far too busy to be inconvenienced by a woman and her small child taking a shortcut across their field. I was actually much more concerned and somewhat apprehensive of our chosen route due to what they were leaving deposited around the field in extraordinarily vast quantities. It was a veritable minefield, full of exceptionally undesirable mines. (Not that there is such a thing as desirable mines, of course, unless they were full of something like marshmallows or feathers, I suppose.)

The hot weather certainly wasn't helping the situation, and the flies were having an absolute ball. Never had I seen so much poo in one place. And judging by its viscous consistency and vile smell, I can only assume that there was some sort of stomach bug going around. Either that, or cows are not actually supposed to eat grass and it doesn't agree with their constitution. Even with only a very basic knowledge of cattle, I think we can probably rule out the second hypothesis.

Some may think I'm being a little over dramatic about the whole incident, but what you have to remember is that I was only a small boy at the time. I was much closer to the offending items than Mum, and the rather pungent aroma would have been far less diluted into the surrounding environment when it reached my nasal passages, than it would hers. I admit the incident did cause me to feel quite nauseous and I came very close to bringing up the contents of my partially digested breakfast. But I didn't. The situation wasn't helped by getting my shoe stuck in one of the disgusting, warm, squishy deposits and then stepping into its equally disgusting, warm, squishy neighbour, in only my sock.

The cow incident story was not only very effective at embarrassing me, it was also told to raise awareness to any listening parties of what a weak constitution I had. In my defence, I would argue that it was rather a long time ago and I was very young. My level of tolerance to such things as an adult had hopefully improved greatly, having now experienced many more of life's gooier and less pleasant moments. Mum didn't seem convinced and reiterated her point. In her opinion, I would not be able to cope with being an undertaker and what the job entailed. Despite Mum's lack of faith in my constitution she agreed to enquire as to whether there were any vacancies, and we left it at that.

Later that day, when I returned from driving through the chaotic streets of London accompanied by the Quasimodo Philharmonic Orchestra, Mum informed me that she had spoken to her boss, Kenneth Mortimer, about whether there were any vacancies. There were none at present, however, Mr Mortimer did say that if I would like to pop down to head office for an informal interview, all being well, he would keep me in mind when the next vacancy arose. Which was better than a no, I suppose.

Kamikaze Tendencies

The pending interview posed somewhat of a dilemma. The rather limited and well-worn selection of clothing hanging in my wardrobe at that point in my life consisted of: black jeans, black T-shirts, black sweatshirts, those lumberjack-type shirts, a well-worn, rather grotty leather jacket, and my bus driver's uniform. Although black might be a suitable colour for an undertaker in general, I'm fairly sure turning up for the interview looking like an extra from a *Mad Max* film would not impress Mr Mortimer at all. And attending the interview in my bus driver's uniform was definitely not an option either. I mentioned my dilemma to Mum as she sat drinking her cup of coffee at the kitchen table, and without warning, like a coiled spring being released, she sprang from her seat and headed for the door. The expression on her face told me that this was not a woman to be stopped in her tracks and questioned. Moments later, I heard the shop doorbell proclaim her exit as she left the premises. I watched from the upstairs window, heart in mouth, as she dodged and weaved between the unyielding volume of traffic on the busy road, like a woman possessed. Oblivious to the near misses I could see from my viewpoint, she headed for the charity shop opposite the undertakers, where she was a part-time volunteer.

How she avoided injury or worse, I'll never know. I nearly collided with her myself on a number of occasions when I was driving the number 13 route, as she darted across the road like she was Wonder Woman, impervious to all that stood between her and her objective – the charity shop. The absurd thing was, there was a pedestrian-crossing only seconds away from the undertakers. But would she use it? Don't be silly – and risk wasting valuable time and missing a bargain in the process?!

Over the years, Mum managed to acquire some fairly decent items of clothing for me from various charity outlets. Although, gone were the days when I would wear anything that would make me look any more eccentric or exotic than I wanted to look. These days Mum's bargain acquisitions for me were mainly jeans and those checked-design lumberjack-type shirts. Comfortable, practical everyday attire, and ideal for the rugged biker image. The thicker lumberjack shirts with the extra padding were particularly good in winter against the cold-cutting wind on the bike. The clothing Mum supplied me with was always a perfect fit. Something I couldn't seem to achieve myself even when purchasing new items which were technically the correct size according to the labels. Which thanks to Mum's expertise and successful purchases within the second-hand clothing sector on my behalf, I rarely needed to do.

Knowing Mum's keenness when it came to bargain hunting in charity shops, I can only imagine her joy when she discovered the undertakers was opposite such an establishment. Let alone her elation when becoming a volunteer. Giving her the opportunity to give something back to an industry she had gained so much pleasure from, as well as its spoils. Her volunteer role would, of course, also give her the opportunity to rummage around new stock before anyone else got their grubby little hands on it.

When I needed a suit for my wedding, Mum managed to source out quite a decent little grey number from the charity shop opposite the undertakers. Once she'd made a few alterations, i.e., removed the shoulder pads, taken up the trouser legs and adjusted the waistband, it looked quite smart. As long as I didn't sit down, raise my arms or make any sudden movements, it was fine. Admittedly, my mobility was slightly limited and my movements resembled that of C3PO from *Star Wars*, much like the cowboy and Indian trousers that Mum had made me with the thick imitation-leather material when I was younger, but all that was a small price to pay after all Mum's efforts to try and make me a little more presentable on my wedding day.

After a short time rummaging around in the charity shop, Mum re-emerged victoriously clutching a selection of miscellaneous garments. Hopefully, something in the tightly clutched bundle would transform me into the perfect undertaker candidate for my forthcoming interview.

Blinkered to the dangers around her, Mum once again dodged and weaved the traffic on the return journey across the road back to the undertakers. At least if she was involved in a collision or fall this time, the bundle of clothing might at least help cushion the blow. I wouldn't be at all surprised if the regulars at the bus stop outside the undertakers had a sweepstake going on the crazy kamikaze undertaker lady, and whether she would make it across the road and back in one piece.

On the Catwalk

On her safe return, looking like the cat that got the cream, Mum laid before me an assortment of clothing which looked like it spanned at least the last five decades of fashion. I tried on various combinations of the hand-me-downs and unwanted garments of the local community.

Walking up and down the narrow hallway of the flat like a model on a catwalk, I scrutinized each ensemble in the full-length mirror at the end of the hallway. My main objective was to not look like someone who had been dressed by his mum in clothes obtained from a charity shop for a job interview, or a trainspotter. No offence to trainspotters intended, each to their own as they say. But some stereotypes do seem to be quite accurate in many ways, don't they? Saying that, many hobbies and interests seem to have a certain dress code or style of clothing that is particularly suited to that specific pastime, whether it be for practical reasons, fashion orientated, or both. It also allows the wearer to be recognised by like-minded individuals, acting as a non-verbal form of introduction. My own style of clothing for riding a motorcycle and fitting into the bike scene is a prime example. Perhaps trainspotters have a certain dress code, for some, if not all of the reasons mentioned above. It just wasn't a great desire of mine to resemble a member of that particular fraternity.

I have to confess, that during my first year at secondary school in Cheltenham, I did actually, on one mad impetuous occasion, through pure curiosity, partake in the act of trainspotting. I was intrigued by the excitement and the hustle and bustle coming from the small group of boys in the corner of the classroom discussing their trainspotting exploits of the previous day, underlining their most recent visual conquests in their handy pocket-sized trainspotter handbooks. My intrigue was duly noted and I was cordially invited to participate and experience the thrills and spills of trainspotting for myself. In order to quell my curiosity, I accepted their kind invitation and the next day after school the four of us cycled to the selected viewing point next to the railway line. An advantageous spot, apparently, where we waited… and waited… and waited, for what seemed an eternity.

I have to say, as excited as my schoolmates seemed to get with every passing of a train, it didn't quite do it for me. Each one that zoomed or trundled by looked very much like the last. An angular tube with or sometimes without carriages, and a great deal of time in between each one passing. I could have understood the thrill and excitement of watching a glorious steam locomotive hurtling by, oozing character and bellowing steam and smoke everywhere. I even tried to spice things up a bit at one point by putting a fruit pastel on the train track to see what would happen to it. Staring at the glittery green sweet on the track, I became concerned that it might somehow cause the next train to derail. My conscience wrestled with itself until I could stand it no longer, removing the sweet and eating it before disaster struck. Which would have been at precisely 17.04, according to my trainspotting companions.

The most exciting thing to happen for me that balmy summer's afternoon whilst spotting trains, was when I discovered that Mum had put pickle in my cheese sandwich without telling me. Bless her! A Wagon Wheel was also present, complementing my savoury feast perfectly. They seemed much bigger back then. Or perhaps my hands were just smaller. Actually, my hands would obviously have been smaller then, and if Wagon Wheels were bigger when my hands were smaller (which I think they were), they would have appeared huge in comparison to today's rather pitiful chocolate-covered offering.

Back on the catwalk, I finally managed to put a little number together that I thought said just what I wanted it to – or at least mumbled it in the right way. Smart but casual and within this decade's time frame. Well, near enough. Nothing too exotic. Just a pair of light-grey trousers, a white shirt and a burgundy tie. Not so much suave and sophisticated, more swerve and suffocated.

To finish the desired look, I wore a jacket I'd found hiding in the wardrobe between the *Mad Max* outfits and the bus-driver section. Which coincidently, Dad had bought for me several years previously for the fire brigade interview. Hopefully, it would bring me more luck this time.

The Interview

The day of the interview had arrived. I decided to make my way to the head office of Mortimer and Sons Funeral Directors, which was in King's Cross, via the London Underground system, my interview attire being quite unsuitable for my usual two-wheeled mode of transportation and probably not conforming to the latest EU safety regulations, i.e., not being fluorescent pink with built-in air bags and sewn-in fairy dust. And as daft as that might sound, it's not far from some of the ridiculous ideas they actually come up with on a regular basis.

I felt uncomfortably self-conscious in my interview attire. If anyone I knew recognised me, they might suspect I was leading a double life, had a court appearance, or had taken up a new interest involving certain modes of transport. I tried to blend in with my fellow commuters as inconspicuously as I could, my actions and suspicious behaviour probably having exactly the opposite effect.

After a short journey travelling through the tunnelled network under London's hustle and bustle and a short walk from the station, I arrived at Mortimer and Sons head office with ten minutes to spare before the arranged time. Good timekeeping is a definite must when it comes to interviews. And most other things, come to think of it. You can miss so much in life by being late. On the other hand, if it were to somehow prevent you from being somewhere at the time of a calamitous event, that in turn spared you from receiving a terrible injury or even saved your life, your lateness would unquestionably have been advantageous and could easily be forgiven. Something to remember if having to apologise or explain your lateness to anyone in the future.

As I opened the front door to the building, a buzzer announced my entry onto the premises. I closed the door initiating a second blast of the buzzer and waited. Initially the property appeared deserted. The silent, abandoned impression was broken by the faint sound of voices followed by movement from above. The buzzer had obviously alerted the appropriate person or persons as to my presence. Now roused they were on their way to investigate. A pair of well-polished black shoes descended the staircase directly in front of me. They were worn by a tall, slim man with short blonde hair, in a smart light-grey suit. He introduced himself politely as Phillip Carter, the office manager. I identified myself to Mr Carter and explained the purpose of my visit. After processing the information, he nodded, smiled, and respectfully invited me to wait in a small room to our left. Although technically it was my left, his right. He then ascended the stairs he had recently descended, to inform Mr Mortimer of my arrival.

In the room I had been directed to wait in, was a pale green armchair and matching two-seater sofa which I sat at one end of. Next to the armchair was an old-fashioned dark wood writing desk with green leather on the section of the table that pulls down. There was also a small round table between the sofa and the armchair. Placed on the table were various brochures relating to prepaid funerals, memorial stones, and bereavement counselling. Not the usual waiting room reading material you might find yourself browsing through. Probably quite inappropriate and even quite distressing in most other waiting rooms, such as a doctor's surgery for instance. I hadn't noticed any similar brochures at Mum's branch. Mind you, I didn't really spend a great deal of time downstairs. As little as possible, in fact.

The small room was curiously familiar. I felt quite at home. Finally, the penny dropped and I realised why that was. The decor was identical to that at Mum's branch. It makes sense, I suppose, having continuity between branches of undertakers, like any other business. And it's generally cheaper to buy the materials in bulk.

Further movement from above was followed by the sound of someone descending the stairs. This compelled me to alter my posture on the sofa and to try and appear more relaxed and more confident, but without seeming disrespectful or arrogant. A slightly taller and somewhat older man than Mr Carter, with brown hair slightly greying at the sides, dressed in a dark-grey suit, entered the waiting room. Offering his right hand out he introduced himself as Kenneth Mortimer. Standing, I reciprocated his gesture and we shook hands. Sitting back into my seat, Mr Mortimer simultaneously lowered himself into the armchair opposite.

He was a courteous, softly spoken man and made me feel very much at ease. It was as he had said it would be, an informal interview; essentially, to meet me in person, as well as being an opportunity for me to find out more about what a career with Mortimer and Sons would entail. After the interview Mr Mortimer reiterated the fact that there were no vacancies at present, but that there may be in the very near future. I was then introduced to Roger Dickinson, the staff manager. Mr Dickinson was a much sturdier chap than both Mr Carter and Mr Mortimer – built like a hooker. A hooker, as in the rugby position, not the sex industry variety. Although, it takes all sorts, I suppose, and who knows what goes on behind closed doors and what skeletons are hiding in whose closet. Especially an undertaker's closet!

Mr Dickinson's commanding manner was accompanied by one of those domineering handshakes that says, my grip is stronger than yours which makes me manlier and better than you. At least that's what I've always been led to believe is the objective of such exhibitions of strength comparisons during introductions. A firm handshake is a good characteristic but there's no need to be a jerk. A limp handshake can be just as bad and a bit disconcerting, instilling all sorts of doubts about a person's disposition. Somewhere in between is good. A matching level of firmness but not trying to outdo the other person's level of firmness, is ideal.

Mr Mortimer asked Mr Dickinson if he would be kind enough to take me to the yard and show me around. The yard that Mr Mortimer was referring to was where the main workshop and vehicles of Mortimer and Sons Funeral Directors were situated, in a mews just off of Camden Road. I was well aware of this from hearing Mum talking about the yard and was not confused in the slightest. Which made a change.

Alas, Poor Yorick

Mr Dickinson and I left head office and drove up to the yard in his car, engaging in the usual small talk that one does in such situations. Once the weather and my travel mode to head office had been covered, Mr Dickinson inquired how Mum was getting on. Having brought him up to speed with Mum's wellbeing he changed the subject slightly, directing it towards my goatee beard. It was a fairly new addition to my facial wardrobe and a subject of conversation that I must say, caught me completely off guard.

Evidently, as Mr Dickinson informed me, it was not permitted for staff to have facial hair at Mortimer and Sons, and if I was indeed offered employment, the goatee would have to go. As future employment at Mortimer and Sons was still very much a matter of speculation at that moment in time, I felt no real need to get into a lengthy debate on the matter. Purely to be polite and to show I had obviously taken the vitally important information on board, I responded with a combined nod and a semi-smile complemented with one of those agreement-type hmmm sounds from the back of my throat. This seemed to satisfy Mr Dickinson's concerns about the future fate of my facial hair, and he turned his attention back to the road ahead. Just in time to avoid colliding with the car in front, which obeying traffic regulations had stopped at the red light.

Driving along Camden Road, we slowed down and turned right, then right again into an L-shaped cobbled mews and parked in front of an enormous pair of black concertina gates. Written on each of the gates in large white letters were the words, 'NO PARKING'. Which I assumed only applied to non-employees or anyone parking without permission. We entered the building via a door of more standard proportions on our right. This took us into a surprisingly large garage area, where it would appear a number of vehicles resided. Nine in total, judging by the painted markings on the slightly oil-stained concrete floor.

"This is where the vehicles are kept," said Mr Dickinson, immediately confirming my suspicions.

There were only three vehicles in the garage at that time, two in what I assumed were their allocated parking spaces – a grey transit van and a large black Daimler limousine. The Daimler was of the same model that the Queen can be observed waving majestically from as she is driven past cheering crowds waving flags, as well as other members of the Royal family, dignitaries, celebrities, and possibly even the odd royal imposter deceiving the innocent and the gullible. The third vehicle, parked next to a battered old workbench at the far end of the garage, was one of the most iconic machines produced by Honda, that in various guises is the most produced motor vehicle in the history of mankind (over 100 million sold), a Honda C90.

There was a great deal of banging coming from an open doorway in the far right corner of the garage, the cavernous expanse of the deserted garage contributing considerably to the impressive acoustics that bombarded our auditory senses. There was also the faint sound of a radio which could be picked up in between the banging, and a rather gruff voice attempting to sing along to the current tune that was playing. Outstretching his left arm, Mr Dickinson indicated that he wished me to head towards the open doorway. His slow, over-exaggerated gestures intrigued me. It was almost as if he were on a stage performing a classic Shakespearian play, rather than giving a prospective employee a tour of the workplace.

'It Wasn't the Cough That Carried Her Off It Was the Coffin They Carried Her Off In'

We entered what appeared to be the workshop area. This, once again, was confirmed by Mr Dickinson. The workshop was much smaller in comparison to the garage. However, it was clear that the limited space had been effectively utilized, with shelving and various storage units placed wherever possible from floor to ceiling. It was nothing fanciful, yet outwardly it gave the impression of practical functionality. A place for everything and everything in its place. There were several coffins on wooden trestles scattered around, exhibiting various stages of construction. Stooped over one of them, hammer in hand, was an old man with his back to us. Conspicuously oblivious to our presence, mumbling various words to the song on the radio, but not quite in the order they were originally performed, he continued hitting his target inside the coffin with great intent.

Mr Dickinson greeted the man, who having been so previously engrossed in his vocational duties, was quite startled by our presence. Hand on chest, only just having averted a coronary, the man was introduced to me as Old Des. He was, by all accounts, one of the company's longest-standing employees. Still standing at the time I was introduced to him – but only just! Old Des was, as his title may give rise to suspect, quite old. His slow, burdened movements and slightly concave stature clear evidence that he had served his time in the workplace beyond retirement age, and for whatever reason he was still doing so.

Mr Dickinson explained that I was Jean's son, and that there might be the possibility of me joining the company in the near future (facial hair permitting, according to Mr Dickinson's remark in the car). Old Des inquired after Mum in his soft but gruff Irish accent that was a little difficult to understand in parts, and told me to give her his regards the next time I saw her. He then wished me luck with my possible future employment, smiled, and returned his concentration and efforts to the construction of the coffin he was working on before he was so rudely interrupted.

The smell of the sawdust-covered workshop took me back to the woodwork rooms at school, the main difference, of course, being the absence of coffins. Mind you, if we had turned up to our woodwork lessons at school to find a selection of coffins on display in the workshop, it may well have made the lessons slightly more intriguing – or completely freaked us out!

The very thought that I may be required to fabricate coffins was not something that had occurred to me. It was a disturbing thought, and had I been prone to panic attacks, I probably would have had one at that precise moment. My woodworking skills left much to be desired. The most successful creation using the medium of timber during my school years was probably the pencil case with a sliding lid. Though the word successful might be construed as being a little misleading. Unfortunately, the lid's sliding ability was slightly flawed and it was a bit hit and miss as to whether you would actually be able to gain access to your pencils at the precise moment you required the use of one, or several. Which was fine if you weren't under any pressure timewise, but rather unhelpful and very frustrating if you were. It would probably have been more effectively utilised as a box to keep valuables safe or items you rarely wanted access to, due to the effort it took to open and close it.

I was always a little too heavy-handed in the planing department when working with wood, and usually ended up with far less wood than was required to fabricate whatever it was we had been assigned to produce. I was definitely much more suited to metalwork where heavy-handedness was often a positive attribute rather than a negative one. I envisaged some rather novel-shaped coffins being turned out if I was to be let loose on the construction side of things, but decided it best not to divulge my concerns as it might affect the decision as to my suitability for future employment. Mr Mortimer hadn't mentioned anything about the need for carpentry skills during the informal interview. I would just have to cross that bridge, if and when I came to it.

Mr Dickinson drew my attention, in his thespian-like manner, to various other items scattered around the workshop that I would be expected to operate should I be taken on. The two dormant engraving machines which sat in the one corner looked likely candidates for the *Antiques Road Show*. Standing menacingly in the opposite corner was a giant paper shredder. Giant in size, that is, not for shredding giant-sized paper.

Pointing to a doorway on the other side of the workshop, announcing it was the entrance to the coffin stores, Mr Dickinson once again ushered me forwards. We walked past Old Des who was unperturbed by our explorations of his work environment, and entered what I can only describe, as complete darkness. Mr Dickinson's mutterings from behind the opened door indicated he was searching for the light switch, and as if by magic, the darkness was banished. Illuminated before us was an area about the size of two badminton courts. I've not actually played a great deal of badminton, it's just a close comparison that comes to mind. Horizontally stacked on wooden racks from floor to ceiling, were row upon row of coffins varying in style and size. It was a macabre and chilling vision that made the hairs on the back of my neck stand on end. It occurred to me, that if I were to be offered employment at Mortimer and Sons, I would probably have to deal with most of the future occupants destined for each one of the coffins I saw before me. A macabre thought, to complement the macabre vision. I couldn't even begin to imagine how many bodies I would come into contact with if I were to stay with the company as long as Old Des. Possibly thousands. Mr Dickinson explained that these days the coffins were not manufactured on the premises as they once were. They were now bought from suppliers with only the furnishings – the handles, ornamental features and the inside material trimmings – that needed to be added. That was certainly a great weight off my mind.

We walked back into the workshop where Old Des was now putting the material lining into the coffin he was working on. As we passed, he glanced up and delivered a knowing wink. Perhaps he knew something I didn't. Actually, he probably knew a great deal more about most things, but he wasn't about to let on. I got the impression that the wink was confirmation that it was up to me to find out for myself through my own experiences, just as he had done a lifetime ago. Mr Dickinson and I continued walking through the workshop towards yet another doorway past a parade of tall, thin grey lockers that stood like a guard of honour either side of us. The doorway led to a T-junction, with toilets to our right, a tearoom to our left, and immediately in front of us, squeezed in between the two like an afterthought, was the smallest office I have ever seen in my entire life. It would probably be more accurate to describe it as a cupboard with a desk in it. Its somewhat restricted dimensions, however, similar to the workshop, had been very effectively utilized to maximise its limited capacity. A multitude of shelves crammed with bulging files and binders surrounded two noticeboards attached to opposite walls. An army of indestructible bulldog clips anchored to each board, gripped on relentlessly to vast numbers of pink cards approximately 5" by 3" in size, which had people's names and other fragments of information written on them.

The minuscule but spatially well-utilised office belonged to Eamon, the foreman. Another ex-pat from the Emerald Isle, similar to Old Des. Eamon was probably in his early sixties, a friendly, balding, rosy-cheeked chap, full of energy and bordering more towards bantam than featherweight. After brief introductions, he too, asked after Mum, and once enlightened said to pass on his good wishes. He then went on to explain some of the workings of his cramped yet organised surroundings. The pink cards which decorated various sections of the office walls evidently held various snippets of information relating to deceased people and their up and coming funerals. Eamon explained at what stages different bits of information might find their way into his compact office, and what he did with that information once he was in possession of it. It was an extremely in-depth explanation, the majority of which, to be honest, I didn't really take in.

All the other staff were out on funerals and removals, leaving Eamon and Old Des holding the fort. Which meant there wasn't anyone else around for me to meet at that point. Eamon asked if I had any questions about what I'd seen so far, but while I was deciding whether I did or not, the telephone sat on the desk in front of him rang requiring his response. He excused himself to answer it, which prompted Mr Dickinson to signal Eamon – through the art of mime – his intention to carry on the tour. We left Eamon in deep discussion with whoever was on the other end of the phone, thumbing through a pile of the pink cards on the desk in front of him.

Room for One More on Top

There was only one part of the tour remaining, which was the mortuary. With Mr Dickinson leading the way across the cobbled mews towards the building opposite in his theatrical fashion, I followed willingly in my supporting role. As Mr Dickinson opened the mortuary door, I prepared myself for what I imagined would be by far the least pleasant part of the tour. Naturally, I was used to the sight of dead bodies, living above the undertakers, but that was after they'd gone through the process of being made more presentable. I wasn't at all sure what to expect at this point of the proceedings, and felt rather apprehensive.

As the mortuary door swung open, we were greeted by the glossy black bonnet of a Ford Granada estate. Not quite what I was expecting, but its presence was quickly and clearly explained by my frustrated thespian tour guide. It seems the old Ford had been acquired as part of a deal when Mortimer and Sons took over ownership of another local undertakers. As space was limited in the main garage, the Ford

Granada, of almost classical status, lodged unchaperoned within the confines of the mortuary. Unless of course you count the other occupants that also temporarily occupied the premises. A Ford hearse had also been acquired through the merger but was fortunate enough to reside in the main garage, unlike its ostracised cousin.

Turning the corner, we entered the main part of the mortuary, a generous amount of floor space besieged by its white surroundings. There was a noticeable drop in temperature that was not unpleasant in the heat of the day. I noticed a familiar odour in the air, a sweet and somewhat sickly smell, which I recognised from Mum's branch. I'd always thought it was a type of deodorising spray or air freshener she used to cover up any unpleasant smells that might sometimes accompany our motionless guests. It appeared I was right.

Along the mortuary wall on our right was a storage rack that was home to an assortment of rather battered-looking grey coffins, as well as a selection of brown fibreglass ones, which also appeared to have seen better days. Apparently, they were used for the collection, transportation, and sometimes storage of the bodies, and were referred to as shells. Next to the rack of shells were a number of wheelie stretchers that were also used for conveying the bodies from one place to another, but generally only on the initial removal from the venue where the deceased had passed away. Along the far wall of the mortuary, directly in front of us, stood a row of large fridge doors. Five in all. Each door had three letters of the alphabet on it running downwards in alphabetical order. There were fifteen spaces in all, my calculations being proof that my schooling, despite my lack of attention, may not have been a complete waste of time after all.

Evidently, there was also storage space available if required during busy periods in what Mr Dickinson described as the cold room, on our right. A board on the wall to our left, similar to the ones in Eamon's office, displayed letters of the alphabet written in black, in the same configuration as the letters on the fridge doors. Securing a selection of pink cards effectively to the board without any sign of a struggle, were the favoured, sturdy bulldog clips.

To the left of the fridges was a door with a decorative copper sign above it which seemed overly elaborate in comparison to its more clinical and very white surroundings. The sign suggested to those not in the know, that beyond it lay the Embalming Room. Mr Dickinson opened the door very slightly, tentatively easing his head through the limited gap he had allowed himself. Returning his head from its reconnaissance mission, I was informed that Marcus, the embalmer, was not available to make an appearance at that precise moment in time. Mr Dickinson, deducing that he had probably taken an early lunch, something he was apparently prone to doing, decided it would be best not to venture further into the embalming room without Marcus being present. It seemed I would have to forgo that little treat for another time. If indeed there was ever to be one.

The tour of the yard completed, Mr Dickinson asked if I required a lift to anywhere that he might be passing. Declining his kind offer politely, I said I was fine to get the bus, having decided a trip above ground in the sunshine would be preferable to another journey underground on such a beautiful day. He nodded, we exchanged farewells, and I made my way to the appropriate bus stop in Camden High Street.

Once again in the land of the living, I watched the world go by as I travelled home on the bus. A rare occasion indeed, being a passenger and not the driver. I pondered the morning's events and the people I had met: Mr Mortimer, Mum's courteous, softly-spoken boss; Mr Dickinson, with his over-theatrical thespian mannerisms; Old Des, the eccentric old coffin maker; not forgetting Eamon, the chirpy red-cheeked foreman, in his minuscule but well-utilised office.

I had a good feeling about the possibility of a new career with Mortimer and Sons. It would certainly be very different from anything else I had ever done. And hopefully, just the change I needed.

Not by the Hair on My Chinny Chin Chin

The day after the interview, I found myself contemplating Mr Dickinson's remark about the no facial hair policy. Strangely, Mr Mortimer hadn't mentioned it during the interview when it was plainly in view. Perhaps he thought it unnecessary to mention unless my future employment with the company was a more definite possibility. I'd been growing the goatee for a while now. Or rather, I was trying to. It didn't seem very enthusiastic to join the other features on my face and was struggling to put in an appearance.

The reason behind the goatee, was an attempt to appear more rugged, more worldly and less baby-faced. It wasn't the most impressive example, I'll admit. I probably could have travelled the world, become more worldly and appeared more rugged on my return by the time it was in any fit state to be classed as a proper goatee. Psychologically though, it was already starting to earn its keep and have the desired effect. At least to me – and that's what really mattered. Even though I thought the job at Mortimer and Sons would be good for me, I decided I wasn't going to sacrifice the new me to get it. If I was actually offered employment, I would politely decline.

A couple of days after the interview, on returning from my day's bell ringing torment on the buses, Mum informed me that Mr Mortimer had phoned to say that a member of staff had left unexpectedly, which meant there was now a vacancy. If I was still interested, would I let him know. Being rather late in the day, I put it at the top of my 'to do list' for tomorrow.

The next morning, I rang head office and asked to speak to Mr Mortimer. Having resigned myself to the fact that the goatee was staying, I started the conversation by thanking him for his kind offer of employment but said that I would have to decline. I mentioned Mr Dickinson's remark about the no facial hair policy on the day of the interview, and that I had decided I really didn't want to get rid of mine as I'd become quite attached to it, in more ways than one. Mr Mortimer, sounding slightly confused about my justification for not accepting his offer of employment, declared he hadn't noticed I had any facial hair. Which I must admit hurt a little, and showed just how pathetic my goatee must have been at the time. He then went on to say that there was no specific policy against facial hair, they just weren't keen on staff being in the public eye during the scruffy stages of early growth. As long as mine was not in those early stages, he couldn't see it being a problem. At which point I said I would be very pleased to accept his offer of employment. I mentioned that with the amount of notice I would have to give my present employers, which was two weeks, I would be able to start on Monday, 28 June. Mr Mortimer seemed happy with this and said he would send me a letter of confirmation that morning. All I had to do now, was hope and pray that the goatee had a miraculous growth spurt to get past the dodgy scruffy stage it was presently at. Which, to be honest, would be nothing less than a miracle at the rate of growth it was displaying at the time.

The following day I received the letter of confirmation Mr Mortimer had promised and it was all systems go! Mum still thought I wouldn't be able to cope with various aspects of the job. Most aspects, in fact. Even so, there was only one way to find out for sure – and that was to give it a go!

A WEEKEND AWAY

By the end of my last week on the buses, living in the bell tower of Notre Dame Cathedral with Quasimodo would have been the epitome of tranquillity! The constant ringing in my ears and the maddening stop-start, stop-start, of the W5 Hopper bus had driven me to my whit's end. My change in career could not have been better timed. I may have just escaped crossing that fine line that separates sanity and insanity. Or at least the varying levels of insanity.

The weekend before I was due to join Mortimer and Sons Funeral Directors, my best friend, Wez, and I took a trip up to Norfolk with the motorcycle club that he and I were members of. At the rendezvous point we met up with Sean, another member of the club, and his other half, Rachel. They were travelling by car having brought their two mini humans along aiming to combine the trip with a visit to the seaside. Also in the car was single mum Sally, a friend of theirs, and her five-year-old boy, Jack. Wez and I were introduced to Sally and Jack via the half open, front passenger window of the rather beaten-up red Cortina estate. After our introductions we then headed off to meet up with the rest of the club members to travel up to Norfolk in convoy.

It was an excellent weekend – brilliant sunshine, great bands, and plenty of amazing custom bikes to scrutinise and get ideas for future projects. I didn't see much of Sean and Rachel or their friend Sally over the weekend. Sally was quite an attractive lady, with her wild shoulder-length blonde hair, and seemed quite nice from what little contact I did have with her. But I really wasn't in the mindset for forging new relationships with the opposite sex, still feeling rather battle weary in the heart department at the time. For me, the weekend was about the ride and enjoying a bit of fun and relaxation with my friends before my new life-changing career debut on Monday. Hopefully, the start of a more positive chapter in my life than the last one.

As I said, I didn't actually speak to Sally much over the weekend, but being the big kids that most blokes are, in between all the bike stuff, Wez and I spent a lot of the time with little Jack. The three of us played with his toy digger, transporting caterpillars from one mound of dirt to the other. We also discovered an old, abandoned tractor hidden in the undergrowth in the corner of the field where we were camping. Little Jack was in his element and his little beaming face was a picture as he sat on the tractor's rusty old seat pretending to drive it. Sally was never far away though, ever the protective mum keeping a watchful eye. And who could blame her, surrounded by all those big, hairy bikers. Well, okay, some were quite short and trying to be hairier.

On the Sunday after the bike show, before heading back to London, Sean, Rachel and their two children, accompanied by Sally, Jack, Wez and myself, went to nearby Great Yarmouth to enjoy a few hours of sun, sea and sand. While the others went to the beach, Wez and I decided to explore the fun fair. First stop, the Wibbly Wobbly House. Trying to negotiate the moving floors and colliding into all the randomly placed obstacles, it was just like a Friday night out in Camden Town. Only without paying a fortune or being inebriated. Although, fairgrounds are hardly the cheapest of places to visit – once you've been on a few rides, won a goldfish, had a hot dog or two, some candy floss, and lost all the change from your pockets on the Waltzers!

Wez and I were in hysterics in the Wibbly Wobbly House. Tears of laughter were running down our cheeks. The crazy mirrors were absolutely hilarious, and we desperately felt the need to share the experience with someone who would truly appreciate it. Returning to the beach where we had left the others, with Sally, Rachel and Sean's blessings, we commandeered their offspring and headed back to the fairground, leaving the adults momentarily relieved of their parental duties lazily basking in the midday sun like lizards.

The youngsters were obviously as impressed with the Wibbly Wobbly House as we were judging by the hysterical laughter escaping from their youthful lungs. It was even funnier watching them, than it was experiencing it ourselves. I don't think I have ever laughed so much.

There's probably a fine line between being childish and keeping in touch with your inner child, but all too often, as we venture into adulthood, life can be painfully thorough at subduing that wonderful childlike spirit. I'm not saying we shouldn't be responsible as adults, but I strongly believe that keeping your inner child close and staying young at heart is key to retaining some level of sanity in this often insane and cruel world. I'm certain the world would be a much better place for all of us, if we did.

As the sun descended into the calm, shimmering sea, and the tears of laughter were dried on our cheeks by the warm summer breeze, we said our goodbyes and went our separate ways via our various modes of transport.

Tomorrow was going to be a big day for me. My first day as an undertaker. Or to use my correct title, funeral assistant. It was going to be an early start and I was going to need plenty of beauty sleep to look my best.

MY FIRST WEEK

DAY ONE, MONDAY

Like any first day, my first day at Mortimer and Sons Funeral Directors was one of mixed emotions. I was excited about my new career but nervous of being the new boy, yet again. Nervous about whether I would fit in and nervous that Mum might be right about me not being able to cope with the job and what may be lying in store for me in this strange new world of the dead.

I'd decided to arrive early in order to make a good impression. Although, I must say, I've never really been much of an impressionist, as anyone who has witnessed my Frank Spencer impression can tell you. However, as I turned into the cobbled mews on my motorcycle, I saw the yard was already in full swing and a hive of activity. The huge black concertina gates of the main garage area were open, and the impressive black funeral vehicles were being washed and polished like enormous circus beasts being groomed in preparation for the day's performances. Coffins were being ferried back and forth to the mortuary over the bumpy cobbles, presumably to collect the main participants of each performance.

As I pulled up in front of the huge open gates, even over the sound of my rattily old bike engine and the almost baffle-less exhaust, I could hear the sound of the relentless hammering from inside the workshop. I wondered if it was Old Des diligently hard at work. The hammering echoed around the large expanse of garage which seemed to be equipped with acoustic capabilities comparable to the Albert Hall. The whole scene was like the Grim Reaper's version of Santa's workshop. With a touch more solemnity, fewer elves, and fewer glam rock Christmas songs. Well, it was late June!

I silenced the mechanical mayhem rumbling between my legs and introduced myself to the member of staff that was washing one of the hearses on the forecourt. He was a well-built chap but with a little more around the waist than he probably would have liked, and he had wavy blonde hair that was thinning slightly on top. I put him to be in his mid-thirties, although I've never been the greatest at judging a person's age and I always seem to upset people with my estimation of the length of time that they have been present on Earth, when challenged to do so. He was wearing a pair of dark-grey, striped trousers and a white shirt with the sleeves rolled up (presumably to keep them dry whilst washing the hearse). A pair of black braces attached to his trousers but uninvolved in their duties dangled at his sides; something you don't tend to see people wearing as often as you used to – which is probably why they caught my eye. Belts definitely seem to be the preferred option for most people's trouser-supporting needs these days. The untethered individual introduced himself as Oliver, one of the hearse drivers, and directed me to park the bike up at the rear of the garage.

"Park it next to the work bench, Bill, behind Eamon's mean machine," Oliver quipped.

Eamon's mean machine was the Honda C90 I'd seen when Mr Dickinson was giving me a tour of the yard on the day of my interview. Starting the bike up again, I rode slowly to the back of the garage and pulled up next to the old workbench. Easing the bike's side-stand down with my left foot, I leant the bike over until it came to rest. Something I hadn't noticed on the day of my interview, that was of particular interest, was the industrial-sized vice bolted to the old workbench. Judging by the unhappy noises the bike had been making recently, extensive repairs were imminent and the vice would be a welcome and very useful addition to the workforce required for the task.

Oliver followed me into the garage and once I'd dismounted and removed my helmet, he introduced me to some of the other staff scattered around the garage who were also busily grooming the regal black Daimlers. Dean, in the far corner behind us, methodically wiping over the bonnet of a hearse with a chamois leather was first on the list. Probably in his late-twenties, like Oliver he was also a hearse driver. Morris, cleaning the windows of the neighbouring hearse, who I would describe as middle-aged, made up the trio of the company's hearse drivers. Each of them acknowledged my presence with a nod after Oliver's introduction but were obviously far too busy to stop what they were doing even for a brief verbal exchange. Ali and Eddie, on the other side of the garage who were also wiping and polishing various parts of large black vehicles, were apparently both limousine drivers. Eddie, a short, stocky man, who again for sake of argument is easiest described as middle-aged, reminded me a great deal of the actor Danny Devito, though Eddie's head of hair was far more abundant than that of Mr Devito, and quite curly. Cleaning the inside of his limousine's rear window he raised a hand and smiled as his name was mentioned. Which was a great improvement on Dean's and Morris's greeting.

Ali, also around the middle-aged mark but a fair bit taller and slimmer than Eddie, possessed the sparsely distributed Danny Devito hairstyle that Eddie was missing – or not missing – so to speak. Ali was what I imagine could be described as olive-skinned and was sporting a rather suave moustache. Something I was sure Mr Dickinson was far from pleased about, going by his concern for my pathetic excuse of a goatee on the day of my interview and the so-called no facial hair policy. Ali remarked jocularly that he was Mortimer and Sons' token ethnic minority representative, which seemed to amuse the others in the garage considerably judging by the accompanying laughter.

Everyone I had met so far was wearing the same grey striped trousers, white shirts, and what appeared to be the compulsory undertaker fashion accessory, a pair of braces. All except Morris, that is, who wore a pair of blue overalls, though, from what I could tell, he appeared to be wearing his undertaker apparel underneath.

I asked Oliver if I'd misunderstood the time I was expected to start work, because it was already so busy. He told me that most of the staff start earlier to get the overtime, and there's always so much to do in the mornings it would be impossible to get it all done in time if they were to only stick to their official hours.

Oliver escorted me through to the workshop, disappointingly a lot less theatrically than my last tour guide, Mr Dickinson, had done on the day of my interview. Another gent in grey striped trousers, white shirt and braces, whose mission in life at that moment in time was to sweep the sawdust on the floor into a neat little pile in front of him, was introduced to me as Reg. Reg was of average build and definitely veering on the upper end of the middle-aged scale. Glancing up from his pile of sawdust as his name was mentioned, he acknowledged me with a sly smirk and a raised eyebrow. I'd met Reg on numerous occasions, as he'd become a friend of Mum's. They went out occasionally and he used to do odd jobs around the flat. I don't think they were any more than friends, although that may well be my naivety getting the better of me, yet again.

One of Reg's little DIY jobs involved the construction of a collapsible table attached to the kitchen wall. It was a very practical idea, the kitchen being so small it made use of the space wisely. The only thing was the collapsible table tended to collapse when you least wanted or expected it to. A number of Mum's delicious home-cooked meals failed to reach the inner workings of my digestive system thanks to Reg's rather deficient DIY skills.

I asked Oliver where Old Des was, as his absence was noticeable by the lack of his presence. Oliver enlightened my curiosity by informing me that Old Des didn't usually start work until about ten-ish, and left about three-ish. Evidently, as well as him not being what you might call a spring chicken, he also suffered from ill health. Hence, there was a certain amount of flexibility within his hours of employment.

In one corner of the workshop was one of the largest coffins I had ever seen. It was one of those titanic, American-style metal coffins. I'd seen them on TV and in films but never realised how colossal they actually were. It was pearl white with gold edging, and like a stretched-limo version of our rather more modestly styled coffins. Oliver told me it had been used to transport a body from abroad but the family thought it was a little on the pretentious side and were allegedly going to scrap it. It seemed they had decided to go for something a little less showy in solid wood. I remarked on what a waste it would be and that it would make a fantastic sidecar for the bike. Oliver agreed and seemed quite taken by the idea.

As Oliver and I headed towards Eamon the foreman's Lilliputian office, we noticed Eamon was having what seemed to be quite a heated debate with whoever was on the other end of the telephone. Oliver suggested a brew and diverted me effectively into the tearoom on our left, where the kettle had conveniently just boiled. The introductions continued in the tearoom with the staff members that were currently occupying it, starting with Mel. Mel was in his late-forties to mid-fifties (I'm trying to be more precise here but could still be way off the mark). Quietly drinking his heated beverage in the corner of the tearoom, Mel was contemplating some information on a clipboard sat on the table in front of him.

"Welcome," he said, in a slow, relaxed tone, simultaneously placing his cup on the table and glancing over at Oliver and me. Visually, Mel reminded me very much of the extremely flamboyant American pianist, singer and actor, Liberace (pronounced – Liberachee). Apparently, the highest paid entertainer in the world at the height of his fame during the 1950s–1970s. But visual resemblance to the famous man himself was definitely where any similarity ended.

Joe, with his short, cropped blonde hair, was the next to be introduced and by far the youngest of any of the staff at the yard I had met so far. Possibly in his early-twenties, at a wild guess, he was actually the first member of staff I had noticed on entry to the tearoom, mainly because he was laying prostrate, face down, on the long cloth-covered bench which followed the perimeter of the tearoom wall, facilitating seating for the two tables, as well as numerous free-standing, grey plastic chairs. Joe acknowledged me with a groan and by slowly raising his right arm, turning his head slightly in our direction and half opening his eyes – almost as if taking a breath during the front crawl swimming stroke. He held the position for a fraction of a second, which seemed to take all his effort, and then letting his arm drop without muscular resistance, resumed his previous face-down pose.

Oliver explained Joe's slight lack of energy by telling me that Joe and two other members of staff had been on call through the night, and by all accounts they had been rather busy. The last call-out, and apparently their fourth, being at about 5 a.m. that morning. By the time they'd returned to the yard, Joe had decided it wasn't worth going back home and crashed in the tearoom in his present position. The other two members of the call-out squad, Frank and Arthur, who weren't in yet, had decided it was worth going home to their beds to try and catch up on some sleep. Perhaps they lived closer than Joe.

The last person introduced to me in the tearoom was Adam, a broad well-built chap, who coincidently was also on his first day at Mortimer and Sons. This surprised me somewhat, as I thought there was only the one vacancy. My concern was short-lived. After all, I had the job I had applied for, and that's all that mattered. Hopefully we'd not been double booked and neither of us would be asked to leave before the day had even begun.

While Adam and I were waiting for Eamon to finish his heated debate on the telephone, some of the others who'd been in the garage cleaning the cars came in to top up their morning brews. I'd already been warned by Mum, and Mr Dickinson, about the merciless mickey taking that goes on between the lads at the yard; though I think that's the case in most work places to a degree. There's nothing wrong with a bit of jovial banter as long as it doesn't go too far. However, I'd decided to start as I meant to go on and nip any urine extracting which headed in my general direction swiftly in the proverbial bud.

Dean, who was now sat in the opposite corner of the tearoom to me, had noticed my lunch box which I'd placed on the table in front of me. I am, of course, referring to the Tupperware variety of lunch box, as opposed to the non-Tupperware variety. Eyebrows would certainly have been raised if I'd placed that on the table; such actions probably ending my undertaking career before it had even begun. Gesturing at my well-packed lunch box, Dean remarked that he hoped I had something he liked in my sandwiches as he was feeling quite peckish. In full bud-nipping mode, I promptly responded to Dean's comment. Selecting a serious tone from my repertoire of vocal options, I looked him in the eye (both to be precise), and informed him that people had died for less. I wasn't aiming for quite such an aggressive response; it just came out that way. I was actually aiming for assertive, with just a hint of psychopathic tendencies. An immediate silence fell upon the tearoom, the expressions on the faces of its occupants clearly indicating their uncertainty as to whether I was being serious or not. Dean's lack of response and somewhat dismayed expression, indicated he, too, had been slightly caught off guard by my riposte and was unsure of how to react. If a clump of tumbleweed had been available to play its part, it would not have been out of place at that particular moment in time had it lazily rolled across the ghostly silent tearoom.

The silence was eventually broken by Eddie asking Ali if he had seen the nature programme on telly the other night about poisonous frogs. Ali replying he had not, vocal momentum was once again validated, and gradually more of the tearoom's participants joined in the conversation about the intriguing little amphibious creatures – with some having actually watched the programme. The tearoom slowly resumed normal service with only a slight undercurrent that something untoward may have just been averted.

Eventually, Eamon emerged from his tiny office, and shaking our hands enthusiastically he welcomed Adam and me to our first day at Mortimer and Sons. He asked us if we'd had a brew and if we had been introduced to everyone. Adam and I smiled and nodded in response to his enquiry, indicating we had. The need to impart any more information than that seemed unnecessary.

Ooooh! Suits You Sir

Eamon turned to Mel and asked him to take Adam and me over to the clothing store and help us sort out something to wear. Mel finished the last few sips of his drink and then escorted us over to the mortuary building where the clothing store was situated. The mortuary was empty apart from the solitary Granada estate, four coffins side by side on trolleys and several wheelie stretchers, being serenaded by the hum of the large fridges. A selection of pink cards attached to the board on the wall indicated a number of prostrate occupants inside the fridges awaiting attention. Mel unlocked the door to a small room on our left and told us to have a rummage through the collection of grey and black clothing hanging on the racks and piled in the cardboard boxes on the floor to see if anything was a suitable fit. He didn't seem over enthusiastic to join us in our search and left us to rummage.

We worked our way through the mass of clothing which Adam and I presumed to be the hand-me-downs from ex-staff over the years or what present staff had grown out of. There was quite an assortment of trousers, jackets, waistcoats and rain macs in a vast range of sizes. Unfortunately for us, there was very little in the sizes that either of us required. We tried squeezing into various articles of clothing that were far too small or were swamped by other items that were far too big. The results from our search were not looking favourable. We certainly weren't going to be very high up in the running for the best-dressed undertaker of the year awards, that was for sure. Mortimer and Sons appeared to have had just about every size and shape of employee over the years, bar ours.

Although on the short side, due to weight training I was quite broad with fairly muscular arms and legs. Not quite a mini Arnold Schwarzenegger, but I was working on it vigorously. This often created problems getting clothes to fit me comfortably that didn't require altering, as Mum was well aware. Thankfully, Mum was extremely proficient with her old Singer sewing machine. Adam was also quite broad for his height – describing himself as big-boned and explaining that he also tended to have problems getting clothes to fit.

Reporting back to Eamon with the few garments that we had managed to salvage from the clothing stores, we informed him that unless Mortimer and Sons were intending to branch out into naturist funerals, Adam and I were in deep trouble. Even joking about it the images that scenario conjured up in my mind still haunt me to this day. Eamon got on the phone to head office post-haste and explained our predicament. After his communications Adam and I were instructed to go and collect a clothing order form from the office manager at head office, Mr Carter, and then head to the Mortimer and Sons clothing suppliers in Charing Cross Road. Which is exactly what we did.

At head office, our new boss, Mr Mortimer, introduced us to his younger brother, Henry, who incidentally and rather interestingly, had a full beard. We were also introduced to Constance, Kenneth Mortimer's wife, and Penelope, his daughter – both of whom worked at head office. Which made me wonder if it would have been more precise to call themselves Mortimer, Sons, Wives and Daughters, Funeral Directors.

After collecting the order form for our new clothing from Mr Carter, we were given instructions on the location of the shop from which we were to obtain the clothing, and the bus fare to get us there. The 24 bus, according to Mr Carter, would deliver us almost directly outside the shop in question.

Eventually, after getting off the bus and taking a bit of a magical mystery tour on foot (because we took a wrong turn), we found the clothing suppliers and eagerly ventured inside. The most authoritative-looking of the shop assistants greeted us courteously as we entered. Adam immediately thrusted the envelope he held authorising the issue of our new wardrobe into the man's unsuspecting hand, accompanied by a brief but extremely detailed account of our predicament. Unsurprisingly, this unexpected bombardment of information threw the man quite off guard. However, he quickly regained his previous air of authority, and clapped his hands twice in the direction of the opposite end of the shop. Before you could say Jack Robinson (an expression apparently originating in the 1700s, referring to a man who paid such brief visits to acquaintances that there was scarcely time to announce his arrival before he had departed, but whose original identity seems to be unknown), four more shop assistants who had been loitering with intent to serve, tweaking bits of garments hanging on racks to look busy, suddenly surrounded us on all sides. Instructions relayed by their superior were direct and brief. Armed and dangerous they got to work with their gleaming metal-tipped tape measures.

Things were measured that I had no idea required measuring for trousers to fit correctly, and tape measures found their way into places that no man had ever gone before except for possibly medical staff within their professional roles. A nudging of my right testicle quite unnerved me, and I'm still not convinced it was actually a necessary manoeuvre to gain an accurate inside leg measurement. The twinkling in the shop assistant's eye did nothing to put me at my ease either. We hadn't even been properly introduced. Some chocolates or flowers at least, prior to such an intimate event, would have been nice!

As quickly as the shop assistants had appeared, after the extremely precise measuring process they dispersed again in all directions of the compass into various nooks and crannies around the shop. After a brief absence they returned laden with clothing which Adam and I were encouraged to try on in the nearby changing rooms. Separate ones, of course. Reappearing like contestants from Stars in Their Eyes, we posed in our new attire for the shop assistants' professional opinions and approval. We got it. A little too approving from some, for my liking.

On our arrival back at the yard, Adam and I caused quite a stir when we handed the invoice for our new clothing to Eamon. We had gone to the wrong shop. It seems we should have gone to the clothing store around the corner from the one we actually did go to. Head office was not happy because of how much more the clothing had cost than if we'd gone to the shop we were supposed to have gone to. Eamon said we would probably have to return it.

The lads at the yard were not very happy with our purchases either, and quite understandably. As well as being a bit on the pricey side, the new boys' kit was very noticeably of a much better quality than theirs. As Adam and I were preparing to head back to Charing Cross Road to return our purchases, or should I say, Mortimer and Sons' purchases, Eamon called us back.

After great deliberation, the powers that be at head office had decided to let Adam and I keep our spoils, on the express condition that we would not be due for replacement clothing for an outstandingly long time. Happily, we agreed to the terms and said we would do our very best to try and avoid any unnecessary wear and tear to the items in question.

Eagle-eyed Joe, now mobile and a good deal more alert than when we had first met, happened to notice that the stripe design on our new trousers was ever so slightly different to everyone else's. The realisation that not only had Adam and I gone to the wrong shop and purchased extremely expensive clothing that we shouldn't have, but that it was also the wrong clothing was a devastating blow to our recent and exceedingly short-lived victory. It seemed we would be returning our ill-gotten gains after all. Joe, seeing our disappointment, took pity on us and pledged he would not utter a word. He suggested the whole episode had already caused enough trouble and it was probably best not mentioned. Agreeing wholeheartedly, a nudge and a wink sealed the deal.

It occurred to Adam and me that we only had one item of each piece of clothing and when they required cleaning this could present a problem. However, we decided not to push our luck and to keep quiet, opting to cross that bridge when we came to it. Which I think was a rather wise move in the circumstances. We were each allocated one of the tall, thin grey lockers in the workshop, where we hung our smart, expensive clothing of discontent, with a hint of relish.

All in all, I think you'd agree it was an interesting start to our first day.

Nice To See You, To See You Nice

After lunch, having eaten all my sandwiches without any assistance from any other members of staff, Adam and I were put to work in the workshop with the coffin master himself, Old Des, to learn the fine art of fitting up coffins.

I'd already discovered, and was greatly relieved to know, that coffins are not generally constructed entirely by the undertakers on their premises these days, but bought in bulk from suppliers semi-finished. According to Old Des, the two most popular types of coffins used today are the solid wood variety for burials, and the chipboard with a wood veneer finish – the cheaper option – for cremations. The chipboard variety is also used frequently for burials, due to the expense of the solid wood coffins. On the odd occasion, a solid coffin might be used for a cremation if that's what the deceased or the family's wishes dictated.

Coffins, whether solid wood or not, come in a variety of styles but are usually a dark wood or a light wood finish, plain sided or panelled. The undertaker will fit the handles and various ornamental furnishings to *the coffin depending on the style of coffin chosen and other factors such as religion, personal preferences, and whether it is a burial or cremation. After explaining which specific fixings were attached to what type of coffin, Old Des explained how the system worked in the workshop.*

Once the family had made the funeral arrangements at one of the company's branches and chosen the coffin to be used, Eamon would put the details of the type of coffin required up on the board on the wall by the entrance to the coffin stores. When the measurements of the deceased had been confirmed, the coffin size was added to the details on the board and the coffin could be assembled.

Old Des proceeded to demonstrate how to 'fit up' a coffin (the term used in the trade for carrying out the process of assembly). Tools required and supplied for the job included: a hammer, a power drill, a manual hand-held drill, a pair of pliers, a screwdriver, a heavy-duty staple gun, and a ruler. Although Old Des did all his measuring by eye, he advised us to use a ruler. At least until we developed an eye for things and reached a certain level of competency. His advice, in order to avoid disastrous and possibly costly mistakes, was duly noted.

Watching the coffin master at work, Adam and I intently scrutinised his every move at every stage of development as he transformed the very plain dark wood coffin shell into the elegant, finished item ready for occupancy. Its shiny brass handles, ornamental fixings and plush white silky lining decorated with gold pins around the edges looked fit for royalty. There was limited commentary during the demonstration process with only the occasional snippet of technical information passed on in his soft, gruff Irish accent. Various tips to assist in the development of our skills in order to become proficient at our craft were thrown in where applicable. On several occasions it was necessary to ask Old Des to repeat his words of wisdom due to their inaudibility. This seemed to test his patience somewhat.

As you might expect, Old Des made the whole process look extremely simple and effortless. In fact, he probably could have done it in his sleep. In his sleep, with one arm tied behind his back, while riding a unicycle, in a tornado. In other words, he was extremely proficient at his chosen craft. When you think how many coffins he'd probably produced over the years, and how many of those would have been built from scratch in the earlier part of his career, it wasn't surprising he made it look so easy.

Finally, it was our turn to try and impress the master. The whole scenario reminded me of *The Generation Game*, one of my favourite TV game shows from my youth. It had a number of hosts over the years, including Larry Grayson and Jim Davidson. But the most entertaining has to be the one and only Mr Bruce Forsyth. In one part of the show participants had to watch an expert demonstrating whatever it was they were an expert in. They used to have people doing all sorts of weird and wonderful things: icing a cake, flamenco dancing, juggling, and even using a potter's wheel. Oh, if only! You name it, they probably had it on the programme over the years the show ran. The contestants, usually a male and female related in some way, had a set amount of time to try and replicate what the expert had previously demonstrated. The resulting chaos was without fail absolutely hilarious, and some of the end results produced by the contestants even more hilarious. Proper entertainment, as Dad would say.

As Adam and I proceeded with our first attempt at fitting up a coffin, the only thing missing from the scene was Anthea Redfern, Bruce Forsyth's assistant and wife at the time, twirling around in her new outfit, as she did on every episode of the show, and Bruce Forsyth darting back and forth taking the mickey out of our efforts shouting 'Didn't they do well?' and, 'Let's have a look at the old score board'. Somehow I don't think Adam and I would have reached the final, missing out on the opportunity to win a cuddly toy, carving knife, coffee percolator, or dinner set, just some of the varied and strange mixture of prizes usually found on offer in the show. There really was no expense spared on quiz shows in those days.

The hardest part of the fitting-up process of the coffin for me, was securing the plastic sheeting inside. An important requirement, by all accounts, in preventing possible leakage of body fluids from the coffin. Nice! If the plastic sheeting was too tight without any give at all, it was very likely to rip as soon as the deceased was placed into the coffin, making the plastic sheeting ineffective in its fluid-retaining capabilities. If the plastic sheeting was too loose, although still capable of carrying out its practical function, it could look very messy and unprofessional. Precision folding was a necessity for a professional finish and correct application of the plastic sheeting's functional role. It certainly made me wish I'd paid more attention to that little Asian chap on TV in the seventies who used to demonstrate the amazing art of origami (the ancient art of paper folding). His wing-flapping swans and jumping frogs were to die for. If you'll pardon the terminology.

In the same time it took Adam and me to finish one coffin, Old Des could have produced at least four or five. Mind you, when learning anything new it can take a while to get the hang of things. Saying that, it certainly looked like we were going to be getting plenty of practice with the amount of names going up on the board in the workshop. It wouldn't be long before we were more than able to impress Mr Forsyth, if not Old Des!

Adam and I spent the rest of the afternoon in the workshop on the coffin production line learning the different types of coffins and fixings and developing our workmanship skills. Equipment wise, the staple guns used for attaching the plastic sheeting were not your average office stationery type. They were heavy-duty items and required the grip of a silverback gorilla to activate and constant hand changes to maintain momentum and alleviate severe muscle cramps. They also had an extremely impressive firing range, as Adam and I discovered – purely by accident. In the wrong hands, if larking around in an immature manner, they could be quite a dangerous device.

We managed to subdue the urges from our inner child who so obviously wanted to utilise the firing capacity of the magnificent staple guns to their maximum, and re-enact that famous scene from history that took place in 1881 in Tombstone between the Earp brothers' law enforcement officers –with support from Doc Holiday – against the Clantons and other members of the outlaw gang, the Cowboys. It was, after all, still only our first day and we were very aware that we needed to give the right impression as we were both on a three-month probationary period.

The use of power tools, for any man, is a very empowering experience that few things in life can surpass within the male psyche, but they *can often create a false impression of the competency of the operative, especially in his own mind. Although not classed as one of the most complex among power tools, the advanced variable speed drill that was now at our disposal would need to be treated with the greatest of respect and used cautiously until we were more familiar with its own particular idiosyncrasies. Being over confident when using power tools, no matter how experienced the operative, can often end in tears. I came very close to amputating my own leg just above the knee once, when using a rotary sander for the first time to sand down the wooden flooring in my sister's kitchen.*

Old Des abandoned us at three o'clock – his usual time of departure from the workplace. So Eamon, darting in and out of the workshop energetically like he was on some energy enhancing substance, made it clear he was available if we got into any difficulty. This was comforting yet unnerving – as being watched in case you make a mistake invariably causes you to make one.

During the day we gradually got to meet the entirety of the yard's workforce, including Frank – a Burt Reynolds lookalike – Arthur, under-foreman and another shorty like Eddie and myself, tall, slender Graham in his Buddy Holly-styled spectacles, and Howard, who couldn't have been far from retirement age at all, an even taller and more slender man than Graham. I remembered Mum used to refer to Howard as the film star because he was always looking in the mirror and combing his luxurious Elvis Presley-style head of white hair. Even more impressive than his fastidiously well-groomed hair was the extremely colourful and elaborate pair of braces that he wore decorated with race horses and jockeys. Very daring, unlike all the others who were obviously playing it safe sticking to drab-coloured braces more traditionally suited to funeral attire. Marcus, the elusive embalmer, also made a couple of appearances, at tea breaks. He was much younger than I was expecting and seemed quite a humorous chap. Not what I envisaged at all.

Funeral crews came and went throughout the day, and in between the funerals the men were sent out to collect bodies from various hospitals, nursing homes and private houses, as well as transporting them to and from the branches for viewing or in preparation for funerals the next day. It was all go! Adam and I were not utilised in any areas other than the workshop. We suspected this was to allow us to concentrate on developing our workshop skills to a competent level, before being let loose into the public domain.

Mr Dickinson dropped by the yard in between funerals that he was conducting to see how Adam and I were getting on, which was thoughtful. It turns out Adam and he were good friends. Which as you can imagine made Adam a bit of a target for a little urine extraction from the guys. Nothing nasty, just a bit of boys' banter – and Adam gave as good as he got. As for me, apparently the sandwich incident raised questions among some of my colleagues regarding my mental stability. Even so, I don't think it's a bad thing for people to be wary of how far they can push you. And it's a good thing if they are encouraged to think twice before they do.

Just before home time Joe appeared with the pony from head office. And before you get on your high horse, the pony was the name for the bag in which the internal post was transported between the various branches, head office and the yard, so named, I presumed, after the Pony Express in the western United States in the 1800s. Granted, this was just an assumption, but a fairly good one I thought, so I didn't bother to ask. The pony was made out of the exact same imitation-leather material that Mum had made my cowboy and Indian outfit from when I was a young boy. As soon as I saw it I started to get flashbacks from my youth; running around like a demented zombie and constantly falling over when I wore the damn things because the material was so thick I couldn't bend my legs properly. Oh, happy days. Perhaps a re-enactment of the gunfight in Tombstone when Adam and I were undergoing our workshop training wouldn't have been totally out of place after all.

In the pony were numerous pieces of paperwork including the next day's orders with information of who was allocated to each funeral, which bodies needed to be where and when for a funeral or viewing, and several arranged collections of bodies from a number of hospitals and the preferred times for those collections to be carried out. Adam and I hadn't been allocated to participate on any funerals or take part in any other of the day's planned events, according to the orders. Which seemed to confirm our presumptions, that before venturing into the various realms of the funeral world, we would probably be assigned to the workshop for a few weeks until we had mastered all workshop-related duties.

My first day at Mortimer and Sons Undertakers was coming to a close, and not so much as a glimpse or sniff of a body, if you'll excuse the expression. It was quite eventful in other ways, of course, but perhaps the less said about that the better. I suspect I may have made a lifelong enemy of Dean over the sandwich incident. I realise my response to Dean's remark, whether he was joking or not, may have seemed a little over the top, but it certainly had the desired effect regarding the safety of my sandwiches. Unless he did something unpleasant to them when I wasn't looking. In which case he'd probably had the last laugh.

Adam seemed a nice enough chap. Apparently, his previous profession before joining Mortimer and Sons was as a turf accountant. Which as he informed me, is not someone who counts turf, but a posh name for a bookmaker.

Most importantly, Adam and I could now fit up a coffin to a decent standard. A coffin you could say, someone wouldn't mind being seen dead in. Furthermore, when the need did arise for us to venture out into the big bad world in our capacity as funeral assistants, even if we may appear confused about what we were doing and why, we would at least be very smart in our new top-of-the-range undertaker's attire.

TUESDAY

On my second day at Mortimer and Sons, I had decided to get ahead of the game and arrived for work at half past seven. As I turned into the cobbled mews, Joe and Oliver were exiting the garage with two coffins on wheelie trolleys heading over to the mortuary. Conveniently, they'd left the giant concertina door open just enough for me to ride the bike through. I rode through the gap cautiously, just in case I met any more coffins on their way out. Parking the bike up next to the old workbench at the back of the garage, I noticed the bike was already starting to leave its unmistakable signature mark, a patch of very well-used, thin black oil.

Eddie and Ali were tentatively rousing the large black Daimlers from their slumber in order to prepare them for another day's work. After greeting me cheerfully they returned their full attention to the needs of the imposing black beasts. Graham and Frank were banging and clattering in the workshop fitting up coffins. The new boys weren't quite up to speed yet and hadn't finished a couple of the coffins that were required urgently that morning. Oops!

Adam was already in the tearoom chatting with some of the others who were also getting their caffeine fix before the day's duties got underway. Eamon was running around like one of those toy rabbits on the TV advert for longer-lasting batteries, handing out lists with the bodies that needed to be boxed up for the day's funerals, and those to be dressed and boxed up ready for transportation to various branches for viewing. Once the caffeine had kicked in and was flowing steadily through people's veins, they started to disperse from the tearoom on their various missions, intently perusing the lists held in their hands.

Wagons Ho!

To our surprise, Eamon asked Adam and I to take two coffins and some clothing over to the mortuary and give Joe and Oliver a hand to dress and box up. We'd obviously been too quick to assume we were going to be limited to only workshop duties for the next few weeks. Taking charge of the coffins Eamon had indicated, Adam and I headed in the direction of the mortuary through the garage, serenaded by Eddie who was in full swing with a rendition of Frank Sinatra's 'I Did It My Way'. Closely followed by Frank and Graham with the two coffins they had just completed, our macabre Wild-West wagon train ventured across the cobbled plains. Ye ha! Except it was more of a north-easterly direction from the garage to the mortuary rather than west and probably not quite so wild. Although, I've heard it can get quite rowdy at the weekends in the local saloons around here – I mean pubs!

I'm convinced that the trolleys used for manoeuvring the coffins around the yard and the branches were designed and constructed by the same company that manufactured supermarket trolleys with the compulsory dodgy front wheel. You know, that one wheel that always seems to want to go in completely the opposite direction to all the other wheels, whilst having some sort of wheel version of an epileptic seizure? Things may have improved slightly nowadays, but years ago there were a lot of shopping trolleys, in various supermarkets, that you had to really wrestle with to complete your weekly shop. There was no need to go to the gym for a workout.

Every trolley at the yard, without exception, seemed to have its rebellious wheel. The uncontrollable wheels combined with the extremely difficult terrain of the uneven ancient cobbles and a few asteroid craters thrown in for luck, made what should have been a very ordinary and uneventful journey from the workshop to the mortuary, and vice versa, into a very challenging one. Trying to steady the coffins and constantly reposition them as they bounced frantically on the bucking bronco trolleys, in order to prevent them from crashing to the ground and shattering into a thousand splinters, or at the least causing quite a nasty scratch, required nothing less than the agility of a circus acrobat and the coordination skills of an ambidextrous psychic.

The scene of our bucking bronco coffins was reminiscent of another one of my favourite TV game shows from my youth, It's a Knockout. All that was missing from the usual antics performed on the show was the wearing of giant cartoon-like heads, buckets of water being thrown from every direction and the hysterical laughter of the game-show host. There's definitely a theme forming here involving my memory pattern, which I've not really noticed prior to writing my memoirs: I obviously watched far too much television as a youngster.

Triumphantly, we finally reached the mortuary door, shaken and a little stirred, but all coffins at least in one piece. Well, two if you count the lid as a separate piece, which technically it is. Adam and I looked at each other apprehensively as Graham unlocked the mortuary door with the sacred master key that opened that and other doors around the yard, head office and the various branches of Mortimer and Sons. All staff were issued with a copy of the sacred key.

As Adam and I hadn't been issued with our sacred key at that point, any time we needed to gain access to anywhere behind a locked door, we had to ask another member of staff to facilitate that objective. An inconvenience for us, and the other member of staff who we would have to burden with the task. Mind you, it was only our second day, we'd probably not gained the appropriate level of trust at that stage of our employment to be permitted possession of such an important item. Either that, or they just didn't have any spare keys available.

I was a little anxious about how I would manage when it came to handling the bodies and tried hard not to display my trepidation. I sensed Adam had similar misgivings, and although I can't say for sure, he certainly gave the impression that he, too, was feeling somewhat uneasy. We entered the mortuary with our unusual convoy and placed the coffins in a row to the right of the bank of large humming fridges. The familiar sweet chemical fragrance that I had become accustomed to at Mum's branch dominated the mortuary, intermingling with a few other odours that were not so sweet that it was clearly struggling to disguise. After a brief bout of jovial banter between Joe, Oliver, Frank and Graham, Frank and Graham returned to the workshop to continue fitting up coffins, leaving the rest of us to get on with the matter in hand.

Nip and Tuck

Joe was sifting through several pink cards whilst simultaneously scanning through a large book to the left of the fridges that was resting on a roughly made wooden shelf; rather like a church lectern but attached to the wall. Hopefully, it was not one of Reg's carpentry masterpieces.

Joe informed me that the pink cards were extremely important points of reference throughout a deceased's journey through the system of Mortimer and Sons, from the name and address of the removal, the recording of valuables retained or returned, and other relevant information up to and including the funeral. All the information on the pink card was used at various other points of call at the yard, head office, and the appropriate branch where the funeral was arranged.

The pink card comes in three parts that are subsequently separated to carry out their specific duties, two smaller sections at each end that fold under the larger main section. The one smaller section with only the deceased's name on it, is attached via a trusty bulldog clip onto the board on the wall next to the letter of the alphabet that corresponds to the fridge the deceased is occupying. The other small section with only the deceased's name on it stays with the deceased, and the larger section of the pink card containing all the other important information is returned to Eamon. The large book on the rustic lectern is for recording information about the deceased and their whereabouts, i.e., in what fridge, at what branch, or whether despatched on the day of the funeral.

Pairing up with Joe and Oliver, Adam with Oliver and myself with Joe, we were ready for our first lesson of dressing and boxing up. Joe informed me that our first body to dress was that of a Mr Jones who was in fridge one on tray B. He told me to put some protective rubber gloves on, indicating in the direction of a stack of small green boxes on a nearby shelf. I first opted for the mediums but they were a little tight. I then tried the large, and although the fingers were a little too long and compromised dexterity, after weighing up the pros and cons of each size I decided that dealing with a little extra length was better than the restrictive tightness of the mediums and the risk of them splitting.

Joe asked me to bring the hydraulic hoist over from the corner of the mortuary and remove Mr Jones from the fridge. While I did this, Joe wrote the relevant information in the mortuary book relating to Mr Jones's destination – which as it happened, was Mum's branch. I wrestled with the heavy and rather cumbersome manual hoist which was clearly more than happy where it was judging by its unwillingness to relocate. Even after releasing the brakes.

Opening the fridge door, a rush of cold air whistled past me like an escaping entity, causing me to shiver. I was greeted by the soles of three pairs of rather pale, wrinkly white feet, at varying levels, complete with stereotypical toe tag tied around the big toe on the right foot of each body. Each pair of feet was protruding from under the edge of a white sheet that covered the contours of the human remains stretching into the depths of the dark fridge. One pair of feet was at eye level, another pair about waist height, and the other pair at ground level. I pumped up the hydraulic hoist to just below the level of tray B, which was the middle tray. The resistance of the hoist lever mechanism was a workout in itself for most of the major muscle groups of my upper body.

As the coldness of the fridge became chilly rather than refreshing, I removed the tray and its passenger from the fridge onto the hoist and shut the fridge door, sealing in once again the Icelandic influence from the more hospitable warmth of the mortuary. I was surprised how much effort it took to move the tray, as Mr Jones did not appear to be a large chap under the white sheet that covered him. The rollers in the fridge and the hoist that facilitated movement of the load should also have made it a much easier operation than it was.

Joe turned towards me from his writing.

"Don't forget to put the safety pin in place, Bill, to stop the tray from rolling off the hoist," he said, pointing to a small metal pin that sat in a hole at one end of the hoist. "We don't want any mishaps."

"We certainly don't," I replied, shaking my head in agreement as I secured the tray with Mr Jones on it safely to the hoist using the small metal pin supplied.

Joe finished writing in the mortuary book and joined Mr Jones and me for the next step of the proceedings. Reaching for each corner of the sheet at the head end of the tray that covered Mr Jones, Joe pulled the sheet down to the level of Mr Jones's waist. The naked, pale body of the late Mr Jones lay partially covered before us. His bald head slightly raised and tilted forwards rested on a block of wood with a semi-circle cut out of it, which neatly supported his head. His eyes were closed and he looked peaceful, albeit very pale and slightly under dressed (except for a toga party perhaps).

"In this job, Bill, there's no such thing as checking too much. Especially when it comes to the deceased's ID and valuables. Check, and double check, then get someone else to check what you've just checked and confirm it. There's no room for mistakes, and you've got to cover yourself."

I acknowledged my understanding at the importance of Joe's statement with a nod.

Mr Jones was the proud owner of four ID tags. Two from the hospital – the plastic bracelet around his left wrist and the toe tag. The other two, supplied by Mortimer and Sons, were the ID bracelet on his right ankle *and the section of the pink card on the tray next to him. Joe asked me to check the details on all the tags, and then double check them. He then checked them himself. Presumably to show me in practice how what he had just explained to me works, just in case I was confused in any way.*

Mr Jones was as cold to the touch as the fridge tray he lay upon. The feel of his cold, clammy skin and the sensation of the relaxed muscles on his lifeless skeletal frame felt similar to that of holding a piece of raw chicken on the bone. I had expected him to be rigid like a shop manikin and was very surprised to discover that he wasn't. I remarked on Mr Jones's unexpected ragdoll mobility. Joe explained that rigor mortis, the correct terminology for the stiffness that takes place after death, is actually a chemical reaction in the muscles. It's often used to determine how long someone has been dead, as the various stages involved in the process of rigor mortis evolve in a fairly precise time frame. However, it disperses naturally after a period of time. If rigor mortis is present, the limbs can be manipulated through their range of movement to work the rigor mortis out, regaining flaccidity. Rather like the stretching movements used to work cramp out.

"That's an extremely severe case of cramp," I said. Much to Joe's amusement.

Mr Jones was eighty-six years old according to his ID tags, and not looking too bad at all for his age. Particularly for someone that had been dead for five days.

"He's got a yellow metal wedding ring which needs to stay on," Joe said, raising Mr Jones's right hand in the air.

"Yellow metal?" I echoed.

"Yellow metal, white metal, yellow metal with stone. It's a simple way to describe the jewellery without getting too technical or overcomplicating matters."

Joe grabbed the bag of clothing that was sitting on top of Mr Jones's coffin. A dark wood, mahogany coffin with plastic brass-look handles. One I made earlier as they say, with my own fair hands. And very nicely finished it was, too.

Mr Jones's family or whoever had supplied his clothing had bought a brand-new set of thermal underwear for him to be dressed in. I couldn't help thinking it was a bit ironic as he was going to be cremated. But I suppose it's the thought that counts, and if that's what he would have worn in life, that's what mattered. It would be a comforting thought to whoever had supplied them, that he was wearing them, I'm sure.

Mr Jones's cold, clammy skin made him difficult to dress. Rather like when you've been swimming and not dried yourself properly because you imagine people are staring at you or you're in a hurry. Your clothes seem to object to being placed next to your skin. Twisting and turning, clinging on like an angry creature being forced to go where it doesn't want to go.

Looking very fetching in his new thermals and a great deal more dignified, Joe and I progressed to the next phase of Mr Jones's dressing process. Arms and legs were fed into, and through, shirt sleeves, blazer sleeves, and trouser legs. Stiff fingers, splayed out uncooperatively as wide as they could be, were grasped firmly but gently and coaxed through the various tunnels of material. It may seem foolish, but the act of holding another man's hand any longer than a firm, manly handshake would take, felt unnatural and made me feel quite uncomfortable. Even a dead man's hand. Or should I say – especially a dead man's hand.

Mr Jones's tight socks put up a real fight, clinging to his clammy feet like two opposing pieces of Velcro. As gently and as respectfully as we were trying to carry out the somewhat awkward task, at some points Joe and I must have looked like a wrestling tag team in slow motion as we rolled Mr Jones back and forward to get his clothing correctly in place. Untwisting and tucking in the bits that required untwisting and tucking in. With his siesta-like expression, I kept imagining him opening his eyes and asking us what on earth we thought we were doing. Of course, if he had, I probably would've had a change of heart about my new career and terminated my employment at Mortimer and Sons rather swiftly, leaving a cloud of blue exhaust smoke behind me as I roared out of the timeworn cobbled mews.

I became slightly concerned at one point in the proceedings and had to ask Joe if we actually had the right clothing, as it seemed far too large for Mr Jones's small frame. Joe assured me it was definitely the right clothing, as he'd collected it from the family himself. He mentioned *that due to Mr Jones's illness he'd probably lost a lot of weight since he had last worn it, and assured me that all would be well by the time the fat lady started singing; a term, I believe, that stems from operatic origins. Although, I think these days the term 'fat' might be classed as a little derogatory, and should probably be replaced with, 'buxom', 'voluptuous', or 'curvaceous'.*

Behind Joe and me, frustrated mumblings from Adam and Oliver indicated they were having problems dressing the recumbent lady on the tray in front of them. Apparently the dress that had been supplied by the family was too small. Radical alterations with the aid of a large pair of scissors would be required in order for the dress to fit, or at least appear that it did. The lady was returned to the fridge from whence she came until the family could be contacted and the matter discussed to find a solution; presumably, radical alterations, or a replacement garment.

I've never really been all that great at doing tie knots on myself, let alone on someone else, so I asked Joe if he would do Mr Jones's tie to avoid embarrassing the poor chap when he was viewed by his family and friends. Joe, placing the tie around his own neck, in an instant produced one of the most impressive tie knots I'd ever seen. A Windsor knot, apparently. Which I'd never even heard of before.

"It's much smarter than the school-boy knot that I do," I remarked. "Mine look more like a sausage roll made of material."

"I can't do a tie on someone else, I have to do it on myself first," Joe stated, placing the perfectly formed tie knot over Mr Jones's head.

Joe centralised the knot and tightened it around the neck of the shirt that swamped Mr Jones's rather emaciated wrinkly old neck and then straightened the collar out. Mr Jones's shoes were causing problems and wanted nothing to do with being on his feet. As with the thermal underwear the shoes appeared brand new. Hard leather ones with absolutely no give in them whatsoever, they seemed far too small. Joe said that Mr Jones probably hadn't worn shoes for a very long time. In fact, he may well have only worn slippers, if anything at all, and his feet had probably spread. They were also quite swollen which didn't help matters, possibly due to his illness or the medication he'd been taking.

Joe thought we should leave the shoes off and ask Jean (Mum) at the branch to explain the situation to the family. They could then decide if they wanted to supply another pair of shoes or whether they wanted us to make a few adjustments to the new ones to get them to fit.

My suggestion that flip-flops should be compulsory coffin footwear appealed to Joe's sense of humour. He wants to be dressed in a scuba-diving suit when he dies, to make things as difficult as possible for the undertakers that have to dress him. An amusing thought that appealed to my sense of humour. Oliver, overhearing Joe's comment, remarked how hilarious that would be to watch and how he would like to be a fly on the wall observing the unfolding mayhem.

Now fully dressed, albeit looking like Ronnie Corbett in one of Ronnie Barker's suits, and minus footwear, it was time to get Mr Jones into his very professionally made coffin. Joe removed the lid revealing the smartly finished inside set with its tastefully and very accurately placed decorative brass pins along the top inside edge of the white silky material. Wheeling the coffin over, Joe positioned it next to the hoist which was currently supporting Mr Jones on tray B. He then asked me to pump up the hoist to elevate the tray and Mr Jones to just above the level of the top of the open coffin – which I did without question. Following Joe's instructions, I leant over the empty coffin to reach Mr Jones on the tray. With Joe taking hold of Mr Jones's upper body and supporting his head, and myself taking hold of Mr Jones at the hips and legs, on the count of three, in unison, we slowly slid Mr Jones from tray B into the coffin, lowering him gently as we took all of his weight. His small, emaciated frame was surprisingly heavy for its size. A dead weight indeed.

Looking a little ruffled at the edges by his latest relocation of resting places, Joe set to work straightening the slightly dishevelled Mr Jones and his clothing. With a few tucks here and a gathering of material there, the ill-fitting shirt and suit were magically transformed to give the impression they had been tailor-made only yesterday. Cunning, even somewhat deceitful some might say. Nevertheless, all done with the right intentions, and I'm sure Mr Jones would have appreciated the effort. He was looking quite dapper now as a result of Joe's care and expertise. The 'buxom' lady began to sing, but was soon silenced as we had not quite finished.

"The pillow's too high. His nose will get squashed," stated Joe. "If we put the lid on now, he'll look like he's done ten rounds with Mike Tyson when it's next taken off. I'll have to lower the pillow. Support his head for a minute, Bill."

While I supported Mr Jones's rather weighty head to hover above the pillow, Joe pushed down the shredded paper that formed the pillow underneath the plastic sheeting, compressing it to a more acceptable level for Mr Jones's head. I had apparently been a little too enthusiastic with my stuffing, according to Joe. I said I'd never had any complaints before. Joe's laughter drew the attention of Oliver and Adam once again, but not for long as they were rather preoccupied with the gentleman they were dressing whose jacket seemed to be proving a bit of a challenge to get on.

Joe gave me the go-ahead to lower Mr Jones's head back down onto the now more appropriately sized pillow.

"Sorted!" he said, looking pleased with himself.

It did look much better. A much more natural position, and most importantly, alleviating the possibility of Mr Jones acquiring the Mike Tyson sparring partner look.

Joe explained that if the coffin pillow was too high the head of the deceased could be angled too far forward, and may also be too close to the lid when it's placed back on the coffin. On the other hand, if the pillow was too low, the head could be angled back too far and the family's last image of Grandad, Grandma or Aunt Maisy could be predominately of their nasal passages. Not the most pleasant last image of a loved one to have imprinted on your mind in your time of grief.

A very useful and important lesson learnt about the art of pillow stuffing. Not too much, not too little – as with many things in life.

The finishing touches were made to Mr Jones in his coffin and a white face cloth was placed over his face. Joe then positioned the lid on the coffin. The pink ID card, which Joe had removed from the committed bulldog clip on the board, that previously indicated the fridge space Mr Jones had occupied, was slipped under one corner of the brass-coloured nameplate on the coffin lid. The unofficial name given to this portion of the pink card by the staff at the yard is the deceased's ticket to ride. Its attachment to the coffin signifies to other staff that Mr Jones is in his coffin and good to go, ready to be viewed by his family and friends to pay their last respects, once the shoe situation had been addressed, of course.

Adam and Oliver appeared to have overcome their difficulty with the gentleman's jacket on the other side of the mortuary and were just placing him into his coffin. Joe, returning to the mortuary book on the lectern, scanned through the pink cards that Eamon had given him.

"Right, stick that tray back, Bill," Joe said, pointing to the empty tray on the hoist. "Mr Lomax, from fridge three on tray G is next."

I did as Joe requested, replacing tray B back into its now vacant space in fridge one. Opening the door to fridge three I was greeted by only one pair of feet this time, once again complete with designer toe tag. Mr Lomax had sole occupancy of fridge three on the top shelf. The penthouse suite. Wrestling the hydraulic hoist into position, I pumped it up to almost its maximum height, level with tray G at the top of the fridge. I then rolled the tray containing Mr Lomax out of the fridge and onto the hoist – making sure I put the retaining pin in place to avoid any mishaps. I was learning fast. Once the hoist was clear of the fridge door I closed it, confining its coldness securely within. Lowering the hoist to waist height, Joe and I carried out Mr Lomax's multiple ID checks. I checked first, then Joe confirmed my findings.

Mr Lomax was a younger old man than Mr Jones, at the age of seventy-five, and was not in possession of any jewellery. According to the information written on the pink removal card it had already been removed and signed for at the nursing home by the family. His clothing was considerably better fitting than Mr Jones's clothing. Which actually made it much harder to dress him, there being much less give or room for manoeuvre as well as the added hindrance of his cold, clammy skin. It was also far more casual, and included a pair of brown trousers, a well-worn beige cardigan (a favourite presumably), a vest, a pair of traditional Y-fronts which were clean but showing indications of high mileage, a pale blue shirt but no tie, and a pair of slippers which did exactly what slippers should do, and slipped on effortlessly. An absolute delight after trying to get Mr Jones's hard leather shoes onto his noncompliant feet.

Some personal accessories were also supplied. A briar, straight-stemmed smoking pipe which was placed in his cardigan pocket, and a leather tobacco pouch with a small amount of rather aromatic tobacco inside (coconut based I believe). Just as Mr Jones's thermal underwear had seemed a little ironic as he was being cremated, so did Mr Lomax's pipe and tobacco. But the thought was there – it was something he enjoyed in life and he would not be him if he was without it.

Some family photos of what looked like a birthday party, possibly his own, possibly his last, were placed around him in the coffin. Presumably the adults were sons, daughters, in-laws, and the children were grandchildren or even great grandchildren. A small picture obviously drawn by a very young child was also placed beside him. I assumed Mr Lomax and the artist were the two people represented in the picture. The clothing on the adult and the object that appeared to be on fire in his right hand seemed vaguely familiar. They stood hand in hand in a very green garden in front of a rather dubiously unstable-looking house which was evidently competing with the Leaning Tower of Pisa for its place in architectural history. Surrounded by a multitude of giant flowers of every colour available in crayon, a huge bright sun beamed above them, suspended in a bright blue sky. Each of the animated characters had a smile that reached from one ear to the other. It was a typical scene produced by a certain age group of our species during the developing stages of their artistic talents. It was simple, from the heart, and spoke volumes of a small child's love. A love for someone they would clearly miss very much.

With Mr Lomax dressed, boxed up and booked out and his pink ticket to ride tucked neatly under the nameplate on the coffin lid, Joe and I only had one more body to dress and box.

The Real Deal

Mrs Collins had been participating in her ninety-seventh year on this planet when she passed away, and was now temporarily residing in fridge two on tray F. Joe started writing in the mortuary book while I did my tray shuffling act. Tray G back into fridge three and then fridge two to extract *tray F. I was becoming a dab hand at manhandling the cumbersome hoist back and forwards now. Even though it looked like I was struggling, it was now a controlled struggle with technique. There's a vast difference. Ask any man. The technique also involved trying to convince any onlookers that the effort required appeared far less arduous than it actually was.*

Not only was I greeted by the now familiar and expected pairs of feet on opening the door to fridge two, a new sight also met my eyes for the first time. That of a large, thick white plastic bag that covered the whole of tray F.

"She's in a body bag," said Joe, stepping from behind me, clearly noticing my look of surprise. "Probably because she had MRSA, according to the pink card."

"What's MRSA?" I asked.

"It's a nasty little bug. Especially if your immune system is low or you're already ill like when you're in hospital."

"Is it still contagious after death?" I asked, with an air of concern in my voice.

"I'm not sure to be honest, Bill. I don't think so. Although Marcus says that every 'body' should be treated as potentially harmful to health and to always use gloves as a minimum precaution. Just because someone died of one thing, it doesn't mean that they didn't have something else that might be contagious, or that there isn't something unpleasant going on as the body deteriorates."

"That makes sense," I agreed.

"More hospitals and hospices are using body bags nowadays. Mainly if an infectious disease is involved, but also because it's a lot more hygienic than handling a naked body or just wrapping them in a sheet. Leaking body fluids can be quite a problem. It's not very pleasant if body fluids start dripping down the side of the stretcher, all over the van, and you."

"I suppose not," I agreed, pulling a face that was supposed to relay my understanding of the useful but rather revolting information relayed to me.

"Mind you, sometimes using a body bag can actually make the problem worse. When you open up the bag, it can be like a flipping tidal wave. It's

swings and roundabouts when it comes to the pros and cons of body bags, but they do generally make our job easier. Especially when dealing with badly decomposed bodies. Sometimes we even have to double bag them. You've got all that to look forward to, Bill," he said, with a smirk on his face.

Carrying on with the task in hand, I removed tray F from the bottom of fridge two with the large white body bag on and then pumped the hydraulic hoist up to waist height. Taking hold of the zip that ran down the entire length of the middle of the bag, I opened up the body bag. Instantaneously, the foulest stench I have ever smelt filled my lungs. I could taste the decay. It was vile. I stepped back turning my head away from the body to try and get a breath of fresher air into my lungs. What little there was in the environment we currently occupied. Turning back towards Joe and the body bag I tried to breathe as shallowly as possible to limit the volume of air I was inhaling, while still trying to gain enough oxygen to retain consciousness. I realised immediately I hadn't dealt very well with the situation. Not quite as calm and controlled as I would like to have been seen to be.

"It's probably a lot worse because the bag's been closed for a couple of days," said Joe. And he asked if I was okay.

"I just wasn't expecting that," I said. "It caught me a bit off guard."

Adam and Oliver looked over.

"You'll get used to it, Bill," said Oliver. "And a lot worse."

Joe was apologetic and said he just hadn't thought to mention that Mrs Collins might not be at her best aromatically. He continued to unzip the bag. Mrs Collins's severely curved spine prevented her head from resting on the wooden head block and meant her head was raised and angled backwards. I studied the contorted, almost skeletal features of the old lady's face, her toothless mouth agape, revealing a thick yellow coating of mucous on her tongue and the inside of her mouth. Her eyes wide open stared out at us. Dehydrated and misshapen they sat deep in the sockets of her skull. A dull cloudy grey, they lacked the lustre they would have once had in life, the last visions of her life lost deep within the stagnant haze.

After a while the intensity of the foul stench became slightly less potent. Released from quarantine like a wild beast, its new-found freedom to assault the senses would eventually be its undoing. Although, even absorbed into the atmosphere and neutralised by airborne chemicals, it was still unpleasant enough to warrant limited inhalation in close proximity to the rather potent human remains.

I was, of course, well aware that if someone was to be viewed after death, a certain amount of preparation of the deceased would be required. But the difference between Mr Jones and Mr Lomax in comparison to Mrs Collins was startling. Joe explained that Mr Jones and Mr Lomax had both been embalmed due to the fact that they were both to be viewed. Mr Lomax was also going to be staying in church overnight. Joe elaborated.

"It wouldn't take long for an unrefrigerated body that hadn't been embalmed to become very unpleasant to be around, especially in the very hot weather we've been experiencing recently."

He went on to explain that embalming is basically the process of sanitising the body inside and out. Making it more hygienic and presentable and slowing down the natural process of decay. Mrs Collins's family didn't want her to be embalmed or interfered with in any way, which was fine because she wasn't going to be viewed and the funeral was going straight to the crematorium from the yard that afternoon.

So, this was death's true face. The real deal. Nature's way. Undignified and unforgiving. Destructive dissolution, assaulting the senses.

Not much more than a skeleton, Mrs Collins had probably been bed-bound and immobile for years looking at the absence of muscle tone and the total lack of muscle on her aged bones, her veins and arteries highly visible with nowhere to hide under the old, saggy, almost transparent skin.

Joe and I checked Mrs Collins's ID tags, and then rechecked them. She had one on each limb from various establishments she had visited recently, including the Mortimer and Sons ID tags which were added when she was picked up from the hospital. As Joe says, 'you can never be too careful', and four ID tags have got to be better than none. As long as they're all the same name, of course. If they weren't, I imagine you might have a slight problem on your hands.

Joe referred to the pink card in his hand.

"She's got a yellow metal wedding ring on that's got to come off to be given back to the family."

Checking her left hand for the ring, I confirmed its presence. Although her fingers were thin and bony the joints were extremely swollen. It didn't look physically possible to me that the ring in question was going to come off unless it was cut off. The ring that is, not her finger.

"I can't see that ring coming off without a bit of a battle, Joe. Will it have to be cut off?"

Joe looked over, smiling mischievously.

"Watch and learn, Billy boy. Watch and learn," he said, raising his eyebrows to accompany his mischievous smile.

With that, he disappeared into the embalming room leaving Mrs Collins and me wondering what it was that he had up his sleeve. Apart from his arm, that is. On his return, he was holding a large, curved needle about 2 inches in length and a piece of string about 12 inches long (that's approximately 5cms and 30cms to those who think in metric).

Joe repeated the advisory sentence about watching and learning accompanied again by his mischievous knowing smirk and raised eyebrows, and once he'd threaded the large, curved needle with the string, like the magician Paul Daniels, Joe proceeded to astound, astonish and bemuse. Unfortunately, though, without the aid of the lovely Debbie Magee's captivating presence.

Passing the needle between the ring and Mrs Collins's finger and then removing the needle from the string but leaving the string in place threaded under the ring, he then doubled the string over. If I've not lost you there, well done!

"Right, Bill, get some liquid soap from the loo," Joe said, pointing to the mortuary's toilet facilities, "and put it around the ring and finger."

I did what was asked of me yet again without question. The liquid soap request being a bit of a giveaway as to Joe's intentions, I was however still a little perplexed with the role of the string, and still far from convinced that it was going to be possible to remove the ring without cutting it off. Gently circling the string around the ring whilst simultaneously applying a small amount of pressure, Joe gradually eased the yellow metal wedding ring very slowly over the swollen, soap-covered finger joint. I would have bet a month's wages that the ring would not have passed over the swollen joint of Mrs Collins's finger. Nevertheless, with a little ingenuity, very little force, and no harm done to Mrs Collins's fragile skin or finger whatsoever, Joe achieved what I would have thought impossible. I was extremely impressed and rather pleased I hadn't bet my months wages on the outcome of the ring removal challenge. Not that I've ever been a betting man. I've never really had the judgement skills, luck, or enough money to be able to afford to lose.

Thoroughly cleaning the ring, Joe placed it into a small brown envelope, ready for it to be returned to the family.

Not being dressed in her own clothes, after placing Mrs Collins into her coffin she was covered with a white shroud. The shrouds come in three pieces – two separate sleeves and the main section that covers the torso and legs. It's a clever idea and involves as little disturbance to the deceased as possible to put it on. A particular advantage according to Joe, in cases where it's not advisable or practical to move them about too much.

The sleeves are placed on first, although I imagine it wouldn't matter too much if the main piece was put on first if the inclination took you to do it that way. But this was the way I was being shown by Joe and I wasn't about to start questioning his reasoning. The shroud was then tucked in and around Mrs Collins to give the impression it was one garment and a perfect fit. Which technically it was. Cunning but effective, and quite becoming in an angelic sort of way. A white face cloth was placed over her face and the lid placed onto the coffin. Last but not least, her pink ticket to ride was tucked under the nameplate on the coffin lid and Mrs Collins was ready to go.

Adam and Oliver had also finished dressing and boxing up their bodies, so using the internal telephone Joe rang Eamon's office and asked him to come and check the bodies before they were despatched to their various destinations. Even with all the checking and double checking carried out by us, no 'body' was to leave the yard without Eamon checking it first.

After Eamon had completed his checks and given his blessings, he told Joe and me to get changed and take Mr Jones to Mum's branch *and Mr Lomax up to the Mill Hill branch. By the time we'd done that, the mortuary would be open at the Central Middlesex Hospital where we were to collect two bodies and bring them back to the yard. My first removal.*

Brace Yourself

Getting changed where the lockers were situated was an experience in itself and quite a challenge. The lockers, as previously mentioned, resided in the workshop and lined the route to the tearoom, Eamon's office, and the toilets. It was an extremely busy and major route of passage. For those trying to get dressed and undressed it was like being in the middle of King's Cross Station during rush hour. A veritable battle at the best of times. Privacy, as in the middle of King's Cross Station, was as you can imagine non-existent. Mind you, it would have been far worse if it wasn't all male staff at the yard. Or more interesting, I suppose!

Due to the limited space restricting normal movement it demanded the use of a variety of skills to actually complete the dressing or undressing process without causing injury to oneself or others. It was certainly a test of agility and coordination skills, and any level of experience in t'ai chi was definitely advantageous. It was also particularly beneficial to be proficient at the swimming-pool-changing-room dressing technique: putting your trousers on without letting them touch the floor in order to try and keep them dry. This was a very important technique in the workshop, not to keep them dry obviously, but to stop them getting covered in sawdust, shredded paper, and any other foreign debris that may have found its way into the building. For those wanting to gain access to or exit the tearoom, toilet, or Eamon's office, with arms and legs coming at you from every angle as people tried to get changed, it was like trying to run the gauntlet against Gladiators, Wolf, Hunter and Saracen.

It wasn't until I was wearing my smart new top-of-the-range undertakers' trousers for the first time, having used the swimming-pool-changing-room technique effectively to keep them clean, that I suddenly realised why everyone wore braces. It wasn't a fashion statement or compulsory undertakers' clothing accessory, it was purely because there weren't any loops provided on the trousers for the application of a belt. A fact that had totally eluded me when trying them on in the shop due to the fact that I wasn't really moving about enough to notice the need for any extra support, as I would be during a vigorous day's work. Perhaps if I'd given a small exhibition of flamenco dancing, with all that stamping about I might have noticed the need for a belt and discovered the lack of belt loops to facilitate such equipment, questioned the staff in the shop at the time, and with the information imparted to me, having been enlightened, sought to purchase a pair of braces.

When I pointed out my predicament to Joe, he said we could stop off somewhere for me to purchase a pair of braces, after we'd dropped Mr Lomax and Mr Jones off at the branches, before going to the hospital. What a gent!

My school-boy mini sausage roll-shaped tie knot having seen me through my earlier years – mainly because I didn't really give two monkeys at that age what it looked like and neither did anyone else, I imagine – suddenly seemed very inadequate to be part of my smart new undertakers' attire. It was, however, the way I had been taught to tie a tie and the only way I knew how to. I was completely oblivious to any alternative methods. At least up until that point in my life. So I asked Joe to show me how to do one of his prize-winning Windsor knots.

I watched intently as Joe gave his tie-knotting exhibition, but after several very poor attempts myself, and the fact that we needed to get on the road before lunchtime, he did the same for me that he'd done for Mr Jones on tray B. First tying it around his own neck, loosening and removing it, he then placed the prized Windsor knot tie over my head, shimmied it into its centralised position, gently tightened it around my neck and folded down my collar. I felt like a little boy being dressed in his new school uniform for his first day at school, by his mum. Mind you, all I would have to do in the future to have a perfect Windsor knot every time, would be to loosen the tie to pass it over my head as Joe had done on himself and Mr Jones, as and when required. Lazy, I know, but the likelihood of perfecting the technique of tying a decent Windsor knot myself was minimal and this way it would save valuable time if

I were ever in a hurry to get changed into or out of my funeral attire. With my smart grey-striped trousers, white shirt, black waistcoat and prize-winning Windsor knot tie, I really looked the part and felt like the dog's knees (to put it politely).

Grey jackets were supplied to wear on removals to prevent the smarter funeral jackets from getting soiled or damaged, but being rather shapeless and rather unbecoming they didn't do much for the figure or the image.

Joe said that in the summer most of the blokes tended to use their smart funeral jackets on removals because they're cooler. I assumed he meant in the temperature sense of the word, not fashion. Although, they were in both senses of the word. Smart jacket it was then, but taking great care to avoid any contact with the outside world that might cause unnecessary wear and tear.

Suited and booted and ready for action, Eamon handed Joe the two pink removal cards with the information required about the bodies we were to collect from the hospital, and two brown envelopes containing money which was payment for important paperwork necessary for the funerals to go ahead. On the way out of the workshop, Joe cut off two large lengths of white plastic sheeting from the roll used for lining the coffins and asked me to check if there were rubber gloves on board the van. The plastic was evidently to wrap around the bodies being collected from the hospital. A sensible precautionary measure according to Joe, reiterating the possibility of various problems with the leakage of certain fluids.

Joining me at the van in the garage, Joe seemed slightly agitated.

"Great!" he said, rather despondently.

"What's up?" I asked.

"Oliver and Adam have taken the automatic van and left us with the manual. It'll be a real pain with all the stopping and starting through hilly Hampstead at this time of day."

"I don't tend have those sorts of problems riding a motorcycle. I can just zip in and out of the traffic willy-nilly, and all the buses I've driven were semi-automatic, which means no clutch; and you often have the luxury of using a bus lane."

"Unfortunately, we won't be doing much zipping in and out of the traffic or using bus lanes in the van, Bill. No willy-nilly-ing this morning, mate," Joe said, perking up a bit. "But we had better get loaded up and on our way. Time's getting on."

Joe jumped into the less favoured manual van and waited as I struggled to open one side of the gargantuan concertina gates of the garage. It didn't exactly glide open. In fact, it felt like it was completely out of alignment and in need of some serious attention, or indeed replacement. It was quite a feat of strength, only moving a few inches before jamming each time I pulled or pushed it with all my might. They should definitely have had it as challenge on the 'Strongest Man in the World' competitions.

Eventually, I managed to get the gate open enough for Joe to squeeze the van out and drive over to the mortuary. With the effort it took to shut the gate again, by the time I joined Joe back at the mortuary he was already wheeling one of the coffins out to the van.

The vans were kitted out inside with a dividing section which basically splits the back of the van horizontally in half. The top section and the bottom section of the van had metal rollers in place to aid the smooth loading and unloading of the coffins. Each van could allegedly carry at least five bodies at a time, if loaded correctly – three coffins on top and two stretchers on the bottom. Eight bodies, if you count the three live ones in the front.

Mr Jones who was destined for Mum's branch and Mr Lomax who was off to the Mill Hill branch, were put onto the lower section of the van. The metal rollers set into the flooring of the van enabled the coffins to slide in with ease. Two collapsible wheelie stretchers required for the hospital removal were sourced from a group of several nestling in front of the rack of rather beaten-up coffin shells. The stretchers were placed on the top section of the van and secured in place using a couple of offcuts of 3" x 2" wedged in between a number of thick metal pins that slotted into a selection of strategically positioned holes.

"We don't want them flying out the back of the van in the middle of Hampstead High Street," Joe stated, checking everything was safe and secure one last time by giving the 3" x 2" a good pull.

"That wouldn't be a good start to the day at all," he added.

An extremely practical piece of equipment in design and fairly simple in theory. Operating the mechanism which controlled the collapsing capabilities of the collapsible stretchers was not so simple in practice. It necessitated a technique that required nothing less than impeccably precise timing between cognitive activity and physical action. Something I seemed to lack judging by the problems I had when trying to carry out the procedure. Joe demonstrated the technique numerous times effortlessly. I, however, struggled repeatedly. If I was to avoid seriously injuring myself or any of my colleagues, I would without a doubt need to master the technique sooner rather than later. Embarrassed by my failings I was slightly comforted by the fact that Joe had apparently witnessed far more disastrous attempts at operating the collapsible stretchers than mine.

Ready for action we set off on our journey out of the cobbled mews and into the busy morning, rush hour traffic of North London, our first delivery, Mr Jones, bound for Mum's branch, which, of course, was also my home.

I was noticing the definite need for some extra support for my trousers while going about my duties and looking forward to picking up a pair of braces on route to the hospital. Or at least before I managed to get myself on the front page of the Sun newspaper for exposing myself to some poor, unsuspecting passer-by as I was unloading or loading the van at the roadside. Not the sort of publicity Mortimer and Sons required or would appreciate, I'm sure.

It was slow-going through Hampstead. Bumper to bumper all the way up the hill. The automatic van would definitely have been a great deal easier on the driver with the amount of handbrake hill starts required as we very slowly edged our way up the hill. Joe really knew his way around London. His knowledge of the backstreets through Hampstead was very impressive. At that time of day, however, no matter how good your knowledge of the area and whichever route you chose, you were going to get stuck in traffic, every backstreet shortcut only bringing you back into another gridlocked main road.

With the location of Mum's shop, unfortunately we had no option *but to park next to the bus stop directly outside in order to unload the van. We certainly got some strange looks from the people waiting there as we wheeled the coffin on the trolley passed them and into the branch. There wasn't a great deal we could do about it though. I'm fairly sure the undertakers was there well before some wally at the council, who probably didn't even know the area, gave permission to erect a bus stop directly outside. Adding to the visual spectacle for our bus-queue audience, the trolley's one frantic wheel, protesting at the demands being put upon it, was going berserk. The other three wheels, clearly embarrassed by their uncontrollable sibling's behaviour, thankfully fought fiercely to keep the trolley travelling in the direction we were trying to guide it in.*

It felt strange being at the branch participating in my professional role for the company, as opposed to being a mere bystander. The first thing I noticed was how efficient Mum was within her work role. Something I hadn't really paid much attention to in the past, for obvious reasons. I was quite impressed, I must say. She was also doing a very good job at embarrassing me in front of Joe. Asking him to make sure he looked after her little baby boy. Joe looked at me sympathetically, like someone who experienced the same from his mum. Mind you, isn't that part of what a mum's job is all about, when you reach a certain age? Among other things, of course.

Joe and I helped Mum set up Mr Jones for viewing in one of the chapels of rest, moving the lady who was currently occupying the chapel into the back room. On our return, Mum was titivating about with Mr Jones to get him ready for his family and friends to view him. Joe asked if Mum had any paperwork to go back to head office – which she did. It was in the pony express bag on the desk in the office. Joe grabbed the pony with the paperwork, we said our goodbyes, and once again joined the morning mayhem on London's overburdened roads, the Mill Hill branch being our next destination, to deliver Mr Lomax.

I didn't know Mill Hill that well so it was a good thing Joe, with his extensive knowledge of London, was driving. Arriving at the Mill Hill branch, it turned out the regular manager was away on holiday and the branch was being covered by one of the managers from head office. As it was still quite early, whoever was covering hadn't arrived yet. Luckily, Joe had his Mortimer and Sons master key so we were able to let ourselves in. Transferring Mr Lomax from the van onto a wheelie trolley we took him into the branch. After an elaborate excursion along a number of passageways and passing through several rooms, including an office, a waiting room and a floral storage area, we reached our journey's end with Mr Lomax – the chapel of rest.

With me pushing at the head of the coffin and Joe steering at the foot there was a fair amount of strategic manoeuvring required to get around some of the tight corners. Joe had obviously done this a few times before and was well aware of the route and angles of trajectory required in order to succeed without any damage to the coffin or property. Once in the chapel, Joe removed the coffin lid and repositioned Mr Lomax a little more centrally in the coffin, straightened up his clothing in a few places and tidied his hair; a necessity, possibly due to some slight movement in the coffin during the journey on some of the sharper corners negotiated along the winding backstreets of Hampstead.

Joe placed a large white lace cloth, about the size of a single bed sheet, over the open coffin. He referred to the cloth as a pall, and folding it back over itself from the head of the coffin towards the foot of the coffin, leaving only the lower half of the coffin covered, Mr Lomax was revealed once more from the waist up. Joe then replaced the white face cloth over the man's face. A respectful gesture and also apparently to help prevent unwanted visitors in the form of insects getting into places you really didn't want them to get into. Not a pleasant thought, but again, a necessary precaution against nature and some of its less agreeable processes.

By the time we'd finished setting Mr Lomax up for viewing, Bradley Masters, one of the managers at head office had arrived to cover the branch for the day. A tall, broad chap, he seemed quite young for a manager. Evidently, he'd only recently been promoted and he and Joe were very pally. Not the usual type of relationship between staff and managers but understandable as he and Joe had once been colleagues at the yard.

Standing in the reception area of the branch, we noticed a traffic warden was taking great interest in the van's unauthorised position on the double yellow lines outside. Looking into the shop he waved to get our attention and pointed at the van. Joe gave him a smile and waved back, but the words that came from Joe's mouth weren't usually accompanied by such friendly gestures. Hopefully, the warden didn't lip-read. Back on the road after thanking the traffic warden profusely for not giving us a parking ticket, we headed back into Central London to the Central Middlesex Hospital. Joe kept his promise and we stopped at a quaint old-fashioned clothes shop in Kentish Town that sold braces. I nipped in quickly as we shouldn't really have been parked outside, once again due to the ever present thickly-painted double yellow lines decorating the roadside.

Kentish Town was where Lesley, my sister, now resided. She'd had quite a turbulent few years after leaving the job that Mum took over, looking after Bibi and Ninka, going back to her roots in Gloucestershire for a while, but returning to London when the relationship she was in didn't work out. She was now a childminder, and a mother herself to a very handsome little chap called Addie – my nephew.

Deciding to follow Howard's lead in the braces department, I went for something a little more daring than grey or black and bought a rather racy pair of red braces with gold clips. They were only cheap but looked like they'd do the job adequately enough. I re-joined my companion just in time to avert another opportunity for a traffic warden to up his quota towards that month's 'Warden of the Month' award. I was quite excited about my new purchase and felt there should be some sort of special ceremony or official inauguration to mark the occasion, although I made no such suggestion to Joe; he might think me a bit odd.

On the way to the Middlesex Hospital, Joe warned me that visits to most hospitals were rarely as straightforward as they should be and to be prepared for a great deal of waiting around. It was quite an old hospital and definitely not designed for the volume of modern-day traffic that was trying to negotiate the limited access to carry out deliveries and collections. In fact, it was complete chaos, and we had to drive around the block to try and let some of the traffic clear as there was absolutely nowhere to park on our first approach.

A short, stocky chap was shouting abuse at various drivers of the trucks and vans that were trying to park or leave. I wasn't sure if he was just some poor unfortunate chap with mental health issues, under the influence of alcohol or mind-altering substances, if he actually worked there, or all of the above. Living in London you get used to people shouting at other people and themselves for no apparent reason, other than perhaps they hadn't taken their medication when they should have done, were high, or drunk. Generally, you try to ignore it as you go about your daily routine, hoping you won't be the one they sit next to on the bus or approach in the street. But you usually are!

It turned out the man did work at the hospital, and it was actually his job to shout at people and deal with the vehicles delivering and picking up. Well, perhaps it wasn't his job to shout, that was just his preferred method of how to get his job done, and he did manage to create a space for us by moving on a disgruntled delivery van driver who was taking his time to move on. It wasn't the most ideal spot but it was better than having to drive around the block numerous times waiting for a better opportunity to present itself, that we might even miss by going around the block. So, well done, that man!

For my own safety, Joe took charge of removing the collapsible stretchers from the top section of the van. Not being one to let others do my share of the work, I supported the weight of the stretcher from the other end as it descended. Which was slightly faster than anticipated due to my slow response and Joe's eagerness to get on with the task in hand. The hospital mortuary was in the basement of the hospital, accessed by a lift. How complicated could that be?

Assigned a wheelie stretcher each, Joe and I manoeuvred the two stretchers through and around an assault course of goods vehicles, towering boxes of supplies, mountainous bags of clinical waste, and a colossal cardboard crushing machine which bore a remarkable resemblance to Optimus Prime from Transformers. Safely completing the hazardous hospital assault course, we eventually arrived at the lift which would facilitate our descent to the desired level within the hospital. The lift not being at ground level, Joe pressed the button to activate the lift's ascent. The response was negative. My confused *expression prompted Joe to inform me that the lift only operated from the ground level to the basement and vice versa. The lift was either out of order or the door was open at the lower level.*

Mingled mumblings and the sound of an object being wheeled in or out of the lift caught our attention. Repeated slamming of a metal-constructed door indicated the lift was not cooperating with the person or persons below requiring its use. The lift's sudden activation into life drew us to scrutinise the lift's door in front of us with great anticipation. Although the lift was only travelling from the basement to ground level it seemed to take forever. On its long-awaited arrival, an inner door screeched objectionably, clearly fiercely resisting the occupant's efforts to open it. The colourful language of the person inside the lift seemed to confirm our suspicions of the struggle within. A solitary undertaker of slightly dishevelled appearance eventually emerged from behind the temperamental lift door, noticeably aggravated by the difficulties he was experiencing. Joe and I assisted him out of the lift with his wheelie stretcher which was visibly occupied. A brief and rather half-hearted thank you was thrown in our general direction, as the disgruntled man propelled the occupied stretcher towards the hospital assault course, we ourselves had only moments before emerged from. Whilst it was an amusing situation to witness, Joe and I quelled the urge to be amused to the point of laughter and acting with the utmost decorum carried on with our own duties straight-faced. As much as our facial muscles would allow voluntarily, that is!

The hospital lift had definitely seen better days. To describe it as ancient would be a compliment of its historical timescale. Only just managing to squeeze ourselves and the two stretchers into the lift, it took several good hard slams of the archaic iron gate, before its timeworn safety mechanism finally engaged and acknowledged that we had carried out the correct procedure in order for it to operate.

As a passenger confined within the lift's temperamental old workings, the jerky and somewhat unnerving journey to the basement seemed to take twice as long as it did waiting for it on the outside. It reminded me of the lift in an old Julie Andrews's film called Thoroughly

Modern Millie. In order to get the temperamental old lift in the film to operate the occupant was required to dance in it vigorously; the movement supposedly encouraging the lift's engineering components spontaneously into life. I think if Joe and I had started dancing in the hospital lift vigorously, not only would we have been dismissed from Mortimer and Sons for gross misconduct if discovered, it probably would have been the end of the lift and its problematic service to humanity.

Once in the basement of the hospital, having prized ourselves and the two stretchers out of the lift, we started our journey to the mortuary. The narrow, winding, low-ceilinged, dimly lit corridors were eerie and seemingly endless. Left then right, right then left, left again, right again. Joe led the way at a good pace but luckily the stretchers were light and easy to control around the tight corners, merely by lifting the front end off the ground to enable a swift and accurate change of direction on the rear wheels. There were numerous doors set back in dark alcoves, displaying yellow and black hazard warning signs. Some clearly indicated warning of possible death by electrocution. Presumably by what equipment was kept behind the door, hopefully not as a punishment for just opening the door. Other signs were a little more ambiguous and suspicious-looking. I dreaded to think what gruesome experiments might be being carried out behind some of those closed doors in the name of progress and the survival of our species.

Arriving at a pair of large, heavy wooden double doors, Joe, with a sudden cessation of movement that almost caused me to inflict serious injury on his person with the stretcher I was controlling, indicated we had reached our destination – the entrance to the mortuary. To the right of the double doors, mounted on the wall, was an old-fashioned black telephone. Taped to the wall, next to the phone, was a series of instructions and a list of telephone numbers on a rather grubby piece of laminated paper. Joe rang one of the numbers – the mortician's pager – then hung up.

After about five minutes the phone on the wall rang, its harsh, loud peal causing us both to jump out of our skin. Joe promptly answered it. The conversation that ensued between Joe and the person on the other end of the telephone, from what I could tell, appeared to be one of a rather witty nature. Which gave me the impression that whoever it was, and I presumed it was the mortician, was quite a comedian.

It turned out that it was the mortician Joe was talking to and he was actually in another hospital as his duties extended between the two. Apparently, it would be at least twenty minutes before he could get from the one to the other. This, according to Joe, would give us time to go to the bereavement office and pick up the cremation papers that were required for each of the bodies we were collecting before the mortician arrived. Leaving the stretchers outside the mortuary we set off to the bereavement office. More narrow, dimly-lit corridors eventually led us to a flight of stairs which delivered us into the heart of the hospital itself. Joe and I seemed to be attracting a lot of strange looks from people as we strolled through the hospital. Not surprisingly, I suppose. Undertakers are probably the last people anyone in hospital wants to see, and it was fairly obvious that's what we were. I couldn't help thinking that perhaps the hospital could have placed the bereavement office somewhere a little more discreet.

When we arrived at the bereavement office, it was closed. Displayed on the door was a phone number and instructions to go to the adjacent office and ask them to call the number which would alert the bereavement officer, via their portable pager device, to the fact that their presence was required. I was beginning to see what Joe meant when he said it wasn't always straightforward with hospital removals. This hospital visit was gradually turning out to be more like a quest for the Holy Grail rather than a trip to a local hospital to collect two bodies and some paperwork. I didn't think I would be getting this much exercise as an undertaker. At this rate I'd be fit enough to enter next year's London Marathon. If I had the inclination to do so!

When the bereavement officer finally arrived, the negotiations and handing over of doctors' fees in exchange for the cremation papers was set in motion. After checking the documents, eagle-eyed Joe discovered that one of the set of papers only had one doctor's signature on it when it required two. The doctor in question was luckily on the premises and paged without delay. More waiting. Half an hour later the doctor *arrived, completed the form and collected his fee. Mission accomplished; it was on with the quest!*

After Joe had finished his flirtatious exchanges with the rather pleasant young bereavement officer Faye, and a slight diversion into the hospital newsagents to purchase a chocolate bar for a well-needed sugar boost, we headed back down into the bowels of the hospital once more and returned to the mortuary. On our arrival we found the old rustic wooden double doors wide open and another pair of undertakers had jumped the queue and were loading up their two stretchers. Apparently, the paperwork for the two bodies they were collecting had been picked up the previous day.

Joe knew the two men and started to wind one up about a car he'd bought (a so-called bargain) that had lost half of its exhaust system whilst on his way home after picking it up. The man was clearly not amused by Joe's remarks, and extremely embarrassed by the whole incident. After the other undertakers had finished and disappeared into the darkness in the direction of the temperamental old lift, it was our turn.

The mortician, Angelo, was a short, stout chap from that wonderful country that has given us some of the world's most mesmerising architecture, incredibly talented artists, intrepid explorers, and iconic sports cars. Not to mention one of the most popular dishes in the world of fast-food cuisine, the pizza. And of course, whatever else the Romans may well have contributed to the world along with the aqueducts, sanitation, medicine, public baths, education, public order, and wine. Although, I suspect public order may have suffered occasionally, due to the wine. Oh! and we mustn't forget about the roads!

Angelo was an extremely jolly man. Almost too jolly. I could immediately see why the telephone conversation Joe had had with him was so comical. Angelo spoke very quickly, hardly taking time to take a breath, and had quite a high-pitched voice for a man. He certainly challenged any preconceived ideas that anyone might have about morticians, in every way. After an exchange of greetings and introductions Angelo thoroughly checked through the paperwork now in our possession before releasing the required bodies. Another set of wooden double doors on our left was energetically opened by Angelo, revealing a small room completely covered with white tiles from floor to ceiling. It was extremely cold, a condition I contributed to the large and very noisy refrigeration unit fixed to one wall – which also necessitated the need to increase the volume of communication to a level just below the level I imagine would be classed as shouting. This not only caused Angelo's already high-pitched vocal tone to increase to a higher level as if he had just inhaled a burst of helium, it also increased the speed he spoke at which made him sound like a very excited small child. It was quite amusing.

The aroma of the refrigerated section of the hospital's mortuary was reminiscent of that of the old lady in the body bag at the yard, though not quite as pungent. In the room were nine large, galvanised metal trolleys. Five of the trolleys were occupied, each occupant wrapped tightly in a white sheet from head to toe resembling an Egyptian mummy. The first of our two bodies was that of a fifty-year-old man, a Mr Edward Harvey. Mr Harvey had died of a heart attack, and looking at the size of him I could see why his heart might have wanted to give up the struggle of its arduous task. The sheet covering him was wringing wet and stained a pinkie yellow from a mixture of various body fluids that could no longer be contained by its human vessel after life had ceased. Relaxation of the muscles and fluid-containing organs had succumbed to the biological side effects of death; evidence that all the talk about leaking body fluids by my colleagues was not just all talk and a definite reoccurring feature of my new career. The white plastic sheeting Joe had brought along to place upon the stretchers became self-explanatory.

Angelo unravelled the well-secured sheet wrapped around Mr Harvey to reveal the man himself. His overweight frame was solid. Not frozen, but the extensive amount of fatty tissue beneath the skin was definitely much firmer than you would normally expect it to be. In all probability, a condition caused by a combination of the cold, and the absence of life. His face appeared unnaturally bloated, even for his size, and was a pale shade of grey with a slight tinge of purple. On his chest were two large red marks consistent with the use of a defibrillator, presumably used by the paramedics to try and shock his heart back into carrying out its previous, although obviously very burdensome, vocation.

Joe, Angelo and I, checked and double checked the hospital ID on the man's wrist. Joe then added the Mortimer and Sons ID bracelet to the man's left ankle. Applying the ID bracelet to an ankle allows it to be covered easily by clothing if the deceased is to be viewed at a later date. Mr Harvey had no jewellery or valuables on him, which had been noted via paperwork prior to entering the Antarctic conditions of the refrigerated room, but he was checked again by all parties to verify that fact.

Having placed a large piece of white plastic sheeting onto the stretcher, Angelo, Joe and I, transferred the portly gentleman from the rather bland galvanised tray to the slightly more upmarket, polished alloy, Mortimer and Sons' wheelie stretcher. Moving Mr Harvey's large, lifeless frame, which was probably exceeding the safe working load of the stretcher by more than a few pounds, even with our combined effort, was quite a struggle. After wrapping the plastic sheeting around Mr Harvey to try and contain any more unwanted leakage, he was secured onto the stretcher. There is a large flap of the same durable, wipeable material that covers the main section of the wheelie stretcher, attached to either side of the stretcher's framework. These run the entire length of the stretcher and when folded in, completely enclose the body. This not only helps to protect the often fragile human remains during transportation, but also helps to keep it safely in position. To fully secure the body to the stretcher, seatbelt-type straps are used and tightened gently but firmly – one across the chest and one across the legs. A grey or black cover is then placed over the top of the stretcher and the body, which cunningly disguises its true nature. Or possibly not!

Our second body for collection was that of a thirty-year-old woman, a Miss Brent. Miss Brent had apparently died of cancer. Angelo unwrapped the white sheet unveiling her body for us to check the ID. Her skin was an unnatural dark yellow known as jaundice; an effect of cancer on the liver. In her battle against the disease, she had also lost most of her hair.

The youngest person I'd ever known who had died was Ninka, the younger of the two sisters Mum and Lesley had looked after. She too had lost all of her beautiful long blonde hair during her treatment for leukaemia, a battle she lost at the age of nineteen in 1992. It was terribly sad. She was such a beautiful person with so much to offer this world that it so desperately needed. At that moment in the hospital mortuary, the fragility of life of all ages suddenly struck me more than it ever had done before.

Although neither of the bodies we were collecting from the hospital had been sanitised in any way, in comparison to Mrs Collins at the yard they both seemed fairly well presented. Their facial features, as in sleep, gave the appearance that they were at peace. The odour of the woman's body was noticeably much stronger than the man's even though there was only a day between their deaths. Something I had noticed when checking the ID tags. Joe told me that cancer has a very distinctive smell of its own. One I would soon become very familiar with.

As refreshing as the cold-room of the mortuary was in the heat of the day, it was starting to get into my bones and was becoming much less welcome. Joe and I were both looking forward to getting back into the warmth of the summer sun and back to the yard for a nice, refreshing cup of tea. Venturing into cold-rooms and walk-in fridges followed by the hot flushes on exit as the rush of blood-flow aims to regain normal body temperature, I started to feel a great deal more sympathetic towards ladies experiencing a particular time of life, than I had previously.

As we were leaving, Angelo called out and asked if he could have a lift back to University College Hospital, the hospital where he'd been when we paged him. Joe said that would be fine. Gleefully smiling, in his high-pitched Italian accent, Angelo said he would meet us at the van after locking up the mortuary.

The wheelie stretchers were not as easy to control with the extra weight on them, particularly around the sharp, narrow corners of the dimly lit corridors. A steady pace and full control of the stretcher was required. After wrestling with the prehistoric lift's problematic door to gain entry, at a snail's pace it groaned every inch of the way to ground level creating doubt as to whether it would complete the journey or not, almost as if trying to make a point of letting us know how much we were adding to its already tormented existence with the demands we were now putting upon it. The thought of being stuck in it with the two bodies, waiting for however long to be rescued, was not one I relished.

Back at ground level we carefully negotiated the assault course of vans and trucks that were frantically loading and unloading at the rear of the hospital and the items they were leaving scattered all about. Once we reached the van, another problem presented itself. The van was completely boxed in by two other vehicles. Another undertaker and a medical suppliers. Sometimes it absolutely astounds me how ignorant and selfish some people can be, without the slightest thought of how their actions affect others. Rant rant, moan moan!

As if by magic, and with perfect timing, the stocky, shouting man appeared once again then disappeared as quickly as he had emerged at full volume into a barrage of vehicles. The driver of the van contributing to our van's confinement surfaced from the chaos. Unapologetic for his actions he boarded his vehicle and drove off in Formula 1 fashion. Baffled by the ignorance of one and saved by the lung capacity of another, once Joe had moved the van forwards a short distance to enable access to the rear, we were able to proceed with our objective and load the stretchers into the van.

As we had to park in the street at the rear of the hospital, passers-by were having double takes at the two men in black and the stretchers with the black covers over them. It didn't really take a genius to work out what we were doing – as clever a disguise as the cunning black covers might be. I suppose it's not something the average person sees every day, so I can understand their intrigue. If the access to the hospital was more suitable, we probably wouldn't have had to load the bodies into the van in the middle of the street. It wasn't the most ideal set up, that's for sure.

I felt quite embarrassed for the dignity of the deceased and for the public to have to witness things that they might find distressing, just as I had done in front of the bus queue at Mum's when dropping off Mr Jones in his coffin. Whether right or wrong, death is still quite a taboo subject in many cultures and generally not something people want to *see or dwell on too much, if at all. Even so, I believe most people would probably be more curious than upset if they did manage to catch a fleeting glimpse of such things; that morbid fascination that we as a species appear to possess.*

Booby-trap Stretchers

Using the wheelie stretchers correctly without doing yourself a serious injury really was quite an art. As I've said before, it was all in the timing. If you got that wrong, you were in trouble. As in many aspects of life, timing was of the essence.

Thankfully, having delivered the two passengers that had previously occupied the lower section of the van, the stretchers containing each of our new passengers were able to be placed on the vacant lower section, instead of breaking our backs trying to get them on the upper section (particularly where Mr Harvey was concerned).

Whether loading the stretchers onto the top or bottom section of the van, the first objective was to get the front pair of wheels onto the van. Taking the weight at the rear of the stretcher, the rear wheels must then be raised off the ground whilst simultaneously pulling the release lever that will activate the collapsible capabilities of the stretcher, thus drawing both the front and rear wheels upwards allowing you to push the stretcher fully into the vehicle; a simple action in comparison to many other very complicated things we humans have to master in our day to day lives, but one that really wasn't as simple as it might at first appear. Or as easy as Joe made it look.

According to Joe, on this occasion, I didn't lift the rear of the stretcher high enough off the ground. Therefore, the mechanism that required disengaging in order to allow the stretcher to collapse and the wheels to rise upwards, did not. Unaware of this when I applied the forward force to push the stretcher onto the van, I kept moving but the stretcher came to a very abrupt halt.

As anyone who knows anything about the laws of physics; 'for every action there is an equal and opposite reaction'. And as Scotty from the Starship Enterprise would say, 'Ye cannae change the laws of physics'.

I was no stranger to the consequences of messing with those particular laws, especially when it came to riding a motorcycle. Kinetic energy – which deals with the effects of forces upon motions of material bodies or with changes in a physical or chemical system – and I, were old adversaries.

It's one of the few things I do remember something about from my science lessons at school relating to actions of motion and velocity, or the lack of it. Why I was paying attention on that particular day God only knows, but it obviously had no impact on how I have been able to apply that knowledge, however small it may be, into situations where it might be advantageous to do so.

On this particular run-in with science, due to the lack of skill and knowledge of the wheelie-stretcher's idiosyncrasies, I managed to severely wind myself and crush my testicles against the stretcher with such a force that not only was it excruciatingly painful, it made me feel quite sick. Although fatherhood was not an imminent prospect in my life at that moment in time, doubts were rapidly forming in my mind as to any possibility of that actually becoming a reality in the future, bearing in mind the amount of pain that I was experiencing in the area involved in such events. In my defence, I did have the heavier of the two stretchers and being shorter, the lift had to come more from the arms than the legs. This requires a great deal more effort as anyone who knows anything about lifting correctly would I'm sure agree. It wasn't so much that I didn't have the strength but lacked the range of movement to get the rear of the stretcher high enough. Even on tiptoes.

The technique required for the smooth action of the wheelie stretchers collapsing and unfolding was very much like mastering the 'clean and jerk' or the 'clean and snatch' movement in weight lifting. Unfortunately named actions, I know, but equally as important safety wise to learn the correct technique and get the timing right in order to avoid unnecessary injury.

A thought has just occurred to me. What on earth is a necessary injury? Is there such a thing? A surgical procedure, perhaps!

Joe, sympathetic to my plight but clearly trying not to laugh (which would have been extremely unprofessional considering the task we were carrying out), seeing I was in trouble quickly came to the rescue and assisted me to get the stretcher into the van. Whilst I was recovering from the little mishap with the stretcher, Joe finished loading the two stretchers and secured them in place with the 3" x 2".

Seated back in the van gently tending my wounds, I realised that the action of rubbing my genitals to ease the pain, though effectively soothing, could easily be misconstrued by any passers-by or the office workers overlooking us from their vantage point across the road, as something far less innocent. Deciding that a certain amount of rubbing was definitely required to ease the pain, I tried to be as discreet as possible.

One, Two, Three, Four, I Declare Bum War

The moment Angelo got into the van I was immediately made aware of yet another design fault of our equipment aside from the lethal collapsing or not collapsing stretchers. No, I'm not referring to the vulnerable position of the male genitalia, though I think possibly a bit more thought could have gone into the positioning of that particular piece of equipment. And I'm aware it may have been a bit of a rush job due to the volume of work involved in the rest of creation over a rather short period of time. Six days in all, I believe. I'm also aware that the testicles need to be at a temperature several degrees cooler than that of the inside of the body because that is best for the sperm. All of which only convinces me more that the location of the vulnerable and very sensitive organs must have been a bit of an afterthought, and not really given the level of attention it warranted. Either that, or our Creator, depending on your beliefs of course, has a rather strange sense of humour!

The design fault I'm actually referring to was the van's seating capacity. Although, I suppose it wasn't really a design fault as such, but rather more of a blatant breach of the Trade Descriptions Act 1968, when that particular model was referred to as a three-seater and so obviously was not. Unless the two passengers sitting on the alleged two-seater section were verging on skeletal, that is. There was absolutely no way two averaged-size adults, male or female, would be able to sit on such a seat without a serious territorial conflict ensuing regarding bottom space, or the lack of it.

I can see how such seating arrangements could easily be used advantageously and even be quite a pleasant distraction in certain situations. However, this was definitely not one of those situations.

Having to share the very inaccurately described seat's limited bottom space with a chubby-cheeked Mediterranean chap, even if he was quite entertaining, was definitely not my idea of fun.

Due to the fact that we would be dropping Angelo off at UCH, to allow ease of his departure from the vehicle I had sat on the inside section of the passenger seat next to the driver. Being of a thoughtful disposition and even though it was only a short journey, I felt it my duty to try and make as much room as humanly possible on the inadequate seating area for two, for our new travelling companion's comfort. Truth be known, I was also not entirely comfortable with that level of contact with another man I hardly knew. Call me old-fashioned, but I believe there's a limit to how much contact two men should have in certain situations. Some situations may unavoidably necessitate more contact than others and should be judged accordingly, or avoided. If it were not for some idiot deeming the so obviously not a two-seater section, to be a two-seater section, I would not have been put in such a predicament in the first place. However, I was.

Sliding as far as I could to the right of the seat, my right buttock hovered in thin air, whilst the left was doing all the supporting work with a great deal of help from other muscle groups that usually have very little involvement in anything for the average person. This balancing act may have created the illusion that I was actually sitting comfortably unaffected by the intrusion of our new guest, whereas in actual fact, I was extremely uncomfortable and still in a considerable amount of pain due to the non-collapsing stretcher incident. Muscles I would usually not be using in this situation were starting to inform my brain that they were not equipped for this level of intense work and wanted to desist as soon as possible.

Angelo, talking for Italy – and his more than ample backside taking up most of the so-called two-seater seat – without a care in the world was clearly oblivious as to how much pain and discomfort I was in, in order for him to be comfortable. My precarious positioning also put me rather close to the gear stick and every time Joe changed gear, he touched my knee. You just can't win!

It was a great relief when Angelo was finally ejected from the van. In the nicest possible way, of course. Well, maybe not the nicest, but no unnecessary force was used and no animals were harmed in the process. Liberated from my physical limitations and discomfort, I savoured the entirety of the passenger seat all to myself. Resting my buttocks contentedly, legs astride, I took up as much of the available space on my side of the van as possible for the rest of the journey.

As we pulled into the cobbled mews back at the yard the huge concertina gates were firmly shut and all appeared quiet. I was now very wary and slightly intimidated by the vicious nature of the wheelie stretchers, so Joe very thoughtfully allowed me get the lighter of the two stretchers off the van. Even with the lighter of the two I still felt quite clumsy and found controlling the stretcher problematic. The unevenness of the cobbles underfoot didn't help with the overall smoothness of the operation, but at least I didn't do myself any more harm in the process. If only I was a bit taller, it would have been so much easier, but then, that's the story of my life. If the vans had been lower or fitted with height-adjustable suspension, that would have been ideal.

Joe made operating the stretchers look so easy: the collapsible legs lowering smoothly and perfectly into place like the landing gear of a Boeing 747 jet plane, the stretcher then gliding off the van and into the mortuary almost of its own accord. My only consolation was that he'd had a lot more practice than me to develop his very impressive, smooth and effortless technique. As with many things, brute force is no match for experience and knowledge. Hopefully I would master the technique before I became infertile or physically impaired in any way.

Size Does Matter

Once inside the mortuary, before placing each of our new guests into their allocated fridge space the very important task of measuring them *for their coffin was to be carried out. A simple and straightforward procedure you would think – but how very wrong you would be.*

Taking the long wooden measuring stick that stood authoritatively in the corner of the mortuary, next to the embalming room door, Joe proceeded to measure Mr Harvey's height. Or length, I suppose, as obviously he was lying down. The measuring stick was basically a giant ruler that made us look like we were a pair of Borrowers moonlighting as undertakers. It was just over seven -feet long according to its numbered markings, and apparently made by Eamon's own fair hands. The giant ruler informed us that Mr Harvey was exactly six feet in length. Joe proceeded to measure Mr Harvey's width. This, by all accounts, is when things can get a little tricky. His shoulder width was approximately twenty-four inches across, but because of his shape and size that wasn't his widest point. His hips measured twenty-six inches across and with his arms by his side it made him even wider at that point. The shoulder width is the widest part of a coffin and from that point it tapers in towards the foot end. This is where the confusion starts, because we had to put down the exact size of coffin required on the pink card and if it was wrong it could cause a multitude of problems.

Coffins are made in standard sizes unless specially made to order, i.e. 5'6" x 20" (5'6" in length, 20" in width), 5'6" x 22", 5'6" x 24", 6' x 20", 6' x 22", 6' x 24", etc., etc. You get the idea. If someone is exactly 5'4" tall x 18" wide, a 5'6" x 20" coffin is by all accounts, going to be the obvious choice and more than a comfortable fit with room for adjustments, according to Joe. It's also the smallest standard-sized coffin that Mortimer and Sons and most other undertakers keep in stock. If however, someone is exactly 5'6" x 20", a 5'6" x 20" coffin is going to be slightly more than a snug fit. Especially if the deceased is to be dressed and wearing shoes. Joe says it's always best to err on the side of caution and overestimate a little when deciding the coffin size. On the other hand, you don't want the coffin so big that the person is rattling around like the last Malteser in the box either. Joe's words, but a good analogy, I thought.

People are all sorts of weird and not so wonderful shapes and sizes and rarely the perfect tapered coffin shape. So a certain amount of creativity and conjecture needs to be applied, but without being too creative and within the realms of sensibility. Caskets, according to Joe, in the case of larger sized clients, can be a wise choice as they aren't tapered like a traditional-shaped coffin and have plenty of room all round.

Joe decided that Mr Harvey would need at least a 6'2" coffin in length, by 28" in width. Which would have to be ordered as that was not a standard size. Alternatively, a casket would be a good option. Even if Mr Harvey had been shorter, the coffin required would have to be large enough to get six men under it to cope with the weight. Joe said a short, wide coffin can look rather strange, resembling the shape of a Mr or Miss Universe contender. The very simple task of measuring a body for its coffin was far more like rocket science than I had previously imagined. However, Joe assured me I would be fine if I just used the measuring stick provided and then aired on the side of caution when adding the extra little bit for the coffin size. Our second body, Miss Brent, was far easier when it came to measuring. She was barely 5' 4" x 17" so a 5'6" x 20" would be just the ticket. Even if dressing and wearing platform shoes.

Over the years Eamon had to all intents and purposes devised and constructed countless ingenious devices in his desperation to help with accuracy and limit mistakes in the measuring process. Some were more successful than others. None it would seem was ever as simple or as fool proof as it first appeared – as the staff repeatedly demonstrated to Eamon's despair.

With Mr Harvey and Miss Brent accurately sized for their coffins – fingers crossed – they were placed into their allocated fridge space. All relevant information regarding each of the deceased was recorded in the mortuary book, and the pink card paper trail set in motion. Our work was done.

I walked over to the main garage for yet another workout manhandling the humongous concertina gates to enable Joe to drive the van in and park up. All of the other vehicles were out except for one of the limousines. The ever familiar sound of hammering being produced from the workshop echoing around the empty expanse of the garage informed us that the yard had not been totally abandoned by the living. Eamon appeared from the workshop entrance telling Joe to have a quick cup of tea because he was going to have to do Eddie's two limousine drives. Eddie had been delayed on a coroner's removal and was waiting for the forensic team to finish before being able to remove the body and take it to the coroner's mortuary. Joe seemed quite pleased about the change to his day's routine.

When Eamon said a quick cup of tea, you knew he meant, 'a quick cup of tea' – or coffee for some – not a leisurely cup and a good old natter for half an hour. Over the last couple of days I had become more familiar with Eamon's unique and subtle way of getting this point across. It was his way of saying, 'I appreciate all your effort and I know you really need a break, but make it a quick one, there's a lot of work to be done and not much time to do it in'. The 'have a quick cup of tea' instruction was his catchphrase, I suppose. The favourable instruction to partake in a hot beverage was accompanied by a rather interesting combination of body movements, which can best be described as a shallow curtsey combined with the actions of a double pistol-wielding gunslinger on the draw. Index fingers, rather than pistols obviously, poised at the point of fire towards the intended recipient or recipients of the well-intentioned message, as well as referring to them verbally by name, just in case there was any confusion who he was actually talking to. And his tongue would touch his top lip as he gave a little nod after the immortal words 'have a quick cup of tea' were uttered – almost like a full stop indicates the end of a sentence.

Joe, being a bit of a comedian and mimic, did a great impression of Eamon and his 'have a quick cup of tea' catchphrase, complete with Irish accent and actions. It really was quite entertaining.

In the workshop Old Des was the guilty party making all the noise, working on a coffin. He greeted us in his gruff Irish accent with words that seemed to mingle into each other making them difficult to decipher. I asked him if he fancied a brew. He declined stating he'd just had one but thanked me for my consideration. While Joe checked over Eddie's limousine making sure it was ready to take out on the funerals, I made him a coffee. His preferred hot beverage. Milk and two sugars.

Marcus the embalmer was in the tearoom having a fresh air break away from the chemicals and the stench of death. While partaking in our refreshments and engaging in small talk we heard someone struggling to gain entry to the premises via the large stubborn garage gate. This turned out to be Oliver and Adam returning from their assignment. Oliver was also instructed to have a quick cup of tea by Eamon, and then to go out on the funeral with Joe in the limousine instead of Frank who was caught up on the coroner's removal with Eddie.

Eventually, it was just Eamon, Old Des, Adam and I left at the yard, and it was back into the workshop for us new boys to work on our coffin craftsmanship skills. Our brief but eventful impersonations of real undertakers now over, at least for the time being, we changed back into our civvies in order to protect our expensive work clothes, knowing it would probably be a considerable amount of time before we would be issued with replacements.

As the day progressed our work colleagues came and went, working between funerals and removals. Passing through the workshop inspecting our workmanship, remarks about crooked handles and uneven head ornaments were generally more to wind us up than helpful or constructive remarks. Once or twice, they may have been correct. A rather fiery debate evolved as to how many decorative pins they would use along the top edge of the inside of the coffin and what colour looked best. Most favoured brass over the silver, but definitely silver for a white coffin or a coffin with silver handles. Even with my limited experience and knowledge in the field of coffin furnishings, I would tend to agree with that.

The number of pins various staff would use varied considerably depending on whether the deceased was to be viewed or not. Generally, it seemed to come down to personal preference. Adam and I both agreed that as the new boys we could not afford to be rebellious or display too much creativity at this stage of our employment, sticking to what we had been told by Old Des and Eamon. Three pins at the head, seven down each edge from the head along the shoulder, and three at the foot for a viewer. One pin in each corner for a non-viewer. No point in being too extravagant if nobody, or 'no body', was going to benefit from your lavish irresponsibility.

After lunch, a generous slice of delicious homemade goat's cheese quiche and some coleslaw, followed by one of Mum's speciality flapjacks for afters, it was back into the workshop once again. Eamon had decided to give us a break from fitting up coffins and show us how to make up the nameplates on the engraving machines. The two engraving machines sat side by side against the wall, next to the door to the coffin stores. Both looked like contenders for the Antiques Roadshow but Eamon assured us that like him, they still had a good few years left in them yet. Eamon sat at the machine on the right nearest the door and talked us through the various components and how to adjust and change the cutters depending on the material that was to be engraved, i.e., plastic or brass. He then set up a template using individual letters, numbers, and various punctuation marks for the nameplate that was required for the coffin Old Des was working on. The information was gained from a piece of paper sourced from a shelf next to the machines.

John Edward Smith

Born 3-11-40 Died 24-6-93

R.I.P.

He then engraved the letters following the guidelines on the template onto a 6" x 4" plastic, brass-coloured plate that was clamped in place on the machine. A plastic plate because it was for a cremation coffin. It took him a matter of seconds to produce a perfectly engraved coffin nameplate, and of course, he made it look extremely easy.

Adam sat at the machine Eamon had been using for the demonstration and I sat at the one next to it. They were almost identical except for a few minor components. After observing our engraving efforts for a short period and with various words of advice and encouragement, Eamon left us to it. It was a good job he did too, because I think he would probably have gone ballistic if he'd seen how many mistakes we were making and the number of plates we'd ruined in the process. As per usual the expert had made the task look incredibly easy, when, in fact, it was not. Again, it was mostly down to practice and getting the knack of things. The engraving needle had to be applied at exactly the right pressure to cut smoothly on the plate. Too much pressure and the cutter would cut too deep and go absolutely haywire due to a build-up of debris on the tip. Usually on the very last letter. Too little pressure and the letters would be incomplete or patchy. This would require them to be redone applying a little more pressure. More pressure would be applied, debris would get stuck on the tip of the cutter ruining yet another plate and rendering all your efforts a complete waste of time. It was all rather frustrating and tested our patience to the limit.

The pile of scrapped plates was rapidly mounting. Adam and I both hoped the cost of them wouldn't be taken out of our wages. If it was, we would probably end up having to pay Mortimer and Sons for the privilege of working for them, rather than them paying us. I suspect Eamon sensed our frustration, possibly due to the barrage of colourful language emanating from the direction of the engraving machines each time one of us made a mistake. Perhaps he was also concerned about the mounting toll of our unsuccessful attempts and the financial consequences.

In his infinite wisdom, Eamon decided to give us a break from the engraving and moved us on to the shredding machine that was used to produce the supply of shredded paper for the coffin pillows. How hard could feeding paper into a shredder be?

It was the king of all shredding machines. A real beast of a thing, standing about four feet tall and two feet wide. Eamon gave us a tour of the shredder and its controls. There were three golden rules when it came to using the shredding machine.

Rule 1. Never put more than four sheets of paper at a time through the shredder.

No more than four sheets at a time for a monster shredder like that? He must be joking. He wasn't.

Rule 2. Remove all staples from magazines and supplements. Rule 2 was common sense really but worth mentioning to the two new boys I suppose, just in case they didn't have any common sense.

Rule 3. Mind your fingers. Which seemed to go without saying but it was said anyway.

Rule one was so important it was repeated for those that might be stupid enough to ignore it. Adam and I acknowledged our understanding of the three golden rules and were subsequently left to develop our paper-shredding skills.

Four sheets seemed to go through the shredder like a knife through butter. It didn't even seem aware anything had been put through it at all. Five sheets were effortless for the monster shredder. Six and seven sheets may have gone through a little slower but I wouldn't say it struggled. Eight sheets... Bang! The shredder came to a sudden and very noisy halt as a mass of shredded paper jammed its layers of shark-like teeth. Eight sheets were obviously too much. Eamon came flying out of his minuscule office like a bat out of hell. Red-faced and performing an angry jig he questioned Adam and I about which part of 'no more than four sheets at a time' did we not understand. It was quite a shock to see him so angry.

Like two naughty school boys in front of the headmaster we knew there was absolutely no point in denying what was staring us and Eamon in the face, i.e., the indisputable evidence of our folly. The king of shredders looked like it had consumed a large quantity of party poppers which had exploded inside its bulking frame and were now being regurgitated from its mechanical jaws.

It took forever to untangle and remove the mass of finely shredded paper from the shredder's complex layout of intertwined and very sharp cutting blades. As ever, my handy multi-tool which I was never without came to the rescue. It normally resided in a small leather pouch that I wore on my belt at all times. Unless I wasn't equipped with a belt, that is.

As the other staff started to filter in from their day's work, they were highly amused to witness our predicament with the shredder, most it would seem having learnt the hard way of the shredder's limitations by ignoring Eamon's no more than four sheets at a time instruction themselves. Every now and then Adam and I could hear the echoing of the words 'No more than four sheets at a time', coming from the tearoom in various imitated versions of Eamon's melodic tones. Some of the impersonations were a lot better than others. Joe's, of course, was by far the best.

It was about twenty to five when Eamon started dishing out his lists for bodies to be dressed and boxed for the morning. En masse, we set across the cobbled assault course with another bucking bronco wagon train of coffins. All that was missing was John Wayne at the head and an Indian on the horizon watching our every move. Although, there was the Indian man who ran the newsagents on the corner who occasionally glimpsed out of the window, but I don't think that really counts.

Getting Carried Away With the Moment

After wrestling with the numerous bodies that required preparing for the next day's funerals and viewings, on our return from the mortuary, the next day's orders had been delivered by Derek Best, one of the managers at head office, a middle-aged Geordie of portly proportions and of average height. Adam and I were very surprised to see we were both out on funerals. This prompted Eamon to initiate a crash course on how to carry a coffin, just in case there wasn't enough time in the morning. Which going by the hustle and bustle of the last two mornings, there probably wouldn't be.

A coffin was brought out from the workshop and put into the back of Dean's hearse which he pulled forward into the centre of the garage to allow more convenient access to the rear of the vehicle. The area in the back of the hearse where the coffin sits is called the bier. It has a beautiful highly polished walnut-type finish with inset rollers for ease of movement of the coffin, as with the vans. I once owned a canary-yellow mini with blue tinted windows which had a dashboard in a similar walnut finish. Very sporty!

Six of us were instructed by Eamon to stand at the back of the hearse in two lines of three facing each other like a guard of honour at a wedding. We were matched in height as best as we could be. The shortest nearest the hearse, which was Eddie and me who would be carrying at the foot end of the coffin. Going up in size, Adam and Joe were in the middle. Furthest from the hearse carrying at the head end of the coffin were the tallest, Oliver and Graham.

Eamon ran through the protocol for carrying a coffin. The important thing, he said, was to use slow, graceful movements at all times. As my opposite number, Eddie asked which shoulder I would prefer to carry on. I said I would prefer to carry on my right shoulder as it was my stronger side. This suited Eddie perfectly as he preferred to carry on his left shoulder. We swapped places to suit our preferences. I was now on the left nearest the hearse and Eddie was on the right.

On Eamon's command we started to feed the coffin slowly off the back of the hearse through our hands. Eddie, looking over the top of the coffin, informed me that the plastic handles were really only for show on the cremation coffins and that it was not a good idea to take the weight of the coffin by the handles but better to support it from underneath. When the six of us had the entire weight of the coffin in our hands and it was clear of the back of the hearse, on Eamon's instructions, whilst trying to keep the coffin as level as possible at all times, we lifted it slowly and placed it onto our shoulders. Still facing the hearse, we now had to turn 180 degrees in order to be facing the desired direction of travel. It had been explained to Adam and me at the start of the practice that we were to keep our arms down with hands clasped in front of us, and not to hold onto the coffin except when turning or when going up or down steps, to help keep it steady. The coffin didn't feel at all safe just balanced on my shoulder and it was very hard to resist the urge to grab hold of it, even though Eddie and the others had assured Adam and me it would be fine.

As our training continued, I was informed by Eamon that the coffin bearer at the foot end of the coffin on the left, which was me, controlled the direction and speed of movement of the other bearers and, ultimately, the coffin. Well, that was just dandy. Now, I was not only carrying my first coffin, but apparently I was fully responsible for its safe transportation from the hearse to its final destination.

The technique for turning with the coffin on our shoulders, involved overlapping the left foot with the right foot repeatedly while simultaneously turning to the left until the correct position had been achieved. My movements felt clumsy and the whole manoeuvre seemed a strange, macabre version of the river-dance technique, but in slow motion. I was far from convinced that the coffin was safe as it balanced precariously on our shoulders, despite my colleague's reassurance, and could not stop myself from supporting the underside of the coffin with my right hand during the turning motion, for fear of it crashing to the ground.

Having turned the required 180 degrees to face the desired direction of travel, on my lead and starting with the left foot as instructed by Eamon, we walked around the hearse and over to a pair of wooden trestles that Dean had placed at the back of the garage. Again, on Eamon's instructions, we lowered the coffin slowly and steadily from our shoulders into our hands and placed it onto the waiting trestles. Keeping the coffin as level as possible at all times was paramount and required the highest degree of synchronisation between all the participants and their movements. Taking one step backwards we bowed towards the coffin. As with every stage of the performance, timing and synchronicity of our actions was of the essence, otherwise our simultaneous respectful bow would look like a complete shambles and appear more like a cranial Mexican wave. Very unprofessional. It was only the first attempt for Adam and me, and we were clearly going to need plenty of practice if we were going to perfect this sombre dance. A great deal of our work seemed to depend on telepathic communication between work colleagues and getting used to each other's body language.

We ran through it a couple more times until five fifteen – time to go home. Joe offered Adam and me some words of encouragement, which the others repeated enthusiastically, the overall consensus being, 'It'll be alright on the night'. To be honest, I was slightly more concerned about the next day rather than the night but didn't want to seem ungrateful for the words of encouragement, which were greatly appreciated.

As we all started to leave, Eamon shouted out for us not to forget there was a coffin delivery in the morning at seven thirty. If anyone wanted some overtime, it was available. The phone rang in his office as he was reminding us of this. He disappeared only to re-emerge within seconds to inform the duty squad that there was a removal pending *from a nursing home in Muswell Hill. Apparently, they were just waiting for the doctor to arrive to certify the death.*

Mel, Ali and Graham were the duty squad that evening, but rather than hang about they each decided to go home. It would seem that doctors can take a while to respond to call-outs to confirm a death – their priority being to those still living. Which I suppose is only right. According to Ali it could be a good few hours before they actually got the go-ahead to collect the deceased.

It had been a fairly busy and eventful second day, with lots of new experiences. I must admit, I was quite nervous about carrying the coffin at the funeral. I didn't want to make a mess of it. Or worse – drop the coffin!

WEDNESDAY

I arrived at seven fifteen in the morning. Eamon, Joe, Ali, Eddie, Oliver, Adam and Dean had already started to unload the coffins off the delivery lorry. I teamed up with Oliver who was the only one going solo; everyone else was paired up. The chipboard coffins weren't that heavy, just a bit cumbersome and awkward to carry on your own, but why work harder than necessary if another pair of hands are available? Many hands make light work as they say. The solid wood coffins were a different ball game and definitely not to be attempted on your own unless you wanted a coronary, a slipped disc, or even worse – to drop it and have the wrath of Eamon to deal with.

Although there didn't appear to be any particular system as to where each coffin was stored, technically there was. It was Eamon's system. The only problem was, he was the only one who actually had any idea how the system worked. It was designed in such an illogical and random way that even staff who'd been working there for years didn't appear to have grasped the theory behind it. Eamon had rather cunningly developed the storage of the coffins in such a way that made him completely indispensable. The man's shrewdness was awe-inspiring. It made no difference if the coffin you had just put away was the same size and type as the next one you had to find a home for, Eamon's system had you absolutely stumped and completely disorientated. It would have driven even the most accomplished of code breakers to breaking point. The man was obviously a genius, completely insane, or both. Which is quite often the case I believe.

Wandering around aimlessly backwards and forwards like lost sheep, carrying the coffins up and down the aisles of the coffin stores, we would search through the racks for each coffin's rightful dwelling place.

"Where's a five-six twenty-two plain-sided mahogany go, Eamon?" would come a desperate plea from a bewildered pair of coffin carriers at their wits end.

"Up the bottom," would come Eamon's reply in his soft Irish accent.

He did, of course, mean at the bottom end of the coffin stores, but his reply entertained everyone so much they would ask the question repeatedly just to hear him say it again. Eventually all the coffins were neatly tucked away in their allocated, if not slightly illusive locations. At least, hopefully they were! Shouts for the kettle to be put on echoed around the coffin stores from every nook and cranny. Ali however, bless his efficient cotton socks, was already on the case. What a star – give that man a cigar.

During our well-earnt refreshment break, Eamon's paper lists began to appear like confetti around the tearoom. Uninterested in relocating from the pleasantness of our present surroundings or the information contained on each scrap of paper, they were quickly passed to the nearest colleague in order to avoid becoming the responsible party for carrying out the instructions upon it.

As time passed and having ignored Eamon's miniature memorandums for as long as possible – like rebellious children pretending they'd not heard their parents tell them it was time for bed – but not wanting to take advantage of his good nature and fairness in his supervisory role, we eventually yielded to his request. A mass exodus of the workforce followed, confetti in hand, and the details of each task tendered was scrutinised intensely before being diligently carried out.

One member of the workforce remained in the tearoom who shall remain nameless (in his blue overalls) but unforgiven by his colleagues for his lack of conviction to the ideology and benefits of teamwork, having claimed he was far too busy carrying out important vehicle maintenance to lend a hand, when he clearly had more than enough time to do both.

As we carried out our instructions, the movement of selected coffins from the stores and workshop area evolved into an eight-coffin convoy on yet another perilous journey to the mortuary across the cobbled plains of the mews. Bodies were checked, dressed and boxed and their tickets to ride secured in an appropriate place on the coffin lid. As we were finishing in the mortuary our next job was already laid out. Graham came over and told Joe and me that the three of us were being sent out on a coroner's removal.

Get a Grip, Lad

Battle commenced with the deluge of passing staff as we got dressed next to our lockers. Today was my first day wearing my flashy red braces with gold clips, and with Graham's kind assistance and expertise they were carefully clipped in place to do their very important job. It took a while to get the adjustment right and was a much more complex procedure than I would have expected it to be. If they were too tight the result was a constant wedgie, which was rather uncomfortable and to be honest would have been an unwelcome distraction from my duties. Too loose, and my trousers felt like they were flying at half-mast just like a circus clown's comical trousers. I might as well have not been wearing any at all. Braces, that is, not trousers!

Eventually, after a great deal of fiddling about with the adjusters, the right level of tension for adequate support and comfort was achieved. It was going to take quite a while to get used to them. The last time I wore braces was when I was about two years old. I have a photo of me as a chubby toddler wearing them, to prove it.

The coroner's removal was that of an elderly lady from a tower block just up the road in Kentish Town. We'd been warned that she was badly decomposed. The police were evidently on scene, as was the deceased's son. I asked Joe what the role of the coroner was and why they might be involved when someone dies. Joe explained that they're involved in investigating deaths that may be suspicious or unnatural. They might also be involved if the death was unexpected or the person hadn't been seen by a doctor recently, or within the last two weeks prior to their death. At least, that's what he thought. Joe also said not to pay too much attention to the badly decomposed alert. It can depend a great deal on the experience of whoever has called it in and who's on scene as to what they deem as badly decomposed. Nevertheless, like good Boy Scouts but without the woggles and not so much dib dib dibbing and ging gang goolying, we needed to be well prepared and make sure we had all the necessary kit on board the van for the worst scenario that we might be faced with.

Stretcher-wise we had one of the collapsible wheelie stretchers and what was called a house stretcher. The house stretcher was basically a fold-up stretcher that was ideal for use in areas with limited space and manoeuvrability, and where a wheelie stretcher could not be used. Some of the wheelie stretchers are actually a collapsible-wheeled base, with a detachable fold-up stretcher placed on top – offering its operatives the best of both worlds. Unfortunately, none of these was available at the time.

The other main bit of kit on board the van was the disaster bag. Not so called because it was unfashionable or difficult to get shoes to match, but because inside it contained the disaster equipment. Or to be more precise, protective clothing for ourselves, and a selection of body bags. It could have been called many things and perhaps the name 'disaster bag' was a little theatrical or inappropriate. However, that's the name it had been given, so that's what we called it.

Coroners' removals were always carried out by a three-man crew, according to Joe and Graham. Graham mentioned that some funeral directors only send two people but you can come up against all sorts of problems lifting-wise and environmentally that could be quite difficult and even dangerous with just two. Obviously Mortimer and Sons were more considerate about their staff's safety. Which was a comforting thought.

Each person on the removal squad had specific responsibilities. Joe was driving, so it was his job to know where we were going and to get us *there in one piece. Graham had the pink card with the address, relevant information about the deceased and attached ID bracelet. This by all accounts put him at the pointy end of our little trio doing the talking to any relatives or official representatives such as the police or medical staff, etc. I was given the very important job of carrying the stretcher, which suited me fine, and was as much responsibility as I wanted.*

In the van, Joe was making the most of his roomy position on the spacious driver's seat, while Graham and I positioned ourselves strategically on the ridiculously and inappropriately named two-seater section trying to avoid any unnecessary contact. And yes, maybe I did have a bit of a bee in my bonnet, but it really did annoy me that they could call it a two-seater and get away with it.

I was quite nervous about how I would deal with my first badly decomposed body, but at the same time I was curious as to what it would be like. That morbid fascination again, I suppose. On the way to the removal, Joe and Graham were giving me a few tips on what to do and what not to do when dealing with a badly decomposed body. Firstly, I was told if I felt like I was going to vomit – don't! Or at least leave the room if timing allows. If I do happen to vomit it may cause a chain reaction, and a trio of vomiting undertakers is definitely not the desired outcome or image that would do any of us any good. Secondly, I was told if the body was badly decomposed, we would use the protective over-suits, masks, and any other equipment required for our safety and convenience that had been provided by Mortimer and Sons at great expense.

The objective is not to hang around any longer than necessary when handling a decomposed body, transferring it into the body bag from its original location swiftly and efficiently without dwelling too much on the unpleasantness of the task. The whole procedure should be carried out professionally and respectfully with no dilly-dallying. I certainly had no desire to dilly my dally any longer than was completely necessary, that was for sure. If the deceased is clothed, grabbing hold of the clothing is acceptable and can be easier and much less unpleasant than grabbing hold of part of the deceased that might rupture and explode, or come away in your hand. With all the helpful tips coming my way I was beginning to wonder if sometimes too much information is not such a good thing. Forewarned and all that, but I think there definitely comes a point when the amount and depth of information you are being given, in many situations, far exceeds the amount you require. Graham's last piece of advice was not to breathe deeply, even with your mask on. They were only cheap polystyrene ones from the DIY shop and more to help prevent breathing in any nasty bacteria than to stop smells. They were also very useful in averting the accidental consumption of flies if there were any hanging about, which apparently there quite often can be. Sometimes in quite an abundance.

I'm sure Joe and Graham meant well, but all the helpful advice got my imagination working overtime and I wondered what we might be walking into and how I would deal with it. I had a sneaky suspicion that they might have been winding me up a little bit as well. Even so, I didn't want to let Joe and Graham down by not being able to do my job because I was too busy bringing up my last meal.

When we arrived at the block of flats, we discovered that vehicle access was restricted and as a result we had quite a walk from where we had to leave the van to the tower block entrance. Graham and Joe went up to reccy the situation leaving me to look after the van. Twenty minutes later and feeling slightly abandoned, I wondered whether I would ever see either of my colleagues again. Then Joe's cheeky boyish face with a beaming smile appeared at the driver's side window of the van.

I was given the bad news first. The lift was out of action and we had to go up to the fifth floor via the stairs. It could have been a lot worse I suppose; the tower block had twenty-two floors! A wheelie stretcher was out of the question, so we would have to use the fold-up stretcher. That meant we'd have a rather long and arduous descent back to the van, carrying our prone guest down a considerable number of steps. The good news was that the deceased was not as badly decomposed as we had been informed and we wouldn't be requiring the use of any of our exotic protective clothing. Just gloves.

By the time we got to the fifth floor, Joe and I were in need of some oxygen and I was feeling a burn in my thighs that any Jane Fonda workout enthusiast would be more than proud of. I felt sorry for poor Joe; he'd already done the trip three times and was about to do it for a fourth.

Graham was talking to a police officer and the deceased's son in the kitchen when Joe and I entered the flat. Even with the news that the body was not as badly decomposed as first thought, I was still feeling apprehensive about not showing myself up or letting my colleagues down in any way. After Graham had finished in the kitchen, the three of us went into the living room where the deceased had been discovered by her son, although, perhaps 'living room' is not the most appropriate terminology to use on this occasion. Mrs Frazer, the deceased, was slumped in an armchair in her nightgown in front of the television. The fragrance of death in the room albeit unpleasant, was not as pungent as I would have expected for the level of decomposition I thought Mrs Frazer was displaying. Her swollen purple face framing her bulging, staring eyes, to me, indicated nature's recycling process was well underway and elsewhere around her body she was starting to turn an interesting variety of ghastly greens. I felt a little queasy but I wasn't going to allow myself to be sick. I was concentrating hard on trying to do everything right and didn't have time for all that vomiting palaver. At least I hoped not! Joe and Graham said Mrs Frazer wasn't looking that bad at all in comparison to many of the bodies I was yet to have the pleasure in dealing with – which was not a comforting thought. The conditions of the bodies I was coming into contact with seemed to rapidly be getting worse as the days went by. A natural progression I supposed, as my time in the funeral business evolved. As this was only my third day, I wondered what gory delights might lie ahead!

Unfolding the stretcher in my charge, I laid it out on the floor. Joe moved it closer to the armchair to minimize the travelling distance from the chair to the stretcher and lessen the possibility of anything untoward happening to the apparently lightly decomposed Mrs Frazer. He then placed the large piece of white plastic sheeting over the stretcher. Graham had already removed the two rings Mrs Frazer was wearing and had returned them to her son at his request. All that was left for Graham to do before we transferred the woman from the chair to the *stretcher was to secure the all-important ID bracelet around her left ankle.*

Between us, Joe supported Mrs Frazer under the arms, I held her legs under the knees, and Graham supported her weight at her middle as best he could at the awkward angle he had positioned himself in. Gently, we lifted Mrs Frazer from the chair onto the stretcher. I was surprised again, that such a small-framed woman could be so heavy. Dead weight syndrome was clearly a very real concept. The rigor mortis phase must have come and gone as there was no sign of stiffness at all in the woman's lifeless limbs. In fact, her flesh felt quite soft and squishy as I took hold of the back of her legs, which made me suspect the stability of the woman's body may be a little more volatile than we had first thought. As we lay her onto the stretcher, a dark, reddish brown liquid bubbled from her swollen purple lips and she let out a ghostly groan. A little disconcerting but quite common apparently. Graham explained that the groaning was a result of the remaining air from the lungs being expelled by the movement. The air mixing with the blood and other redundant body fluids caused the bubbling effect from her mouth. The smell of stagnant air escaping from her lungs and whatever other noxious gases were mixed with it rapidly found its way into our nasal passages for analysis, causing each of us to grimace.

In theory, when we use our sense of smell it involves the actual absorption of the odour molecules which then stimulate various cells that process the information. Not a particularly nice thought, I must say! Although fortunately, it is a separate process to taste, even if the two senses are inwardly intertwined and very much reliant on each other for a complete and accurate analysis of smell and taste.

We wrapped the plastic sheeting around Mrs Frazer to help contain any fluid that may try to escape her lifeless and slightly unpredictable frame. The foot end of the folding stretchers have a large pocket that the deceased's feet are placed into in order to prevent them from slipping off the end of the stretcher, should it be necessary to position it at an acute angle at any stage of the removal. Four large flaps of material, as with the wheelie stretchers, but this time there is one attached to each end of the stretcher as well as on each side, completely enclose the body, restricting its movement and protecting it. To fully secure the body to the stretcher, the seatbelt-type straps are once again employed. Finally, to complete the ensemble a grey or black elasticated cover is respectfully placed over the stretcher and the deceased. A grey corduroy cover was used on this occasion.

Once Graham had informed the police officer and Mrs Frazer's son that we were ready to leave, he returned to assist us with our epic journey down the ten flights of stairs to the bottom of the tower block, back to the van. As I squatted down to pick up the foot end of the stretcher, without any warning, I was viciously attacked from behind. The clips of my braces attached to the back of my trousers had decided they'd had enough and could not cope with the extra strain caused by the stressful dynamics of my new position. Their reaction to my action, was to release themselves from their bondage at a rate of speed probably only known to those who travel in vehicles able to break the sound barrier or who are involved in space travel. The resulting collision with the back of my head and the detached part of my braces, equal to the impact of a stone released from a catapult at close range, was a tremendous shock and extremely painful. My thoughts turned to Goliath and how he must have felt at the conclusion of his little 'tête-à-tête' with David. Except he was hit from the front and from what I remember about the informative biblical account, died instantaneously. So, in actual fact, I may not have felt more pain than he did, but I probably felt it for a longer period of time and was able to remember it. Joe's and Graham's immediate thoughts were that I'd slipped a disc or pulled a muscle. When I told them it was my braces that had just assaulted me on the back of the head, they could barely contain their amusement.

"Do you want me to clip them back on?" Joe asked, with a smirk.

"No thanks, let's just get going," I replied, gesturing towards the door with my sore head.

As I stood up, Graham, being the thoughtful, caring kind and having concern for my safety and modesty, without any prompting reattached the braces to my trousers. Being on the foot end of the stretcher meant I had to walk backwards down the ten flights of stairs, which was no easy task carrying a stretcher with a body on it, and made worse by my Goliath-type injury. That's when I discovered how important it is to have a third person on the team to guide and support you as well as inform you of any obstacles or environmental hazards that may be a danger or cause any problems. It was a simple but effective technique that Graham used, and was not unlike doing the conga party dance, but in reverse and without the music. With his hands around my waist – in a manly sort of way, of course – and applying a slight amount of pressure, he was able to guide the speed and direction of my descent, physically and with verbal instruction. This helped me to feel more stable, at least physically if not mentally. Joe had to raise the head end of the stretcher above his head each time we turned a flight of stairs in order to get around the tight corners. In response, while still walking backwards, I had to lower the foot end as much as I could to counteract Joe's raising of the head end. The whole process was extremely awkward and put a lot of strain on my lower back. A challenging workout for all concerned! Except one, of course!

It seemed to take forever to get to the bottom of the tower block. Numerous short breaks were required along the way to both catch our breath and adjust our grip on the stretcher. Once at ground level, Graham was able to take one side of the foot end of the stretcher and help carry it the last part of the way to the van. His contribution however small was greatly appreciated. By the time we got to the van my grip on the stretcher was becoming quite a struggle and my forearms felt like they were going to explode. I was completely exhausted and sweating like I'd just come out of a sauna. Poor Joe was in a similar state. It just goes to show, even with all the weight training I did, I wasn't really that fit. But then I didn't do anywhere near as much cardiovascular work as I should have done.

The white powder in the latex gloves we used got everywhere. Black definitely wasn't the best colour to be wearing when using them. The three of us looked like we'd been in a flour fight. Graham did mention that the lads at the yard had been asking to be supplied with gloves without powder in for quite a while, but with no response from head office regarding the matter.

On our way to the coroner's mortuary in King's Cross we had all the van's windows fully open in an effort to create a decent breeze *going through the van to help cool us down. By the time we arrived at our destination our heart rates and oxygen saturation levels were just returning to normal, the sensation to our hands and forearms had been resumed, and the sweat from our troubled brows was gradually evaporating.*

The mortuary was part of a group of what looked like an assortment of periodic building extensions. Standing next to the rather less modern and more Gothic-styled coroner's court, the mortuary had a long, steep wooden ramp, leading to a stage-like platform and a pair of glass double doors (the heavily frosted type with the square-patterned wire inside the glass). Joe reversed the van up to the wooden platform. When the noise of the van's engine was silenced, we could hear a high-pitched sound coming from inside the mortuary like an electric drill or cutter of some kind. I was duly informed by Joe that it was the latter, probably being used to cut through the thick bone of a skull in order to remove the brain as part of the post-mortem examination. I pictured a Dr Frankenstein-type laboratory with various bits of bodies being removed and scrutinised under various microscopic devices.

A post-mortem is basically an investigation in to what has caused a person's death. The body is dissected and examined meticulously in order to determine if death occurred naturally or unnaturally. Unnaturally, possibly indicating foul play.

Unloading the stretcher from the van we walked up the steep wooden ramp to the mortuary entrance. The ramp had a wonderful deep bass drum tone due to its hollow construction. Perfect for tap dancing or any type of dancing which might benefit from good acoustics. Clog dancing would have sounded incredible. As we placed the stretcher onto the ground outside the mortuary door, the clips on my braces decided I needed yet another lesson on their inadequacies, whacking me on the back of the head in exactly the same spot as before. After this second assault, I was seriously questioning the clamping capabilities of my new braces, wondering why they had not come with a health warning informing all new owners of the possibility of serious injury. Data explaining their limitations should surely have been supplied as a requirement at their purchase, declaring that if the braces were to be stretched beyond a certain maximum 'pounds per square inch', 'newton per square metre' or whatever the correct measurement is with reference to Hooke's law of elasticity, that the end result may be more than just being disappointed in the braces' trouser-supporting capabilities.

Caught off guard, having already forgotten the last assault, a 'b' word referring to fatherless children escaped my lips embarrassingly and rather louder than I would have liked it to. Luckily it was timed perfectly and bleeped out by the very loud severe ring of the mortuary bell that Graham had just activated. Hopefully, it was loud enough to adequately mask the sound of my obscenities to anyone inside the mortuary! While we were waiting for a response to Graham's activation of the mortuary bell, Joe kindly reattached me once again to my braces. A thoughtful act, but one I felt would soon be classified as pointless due to their complete lack of interest in carrying out the only job they were created for and that was required of them.

The high shrill of the cutting tool ceased inside the mortuary. Shortly after, a fuzzy figure passed behind the reinforced frosted glass of the door before opening it. Duncan, the mortician, who must have been anywhere between the age of thirty and fifty at a very wild guess, greeted us with a smile that had lost more teeth over the years than it had retained. With his green PVC laboratory apron, toothless smile and limp, he reminded me, very appropriately, of the character Igor – the trusty and faithful servant of Dr Frankenstein. Or was he Dracula's trusty and faithful servant? I'm not entirely sure. To be honest, he'd have been perfect in either role without any help from the make-up department or any special effects should he have ever had the urge to pursue a career in acting and considered auditioning for either part. Duncan, like Angelo the mortician from the Central Middlesex Hospital, was quite a jovial chap. A much thinner man than Angelo – almost to the point of looking ill – he would have easily fit onto the two-seater section of the company's van without causing any distress or interfering with its second occupant's comfort whatsoever.

The foul odour emanating from the coroner's mortuary was rather more potent than anywhere I had ventured so far in my new career. This was presumably due to the number of bodies on the premises that *were likely to be far from at their best. There's clearly only so much that adequate ventilation and an industrial air freshener can cope with. We could see into the part of the mortuary where the bodies were examined. Two people dressed in green gowns, similar to those that surgeons wear, were leaning over a cadaver lying on a steel table. Their faces were masked and shielded by visors, no doubt to protect them from being splattered by blood or other body fluids during the dissection of the human remains, as well as limiting the foul odours, of course.*

The usual undertaker and mortician banter between Duncan, Graham and Joe flowed and was fairly continuous throughout our visit. Mrs Frazer was transferred from the stretcher to a fridge tray. Joe then helped Duncan to put the body into one of the fridges while Graham and I sorted the stretcher out. Duncan also measured the body, using a very similar instrument of design and construction to the one we had at Mortimer and Sons. A heads-up on the size in case we got the funeral. By all accounts, just because we'd participated in the removal on behalf of the coroner, it didn't mean we would automatically be doing the funeral.

The 'F' Word

Back at the yard there was just time for a quick cup of tea and a bite to eat before getting smartened up for my first funeral. A good polish with some of Joe's parade gloss on my trusty Doc Martens, a thorough brush-down of my smart new undertaker attire, and I was ready for action.

The body for the funeral was at head office in one of the chapels of rest. The family and friends had been viewing the deceased over the last couple of days. Oliver was the hearse driver and there were three limousines. Eddie, Ali, and a chap called Burt were the limousine drivers. Burt, who was well into his seventies, didn't work for Mortimer and Sons but was hired in using his own limousine when it was busy and extra cars were needed; a common practice with most funeral companies. Old Burt, as he was affectionately known, didn't carry coffins at the funerals, mainly because he wasn't up to it physically. Plus, he wouldn't have matched up height-wise with anyone as he was even shorter than me! Graham, Joe and I were the other three bearers aside from Oliver.

Joe travelled down to head office in the hearse with Oliver, I went with Eddie in his limousine and Graham travelled with Ali. Which left Old Burt flying solo at the rear.

The Daimler DS 420s really were built like tanks, with a bonnet that's as long as a wait in your local A & E department and a throbbing 4.2 litre, straight six Jaguar engine under it. The DS 420s were the limousines you usually saw the Queen and other royals, various dignitaries and some celebrities waving from. And occasionally the odd suspected royal imposter trying to fool some poor innocent nursery school children that they were having a visit from a member of the royal family.

Sitting on the huge double passenger seat in the front of Eddie's limousine, my proportions were swamped by its size like a small child in an adult's armchair. It was definitely a double seat, no question about that. You could get two very ample-sized bottoms next to each other on one of those seats and still have plenty of room to manoeuvre.

We drove through Camden in convoy. The shiny black beasts staying closely together almost as if one were towing the other, resembled a giant black snake winding its way through a concrete jungle. People seemed intrigued by our presence, peering keenly inside the vehicles to see if there was a coffin on the hearse or perhaps someone they knew in the limousines. The smoothness and power of the Daimlers were extremely impressive. Even the gentlest action on the accelerator by the driver raised the front of the car upwards and changed the gentle purr of its massive beating heart into an adrenalin-stirring roar. When the accelerator was relaxed, the beast under the bonnet would be subdued once more.

We arrived outside head office and were greeted by a large gathering of people congregating outside the front of the building. Surrounding them, countless bouquets of flowers were scattered along the edge of the pavement. Some of the people were crying and hugging one another. It was a very emotional scene, the sadness quite overwhelming. There were a large number of teenagers in the gathering which made me wonder if the funeral was for a young person. I asked Eddie if he knew. He told me the funeral was for a nineteen-year-old lad that had died in a car crash. He must have been a very popular young man judging by the number of people that had turned up for his funeral.

Oliver reversed the hearse around to the rear entrance of head office and the three limousines parked up outside the front entrance on the main road. Eddie first, then Ali, followed by Old Burt. Excusing ourselves through the mass of mourners we entered the building. Greeting us as we walked in was the overpowering perfume of yet more floral tributes of all shapes and sizes. Everywhere we looked there were flowers. Mr Dickinson was showing some very tearful mourners into the chapel of rest where the young lad was lying. He was using the same theatrical body language he had done on my tour of the yard which had amused me as it seemed so out of place. Now, it seemed quite appropriate, his unhurried, meaningful actions communicating care and calm.

When Mr Dickinson resurfaced from the chapel alone, he asked us to start loading the flowers onto the hearse and limousines. I'd never seen such a variety of flowers or so many in one place, not even in a florist. Not that I tended to frequent those particular establishments very often. Perhaps my relationships might have been blessed with slightly more longevity if I had!

Floral tributes filled the shelves to bursting in the small room used to store them before the funerals, and occupied every inch of space on the floor either side of the long, narrow corridor that led to the back door. Some were traditional bouquets and wreaths, others were much more elaborate botanical works of art. One was the Arsenal Football Club emblem which stood about three feet tall. Not everyone's favourite maybe, but obviously the young lad was a fan. The detail in it was incredible, particularly considering it was completely constructed of flowers. There was also a floral display in the shape of a dog that stood about two feet high. These accompanied various name tributes on large wire frames such as Son, Brother, Grandson, and Best Friend.

As the family and friends said their last goodbyes, we loaded up the hearse with the various floral tributes. Mr Dickinson instructed us to leave the 'Son' tribute until last which was to go at the back of the hearse at the head of the coffin. The Grandson and Best Friend tributes were almost as long as the hearse itself and were hung on the outside of the hearse on metal hooks. The same type as the ones you see in butchers' shops. Oliver was being very careful not to scratch the pristine black paintwork on the hearse and strategically placed small pieces of black cloth between the wire frames of the floral tributes and the bodywork.

As many of the bouquets as possible were placed on the tops of the hearse and limousines and were strapped down with bungee straps to prevent them from being blown away. The more delicate floral tributes, which were more likely to get damaged, were placed inside the hearse. Dealing with such a volume of flowers left our black suits looking like we'd been in a paintballing battle. A battle we clearly hadn't won judging by the amount of colour splattered all over our once black attire. Although only a few days in and with limited experience wearing my undertaker apparel, I could see that black really wasn't the most practical colour to be wearing in this job. Black is obviously the conventional colour assigned to mourning and traditionally worn by undertakers, but to be honest, woodland camouflage with the occasional splash of colour would be far more practical in many ways.

Another good brush-down however, with the use of a handy clothes brush, and we were transformed once more to our smart all-black status, no longer resembling a group of escaped harlequin clowns. At least not clothes-wise.

Once the last of the family and friends had finished viewing, Mr Dickinson gave us the all-clear to move the coffin from the chapel into the back room, ready for the final checks to be carried out before the coffin lid could be screwed down. Everything that had been placed in the coffin was to remain in the coffin: the photos, the trinkets, and the yellow metal cross and chain around the young man's neck. The deceased had received horrendous head injuries in the accident that had taken his life and Marcus had been required to do some very intricate reconstruction work in order for the family to view him without it being even more distressful than it already was for them. He had done an amazing job. You would never have known by looking at the young man that he'd suffered such horrific injuries. Apart from a slight hint of foundation-type make-up that Marcus had used to cover up some superficial wounds on his skin, he appeared uninjured.

The photos placed around him in the coffin were of himself with his family and friends at parties and on exotic holidays in the sun. He *had obviously been someone who enjoyed living life to the full and very much looked like he was generally the life and soul of the party. It all seemed such a tragic and terrible waste of a young life. A young life – now gone forever. A void for those that loved and knew him that would never be filled. It reminded me of what someone had once said to me about never leaving things on a bad note with those you love. Saying things you might regret, don't mean, or perhaps should have said but didn't. You might never have a chance to put things right.*

Mr Dickinson placed a face cloth over the young lad's face before Oliver and Joe put the coffin lid on and screwed it firmly down. A thin piece of green wire was attached at each end of the coffin lid via a decorative gold pin. This was used to secure the large floral tribute from the family firmly in position, the green wire being cleverly camouflaged by the green foliage of the floral display, magically disappearing from view.

Oliver, Joe, Eddie, Ali, Graham and I, wheeled the coffin out to the hearse, and on Mr Dickinson's order, the six of us lifted the coffin ceremoniously from the wheelie trolley which Mr Dickinson then removed. Placing the coffin gently into the back of the hearse we fed it slowly forward across the rollers. The coffin finally coming to rest against the ornate chrome stopper at the other end of the bier, Oliver then clamped it safely in place and leant the large 'Son' floral tribute against the head of the coffin at the back of the hearse. Oliver got into the hearse while the rest of us, including Mr Dickinson, returned to the front of the building where the mourners were now gathered.

The vicar from the local church, a tall, young, scholarly-looking chap, had arrived and was talking to the family. Mr Dickinson began to tactfully usher the family members into their designated limousines like a farmer rounding up his sheep. He then asked the remaining mourners who were travelling in their own vehicles to get ready to follow the funeral cortège. That's the posh name for the funeral procession. French, I believe. Why is it that everything sounds so posh when you say it in French? Even, 'I have a boil on my bottom', 'J'ai une ebullition sur le fond', sounds posh when you say it in French.

The immediate family was travelling in the first limousine. Further down the family tree were in the second and third limousines. Eddie, Ali

148

and Old Burt, assisted by Graham and me, helped the mourners into the correct limousines. An important safety measure carried out during this supportive role is to put your hand against the top of the inside part of the door frame, to cushion the blow in case they hit their head on entry. Quite a common occurrence, apparently. Even when vocal instructions to mind their head are given before entry. Further physical assistance may also be required depending on the mourner's mobility or lack of it. However, I was advised to assess the level of assistance offered very carefully as some mourners can be offended easily, taking it as an insult of their own capabilities rather than a polite offer of assistance. What a strange species we are.

For a large, impressive car it was incredible how cramped the Daimlers were on the inside. The complete opposite to Dr Who's TARDIS. Legally, according to Eddie, you could only seat six people in total in the back. I was warned that some mourners might try and get you to squeeze an extra one or two in if they could. However, if you did succumb to their persuasions, it could void the vehicle's insurance in the event of a claim. The fairly decent-sized back seat would comfortably seat three average-sized adults. Then there were what was called the occasional seats that pulled down from the front. There were two occasional seats which technically three people were able to sit on. The problem with the occasional, bench-type seats, was that where they met in the middle there was a slight gap. This meant that the person sat in the middle often had one bum cheek on each seat with their genitals in limbo poised over the space between the two seats. A 'mind the gap' sign would not have been out of place, and a specific warning to kilt-wearers completely appropriate – if not a necessary obligation. Although quite roomy on the back seat without the occasional seats pulled down, once they were it became rather cramped leg-room-wise for anyone over five feet tall in the front or the back.

With everyone seated in the vehicles Mr Dickinson and the vicar stood at the side of the road and waited for Oliver to pull up in the hearse. As he did so both men bowed gracefully towards the coffin. Walking side by side in front of the hearse they led the cortège. First the hearse, then the three limousines followed by an endless stream of private cars. I was now sat in the third limousine with Old Burt, Graham was in the second with Ali and Joe was in the hearse. Apparently, the vicar would eventually join the immediate family, in the front of the first limousine. Normal funeral logistics, by all accounts.

It was all very solemn as you would expect. Mr Dickinson's theatricality perfectly befitting the occasion, he resembled a circus ringmaster in his tails and his shiny black top hat held at waist height like some family heirloom on display. He certainly looked the part. I was quite impressed.

Follow the Leader

After walking a short distance up to the first traffic lights, which just happened to be on red, Mr Dickinson and the vicar moved to the left and bowed once more towards the coffin as the hearse drew level with them. With the vicar placed in the first limousine and Mr Dickinson sat in the front of the hearse, once the lights gave permission, we headed off to Golders Green Crematorium. The drivers of the private cars were asked to put their headlights on so the hearse driver and limousine drivers could keep an eye on them and try to keep everyone together, pulling over if necessary to allow any vehicles that got separated, to catch up and regain their position in the funeral cortège.

It was a baking hot day. An unfortunate term of phrase bearing in mind where we were heading, but nevertheless an accurate description of the weather. Being dressed in a black suit travelling in a black car didn't help to avert the sun's attentive rays in any way.

The dividing window between the front and back of the limousine was up, to give the mourners some privacy. It also meant that Burt and I could chat without appearing disrespectful. Just to make the journey a little more Sahara-like, I noticed that the heating in the limousine was on full blast. Somewhat puzzled, when I questioned Old Burt about the matter, he answered my query by informing me that it wasn't by choice, the heater control was broken and stuck in the full-on position. Marvellous! A mobile sauna. Just what we needed.

Burt offered me a boiled sweet from a small white, well-crumpled paper bag as compensation for the uncomfortable journey ahead. I declined politely, having been very successfully brainwashed as a child about accepting such things from strangers; even if strangers are just friends we haven't met yet – so they say! Although, I'm fairly sure not all strangers are destined to become our friends. At least I hope not! Some are a great deal stranger than others and definitely to be avoided.

Winding through the busy streets of London, the funeral cortège calmly and steadily made its way through the madding traffic, occasionally having to stop and pull over to wait for those that were temporarily delayed for various reasons. With the heat and the slow, smooth, bouncy action of the vehicle I could feel myself starting to nod off. It became harder and harder to fight the induced siesta and at one point my nodding-dog impression was in full swing. A large pothole in the road that was unavoidable, according to Old Burt, startled me into renewed alertness, putting an end to my drowsy canine impression. Old Burt made comments about what he thought the government did with all the road tax we paid and how it certainly didn't seem to be used to repair the roads. Thoughts I often have and comments I often make myself.

Heads turned, tongues wagged and fingers were pointed at the funeral procession as it passed by. It was like being a celebrity on the way to a première performance, except I wasn't the celebrity, of course. The celebrity, rather sadly, was inside the coffin.

During our solemn journey, I was absolutely astounded by the sheer ignorance and insensitivity of some road users. Other vehicles cut in between the hearse and the limousines and blasted their horns in anger because we were holding them up. One man even gave us a two-fingered salute as he zoomed past. Obviously late for a very important meeting! Old Burt said it was nothing out of the ordinary and that I should try not to get stressed out about it. Apparently, there's a lot of armholes out there, according to my spell check, that is! Clearly programmed by someone very polite, and not quite what Old Burt actually said. But I'm sure you get the gist.

Eventually the crematorium came into view, an intriguing-looking red brick building, hidden away in the back and beyond of Golders Green opposite a Jewish cemetery. A cemetery that according to Old Burt, was off limits to gentiles (someone that's not Jewish).

A short distance from the main entrance of the crematorium the cortège came to a halt in the road. Top hat in hand, Mr Dickinson got out of the hearse and stood beside it. He looked thoughtfully at the coffin for a moment as if pondering the meaning of life. Perhaps he was. Or perhaps he was trying to remember what his wife had asked him to get from the shop on his way home from work that evening. Whatever his private thoughts may have been, visually it was very effective and his presence portrayed dignity and commanded respect as he bowed reverently in the direction of the coffin. He walked slowly to the front of the hearse and after a brief but sombre walk he guided the cortège through the tall black gates of the crematorium. The hearse, following Mr Dickinson, drove under a small archway and stopped only moments before the act of stopping would have been initiated by the brick wall in front of it and not by the action of Oliver's foot on the brake pedal. A strategic manoeuvre apparently devised to allow the limousines to pull up under the archway in front of the chapel doors to enable the mourners to alight, and not due to any lack of concentration on Oliver's part. Once empty, the limousines could then drive past the hearse and park up.

Without delay the first limousine drove forward and came to a halt outside the chapel doors and the second pulled up behind it. Due to a lack of space behind the second limousine, the third, driven by Old Burt, in order to avoid blocking the entrance to the crematorium, drove to the right into the car park. The private cars following the third limousine also dispersed into the car park, and suddenly it was every man (or woman of course), for themselves.

Old Burt and I got out of the limousine and assisted the passengers to alight. Joe, Ali, Graham and Eddie, assisted the mourners in the other limousines, which were waiting outside the chapel, to do the same. Heads were protected from possible injury as the mourners exited the vehicles. Some of the taller passengers almost needed to be prized out of their seats as their long legs had gone to sleep having been starved of oxygen on the regal but rather cramped journey. I couldn't help but notice as I assisted people out of the limousine, that some members of the fairer sex appeared to find it quite difficult to exit the vehicle in a dignified and lady-like manner. Particularly if wearing a short skirt. Being the gentleman that I am, I had to avert my gaze skyward a number of times in order to protect the honour of a few of the female passengers. Luckily, there were no kilt-wearers. Once empty of mourners the limousines outside the chapel drove past the hearse and parked up. Mr Dickinson, still exuding a respectful and demure manner, led the family followed by the rest of the mourners into the chapel.

With the volume of mourners attending the funeral Joe and Graham were commandeered to help the chapel attendant Mark, a balding middle-aged chap of average build, to hand out the order of service sheets as the mourners entered the chapel. Due to such a large number of mourners quite a few had to stand at the back of the chapel. Having completed their duties assisting Mark, Joe and Graham re-joined Ali, Eddie, Oliver and I at the back of the hearse. Oliver, having reversed into a more advantageous position closer to the chapel doors, had opened up the back of the hearse and unscrewed the shiny chrome stopper that was keeping the coffin securely in place. Not wanting to tempt fate, rather than removing the stopper completely, he had left it in situ until the actual moment we would be required to remove the coffin. I don't think it would have gone down very well if the coffin had rolled off the hearse and crashed to the ground just before we were about to carry it in. An undertaker's worst nightmare, I would imagine. Although, I'm sure I could think of a few other unpleasant scenarios that could be as equally nightmarish!

Standing in guard of honour formation at the back of the hearse, in two columns of three, each of us faced our opposite number. As the shortest of the bearers, Eddie and I stood nearest the hearse in order to carry at the foot of the coffin, Joe and Ali were beside us which put them in the middle, and Oliver and Graham being the tallest were next, carrying at the head. Oliver, Joe and I stood to the left of the coffin to carry on our right shoulders, and Eddie, Ali and Graham stood to the right of the coffin to carry on their left shoulders. And if all that doesn't confuse you, I don't know what will! Continuing to present our funeral faces, as Eddie described it, but trying not to look suicidal, a sombre facial expression befitting our role was displayed by all. Hands clasped in front of us at arm's length, like a group of footballers protecting their genitals from a ball being kicked directly at them from a penalty shot, we waited in anticipation for Mr Dickinson to reappear from the chapel.

Eddie very quietly and almost using the art of ventriloquism, informed me that it's considered very unprofessional to make eye contact with the mourners, and I should try and remain as inconspicuous as possible. A very important skill for any undertaker to master, according to Eddie. I assured him I would try my best to be as inconspicuous as I possibly could and I would avert my eyes as soon as any eye contact looked at all likely between myself and anyone even resembling a mourner. Eddie asked me if I was sure I was happy carrying on my right shoulder. I confirmed that I was and that it was definitely my preferred side to weight-bear.

In my head I was going through the practice run we'd had with the coffin at the yard. While trying to remember all the intricate manoeuvres, I realised my body was moving in conjunction with my thoughts and it probably looked like I was desperate to go to the toilet, my legs involuntarily practising the movements for the 180-degree turn that I was about to attempt in public for the very first time. I was hoping and praying I wouldn't make a complete hash of it all and humiliate myself and my colleagues. I could see the headlines in the Funeral Directors monthly journal. 'Mortimer and Sons coffin-carry a shambles', with the story expanding on the headline proclaiming that our footwork resembled that of an inebriated aardvark and that our bowing was as synchronized as a flock of epileptic chickens at a barn dance. On the other hand, of course, if all went well there might be a talent scout amongst the mourners to notice our smooth, faultless, almost ballet-like grace and subsequently offer us the opportunity to represent Great Britain in the next coffin-carrying championships. And if such competitions don't exist, perhaps they should. There's nothing like a bit of healthy competition to keep you on your toes, improve your skills and encourage pride in performance.

Eddie, noticing my strange body language, must have sensed my nervousness and gave me a reassuring nod and a smile. That or he was experiencing the side effects of wind or indigestion. Joe and the others also showed their support with various nods and winks, gestures which when displayed usually indicate that someone is right behind you in a supportive role. If anyone had been watching they'd have probably thought Mortimer and Sons employed a large percentage of people with nervous twitches or who suffered from involuntary athetoid movement of the limbs. It was nice to know the lads were right behind me though, in more ways than one. All except Eddie of course, who was right behind me and beside me, in his allocated position on the other side of the coffin. If nothing else I felt extremely well supported. Except by my braces, that is, that were playing up something chronic and far from fulfilling the role they were designed for.

I noticed a couple of the lads had small pieces of grey material that they had placed onto the shoulder they would be carrying the coffin on. I was informed that this was to prevent any splinters from the underside of the coffin imbedding themselves into the material and damaging the jacket. A little trick to keep it looking smart and help increase the jacket's longevity. Adam and I were definitely going to need to get hold of one of those little gems.

Time Gentlemen, Please

Mr Dickinson, with top hat in hand, emerged from the chapel accompanied by the vicar and approached the back of the hearse with all the anticipation of the first night of a new West End musical. Pausing for a moment in front of us, Mr Dickinson, as lead man, gave us the nod.

"Thank you, gentlemen," he said expressively, which by the shuffling movement of my colleagues was clearly an indication we were on the move and not just Mr Dickinson thanking us for being gentlemen.

Eddie removed the chrome stopper that was preventing the coffin from prematurely ejecting from the hearse, and slowly and steadily we started to feed the coffin into our hands from the back of the hearse. First Eddie and I, then Joe and Ali as more of the coffin was accessible, and finally Oliver and Graham. Once the coffin was clear of the back of the hearse and the six of us were supporting all of its weight, trying to keep it as level as possible, we slowly raised it and placed it on our shoulders. The coffin at that point naturally took a slight downward slant at the foot end due to the gradual decrease in height of each pair of bearers and their position under the coffin. It was much heavier than the empty coffin that we had practised with the previous day. Probably pointing out the obvious I know, but it felt much more stable and secure on our shoulders with the extra weight, which was quite reassuring. After some strategic repositioning of our shoulders in order to get comfortable under the weight of the coffin, poised and ready we awaited further instructions from Mr Dickinson. From that point on, due to my position under the coffin, it was up to me to lead the way and keep the pace. Very carefully and sticking to the slow-motion tempo I had learnt the previous day, I overlapped my left foot with the right foot in a repetitive motion. As my colleagues followed my lead, the coffin with us under it started to rotate in an anti-clockwise direction. Carrying out a slightly slower version of the Riverdance technique than Mr Flatley so impressively demonstrates, we turned the 180 degrees required to face Mr Dickinson and the vicar who were stood in the direction of the chapel. So far so good! During the turn, unable to quell the urge to support the coffin on my shoulder with my left hand, I succumbed to my natural instinct. Due to the large object resting on my right shoulder limiting my field of vision, I was unaware whether any of my fellow bearers felt the same need.

Mr Dickinson nodded once again before he and the vicar turned about face and proceeded to walk at a leisurely pace towards the open chapel door. On my lead, left foot first and best foot forward, we followed in hot pursuit. Or more appropriately, we followed 'hot in black suits'. At the entrance to the chapel three steps presented themselves. Taking my first step up, again supporting the coffin with my left hand, I felt confident that they would not present a problem in any way. However, a sudden boost from the rear of the coffin, like a turbocharger kicking in, caught me completely by surprise. Particularly as I was under the impression that I was the one who was supposed to be dictating the speed of the proceedings in my key position under the coffin. Fortunately, it wasn't a drastic change in velocity and it certainly provided the momentum required to get us up the steps without any hesitation. That said, I would have appreciated being forewarned about the pending action prior to its activation. Although, I suppose not all information can be given prior to an event and all jobs have a certain amount of on-the-job training.

Perhaps the use of words like velocity and turbo boost are slightly misleading. It would probably be more appropriate to describe it like the feeling when you are changing down a gear in a car, or on a motorcycle, to go uphill. The revs go up and you get that bit of a jolt as the extra torque kicks in. It's the feeling of extra power but you're not actually going that much faster except perhaps during the initial change. To the casual observer or mourner, it wouldn't have been that noticeable an increase in speed at all. However, when you're one of the participants actually carrying the coffin on your shoulder, it was. Or at least it felt like it was and it can be quite a shock if you're not expecting it.

Almost immediately after our turbocharged entrance into the chapel, without any warning whatsoever, a sudden need to stop presented itself – Mr Dickinson and the vicar coming to a rather abrupt halt directly in front of us, to be exact. Something, to be honest, I was expecting even less than the turbo boost at the steps. Swerving quickly to the right I managed to avoid what could have been quite a serious collision involving the foot of the coffin and the back of the vicar's head, mostly thanks to the masterful grip and stabilising capabilities of my trusty Doc Martins' air-cushioned soles. I suspect a bit of quick thinking on Eddie's part may have also helped to circumnavigate the coffin, averting tragedy and what could have been a rather severe headache for the vicar, or worse. Eddie, in conjunction with my quick thinking and physical reaction, helped to guide the coffin on its very sudden newly directed course like a driving instructor with dual controls would, to correct the learner's mistake. In fact, I believe he told me he'd once been a driving instructor for a short time. Perhaps he never got out of the habit. Something I was indeed extremely grateful for.

The mourners were asked to stand, by the chapel attendant, which they did. All except one old lady at the back of the chapel in a wheelchair who I presume was excused this show of respect for obvious reasons.

Guns 'n' Roses, 'Don't Cry', started playing on the chapel's music system. I was quite partial to a bit of Guns 'n' Roses, my taste in music being fairly broad ranging, and this was a song of theirs I particularly liked. The lyrics, however, had never quite touched me or seemed as appropriate as they did at that moment in time. The volume of Guns 'n' Roses lowered slightly, and the vicar started to recite something from the Bible about the resurrection and the life. On the move once again, we slowly carried the coffin up the aisle towards what looked like an altar at the top of another set of steps. To the left of the altar was what looked like another altar, but was actually the catafalque. The catafalque, as Eddie had previously informed me, is where the coffin is placed during the funeral service. Not to be confused with a catapult, which would definitely be an entirely different type of send-off for a loved one. In the wall at the one end of the catafalque was a small door rather like a serving hatch which was where the coffin would make its exit at the designated time.

As we passed each row of mourners with the coffin, the volume of crying and sobbing on that row became more prominent and louder. Eventually, the volume of the crying in the chapel made it almost impossible to hear the music or the vicar's biblical recital. We gradually approached the steps which led up to the catafalque. This time I knew what was coming and was ready to support the coffin with my left hand. As soon as I'd taken my first step up, the turbocharger kicked in from behind and without delay the coffin was confidently encouraged forwards on the incline. Once at the top of the steps a sharp but steady turn to the left was required in order to approach the catafalque head on with the foot of the coffin. Positioned in front of the catafalque I heard the familiar voice of Mr Dickinson utter what I thought were the words, 'In Hans'. My thought processes reacting like lightning came up with two options. Mr Dickinson was either addressing a man called Hans in the congregation who was attempting to leave and instructing him to return to his seat, or he wanted us to lower the coffin from our shoulders into our hands and onto the catafalque. The second option made much more sense, although the first option could not be totally ruled out. Movement from my fellow bearers starting to shuffle about as if preparing to lower the coffin from their shoulders reinforced my instinct to go for the second option, which luckily was the right option. The delay and questioning involved in these thought processes was minimal, even for my standards, and I believe I adequately disguised my initial confusion. Despite my slightly slower reactions in comparison to my colleagues, the coffin was lowered from our shoulders steadily and smoothly. Little effort was required to roll the coffin gently onto the catafalque which was equipped with the ever trusty rollers. Apparatus that seemed to play an extremely important part within the funeral industry by enabling smooth movement of coffins on and off various objects.

As the coffin gently glided forward on the catafalque each pair of bearers having completed their supporting role released the coffin and took one step back, allowing the next pair of bearers still supporting the coffin to move forwards unimpeded. Mr Dickinson who was at the head end of the coffin and the last person to have contact with it, gently eased it to a halt in position on the catafalque. Facing the solitary coffin that lay before us, after a momentary pause we bowed our heads in unison. Not a full bent over stage-type bow that is usually accompanied by rapturous applause, but a respectful semi bow. To be more precise, it was probably more of a quarter of a bow involving a very slight tilt of the upper body just below the ribcage. Mr Dickinson's bow was far more theatrical than ours of course. The sort of bow that would usually be accompanied by rapturous applause. But that was to be expected with his obvious desire to untether the frustrated thespian deep within his psyche. With all the constant nodding and bowing, I wondered if repetitive strain injuries relating to the neck might be a common complaint that those in the funeral business suffer from.

Like most actions during a funeral, the synchronisation and timing between bearers while bowing is paramount. A Mexican cranial wave really just won't do. With no specific time structure or indication of when anyone else was going to bow and telepathy being limited to the chosen few, it would have been a good idea to have had some sort of secret signal instead of trying to read each other's body language. Which is an art in itself and to be honest is much harder than it looks, especially with more subtle movements. You have to know your colleagues really well to be able to anticipate their actions. There is an element of learned timing involved, certainly, but that can be a bit hit and miss as I quickly discovered.

After the bow the others turned and walked slowly towards a door in the far left-hand corner of the chapel, located just behind the organist who was operating the sound system. I thought it best to follow and tried to make it look as if I had always planned to do so. It was as if we were exiting a stage via the wings after a performance. Without the applause.

I think I may have resembled Corporal Jones from Dad's Army on more than a couple of occasions with my delayed reactions. I always seemed to be one step behind the others. I was reassured by Joe that the mourners probably wouldn't have noticed the fact that my timing was slightly out of sync, due to the tears in their eyes. It was still early days, as he said, and he was sure as time passed I would get more in tune with my fellow bearers and develop the skills required. It brought to mind something that had been mentioned to me a few times over my life that I thought I might need to apply to the situation. In short, I would try harder, endeavour to avoid being distracted, and pull my socks up to a level that demonstrated my determination to succeed in every aspect of my role as a funeral assistant.

Perhaps telepathy should be a requirement for all future employees of Mortimer and Sons. The synchronicity of every action between bearers would be impeccable. A harmonious display of Homo-sapien locomotion!

Once the chapel door had shut behind us, our funeral faces came off and our normal speed of body movements was resumed. All of us back in real time instead of slow-motion mode, just as if a switch had been flicked on our backs like a robotic toy. Behind the scenes at the crematorium there were a number of coffins on trolleys which were presumably waiting to be cremated. The attendant, Chris, a tall, pale-faced, ginger-haired bloke in his early twenties, started chatting to Joe about the Tottenham Hotspur game a few nights previously. Apparently they were both avid fans of the North London club, but judging by some of the comments being shared by the two fans both seemed to feel they could do a far better job managing the team than the current manager.

A number of small hatches along the two inner walls in the L-shaped building were evidently the entry points where the coffins were placed into the cremators. Joe and Chris walked around the corner into an area that was on the other side of the cremators. With a quick tilting of his head in the direction of travel they were headed, Joe beckoned me to follow them. The area we entered was not that dissimilar to what I would imagine a ship's engine room might look like. Switches and dials everywhere you looked, with the dull roar of the cremators just like a ship's engine humming away in the background. The warmth and smell of ash completed the sensory effect perfectly.

Chris explained that each cremator was capable of reaching temperatures of between 870 and 980 degrees Celsius during the cremation process. Which in my book, is exceedingly hot on any scale. In order to deal with increasingly strict regulations on the emissions generated from each cremator, they had become a great deal more sophisticated and as a result were an extremely expensive bit of kit.

Chris asked me if I would like to see a cremation in progress and pointed towards a small inspection window on one of the cremators. Using what is obviously the preferred form of communication within the funeral business, I nodded in reply to Chris's question. On closer investigation, the small window looked exactly like one of those small peepholes you get in a front door that allows you to see who's on the other side before you open it. An extremely wise safety feature in any home if you ask me, and very handy when being visited by unwelcome callers, enabling you to pretend you're not in if it's someone you want to avoid. As long as they don't notice your beady little eye spying on them from the other side of the door, that is.

Cautiously, I edged forward towards the inspection window and offered my right eye up to it whilst closing the left. I was surprised that even through the thick metal door I could feel the heat on my face. However, that was not the most interesting revelation of the day. Inside the furnace in clear view, surrounded by the red-hot glowing bricks, lay a cleanly picked skeleton. Captivated by the image, I watched intently as the flames danced and licked at the remaining bones searching for any flesh or gristle that earlier flames may have missed; but there was none visible. Where the coffin once stood, only a thin line of ash surrounding the skeleton outlining the coffin's previous position was proof it had ever existed at all. Almost as if it had been zapped by a magician's wand. Apparently, on average it can take from two to three hours to cremate human remains.

As I continued to watch the dancing flames, the skeletal structure eventually surrendered to the continuous and unforgiving bombardment from its unceasing foe, and unsupported by the softer bones and cartilage that had already succumbed to the flames, the bony framework finally collapsed. The skull, free from its anatomical constraints, unexpectedly rolled to one side which startled me and caused me to jump back. Chris and Joe drawn to my sudden movement asked me what was wrong and were highly amused when I explained what had made me jump. Returning to my observation point at the small inspection window, the angle of the skull, having turned, gave the impression that it was staring back at me. It looked angry and displeased with my rude and uninvited interruption into its final moments of existence.

It was a sobering vision. Not that I'd been under the influence of alcohol prior to the experience, of course. Although after such a thought-provoking image, I wouldn't have turned down a sip or two of something a little stronger than a cup of tea, to help calm the nerves. Soon to be nothing more than ash, it was strange to think that the skeleton disintegrating in the flames in front of me was a living, breathing person only a few days prior to the event that I was now witnessing. My own mortality had never felt so temporary and insignificant. A mere intruder passing through for a fleeting moment on this mysterious and ancient planet, as it spins relentlessly through an infinite and unfathomable universe. Or something along those lines!

It wasn't quite as romantic as a Viking send-off – no flaming longboat drifting out to sea – and not as spiritual or as dramatic as a blazing pyre on a mountain top. However, modern technology applied to the cremation of human remains, although a little clinical, was extremely efficient at completing the task it had been presented *with. It was also a far more practical way of coping with the increasing demands of a growing population that will inevitably put more strain on crematoria, which as a result will undoubtedly have to deal with tougher environmental regulations.*

Chris and Joe entered an adjoining room which was full to capacity with bronzed-coloured plastic containers. These were the urns provided by the crematorium for returning the ashes to the undertaker or family of the deceased. They were very similar in shape and size to the glass jars they used to have in sweet shops when I was a boy. Some places still use them but not so much nowadays. Although, the contents were not nearly as desirable on this occasion.

I watched as Chris transferred the ashes of one of the temporary residents of one of the furnaces, from a metal box about the size of a large biscuit tin, into one of the plastic bronze containers. I was amazed at the volume of ash and commented on how much more there was than I had expected. Chris explained that the term ashes was a little deceptive and that the newly homed contents of the bronze container were mainly crushed bone and not ashes as most people believed them to be. Unlike the soft tissue and cartilage, the more densely composed bones are not burnt and transformed into ash by the heat, but calcified. He pointed to a machine resembling a tumble dryer, which was relentlessly clattering and rumbling noisily behind him, explaining that the remaining calcified bones are placed into the machine with a number of heavy metal balls. Not unlike old-fashioned cannon balls in size and weight, the balls break down the bones until they bear a resemblance to a fine gravel-like compound. Chris handed me the urn containing the ashes/ crushed bone, noting that an adult, once transformed into the basic elements in hand, averaged between four to six pounds in weight. The ashes that Chris had handed me, definitely felt on the upper end of that range.

"Perhaps they're referred to as ashes because it's a more sensitive term to use rather than saying, here's your loved one's crushed bones!" I suggested.

"You could be right there, Bill," Chris said, checking the cremation in progress through the inspection window.

Leaving Chris to his work, Joe and I re-joined our colleagues at the hearse and limousines who were unloading the mobile version of the Hanging Gardens of Babylon.

"Nice of you to join us, ladies," said Oliver, playfully.

"Just showing Bill around, Olivia," Joe responded, equally as playfully, as we both took up our floral relocating responsibilities.

The flowers and tributes were placed in the cloisters at the back of the crematorium, the designated area for them to be displayed. Each funeral had an allocated plot indicated by a name card on a metal stand. In order to fit all of the floral tributes from our funeral in, we had to move a number of the neighbouring name stands and flowers along slightly. This seemed a little cheeky, but was apparently common practice, as some funerals could have a considerable amount of flowers, while others might only have a few or none at all.

As Ali was removing a large wreath from the roof of the hearse, he looked up and made an observation.

"They haven't chosen a new Pope yet then."

Confused, I wondered what on earth he was talking about, exclaiming such random information. I wasn't aware that the previous Pope had died. Then it clicked and I realised what he was referring to. Thick black smoke was bellowing out of the tall crematorium chimney. The usual sign from the Vatican to indicate that a new Pope had not yet been chosen. (White smoke would have indicated that one had.) I had been formally introduced to Ali's dry, undertaker humour.

"It can't be very pleasant living around here with all that smoke containing particles of deceased people getting into your lungs or mingling with your undies on the washing line," I said, screwing my face up as if I'd just eaten a sour grape.

"Most people in this neighbourhood have probably got tumble dryers," he replied, rather sarcastically.

"You're probably right there, Ali," I agreed, removing the last bouquet of flowers from the roof rack of Old Burt's limousine, before following Ali through to the cloisters.

The grounds of the crematorium were very well kept and the building itself was an interesting design based on North Lombardic architecture.

That's impressed you, hasn't it! It's amazing what you can learn if you take the time to read a few informative signs.

Once again, we managed to get absolutely plastered in pollen. Like alien beings spreading infectious spores in order to colonise the earth the floral displays disseminated their pollen onto our solemn attire – lilies being the biggest culprits and worst offenders! Pollen wasn't our only challenge when handling the floral tributes – there was another hidden hazard. All too soon I learnt to watch out for buzzing stowaways who were attracted by the floral extravaganza and that seemed to relish in revelling in insect-utopia. On this occasion one such stowaway, a very plump bee, scared the living daylights out of me as it exited angrily from a floral tribute I picked up. Buzzing loudly, cursing me in bumble bee no doubt, it flew straight into my face and then drifted off aimlessly into the distance like a helicopter pilot on their first lesson struggling with the controls.

After laying out all of the flowers from our funeral in the cloisters, Oliver, Joe, Graham and I jumped into the hearse and headed over to the North Finchley branch of Mortimer and Sons for our next funeral. This left Eddie, Ali and Old Burt to wait for the service to end, after which they were to return the mourners to a pub in Camden and drop Mr Dickinson and the vicar back at head office. As it was a double service due to last approximately forty minutes, those waiting on ventured over to the crematorium tearoom where the delectable Fran and Edith reputedly served a selection of tasty snacks and hot and cold beverages, as well as irresistible home-cooked meals throughout the day.

A Man with One Leg Remarks on the Climate in Brussels

The North Finchley branch was co-managed by Richard Barker and Henry Mortimer's wife, Frances. I was given this information before entering the branch just in case I felt the need to say or do something that might put my three-month probationary period in jeopardy. As if I would!

Oliver parked the hearse directly outside the branch and once all on board had disembarked, we entered the establishment. Mrs Mortimer and Mr Barker at first glance appeared to be absent from the office, however, further inspection revealed the two sitting in the garden at the rear of the premises, enjoying the sunshine. They were engaged in a cryptic crossword puzzle in one of those large, posh newspapers. You know the type – you can just about open the pages fully if you have your arms extended out on either side and in doing so block out the rest of the world around you. The type that makes you feel you're in a wrestling match every time you try to turn one of the oversized pages, with the added bonus that if even the slightest breeze catches the sail-like broadsheet, you'll end up wearing it as a blanket. And if you're not the first person to read it in its crisp, straight-off-the-press state, you can never find the page you want because the previous reader has been practising the art of origami with it and muddled them all up. Thank goodness for the far more sensibly constructed and more manageable smaller sized tabloids where you only have to turn one page to get to the next enthralling feature. I rarely partake in reading them myself, but it's nice to know they're out there if you want a paper that you don't have to do battle with in order to read it. And the crossword puzzles are generally a little less taxing and far more doable for someone like me.

Eating cherry tomatoes that had allegedly been grown by their own fair hands in that very garden (a claim substantiated by a number of cherry tomato plants growing in the flower beds, bearing the small red fruits), Mrs Mortimer and Mr Barker offered each of us a sample. And very tasty they were too. You really can't beat home grown!

The atmosphere was calm and relaxed at the North Finchley branch. Mr Barker had already very efficiently checked the body, sealed down the coffin and secured the coffin flowers, a beautiful large display of yellow roses. I sensed that this was going to be a very different affair compared to our first funeral. Just the hearse from the house with only one or two private cars following, according to Mr Barker. Our destination was St Marylebone Crematorium, which was actually situated in the grounds of East Finchley Cemetery, just a short drive from the house.

After a good brush-down to remove any remaining pollen stains from our previous funeral, the four of us and Mr Barker wheeled the coffin out to the hearse on a trolley and loaded it into the hearse. Two more floral tributes were sat on the floor in the hallway of the branch. One from a nursing home offering their condolences, and the other from someone called Mavis who had written on the card, 'At peace, dear friend, see you anon'. A far cry from the mass of flowers at the previous funeral, yet it seemed to say just as much in its simplicity about the love and respect felt for the deceased. It was also a great deal easier on the black suits pollen-wise.

Unlike Mr Dickinson, Mr Barker wasn't dressed in traditional hat and tails as I had expected him to be. Instead, he wore a plain navy-blue suit. He seemed a very easy-going man. In fact, if he were any more laid back, he would probably have been the passenger lying in the back of the hearse. He seemed a very genuine type of chap but came across more like someone you would expect to find working in a bank or an office rather than an undertakers. Although he did have an office in the undertakers, of course.

Leaving Frances Mortimer dealing with a prospective customer on the telephone, in order to meet up with the family we headed off in the hearse to the house. Graham and I were in the back, whilst Joe shared the large front passenger seat with Mr Barker.

At the house Mr Barker dealt with the family respectfully, omitting the fuss or theatricality that Mr Dickinson may have displayed. Neither was right nor wrong in their approach, I'm sure, they just used different methods when performing their professional duties. One was very natural and relaxed in his manner, the other was the epitome of showmanship and favoured the use of melodramatic body language and props. It was an interesting contrast to observe in action.

Two bouquets of flowers at the house which were from neighbours were placed in the hearse on either side of the coffin, joining the ones from Mavis and the nursing home. The family and other mourners got into three private cars, and with headlights on as instructed, they pulled up directly behind the hearse that was now blocking the rather narrow residential road. Mr Barker paused at the side of the hearse and gave a bow towards the coffin (although, it was definitely more like a nod). He then walked in front of the hearse for a short distance before getting back in. Not quite the show I suspect Mr Dickinson would have put on, but respectfully done, nevertheless.

It was a steady drive to the crematorium and keeping together was much easier without the large convoy of cars. There was no need to pull over and wait for stragglers as the roads around the area were far less busy than Camden and Hampstead, helped in part by it also being later in the day.

East Finchley Cemetery was a fair size and possessed the most varied assortment of gravestones and monuments I'd ever seen, from small, simple granite slabs to elaborate life-size angels guarding colossal stone tombs; the diverse and eclectic cenotaphs each as individual as the person they commemorated.

As we got closer to the crematorium building, we noticed there was already a hearse and a limousine waiting outside the chapel entrance. The previous funeral was apparently running late. Mr Barker instructed us to hang back and wait where we were, while he went to speak with our mourners. Observing from our position in the hearse, my colleagues and I watched as Mr Barker directed the mourners where to park. Once they were out of the vehicles, he escorted them to a picturesque spot away from the main crematorium building where he waited with them for the funeral service currently underway to finish. Which was all he could do really, under the circumstances.

It was incredibly hot sitting in the hearse. It was like a mobile greenhouse, with all those large windows inviting the sun's intense rays to shine through. Which might have been bearable if we were wearing shorts, a T-shirt and flip flops, holding a nice cold drink in our hand, but not when wearing black suits with a waistcoat and a tie, with only thoughts of a nice cold drink. I was dripping with sweat, as were my colleagues. As the sweat ran down my face, I can remember thinking that in the future I would have to start carrying a handkerchief in order to wipe the sweat away. Or even better, I wondered if I could get away with having one of those mini hand-held fans. I could keep it out of view and just give myself a sneaky blast of air with it now and again to cool myself down.

Eventually, the funeral that was running late finished and Mr Barker signalled to Oliver with a nod and hand gesture to drive the hearse up to the chapel doors. The doors were under the cover of a long drive-through arch, or perhaps it was more of a porch. Either way, the cool shade was more than a welcome break from the heat of the sun intensified through the glass. Exiting the vehicle at the earliest opportunity – in order to escape our roasting – Oliver, Joe, Graham and I stood at the rear of the vehicle in our columns of two, with our hands clasped in front of us awaiting further orders.

The 5'6" x 20" coffin only required four bearers, so Joe, who wasn't that much taller than me was carrying at the foot end of the coffin opposite me, and Graham and Oliver who were of a similar height to each other, were carrying at the head end. Joe had been having problems with his left shoulder so asked me if he could be on the left of the coffin in order to carry on his right shoulder. I wasn't very keen to change positions because I find it quite awkward to weight-bear on my left shoulder, a condition I generally attribute to several historical road collisions on my motorcycle and numerous confrontations on the rugby pitch from my younger days, which left me with a variety of injuries to my upper torso. But being of a thoughtful disposition (at least I'd like to think I am) I didn't really like to say no.

It was to be a Humanist ceremony, as the deceased was not a religious person and apparently didn't want any form of religious service. I have to admit my ignorance and say that I had never heard the term Humanists before and therefore didn't have much of an idea what they did or didn't believe. I just assumed they didn't believe in a God.

Malcolm, the chapel attendant, a stout, balding gentleman in his early-ish fifties, enquired as to everyone's health and welcomed me to St Marylebone Crematorium. Which was thoughtful. Mr Barker in the meantime was showing the mourners and the Humanist minister into the chapel.

It was a very different atmosphere from our previous funeral, perhaps because the deceased was a much older person who had lived out their life, and death was not as unexpected. It was still a sad occasion but obviously more natural in the order of life's events.

Mr Barker and the Humanist minister, although I believe he preferred the term celebrant, re-emerged from the chapel and joined us at the hearse. A nod from Mr Barker, and we were on the move again. Withdrawing the coffin from the back of the hearse slowly, once clear of the vehicle we placed the coffin onto our shoulders. After a quick but subtle shuffling of shoulders to get the coffin positioned comfortably and distribute the weight fairly, the words 'Thank you, gentlemen,' from Mr Barker acknowledged participation in my second funeral. Having changed places with Joe for him to be able to carry on his right shoulder, Joe was now officially lead bearer. Under Joe's directorship the carry felt much more controlled than when I was leading. Smoother, more positive movements and changes of direction. Mind you, having been in the job for a couple of years he'd had slightly more practice than I had.

St Marylebone Crematorium's chapel was somewhat larger than the one at Golders Green, but decoratively it was a very similar layout with its church pew seating, plush, deep-pile red carpet and the catafalque situated at the top of several steps. The small gathering of mourners seemed quite lost within its walls, only taking up the first three pews in front of the catafalque.

As we started the long journey down the aisle along the plush red carpet towards the catafalque, a piece of classical music began playing quietly in the background. I've no idea what it was, not being very educated in the area of classical music, but it was very peaceful and calming, a flute notably being the most prominent instrument. As we negotiated our way up the steps to the catafalque, I knew now from my previous experience to expect the change down in gear and so was fully prepared when the sudden surge in power was delivered from behind.

Arriving safely at the catafalque we placed the coffin in position and took one step backwards before pausing and bowing. Slightly premature with my bow, I bowed alone. The others bowing in unison immediately after my solo performance, I quickly bowed again trying to make it look like I had only performed one bow but with the addition of a theatrical embellishment that to the untrained eye might look like I had only bowed the once. Whether I managed to cover up my untimely mistake convincingly I can't say for sure, but it was probably dependent on how much attention any particular mourner was paying to the proceedings at the time, or if they had tears in their eyes. There really should be some sort of secret signal or specific lapse of time between placing the coffin on the catafalque before the bow is performed, in order to achieve maximum bowing synchronisation between bearers. I contemplated suggesting it, but decided against the idea. As the new boy it would probably be wise to at least wait until my probationary period was completed before trying to encourage any changes to working practices.

Unlike Golders Green Crematorium, the absence of a convenient exit behind the catafalque allowing us to disperse inconspicuously after the completion of our coffin-carrying duties, meant at St Marylebone we had to promenade back down the centre aisle and exit through the same door we had used to enter. I wouldn't imagine it makes a great deal of difference to the mourners, but I much preferred being able to disappear into the shadows unobtrusively. Making your way to the exit, facing the mourners, trying to avoid eye contact because it was unprofessional to do so, and averting one's gaze southward while trying to remain inconspicuous and respectful, tended to make you look like you had autistic tendencies or a severe lack of social skills. At least that's the way it made me feel.

The funeral flowers at St Marylebone were placed in a large quadrangle behind the main building. The outer perimeter of the quadrangle, where the flowers were put on display, was under cover, and the middle section was open and sported a small fountain adorned with cherubs, although they could quite as easily have been described as Munchkins. All in all, it was very quaint and picturesque and would have been an idyllic place to sit and reflect, had it not been for the constant trickling of water from the fountain which just made me want to go to the toilet. With only a small amount of flowers to deal with, minimal pollen migration from the flowers to our suits meant we remained quite respectable. Clothing wise, at least!

Mr Barker had asked Joe to collect the ashes of a Mr Campbell from a funeral earlier in the week. I went along with Joe, at his suggestion, in order to familiarise myself with the layout of the place for future reference. First stop was the main office. The three ladies busying themselves in the office, seemed pleased of the intrusion and were very welcoming, especially so when it came to Joe. Once I had been introduced to Dawn, Grace and Lisa, Joe's attentions for some inexplicable reason (although maybe not that inexplicable) appeared to be drawn to Lisa, the younger and more attractive of the three ladies sat at her desk typing. Her shoulder-length dark hair, stunning blue eyes and pale but perfect complexion, put me in mind of the 'Brothers Grimm' fairy tale character Snow White.

Joe didn't give all of his attention to Lisa; he very diplomatically drew the other two more middle-aged ladies into the cordial exchange too. As the song goes, he was a smooth operator. His cheeky, boyish good looks combined with his gift of the gab seemed to be just the ingredients the ladies liked. Especially going by the now blushing 'Snow White' who was still tapping away on her keyboard while trying to avoid looking Joe in the eyes, no doubt making a few more typing errors than she was five minutes prior to our intrusion into her work environment. Joe reminded me very much of the character Alfie, as played by Michael Caine in the 1966 film of the same name. Joe was a cocky fellow, in a warming sort of way rather than an annoying one. Very much like the Alfie character in the film.

Bidding farewell to the St Marylebone ladies we ventured forth to another part of the building to collect the required ashes. The ashes were stored behind the scenes as they were at Golders Green, in the same area as the cremators and in the familiar plastic, bronze-coloured containers. It was Malcolm, the attendant that had greeted us on our arrival, that dealt with the ashes. He appeared to wear many hats. Not at the same time but metaphorically speaking, in his various duties around the crematorium. Having said that, who's to say he didn't actually own many hats? He may well have done.

Paperwork was exchanged and names checked (the deceased's, not ours), and taking possession of the ashes of Mr Campbell, Joe and I returned to the hearse. The hearse was now parked at the rear of the crematorium out of sight of the next funeral which was now approaching the chapel. Oliver and Graham were waiting in the hearse passing the time with idle chit chat, which Joe and I were more than happy to join in with while we waited for Mr Barker.

After the service, Mr Barker, along with the chapel attendant Malcolm (wearing his other metaphorical hat), led the mourners out of the chapel to the sparse but nicely put together floral tributes at the allocated spot, as indicated by the crematorium's wire-framed name plaque. After the mourners had ceremonially viewed the flowers and spent a few minutes mingling and chatting, Mr Barker removed the small message cards attached to each floral tribute and gave them to the family. Once all the mourners had made their way back to their vehicles, Mr Barker joined us at the hearse. Then, accompanied by the ashes of Mr Campbell, he was chauffeured back to North Finchley, no doubt to carry on with his cryptic crossword and sample the latest crop of cherry tomatoes. As well as all his other very important professional duties, of course.

Do Not Resuscitate

On our return to the yard, as we were walking through the workshop towards the tearoom, Eamon emerged from his kiosk-like office. His body language completely giving away the motivation behind his appearance and what he was about to say, before anyone could utter a word in protest, those immortal words, 'Have a quick cup of tea' left his lips and were effectively delivered to our brains via our unprotected auditory senses.

So, after a quick cup of tea, or coffee in Graham's case, our day's work resumed. Oliver and Joe were sent out to deliver two bodies to branches for viewing, while Graham and I, joined by Eddie, were to attend a coroner's removal. A suicide apparently. Eddie having returned earlier from the funeral he was on, had already been given his orders to refuel quickly with a hot beverage, and having completed that objective, had then loaded up one of the vans with all the relevant equipment we might require on the removal. Rehydrated and bladders emptied the three of us headed off to a hotel in the West End where the police awaited our attendance.

Out of our little trio Eddie was the one in possession of the pink card and consequently would be doing all the talking. Something I gathered he quite liked doing (although singing was definitely his preferred form of communication). Gentleman Graham had sneakily but politely nominated himself as driver and once again I was in charge of the fold-up stretcher. An outcome, as usual, that I was more than happy to endure as I had no real desire to talk to anyone. Particularly someone who might ask me questions about what we were doing, why we were doing it, and what they should do next in relation to legal requirements or funeral arrangements. That said, I wouldn't have minded doing the driving – if only for the luxury of ample seating! Some assistance with the navigating may have been required.

On our arrival at the hotel the manager was called. He didn't seem at all pleased to see us waiting at the reception desk in his lavishly decorated reception area. Immediately questioning us, he wanted to know why we hadn't used the tradesman's entrance as instructed. We avoided an in-depth debate, in part, because we hadn't actually been given those instructions but predominantly because his derogatory manner and belittling tone clearly indicated he was not a man who was going to listen. The reason we hadn't used the tradesman's entrance, was because a large vehicle with 'Manson's quality meats' displayed on its side was blocking the access. Agreeing it would be unfitting parking next to a meat delivery vehicle we subsequently chose to enter the building via the least inappropriate of the two scenarios – which in our view, was the main entrance.

The grey Mortimer and Sons vans were not obviously undertakers' vehicles. It was in all probability only when we were stood next to them in our black suits that people would start to put two and two together. If we were carrying a stretcher with a suspicious-looking bundle shaped like a body on it, they might even put three and three together.

The manager, still displeased and sour-faced, before leaving, delegated the job of escorting us up to room twenty-nine on the third floor where the police were waiting for us with the body, to Adriana, one of the two young ladies carrying out their duties behind the reception desk. Eddie asked Adriana if she thought we would be able to use a wheelie stretcher to carry out the removal. After Eddie's brief description of a wheelie stretcher and its capabilities, Adriana was quite positive the *lift would be far too small to accommodate its dimensions. I believe she was of East European extraction, going by her accent, but her English was excellent.*

Leaving my colleagues chatting to our guide Adriana, I went back to the van to collect the ever-trusty folding house stretcher. On my return, Adriana shepherded my colleagues and me towards the three hotel lifts just around the corner and to the right of the reception desk. Our guide summoned the centre lift, due to it being the closest to the ground floor as indicated by the illuminated number- two above its doors. Entering the lift on its arrival, it was clear that Adriana's doubt as to whether we could have used a wheelie stretcher or not was well founded. With the four of us standing in it, it was without a doubt clearly limited to vertical use by four, or maybe five persons at a push (and probably a bit of a shove). Though a fifth person of even ample proportions would have definitely caused serious territorial issues and possibly accusations of inappropriate behaviour.

I could certainly see where Joe's gift of the gab came from. Eddie was very chatty with Adriana. Not in a chatty-uppy sort of way, but more out of gentlemanly politeness. At least that's the impression that I got. I assumed he was trying to avoid that awkward silence you often get when standing in a lift with strangers. Although, I don't suppose anyone wants every Tom, Dick or Harry listening in on their conversation. Unless, of course, they're in the lift with their good friends Tom, Dick and Harry and there is important information to be passed on.

It was a long walk from the lift to room twenty-nine, along numerous red-carpeted corridors lined with multiple numbered doors. A typical hotel layout, I suppose. Eventually arriving at room twenty-nine, Adriana excused herself and handed us over to the fresh-faced young policeman who was patiently waiting outside. The room was extremely small, sparsely furnished and painted in duck egg blue. My fastidious reference to the exact type of blue, rather than just saying light blue, no doubt derives from my time as a young model maker. The colour of the hotel room was a perfect match to the duck egg blue I was instructed to use by a specific manufacturer of plastic models, to paint the underside of various WW2 aircraft. With the amount I made and painted during my modelling years, it's not surprising that it's such a prominent childhood memory.

Glancing around the room it looked more like a prison cell rather than a hotel room. Not quite what I was expecting at all after seeing how lavishly the majority of the hotel was decorated. Perhaps they'd gone over budget with the rest of the hotel and had to be a little more frugal with their money when it came to decorating the rooms. On the other hand, it may have been that the woman had only asked for the economy accommodation. Bearing in mind her objective, she probably had little concern for its overnight amenities, comfort or colour scheme.

A red blanket, which the ambulance crew had left behind, covered the woman on the single bed against the wall. A considerate gesture on their behalf, I thought. The empty bottle of vodka sat on the bedside table next to an empty container of pills, appeared to confirm the suspected suicide, although the evidence in front of us would apparently not be seen by the coroner as concrete proof of the purposeful choice the woman under the blanket would appear to have made.

Graham partially pulled aside the red blanket to reveal a bare-breasted woman who looked to be in her mid-forties. Written across her chest in large bold letters in what appeared to be permanent black marker pen, penned by her own hand presumably, were the words, 'DO NOT RESUSCITATE.' Clearly more an instruction than a request, I wondered if the paramedics had tried to resuscitate her or if she was already long gone by the time they had arrived. Would they have been obliged to take any notice of the strikingly explicit message or not?

Unfolding the stretcher, I laid it next to the bed topping it with the white plastic sheeting that had been neatly and compactly folded in the inside pocket of my jacket. Once Eddie had attached the ID bracelet around the woman's left ankle, Angela Susan Bishop was transferred from the bed to the stretcher, covered with the plastic sheeting and strapped securely in. She was not a small woman in any sense of the word, a statement my lower back would willingly confirm. With limited space available to manoeuvre the stretcher that the deceased now occupied, exiting the room demanded a combination of strenuous vertical and horizontal operations which took all of our combined strength. Carrying the heavily laden stretcher, the walk back to the lift seemed twice the distance we had covered in the opposite direction to the room. Graham and Eddie shared the workload at the foot whilst I contended with the head end. In order to facilitate use of the lift for our descent, the stretcher and its occupant had to be supported in an upright position. The stretcher actually required little physical intervention to aid stability, as it was thoroughly wedged between the three of us. A veritable group hug!

Walking through the reception area of the hotel we tried to be as discreet as possible but I think it was fairly obvious to the two guests sat with their luggage waiting for a taxi, that the lumpy stretcher being supported by the three men in black suits, was not the hotel laundry.

Sat in the van travelling along a hectic Euston Road, I contemplated the 'DO NOT RESUSCITATE' woman now lying in the back of Mortimer and Sons' grey van. What a terrible tragedy it is for someone to feel such despair. To consider death a more favourable option than life. Undeniably, there are many reasons why someone may feel that way. Life can often seem very cruel and extremely unfair at times, even to the more robust of spirit. But had Angela Susan Bishop really wanted to cease to exist forever, or did she just want her life to be different? Sometimes it can be extremely difficult, even painful, to make the changes we know we should. Was death really her only reprieve from the torment she was experiencing? Was she now at peace, or a tormented spirit searching for serenity?

Over the years I have often wondered if we are at times too sensitive for our own good and ultimately do we end up paying the price for our over-sensitivity as a consequence? Then again, a world without sensitivity would undoubtedly be lacking in compassion and a great deal harder and unbearable in times of need for many of us.

Following a short drive to the coroner's court in King's Cross, we chaperoned our poignant passenger into the mortuary, admiring the impressive acoustics of the steep wooden ramp which led the way up to the entrance. Protocol was followed, booking in the mortuary's most recent guest and the usual jovial banter ensued between Duncan the mortician and my colleagues and me. The jovial banter appeared a vital part of the mechanism that enabled us to cope with being surrounded by death on a daily basis, but for some reason it felt wrong amidst the sadness of someone that felt so alone and desperate that they had taken their own life. Perhaps the banter was even more essential in such circumstances, in order to protect ourselves from that despair.

"Don't take it all on board, Bill," Eddie advised, as if reading my thoughts. "We see so much of this, it doesn't do any good to dwell on it. And the banter just helps us to cope. It's not out of disrespect."

I nodded in agreement, but all the way back to the yard I couldn't help wondering what had driven Angela Susan Bishop to take her own life and what the consequences would be for those she had left behind.

It wouldn't be long before it was time to go home once we got back to the yard. Just time for a nice, slow cup of tea and to get changed back into our civvies.

To Pull or Slide, That is the Question

When we arrived back at the yard, Eamon was on the hunt for a sixth man for a church take-in. (That's when a coffin is taken into church for a service prior to the funeral and stays there overnight, ready for the funeral service the next day.)

Dad used to say that one of the most important things he had learnt during his time in the forces, was never to volunteer for anything. Even though the words were wrapped in mirth, which was just his way of imparting those particular words of wisdom, I believe the advice was given with serious intent. Unfortunately, like many things our parents say or do to try and help guide us successfully through life, it's not usually until we have learnt things the hard way ourselves that we realise they were generally right about most things and knew exactly what they were talking about. Despite being mindful of Dad's words of wisdom and eternally grateful for his parental concern, without hesitation, I volunteered my services for the church take-in.

I hadn't done anything churchy so far and was curious to see what went on, as well as it being an opportunity to work with some of the other staff that I hadn't had much to do with yet. Plus, the chance of overtime *in any work place to boost monetary funds is generally greeted with enthusiasm, especially within the lower ranks whose financial rewards for their time are often, how shall I put it, a little on the stingy side? Not that the wages at Mortimer and Sons were that bad, particularly in comparison to some undertakers, but every little helps, as they say. I was also hoping that my eagerness to offer my services might earn me a few well-needed brownie points with Eamon, following the dreaded paper shredder incident.*

It was Mel, Ali and Graham's out-of-hours duty week, which meant they were doing the take-in because it would run after five fifteen, Mortimer and Sons' official finishing time. Dean was driving the hearse, Howard made the crew up to five, and my offer of help brought the team up to the required six. If only Mr Wise, my teacher in Class 2b, could see my mathematical genius at work. He would be so proud.

The actual take-in was at six o'clock and with the church being very close to the Tufnell Park branch, where the body was lying, it meant we had time for another quick cup of tea. The kettle was duly filled and switched into action. During refreshments, a general sprucing up, brushing down and polishing of shoes was carried out, removing any missed bits of pollen, sawdust and other foreign bodies that may have hitched a ride on our smart black suits from the day's activities. A mass scrounging of Joe's parade-gloss shoe polish ensued, like a frenzied seagull attack around a fish and chip shop at the seaside.

So frequently used by so many, the contents of the tin at the time would have been more appropriately described as essence of parade gloss. Joe had to heat the bottom of the tin with his lighter to encourage the remaining residue into a usable consistency. As it cooled to a workable temperature the frenzied attack on the tin continued. With the sorry-looking quantity of polish that was available, it made the feeding of the five thousand with five loaves and two fish seem quite doable. It appeared Joe possessed the only source of polish on the premises, which I thought was a little bizarre considering the vast number of times everyone's footwear required a rejuvenating coat of polish throughout the day. Further investigations into the shoe polish situation educated me to the fact that staff took it in turns to purchase the product in question, as and when stock required replenishing. Surely it would have made much more sense for everyone to have their own supply, if only for convenience, but I wasn't about to start making waves or poo pooing time-honoured traditions. I did however promise myself that I would purchase some polish at the earliest opportunity in order to alleviate my reliance on others. As well as supplying a tin for all to use when it was my turn.

At twenty to six Dean, Ali, Graham and I, travelled up to the Tufnell Park branch in the hearse with Mel and Howard following closely behind in a limousine. It was thought the limousine might be required to ferry some of the older and less mobile members of the family between the branch and the church, even though the church was literally just across the road from the branch.

There was quite a gathering when we arrived at the Tufnell Park branch, with people lining the pavement and surrounding area on both sides of the road. Mr Best from head office was the funeral director in charge of the 'take-in' and was standing outside talking to some of the mourners. Mr Best was from Newcastle and spoke with a wonderful Geordie accent, as did his partner, Rose, who I mention because she was the manageress of the Tufnell Park branch and also in attendance.

As we pulled up outside and exited the vehicles, our funeral faces automatically appeared and our body movements instinctively selected undertaker mode. Every movement now appeared almost robotic as we enacted the slow and methodical aspects of our job with dignity and grace. I had noticed that even when not carrying out specific funeral duties, most things my colleagues and I did in the public domain naturally seemed to be performed at a noticeably slower pace. I think the perception that moving slower is more respectful and compassionate may be the reason why this happens. Which I suppose in many ways is true and something I found I was doing already, without even thinking about it.

While the last of the family and friends were viewing the deceased in the chapel of rest, I decided to take the opportunity to answer nature's call. A call that was quickly becoming a shout of desperation from my bladder with an increasing sense of urgency. I really shouldn't have had that last cup of tea before leaving the yard, or perhaps the other however many prior to it! The toilet was situated halfway down the narrow hallway to the rear of the building just past the chapel. Finding the door closed, I attempted to open it. Unwilling to cooperate with my efforts I came to the conclusion that the door must be locked and the facility for performing bodily functions was occupied. I enquired politely and discreetly in order to confirm my suspicions but there was no reply. I could clearly see that the light was not on, which to be honest due to the rather severe lack of natural light in that particular part of the building would have been a definite necessity. After all, seeing what you're doing with regard to directional responsibilities, particularly when standing as men generally are, is not only quite an important factor to carrying out your objectives in a civilised manner, but also an obvious courtesy to the toilet's owner, caretaker, and fellow users.

Out of desperation and a lack of response from any possible occupant, I concluded the room was vacant and having operated doors successfully most of my life and possessing what I considered to be a fairly good working knowledge of how they functioned, I decided a little more force was required to free the obstreperous wooden obstacle from its bondage in order to relieve my aching bladder as soon as possible. That's when I discovered – to my surprise – that the door I was so urgently trying to open in the conventional manner, was actually a sliding door. Regrettably, this little gem of knowledge came a little too late and there was an extremely loud bang as I pulled the toilet door off its rails. Alerted to my plight, an audience of curious staff and mourners soon gathered to witness my stupidity. Rose, who you may remember me mentioning was the manager of the Tufnell Park branch, didn't seem at all impressed when she saw me standing there clutching her toilet door in my hands. If looks could kill, I'm fairly sure I wouldn't be here now to tell the tale. To be honest, I felt a bit of a dick. And although it would be an essential part of my anatomy to handle in order to carry out the call of nature, it certainly hadn't been my desire to look like one!

After standing there for what seemed like an eternity with the dislodged sliding door in my hands wondering what to do about the result of my recent role in demolition, Graham very kindly came to my rescue. Thankfully, due to his advantage in the height department, he was able to assist me in reuniting the door with its overhead tracking without too much difficulty. Grateful that I had managed not to wet myself during the rather prolonged delay and that I was now able to use the facilities and perform the function I so desperately desired, I subsequently made use of the small but adequately furnished toilet with recently reattached sliding door. What a relief, for all!

With the urgent bladder situation now appeased and calm restored all round, I re-joined my colleagues and assisted in taking the funeral flowers from inside the branch out to the hearse. Due to the nature of our current undertaking, my colleagues were unable to give me the ribbing I knew they so desperately wanted to, but I was fully aware that as soon as the opportunity presented itself, I would get it with both barrels.

Dean, Graham and I accompanied Mr Best into the viewing chapel where he carried out the last-minute checks on the deceased, a Mr Murphy, aged sixty-three. Dean and Graham then secured the lid of the coffin. An impressive display of team work if ever I saw one. A magnificent arrangement of majestic white lilies that almost covered the entire length of the 6'4" x 24" coffin, was secured using the green wire which became virtually invisible amongst the decorative vegetation. The large coffin on the wheelie trolley was far from easy to manoeuvre around the tight corner of the rather narrow chapel doorway, but once achieved and in the hallway, we took up our appropriate positions around the coffin and lifted it onto our shoulders. Rose moved the trolley aside, its part in the proceedings having come to an end and its present position now presenting a significant obstacle. After a short pause and a quick shuffle to get the heavy coffin comfortable on our shoulders, the words 'Thank you, gentlemen,' were uttered by Mr Best and we followed his lead out of the building through the now open double doors of the entrance to the branch. Slowly and solemnly, we walked with the coffin on our shoulders out to the hearse.

Once the coffin was placed into the hearse the mourners that were sporadically positioned outside the branch, around fifty in total I would say, started to gather closer. As a mark of respect for the deceased, the family and mourners had decided to walk behind the hearse to the church. Fortunately, the church was only a short distance away, about a hundred metres at most, which was just as well really because many of the mourners were very old and a few looked decidedly dodgy in the health department. Not wanting to appear insensitive, some of them looked like they might be requiring Mortimer and Sons' services themselves in the not too distant future. I tried to remember the breaths to compressions ratio of the resuscitation technique, just in case I might be required to perform CPR. That would be an interesting headline in the local paper! 'Undertaker resurrects mourner at funeral!'

Mel, Ali and Howard had already made their way to the church on foot once the coffin had been placed into the hearse, leaving the limousine outside the branch as it was not required. Escorting the coffin on its journey to the church, Mr Best was to walk in front of the hearse, Graham and I were to walk either side of the hearse out on the wing, and the mourners would follow behind.

A bow towards the coffin and a nod in Dean's direction from Mr Best initiated the start of the procession. There was a slight hint of a waddle incorporated into Mr Best's walk, possibly due to a leg or pelvic problem. However, it was no less respectful or solemn. It was an extremely slow trek, not just because of the customary slow funeral pace but mostly because of the even slower and lesser-able mourners following behind.

The first thing I noticed about the church, which caused me some concern, was the vast amount of steeply inclined steps leading up to the large arch-shaped doors of the entrance. Even with my very limited experience I could see the coffin was going to be at quite a precarious angle on our shoulders and would require a good surge of power to get to the top of the steps.

At the church, while we were waiting for the vicar, we unloaded the flowers and placed them inside the church at the altar. The highly polished tiled flooring inside was incredibly slippery. Fantastic for sliding on in your socks, if you felt the urge and were of an age that wouldn't draw too much attention, but I could see it making things a great deal more exciting than we might want them to be if we weren't very careful while carrying the coffin. Everyone's shoes were squeaking loudly as they walked on the shiny slick tiles, which wasn't exactly conducive to the solemnity of the occasion. It sounded like an invasion of squealing rats as it echoed around the vast expanse of the church.

The outside of the building was quite deceptive, giving little indication of the enormity of the inside. The distance from the main entrance to the altar was almost as far as it was from the branch of Mortimer and Sons to the church. It was probably the largest church I had ever seen. Although admittedly that list was not the most extensive of lists at the time. The hallowed structure was a true testament to mankind's architectural abilities and craftsmanship. It was also the first Catholic church I had ever entered and was apparently run by an order of Dominican monks.

The trestles which the coffin was to be placed on overnight and during the service the next day, were put in position in front of the altar. Unlike the rough and ready ones we used at the yard in the workshop, these were very posh, dark wood that stood about four feet high. They also had velvet covers; vivid purple, embellished with gold edging. Very classy!

Apparently, different venues prefer different heights of trestles for various reasons. Here they preferred the taller ones. Once the trestles and flowers were in place at the altar, back at the hearse we stood in our usual regimented formation; hands clasped in front, funeral faces on, facing our opposite number and averting our gaze from any passing mourners. You can understand why people might think undertakers are a bit strange, can't you?

Eventually, one of the friars appeared, a very tall, elderly man dressed in a white hooded robe. Not a vicar as I previously mentioned. The friar was carrying a small brass bucket containing what looked like a baby's rattle, also made out of brass. Stood in front of the tall, robed figure, as a result of me being a bit of a short arse, I felt like Bilbo Baggins in the presence of Gandalf the White.

On Mr Best's instruction we removed the coffin from the hearse and rested it on our shoulders. Mel was on the foot end with me, Ali and Dean were in the middle, and Graham and Howard were at the head. As we paused at the hearse and waited for the friar to bless the coffin, we took the opportunity to carry out the usual repositioning procedures.

The coffin was quite a weight and had already started to dig into my shoulder. Even the high-quality shoulder pad of my expensive jacket didn't help and I was experiencing a great deal of discomfort.

The friar moved forward and began speaking in what I assumed to be Latin. At the same time he extracted the brass baby's rattle from the brass bucket and proceeded to vigorously wave it in our direction. Large droplets of water, like those of a tropical rainstorm, came hurtling towards us, each droplet splashing and dancing over the coffin and us. The brass instrument was obviously no baby rattle, but a cunningly disguised implement used to distribute water over undertakers. Even in my ignorance I knew we were probably being dowsed with holy water and not just your ordinary out of the tap heathen H_2O. If any of us had been vampires or possessed by demons we'd have been sizzling in our shoes. The friar dipped the brass implement into the brass bucket replenishing its supply of righteous liquid, and with another bout of vigorous waving accompanied by more Latin incantations he released a second tsunami of holy water. I remember thinking that the most probable reason for the second bombardment was to drench any part of the coffin and us that might have escaped his first attempt. He succeeded!

The friar turned and ascended the steep set of steps towards the huge ancient-looking double doors of the church which were now open. Holding onto the coffin we followed in hot pursuit at a pace not entirely appropriate for carrying a coffin, but very necessary in order to reach the summit of the steep steps. Mr Best supporting at the rear added an extra pair of hands to steady the coffin. Thankfully the flowers were well secured on top of the coffin, which would have otherwise been doomed sitting on any surface at such an extreme angle. Once at the top of the steps and on the flat, the friar who was once way ahead of us suddenly became very close; directly in front of us, in fact, and stationary. (I have come to notice that it seems to be a particular trait of religious people carrying out ceremonial duties on the move, to abruptly come to a standstill without forewarning those following behind.) Our response to the unexpected hazard in our path on this occasion, involved a slight but very quick detour to the right of the stationary friar in order to *avoid contact, but without actually overtaking him. The highly polished flooring came in very handy and assisted with the urgent change in direction superbly. All was well, hearts were thumping rapidly, but a tragedy had been averted and hopefully not a soul was any the wiser that our elaborate manoeuvre was not part of the organised choreography. We used the pause at the top of the steps to once again make fine adjustments to our positioning under the coffin and regain composure, the rather turbulent journey preceding our resting position having left us slightly dishevelled.*

The friar assumed a leisurely pace as he made his way towards the altar reciting his biblical message to the congregation and the large number of mourners following us up the aisle. This did little to alleviate the excruciating pain in my shoulder and neck due to the weight of the coffin. We plodded so slowly towards the altar, it appeared to be getting further away rather than closer, and just like a mirage in the desert I wondered if the altar actually existed or was merely an illusion.

As more mourners entered the church the squeals and squeaks from the magnitude of shoes on the highly polished flooring almost drowned out the friar's religious incantations, requiring him to increase his volume to almost a shout in order to be heard. Behind me, I could hear one of my fellow bearers starting to huff and puff heavily like a steam train, under the weight of the coffin. I suspected it was Howard, being the oldest and most battle-weary of our little crew, but that was purely speculation.

As we approached the tall trestles in front of the altar, Mr Best pulled the first set of trestles away to the side. I'd not been informed that this or any other action with the trestles would be taking place and assuming I was meant to proceed to the front set of trestles, I did so. More on the job training! Mr Best then returned the absent trestle under the head end of the coffin and on his instruction we lowered the coffin from our shoulders onto the pair of waiting trestles. Each taking one pace backwards, we bowed respectfully – the illusion of being in unison with my colleagues, almost achieved on this occasion. We made our exit in the darkness of the outer edges of the church whilst trying to be as quiet and inconspicuous as possible so as not to disturb the service which was now in progress. Unfortunately, as I mentioned earlier, the highly polished flooring of the impressive church had other ideas. With every step we took, it sounded like some poor squeaking rodent was in distress. In an attempt to alleviate the annoying and very disruptive high-pitched sound, I tried walking on tiptoes, then on the outer edges of the soles of my shoes, then the inner edges and then on my heels. No technique applied seemed to thwart the incessant shrieking or decrease the volume of my rodent-imitating shoes. Anyone witnessing this bizarre display of footwork could easily be forgiven for thinking I was suffering from any number of severe physical ailments, trying to re-enact the famous warehouse dance scene from the film Footloose, or that I'd totally lost the plot.

After carrying the weighty coffin on the marathon-like trek to the altar, my shoulder, or rather the trapezius muscle that travels from the neck along the top of the back, was extremely tender. It felt like I had just received an intense deep tissue massage. You know, the painful kind of massage where the sadistic sports therapist uses their whole weight to burrow into the muscle with their bony elbow – not the nice, gentle kind of massage with strawberry-scented body oil applied by a six-foot blonde called Candy who asks if you require any extras – or so I've been told!

Looking at my colleagues they appeared to be suffering the same kind of fate. We were fairly well matched size wise, the weight distribution should have been fine. Mind you, it was a solid wood coffin, which are far from light even when empty. The other bearers informed me that even when you're well matched, positioning will have a lot to do with how much weight is put onto each bearer's shoulders. The smallest change in position can make all the difference. Sometimes there's just not the time to make those fine adjustments and you just have to grin and bear it.

As we continued to chat, I mentioned my confusion with Mr Best's actions regarding the trestles. My colleagues offered their apologies for not informing me of the likelihood that this would happen and went on to explain that various conductors do things differently depending on their own preferences. Some leave both trestles in place, in which case the bearers will walk alongside the trestles – usually to the left – come to a halt, and then take the coffin off their shoulders before placing it onto the trestles. After listening to a variety of scenarios and quite extensive explanations into the pros and cons of each method, I decided I preferred Mr Best's technique. It was simpler, involved a lot less shuffling about for the bearers and was far less likely to invite complications.

When we arrived back at the yard, we found Adam and Joe had stayed on to do a bit of overtime and were just finishing off some coffins that were needed first thing in the morning. In our absence, the pony had also been delivered from head office containing Thursday's orders. Like a group of excited school boys clambering to see whether we'd been picked for the school rugby team, we eagerly looked through the orders to see what we would be doing. There were eleven funerals and I was on four of them. I wasn't sure whether to laugh or cry when I saw my first call of the day would be to attend the funeral at the church where we had just carried out the 'take-in'. Lucky me, another shoulder-crippling marathon and tenderising sports massage to look forward to! According to the orders it was to be a horse-drawn carriage taking the coffin from the church to the cemetery. That should be interesting. Elsewhere, aside from the other funerals and removals, Eddie and Frank were off on a road-run to Wales to collect the body of a climber that had made an unplanned and rather speedy descent from a mountain.

All in all, it had been a fairly hectic day, with plenty of food for thought. Those obstreperous braces were a complete pain in the derrière. Not only were they uncomfortable and useless at carrying out their designated duties but they were downright dangerous and would have to go if a serious injury was to be averted. No one else seemed to have any problems with theirs. Perhaps I'd bought a duff pair. And white shirts for undertakers are definitely not the most sensible choice. I won't even try to describe the colour of my collar after just one day's use, but it certainly couldn't be described as white any more. It would take a real bio-chemical reaction to get that shirt clean and bluey white. Although to be honest, I find the whole concept of washing powder manufacturers claiming that their products will get your whites, 'bluey white' or 'whiter than white' quite bizarre. Famous advertising slogans used by particular manufacturers over the years. Thoroughly clean and as white as when the item was new would impress me, and be more than adequate a statement from any manufacturer to tempt me to buy their product. Personally, if I wanted any item to be bluey white, I would probably have bought it in a light shade of blue to begin with, and if I wanted my whites whiter than white, I would without a doubt be any shop assistant's worst nightmare who was trying to sell me something white that I considered not to be white enough.

THURSDAY

Having arrived bright and early on my fourth day at Mortimer and Sons, I started the day by making a complete fool of myself, by pulling the handle off the false drawer under the sink in the tearoom during my search for a teaspoon. It would be some time before I lived that one down! Why do they make it look like a drawer if that's not its purpose in life? No doubt to make people like me look stupid when they foolishly perceive it to be what it is not and try to open it. Now, my catalogue of clumsiness at Mortimer and Sons not only included ripping the sliding toilet door from its tracking at the Tufnell Park branch but it also featured the blundering non-opening drawer incident. If I wasn't careful, I'd be getting a new name for myself – and that name would be Wally.

Fortunately, a busy day lay ahead and there was a good chance I may escape the mickey-taking I could expect due to my stupidity, at least for a short time. It was going to be so busy, that even blue-arsed flies would find it hard to keep up with us.

Eddie and Frank had prepared the Granada estate for the trip to Wales. Apparently, wheelie stretchers and some of the lengthier coffins are slightly too long to fit in the back of the vehicle unless they are positioned at an angle. The trouble with that is the front passenger seat has to be so far forward in order to accommodate the stretcher or coffin that there's hardly any leg room, even for the shortest of the staff like Eddie and myself. More importantly, with the vehicle not being properly adapted in any way to carry such items, if at any time the driver was required to brake hard for any reason there was nothing to *prevent the stretcher or coffin from being propelled rapidly forwards and joining the passenger in the front seat, thus leaving them with a rather severe headache or worse. Still, at least Eddie and Frank would have a nice ride out in the countryside and get to see some beautiful scenery. Even if there was a strong possibility one or both of them might end up requiring medical attention in a Welsh A & E department.*

Joe and I were assigned to dress and coffin-up some bodies for viewing and after the first caffeine requirements of the day had been satisfied, therefore initiating more efficient brain to body neurological communication, we were able to start work on our first task of the day. Sadly, our first client was an eleven-year-old boy. As we dressed his delicate, pale, lifeless frame in his Man United football kit, I couldn't help but notice how much smaller he seemed in comparison to most eleven-year-olds. Perhaps this was due to illness. After gently placing him into the white coffin with silver fixings and light-blue inside trimmings, as requested by his parents, we then surrounded him with the family photos supplied and placed a small teddy beside him that was also in a Man United football kit.

The silence between Joe and I during that time said more than any words could have about how it made us feel. And besides, what could we possibly have said that would have had any worth? There is something exceptionally tragic about the loss of a child. So much so, I couldn't even begin to imagine what the boy's parents were going through. Looking back, I can clearly remember hoping and praying, that if I ever became a parent, to never experience such pain.

At times like these, it makes me wonder about the concept of a loving God. Why would a loving God want us to experience such heart-breaking misery in our lives? Personally, I'm not so sure about the theory that in order to become a better person you have to suffer. The pain of losing a loved one can undoubtedly change a person forever, but what lesson is being taught when we grieve, apart from how fragile and unfair life can be. It's certainly a harsh way to learn such a lesson, and a very cruel way to teach it. And ultimately, I'm not so sure we become better people, just people learning to live with loss. Perhaps the most valuable lesson any of us can learn through such things, is to make the most of the time that we have with those we love and not to take them, or the time we might have to be with them, for granted.

After Joe and I had finished in the mortuary, Graham and I were sent down to head office with the young boy. Joe had to stay and get Eddie's limousine ready as he was doing his dad's drives for the day due to Eddie's trip with Frank to the land of daffodils, sheep and leeks. Among many other things, of course.

On our return to the yard, Graham and I had just enough time for a 'quick cup of tea' and to get smartened up before setting off with the others on our first funeral of the day. Morris was going to be the hearse driver. Even though the coffin would be on a horse-drawn carriage from the church to the cemetery, the hearse was to be used to transport some of the many floral tributes. Mel, Ali and Joe were the three limousine drivers. Graham and I, mere menial bearers, making up the six-man crew.

On the way to the church, where the coffin was placed the night before, we stopped off at the Tufnell Park branch to pick up a few more flowers that had been delivered that morning. Mr Best had made his own way to the church and was already there when the mass and combined funeral service got under way. As we pulled up outside the branch, we could see the two magnificent black horses and the old-fashioned carriage-hearse standing in front of the church. We gathered the remaining flowers for the funeral and made our way over to the church in the cars.

The service would be a good forty to forty-five minutes according to the lads, so we used that time productively and loaded the flowers that had accumulated at the back of the church onto the hearse and limousines. Even though we tried to be as discreet and as quiet as possible, the highly polished flooring with its high-pitched squeaking tendencies made this an almost impossible task. We were only able to limit the off-putting high-pitched squeaks to a minimum by reducing the speed of our movement to an even slower pace than normal. Seriously, a snail could have overtaken us! Once the flowers from the back of the church were loaded and secured onto the vehicles using the faithful old bungee straps, the traditional de-pollinating ceremony of our funeral attire was diligently carried out.

Outside the church, Dave, one of the coachmen, was adjusting the position of the coffin stops inside the immaculately restored ornate Victorian carriage. Chris, the second coachman, was tending to the horses and stood grooming one of the animal's shimmering black coats. Adorned in traditional livery, the black ostrich feathers embellished the poised animal's head harness gracefully and danced in the slight breeze, adding an almost ghostly elegance to the occasion as the noble creatures stood proudly and patiently while waiting to do their duty. As we marvelled at the impressive equine beauties in front of us, Chris began chatting and informed us that the horses were known as Belgian Blacks. He told us that the Belgian Black's ancestors were originally from Friesland in Holland and were used as war horses by medieval knights. Later, due to their grandeur, they became very popular with circuses, the film industry, and were also widely used to pull carriages.

Drawing closer to the animals, I asked if I could stroke one of the horses. Acknowledging my request, Dave nodded. Cautiously, I reached forward and lightly stroked its muscular shoulder. I've been nervous of horses ever since I was a small boy, mainly due to a biting incident following an unsuccessful attempt at giving an apple to a horse. (Just in case there is any confusion, it was the horse that bit me, not the other way around.) So, for me, this was a bit of a face-your-fears moment. The magnificent black horse, with a disgruntled snort, turned its head towards me quickly, making me jump. I think he sensed my nervousness. Animals always can. Perhaps I'll stick to cats and dogs to practise my Dr Doolittle techniques in future!

Leaving Dave and Chris in peace to get on with preparing the carriage and grooming the horses, as the church service continued, my colleagues and I decided to retire to the comfort of the vehicles. Morris and Graham sat in the hearse, while Joe, Mel, Ali and I sat in the third limousine. It was during this time that my fellow workers felt the need to educate me in the art of burial protocol and advised me on how to tackle some of the trickier elements of a burial that may arise. It was mostly the usual follow-my-lead sort of stuff, do what we do with a level of telepathy thrown in. However, the main lesson of the morning concentrated on how to correctly lower the coffin into the grave using the canvas straps. Or webbing, to use the correct terminology. Mel initiated the conversation.

"Invariably, Bill, you'll be balancing on the very edge of the grave quite precariously on unstable wooden boards hidden under green matting. Terra firma that's not so firma," he added with an element of wit.

He continued to explain that prior to lowering the coffin into the grave it is placed in front or beside the grave on the ground, usually on top of the canvas webbing which is then fed through the handles on each side. Two or three webs will be used, depending on the number of bearers. Occasionally the coffin will be placed on Putlogs prior to being lowered (wooden, beam-like supports that lie across the top of the open grave). Each bearer holding onto their length of webbing and taking up the slack, waits solemnly, ready to mirror their opposite number's movements when given instruction to do so by the minister or presiding official. A shoulder-width stance – good for balance – keeping your body nice and rigid and slightly leaning backwards to counteract the weight of the coffin during its descent, is recommended in order to avoid the possibility of accompanying the coffin into the grave. It's important for all the bearers to try and lower the coffin at the same speed in order to maintain as perfect a horizontal position as possible continuously throughout the whole of the lowering process, and the slower the better. A descent into the grave at an angle, particularly an acute angle, and especially head first, is not desirable or very dignified. Apparently, on occasions when a framed structure has been used inside a grave to prevent it collapsing due to various environmental conditions, angling the coffin to negotiate the framework may be unavoidable, but should be kept to a minimum and carried out as gracefully as possible.

Joe mentioned that when lowering the coffin, the best technique with the canvas webbing is to let it effortlessly slide through your hands in a slow, deliberate and controlled manner, gripping it or releasing it gently to control the speed. Unless, that is, it's the coarse type of webbing or it's been lying in the sun and covered in dried mud. Letting webbing in that condition slide between your hands can lead to some *nasty friction burns. On those occasions, you need to feed it through each hand gradually, a little at a time. Joe imitated the actions, while describing each technique.*

Having experienced the level of pain that friction burns can inflict, at various points in my life, Joe's advice was intently listened to and greatly appreciated. And while some of the incidents when I have sustained such injuries are best not talked about, there is one occasion that I do feel able to share without fear of damaging my 'so far' choirboy image.

It took place one balmy summer's afternoon in Golders Hill Park, Golders Green, whilst walking a canine companion called Fred. Fred was Ninka's dog, and after Ninka passed away, Mum occasionally looked after him. He and I were happily roaming the picturesque grounds enjoying the serenity of the park. Unfortunately, our peaceful stroll was abruptly interrupted when Fred saw something on the other side of the park that he felt the sudden need to investigate further. Connected together via one of those retractable dog leads, which at the time was set on freedom of movement mode, without any delay or hesitation and with the speed and tenacity of a greyhound being released from its trap, Fred, focused on only one thing, shot off across the park.

As wonderful an invention as the retractable dog lead might be – enhancing the walking experience between owner and canine companion – it was a piece of equipment that I was not familiar with, nor had any experience of at the time. Panicking, I grabbed the extending nylon cord with my left hand as it rapidly unravelled itself from the device in my right hand. Had I been more adequately trained or more experienced in the use of retractable dog leads, I would have probably just calmly locked the nylon cord by pressing the appropriate button and subsequently stopped Fred dead in his tracks, before he had time to cause even the slightest of interruptions to any innocent bystanders on that balmy summer's afternoon. Sadly, I was not and I watched in amazement as the smoke rose from the burning skin on my left hand that had grabbed the speeding nylon cord with Fred running amok attached to the other end. My cries of 'Come... back... Fred' went unregistered by their intended recipient, although, Fred being of Italian origin, he was probably not acquainted with the lingo of our fair land at that point in time, so he can't be totally to blame, I suppose.

A scene of pandemonium unfolded before my eyes as picnickers, siblings playing, ice-cream lickers in mid lick, and a fast-paced game of rounders being played by a group of Brownies became casualties of Fred's mutinous behaviour, the intrusive nylon line now imposing itself like a border-crossing between them. The pain of my injury somewhat delayed by the fast-moving pace of events, once acknowledged by my brain via the appropriately effected nerves, registered as excruciating.

My lesson on burials was interrupted by Mr Best's head appearing from around the door of the church. The men in black were required back inside the church and therefore duly summoned.

As the service drew to a close, we edged our way stealthily along the outer perimeter of the inside of the church. Trying to blend into the shadows like ninja assassins, we would probably have been a lot more stealth-like if the squeaking of our shoes had not alerted the congregation to our presence. Gradually we made our way towards the coffin in front of the altar and waited statue-like in the wings for our cue to leap into action. Well, not leap exactly. That would definitely have altered the mood of the occasion and probably caused a bit of a stir.

After the final blessing and yet more splattering of holy water, we got the nod we had been waiting for from the friar and moved collectedly into our positions around the coffin. A second friar started enthusiastically swinging a smoking brass receptacle supported by long chains to and fro in the vicinity of the coffin. The incense, as I later discovered it to be, was quite overpowering and managed to produce an incredible amount of smoke that dispersed rapidly around the church. It was so dense that it became quite difficult to see your hand in front of your face. It was at that point that my thoughts turned to any asthmatics in the congregation, or anyone with any sort of respiratory problem, and the likelihood of them having a bad reaction due to the overpowering smokescreen that was expeditiously engulfing every inch of the inside of the church.

Standing beside the coffin, trying to ignore the bellowing smoke, we bowed and then proceeded to carry out the undertaker shuffle into *position under the coffin, resting on the tall, ornately robed trestles. Raising the coffin off the trestles we took its full weight onto our shoulders. Mr Best, starting at the trestle nearest the altar, then removed each of the trestles one at a time and placed them to the side of us. Still facing the altar, a 180-degree turn was now required in order for us to exit the church. I hadn't heard the usual 'thank you, gentlemen' from Mr Best, so I was a little confused when Mel started to move to his left in true Michael Flatley style, as it should have been me that initiated movement due to my position on the left of the coffin at the foot, designating me as lead bearer. Not wanting to be the cause of a coffin-carrying catastrophe, and being the new boy, I thought I'd better just go with it.*

The friar with the smouldering incense in charge of producing the diversionary smokescreen continued to dispatch copious amounts of smoke in all directions, just in case we could see where we were going. Visibility now bordering on impossible, as we followed the three blurry figures in front of us along the extensive aisle towards the exit, I couldn't help but think how useful it might be to have fog-lights mounted on the front of coffins in such hazardous conditions. Finally, and extremely relieved nothing untoward had occurred during our visibly obscured journey, we hit daylight and encountered a very welcome rush of fresh air into our oxygen-starved lungs. It was at that point that we were greeted by our next challenge.

The steep decline of the church steps made for an interesting exit from the building. It was not the most graceful of manoeuvres, but it would not have appeared unprofessional or uncontrolled to the untrained eye. The main priority was to prevent the coffin travelling faster than the people carrying it! Due to the quite severe angle a number of tactics were required, including an all-hands-on technique. Mr Best helped to maintain the coffin's steady descent by supporting the foot end of the coffin as he walked backwards down the steps. This was helpful, although his exceptionally worried expression during a moment he looked like he was going to lose his balance and do a back flip, did little to help ease our concerns at the time. The whole experience certainly increased my heart rate by more than just a few beats per minute, as it did for my colleagues judging by the look on their faces after we had placed the coffin safely on the horse-drawn carriage. The trusty and ever-reliable green wire securing the large spray on top of the coffin, as ever, did an award-winning job of avoiding the unwanted distribution of funeral flowers at an untimely moment.

The actual carry had been a great deal more comfortable than the previous night's 'take-in' which had left me battered and bruised, perhaps due to being slightly better matched height wise, our positioning under the coffin, or a combination of the two. Eddie, had warned me that some unscrupulous bearers will position themselves under the coffin in such a way that it can shift the weight from their shoulders onto one, or more, of the other bearer's shoulders. A rather crafty move by all accounts, and one that can be rather difficult to determine whether done accidentally, out of ignorance, or intentionally out of malice. Who'd have thought such intrigue and sinister acts might manifest themselves during the carrying of a coffin? Clearly, nothing is sacred!

I was put a little at ease by Eddie who during this enlightening conversation explained that it is probably a rare occurrence and that very few people would do it intentionally. Nevertheless, it had been known, and if anyone was discovered committing such a dastardly deed, they would be severely chastised and face dire consequences, as it can be quite dangerous. Fortunately for me, I appeared to be working with conscientious professionals, so the likelihood of me encountering this problem was very unlikely.

After the coffin had been secured in place on the carriage by Dave the coachman, the limousine drivers, Mel, Ali and Joe made their way to their vehicles and awaited the arrival of their allocated mourners. Graham, Morris and I went back into the church to collect the trestles and the floral tributes which were to be placed into the horse-drawn carriage with the coffin. On our return the mourners were still milling around and chatting. When it came to guiding or directing the mourners, Mr Best, although a pleasant enough chap and very knowledgeable in his chosen career, was not the most authoritative or assertive of men. Luckily, Mel was, and he was diplomatically able to motivate the mourners to move towards the cars in order to proceed with the funeral's timetable.

With all bodies accounted for on board their allocated vehicles, the funeral cortège was ready to leave for the cemetery. The unavoidable hilly route ahead was going to be a hard slog for the poor horses. Chris the coachman mentioned earlier that the main problem for the horses is having to stop on a hill and then subsequently having to regain momentum. Unfortunately, the sheer volume of traffic on modern roads and the ever-increasing need to stop and start repeatedly, can often make a journey a lot more strenuous for the horses than that same journey would have been in the past.

A large number of mourners in private cars, who clearly had no intention of hanging about to be part of the funeral procession up to the cemetery, rapidly began to make their exit. With so many cars leaving all at once at such a pace, it resembled the starting grid of a Formula 1 race. Once the mad rush was over and calm was restored, the funeral procession could begin. Mr Best and the friar walked in front of the carriage for a short distance before the friar, clutching his brass bucket of holy water and baby-rattle sprinkler, was assisted into the front of the first limousine with the family, and Mr Best got into the front of the floral hearse behind the carriage. I travelled with Ali in the front of the second limousine.

The magnificent Belgian Blacks pulling the ornamental carriage proceeded steadily on their way up to St Pancras Cemetery in East Finchley, followed by the floral hearse, the three limousines, and a cavalcade of private cars.

Apparently, the cemetery at St Pancras was named after a fourteen-year-old Roman boy who had converted to Christianity in 303 AD and consequently was martyred. Not to be confused with St Pancreas, as some people pronounce it, the patron saint of glandular organs.

Ali made sure the mourners in our car were comfortable and thoughtfully explained where various electrical controls that they may require the use of were situated, especially pointing out the obscure ones that the designers of the Daimler limousine seemed to want to remain a mystery. He reminded me of an air hostess giving pre-flight instructions and I was very impressed with Ali's display of limousine-driver etiquette. As we made our way in convoy, the mourners in the back of our car seemed to be having quite a laugh, swapping amusing stories and anecdotes in which the main character was mostly the deceased. Ali politely informed the mourners that he was about to initiate closure of the partition window between us in order to give them a little more privacy, adding that if at any point they required anything they should knock on the window to gain his attention.

The majestic Belgian Blacks and the Victorian horse-drawn hearse were attracting a great deal of attention as the funeral cortège made its way through the hilly streets of Hampstead. The coachman Chris, through his foresight and judgement, managed to keep the funeral procession moving at a steady pace. That is, until the red lights caught us at Whitestone Pond bringing the entire funeral cortège to a sudden halt.

Whitestone Pond, for obvious reasons, was not my favourite North London landmark and flashbacks from the accident on my motorcycle there, even though I escaped the incident fairly unscathed, are as vivid today as they were back then. Luckily the incline of the hill was only slight at that point and the horses were able to regain momentum without too much of a problem once the traffic lights changed to green. Continuing our journey, even with the large volume of traffic and numerous red lights on route trying their best to sabotage the momentum of the cortège, Chris managed to keep the horses on course at a good pace until we finally reached our destination.

As we entered St Pancras Cemetery, gravestones, old and new, large and small, lined every route we turned down and covered the extensive area of land as far as the eye could see. Many of the very old stones, timeworn and only partly readable, were almost hidden, dressed in gowns of undergrowth and guarded by aged trees. I couldn't believe the enormity of the place. A bona fide city of the dead. I didn't think I would ever be able to remember my way around. Not with my hamster-like memory (the hamster now officially overriding the goldfish as having the worst memory, if I remember rightly!). As we continued to make our way through the maze of winding roads, I imagined us stumbling across long-lost funeral processions of dishevelled undertakers and mourners that had been driving around for days looking for elusive gravesites.

Eventually emerging into a vast open expanse within the cemetery, the sea of green now lying before us was broken only by a large, regimented display of grey and black gravestones sweeping towards the horizon. In the distance, two men, one appearing to be holding a shovel, were discreetly gesturing to us. They were standing next to two mounds of what I assumed to be earth. Both mounds appeared to be covered in the false grass you often see in the greengrocers. I suspected that the two men standing next to the grave were the cemetery's gravediggers waiting there for our funeral, hence the gesturing. Of course, there was a good chance that I could have been completely mistaken, however, Ali soon confirmed my suspicions and informed me that they were indeed the gravediggers and they were waiting for us. I could also see some of the private cars that had been so impatient to get away from the church already parked up near the gravesite, and noticed a few of the cars' previous occupants using the additional time they had gained to top up their nicotine levels to a satisfactory level before our arrival.

The procession of the horse-drawn carriage, floral hearse, limousines and private cars snaked its way through the expanse of gravestones via the network of small connecting roads, gradually coming to a halt adjacent to the gravediggers and the grave with its cunningly disguised mounds of earth. The two Belgian Blacks were steaming, as the sweat pouring from every part of their muscular, sweaty bodies evaporated. They appeared absolutely exhausted after their epic journey, which had been almost totally uphill. To put them through such an ordeal seemed almost bordering on abuse.

The grave was situated in the middle of one of the long rows of graves that engulfed the cemetery grounds and was a fair walk from where we had stopped. My colleagues and I helped the family and other mourners out of the limousines, and while we were waiting for those who had been following in the private cars to park up and make their way over to us, we started to unload the flowers off the carriage and place them near to the grave. Acknowledging our presence and seeing that the funeral was about to continue, the group of smokers inhaled deeply from their cigarettes as though it were their very last, before putting them out under foot and joining the rest of the mourners.

All mourners accounted for, the coffin was removed from the carriage and placed onto our shoulders. After another good soaking with holy water, for good measure, the friar and Mr Best led the way to the grave through the corridor of existing graves and the mourners followed behind the coffin. The grass-covered route to the grave, although visually flat, was deceptively uneven which led to quite a precarious carry with the heavy coffin. I felt a couple of my colleagues falter on a number of occasions as their footing met with uneven ground. Thankfully we managed to make it to the grave avoiding any disasters and gently lowered the coffin from our shoulders to its penultimate resting place in front of the grave. The imitation grass matting had not only been used to cunningly disguise the large mounds of earth either side of the grave, but it was also placed around the edges of the grave and surrounding area. No doubt for aesthetic reasons as well as practical ones.

Three long pieces of canvas webbing which were to be used to lower the coffin had been strategically placed on the matting in front of the grave. With the coffin resting on top of the webbing, the webbing now lined up perfectly with the three handles on each side of the coffin. Following Mel's lead, who was my opposite number on the other side of the coffin, I threaded my piece of the webbing through the metal handle on my side of the coffin. The webbing, approximately two inches wide, was coarse, dry and dusty. Perfect for producing friction burns on unsuspecting newcomers into the funeral business. Especially ones who were unaware of specific safety precautions in order to avoid such injuries!

The large floral tribute was removed from the top of the coffin and a single flower taken from it was placed beside the nameplate on the coffin lid. A small but poignant gesture of love. The six of us stood solemnly either side of the coffin with webbing in hand and heads bowed as the friar continued with his Latin incantations and biblical references. Yet another torrential distribution of holy water came our way that even the most determined demonic spirit possessing any of us would be incapable of battling.

At the appointed time the friar looked in our direction, nodded, and gestured for us to move forward with the coffin. Lifting in unison we raised the coffin using the canvas webbing and moved carefully towards the grave with a side-stepping action. The wooden boards around the edge of the grave, under the green matting – which in theory were placed there to aid stability and help prevent the edges of the grave from giving way beneath us – were quite unstable and only made things more precarious. Something Mel had pre-warned me about earlier. I could just picture myself losing my balance and following the coffin into the grave. Not something I really wanted to do on my first burial. Or any other come to that!

After a momentary pause we started to lower the coffin inch by inch into the depths of the grave. From where I was standing, it didn't look the most inviting place to be resting for all eternity, though I doubt it would have been a great concern to the coffin's resident at that point in the proceedings. The dry webbing made it extremely awkward to lower the coffin smoothly, as it was far too dry and coarse to slide through our hands freely without removing a layer of skin. Mimicking my colleagues, I fed a section of the webbing alternately through each hand as instructed during my pre-burial tutorial in the back of the limousine. The technique allowed for us to experience an injury-free descent as the coffin made its way to its final dwelling place. Once the coffin was at rest, we placed the surplus webbing in our hands onto the ground, bowed and then ceremoniously walked away from the graveside. Duplicating the movements of my colleagues as synchronously as I could, I attempted to look like I knew what I was doing.

As part of the funeral ritual, the mourners were given the option of throwing a handful of soil into the grave, which most of them did, one by one. After the service they mingled and perused the floral tributes that now surrounded the grave. We collected the rest of the flowers that had been put on the other vehicles and placed them alongside the others. Many of the mourners commented on how beautiful the flowers were. My colleagues and I loitered with intent in the background giving the impression that at any moment our services would be useful once more.

As the mourners filtered back to their vehicles, Mr Best asked Morris, Graham and me to collect the cards from the flowers. The three of us *sprang into action committed to retrieving every last card from the floral tributes without delay. Although, physically there was far less springing involved, with more sloth-like movements being incorporated into our actions in order to retain the slow and dignified manner expected of our profession going about our duties.*

Ali, Mel and Joe assisted the mourners back into the limousines, their destination a pub in Kentish Town. Mr Best and the friar were to be dropped off at the church on the way. Most of the mourners in the private cars had dispersed soon after the coffin entered the grave and were most likely already ordering their first drinks at the bar.

Our clothing was displaying the rigours of the day, and if this was anything to go by it wasn't going to be an easy task to make the expensive suits Adam and I acquired last as long as Mortimer and Sons might like us to be able to. With the dried mud from the webbing on our black suits combined with the pollen from the flowers and the wood splinters from the bottom of the coffin on our shoulders, we looked like we'd been in a brawl at a flower show held in a Wild-West saloon. Definitely not the desired look for an undertaker!

After leaving the cemetery, Morris, Graham and I headed directly over to the Mill Hill branch for our second funeral of the day. Our fourth man, Arthur, was meeting us there in a limousine. David Thomas, the manager of the aforementioned branch, was back from his break in the Welsh Valleys. Blunt and to the point, he was an outspoken man. Not always endearing qualities but refreshing in a world where you're often left guessing people's true intent. He described his escape to the wilds in his new motorhome passionately and of his disappointment at having to return to what he described as the madness of the concrete jungle. A feeling I'm sure most people would share after returning to work from what sounded like an idyllic break from the daily grind. And being a country lad at heart, I agreed wholeheartedly with Mr Thomas's sentiments.

Mr Thomas told us quite a humorous tale of an event that took place during his touring adventures, that involved an altercation between two rather inebriated Morris dancers outside a country pub. Thankfully neither party was seriously injured, as apparently it involved a great deal of handkerchief-waving rather than sticks (traditional Morris dancing props). Not to mention the musical accompaniment of clusters of jingling bells attached to the duelling men's limbs. A tale that even now, makes me chuckle and conjures up some very amusing images.

Carrying on with the task in hand, we made our way to the chapel of rest to carry out our duties in accordance with company procedures. All was as it should be, and the deceased Mrs Unwin was sealed into her very tasteful mahogany-finish solid wood coffin with solid brass handles and carried out to the hearse. One of my coffins, in case you hadn't guessed!

The family, who had been to see their loved one for one last time before the coffin was sealed down, had chosen to wait in the limousine until we were ready to depart. Taking place at Hendon Cemetery, this funeral was also a burial but with a much smaller gathering than the previous one. It was just the family in the solitary limousine following the hearse from the branch going direct to the cemetery, with a few more mourners joining them at the cemetery chapel. The vicar taking the service was making his own way and meeting us there.

Although Hendon Cemetery was much smaller than St Pancras it was decidedly more picturesque. After taking in the surroundings, I watched as Mr Thomas walked in front of the hearse to the crematorium chapel. It was then that I noticed Mr Thomas possessed quite a prominent limp. A factor that I believe may have contributed to the much shorter walk on this occasion in comparison to some of the other conductors I had witnessed so far.

Even though it was a burial, the funeral service was going to be held in the crematorium chapel, with the coffin being placed on the catafalque during the service instead of on trestles. It was a short walk into the chapel from the hearse – through the chapel doors, an immediate turn to the right, and Bob's your uncle, Fanny's your aunt, onto the catafalque. The task was almost effortless. Even though it was a solid wood coffin, Mrs Unwin was such a frail old lady, it was without a doubt, the lightest coffin I'd had to carry so far. Supporting us in his role as crematorium assistant, was Leo. Leo was a friendly, lively chap whose wonderfully unmistakable Liverpudlian accent left you in no doubt as to his origins.

In the crematorium waiting room we managed to grab a quick cup of 'hot water' that the vending machine claimed to be tea. It was more of an assault on the taste buds and clearly a blatant lie under the Trade Descriptions Act 1968, if you ask me. Definitely the worst hot beverage vending machine I've ever had the misfortune to insert my hard-earned cash into. I know when asked, some people jokingly say they like their tea or coffee, wet and warm. However, like me, I'm sure their expectations are a little more than that realistically.

The funeral service was short and sweet – about twenty minutes in all – after which we carried the coffin back out to the hearse and then made our way to the grave on the other side of the cemetery. Mr Thomas and the vicar walked in front of the hearse, with the mourners following behind. Morris was driving of course, which once again, left myself and Graham chaperoning the hearse on each side. Following at the rear, Arthur was left to chauffeur one old lady who wasn't up to the walk. She looked just like the Queen Mother sat there in the back of the limousine. Without all the hand-waving actions, of course.

At the graveside, everything seemed to be going smoothly until we started to lower the coffin into the grave and it got wedged halfway down the hole. Responding to our looks of dismay, the gravediggers, who only moments earlier had been relaxing under the shade of a nearby cedar tree, suddenly looked a lot less relaxed and came scurrying over. With the gravediggers help, we were able to release the coffin from its sticking point and extract it from the grave. It would appear that measurements are not always as clear cut as they might seem at first. Something I had learnt quickly when trying to measure bodies for their coffins accurately. As for the grave, I felt sure that the gravediggers would normally err on the side of caution and add a few inches to whatever size they had been given by the funeral director, in order to avoid the embarrassment of exactly such situations. After all, adding a few inches in many aspects of life is generally the norm for most men. Fishing, and the one that got away scenario, being just one of many examples of measurement exaggeration in a man's world, that comes to mind.

This time however, something had clearly not gone to plan, and so, with shovels in hand, the two – now not so relaxed – gravediggers, jumped into the inadequately sized excavation to make the necessary adjustments. An embarrassing moment for everyone concerned and once again proving that sometimes, size does matter. Luckily the family saw the funny side of things, saying how Edna, the deceased, would have loved the drama of it all and found it absolutely hilarious.

Fortunately, the second attempt to lay Mrs Unwin to rest was effortless in its execution and a smooth and graceful descent. Like pieces of silk, the obviously well cared for, or possibly brand new canvas webbing, glided through our hands with ease and was an absolute delight to work with. No chance of any unwanted friction burns on this outing. As the family had asked people to give donations to the Macmillan Nurses charity in lieu of flowers, there weren't many floral tributes to place around the grave once the service was over. This meant our work here was done and it was time for me, Morris and Graham, to head off to our next job.

After our little adventure at Hendon, it was back over to Mum's shop for our next funeral – a cremation at Golders Green Crematorium. Mum did her usual bit to embarrass me in front of the lads by calling me her little baby boy, grabbing my face in both hands and kissing my smooched-up cheek. As you might imagine, this seemed to greatly amuse my new workmates.

Although Mum was involved in organising funerals and all other aspects concerning the aftercare of the deceased, she didn't actually conduct funerals. The funeral would usually be conducted by one of the many managers from head office. The same went for any of the other branches run by managers who didn't conduct funerals. On this particular occasion, it was Bradley Masters who would be conducting the funeral that Mum had arranged. Reg, designer and builder of collapsing tables, was meeting us at the crematorium as the fourth bearer.

Prior to our arrival, Mum had received a message from head office, to make Graham and myself aware that after our last funeral at Golders Green, the three of us, Reg, Graham and myself, would be going on a

removal to a nursing home in North Finchley for the Finchley coroner.
Then, after taking the deceased to Finchley Mortuary, there would be
two bodies to collect from there to bring back to the yard. No peace for
the wicked, as they say.

Watched intensely by the queue of people at the bus stop directly
outside the shop, once the coffin and flowers were on board the hearse
we made our way to the family home of the deceased, which was just
the other side of Hendon Way. The family and friends who were waiting
then followed the hearse to Golders Green Crematorium in their own
cars. The service was held in the East Chapel. A smaller chapel than
the West but much cosier and more suitable for a funeral with a small
number of mourners. Having travelled up to the crematorium in the
van that we would need for the removal, Reg was already waiting
outside the chapel when we arrived.

After we'd carried the coffin in, Morris headed back to the yard in
the hearse. Bradley Masters headed back to head office in his own car
that he'd left at the crematorium before meeting us at Mum's. Graham,
Reg and I, waited for Dean who was coming directly from the yard in
his hearse with the coffin for our last funeral of the day. The family for
that funeral, not wanting to follow the hearse, had arranged to make
their own way to the crematorium.

As we had approximately fifteen minutes before Dean's arrival,
Graham suggested we head over to the tearooms to quench our thirst
and seek nutritional sustenance. Reg said he'd prefer to have a wander
around the gardens of remembrance and meandered off through the
cloisters.

The tearooms at Golders Green were divided into two separate
sections, one for the mourners and funeral functions and the other for
funeral staff. It was here that I was introduced to Fran and Edith and
their tempting choice of hot and cold snacks, as well as a selection of full
cooked meals. All that I desired was a nice cup of 'Rosie Lee' which was
served with a smile and just what the doctor ordered. Graham fancied
some of the apple crumble, and judging by the size of the portion Fran
served him and the fluttering of eyelashes going on, I'd say that she
definitely had a soft spot for our Graham. And who could blame her,

he's such a nice bloke and quite handsome too, I suppose. Not that he's quite my type. Call me old-fashioned, and not that I'm a prude or narrow-minded, but I tend to prefer my significant other to have a much higher percentage of oestrogen in their biological makeup, and rather less bulky equipment below the waistline.

Arriving at the crematorium early, Dean, poking his head around the tearoom door, alerted us of his arrival and requested our presence over at the West Chapel. Hurrying our nutritional purchases, we bid Fran and Edith 'au revoir' and made our way over. Mr Dickinson, having travelled with Dean from the yard, was standing at the entrance to the chapel waiting for the family to arrive. Applying our funeral faces once again, Graham and I joined Dean and Reg who were already standing in readiness at the back of the hearse. Adjusting our positions at the hearse height-wise in preparation to carry the coffin, Reg and I stood nearest the hearse in order to carry at the foot of the coffin, and Dean and Graham stood behind us to carry at the head.

Keeping our empathic funeral faces on show we waited for the mourners to arrive. Emerging in dribs and drabs a number of them handed us floral tributes which we then placed in and around the hearse. As we continued to collect and distribute the arrangements, my attention was drawn to the roar of a Triumph Bonneville as it entered the crematorium and parked up outside the crematorium office. It wasn't just the bike that impressed me, but the fact that its proud owner was a vicar; the vicar officiating on our funeral, in fact. Quite a jolly chap, he seemed very young to be a vicar, but that made quite a refreshing change. Not that there's anything wrong with older vicars, of course. Their life experiences and knowledge obviously make them good candidates to help and guide the rest of us about worldly and spiritual matters. It was just nice to see a youthful man with spiritual belief and commitment, embarking on his journey to help mankind. And womankind, of course. Especially, someone with such good taste in motorcycles.

Once all the mourners were seated and the minister was out of his leathers and into his ecclesiastical vestments, it was time to get the show on the road. Synchronised nods from Mr Dickinson and the vicar motivated us into action and the coffin began its slow, steady and dignified journey on our shoulders from the hearse to the chapel. It started with the usual pause for reflection and a subtle shuffle of shoulders to get comfortable. It was then followed by a perfectly executed 180-degree turn performed with such smoothness and poise, that even the Strictly Come Dancing judging panel would have found it hard to find fault. I really felt I was starting to get the hang of things.

Our carefully choreographed journey continued as we walked into the chapel behind the vicar and Mr Dickinson, to Frank Sinatra's 'My Way', a song, according to Graham, that is a popular choice at funerals of the older generation. I felt a gentle swagger develop during the carry, probably unnoticeable to the naked eye, but a swagger none the less, 'Old Blue Eyes' obviously inspiring a bit of rhythm to our step as we made our way towards the front of the chapel. Our perfect performance continued as we placed the coffin onto the catafalque and bowed with such perfect timing and graceful poise that it couldn't have been better if we had tried. An Olympic synchronised swimming team would have been envious. As we exited the chapel via the door behind the organist, a wave of complete satisfaction came over me. It was an Oscar-winning performance by all concerned. After a passing chat with Chris the chapel attendant, and placing the floral tributes in the cloisters for the mourners to view after the service, Reg, Graham and I hit the road and headed off to the nursing home in North Finchley to carry out the coroner's removal.

Up until that point in my life the only experience of nursing homes that I'd had, was of the one in Cheltenham where I used to visit Nan in my late teens. To be honest, it was always such an emotional experience, I never really took much notice of the place itself, or the staff. Except for the manager who was a complete idiot, and seemed to take an immediate disliking to me for some reason. Or perhaps he was like that with everybody.

Nan had severe dementia and was so confused about everything. I don't think she even knew it was me half the time. She was always in the communal lounge when I went to see her, no matter what time of day it was, sat in the same armchair by the window, facing into the room. Dotted around the room, there would always be several of her fellow residents, some a little less confused, and some that I wasn't sure whether they were alive, or not. Nan rarely spoke or looked at me during my visits, and would only occasionally look in my direction to give me a vacant stare, as if to say: 'Who the hell are you?'

I remember when she first became ill. I would ride up to Cheltenham from London on my motorcycle (with my then girlfriend Laura), and cook Nan a Sunday lunch. Sadly, on many occasions she wouldn't eat it because she thought we'd poisoned it – saying we were only after her money. The fact that she was almost penniless seemed inconsequential. Also, whilst I know my cooking probably wasn't up to much back then, I don't think it was quite so bad that it would have poisoned her. After all, how wrong can you go with a Fray Bentos pie, some frozen veg, and tinned new potatoes? And Laura would open those tins so beautifully, with the expertise and finesse of one who'd obviously opened quite a few tins in their time.

As my colleagues and I entered the nursing home in North Finchley, the first thing that I noticed was the overpowering odour of stale urine. Facial expressions exchanged between my colleagues and me confirmed that I was not alone in my disgust. I know a lot of old people might have problems with the downstairs plumbing (if you know what I mean), but surely nothing a good standard of personal hygiene and regular washing of their clothing wouldn't improve. Not to mention the use of modern-day cleaning products and possibly a few strategically placed air-fresheners as a precautionary measure. Just in case any little mishaps go unnoticed or staff are unable to attend as quickly as they might like, for whatever reason. The neglected public lavatory aroma was definitely not a great first impression, and I must say it gave little confidence in the level of care being given to its residents. I certainly wouldn't have wanted to live there, or have any family member of mine live there. Not even a pet of mine!

An old lady sat in the hallway – clearly one of the residents – asked if we had come to pick her up, and seemed very disappointed when we told her we hadn't. Perhaps if she'd known who we were she might not have been so disheartened. Or maybe she would. The member of staff *that had facilitated our entry onto the premises was a short, heavy-set woman in her fifties with very obviously dyed black hair that was clearly in need of the next application of colour, particularly to the roots. She had a strong foreign accent which I could not place or even hazard a guess as to its origin, and we understood very little of what she said. On top of that, her goatee beard was in a far more advanced state of growth than mine – I was quite jealous.*

Just as we were about to be shown to the deceased's room, I was set upon by another old lady who had ventured from a room on our left, who felt the need to embrace me with an extremely impressive bear hug. There was nothing I could do to break free that would not have been judged as brutish or improper, so I just stood there. Moments later a member of staff came over and made the first rescue attempt, but to no avail. The old lady, Gladys, just tightened her grip. Negotiations underway, a cup of tea and a pink wafer biscuit were offered up to try and entice my captor away. Clearly, she was not impressed. In the end it took two pink wafer biscuits, a custard cream and the promise of her favourite Des O'Connor CD being put on in the lounge, to finally get her to release her bear-like grip. Whatever does it for you, I always say, and at least now I know how much I'm worth! I could see my predicament amused my colleagues immensely and I sensed a few jovial quips were destined my way at the nearest opportunity. The price to be paid for freedom!

Once released from the grip of my captor, we were led away via a vast network of narrow corridors and winding staircases to the location of the deceased. I was getting flashbacks of the Wibbly Wobbly House Wez and I had been so impressed with at Great Yarmouth at the weekend. In fact, I'm sure the home could easily make some extra money on weekends masquerading as a Wibbly Wobbly house. A few well-placed crazy mirrors here and there might even give the residents a bit of a laugh. Although, I suppose that could possibly add to an increase in bladder activity to deal with which might not be the best scenario for the residents or the staff.

Without so much as a by your leave, the member of staff having shown us to our destination vanished into the abyss, leaving us to carry out our duties without her. I was surprised that she had left us unsupervised, and when I asked Graham if that was usual, he said that it was quite rare during the day, but not at night when there were usually very few staff on duty. Perhaps they were particularly understaffed. I had got the impression that she wasn't really in her dream job. But then – how many of us are? Maybe she was, but it was just one of those days.

The deceased's room was tiny but quite homely in a claustrophobic sort of way. A small picture of some flowers in a vase hung on the one wall (a print of a Van Gogh, I believe), and the smallest wardrobe I have ever seen sat against the opposite wall. A solitary black and white photograph of a rather handsome young soldier rested on the bedside table. A light breeze came in through the open window and did its best to freshen the room. Unfortunately, the clean air entering via the glazed aperture already had more than its work cut out for it dealing with the pungent stench of urine that swept through the nursing home. Death's unsavoury scent adding to the burden, the breeze was without a doubt fighting a losing battle.

We checked the deceased, Marjorie Anne Porter, for valuables, but there were none. Not that anyone could bear witness to that fact as our guide had vanished without a trace. After Reg had applied the ID bracelet around the old lady's ankle, we gently transferred her frail skeletal frame from the bed onto the fold-up stretcher on the floor. We then wrapped her in the plastic sheeting and strapped her onto the stretcher securely. She was now ready for what was going to be an interesting return journey back through the winding narrow corridors of the building to the front entrance.

With only our own feeble memories of the route taken to get to where we were presently positioned, navigating our way back to the front door through the labyrinth of corridors and dead ends was going to be quite a challenge. None of us had been paying a great deal of attention to the route taken, due to the fact that we all assumed we would be escorted to and from the location of the deceased by the member of staff. Fortunately, we only managed to get lost twice.

The narrow staircase with the stairlift was by far the most awkward part of the journey. Trying not to dislodge any of the pictures and hanging knick-knacks on the wall with the stretcher as we lifted it above the stairlift mechanism was far from easy. (I hadn't seen those three 'ducks in flight' ornaments for years.) As much as we tried to negotiate the narrow stairways in as dignified a manner as possible, it was like trying to do that challenge that you often get at summer fêtes – or at least you did when I was a youngster. You know, the one where you have to get a circle of wire around a wire frame of twists and turns without letting the two metal surfaces touch. Failure to do so would mean setting off a buzzer that would scare the living daylights out of you.

The woman with the impressive goatee that had previously deserted us in our time of need on whatever floor it was, appeared again from the communal lounge where a number of residents were sat listening to a Des O'Connor CD. Most seemed quite oblivious to what was going on around them. Clearly disgruntled that she was required to come to our assistance yet again, the woman aggressively punched the numerical code into the security device positioned beside the front door facilitating our departure from the premises, the security device presumably installed to prevent the residents from escaping and terrorising the indigenous population of North Finchley; as well as for their own safety, undoubtedly.

The journey to Finchley Mortuary felt like a bit of a magical mystery tour. It's a good job the others knew where they were going, as it turned out to be tucked away quite surreptitiously at the end of a cul-de-sac, 'cul-de-sac' being a French term we use for a dead end. How appropriate!

Driving into what appeared to be the driveway of a private house, the mortuary, a small red-brick building surrounded by trees, sat opposite the house. The house was apparently the living quarters of the mortician and his family. After Reg had reversed up to the double doors of the mortuary, Graham exited the vehicle and rang the mortuary bell alerting any occupants of our arrival. A wait of about five minutes followed, before one of the wooden double doors was opened just enough for a head to appear. The head belonged to Greg the mortician, and was extremely abrupt. Quite rude, in fact. He told us that he was extremely busy and it would be at least ten minutes or so before he was available. I immediately took a slight disliking to the head and its owner. If there's one thing I can't stand its rudeness, especially with no apparent reason or justification. After all, it wasn't down to us that he was so busy. Although, we were delivering another body requiring his attention, which obviously wasn't going to ease his workload.

As well as giving the impression that Greg might need to improve his people skills somewhat, he appeared to be a rather fastidious person, bordering on the obsessive in his approach to everything. Not particularly appealing qualities but such attributes obviously paid off professionally, as the mortuary was immaculate. I'm fairly certain you could have eaten your lunch off any of the stainless-steel trays that the bodies lay on in Greg's mortuary fridges, without any fear of endangering your health whatsoever. Not that you would want to, of course. Everything had its place in Greg's mortuary, and everything was in its place. Unless it was being used at that precise moment in time.

Greg's attitude had not endeared me towards him at all, not that that would have bothered him in the slightest, I'm sure. But his pristine mortuary and his attention to detail was extremely impressive and an absolute privilege to witness and a joy to experience. Mortimer and Sons' embalmer, Marcus, was far from being a slob and his embalming room came a close second to the level of cleanliness and tidiness of Greg's mortuary, but with perhaps a slightly lesser degree of obsession involved.

Having concluded our business at the Finchley coroners, seated in the van, I think Graham sensed that Greg's attitude had got to me a bit.

"Don't mind Greg, he's always like that, it's just his way. He's actually quite a nice bloke when you get to know him."

I thanked Graham for his concern and assured him that I was fine, and that I'd just found Greg's rudeness a bit annoying. Undoubtedly, he was under a lot of pressure, and I was happy to give him the benefit of the doubt.

Back at the yard, the two bodies collected from Finchley Mortuary were unloaded, booked in and measured, before being appropriately stored within the refrigerated appliances. That done, I was just about to wrestle with the cantankerous old concertina gates of the garage, when Eamon shouted over to leave the van outside the mortuary. Eddie and Frank had returned from their globetrotting adventures in Wales, without anything untoward occurring or being kidnapped by the Welsh Liberation Front. Accompanied by Adam, their next job was to take a couple of bodies to the Holloway branch and one to Mum's.

Inside the garage some of the black beasts were being washed and groomed by their keepers after an arduous day of numerous performances, the radio playing in the background helping to sooth and de-stress them and their hard-working keepers. The hammering noise emanating from the workshop which turned out to be Oliver and Howard fitting up coffins, was accompanied by the shrill of an engraving machine operated by Arthur carving details into a brass nameplate. The Grim Reaper's workshop was in full swing.

Reg returned the pink removal cards to Eamon in his little cubbyhole, by which I mean his office, of course. Acknowledging the information presented on the cards, such as coffin size and nameplate information, Eamon immediately went about transferring the new data to the various ports of call around the workshop. He then got on the phone to relay that information and inform Mr Carter at head office about the arrival of the bodies.

It was at that point that Graham suggested we venture to the tearoom for a well-earned brew. Shouts from around the workshop alerted us to the fact that a large majority of the staff on the premises thought that this was a splendid and most intuitive idea. Joining Graham and I in the tearoom, they reminded us of how many sugars they required and whether or not milk was an important additive for them to enjoy their hot beverage to the full.

As we sat with our colleagues, tales of the day's adventures, good and bad, were exchanged. A coroner's suspicious death fished out from the canal in Camden, a hanging from a flat in Cricklewood, a collection from a rather aromatic nursing home in North Finchley, a climber from Wales, or should I say faller – and a total of seven other removals from various local and a couple of not so local hospitals. Not to mention the eleven funerals that had to be carried out in between *and the transferring of bodies to and from various branches and other ports of call.*

It wasn't all work talk – far from it. The conversation also contained irrelevant snippets of inane drivel; debates about television comedy shows past and present, speculation on the outcome of various forthcoming sports events, and a remark from Joe about a rather stunning young lady he had spotted crossing the road in Hampstead High Street. Trust him!

Our therapeutic wind down was interrupted by the realisation that there was still work to do and all too soon it was time to wind up again and venture over to the mortuary to dress and box up the bodies for some of tomorrow's funerals and viewings.

The body that Oliver and I had to dress and box up which was due to be viewed early the next morning, was still on a table in the embalming room. Marcus had not long finished embalming the gentleman, and due to our untimely interruption, was not a happy bunny. He went on to explain that after the embalming process has been carried out, ideally the body should be left undisturbed for a period of time to allow the embalming chemicals used to take full effect, especially regarding the facial features. Still grumbling about being rushed and not being able to do his job properly he moved over to the second mortuary table on the other side of the room.

Pulling back the white sheet in front of him, he uncovered the body of the man he was currently working on. Shocked at what I saw, I can honestly say it was the most gruesome sight I had ever seen. The man that lay before us had undergone a post-mortem, and in many ways could easily have been mistaken for one of the carcasses that you see hanging on display in a butcher's shop window. The main torso of the man was sliced open down the middle from neck to pelvis. Large sections of red meat and thick creamy-coloured layers of fat were splayed open like wings on either side of the torso, revealing an empty cavity inside the ribcage and abdominal area. A small pool of blood was all that remained at the bottom of the void where once upon a time the organs had been. The sternum, having been cut out to gain access to the upper body's organs, lay to one side next to the body. Looking like a skinned rabbit, the man's face was not spared the ordeal and the skin from the top of the forehead was folded over onto his chin like a rubber mask turned inside out and upside down, exposing the macabre sight of individual layers of facial muscles. The neatly cut top part of the skull, like the top part of a boiled egg, sat in the large white Belfast sink which stood behind Marcus. In a bucket on the floor, just to the left of Marcus, were the man's internal organs soaking in a cocktail of sanitising chemicals, before being placed back into the empty cavity of the torso.

Although it was a repulsive sight to see, it was fascinating at the same time. Another thing that struck me was the smell, the unpleasant aroma coming from the dissected human carcass was indistinguishable from the aromatic waftings one might experience coming from a butcher's shop. The raw basics of the human body's structure and its resemblance to what you see displayed in a butcher's shop window appalled me. It was a realisation I had never really contemplated to such a degree before. The real connectivity between human beings and the animal kingdom. A vegetarian diet from that moment on, seemed very appealing!

My fourth day as an undertaker ended in the workshop fitting up the coffin for Mr David Mead, aged forty-five years, the gentleman I had seen on Marcus's embalming table, in his dissected state.

A week ago, Mr Mead's life probably consisted of a complex variety of things going on that may have caused him concern or triggered any number of positive or negative emotions. Then, out of the blue, a brain haemorrhage came and took all those concerns and thoughts away. Life's delicate balance tipped, and in two days' time he would be no more than ashes and crushed bone. Quite a sombre thought.

With only five minutes until home time the phone in Eamon's office rang. An echo of voices from various nooks and crannies around the yard shouted in a jokingly yet taunting manner.

"DUTY SQUAD!"

Unluckily for the duty squad, it was no joke. You could almost guarantee that around that time of day a call would come through from head office informing the duty squad about a removal or pending removal. It was as if the Grim Reaper himself waited specifically until then to tease and torment the poor lads on call-out. Mind you, as the lads said, they'd rather get the call then than just as they got home. To them there was nothing worse than being disturbed when they were in the middle of their evening meal, or in bed asleep. Although, that's often what did happen when on call-out. Often more than once. Sometimes several times.

So, while the rest of us called it a day and headed off to our various destinations of relaxation and leisure, Mel, Ali and Graham loaded up the van and headed off to St John's Wood to pick up a body for our local jolly coroner. A suspicious death, apparently.

Thought for the day (without the aid of an alcoholic beverage in sight).

I can't believe for one minute, that with the complexity of mankind, all we end up as is what I saw on Marcus's stainless steel table today. Are we really no more than a piece of meat, blood and guts? Surely there's so much more to us than that. Just because the blood stops pumping and the brain stops thinking, does the essence of life, the spirit, the soul, or whatever you like to call it, cease to exist? The life force that makes us the unique individuals that we are – how can it just stop? Surely it can't? Can it? Does it?

Science shows us that nothing in creation is truly destroyed. It just changes form. Although, perhaps scientists today with their incredible knowledge and amazing technology can completely obliterate something that once would have gone on forever in some shape or form. Nothing would surprise me! Proof I think that we ourselves will undoubtedly be the cause of our own demise, as we have been the cause for so many other creatures that we share or once shared this amazing planet with.

On a slightly lighter note, eight funerals tomorrow and I'm on three, two burials and a cremation. And who knows what else might be in store for us lurking around some dark corner. Particularly if those damn braces continue to launch surprise attacks. I'm starting to develop a nervous twitch. They will definitely have to go!!

TGI FRIDAY

Starting early, for our first jobs of the day Oliver and I were to take one body to the Tufnell Park branch and collect one from the Highgate branch. As the one we were delivering was already boxed up, it was just a matter of loading up the van and hitting the road, once we'd rechecked IDs, valuables and obtained Eamon's blessing, of course.

The Tufnell Park branch, you may remember, was where I'd unwittingly been a victim of a technological misunderstanding with a sliding toilet door, brutally removing it from its runners because I foolishly expected it to open in the traditional manner via hinges. Not the best first impression I could have made in front of Rose, the manager.

On the way there, Oliver told me a rather interesting story. Apparently Rose was psychic and once informed him, quite seriously, that one of his cats had fur balls. Naively, I asked him if she knew that his cat was male. Smiling, Oliver corrected my misinterpretation of the statement. Rose had of course been referring to the type of fur balls that are caused by the build-up of hair in a cat's stomach from grooming itself. The fact that when Oliver returned home that evening and his cat had left him a little present in the middle of the kitchen floor which just happened to be a regurgitated fur ball, some might say could easily have been coincidental. Or possibly not!

I'm certainly not one to dismiss ideas of the supernatural and people's abilities in relation to it, in whatever shape or form. I am a firm believer in such things. Although, problems regarding the digestive system of a cat does seem a rather strange snippet of information to be given insight into. But ours is not to reason why as they say, and personally I find it quite comforting to know that even in the supernatural world, little things still matter. Even the wellbeing of a cat.

In actual fact, my sister Lesley is quite psychic and has passed on various messages to me in the past, that due to their content could only have come from a spiritual realm and not via any other source. Often, when visiting Mum at the undertakers, Lesley would receive messages from one or more of the horizontal guests residing in the chapels of rest. This would usually be information that the deceased wanted passed on to a relative or friend. Whether Mum ever did pass any of the messages on or not, I'm not certain. The sceptics among you may mock, but I certainly have no doubts. Hence, I had no reason to doubt Rose's psychic abilities or her feline revelations.

When we arrived at the Tufnell Park branch, Rose was waiting at the entrance and opened up the double doors (she obviously knew we were on the way). Unloading the coffin onto a wheelie trolley Oliver and I took the coffin through to the chapel of rest. It was quite a challenge manoeuvring the fairly long coffin around the tight corner into the chapel without damaging the coffin or the doorway. Once the Krypton Factor-style ordeal was accomplished, we assisted Rose to set up the deceased for viewing. Rose brought in a bag of makeup that the family of the deceased had given her with instructions on how the woman would usually apply it. Thank goodness it was her job to apply it and not ours. The poor woman would have ended up looking like a circus clown.

For the most part, Rose seemed pleasant enough and at a rough estimation was somewhere in her late forties. Quite petite, she had a very gentle and calming manner which her soft Geordie accent complemented perfectly. Ideal qualities for her job role. Even so, you sensed she was not a woman you wanted to get on the wrong side of, and if I'm honest, I was very pleased there was no mention of the sliding door incident! Regrettably, Rose had no messages of a supernatural nature for me during our visit. Maybe next time.

Leaving Rose to her role as beautician, Oliver and I were once again journey bound. This time we were off to the Highgate branch. Jeremy Wainwright managed the Highgate contingency of Mortimer and Sons. I'd met him once before at Mum's shop one summer during the time that Emma and I were living there when she and I were first married.

Mr Wainwright recalled our first meeting. Apparently, I had returned from a cycle ride and was wearing a pair of shorts that were a bit on the tight side, so tight by all accounts, that I had caught his eye and got his heart racing (I think I may well have blushed at that point in the conversation). I noticed the same twinkle in Mr Wainwright's eye when he was recollecting the occasion, that the assistant in the clothes shop had when measuring my inside leg for my Mortimer and Sons' *work attire. Initially I felt a little uncomfortable with Mr Wainwright's declaration but I soon realised that it was more of a wind-up than a come-on. And to be honest, I should never have been allowed out of the house in those shorts. What was I thinking? I definitely should have opted for the tracksuit bottoms, if only for decency's sake.*

Back at the yard and with our delivery and collection completed, Oliver and I had just enough time for a quick cuppa and a bite to eat, after which it was going to be all hands to the pumps for the rest of the day. That morning I'd forgotten to pick up my lunch box with my day's nutritional supplies so lovingly put together for me by Mum. This however, according to Oliver, was not a problem but rather an opportunity to broaden my culinary horizons and experience the delectable delights of Ron's Cafe. Evidently, one of Camden's premier eating establishments which dealt in traditionally cooked English cuisine for breakfast, lunch and dinners, and it was only a two-minute walk around the corner from the yard.

On the outside Ron's Cafe looked like any other traditional English cafe and there was nothing in particular that was out of the ordinary on the inside. The familiar set menu displayed on the one wall, although extensive, held no surprises and the selection of condiments on each table, including the brown plastic squeezy bottle for brown sauce and red plastic squeezy bottle for red sauce, was all one needed to complement any of the culinary options available. Asking for mayonnaise in Ron's Cafe was a definite 'no-no', if you knew what was good for you. Cafe traditions aside, on the inside of Ron's Cafe, there was a whole new magical experience awaiting the unsuspecting clientele.

Entering Ron's establishment, we were greeted by the evocative sounds and smells that only exist in a true traditional British cafe; the smell of the food; the clink of a spoon having completed its duties stirring a hot beverage, being placed on a saucer. The sound of a radio in the background, and the chitter chatter of its patrons. There were a number of people sporadically placed at red and blue-topped tables, seated on classic, spindle-back wooden chairs. Two separate individuals and two small groups. Closing the door behind us we walked up to the counter, Oliver leading the way.

An elderly, balding man standing behind the counter, possibly Ron himself, pencil poised over his small notepad obviously waiting for our order, gave us a rather half-hearted smile but no other communication was offered. Two more gentlemen of later years were milling around behind him in the small kitchen area on view, each clearly allocated certain responsibilities in the process of supplying the cafe's clientele with their chosen meal, and going about it with an equal amount of zeal as Ron's greeting.

Oliver had undoubtedly already given a lot of thought as to what he was going to order – either that or his choice of cuisine procured from Ron's cafe had little or no variation – and without hesitation he relayed the relevant information to the man behind the counter.

"I'll have a full English with extra fried bread, extra mushrooms, two slices of bread and butter, and a milky coffee, please, Ron."

Ron wrote the information on his notepad. Clarification as to Ron's identity made further questions on the matter from myself unnecessary.

Taking note of Oliver's rather extensive order, I questioned him as to whether we had time for such extravagant feasting, given that our pending funeral was approaching fast. To which he replied, with a smug look on his face, "No worries. What you having, Bill?"

I was worried, I couldn't help it. Generally, I do tend to be one of those cup half-empty types. I don't know why, I just am. I try not to be, but to no avail. You can't be what you're not, as they say. Not convinced we would have time to wait for and consume such a large order of gastronomical proportions in the time we had available (without giving ourselves severe indigestion) I erred on the side of caution. Ron, pencil poised, and void of emotion looked me in the eye, clearly awaiting my own choice from his extensive range of culinary delights.

"And... I'll have a fried egg sandwich and a cup of tea, please."

Without vocal acknowledgement, but at least accompanied by another half-hearted smile, my order was written underneath Oliver's order on the small notepad. The solitary sheet was then torn from the pad with a level of passion I was not expecting, and passed to one of the other elderly gentlemen in the kitchen behind him.

Having paid for our order and being issued with our choice of hot beverage we turned and walked to a vacant table at the front of the cafe by the window. Just as we were extracting the chairs from under the table in order to sit down, as if by magic, both of our orders appeared on the table in front of us. One full English with extra fried bread and extra mushrooms, two slices of bread and butter, and one fried egg sandwich. Oliver looked at me and raised his eyebrows knowingly.

"Plenty of time, Bill," he said, and sat down to his rather substantial fried banquet.

Speechless, I sat and stared at my solitary fried egg sandwich. In comparison to Oliver's banquet it was not quite as impressive, but I was equally as amazed at its incredibly speedy construction.

"How... the... hell?" I said in amazement.

"Don't know, don't care," Oliver stated, just before making a portion of sausage covered in dripping egg yolk disappear into his mouth.

"Surely there's only so much a meal can be pre-cooked," I said. "Some things have to be prepared and cooked as and when they are required, don't they? Even if all the necessary components of the meal are ready and waiting, there's the logistics involved and the time it takes to gather them all together on one plate in an orderly and appropriate manner."

Oliver's concentrated efforts of mastication were unperturbed by the uncertainties surrounding the production process of the food that lay before us, whereas I was completely mystified as to how this remarkable feat of culinary magic was achieved. Maybe there was a magician's wand hidden in amongst the kitchen utensils!

The food itself was not of the highest quality but it was more than adequate in its capacity to entertain the taste buds and satisfy the stomach. And even if its nutritional value may have been a little suspect, at the time it certainly seemed to tick all the boxes that mattered. The only real complaint I had, and I'm not someone who generally likes to complain, was something that I noticed when I unveiled the fried egg between the two slices of buttered white bread in order to disperse the complementary condiments to season the food to my personal liking.

The item in question was a dubious-looking curly black hair, staring up at me from the slightly, but only slightly, undercooked fried egg. Although I suppose it very much depends how you like your eggs done as to whether everyone would have considered it undercooked or not. For my taste it could definitely have done with spending more time participating in the cooking process. More importantly, I do tend to prefer my eggs, however they are cooked, without the added complementary garnishing's of what looked suspiciously like a pubic hair. According to Oliver this was no rare occurrence and one that the lads had come to expect from this particular establishment. Yes, that's right, I said expect.

I discreetly observed Ron and the two other gentlemen unconcernedly busying themselves behind the counter and what I could see of the kitchen area from where I was sitting. There was very little going on in the hair department head wise, and what hair any of them did have was grey and wispy, not curly and black. That said, each of them did appear to have an abundance of nasal hair, but nasal hair isn't generally curly and after one more subtle glance at the nostrils of the gentlemen in question, although some appeared quite dark, hair from that vicinity of the body was definitely ruled out.

I debated the options on offer with Oliver as to the possible origins of the little curly visitor bathing in my egg yolk and weighed up the choices that now lay before me. As I was hungry and not brought up to complain, an executive decision was made. I decided to remove the uninvited follicle and wrapped it in the napkin that had been supplied with the meal. This was not for forensic examination at a later date, but for disposal at the earliest opportunity.

'That which does not kill us makes us stronger'; that's what they say, isn't it? Though I'm not entirely sure who said it or whether it can in fact, be applied to every situation in life that might not kill us. For example, if you were hit by a bus and it didn't kill you, it wouldn't necessarily make you stronger. In fact, I imagine it could be very detrimental to your long-term health both mentally and physically and make life extremely difficult in many ways.

My digestive system not being without its own problems already, having been diagnosed with suspected Irritable Bowel Syndrome in my early twenties, I decided to throw caution to the wind and take a chance. As I ate the slightly undercooked and now de-haired fried egg sandwich, I did my best to enjoy it for what it was. There were only a few mouthfuls that caused me to question my decision but I felt no adverse reactions during the actual devouring process. Only time would tell if it was the right decision or not in the long term, and hopefully I would be close to toilet facilities if it turned out to be the wrong decision.

Upon our return to the yard, the usual quick brush up, shoe shine and shake down of funeral attire was carried out before we headed off to the Holloway branch via head office to pick up Mr Dickinson, who was due to be conducting our first funeral of the day. Oliver was at the wheel of the hearse, Eddie and Ali were the limousine drivers and I was the lone menial bearer making up the four-man crew.

Lucy Button was the manager of the Holloway branch, and like most of the managers she lived in the flat above the shop. Her partner, Gary, who often helped out as a casual bearer on funerals for Mortimer and Sons during busy periods, shared the flat with her. And when I say he was a casual bearer, I am of course referring to his attendance on funerals being of a casual nature, not that he dressed casually when carrying out his supportive role. Lucy was the company's youngest branch manager and quite an attractive lady. It was quite amusing watching my colleagues and their flirtatious behaviour when in the presence of Lucy – particularly the older ones. Naturally, I was merely a conscientious observer and did not partake in such frivolous behaviour.

As Mr Dickinson entered the office there was an immediate change of atmosphere. Suddenly everyone became more proficient and focused on the various tasks in hand that needed to be completed before the pending funeral. The usual checks were carried out on the deceased, a woman of sixty-six according to her brass nameplate. The yellow metal ring on her wedding finger, left on for the viewing, had already been removed and given back to her husband, at his request.

Thoughtfully, Lucy polished the light-oak-finished coffin and then Oliver secured the coffin flowers onto the lid with the ever faithful green wire. Once the coffin was in the hearse the other main floral tributes were strategically placed around the coffin under Mr Dickinson's professional, artistic guidance. The remaining flowers were then placed on the roofs of the hearse and limousines.

It was only a short distance from the Holloway branch to the family home of the deceased to pick up the family, and an even shorter journey to the church, which was literally just around the corner from the house. It was a Greek funeral and I recognised quite a few of the mourners from my time as an instructor at the local gym. With all the black suits, dark sunglasses and olive-skinned Mediterranean gentlemen, the occasion had a somewhat Mafia-type flavour. Especially as some of the big lads from the gym looked like menacing bodyguards. Come to think of it, quite a few of them actually were menacing bodyguards.

From the outside, the church was a small, unimpressive building. I'd walked past it many times over the years without ever giving it a second glance. Inside however, it was a completely different story. I had never seen such ornate décor and use of such vibrant colours to depict holy images. It really was quite impressive. The priests, with their long grey beards and elaborate robes looked like they had just stepped off the set of a big-screen Old Testament biblical epic. In the Greek church, they seemed to be as keen on the old incense as the Catholics were, but the monastic-like chanting of the priests was a nice touch. The deep base tones that the one priest managed to produce went right through you and was quite haunting.

For some reason, of which my colleagues were unable to enlighten me, the preferred method for transporting the coffin into and out of the Greek church was not to carry it but to use a trolley. Personally, I don't think it looks quite right or as respectful. But what do I know! Besides, we weren't about to complain, particularly as it was a solid wood coffin and the deceased was far from on the light side. If that was the way they liked to do things there, who were we to argue. And it wasn't one of the dodgy wheelie trolleys from the yard being used, it was a posh collapsible chrome one. Very upmarket.

Once the coffin was in church and the service was underway, we loaded up the vehicles with the floral tributes that had been placed outside and at the back of the church. Afterwards we sat in the back of one of the limousines contemplating life, chatting about various theological issues, and indulging ourselves in a discussion about the extremely funny episode of Only Fools and Horses that had been on the television the previous evening.

At the end of the service, back inside the church we waited in the wings as the mourners lined up along the centre aisle. One by one they walked up to the coffin to pay their last respects. Rested on top of the coffin was a large gold cross which each person kissed before returning to their seat. After the service was over, there was a large amount of mingling between the mourners outside the church, before we were successfully able to usher them into their respective cars.

As the funeral cortège wound its way unhurriedly along the selected route to Southgate Cemetery, we encountered the usual looks from the general public that our presence seemed to invite. This was accompanied by pointing fingers from little children and raised cans of Special Brew from a small gathering of rather inebriated individuals sat in a closed-down shop doorway. Several motorists that we encountered along the journey shared a few choice words about our apparent inconsiderate lack of speed. A sentiment shared by a surprisingly large number of motorists, and one that I was sadly becoming all too familiar with. Nobody wants to get stuck behind the funeral procession, but a little bit of respect costs nothing.

The Greek section of the cemetery, or Brighton beach as my colleagues affectionately called it, due to it being entirely covered in shingle, was quite a picturesque part of the cemetery. It definitely had more of a Mediterranean feel to it than the rest of its surroundings. All that was missing from the scene from my own memories of such underfoot beach dressings, was the pain of walking on it in bare feet, the fresh salty sea air, the sound of scavenging seagulls, Dad grappling with uncooperative deck chairs, and a '99' ice cream with a double flake, dripping down my arm. Happy days!

Using the trolley with its small, inadequate, off-roading wheels to transport the coffin over the shingle was definitely out of the question, and would only be inviting a plethora of disastrous consequences. Carrying the coffin on the shingle, however, required a great deal more effort than if we had been walking on more stable compounds. My understanding of how muscle groups work, added some insight into why the struggle was inevitable. The unfamiliar demands on the muscles caused by the unpredictable surface, particularly on the smaller muscle groups, can make even the simplest of manoeuvres quite problematic. Subsequently, the actions of walking on shingle is not too dissimilar to those of someone under the influence of fermented refreshments, staggering home from the pub after a good session on a Friday night.

Digressing slightly, as I tend to now and again, this little episode reminded me of my first weekend away with the London Scottish Regiment of the Territorial Army. Over the course of the weekend my new comrades in arms and I were given many challenging and character-building assignments to complete to show what we were made of. One particularly gruelling task involved running around an area of fine sand (about half the size of a tennis court), in the middle of dense woodland with a discarded telegraph pole supported on our shoulders. As with shingle, walking on fine sand can be quite challenging in itself, let alone when having to carry a discarded telegraph pole. Being the shortest among my new comrades my shoulder was about six inches or so shy of the telegraph pole, when it was resting on their shoulders. The sergeant, in his delicate manner, advised me to put as much input into the event as I could and to run beside my brothers in arms shouting words of encouragement. So, at the risk of becoming as unpopular with my new comrades as I had done when I scored three own goals in my first football game at my secondary school in London, and not wanting to disobey this new authoritative figure in my life who seemed to wield so much power over whatever I said and did, I thought it best to do exactly as I was told.

It was a tough but extremely enlightening weekend and highlighted what being part of a team is really all about. Even if you're not all the same height. We also learnt a great deal about our own capabilities, strengths and weaknesses. There was a great mix of characters from all walks of life that like me were looking for a bit more of a challenge and possibly some excitement in life, too. As well as the added bonus of being paid for it, of course. Although at one stage during that first weekend, when we were nearing the point of mental and physical exhaustion, my comrades and I did start to wonder if it was possible that we had been deceived at the open day at the Duke of York Barracks in the Kings Road and had unknowingly signed up for the Foreign Legion by mistake.

I would also like to add, that although lacking in height somewhat, I was not a totally useless cog in our newly formed future defence-of-the-realm fighting machine. During some of the other gruelling tasks that thrilled us on that character-building weekend, I feel I more than redeemed myself for my lack of participation in the relocation of the telegraph pole, thus proving I was still a viable member of the team with some worth.

Back on Brighton beach, once my colleagues and I had lowered the coffin into the grave, we walked back to the hearse and waited. Throughout the graveside service various items such as oils and food were placed into the grave. And when I say oils, I'm naturally referring to the extra virgin olive type, rather than the motorised variety. I presumed these oils and foods had religious connotations and formed part of burial rituals and various beliefs about the afterlife. Conformation that I was thinking along the right lines, given by Ali.

After the burial a small group of women mourners rummaged around in the boots of two of the private cars and subsequently extracted a pair of collapsible tables. The tables were of a very similar construction to the ones used when decorating, in the process of applying the glue onto wallpaper before hanging it on the wall. As a matter of fact, judging by some of the brush-like markings on the table tops, I suspected they probably performed that role when not involved in their funeral duties.

The women proceeded to wrestle with the folded tables vigorously in order to transform them into their usable configuration. Seeing the ladies struggling, Ali being the true gent that he is, offered to help. However, the proud ladies in black shook their heads and unanimously declined his offer of assistance, smiled, and then continued with increased vigour with their own efforts to achieve the task. They were clearly not going to be beaten by the fragile yet obstinate items of furniture and definitely did not need any interference from any man, in any way shape or form. Eventually, after a fine display of furniture manipulation, the table-wrestling tag team was victorious and the tables were up and ready for the next stage in the campaign.

White table cloths were unleashed through the air like billowing sails, landing precisely on the fragile wooden frames and needing only minimal adjustment to remove unwanted wrinkles. If only all wrinkles were so easily dispersed!

As time passed, it became apparent that this was not a random opportune car boot sale being set up, but as Ali informed me, a feast for the deceased. Or to be more precise, a feast on behalf of the deceased for the mourners. We watched as a selection of foil-covered dishes were produced from various car boots and carefully unveiled once in place on the table tops. Each unveiling revealed either whiter than white cheese, black and green olives, or some bread of varying descriptions. These were accompanied by three bottles of red wine, a pile of paper plates, some napkins, and a tower of plastic throw-away cups.

With all the food in place on the collapsible tables, the stability of their somewhat flimsy metal framework became questionable and caused me some concern. My slightly over-imaginative mind conjured up images of a calamitous funeral buffet, after the laws of physics, specifically of gravity, had cruelly taken advantage of the inadequately structured tables on the rather unstable ground. The vision in my mind became more elaborate as the imagined disaster unfolded. I pictured the devastated ladies in black scrambling around on the ground trying to salvage what they could from the carnage of the scattered grit-covered cuisine. I hoped for their sake that my vision was not a psychic revelation but merely my over-active imagination running away with itself.

As the host of the banquet is technically the deceased, I was made aware by my colleagues that it is considered disrespectful not to participate in the food and drink's consumption. Even though my digestive system was still more than satisfied from the gastronomic delights I'd had earlier during my ultimate fast-food experience at Ron's Cafe, like my colleagues, I certainly didn't want to offend anyone or seem disrespectful in any way. And like most people, the prospect of some free grub and refreshments, was something I would rarely say no to.

As I fulfilled my duty and sampled the food on offer, I have to admit, the cheese was a tad rubbery for my liking. As for the olives, they are something that my palate has never found good reason to endure. The bread however, and a smidgen of the red wine, went down a treat.

When Emma and I were married, for a period of time we had rented a flat in North London which was situated at the top of a Greek family's house. They were lovely and treated us more like part of the family than tenants. Particularly the mother, Elene. It was a common occurrence on entering the household via the front door to be greeted by Elene's smiling face from her kitchen at the end of the hallway and to be invited in for a cup of tea. Not wanting to appear rude, it was very hard to refuse. However, the cup of tea would invariably end up being a five-course meal as more and more items of food were placed in front of you. On many occasions, Emma would return home from work only to find me gorged out on homemade Greek cooking and unable to eat the meal she had planned for us both that evening. This, as you can imagine, did not make me Mr Popular.

Oliver and I passed on our gratitude to the ladies in black for the nutritional sustenance and headed back to the yard in the hearse, leaving Mr Dickinson, Eddie and Ali to enjoy their mobile delicatessen offerings. On our arrival back at the yard we were greeted by the appearance of Eamon's head poking intently out from his small office window on the outside of the building. With the sun gently reflecting off the sparsely covered flesh, it disappeared again almost as quickly as if to attend a most urgent matter that our appearance had either reminded him about or distracted him from.

After parking up the hearse in its allocated bay in the garage, and finally getting out of the car, Oliver and I proceeded with the usual stretching movements and vocalised moans and groans that finally being set free from a small space that restricts your movement for a long period necessitates.

Unfortunately, our sense of freedom was short-lived, and in the same way that the shopkeeper used to appear in Mr Ben, 'as if by magic' (for those of you old enough to remember), we were suddenly greeted by a very intent Eamon who was now standing in the workshop doorway doing his semi curtsey, tongue out, 'have a quick cup of tea' routine. Politely, he informed us that our presence was required post-haste, and *that we were needed to attend a coroner's removal at Arlington House. The flash of cranium from the office window earlier had been to check to see if the vehicle approaching the yard's gates contained prospective candidates to go out on the removal. The equally lightning disappearance of the same cranium had been Eamon's efforts to get the kettle on in the tearoom. In his mind, this would allow the chosen candidates to partake in some speedy refreshments, and ensure sufficient hydration to those concerned before being sent back out into the big, bad world. I wonder how many other foremen would have been so thoughtful. None that I have ever come into contact with, that's for sure. Apologetically, but with respectful authority, Eamon went on to explain that there were no other staff available as they were all out on funerals or removals themselves. He'd even had to call on Bradley Masters from head office to make up the three-man removal crew that was required.*

The Arlington House we were to attend was the same Arlington House that featured in the 1984 Madness song, 'One Better Day'. One of my favourite, more mellow songs of theirs. It was a hostel for homeless men and was located in the heart of Camden Town close to the famous Camden Lock. With limited parking facilities directly outside the hostel, our objective, as was often the case, was to avoid a major hike back to the vehicle. Especially in cases when it was difficult or not possible to use a wheelie stretcher, as was the case at Arlington House. So, Oliver, our designated driver, did what we often had to do in these situations. Throwing caution to the wind with a devil-may-care glint in his eye, he parked the vehicle as close as he could from the main entrance of Arlington House on the exceptionally decorative yellow markings that so artistically line so many of the streets in this fair old city of ours. But not, I might add, before checking very carefully in the shadows and darkened doorways of nearby buildings for any skulking traffic wardens. It's always advisable to keep a little caution out of the wind, in reserve. Just to be on the safe side.

Feeling fairly confident that the area was traffic warden free (at least as confident as you ever can be about such things), we exited the vehicle and headed into the main reception area of the sizeable red-brick building and reported to the duty manager who was busily tapping away on his computer keyboard in his sparsely furnished, but more than adequately sized office. Bradley, guardian of the pink card, did the talking, Oliver carried the fold-up stretcher, and I was at the ready to support each of them in their given role to the best of my ability, if required to do so.

Our presence had attracted a trio of rather shabbily dressed, unkempt gentlemen who looked like they might be off to, or returning from, an audition for the role of Fagin in an Oliver Twist production. Standing in earshot, they were taking a great deal of interest in our conversation with the duty manager and appeared noticeably unhappy and slightly agitated by our presence. I sensed some rather hostile vibes emanating from their direction and it looked like things could kick off at any moment. Particularly from the one gentleman who appeared to be talking to somebody on his left who wasn't there. It was quite unnerving.

I tried to give the impression that I was not fazed by their threatening stares and chose to avoid making eye contact as much as possible so as not to aggravate the situation any more than my pure existence seemed to have already succeeded in doing. I doubt very much whether undertakers are ever going to be the most popular people to enter a room, particularly if it's in their professional capacity, but I'd never experienced such hostility towards my person just because of the job I did. It was a whole new experience, and not a pleasant one at all.

The duty manager escorted us past the mumbling Fagin lookalikes and to the room where the deceased awaiting our attention was lying. An assumption at the time, as he may have been sitting, crouching, or otherwise positioned for all I knew. Our journey took us along an endless network of corridors and several flights of stairs. Each corridor lined with a multitude of small dark rooms, it was almost prisonlike in its layout but with fewer bars. There was also the notable absence of white-shirted staff members poised to wrestle you to the ground at any moment for any infringement of the rules.

As we strode down the corridors, faces stared out at us from the darkness of several of the tiny rooms. Blank, soulless expressions common to each. Alerted to our presence, a group of rowdy young men were distracted from their game of pool in what appeared to be a games room. They shouted out various supposedly witty quips, including that hilarious old adage about undertakers having dead end jobs. The duty manager responded to the various interruptions in the same way a teacher would when addressing a group of unruly teenagers in class. They seemed unimpressed and responded to his pleas for decorum with contempt.

The small, dark room that we were eventually directed into smelt stale and musky. In fact, it was hard to determine just how much worse it smelt then, than it might have done before, due to the newly present aroma radiating from the dead body. Of course, the stale and musky smell may have been partly down to the fact the late occupant had been a smoker. This was evidenced by an empty cigarette paper packet and a comparatively full plastic pouch of Old Holborn that lay next to an ashtray on the bedside table. The ashtray was overflowing with ash and roll-up butts by at least three times the amount it was designed to hold, the butts piled within it clearly having been smoked to their absolute maximum; finger and lip-burning maximum. The co-habiting flies may or may not have been new tenants. In all probability, the impressive collection of large, empty plastic cider bottles, crushed beer cans and other food and drink-related waste scattered around the room in vast quantities, had probably enticed them to investigate the premises long before the benefits of a corpse were on the menu.

In amongst the debris that littered the room there lay on the bed in front of us, curled up in the foetal position as if to ease pain, a man in his early thirties; thirty-three to be exact. He was fully dressed and despite his more than adequate layers of clothing for the time of year, he was also wearing a thick black winter coat. Closer inspection revealed the man's greyish purple complexion, which indicated he'd probably been dead for some time – the left side of his face marinating nicely in a pool of thick, dark, reddish brown goo on his pillow. Moving the man from the bed to the stretcher, the room's pungent aroma intensified further as the taste of death's odour spread via newly released gases from the disturbed body. There was a sense of despair and tragedy about the whole scene that was quite overwhelming.

Carrying the now laden stretcher back through the building, we were watched again by the lost faces that had surveyed us on our way in. Although they were aware of our presence, they seemed to look straight through us as if we didn't exist, no more interested in us than they were when we first entered their world. The group of rowdy lads in the recreation area, absent of witty remarks, fell silent as we passed, their eyes briefly falling in the direction of the stretcher before turning away and returning to their game of pool. As we walked through the corridors, the sense that the man on our stretcher had led a very solitary existence became all too apparent. No one seemed connected in any way at all to the deceased male now lying on our stretcher. The faces that looked blankly on were not friends or acquaintances wanting to bid him farewell or even faces that showed any concern at his departure.

It was a relief to step back into the daylight and breathe in the fresh warm air. Leaving the gloominess and volatile residents of Arlington House as far behind us as possible, I hoped visits there would be few and far between. It had been an insight into a sorrowful and depressing world that up until then I had been able to ignore or at least cross the road to avoid. The experience left me feeling quite melancholy.

We escorted our lonesome passenger to the coroner's mortuary in King's Cross, a visit that was short but not so sweet. A badly decomposed body taken in the previous day by another firm of undertakers was causing a most unpleasant stench throughout the entire building.

After dropping Bradley Masters off at head office, back at the yard we had just enough time for a quick cuppa while we smartened ourselves up before heading off to the Mill Hill branch for our next funeral, Oliver and I in the hearse and Eddie and Frank in the limousine.

The Mill Hill branch manager, Mr Thomas, was a tad flustered when we arrived and not in the best of moods. It seemed he had just had a particularly heated discussion with his wife about a situation involving their daughter and her rather aggressive partner. The partner was about to get a good talking to by all accounts and put straight on a few things. A talking to which I was glad I wasn't going to be on the other end of. Based on my brief observations so far, Mr Thomas didn't seem the type of man to let anyone mistreat or take advantage of his daughter. An attribute and quality I would admire in any man.

Followed by Mr Thomas, my colleagues and I ventured up to the chapel of rest where the deceased, Mrs Danby, an old lady in her eighties, was lying. The usual mandatory checks were carried out with due care and attention before the coffin lid was placed on top of the coffin. The lid was not sealed down as the coffin was to be open during the church service. However, to keep the lid secure during transportation, one screw either end was fixed in place. The coffin was placed into the hearse and the floral tributes were positioned around the coffin and on top of the hearse. The hearse and limousine then made their way to the family home in Hendon where the immediate family was waiting to be collected before travelling to the church.

Followed by several private cars, the funeral cortège travelled slowly from the house to the small church in Mill Hill. On the journey we passed the army barracks. I hadn't been up that way for years. I used to hang around with some of the squaddies from there back in the eighties. We would often meet up at the weekend on our motorcycles at 'Ye Old Bull and Bush' in Hampstead. (Yes, the one in the song.) After closing time we would head down to Chelsea Bridge, a favourite meeting place for bikers. That is, until the police decided to clamp down because of all the accidents. Allegedly, unlawful speeds were being reached and dangerous stunts being performed by unruly motorcycle gangs. They were carefree days, with little to trouble my mind. No plans or ambitions, just living day to day. 'Cigarettes and whiskey, and wild, wild women'. Well, cigarettes and cider, and anyone that would have me!

Once past the barracks, the old church appeared companionless in its position on the long and winding country road. Just a few sporadic dwellings in either direction to save it from complete isolation. We pulled up outside and began to ready the church to receive our principal passenger. Inside the church, it was very cool in comparison to the heat outside, and it took a while for our eyes to adjust to the darkness after being in the bright sunlight. Oliver and I took a pair of low trestles with purple velvet covers and placed them in front of the altar. Apparently, they weren't keen on the tall trestles at this church and it wouldn't have been very practical either. Only the members of the congregation who were well over six feet tall would have been able to actually see the late Mrs Danby in her open coffin and witness Marcus's magical skills in the field of embalming.

When all the mourners were in the church, the service began. The minister, walking in front of us as we carried the coffin into the church, recited a passage from the Bible which included a reference to 'walking through the valley of the shadow of death and not fearing evil because God is with us'. Psalm 23, I believe. Quite poetic and very apt for a funeral.

After placing the coffin onto the waiting trestles in front of the altar, we remained in our positions next to the coffin. Oliver removed the two screws holding the coffin lid securely in place. The lid was then moved about a third of the way down the coffin and left in situ. Mr Thomas and Oliver placed a large purple and gold cover, the pall, which was about the size of a king-size duvet cover, over the coffin – leaving Mrs Danby in full view from her waist up. Oliver gently brushed aside some strands of hair from her face that must have relocated themselves during the slow but somewhat turbulent journey over the many speed bumps that we had to negotiate along the way. Mrs Danby was now ready to be viewed. Having fulfilled our role up to that point, we bowed and solemnly made our exit.

During the service we could hear the hymns being sung from inside the church. I recognised two out of the three from my primary school days. Emma and I also went through a churchy period, so I'm not a complete heathen or totally lacking in my knowledge of some aspects of the Christian faith.

A reconnaissance mission was carried out in order to locate the whereabouts of the grave in the churchyard. As it turned out, it couldn't have been in a more awkward position – squeezed between two existing graves at the far end, and in the corner. To reach it, with no pathway or clear route to the grave, we were going to have to battle through an assault course of very closely packed gravestones and memorials.

As the service was coming to a close, Mr Thomas called us back inside the church. The congregation at that point were shuffling up to the altar in a disorderly fashion. Their movements were snail-like as they ebbed slowly along the left side of the centre aisle in order to get one last look at Mrs Danby and pay their respects. Once satisfied, they shuffled past the coffin and back down the right side of the aisle before returning to their seats. After a few last words, the minister gave the traditional nod and a wink indicating he was ready for us to continue with our duties. Resuming our previous positions around the coffin, Eddie, Frank and I stood almost statue-like as Oliver and Mr Thomas ceremoniously removed the large purple pall that had partially adorned the coffin during the service. Next, they sensitively reunited the coffin with its lid and Oliver inserted a screw into each hole on the lid, six in all, two at each end and one either side in the middle. He then proceeded to secure the screw in front of him with an old-fashioned wooden-handled brace. I couldn't help but notice that it was exactly like the one Dad used to have hanging in the garden shed, amongst numerous other tools that I generally only ever see nowadays if I'm channel surfing on the TV and accidently come across an episode of the Antiques Road Show.

Oliver, having secured the screw in front of him at the head of the coffin, using the antique-type brace, passed it to Eddie, my opposite number at the foot of the coffin. Oliver's screw had gone in fairly smoothly with little resistance; Eddie's however, was putting up much more of a fight. It was at that point that alarm bells began to ring in my head. No one had mentioned or consulted me about my willingness or ability to undertake such a task so publicly. My heart rate increased considerably as I started to panic at the thought of performing the art of antique brace operation in front of such a large and emotional audience, who would probably be watching my every move in relation to the coffin that stood before me. This was on-the-job training I could have well done without.

To make things worse, Eddie was starting to get flustered and I watched as a bead of sweat ran down his troubled brow. Eddie's sense of relief was felt by us all when finally the screw came to a halt. Now evident that the brace was going to continue its journey around the coffin and eventually arrive at me, it was beginning to feel like we were playing DIY Russian roulette. My panic and fear intensified further *when I looked down and realised that the screw to be secured was a slotted screw and not cross-headed. I've always found the slotted ones more of an ordeal and much harder to control. In my hands, there was nearly always a severe lack of cooperation between a slot-headed screw and the end of a screwdriver, usually ending in disaster for both the screw and its intended dwelling place. So, as Eddie handed me the brace, I began to feel as though I was destined to lose this particular round of roulette.*

Introducing the brace to my allocated screw, I started to turn it clockwise into the hole on the coffin lid. To say that my experience of using any type of brace was limited would be a massive understatement, and mostly involved removing or replacing wheel nuts when I was a trainee mechanic. As I recall, this wasn't necessarily a skill I'd mastered and I would invariably end up snapping them off or rounding them to such an extent that they were impossible to loosen or tighten, thus rendering them useless and in need of time-consuming intervention and sometimes costly corrective engineering.

With no time for either of the previously mentioned procedures, my focus on the brace's interaction with the screw was intense, with extreme caution being taken at every turn. When the screw began to stubbornly resist my efforts, I stopped. After all, it was sufficiently tight enough to secure the lid, clear of the decorative brass cover it was required to sit flush within, and I wasn't going to tempt fate by forcing it any more than necessary. My ordeal was over. My heart rate searching to regain its natural rhythm once again, I wiped the sweat from my forehead as discreetly as I could before handing the brace to Frank to complete his part in operation screw-down.

Frank was absolutely faultless in his execution of the task and made it look completely effortless. Cool as a cucumber, like a true professional, he calmly and without any outward signs of pressure or stress screwed that sucker well and truly down. Such a performance would usually have demanded an applause but under the circumstances I felt it wise to resist. As we were only a four-man crew, with six screws to secure, Oliver stepped up and thankfully tightened the middle screw each side of the coffin. Nods were exchanged between the appropriate officials and as the congregation sang the hymn 'Jerusalem', with a fair amount of gusto for the amount of people present, we carried Mrs Danby out of the church.

Once outside, taking Mrs Danby to her final resting place, we began our trek across the rather overcrowded graveyard. Tentatively, we ventured through the snugly-spaced graveyard with the coffin on our shoulders for as far as we could, only taking it into our hands when the passing became more precarious. We then manhandled it over, around, and in between the closely packed gravestones and higgledy-piggledy monuments. After a while, due to the ever-shrinking availability of somewhere to place our feet, it became apparent that a new tactic was needed if we were to reach the intended grave without anything untoward occurring. That's how Oliver and I ended up carrying the coffin between the two of us, Oliver at the head of the coffin and me at the foot. There were a few heart-stopping moments along the way when footing was lost and a secure grip on the well-polished coffin was hard to maintain, but all's well that ends well, as they say, and we successfully made it to our desired destination.

At the graveside we resumed our professional demeanour as we waited for the mourners to gather. Outwardly we looked calm and poised; inwardly our breathing rhythms were a tad more erratic than before and our sweat glands far more active. Once all the mourners who were able had negotiated the graveyard obstacle course and positioned themselves as near as humanly possible to the grave, the minister continued with the graveside service and the committal of the coffin. As the minister spoke, my focus was drawn to the thickness of the roots that lined the walls of the grave; they appeared to belong to the ancient cedar that encompassed that edge of the graveyard. The gravediggers would have had their work cut out for them digging that grave, and with no room for a mechanical digger to share their workload, I expect their breathing rhythms were more than a tad erratic, too.

After lowering the coffin into the root-lined grave, we made our exit. While the graveside service continued, we collected the flowers from the vehicles and from inside the church and placed them in the graveyard along the outer wall of the church building. The assortment of vivid colours fluttering in the bright sunshine and the blend of the flowers' sweet scent was quite mesmerizing. A treat of nature I and many of our species unfortunately rarely take much notice of in our usual daily haste to get from A to B, and getting caught up in all the frantic activity in between. With the vehicles now free of their floral tributes, Oliver, Frank and I left Mr Thomas and Eddie dealing with the mourners and headed back into town in the hearse for our next funeral.

Next on our list was a Hindu funeral, but before we could get started there were a few stops we had to make. Our first port of call was the yard to pick up our fourth man, Graham. Our second stop was head office in order to collect our conductor, Mortimer and Sons' very own would-be BAFTA nominee, Mr Dickinson. With our entourage complete, we made our way to the deceased's family home in Finchley. The deceased, a lady in her fifties, had been taken there earlier in the week by Mel, Ali, Graham and Dean for the various religious ceremonies to be performed before the funeral.

On our arrival there was a large contingency of mourners entering and exiting the house; family and friends of the deceased saying their last goodbyes. As we entered the house we were asked to remove our shoes. This was not something we were used to doing, however, under the circumstances and out of respect, we were happy to oblige. Looking down at my shoeless feet, I wished I had been forewarned about the possibility of such an activity, and regretted the choice of socks that I had chosen to wear that morning, my big toe now protruding rather embarrassingly from its well-worn cotton sheath, for all to see.

After the Hindu priest had finished his prayers, we were permitted to seal down the coffin. The woman's body, clothed in white, was surrounded by an abundance of multicoloured petals with a beautiful garland of flowers placed around her neck. Scented candles scattered around the darkened room added a radiance to the woman's face as they performed their mournful dance. A wave of emotion overcame the mourners who stood before us, as they stole one last vision of the woman's physical form before the coffin lid was secured in place.

At the site of the brace, my heart raced as panic seized its opportunity once more. Closely watched, in turn we secured the screws positioned in front of each of us to fasten the lid in place. To my relief, being a cremation coffin the screw gave little resistance as it entered the veneer-covered chipboard – unlike the solid wood coffin at the church earlier. One of Eamon's many useful tips to make life easier for us in our daily work, was to wax the thread of the screw, thus allowing ease of entry into the solid wood. Apparently, Oliver had followed Eamon's advice and waxed the screws used on the solid wood coffin at the church, but it had still been quite a troublesome task to complete.

Carrying the coffin out of the house was a real challenge. At one point we even had to stand it on end to negotiate the rather tight corner leading out from the room we were in into the hallway. Mr Dickinson had already removed the wooden trestles from the room where the deceased was lying and had positioned them in the hallway, giving us somewhere to rest the coffin while we put our shoes back on. With our footwear on and embarrassing socks and my big toe out of sight once again, we took the coffin outside and placed it into the hearse.

The journey to Golders Green Crematorium was slow and disrupted, with us having to pull over numerous times to wait for mourners in private cars that were getting caught up in the volume of traffic, and by red lights demanding cessation of movement. Once at the crematorium, cars headed in all directions searching for a place to park. It was like a scene from the Wacky Races with us as the Anthill Mob in our big black car. Limited parking spaces and a high volume of private cars meant many had to leave the crematorium again and park up along the road outside. Fortunately for us our parking spot was secured, and with the hearse now outside the West Chapel we were ready to carry out our duties.

I was informed by Oliver that the family and friends of the deceased would be carrying the coffin. We were to follow closely and be ready to step in if anything untoward happened, such as someone not being able to handle the weight or becoming too emotional. What followed was a sight to be seen. About twenty volunteers from the crowd of mourners stepped forward to carry the coffin into the chapel. Expecting only a select few to be chosen, you can imagine my surprise when the entire group gathered at the back of the hearse raring to go. Non-verbal communication from my colleagues indicated clearly that this was the norm.

The Hindu minister announced his readiness to proceed and a subsequent nod from Mr Dickinson in our general direction indicated movement on our part was required. Once we had assisted with the safe removal of the coffin from the back of the hearse, intrigued, I watched in amazement as the coffin was transported into the chapel on a writhing human wave. It was impossible to determine who, out of the chaotic mass of energetic bodies completely surrounding the coffin, was actually supporting it, although it was clear that someone obviously was. In comparison to the almost regimentally carried out ceremonies that I had experienced so far in my new career, the absolute chaos I witnessed before my very eyes left me speechless. Something of a rarity I must say! As we had in the beginning, my colleagues and I assisted towards the end of the carry to ensure a safe landing and a securely positioned coffin on the catafalque.

Although it was a rather anarchic affair and visually disorganised, there was something quite appealing about everyone wanting to do their bit and getting stuck in. Being cremated in a furnace at a crematorium in North London may not be quite as spiritual as a flaming pyre next to the Ganges or as picturesque as a devouring blaze on a mountain top, but regulations and legal requirements regarding cremations in this country are a little more stringent than in some other countries around the world. Despite the restrictions, the spirit of the volunteers carrying the coffin and the overwhelming feeling of family and celebration of life, it really was something quite special.

Back at the yard, Eamon was busy in the workshop sewing together a protective cover of coarse hessian material around the outside of a coffin. Using a large, curved needle identical to the one Joe had used to remove the old woman's wedding ring, he was sewing it tightly together with string. Hessian is a versatile and dense woven fabric, usually produced using the skin of the jute plant combined with other vegetable fibres. Being strong and resilient, it's widely used to make netting, bags and sacks, amongst other things. Aside from the egg and spoon race and the three-legged race, no childhood sports day would ever be complete without the bizarre sight of a multitude of excitable children jumping frantically towards the finishing line in a hessian sack. The memories of participating in such events myself, as a child, conjures up wonderful memories of the madness and mayhem, and how difficult it actually was to project oneself at a decent speed to have any chance of finishing in the top three and receiving recognition for your efforts.

The coffin was being treated to its shroud-like garment in order to protect it on the plane journey to Ireland. According to Eamon, many older Irish people request to be flown back to their ancestral home after death, to be buried in their native soil. A funeral service would usually be held in the UK, for family and friends here to attend, before the deceased's journey home for burial. Eamon refers to them as salmons – which I think he's allowed to do being Irish himself. A reference, I believe, to do with the life cycle of salmon and their arduous quest as adults to return to their birthplace.

With the coffin snuggly wrapped in its protective sackcloth garment, the duty squad, consisting of Mel, Ali and Graham, loaded it into the van and headed off to Heathrow Airport in readiness for the next part of its homeward journey. It looked like they may be in for a busy evening, as just before they left, the phone rang. The call was from head office informing Eamon about a pending removal from a block of flats in King's Cross.

The rest of us changed back into our civilian attire, the rather limited space around the lockers once again the location for the now customary battle between numerous partially dressed colliding limbs. The ensuing skirmish only confirmed that there really wasn't enough room in there, as the saying goes, 'to swing a cat'. Although, I must say, it's not a saying I have ever been very keen on or ever felt the inclination to use myself, as a lover of animals – particularly of our fury little feline friends. There are definitely many items that it would be possible to swing to effectively determine whether an area is limited space-wise or not, that would be a great deal more humane and far less likely for the swinger (not meant as a sexual reference, yet it may also apply) to end up being scarred for life. However, in my view, anyone with even the slightest thought of carrying out such a barbaric act would more than deserve to suffer the painful consequences delivered by the angry feline.

Once changed and with peace restored, we were ready to leave the death and sadness of the working week behind. The slamming of the garage door, like a symbolic full stop to the end of our week's toil – except for the duty squad, of course – echoed in the vast space behind it as Eamon closed up for the weekend. Venturing forth, those of us lucky enough to be temporarily free from our labour, were now ready to participate in life's many distractions. A few of us decided to go for a pint, or two, in the local pub. A traditional end of week activity for many workers from all walks of life.

Walking away from the yard, we left behind the silent darkness where the black beasts lay motionless, and the coffin store's macabre commodities waited patiently for the next week's customers. The incessant noise of hammers, drills and Capital Radio that usually echoed from the workshop, was now replaced by a tranquil hush. In the mortuary across the well-travelled cobbled mews, every tray in the fridges was occupied by a silent transitory resident. As the appliances worked tirelessly to keep their lifeless occupants comfortably chilled, the monotonous pulsating hum was the only sound to be heard this side of life. All in all, it had been a busy week, now it was time for the Grim Reaper's workshop to rest.

As for me, I had learnt much and now had many things to ponder that had certainly not been on my pondering list at the beginning of the week. It had been an interesting five days to say the absolute least, and I had a feeling that being an undertaker was definitely going to be a challenging career in more ways than I could have possibly imagined. Fortunately, from what I'd seen so far, the lads were a fairly good bunch. I was looking forward to getting to know them all better. Maybe even improving on certain relationships that might not have got off to the best start.

For now, I was happy to find out, after a week of being assaulted by my braces, much to my colleagues' amusement, that you can actually get button-on braces. Information very thoughtfully passed on by Joe.

Now he tells me!

AFFAIRS OF THE HEART

Outside of work things were changing too. Speaking to Sean at the bike club meeting on Thursday night, he mentioned that he and his other half, Rachel, were taking the children up to the Olympic-size paddling pool on Hampstead Heath on Saturday. He asked if I would like to join them as Sally and her little boy Jack were going to be there too. Apparently, Sally had mentioned how impressed she was that Jack and I got on so well at the bike show, and suggested that it would be nice for us to meet up again under slightly less lively circumstances. A meeting where we might even get a chance to have a conversation. It seemed like a pleasant idea and it would be a welcome distraction from the past week's interesting, yet rather less cheerful activities. It would be good to get out in the sun in something other than a black suit. Or out of a suit at any rate, as I have to admit that most of my clothing at the time was black. However, it was a little less formal and a great deal more comfortable. The absence of trouser-supporting equipment with psychotic tendencies was an added bonus.

So, on Saturday afternoon I made my way to the appointed meeting place on Hampstead Heath to meet up with Sean, Rachel, Sally and the children. As I arrived, I was thankful they were already there so I didn't have to hang about on my own looking decidedly dodgy while lurking around the children's play area. Sean and Rachel were lazing in the hot midday sun on the grass by the playground, while Sally kept an eye on the children in the huge paddling pool. They appeared to be having the time of their lives splashing away under the heat of the sun, without a care in the world.

At first things seemed to be going fairly well and conversation flowed, flowed that is until Sally appeared to take offence at something I said. I'm not exactly sure what I'd said to upset her but whatever it was she had suddenly become very defensive and looked extremely annoyed. I suspect it was my sense of humour she didn't understand. Sometimes it can take a little time for people to get tuned into my rather unique comedic quirkiness. That said, I can honestly say I've never had anyone respond quite like that before. From that point things seemed to go decidedly downhill and with no improvement on the communication front as time went on, I thought it best to make my excuses and leave.

I hadn't been walking long when the familiar long red bonnet, with more than a hint of rust, of Sean's old Ford Cortina estate pulled up beside me. Sean said they were heading back to Islington to pop in to their local pub for a few bevvies and was wondering if I fancied joining them. As I contemplated the offer for a moment, I noticed Sally's still rather annoyed facial expression in the back of the car. However, I decided that the invitation to partake in a few alcoholic beverages on such a lovely summer's day was far too tempting and without further ado I jumped into the vacant passenger seat in the front of the car.

It was very pleasant sitting outside the pub in the warm breeze of the balmy summer's evening. Earlier misunderstandings seemed to fade and the lines of communication aided by a little alcoholic lubrication, appeared far less confused. As darkness descended, Sean and Rachel decided it was time to head home and get the little ones to bed. Rather conveniently, Jack was invited to have a sleepover with them. A somewhat transparent move I thought, on Sean and Rachel's part, but one I was more than happy to go along with as Sally and I seemed to be getting on quite well.

Pleased that the evening could continue in her company, time seemed to fly by as last orders came and went. With our thirst-quenching pleas to the bar staff for just one more drink falling on deaf ears and being the gentleman that I am, I was ready to walk Sally home. However, Sally being the woman she was (as I was soon to learn) had other ideas, and was having none of my defeatist attitude. Taking me by the hand she whisked me off into the night, just like the young boy from the story of *The Snowman*, in search of a venue to continue the night's frivolities. You may find it hard to believe, that even though I was the ripe old age of twenty-nine, I had never before participated in the activity of illegal after-hours drinking. This woman was quickly becoming the sort of woman that my mother had warned me about. The type that leads poor defenceless young men like me astray. At least I hoped that she was!

Like an Apache Indian tracking buffalo on the Great Plains of North America, Sally listened intently for the sounds of merriment, tomfoolery and the clinking of glasses. She inhaled the warm summer breeze that gently caressed our red-cheeked faces, in search of the aroma which radiates from alcohol-soaked wooden flooring. Obviously, that's not what the Apache Indian would have been sniffing for in his hunt for buffalo. If he had got a whiff of such things, I'm fairly sure he would have abandoned the buffalo hunt rather sharpish.

Hand in hand we wandered through the darkness and eventually arrived at a small but pleasant-looking public house which Sally assured me participated in the act of illegal after-hours drinking. Shame on them! From the outside there were no visible signs that this was the case, no signs of life at all, something my first week in undertaking was already sharpening my skills at detecting. As we stood in the doorway, Sally assured me once again that our quest would not be in vain at this particular watering hole of fermented beverages. I suggested that perhaps the people inside had been alerted to our presence by a lookout and were instructed to cease from their frivolousness until we had given up and moved on. Unresponsive to my suggestion, Sally knocked on the pub door purposefully in an effort to gain entry. I asked her how well she knew the landlord of the pub. It was at this point that she informed me she had never actually frequented this particular public house herself. She had, however, heard from some of her friends and acquaintances that occasionally indulged in the activity that we were in search of and who she considered to be reliable sources, that this was indeed such a place. Sally continued to bang on the pub door with such tenacity and determination that the increased volume should surely have been heard by even the hardest of hearing landlord and clientele. Confirmation that this was the case came from the sound of hefty door bolts being withdrawn from their fixing points on the other side of the door. Sally ceased knocking as the door opened very slightly. I watched as she pleaded our case convincingly with the nose and one eye that were visible from our side of the door, stating our desperation and dire need to enter their inviting establishment that we had heard so much about. Her pleas were not in vain and in two shakes of a lamb's tail we were sat at a table for two in a corner of the pub at a quarter past midnight, enjoying the delights of yet another thirst-quenching alcoholic beverage.

The pub seemed to be doing extremely good business at this ungodly and unacceptable hour for alcoholic consumption, according to the powers that be, that is. Although, judging by the number of customers enjoying their extra quota, a large number of people similar to ourselves obviously disagreed with the government's idea that we should all stop drinking in public and go home at 11 p.m. Never had a pint deemed so wrong, tasted so good. Bring on prohibition, that's all I can say. Bring it on.

On a slightly different note, why would anyone ever want to shake a lamb's tail twice as a method of time keeping? Unless, of course, they were a shepherd who had no other way of measuring the passing of time. Whether it is an accurate method of time keeping or not, I have no idea, but I don't suppose there are many other things in a field full of sheep to use. Either way, who am I to question such things? If sailors can use the stars to chart their course, I suppose it's only right that a shepherd is entitled to deduce time by shaking a lamb's tail. Digression over.

I have to say, that even though I was slightly shocked by Sally's behaviour, at the same time I was also immensely impressed. Not only had this woman gained me access to a locked public house, when the powers that be had told me I couldn't be in one, she drank bitter. I'd never met a woman that drank bitter before. So far in my life this new type of woman had eluded me and I have to confess to being totally in awe of her real get up and go. Most of the women I had known thus far, had just got up and gone!

The evening, or rather early morning, ended cordially and after walking Sally home I took a short taxi journey back to the flat above the undertakers. I sneaked back into the flat, desperately trying not to disturb Mum. No mean feat given that the wafer-thin partition wall, which divided the once one large bedroom into two smaller ones, was all that separated us. Lying contentedly on my bed, I stared up at the familiar old cracks in the ceiling and contemplated the evening's events. For the short time it took me to fall into a deep and happy slumber, that is.

BACK ON THE JOB

The first week in my new career at Mortimer and Sons Funeral Directors had shown me that there was a great deal more to being a funeral assistant than just carrying a coffin on your shoulder and driving a posh car around all day. My second week was very much more of the same. Developing my skills in the workshop, broadening my knowledge in the correct etiquette on funerals, carrying out removals and getting to know the many new places and people that were connected to this new and somewhat strange domain. All that said, it was still early days and my first badly decomposed body was still to transpire. Unsurprisingly, I wasn't in any rush to experience that particular delight.

I had also purchased my own shoe polish, which seemed to have replaced Joe's as the communal offering. You'd think it would make sense for everyone to have their own. Perhaps it was a social thing among undertakers, like offering a cigarette to another smoker.

The psychotic self-releasing braces had also been disposed of and had been replaced by button-on braces. Mum had sewn the buttons on to my trousers with extra strong thread in order for them to cope with the level of stress they had to deal with throughout the working day. Overcoming the nervous twitch that I'd developed as a result of the constant brutal attacks from their predecessors, was going to take a while.

THE PATH OF TRUE LOVE IS NEVER SMOOTH

At the end of my second week at Mortimer and Sons, a telephone conversation with Sean alerted me to the fact that Sally was a bit put out that I hadn't called, especially as things had gone so well the previous weekend. Once the lines of communication had been improved, that is.

It had occurred to me that perhaps I should have called. In all honesty I had meant to, but I'd got so wrapped up in my week's work that I just hadn't got around to it. I know that sounds a bit lame but the week seemed to go by so quickly. Feeling quite bad about having let Sally down, even though I hadn't meant to, I rang Sean back for Sally's phone number to give her a call, because I couldn't find it anywhere. On the other hand, I couldn't actually remember her giving it to me, but having witnessed her attack on the pub door the previous weekend, I was fearful that my attempts at an explanation to cover the oversight would be seen as weak. Thankfully, my genuine apology about not contacting her sooner and a little bit of sweet talking seemed to do the trick and I was quickly forgiven my indiscretions. The following week was to be the setting for our first official date.

Our First Official Date

As arranged, I met Sally outside South End Green Railway Station in Hampstead. Since our last rendezvous, that almost wasn't, she'd given her shoulder-length blonde hair a slightly wilder look. She was wearing a snazzy, short black velvet jacket covered in multicoloured gems.

It's fair to say that this was the first time I had actually noticed that she had quite a nice figure, a figure which I hadn't really appreciated before. Perhaps I had been distracted by other things or maybe the clothing she had been wearing on previous occasions hadn't really done justice to her figure. Either way, I think I'm going to stop there before I dig this hole any deeper!

As she stood waiting for me outside the railway station, clutching her handbag in front of her, she looked quite stunning in the early evening sunlight. The bright red lipstick decorating her beautifully shaped lips, complemented her welcoming smile perfectly.

We enjoyed our first drink of the evening at the Freemason's Arms opposite the heath. Sat outside in the warmth of the early evening sunshine, it was all very relaxed, with no communication problems whatsoever. After a few drinks, and a lot of talking about life in general – with the occasional snippet about ourselves thrown in for good measure, as you do on first dates – hunger dictated that we move on to a restaurant. As part of our date, I took Sally to a place called Old Orleans which was a little further up the hill in the high street. I was sure they would be able to cater for our nutritional requirements that evening, as they had a rather interesting menu which specialised in Cajun-style food from the Deep South that was absolutely delicious. FYI that's the Deep South Louisiana I'm referring to, of course, not the deep south Bognor Regis.

As the evening went on, I noticed Sally's eyes seemed to be irritating her and were looking quite red. Enquiring if she was all right, she explained that she was wearing contact lenses but wasn't used to them and was finding them very uncomfortable. In an effort to make her feel better, I mentioned how I thought glasses on a woman could be quite sexy, and while she seemed quite pleased by this remark, I sensed she was also slightly annoyed. She had gone to all the trouble of wearing contact lenses to look nice and was suffering for her efforts, when she obviously needn't have bothered.

It was an enjoyable evening and for the most part it seemed to go well. Sally politely laughed at my jokes and I tried my best to compliment her in all the right places. Within the conversation that is, not geographically.

Time seemed to fly by, and as we walked back through Hampstead High Street, I realised it was getting quite late. I couldn't be too late as I was working the next day but concern for Sally's wellbeing took priority and making sure she had a safe journey home suddenly seemed paramount. Seeing a vacant taxi about to pass us by and knowing from personal experience how long it would likely be before another would appear, I decided to seize the opportunity and hailed it.

"TAXI!"

As quick as a flash, the taxi swerved towards us and came to a screeching halt with the back door in an almost perfect position for Sally to enter the vehicle. Being the gentleman I am, I opened the cab door and thanked her politely for a lovely evening.

In my mind, I had achieved my objective, sending Sally safely on her way homeward bound in one swift and efficient hailing of a taxi. And even though I may have taken her a little by surprise with my sudden and spontaneous actions to facilitate her safe journey home, I was confident that she would think my actions and concern for her safety both chivalrous and gallant.

Good Intentions

Sometimes our actions and intentions are not always taken as well as we might perceive them to be, a lesson I was soon to learn. At the weekend, still convinced that my date with Sally had ended well, I met up with Sean and Wez. As you might imagine, the topic of conversation soon turned to my romantic evening with Sally, and it was during this mocking repartee that my delusions of chivalry and gallantry were ousted. It would appear that I had caught Sally more than a little off guard when I so hastily hailed the taxi at what I deemed to be the end of our date in Hampstead. In fact, she was convinced that I'd suddenly had enough of her or that she had said something to offend me; 'Bundling her into the taxi without any prior warning and sending her into exile', to use Sally's own words. Up until that point she'd thought it was all going so well. However, neither the impromptu hailing of the cab or the chivalrous opening of the door had been recognised as the act of concern and kindness that it was, and had instead been interpreted as a means of escape.

When I called her to explain that my actions had been fuelled only by good intentions, she was surprised to hear from me. She was convinced she would never hear from me again. It just goes to show how people can interpret things differently. I will endeavour to consider the consequences of my actions a little more thoughtfully in future, or at least explain them in order to avoid misinterpretation. Thankfully, after explaining the motives behind my conduct on this occasion, I was yet again graciously forgiven and invited to join Sally and Jack for lunch that Sunday.

Sunday

The day spent with Sally and Jack was definitely the highlight of my week, Sally working her way into my heart with her delicious home cooking. After lunch we went to the local park. Jack, peddling his go-cart hell for leather, unhappily only managed to get to the park and halfway round before he was exhausted. With Jack on foot, I became official go-cart carrier for the remainder of the journey. Renewed energy was found as we approached the adventure playground, Jack racing off towards the intricate, multicoloured climbing frame and throwing himself at it. It was really nice to see him having so much fun. We were quite the little family.

Illuminating

Shortly afterwards Sally and I went on our first excursion together; a wee jaunt up to Scotland on the motorcycle, with the bike club. Our destination for the weekend was a little place called Dunbar, approximately twenty-eight miles east of Edinburgh. If I'm honest, I thought her very brave considering her very limited experience on the back of a motorcycle and was extremely impressed with her sense of adventure. Mungo Jerry was headlining the weekend's band line-up, which was quite entertaining, and well worth the long haul in itself.

Sally and I learnt a valuable lesson in camping etiquette that weekend. The lesson being, do not leave your torch on inside the tent at night when participating in amorous activities, as it produces the same effect as those silhouette puppet shows; only slightly less suitable for younger viewers. Oooops! The applause from the rest of the campsite on exiting the tent the following morning caught us quite by surprise. Apparently, our unintentional performance had been seen by a fair few of our fellow campers. Who'd have thought that we would be part of the weekend's entertainment line-up too?

Family Life

In the weeks and months that followed, Sally, Jack and I spent more and more time together doing the sort of things that families do and having lots of fun, and it wasn't long before Sally and I decided it was time to step things up a notch by means of co-habitation. The move to the one bedroom, second-floor flat in Islington, was not complicated logistically. Excluding my motorcycle, everything else I owned fit into one rucksack and two black bin bags.

Up until that point Sally and little Jack had been sharing the only bedroom. So with his best interests at heart, it was decided that Jack should stay put. This meant that Sally and I would have to be a little more creative at bedtime in the lounge (sleeping-wise that is), using the cushions from the sofa and armchair to construct a makeshift bed on the floor. We did this for quite a while, until eventually deciding to invest in a Futon. If I'm honest, the cushions were a lot more comfortable than the Futon, but the Futon was far more practical than putting the cushion puzzle bed together every night. Mind you, there's quite a knack to unfolding a Futon without doing yourself a serious injury, as we both found out on more than one occasion. Our nightly wrestles with the Futon proved that they can be quite an aggressive piece of furniture during the transformation process from sofa to bed, and vice versa!

With our living arrangements taken care of, the next step was to address our transportation needs. My two-wheeled mode of transport was far from ideal for three. Of course, there are some countries where you can often witness the whole family, several chickens and a goat balancing on a moped, but somehow I didn't think we'd get away with that in this country – especially not around London. I didn't want to get rid of the bike; to me it was more than just a form of transport, it was my way of life. The addition of a sidecar would have allowed for more room to balance the family, several chickens, and a goat – and one was actually purchased for the princely sum of £200. However, on closer inspection the sidecar was found to require far more extensive renovations to make it roadworthy than was originally thought. To be honest, it really wouldn't have been that practical for everyday use anyway and being the size of a small boat, the bike, which was only a 650 cc engine, would probably have really struggled with the weight of it on its own, let alone with anyone in it. With that idea out the window, it was clear that the time had come to invest in a more suitable mode of transport for everyday family use, and something that would be more suitable for Sally's driving skills. The motorcycle remained unhindered by boat-like add-ons and was clearly pleased at this outcome, and the sidecar was eventually disposed of once it had been reduced to more manageable pieces for the process of disposal.

After perusing the small ads, I found a very promising Ford Sierra in a garage just around the corner from my sister's in Kentish Town. We didn't really need such a big car but it was a decent price and in good condition for its age. It would also be more comfortable on longer journeys, for going on holidays, and with all that space inside we wouldn't have to worry about balancing the chickens or the goat – they could share the back seat with Jack.

As I was showing Jack our new car from the kitchen window, he and I decided it would be fun to play a little joke on Sally. So, when she came to the window to see our new mode of transport, we pointed to an old rusty blue Escort van. Telling her that this was our new car, I was surprised that Sally's excitement and enthusiasm was in no way dampened by the prospect of it being the rusty old van that Jack and I had just pointed to. Enthusiastically, we all went downstairs to have a closer look at our newly acquired family transport. Sally walked straight up to the old blue wreck and like a young child on Christmas morning receiving the present they'd been wishing for all year long, she began her inspection of it. To Sally's surprise Jack and I had continued past the rusty blue wreck and only stopped when we got to the shiny white Sierra parked slightly further down the road. Keeping my eyes on Sally as I opened the car door, realisation dawned and Sally's jaw dropped. Jokingly she waved her clenched fist at the both of us. I felt so mean at having teased her but Jack thought it was hilarious. I was so touched that Sally would have been pleased even if it had been the dilapidated old blue wreck. Bless her little cotton socks!

The Sierra served us well for the short time we had it. Short because the dreaded rust underneath, unseen on the day of purchase, had started to eat away at parts of the car that were just too expensive to repair. It was time to look for another car. Sally had always promised Jack that one day, when she could afford it, they would have a Mini. With that in mind, I searched the classified ads once again and went on the hunt for an appropriately priced bargain, and in no time at all we were the proud owners of a smashing little 1000 cc beige mini. Not my first choice colourwise, but you can't have everything, as they say.

After spending an extra £500 on undetected but much needed work (one of the many joys of buying second hand), the Mini turned out not to be quite the bargain I had originally thought it was. It was, however, far more practical for our everyday needs than the Sierra. Less comfortable on the longer journeys to Gloucestershire to visit Dad and down to Essex to see Sally's family than the Sierra, but it was great fun. Every journey was like being in a scene from the film, *The Italian Job*. The original film that is, with Michael 'You're only supposed to blow the bloody doors off' Caine. Not the second one with the imitation Minis produced by BMW.

Emma had left me to go off travelling and find herself. Sally had already done the travelling bit and already knew who she was. She'd lived in the mountains of India, been lost in the jungles of Thailand, swam in shark-infested waters, and escaped with her life from a maniac in Morocco. In fact, I felt quite unworldly and extremely boring in her presence. I keep telling her she should write a book.

Life continued in the little one-bedroomed second-floor flat in Islington with the usual family trials and tribulations. Life as an undertaker also had its fair share of surprises and was giving me some interesting tales to tell on those wet and windy nights.

I must stop drinking that gassy cider.

The Pitter-Patter of Tiny Feet

In the early part of '95, Sally became pregnant and as the bump grew bigger names for the new addition to our family became a subject of some importance. How hard can it be? There's certainly enough to choose from. However, when it's your child, suddenly it's not so easy. The names you think of remind you of people you know, once knew, or have heard of that you don't want your child to be like. Even if only in name.

We attended the local anti-natal clinic and were shown all manner of medieval devices that might be used to extract a baby in the eventuality of various difficulties or complications that may arise during the birth. Which, to be honest, was a far more unnerving experience than it was educationally comforting. Trips to King's College Hospital in south London on a motorcycle absent of rear suspension and with minimal seat padding, became a regular occurrence for mum and the tiny being growing inside her. When we were asked if we wanted to know the sex of the baby, we said no. Surely that's the most exciting part of it all! Finding out at the birth whether it's a boy or a girl. I'd always been led to believe that was the case. And I still do.

Zero Hour

It was 4.30 a.m., Monday, 11 September 1995, when Sally calmly woke me.

"Bill, Bill, I think the baby's coming, we need to get to the hospital."

I have never become so alert so quickly from my slumber. Luckily, Sally with some forethought, and possibly a certain amount of woman's intuition, had started to put a bag together of items she would require in hospital when this moment came.

"Don't forget the TENS machine," she called out from the bathroom.

The TENS machine had been delivered the previous day but we hadn't even taken it out of the box yet, let alone read through the instructions. Basically, it's an electrical device that if used correctly is supposed to help with pain relief by the use of electrical impulses. It looks a bit like the control unit for a model train set. It seemed like a good idea at the time when we saw the advert for it, so we ordered one.

We delivered a half-asleep Jack to the downstairs neighbour Annabelle who was a good friend of Sally's. Then, with plenty of haste and as much speed as the law would allow, like a championship rally team we sped off into the wee small hours in our little beige Mini. (Not quite so many speed cameras in those days.) Our destination was the Whittington Hospital in Archway, or Lower Highgate as some people like to call it, our designated hospital and where coincidently Jack and many of Sally's family had taken their first gasps of air outside the womb for themselves.

I'd like to say I screeched dramatically to a halt outside the entrance to the maternity unit, but being the thoughtful and safety-conscientious chap I am, it was more of a smooth positive action on the brake pedal that brought the Mini and us to a gradual halt in an allocated parking spot thoughtfully provided by the hospital for just such occasions.

Sally was settled into a room and immediately instructed me to get the TENS machine out of its so far unopened box and read the instructions. She became very impatient with me as I tried to follow the rather complex instructions whilst simultaneously fiddling with the machine as per the instructive guidelines. Her impatience soon turned to anger and doing a perfect impression of the possessed girl from the film, *The Exorcist,* she told me to 'put the bloody thing down for God's sake and just rub my thighs'. I did as instructed without question or hesitation, the thought of the consequences of any pause between the instruction being given and me carrying it out, being more than enough to cause a swift response. The rubbing of Sally's thighs was something she'd discovered helped relieve discomfort in them that she experienced during the pregnancy. I had been fully trained in the technique involved under strict supervision. Sally was also given gas and air, which was a relief not just for her but also for me. I don't think my thigh rubbing on its own was quite hitting the spot on this particular occasion.

Various medical staff came and went uttering words of comfort and encouragement – regular checks being carried out at each visit to clarify how the impending birth was progressing. At about 7 a.m. things seemed to start moving along very quickly and a decision was made to move Sally swiftly to the delivery room. Along the way I was diverted into a changing room by the midwife to put on a green gown and matching rubber clogs. I re-joined Sally and the medical staff, looking like a reject from the seventies' satirical comedy *M*A*S*H*, about a medical army unit during the Korean War. The room we now occupied was apparently not the delivery room but a room on the way to the delivery room, a slight diversion having been made on route during my departure because the baby had decided it had waited long enough and was coming out now, ready or not.

At 7.24 a.m., complete in amniotic sac – the fluid-filled sac that contains and protects the foetus in the womb that normally bursts but had not – like a cannon ball being shot from a cannon, the baby was born. I won't say effortlessly – that would probably be more than my life is worth and incorrect – but there was none of the 'I can see the head' business, or 'here comes a shoulder'. There was certainly no need for any of the medieval extraction devices we had been shown at the anti-natal sessions prior to today's big event. Thank goodness! This baby was on a mission, with a life to get on with.

It's said, sailors consider it to be lucky for a baby to be born still contained within the amniotic sac and will keep it and hang it around their neck for luck. Presumably not straight away. I imagine it would have to be dried and treated in some way before becoming an ornamental lucky charm adorning even the most rugged of sailors.

"Is it a boy or a girl?" Sally asked, exhausted.

"It's a beautiful bouncing baby girl," replied the midwife who was carrying out some initial medical checks on the new edition to the human race.

I kept a close eye on the midwife from that moment, making sure she had no inclination to check the bouncing abilities of our newborn daughter. However, I thought it wise not to aggravate the midwife by getting into a lengthy discussion about my opinions on newborn terminology, at that point in the proceedings.

I was handed my baby daughter, who bore a close resemblance to a little wrinkly blue monkey at that moment in time. But she was a beautiful little wrinkly blue monkey, and she was our little wrinkly blue monkey.

After great deliberation, when we were thinking of names for our unborn child, we had agreed if it was a girl we would call her Rosanna. So, Rosanna it was. Baby Rosanna was slightly on the small side at 5 lb 6oz, the most important information it would seem, to pass on to family and friends after whether it is a boy or a girl. Due to Rosanna's compact dimensions, Mum and baby were required to spend a few days in hospital just to make sure all was well. I was sent on my way to allow Mum and baby to rest and recover from their ordeal, having been designated the joyous task of informing family and the rest of the world of Rosanna's arrival. Something I wasted no time in doing, rousing family and the rest of the world from their sleep.

That night I took Jack out to get a pizza with quadruple extra toppings of his favourite food, olives. Strange boy. I don't think I'd ever eaten an olive until I met Sally and Jack. They're certainly an acquired taste. And so are olives! Jack wasn't over the moon that he had acquired a baby sister instead of the wished for baby brother. Hopefully he'd come around to the idea in time.

Over the next few days we visited Mum and baby in the hospital who were doing fine and would be allowed home very soon. Because Rosanna was so small they had to keep checking her blood sugar levels. To obtain the blood sample they would jab her tiny little heel with a needle to make it bleed. This made her cry, which was quite upsetting to see. What a horrible introduction to the world outside the womb. Poor little thing.

The compact beige Mini soon had to be upgraded to something slightly larger and more practical for a family of four. Or should I say, a family of four and all the accessories that are required when you have a new baby. An old but fairly well-presented royal-blue Escort estate was seemingly destined for that role and purchased at a bargain price of £900.

Rosanna

When Rosanna was about four months old she was very poorly. Limp like a rag doll, her eyes staring into nothing, we rushed her to the Whittington Hospital. The staff there were brilliant and wasted no time to find out what was wrong with our little girl. Meningitis kept being mentioned – which had been in the media a great deal recently due to a number of cases being missed and some children even dying. Scary stuff! After various tests including a rather unpleasant procedure called a lumber puncture where they extract fluid from the spine, thankfully the meningitis scare was ruled out. It turned out to be a flu-type virus, which although not very pleasant for Rosanna, was a relief to hear.

It just so happened that a heart specialist from the Royal Brompton was attending the hospital on one of his routine visits at the time Rosanna had been admitted and for some reason he had become involved in her case. During his examination of Rosanna, he discovered a slight irregularity in her heartbeat. We were told not to be too concerned and that it was probably nothing, but he would like to see her when she was a year old at the Royal Brompton for a check-up. Relieved that Rosanna's diagnosis was not anything serious, we took on board what the specialist had said and as he didn't really seem too concerned himself, we gave it little thought.

Tying the Knot

In the July of '96, Sally and I got married. Having experienced a registry office ceremony, I wanted to get married in church this time. Sally also preferred the idea of a church wedding. The vicar of our local church was away in America at the time but the churchwarden said if we could supply our own minister, he could see no problem. Well, I certainly knew a few vicars by that time and I knew exactly who I was going to ask to perform the ceremony. Father Paul, from St Pancras Old Church.

Because I'd been married before, some churches would not have permitted me a church ceremony. However, so I was informed, they can't refuse use of your parish church if you have a minister that will perform the marriage. Father Paul saw no reason for me to be ostracised from having a church wedding because things had not worked out for me in the past. After all, as he said, 'Isn't the Christian faith all about forgiveness and new beginnings?'

The wedding was a small affair, partly because Sally's mum was very ill at the time and couldn't have coped well with a lot of hustle and bustle. Sally and I had also agreed that that's the way we both wanted it to be. No problems with a badly fitting suit this time, being half Scottish I decided to wear a kilt, and Sally looked lovely in her favourite summer dress, which was a beautiful bright floral design. Jack also wore a kilt, although I don't think he was very pleased with the idea. Rosanna, whose name had now been shortened to Rosie, at ten months old, in a little red and white spotty number, easily stole the show. Just slightly outdoing Wez, my best man, with his bright red Mohican hairstyle.

The wedding could be described as a little unorthodox. Old Burt kindly let me use his Daimler limousine, and I drove Sally, Jack and Rosie to the church. After the ceremony we went back to Lesley's for drinks and nibbles. Mum, bless her, made us a very impressive three-tier wedding cake. It was strange to see Mum and Dad in the same panoramic view after all these years, but Dad didn't come back to Lesley's after the church. Which was understandable, I suppose, and probably for the best.

THE POINTY END

With eight branches of Mortimer and Sons to work between, our days were often quite hectic. We were used to running around like headless chickens and had become rather adept at doing impressions of blue-arsed flies. It could be a real juggling act to get everything done on time, with funerals to attend, workshop duties to complete, vehicles to clean, bodies to dress and box up and removals to carry out. Nevertheless, this was done with the decorum that you would expect from a well-respected independent funeral directors. We were very much like the graceful swan gliding effortlessly and gracefully across the water. Of course, a peak under the surface would reveal legs and webbed feet that were frantically going ten to the dozen as they propelled the graceful image above.

As with most jobs, if you've not been directly involved in its day-to-day goings-on, then you'll have little or no knowledge of what the job actually entails, what goes on behind the scenes, or which is the most challenging part of the job. The funeral business is no exception.

Out of all aspects of the funeral business, the least known about part and definitely one of the most challenging, is the removals. And it's fair to say that they could also be the most gruesome. Removals, either planned or unplanned, had to be achieved by working them in and around the day's funerals and our mandatory day-to-day duties. Not the easiest of tasks, and at times a logistical nightmare. Fortunately for my colleagues and me, the responsibility for this planning fell to Mr Carter, the office manager, as it was his job to organise the day's diary. At times he must have felt as though he were playing Tetris with time – trying to redeploy staff in order to make sure that the right people were in the right place, at the right time. A task which didn't always make him very popular, and due to added pressure on us, we were often in conflict with Mr Carter and his reshuffling of personnel.

To give you a bit more insight into how difficult our job could be, I need to explain how it all worked, in a little more detail. Planned removals were easier as they could usually be scheduled in without too much disruption. However, unplanned removals meant we could be called upon at any time, without much warning. In the daytime, fitting in any unplanned removals was a bit of a test as we were often restricted by other people's schedules. For example, the police, forensic scientists, the coroners, hospital and care-home timetables, and of course, the bereaved – who often, and understandably would not always be concerned with the passing of time.

Due to the nature of their work, it was essential that coroners' removals were carried out with as little delay as possible. Not only to preserve important evidence and possible crime scenes but because they often involved the removal of a body from a rather precarious or unorthodox location within the public domain.

And then there were the out-of-hours removals, carried out by the duty squad, who in addition to their normal working week, were responsible for removals during the hours of 5.15 p.m. until 8.30 a.m., seven days running, from Monday to the following Monday. The duty squad was usually a team of three and their purpose was to facilitate any after-hours removals, church take-ins, airport runs, or indeed any other duties that fell outside of the working day.

A coroner's removal would always be taken to the coroner's mortuary, day or night. Other out of hours removals, i.e., hospitals, care homes, private homes, etc., would usually be taken to the yard mortuary or possibly to one of the other branches' mortuaries, where they would stay until the necessary arrangements could be made the following day.

When it came to removals, the vans were the preferred mode of transport. Ideally, we didn't want to draw too much attention to ourselves. A van driving through hospital grounds, parked outside a nursing home, or on someone's private driveway, was slightly more subtle than a big black Daimler hearse. However, on the occasions when a van wasn't available and a removal had to be done as soon as possible, we would use a hearse, but only as a last resort. That said, despite all our efforts to be as discreet as possible, three men in black suits in a van can be a bit of a giveaway as to their profession and the task they are probably carrying out. After all, I'd say it was fairly obvious that we weren't there to deliver a washing machine. Well, unless you'd ordered it from Harrods, perhaps?

If a removal had to be carried out in between funerals and time constraints didn't allow a trip back to the yard to collect a van, obviously we would have no choice but to use a hearse. The reality of the undertaking world is that you can only do so much to keep a low profile. Our main priority was always to be as respectful and as low key as we possibly could, in often rather difficult circumstances.

Some undertakers have the words 'Private Ambulance' displayed on their vehicles. Personally I've always thought this rather odd. It may be a private vehicle but the word ambulance seems a little inappropriate and not a very accurate description of an undertaker's vehicle. Perhaps it's their subtle way of alerting people as to their purpose, like the police or traffic wardens, if they were parked somewhere they shouldn't be whilst in the process of carrying out their professional duties. Although, in my personal experience, traffic wardens don't generally care who you are or what you're doing, they just give you a ticket anyway. On one occasion we had a traffic warden issue a parking ticket on a hearse that was parked outside one of the branches, as we were carrying the coffin out to load up. I kid you not!

The other reason the vans were more practical to use for removals than a hearse, was the number of passengers that they could carry. You could get five bodies in the back of a van by using a combination of shells and stretchers strategically positioned, as opposed to two on a hearse – one on top of the bier, and one below. The only problem space-wise with the vans, was the seating for the two live occupants on the unsuitably described two-seater passenger section in the front (as mentioned earlier in the book). Vans were also more suited to off-road situations. A trip over Hampstead Heath to collect someone who had decided to end it all by hanging themselves from a convenient tree, was not as rare an occasion as you might think. An excursion that could be extremely difficult in one of the large, heavy, low-slung hearses with their minimal ground clearance and soft suspension. In fact, it was often a bit of a struggle in a van – a 4x4 would have been a far better option at such times.

Removal Equipment

With the development and use of lightweight, fold-up stretchers and wheelie stretchers, the job of an undertaker was a great deal more manageable than it used to be. The lightweight, fold-up stretchers were an absolute blessing in environments where space was limited and complex manoeuvres were required. The wheelie stretchers really came into their own when visiting hospitals and were particularly useful when having to negotiate an endless maze of corridors or cover an extensive distance.

There really was no comparison between the versatility of modern stretchers to the coffin shells that were once the only options available. Of course, there were a few occasions where the shells were still used, but this was usually only if the stretchers were not available. Whenever we did have to use a shell, it was often rather a precarious operation and it certainly made us appreciate our newer technology. It's fair to say that we were all very grateful that we didn't have to use the shells all of the time, and we had a huge amount of respect for our predecessors and elders still in the trade who once had no choice.

During my time as an undertaker, when collecting bodies that were infectious, some hospitals and hospices insisted on the use of a shell, the reason being, that there was a much lower risk of body fluids escaping from the more enclosed structure. It was a policy we agreed with wholeheartedly and tried on many occasions to convince those establishments that didn't have such a policy at the time, to put one in place. Shells were also handy for use during busy periods, in order to store bodies in the cold room if there were no fridge spaces available.

Eventually, I developed the knack of the collapsible stretchers and their wicked and wily ways, only periodically doing myself an injury when not focusing properly on the complex and intricate procedure involved in their correct operation.

PPE

When it came to removals, the most essential Personal Protective Equipment or PPE for short, was a pair of rubber gloves – or two pairs in the case of a badly decomposed body. In the earlier days of my undertaking career the gloves that we were issued with had a powdery content inside. This was a useful addition when putting them on, especially if you had sweaty hands, but not so great when you removed them if you were wearing a black suit. Fortunately, after much pleading with the powers that be, we were issued with the powderless variety which didn't leave copious amounts of white powder over anything which we happened to be wearing. These were much better and prevented us from looking as though we'd been rolling around on the floor in a bakery.

On the more unpleasant and messier removals, as well as our two pairs of gloves, we were also given more substantial PPE. This included: disposable white over-suits, blue overshoes, and polystyrene face masks. These items were kept in the 'disaster bag' – as we called it – and there was one on each van. Or at least, there was supposed to be one on each van. The over-suits supplied were purchased on a one-size-fits-all principle, but invariably didn't. Sometimes it could be quite comical watching one of the larger staff members trying to squeeze into an over-suit that was way too small. As it was in reverse, when one of the smaller staff members was wearing one that was far too big.

Hospitals

As a species we have, without a doubt, completely mastered the art of over complicating the world we live in, often turning the simplest of tasks into a full-length drama. It's almost as though we enjoy being confused. Technology, as wonderful as it may be in many ways, has undoubtedly contributed to this complexity, but mostly, I believe it is mankind's incessant obsession to make things harder than they really need to be. If the answer is simple, for some reason we seem to doubt it's correct. When it comes to removals, collecting bodies from hospitals is a prime example of this innate Homosapien talent.

In London, the hospitals are like pubs. And when I say that, I don't mean they are full of inebriated people – although for many hospital A & E departments, particularly at the weekend, that may be a fair comparison. What I mean is, there's literally one on every street corner, and quite often one in between as well. This not only produces a great deal of career opportunities for medical professionals, but also inevitably, due to the law of averages and nature being what it is, also generates a great deal of work for the funeral business. I think it's fair to say that we spent a great deal of our time during the day, and the night, travelling to and from various local hospitals – as well as a few that weren't so local – collecting those that had passed away whilst in their care.

As an undertaker I discovered very early in my career, the second day in actual fact, that collecting a body or multiple bodies from a hospital was rarely a simple or straightforward affair. The general layout of the majority of hospitals, as most of us will have discovered at some point in our life, is usually far from user friendly and a challenge for even the most accomplished orienteer. Even when, or should I say, especially when, following the directional signs put in place that are allegedly there to help you find your destination.

The location of a hospital's mortuary is undeniably one of its most closely guarded secrets. Usually, and with only a few exceptions that I can think of, it is located in one of two places, either deep within the darkest depths of the hospital's foundations, or miles away from the main building in some desolate spot in the far-flung reaches of the hospital grounds. Each location presenting its own challenges to overcome in order to gain access, like Indiana Jones and Miss Croft, our quest was often a long and arduous one thwart with dangers, mythical creatures, cryptic clues, and villains that would stop at nothing to throw us off the scent to prevent us from achieving our objective. Well, maybe not quite that elaborate, but there were certainly numerous physical and mental challenges to delay and distract us from our purposeful undertaking.

The first of the two possible locations mentioned for the hospital mortuary – deep in the darkest depths of the hospital's foundations – was usually accessed via an underground car park or by the use of a lift. On some occasions, it could be both. Some of the lifts we had to use, I'm fairly certain pre-dated the Roman occupation and would have been condemned in any other working environment. The adventure of the lift would often be followed by an epic journey through labyrinths of endless narrow, winding corridors. Dimly lit and adorned with a mass of tangled wiring, puzzling pipework and humming air conditioning duct, the route to the mortuary often felt like we were heading towards the earth's core. In addition, there were often ramps with gradients that would test the fittest and strongest of Olympian athletes when in control of a laden wheelie stretcher, let alone a rabble of unfit, decrepit undertakers, afflicted with irritable bowel syndrome, dodgy knees, sciatica, heart conditions and various other ailments that usually accompany those affected by the ravages of time, and who often neglect to do what you should or shouldn't do in order to maintain good health.

The second most popular location of a hospital mortuary, although above ground, wasn't any easier to find and generally demanded the orienteering skills of an aboriginal tracker to locate it. Usually situated as far away from the main building as possible, it would invariably sit disguised as an obsolete and unimportant outbuilding. A number of dummy buildings would often be erected willy-nilly around it to throw us off the scent and send us on various time-consuming and unsuccessful detours.

Fortunately, as time went on, I learnt that on many occasions a fairly reliable guide to the mortuary's whereabouts – above ground – would often be to look for the building with the tall chimneys, which I believe belonged to the incinerators. This theory was supported by the fact that the tall chimneys would regularly be used as a landmark by individuals we asked for directions, of whom we suspected were hospital staff and privy to such information. In an effort to remain as inconspicuous as possible, directions were only sought once all other options were exhausted and after circling the hospital's one-way system at least three times.

I can only presume that the reasoning behind such obscure locations for the hospitals' mortuary is not just to make life as hard as possible for undertakers, which it consistently does, very successfully, but to try and keep death under wraps and attempt to avoid distressing patients or visitors unnecessarily, by its and our presence. Fair enough I suppose, and quite thoughtful if that is indeed the reasoning behind it all. However, this cunning and well-intentioned plan, if indeed it ever is actually planned, invariably means that undertakers have to drive their vans – or on occasion, a hearse – around the hospital grounds several times thus completely defeating that objective. It's like being on the Grim Reaper's version of a merry-go-round.

Once we had located the hospital mortuary, our next challenge was to gain entry. This would usually be achieved via the use of an intercom system, a bell, or a good old-fashioned bang on the door. However, if our efforts to gain entry through any of these methods failed, we would have to resort to seeking out either the mortuary technician or a hospital porter. Both were usually contactable using a phone conveniently provided for that very purpose positioned nearby, searching out the nearest occupied office and asking them if they would be kind enough to contact the bereavement officer or a member of the mortuary staff on our behalf, or thanks to technological advancement, by using a mobile phone in our possession.

The first exchange of communication would always involve finding out if the required paperwork was in the possession of the mortician, or whether we needed to collect it from elsewhere. Unfortunately, the answer more often than not would be 'No', they didn't have it, and 'Yes', it did require collecting from elsewhere. You could almost guarantee that wherever the mortuary was located, in or around the hospital, the bereavement office – which is where you usually have to go for the required paperwork – would be at the furthest point within the hospital grounds from where you were. This would raise the question, yet again, about the level of thought and planning that had gone into the whole keeping death under wraps scenario. A conversation which my colleagues and I would often engage in as we hiked around the compounds of the hospital in search of the paperwork. Logistically, more often than not, we could not have been made to cover more ground from start to finish, by vehicle or on foot, in and around the hospital if they had tried. Probably being seen by most of the hospital staff and its patients. A rather unnerving vision in the circumstances, I would have thought.

Once at the bereavement office, the illusive lesser-spotted bereavement officer would rarely be found within it. I know how busy hospitals can be, and that it's quite conceivable that the bereavement officer had other duties to attend to in other parts of the hospital – and possibly even more than one role – but it was extremely rare for them to actually be found in the bereavement office. Following written instructions strategically placed on the locked office door, to try and contact the bereavement officer via phone or by getting them paged was usually the next step in the quest. It's fair to say that generally there was a great deal of waiting around for either paperwork or people as an undertaker, but never more so than when you were in a hospital.

Once the bereavement officer appeared, there was usually a polite exchange of pleasantries followed by the trading of monetary funds for the paperwork. Unless, that is, the documentation wasn't completed, in which case you would have to wait while the relevant doctor was contacted. If we were lucky, they would be on duty in the hospital. If not, another trip back to the hospital for the paperwork may be required.

Masters of Disguise

Of course, it wasn't always about the mortuary not standing out; at times we were the ones required to blend in and go unnoticed. I can remember at one rather posh hospital in the West End, we were expected to put on white coats and cover the wheelie trolley with a white sheet. The subterfuge was a somewhat bizarre plan that was supposed to enable us to blend in more within the hospital environment. Interestingly, it wasn't at the hospital's request that we adorned such attire; that honour was held by one of our newest managers – Mr Haughton. If I'm honest, it all seemed a bit pointless, as most of the time when there we would go directly to the mortuary and the only people we actually came into contact with were the porters – and we certainly weren't fooling them with our cunning disguise.

On rare occasions, we were asked to collect the deceased directly from the hospital ward. I personally felt that this was quite insensitive, as did many of my colleagues. It seemed strange that the hospital porters hadn't taken the deceased to the mortuary or at least somewhere a little more private so that we could collect them without our presence being quite so noticeable. But ours was not to reason why, as they say, ours was just to collect those who'd died, and if we were required to go onto the ward, I could see that the white-coat scenario might be a good idea and a little less alarming than three men in black suits.

It's amazing how by putting a simple white coat on, a person's whole outlook can change. Especially, when in a hospital. Suddenly you feel a great deal more important to humanity and it's very easy to get ideas above your station. I can only imagine how the added accessory of a stethoscope draped around your neck must feel.

A Bag for Death

According to Marcus, when handling the dead, the same level of caution should be maintained at all times. The reason being, that no matter what the cause of death might have been, there's always a chance that potentially harmful bacteria may have developed, or an undetected viral infection unrelated to the cause of death may be present. Therefore, it made sense to take the appropriate safety precautions at all times. It's better to be safe rather than sorry, as the saying goes.

When I first started with Mortimer and Sons back in '93, different hospitals had different ways of treating the bodies when placed in cold storage. Some covered or wrapped them in sheets, some left them in those rather badly designed hospital gowns that never seem to fit properly, exposing a person's derriere, and some even used a plastic version of those awful gowns. More often than not, the bodies would be *au naturel*. One of the main issues with transporting bodies in any of these circumstances, is the possibility of having to deal with the leakage of body fluids. Plastic sheeting wrapped around the bodies was an essential part of our PPE and generally quite effective in most cases.

In the early days, we only used body bags when dealing with decomposed bodies or highly infectious cases. Hospitals and hospices would generally use them where the deceased had died of a highly infectious disease, but increasingly they became more the norm due to their practical nature. Using a body bag is far more hygienic, and generally, because of the extra support, it's also much easier to move the deceased in a gentler, more controlled, and respectful way. Body bags can be particularly useful in cases where there is excessive leakage of body fluids, but there is also a downside. By containing these fluids, in extreme cases, it can often mean that the deceased literally ends up marinating in their own urine and blood. Not a very pleasant thought. Having to deal with a large amount of body fluid when opening a body bag is never going to be easy and can get quite messy.

Some hospitals were able to overcome this problem quite easily by using large amounts of wadding or cotton wool to soak up the fluid, whilst others didn't seem to make a great deal of effort to resolve the issue at all, and no amount of moaning or complaining from us at the pointy end or from the powers that be at head office, seemed to make any difference. In general, using body bags is an advantage, but sometimes the build-up of fluids is so excessive that it can seep through the cloth part of the zip. If we knew we were going to one of the hospitals that seemed unable to deal with the problem, extra plastic wrapped around the body bag was often a wise move.

However, that didn't always help and a good hose down of the vans and stretchers was often needed on our return to the yard. Not to be mistaken for 'A Good Hoe Down', which I'm fairly sure would probably have been totally inappropriate altogether.

During the nineties we saw an increase in AIDS-related deaths, which was a bit of a concern. At that time there were many misconceptions – due to the lack of knowledge and information available – about how it was contracted and also about how infectious it could be even after death. Patient confidentiality meant we were often given limited information, if any, about the cause of death, or even if the body was infectious. Such information might only come to light after we had already been in contact with the body. Which only goes to support Marcus's point that all bodies should be treated as potentially harmful when first dealing with them.

The right to patient confidentiality is fair enough, but surely people on the frontline who are putting themselves at risk every day also have a right to know what they are dealing with, in order to keep themselves and their families safe. Fortunately, a nod and a wink from a considerate mortician along with a remark to be extra careful was always understood and greatly appreciated. That said, some morticians were more helpful than others. Hopefully, things are more transparent today.

Dr Who?

One of the strangest removals that I ever attended was one where Eamon, Oliver, Dean and I were sent to a hospital for tropical diseases in Muswell Hill. As it turned out we were there to collect someone who had died from a rather nasty virus, known widely around the world, called Ebola. Not to be mistaken for tombola, which is a very different thing altogether. Tombola victims often suffer more from disappointment, rather than serious illness or death.

On arrival at the hospital, we were directed to the rear of the building, as was often the case, towards a small outbuilding away from the main hospital (presumably one of the dummy mortuaries).

Awaiting our arrival was a hospital porter who was standing under a gazebo-type structure erected next to the outbuilding. As we got suited and booted into our white protective over-suits, over-boots, masks and two pairs of rubber gloves, it dawned on me that this was going to be far from an ordinary removal. Resembling extras from a sci-fi movie, we continued with the task in hand.

Due to the nature of their death, the coffin that was to hold the remains of the Ebola victim was zinc lined. (This was achieved by the use of a thin zinc coffin-shaped insert that was placed into the main coffin, which for safety and strength was usually made of solid wood, as it was in the case of the Ebola victim. In the lid of the zinc lining, at the head end, there is usually a window which enables the deceased's face to be seen, unless the face is covered or if a body bag has been used, of course.)

Once the double-bagged body had been placed into the zinc-lined coffin, it was taken out of the hospital mortuary and positioned underneath the gazebo away from the main building ready for us to seal it down. I'm not really sure why we had to perform the sealing down process outside rather than inside the mortuary – perhaps it was something to do with Eamon's explosive equipment. His soldering equipment, that is! Blow torch in hand, Eamon carefully melted copious amounts of solder into every inch of the gap between the zinc lid and the zinc lining. It had to be completely air tight. Not so much to keep the air out, but to keep the Ebola virus in.

Eamon was meticulous and efficient in all he did – he was a jack of all trades and master of many. He was like a human dynamo. A man with half a stomach and a full set of false teeth by the age of nineteen (the teeth removal occurring in an effort to avoid further trips to the dentist in later life, apparently). He was a man who made his own bread and who would have at least half an inch worth of butter in a sandwich with no other filling. A man who was to shelving design and construction, as Geppetto was to puppet-making. Teetotal all his life, and proud of it, Eamon was a man who did not require the use of an alcoholic beverage to let his hair down – if he'd had any, that is. A true family man, he seemed to enjoy life with great enthusiasm and was always the life and soul of any work parties or outings. As a foreman, he was fair and cared about our wellbeing, managing to keep us all on track at the yard, encouraging us to move in the right direction, and all without losing his cool (most of the time, anyway). Riding his trusty Honda C90 through hell or high water to get to work, he was a man for whom I have nothing but admiration.

With the zinc-lined coffin well and truly hermetically sealed and the body secured within the solid oak coffin, our protective clothing was safely placed into clinical waste bags ready for incineration. Driving back to the yard with the human remains and its deadly visitor, we watched the hustle and bustle of people going about their daily lives around us, obliviously safe from our potentially deadly cargo.

The Fragility of Life

In London there are a large number of specialist children's hospitals. This inevitably meant that we were involved a great deal more than we would have wanted to be with the funerals of the young. Heart-wrenching, it was without a doubt the worst part of the job, as no matter how hard you try, there can be no satisfactory reasoning or way to understanding the loss of a baby or child. Life can be so resilient but in the same breath it can also be so fragile. Nature in all its wonder and incredible complexity, can sometimes seem so cruel and callous. But no more so than when a child is taken from its parents.

The reality of holding a lifeless baby or child in your arms, even if it is not your own, is heartbreaking. Nothing anyone can say or do can make any sense of it or ease the pain of others. As an undertaker, the sad reality was that all we could really do was to try and support those who had lost their child as best we could, and hope and pray that we never had to experience that pain for ourselves.

NVF

It's sad to say that death can occur even before a child is born. I'd only been with Mortimer and Sons for a couple of weeks when Joe and I were sent to collect two adults and a NVF from one of our local hospitals. (NVF is the abbreviation for a Non-Viable-Foetus.) My ignorance of foetal development, meant all I'd expected to see was a blob of jelly, possibly with some small signs of it starting to develop into something more. It's fair to say that I could not have been more mistaken or more shocked with what I saw when we had to check the contents of the A4-sized body bag.

Inside one of the smallest body bags I had ever seen, lay a twenty-week-old, tiny little human. Like a lifeless doll its miniature hands and feet were perfectly formed. What really shocked me was not my ignorance about the stages of development of a foetus, but the fact that at twenty-four weeks it was still legal to terminate the life of such a developed human being. I later learnt, that at twelve weeks old, a foetus has fingerprints, its own personal identity, it's unique individuality. At twenty-one weeks, babies born prematurely have survived and gone on to grow into healthy children. These babies were younger than some of the NVF's we were being asked to collect and bury or cremate. It was an extremely thought-provoking experience.

Hospices

As well as hospitals, there were a number of hospices that we regularly attended. Our visits to these were very different to the lengthy and often complex expedition that occurred at most hospitals. There was a strange sense of peace that seemed to emanate from hospices and from their staff. It was as if the chaos and rushing about had turned to calm and the fear of not knowing had turned to a peaceful acceptance of the inevitable. That may not always be the case, of course, or true for everyone's experience, but it was the feeling I got when I visited such places. The care that is given, and the power of love that breaks through the sadness, is quite overwhelming. Not that the same level of care and love is not to be found in hospitals amidst all the hustle and bustle – far from it. Hospitals and hospices are very different in many ways, I suppose.

The hospices in London were generally quite modern purpose-built buildings. Not all, but it's fair to say that most of the ones we went to were. They were also typically quite easy places to find, with good access. Hospice removals were ordinarily the easiest of all removals in every way and usually required the least physical exertion. With this in mind, it's understandable why volunteers were never in short supply when Eamon needed a crew to go to a hospice. Removals from hospices were generally done during the day. Rarely were we called out in the middle of the night to a hospice, as most would have their own mortuary, albeit typically quite a small one.

Care Homes

In my capacity as an undertaker, visits to care homes were frequent. Many were large old houses that had probably been quite grand in their day. Since then, these had been converted into homes to care for our aging and sickly population, a decision that had been rather lucrative for their owners, from what I gather. Even some of the smaller care homes were like rabbit warrens, with a bedroom squeezed in at every turn to ensure maximum occupancy. The lifts in these places, if fitted, were usually extremely small and of little use for our needs, meaning the fold-up stretcher was an absolute godsend. The more modern purpose-built establishments were generally much easier to get around. It actually seemed like a bit of thought had gone into their construction and a decent-sized lift was usually installed, though rarely were they large enough to accommodate a wheelie stretcher.

In all fairness, I suppose what really makes a good care home, above anything else, is the quality of the care, not the layout of the building or how grand the décor might be. Saying that, there were a few places we went to where the cleanliness of the building and quality of the care was definitely questionable. Places that I wouldn't have let care for my cat or dog for a few minutes, let alone a relative of mine for the rest of their life.

A residence full of old people with dementia is always going to be a recipe for some comical happenings, that's for sure. One of the funniest moments I can remember, as an undertaker, was the time when the old lady was giving me a bear hug and wouldn't let go until she was tempted away with some biscuits and the promise of her favourite Des O'Conner CD being played. At the time, I felt quite helpless and didn't have a clue what to do, much to the amusement of my colleagues. Thank goodness for Des O'Conner and biscuits. On the other hand, there always seemed to be an old woman sat next to the front door asking if we were the taxi she had ordered to take her home, or who thought one of us was her son or her dead husband come to visit. It was quite sad to see the disappointment on their faces, as they returned a watchful eye to the door. It was also quite common to have one of the more able residents hovering around the front door, slyly waiting for an opportune moment to make a dash for it, if the door was left open long enough.

When it came to explaining why we were actually there to any of the residents, there was rarely any attempt by the staff to cover up who we were or what we were there to do. There was no creeping about via secret passages or dressing up as doctors or plumbers. On some occasions, we would even be guided through the communal lounge to exit the building with the recently departed resting on the stretcher, as the other residents and staff sat sipping or slurping their cups of tea and eating various pureed delights. Although, in many situations, that may well have been more down to the architectural layout of some of the buildings rather than anything else. Many of the residents with severe dementia would probably have been oblivious to our true identity and of what we were up to. That said, some of the more compos mentis residents who were more aware and accepting of nature's way, would often bid their old companion a fond farewell with an added 'See ya later, ducks' thrown in for good measure.

Enlightened

Haunted by unpleasant childhood memories of my nan in a care home, I always found them quite sad and depressing places; old people locked away vegetating – just waiting to die – in what always seemed such an unnatural and institutionalised environment. It's only really now, having experienced first-hand the need for 24/7 medical care for both Mum and Dad, that I truly appreciate how important these places are and how dedicated the staff are to looking after those in their care. Neither my sister nor I could have provided the level of care that either of our parents needed. It was a tough call at the time and not really what either of us would have wanted. If there had been any other viable options I'm sure we would have chosen them, but unfortunately there wasn't.

It was Mum who needed full-time care first, as after having had several serious strokes, she was bed bound and had severe dementia. The true tragedy being that during the last couple of years of her life, when visiting her in the home, we didn't even know if she was aware we were in the room. After being such a vibrant, lively soul most of her life, even in the earlier years of illness, it was so sad to see her reduced to such a joyless, unanimated existence. In later years Dad also required nursing-home care after he was diagnosed with Parkinson's and dementia. Trying to retain some level of normality for him during the four years he was in the home, thanks to the care that he received that kept him as well as he could be, we were still able to take him out regularly. When the weather was nice, we would drive to a nice country pub, and Dad was able to attend various family get-togethers, including Christmas and birthdays. Our main port of call on our excursions, which were at least once or twice a week, was the 'Cotswold Inn' public house, where Dad had been a regular for the last fifty years of his life. On a good day he could still manage to down a couple of refreshing pints of IPA, his favourite alcoholic beverage. The 'Cotswold' also held many wonderful memories for us, spending time with Dad as a family, and the regulars at the pub, as you can imagine, were like Dad's extended family. It was the one place where he really seemed to be settled, and be more like the man he once was. At least for a time.

Both Mum and Dad, as they suffered with their respective illnesses, could often display quite challenging behaviour. At times they could each be quite a handful and they certainly gave their carers at the nursing homes a run for their money. Mum particularly so – as one of the front door hoverers – with a number of quite daring escape attempts, before she was sadly confined to her bed towards the end of her life. She did manage one successful dash for freedom that luckily and quite bizarrely coincided with a visit we were making to the home and I spotted her happily walking up the road in her nightie. We couldn't believe it!

Eeny Meeny Miny Moe

A very high percentage of our nursing-home removals were carried out during the night by the duty squad on call. Death obviously had some logistical reason for this particular time preference, the reasoning of which I can only surmise. Perhaps Death has a day job to earn a little extra cash.

One particular balmy summer's night, Joe, Eddie and I were sent to a nursing home in Muswell Hill. I say night, but it was actually about 3 a.m. if I remember correctly. It was a grand old building that had once probably been home to a very well-to-do family. Alerting the staff to our arrival by ringing the bell, we waited patiently to be let in. After a rather lengthy wait, through a narrow panel of coloured glass in the solid oak door (I was getting to know my timber by that point), we could just about make out a small figure wrestling with the lock and security chain on the other side of the door. Once opened, a short Asian lady beckoned us inside hurriedly. We entered the large expanse of hallway in the once grand house that now showed signs of institutional décor, and displayed signs alerting visitors to the various amenities, events and fire exits.

Standing in front of a huge decorative dark-wood staircase that itself stood in the centre of the vast area of the hallway, we waited expectantly for our instructions, looking just like three new boys at Hogwarts. Our seemingly rushed host closing the door behind us, pointed towards another door on our right.

"She in there, you go, I busy," and with those very brief instructions still echoing around the corridors, off she scurried up the grand old staircase into the shadows and out of sight.

It wasn't unusual to be met at the entrance to such an establishment, shown to where the deceased was and then be left to our own devices.

With so few staff trying to deal with goodness knows how many residents and however many chores they were allocated to carry out through the night, it couldn't have been easy.

So, as instructed, we ventured forth through the door on our right and into the room where the deceased apparently lay. On entering the large high-ceilinged room with its ornate cornice and massive gold-framed wall-mounted mirror, we were faced with not one bed, but four. Each bed contained an old lady, who to be honest, at first glance didn't appear to have a great deal of life in them, or in fact to be breathing. This caused us somewhat of a dilemma. We felt it would have been inappropriate for us to go wandering around the premises unattended to search for our host, even though in theory the three of us were already doing just that. Having ruled out the 'Eeny-meeny-miny-moe' technique due to its marginally unscientific nature, we instead opted for 'the one who is breathing the least' technique, carefully listening to each one of the candidates for signs of breathing while simultaneously watching for chest movement. Two fairly reliable signs of life.

Unfortunately, this method of detection only ruled out two of the four women, so further tests were required on the remaining two. Trying not to disturb the sleeping candidates for fear of giving the living a heart attack, I asked if anyone had a mirror on them to do the mirror mist test. (Even the slightest breath will create a mist on the mirror.) I ignored the sarcastic replies from my colleagues which I suppose I justly deserved. The huge, gold-framed mirror on the wall was obviously out of the question. For a start we didn't have any tools to remove it from the wall and the risk of dropping it on top of one of the slumbering ladies while trying to get a result was far too high and only asking for trouble. I'm not serious, of course. You really should know me by now.

It was at this point that the carer reappeared. Surprised to see us still on the premises and standing in the middle of the room doing nothing, she questioned our presence in the same hurried manner that we had been greeted with on our arrival. Sheepishly, we tried to explain our predicament. She didn't seem impressed. Walking over to the bed nearest the window, appearing quite annoyed, she pointed accusingly at the old lady that lay beneath its floral design bed covers.

"She here, you take," the rather annoyed carer exclaimed.

Our predicament resolved, we removed the deceased from the premises as swiftly and respectfully as we could and went on our way. And you'll be pleased to know, that none of the other ladies was disturbed in any way or woke during the process of removing their roommate.

Looking back, and in our defence, the room was extremely dark and all four ladies were doing an amazing impression of someone who was no longer with us in spirit. Although, technically, one wasn't actually doing an impression and therefore had an advantage over the others. I've been told that even medically-trained professionals can have problems detecting signs of life sometimes. So what chance did we have?

I would of course like to put to rest any concerns for those of you who think we would have even considered the 'Eeny-meeny-miny-mo' technique. Or that we would have continued in our endeavours and just chosen the most likely candidate, without searching for a member of staff to assist in our enquiries and clarify the identity of the lady in question.

Moving on…

Stuck in the Mud

On another occasion, during one stormy autumn night, somewhere around midnight, Oliver, Eddie and I were called out to a nursing home in Hendon. The nursing home was one we hadn't visited before, but Oliver said he was fairly sure he knew where it was – famous last words. Once we'd loaded up the van with the necessary equipment and received the removal details from head office, we headed out into the cold, wet, blustery night. It was my turn to drive, and clutching the pink card tightly in his hand Eddie was in charge of the communication side of things. Oliver, 'fairly certain he knew the location of the nursing home', was navigating.

I followed Oliver's instructions without question or hesitation, confident in his abilities to get us to the nursing home safely. It was only when he told me to head down what appeared to be a single-track road after our deviation from the main road, that I began to suspect that Oliver's knowledge might not be quite as reliable as first hoped. Convincing me that I should have more faith in his navigational abilities, I drove on. A short distance later the single-track road became narrower and narrower and eventually turned into what would best be described as a wide, slightly overgrown footpath, the van's mirrors clipping the foliage on either side. By now my faith in Oliver's knowledge of the whereabouts of the nursing home was dwindling rapidly, and by the look on Eddie's face, he also had his doubts.

Oliver was a product of our public-school education system, though there were no outward signs of any permanent damage and generally he appeared quite normal. The education he received meant that he was quite a clever chap, however, his proudest achievement – learnt at great expense to his parents during his time with the toffs – seemed to be having mastered the art of setting light to his farts. His other half, Sue, also a product of public-school education, by all accounts, had also mastered the same conversation-stopping skill. They were obviously a match made in heaven and a godsend at any social function if the entertainment failed to show up.

Oliver continued to insist with increasing animation that he knew where we were and that he was sure we were heading in the right direction, and therefore we should carry on. As neither Eddie nor I had a clue where the nursing home was, we had little choice but to put our faith in Oliver's alleged knowledge of the geographical location of the nursing home and continued our search for it under his guidance, albeit with a smaller amount of trust and with a slightly larger amount of trepidation than before.

As we continued with our drive, the overgrown path widened giving way to an expanse of grass which was surrounded on all sides by residential dwellings. Apart from the newly present Mortimer and Sons grey van, the grassy area contained an excellent section of grass for ball games and a small, enclosed playground. Numerous signs forbidding ball games were dotted around the inviting ball-game area, obviously aimed at the rebellious that may have been tempted to partake in such anti-social activities.

As we looked around, it became apparent that the only exit from this oasis in a concrete jungle was back the way we had come. Due to the incessant rain the area of ground the van was occupying was extremely waterlogged and as I tried to manoeuvre our way back to civilisation the van became stuck in the mud. The subsequent commotion we caused as we tried to free the van from its captive quagmire started to draw attention to our plight. Lights began to illuminate the surrounding dwellings, curtains twitched and curious faces appeared at the windows in time to watch a comical display of three men's futile battle against the elements.

The ensuing performance included advice from Oliver and Eddie about high revs, gears and clutch control. Uncontrollable laughter from them as they saw how stressed I was becoming did not help the situation and a self-styled monologue which included an assertion that 'Now was not the time', and an insistence that they should try and be more helpful, was frustratingly aimed in their general direction.

The second act in the performance included Oliver and Eddie scrambling over each other to get the van door open as quickly as possible, as though they were trying to escape a psychopathic killer. During this hasty exit from the vehicle, they informed me that they were going to try and help resolve our predicament by pushing down on the front of the van. The theory being, that action, if timed correctly in conjunction with my efforts to engage movement of the van, would hopefully assist in the wheels being able to gain traction.

Positioning themselves at the front of the van they placed their hands on the bonnet, their smirking faces lit up by the headlights of the van like scary torch faces. Stood side by side, they reminded me of the comedy duo Little and Large, performing under the spotlight at the Bournemouth Hippodrome. I once saw the real Little and Large supporting Val Doonican there when I was about eight. Not because he couldn't stand up on his own; they were his support act. Looking back, it's the only family holiday I remember. Probably because as far as I can recall, it was the only family holiday we ever had.

Our rather bewildered audience was quickly growing in size, intrigued, no doubt, to witness the outcome of the currently unfolding drama. At the front of the van, Oliver's and Eddie's illuminated faces were still giggling as they reiterated their advice on clutch control, correct gears and the appropriate revolutions per minute to the stressed-out driver who still saw nothing humorous about the farce now taking place. The van seemed to be going nowhere fast, other than digging itself deeper and deeper into the mud. Then, all of a sudden, the final act was upon us, and rather unexpectedly the wheels seemed to get a grip (which was more than could be said for the driver at the time).

Fast and furious, and without warning, the van shot backwards rapidly. Eddie and Oliver, losing the object of their support and looking somewhat startled, fell front facing and equally as rapidly in a downwards direction, their illuminated faces clearly indicating it was not an outcome they had anticipated when volunteering themselves as instruments of human propulsion. Oliver being taller, instead of vanishing totally out of view like Eddie, smacked his head on the bonnet of the van as he ventured southward to meet the muddy terrain underfoot more intimately. Watching the whole affair unfold in the glare of the headlights, although I was obviously concerned about both my colleagues' wellbeing, I'm sure I smiled as I experienced what I think is described as, 'the last laugh'.

With the show now over and the van mobile once again, we eventually managed to find the nursing home in question, which was actually on the other side of the housing estate. Oliver was adamant that he was fine to carry on with the removal, despite the rather nasty lump forming on his forehead after his vehicular assault, and considering the amount of mud that he and Eddie had to battle to help free the van, they both appeared to have got off miraculously lightly. After a little attention with a damp cloth to their mud-splattered trousers and muddy footwear, in the light of the dimly lit nursing home any sign of their earlier swampy exploits was hardly noticeable on their clothing at all.

I would however like to take this opportunity to pass on belated apologies for the slightly muddied beige carpet in the reception area of the nursing home. I'm sure it brushed out without too much trouble when dry.

A Comedy of Errors

Another care-home removal in the small wee hours, or is it the wee small hours? If I'm honest I'm not entirely sure. And are they called that because you often need to get up to have a wee at that time? Back to the removal – Eddie, Joe and I were on call that night, but as Eddie wasn't feeling well, Joe and I offered to cover for him so he didn't lose out moneywise. We just had to hope that we didn't get a difficult removal. As luck would have it, we only had the one that night, from a care home in Swiss Cottage.

As it happened, the nursing home was only a five-minute drive from the yard and removals from that particular home were usually fairly straightforward, and we were able to use a wheelie stretcher on most occasions. Joe and I arrived there at about three in the morning – a response from the out of hours doorbell came about ten minutes after pressing it (longer than it had taken us to get to the care home from the yard in the first place). The response came in the form of a garbled vocalisation that was completely inaudible, booming out from the intercom on the wall. I can only assume that our response was more decipherable, as after stating our business the door buzzed angrily as the locking mechanism unlocked, and we were permitted to enter.

Joe, from day one of my career with Mortimer and Sons, had taken me under his wing and had become my unofficial mentor. Most of the other guys would impasse snippets of advice and information if and when they thought it necessary, but not in quite so much depth. Joe always seemed to go that extra mile to make sure I had all the facts and knew what to do with them and when.

Joe was one of those annoying blokes that seemed to be good at everything they turned their hand to. You know the type; they can throw a cricket ball miles and catch one without a hint of wincing; they can skim a pebble out to sea that will seemingly bounce for an eternity on its watery surface, or at the very least until it's out of sight, and they can do any DIY job under the sun as good, if not better, than a professional tradesman. Even so, as inadequate as Joe made me feel at times, he and I became good friends over the years and had many hilarious outings which usually involved the consumption of alcoholic beverages in establishments in and around Camden. Our self-counselling sessions, as we used to call them. Joe was a diamond in the rough. Although, I suspect not as rough as I think he liked others to believe, he was just rough enough for survival purposes.

We loitered in the reception area of the care home for what seemed an extremely long time, patiently waiting to be met by a member of staff and shown to the room where the deceased was awaiting our services. In the absence of staff to give us any formal direction, Joe and I decided that they must be expecting us to make our own way up to the room, so off we went. Checking the pink card once again to clarify the room number, we entered the lift on our left with the wheelie stretcher in readiness to begin our ascent to the second floor. This was where we would find room 34 according to the sign on the wall placed to the left of the lift.

An automated female voice alerted us to the fact that the doors of the lift were open; something we could clearly see for ourselves. As a matter of fact, we were alerted to the doors' open state repeatedly for the next five minutes. With no sign of the lift doing anything else other than sitting at ground level with its 'doors open' for the rest of the night, Joe and I exited the lift and decided to use the stairs instead. Fortunately, the stretcher we were using that night was one of the wheelie ones with a detachable folding stretcher. This was subsequently removed from its mobile base unit to facilitate its even more mobile state of being carried.

Approaching the door to the stairs we heard the automated female voice from the lift behind us, informing goodness knows who that the doors were now closing. Once on the second floor, with the lift having travelled up to the second floor as we had originally requested it to do, we heard a familiar voice echoing down the corridor letting us know, once again, that the lift's doors were open. The wonders of modern technology and how it is supposed to make our lives so much easier, never ceases to amaze me!

As there was still no sign of any staff, we made our own way to room 34. Standing outside the door, Joe and I simultaneously straightened our ties and neatened ourselves up. As the frontline representatives of Mortimer and Sons Funeral Directors we always tried to look presentable and at our best at all times, day or night. I knocked gently on the door so as not to disturb any of the other residents in the nearby rooms. With no response, after a few moments I knocked again, but this time with a little more force. This knock triggered movement and the faint sound of shuffling coming from the other side of the door caught our attention. To reiterate our desire to enter, I knocked again – this time stepping the level of force up a notch and in turn the volume of the knock. The shuffling noise from the other side of the door indicated no sense of urgency from whoever or whatever was approaching it. The thought crossed my mind that perhaps they were unable to move in rapid response to the knocks being rained upon their door at such an ungodly hour. It was at that moment that another more worrying thought flashed into my head and I began to question one particular aspect of the situation we were now in. So, with more intensity than I had previously, I decided to scrutinise the details written on the pink card once more. My findings were as I had feared. I'd been looking at the nursing home's street number, not the room number. The room we should have been at was on the next floor down and was actually number 24, not 34. I looked over at Joe anxiously.

"What?" Joe asked.

"It's the wrong room," I whispered.

"What?" he replied, looking for verification of my previous statement.

"It's the wrong room," I repeated in a quieter voice but this time exaggerating my mouth's movements in order to pronounce the words as clearly as I could at the lower volume.

The shuffling from behind the closed door was getting closer and whoever was on the other side would soon be opening it. Two scenarios ran through my mind like two very short film clips on fast forward.

Scenario 1

Whoever was on the other side of the door would open it and find two men in black standing in the doorway – one holding what looks like a fold-up stretcher. The two men would subsequently try to explain to the surprised, confused, and very sleepy resident, their reasons for this late-night interruption, trying not to highlight their incompetence at following simple instructions. A stressful outcome for all concerned and one that should ideally be avoided at all costs.

Scenario 2

Whoever was on the other side of the door would open it and *not* find two men in black standing in the doorway – one holding what looks like a fold-up stretcher. The person in question, probably half asleep, would, of course, still be surprised and confused but any other complications and unpleasantness that might have arisen from Scenario 1, would thankfully have been averted. The person would then probably return to bed thinking they had dreamt or imagined someone knocking at the door, and in all likelihood would not even remember the incident when they woke up in the morning. They may even pop to the toilet on the way back to bed, consequently avoiding a mishap during sleep, and therefore avoiding discomfort and embarrassment.

It seemed clear to me which scenario was going to be best for all parties concerned and an executive decision had to be made, and made quickly. The solution was obvious – not to be discovered at the door in the first place. With this in mind I turned to Joe and hastily suggested what I thought our response to the situation should be.

"RUN!" I shouted in a whisper (it is possible, try it).

An initial split second of panic followed as we surveyed our choice of escape routes, then in unison, as if telepathically in tune, we both bolted halfway down the corridor in the same direction. With more luck than judgement, we simultaneously dived into the shadows of a handy alcove on our right. From the safety of our hideaway, Joe and I heard the door open to room 34. Faint indistinguishable mumblings emanated from the figure now stood in the doorway who clearly could not understand where the knocking had come from. Listening from our vantage point, we waited for the sound of the door being returned to its original closed position. Taking a moment to regain composure and get our breath back from the sudden demands put on our cardiovascular systems, the silence was broken by a familiar automated voice from the other end of the corridor, politely informing us that the lift door was open.

Pulling ourselves together we ventured back down to the first floor via the stairs and arrived at room 24. Our delay was not questioned and neither was an explanation offered as we carried out the removal with the usual professionalism, dignity and care befitting our profession.

Via these writings, I would like to take this opportunity to offer a most sincere apology to whoever was behind door 34 that night. I apologise for the intrusion to your slumber, for the obviously quite strenuous and wasted journey that you had to make to open the door and for any confusion that came as a result of our disappearance. That said, I must admit to having doubts about which side of the veil you now reside on. However, whether you are in this world or the next, once again, please accept my most sincere apologies. Hand on heart, to this day I can honestly say with total confidence that I still feel scenario 2 was definitely by far, and without a doubt, the better of the two outcomes on that balmy summer's night.

Of course, an even better scenario than scenario 1 and 2, would have been scenario 3. Whoever was on the other side of the door would open it and find two men in black standing in the doorway – one holding what looks like a fold-up stretcher. Realising their mistake, one of the men in black raises his Neuralyzer and in true

'Men in Black' style, the person's memory of the incident would be completely erased. Sorted!

A Little of What You Fancy Does You Good

Although not always as dramatic, other removals were just as memorable. I remember one removal from a nursing home in Highgate. The lady who had just passed away had very recently reached the grand old age of one hundred. Apparently a very spirited woman, the staff said she was determined to get her telegram from the Queen and had held on to life until she had achieved that specific goal. The proof sat framed and proudly displayed on her bedside table. Also on the table was a half-empty bottle of whiskey, or half full depending on your outlook. Seemingly spirited in more ways than one, this was the old lady's secret to longevity according to the staff at the nursing home. A proud Scottish lady, her motto of, 'A dram a day keeps the doctor away' certainly seemed to work for her, that's for sure.

Arlington House
(Address: No Fixed Abode)

Arlington House was a hostel for homeless men, built in the early 1900s. It was a large red-brick building in the middle of Camden Town.

Our visits to Arlington House always depressed me. The whole place oozed despair and the majority of the individuals who frequented it always seemed so hostile. Those that lodged within the walls of Arlington House were often described as society's outcasts, losers, drunks, junkies, shirkers and failures. They were generally the sort of men that if you saw them on the street, you would go out of your way to avoid, especially if there was a group of them. That said, these men were obviously in need of help and the people at Arlington House seemed to spend a great deal of time and effort encouraging them and supporting them to get their lives back on track.

Each resident came with a unique story that depicted numerous challenges which had reshaped their life, their stories laced with tales of tragedy and cruel twists of fate. For some, pure bad luck had played its part, for others, poor judgement had been thrown into the mix and their upside-down worlds and tumultuous existence had left them at Arlington's doors. I wouldn't necessarily have described Arlington House as an oasis in a concrete jungle, but it did offer the men who stayed there some home comforts, shelter from the elements, hot food, and companionship, as well as practical advice and support. None of us knows what's lurking around the next corner and how we will deal with life's ordeals, and none of us has the right to judge others who for whatever reason have not coped well.

Strangely, I often envied the simplicity of their lives. I can remember watching them in their little groups sitting on a park bench in the summer sun, laughing and sipping their cider without a care in the world, while I was caught up in the rat race grabbing what overtime I could for an extra few pounds to make ends meet, towing the line whilst trying to be everything to everyone and always feeling that I had no time for myself. Slowly ebbing towards the day where I would be the occupant of tray B in fridge one. In reality, of course, I wouldn't want to walk one step in their shoes and I was probably just feeling sorry for myself. At times, it can be all too easy for us to get caught up with the negative things in life and literally worry ourselves sick about things that don't really matter. I'm not saying that there won't occasionally be worrying times that may test us in many ways, but so often we can lose sight of all the positive things in our lives – and the most important – our family and friends.

House Removals

Although removals from hospitals, hospices and care homes weren't always straightforward, most of the time they tended to be fairly undemanding physically. Some of the smaller house-conversion care homes occasionally required a bit of muscle and a certain amount of precision manoeuvring, but generally there was nothing too precarious involved and sometimes they even had a lift. In most cases the lifts were a little on the small side, but with a little ingenuity and vertical thinking, more often than not, it was possible to utilise them in the process of the removal.

Removals from people's private homes, whether a house, a flat, a tower block, a riverboat, or a shed at the bottom of the garden, were on the whole rather more problematic than removals from institutions of care. When carrying a body on a stretcher, not only could the architectural layout of many residential settings cause problems but there was often an array of obstacles and hazards, in the way of furniture, shelving, photos, pictures, ornaments and various knick-knacks, large and small, strategically scattered around every available surface. This could effectively convert the cosiest of dwellings into an elite fighting force's assault course that would test the fittest military personnel to the limit. The old couple that had been crushed to death while they were lying in their bed, by all the newspapers and magazines when the shelving collapsed, is probably the most extreme case of obsessive hoarding I've ever seen, but it wasn't uncommon to see, especially in older people's homes. The agility of a gymnast, the flexibility of a contortionist and the strength of a superhero are just some of the desired qualities that serve you well on the majority of removals from people's own homes.

To complicate matters further, people didn't always die in the most convenient or accessible of places, such as in bed or in an armchair in front of the TV (although, admittedly, both are fairly popular for many of the population to take their last breath). In reality, some people were in the habit of dying in the most inconvenient and least accessible of places. Having said that, I suppose you can't really get in the habit of dying, can you? Unless you believe in reincarnation, that is!

Bathrooms and toilets, due to the general lack of space, were probably the two most awkward places in a home we were required to extract bodies from. Often it could be a major operation just to get into the room, as frequently the deceased was pressed up against the door, effectively restricting our entry. It does tend to be quite a high percentage of the older generation that are particularly susceptible in taking their last breaths in these rooms. Though, bathrooms can be quite dangerous territory for most of our species, whatever their age or physical prowess, due to it typically being quite a wet and slippery environment. You can sustain quite a nasty bash on the head on a sink or a bath. And when I say nasty, I do, of course, mean fatal.

Digressing for just a moment, it's fair to say that many of these deaths might be prevented by the installation of grab rails, a handy little piece of apparatus which can easily be incorporated in and around the home. In fact, I think they should be compulsory fittings. Not just in bathrooms or for the old and less stable among us; they'd also be very handy to have around the house for those times when you may have partaken in a few too many alcoholic beverages. As well as reducing fatalities, it would also most likely reduce the number of nasty accidents that can occur in the home at such times quite considerably. Reducing even just a small percentage of those injuries, surely being an added bonus for our very overstretched National Health System.

Even sitting down on the toilet, for some of us, can be a risky business. It's not an uncommon occurrence for undertakers to have to remove someone off the toilet, having passed away whilst attending to their bodily functions. It's worth noting, that constipation can increase with age and often coexists with cardiovascular risk factors, and excessive straining during the elimination process can cause a rise in blood pressure, which in turn can trigger heart failure. Elvis, the king of rock and roll, apparently breathed his last on the porcelain throne, leaving the building for the very last time on a stretcher.

In relation to problematic bowel movements, eating a well-balanced diet is an important part of maintaining good health, and plenty of high fibre food such as fruit, vegetables and whole grains will help to increase the weight, size and softness of your stool. I'm talking poo, of course – not about household furnishings. A soft bulky stool is easier to pass, decreasing the chance of constipation and the need for straining. Staying hydrated is important too, and generally, 1.5 to 2 litres of water is recommended as a daily intake for good health. That's approximately eight cups a day.

Regular exercise helps to reduce the time it takes food to move through the large intestine, thus limiting the amount of water absorbed from the stool and maintaining a soft consistency. If mobility is a problem, just moving about a little can help. However, if you do happen to experience times when constipation becomes a problem, I hear prune juice can work wonders. Correct positioning can also make all the difference when sitting on the toilet. The knees should be at a slight angle above the hips which allows for a more natural position similar to squatting, promoting a more trouble-free evacuation.

Logistically, removing a body from a small bathroom or cubicle-sized toilet is never going to be an easy task, or very dignified. Correct lifting techniques are often impossible to carry out in such situations, but luckily, we had those previously mentioned contortionist and gymnastic skills to fall back on. I would like to say, that in my experience, no matter how difficult a removal might be, you can rest assured that any undertaker worth his or her salt, will always endeavour to carry it out in the most respectful and professional manner possible.

So, remember, folks, 'Relax, don't do it, if you want to live through it', a little reminder that straining is definitely not for the faint-hearted.

Stairway to Heaven

Of course, bathrooms and toilets weren't the only places where complications could arise. Stairs usually required a whole new level of problem solving, and it's fair to say that they were by far one of the trickiest and more precarious elements of many removals, highlighting the need for both brains and brawn. When it came to negotiating stairs, the lightweight folding stretchers were an absolute blessing and made things a great deal easier than they would have been in the days where all they had to use were the rather cumbersome coffin shells. I dreaded using the shells on the odd occasions when stretchers were in limited supply and I was always grateful that we didn't have to use them all the time. As were my colleagues.

Staircases were one thing, but a staircase with a stairlift was something else. This useful piece of equipment may have enabled the individuals who lived there to ascend and descend the stairs with ease, but to an undertaker they were just another obstacle to overcome when it came to going up or down the stairs, especially when carrying a body on a stretcher or in a shell. If only we could have utilised the stairlift in some way to our advantage – it might have been quite useful. But alas, in the undertaking world, this would not have been an acceptable use of modern technology, or so I was informed. I'm just kidding, of course – such a thought would never have entered our minds. Honest!

During my time as an undertaker, I left my carbon footprint on a considerable number of staircases. Some were very grand, some were rather grotty, and some were downright dangerous. Then there were those that seemed to go on for an eternity and that demanded every last ounce of energy and strength that we had. These would leave us with sweat dripping from our troubled brows, our grip at breaking point and with the muscles in our forearms screaming out in agony for us to end the pain and let go of the stretcher. A little too dramatic, you think? You try carrying a twenty-stone body on a stretcher down ten flights of stairs and see how you feel afterwards.

Fewer than three of us on a house removal was a definite no-no at Mortimer and Sons and made all the difference safety wise. Most undertakers only tend to use two people on house removals. That third person though, on many occasions, was an absolute godsend, particularly when assisting in guiding whoever was carrying the stretcher down any stairs backwards, as well as helping to lift and negotiate some of the trickier manoeuvres that would often present themselves in even the most sensibly laid-out homes. Many a serious injury was averted thanks to a diligent third person.

Around the Twist

The most complex of staircase designs and by far the most problematic even with only your own body weight, is without a doubt, a spiral staircase. Before becoming an undertaker, my first encounter with a spiral staircase came when I was in my early twenties, in a gymnasium that I used to work in as a gym instructor in North London. The staircase led from the reception area to the upstairs office and storeroom, and was an intriguing feature in what would otherwise have been a somewhat unimaginative reception area. Anyone who has ever used a spiral staircase in its functional capacity, would I'm sure agree that it's not just a matter of putting one foot in front of the other as you do with normal stairs. For a start, the steps are narrower on one side! Intricate skills are needed to limit the risk of injury and can only be developed by regular practice. I think it's fair to say, that despite the copious amount of practice I had going up and down that spiral staircase each shift, I don't think I ever really mastered the skills required to use it safely, as the scars on my shins and my misaligned coccyx will bear witness to.

So, when Eddie, Joe and I first arrived at the house in Highgate and I saw the spiral staircase in the far corner of the living room, my heart sank and a feeling of dread came over me. Ever the pessimist, I just knew that the removal of the deceased was going to involve that spiral staircase. And sadly, I was right! As we were led up the ornate, twisting wrought-iron death trap by the son of the deceased, Joe and Eddie stared at me wide-eyed. Our minds were in tune with only one thought. How on earth were we going to maintain a dignified descent for the deceased, without breaking our backs in the process?

Well, manage it we did, thank goodness. Although, as we had suspected it certainly wasn't the easiest of descents or without its heart-stopping moments. It was quite a struggle to guide the stretcher gently down the twisted metal structure with its rather weighty passenger aboard. Nevertheless, with a little application and a great deal of professional expertise and care, a dignified removal under very difficult circumstances was achieved.

Back in the van, our synchronised sighs of relief and the wiping of sweat from our extremely relieved brows, was affirmation of our success. Content with a job well done and having quite impressed ourselves, we drove slowly away, disappearing into the intense brightness of a fiery sunset. The end of another day, and another life.

Behind Closed Doors

You've all no doubt heard the saying, 'You never know what goes on behind closed doors' and over the years I've had to venture into environments I wouldn't have let an animal live in for fear of their health, let alone a human being. Yet some people are existing in the most atrocious conditions and often in the places where you would least expect. Sometimes in your own neighbourhood, or even next door to where you live. The small ground-floor flat on the quiet little estate in Kentish Town, just around the corner from where my sister lived, was a prime example of this.

As we pulled up in the van outside, Oliver, Ali and I were greeted by a rather enthusiastic police officer.

"You're going to need your over-suits for this one, lads," he said, in his deep, Barry White tone.

"Bad, is it?" enquired Oliver.

"It's the flat you're going to need the suits for, not the state of the body," replied the officer, pulling a face of disgust mid-sentence.

Approaching the open front door, we could see exactly what the police officer had meant about the state of the house. The entire floor space was covered with discarded waste. Firmly compacted, it must have been built up over a period of years, evident by the fact that as soon as we stepped into the house, we were at least six inches or so higher than the original flooring would have been. There were also definite signs of infestation and insect activity under foot. Blue overshoes from the disaster bag were swiftly utilised. Although, to be perfectly honest, in terms of protective coverage, they were generally about as much use as a chocolate teapot.

As we walked into the living room area we were cheerfully greeted by a grey-haired chap who looked to be in his seventies, sitting on the sofa watching TV. Having noted our presence, the elderly gentleman promptly returned his full attention to his programme – *Supermarket Sweep*, presented by Dale Winton – that had obviously reached a nail-biting finale. Behind the man on the sofa, standing at an ironing board and shimmying an iron over a white shirt, was a rosy-cheeked middle-aged lady with long dark hair. She also greeted us with rather more cheer than we were generally used to when entering someone's home in our professional capacity. To the woman's right and the cheeriest of them all, was another rosy-cheeked individual, a boy in his mid-teens wearing a grin like a Cheshire Cat. He was sat at a small round table putting together a plastic aeroplane kit. Very keen for each of us to inspect his handy work, he proudly held the model aloft, as though it were in flight. In turn, we examined the three-dimensional scaled-down representation of the Lancaster Bomber, complimenting him on his skill and patience, his Cheshire Cat grin expanding further with each compliment.

The woman, who diligently carried on with her ironing, was very chatty. She asked how we all were and if we would like a cup of tea, which we declined politely. As fond as we were of 'a quick cup of tea', the state of the kitchen and its contents, which resembled a developing eco system in its own right, made us feel that it was a risk we shouldn't take. It was very evident that something was not quite right with this picture.

The policeman who had come in behind us, directed us to the bedroom where the deceased was lying, which was located behind the woman ironing. We excused ourselves past the woman and entered the bedroom, leaving the rather unusually normal family scene behind us.

The deceased, who was in bed, was a man in his mid to late-fifties – the woman's husband, we assumed. The state of the floor in the bedroom was similar to that of the rest of the flat, so we had to watch our footing, but logistically the removal was fairly easy. Walking back through the living room with the body on the stretcher, the woman continued ironing, the boy concentrated intently on his model and the old man carried on watching the TV. Smiling, they each waved us goodbye as if they were totally oblivious to the fact that we were in the process of removing the body of one of their family members.

In a rather bizarre twist of fate, only a few months later, Oliver, Ali and I were called back to the same address. We were all expecting to be picking up the old man that had been watching the telly on our previous visit or possibly the rosy-cheeked woman. We were all extremely shocked to find out that it was actually the young lad that had died.

As we entered the flat, the scene was reminiscent of our previous visit. The old man was sat in the same place in front of the TV and the rosy-cheeked woman was stood ironing in exactly the same spot she had been only a few months earlier. The now completed model aircraft lay in the middle of the small round table where the young lad had sat proudly putting it together on our last visit. I couldn't help but wonder if the rather unhygienic conditions of the place had contributed to the two deaths. Or whether it was purely coincidental. There were clearly mental health issues and I wondered what sort of support they were getting, if any. If I'm honest, I'm not convinced they were being adequately cared for and I'm fairly certain they weren't aware of the impact that their neglected dwelling could have on their health.

Keep the Home Fires Burning

Sometimes it wasn't just the way in which people lived that was a real eye-opener, it was also the places where they lived. A coroner's removal from a squat in Crouch End one afternoon proved itself to be one such removal. It also turned out to be one of the most challenging removals during my time at Mortimer and Sons, which tested mine, Joe's and Frank's skills of agility and balance to the limit.

On our arrival we were greeted by a house almost derelict in appearance. The windows were boarded up, which made it extremely dark once we were inside. The only natural light came from a few rogue beams of sunlight creeping in through the gaps in the boarded-up windows, illuminating small sections of the house like lighting on a stage. The small amount of natural light that had managed to penetrate the darkened house's fortified exterior was greatly appreciated, as there was no electricity supply. As usual, the torches kept on the van for such occasions were about as lively as the majority of our passengers. To make the removal even more exciting, most of the floorboards on the premises were missing which meant we had to balance on the supporting joists and beams – tentatively stepping from one to the other in order to get across each room.

Downstairs, evidence of charred wood in the fire grate that closely resembled the dimensions of missing floorboards, banisters and wall panels, and a makeshift camp fire in the centre of the large room with similar remains, suggested that the occupants of the house had cannibalised almost all of the available wood from wherever they could for warmth and cooking. All that was left holding the house together, was a carcass of beams and joists with only a few essential sections of flooring and ceiling remaining. Presumably, to retain some sort of living space that didn't require numerous circus skills to occupy.

It was, however, circus skills that we would need to employ if we were to scale the rather dodgy looking skeletal framework of what was left of the staircase. Which unfortunately, was the only way to get to the first floor of the building where the body was precariously positioned on one of the remaining sections of flooring. Or ceiling, of course, depending on where you were standing in the house at the time. It was quite a drop if we were to lose our footing, and when Joe said don't look down through the gaps in the joists, I probably should have listened. But what's the first thing you tend to do when someone tells you not to do something? You do it, don't you?

Trying not to focus on the missing floorboards, we surveyed the area where the body lay. Hypodermic needles were scattered all around the shabbily clothed body that lay on a small section of remaining floor. Hypodermic needles were something we had to be very aware of on many removals, particularly when searching the bodies. The police were technically supposed to search the bodies but often didn't due to the state that many of them were in. (The bodies that is, not the police.) In all fairness, we didn't mind doing it if they asked nicely and stayed in the room. We needed their presence to avoid allegations arising at a later date, of us taking any missing items.

I can remember one occasion where a young officer was very rude to Eddie. He ordered Eddie to search a very badly decomposed body that he so obviously did not want to search himself. Eddie's very polite answer to the young fledgling constable, whilst reminding him of his responsibilities, was, 'Actually, officer, it's your job to do that, so we'll just wait over here until you've finished'. The young constable's face as he rummaged around the pockets of the maggot-ridden body was a picture, and looking rather nauseous he made a speedy exit from the room once he'd completed the task in hand. The older and more experienced officer that had accompanied him, seemed to be happy for his younger charge to learn a valuable and very much needed lesson in people skills. After all, a little respect for others can go a long way and makes life a lot less unpleasant for us all.

While the removal from the squat in Crouch End was quite a challenge, it certainly wasn't the only time we had to venture into such a hostile environment or carry out a removal in difficult circumstances.

A Bit of Argy-Bargy

As well as environmental and biological issues that can make the job of an undertaker quite challenging, at times, people can also be rather unpredictable and occasionally aggressive. It is, of course, quite understandable that people are going to be very emotional when grieving the loss of a loved one, and as an undertaker it's important to be empathetic and open to people's needs at such times. Saying that, society has become increasingly more cosmopolitan over the last few generations – with cultures that don't tend to subscribe to the old British principle of, 'get the kettle on, keep a stiff upper lip and bottle it all up' type of attitude. A philosophy that admittedly may not always be the best approach, but is what we've been used to for many generations and has helped this country through many a sticky situation in its fairly sticky history. It can be quite hard for some of us, due to our upbringing, not to naturally apply this philosophy at stressful and emotional times.

Agreed, bottling things up is definitely not the best long-term strategy, but there's a time and a place for letting your emotions get the better of you, particularly when it involves a lot of angry shouting and waving of arms in an over-theatrical manner that is likely to unnerve the undertakers.

It has to be said, that hostility towards undertakers is generally quite a rare occurrence, and when it does happen it's often due to the influence of alcohol – or other less legal mind-altering substances – added to an already heightened emotional situation, that can be a large contributory factor. However, whatever the reason, more frequently we were very grateful for the presence of the boys and girls in blue, who were always on hand to keep things under control should we need them.

I can remember one time, when Eddie, Joe and I were sent out on a coroner's call to a new housing estate in Chalk Farm. It was there that a young Somalian man had died at home. The family weren't at all happy about him being taken away to undergo a post-mortem, and the police, sensing that the situation could escalate as more friends of the family and Somalian community arrived, had already called for backup by the time we were on scene. A wise decision on the part of the police, as it turned out.

A group of about twenty or so very hostile young Somalian men who all seemed very determined that we were not going to be permitted to enter the house, let alone remove the body, was growing in number by the minute. To be confronted by such a gathering was quite disconcerting, and it was a rather tense situation. They just couldn't seem to understand that it wasn't up to us to decide whether or not the body stayed. The young lad had apparently had an unexpected brain haemorrhage, so the coroner was automatically involved. Under the circumstances, not removing the body was not an option.

Eventually, with no other option, and a little more understanding of why the deceased needed to be taken to the coroner's mortuary, the family agreed to let us take the body. The growing number of angry onlookers were not as easily convinced, and it wasn't until the police reinforcements arrived and were able to contain the hostile crowd at a distance, that we were eventually escorted into the house by the police to carry out our duties. The police also accompanied us to the coroner's mortuary in King's Cross – not usual practice – but under the circumstances, we welcomed the company.

NATURE'S WAY

Like any other living organism, we will all eventually die. In death, Mother Nature will take back control of our bodies and in turn the ultimate recycling process will begin. As Mufasa explained to a wide eyed Simba in Disney's *The Lion King*, it's the circle of life. Such a wonderful and almost romantic concept, returning to the earth to give birth to new life. However, the reality is it's a rather unpleasant biological process that doesn't even bear thinking about, let alone witnessing.

From day one Adam and I were only too aware that we were on standby and would be expected to deal with our first decomposed body as soon as one was called in. Preparations for such a task came thick and fast in the form of gory stories from all the lads, and although we had no way of knowing what was fact and what was fiction, we weren't exactly in a rush to find out. On the other hand, with that natural morbid fascination that our species seems to have for such things, the anticipation of our first badly decomposed body created a variety of mixed emotions. Our biggest fear was that we would expel the contents of our stomachs involuntarily, embarrass ourselves, let our colleagues down and become more of a hindrance than a help.

Looking back, there was certainly no shortage of disgusting images racing through our minds. All the unpleasant stories the lads had been so thoughtful to share with us manifesting themselves into visions of green rotting flesh that could peel away in your hands, dismembered limbs, legions of wriggling maggots, swarms of frantic flies, and overflowing insect infestations that crunched under foot, each accompanied by the fear of how we would react to the unimaginable stench generated by these sights. And while these were just a few of the gruesome images fed to our gullible and over-imaginative minds in the days and weeks before we attended the removal of our first decomposing body, they in no way prepared us for the many macabre revelations that lay ahead in our newfound career.

Raiders of the Lost Ark

It was a Friday afternoon, about four o'clock, when a call from head office alerted us to a coroner's removal from a flat in Summers Town, Camden. Evidently, the body had been patiently decaying for several months, while waiting to be discovered. As anticipated, it was time for Adam and me to do a little more on the job training and as novices we were to be supervised by Joe.

Adam and I had started our journey with Mortimer and Sons on the same day, so you could say that we had a sort of new boys' bond. Previously a bookie, jokes about dead certs from would-be comedians were as common as horse poo and about as humorous, too. His response to such remarks were always more than adequate to deal with the comic wannabes.

Adam did have a tendency to elaborate the facts about most things rather colourfully. Presumably to impress – which I suppose many of us do on occasion, but not quite as colourfully. If I'm honest, there was really no need for him to do so as he was a very likeable chap, whatever his story, and a genuinely nice bloke. If you were in need of help, and Adam was able, he would go out of his way to lend a helping hand.

Pulling into the inner road system of the housing estate in Summers Town, we could see the police and a small gathering of inquisitive onlookers standing on the outer walkway of the third floor of the extensive red-brick building, this collection of people, highlighting the location of the deceased that we were required to transport on behalf of the coroner. In readiness for the unenviable task ahead we decided to put on our disaster suits at the van. This was mainly because we didn't want to make a second journey back up to the third floor in order to retrieve our jackets after we had completed the removal. Some of the local children were intrigued by our Arctic-look fashion accessories and others decided we were fair game for some entertaining mickey taking. Of course, we kept our cool and ignored the infantile taunts; mainly because we were professionals and definitely not because we couldn't think of anything verbally to throw back at them at the time.

With no lift to take us to the desired level of the building where our services were required, we used the stairs. It seemed the most sensible route, particularly as our Spiderman outfits were at the dry cleaners and we would obviously have looked quite ridiculous scaling the walls of the building in our disaster suits. Joe, pink card in hand and the most senior and knowledgeable of our trio, acted as our representative and did all the talking. Adam carried the disaster bag containing a selection of body bags, overshoes and masks. You could say, there was something for all occasions. As for me, I was left in charge of the stretcher. Gowned up and looking like something from the set of the *E.T.* film, we were ready for anything. Well, almost anything.

After climbing six flights of stairs, we reached the flat on the third floor and were greeted by a rather attractive female police officer who reliably informed us that we'd got all dressed up in our very fetching protective outfits for nothing. The body, an elderly man, having been dead for such a long time had gone through all the disgusting stages of decomposition and was now nothing more than a dried-out carcass. Obviously, he hadn't been the most sociable of people or had regular visitors, for whatever reason, but you'd have thought at least one of his neighbours might have been a little suspicious about his total absence from the scene for so long. At some point, as Joe mentioned, there would definitely have been quite a strong and rather unpleasant odour, but the windows and front door of the flat seemed well sealed against the elements which probably kept the malodour from escaping and alerting the neighbours that something was amiss.

Once inside the small, gloomy flat, we saw exactly what the officer had meant. Not a hint of an offensive aroma or even the slightest sign of any unpleasant gooey substances whatsoever. The body was completely dehydrated and all that remained was a skeleton covered in a thin layer of hard, dry, leathery skin, dressed in rather baggy clothing, probably due to the crash diet the deceased had recently been on. Any insect infestation that there may have been, was now reduced to a few rogue flies. Seemingly inquisitive about our presence, they were the only signs of any insect life apart from a few dried-out maggot encasements – post-metamorphous stage – scattered around the edges of the body.

Prior to our arrival, the police had thoroughly searched the dried-out remains and found bundles of cash about his person during their investigation. With the crumbling mummified remains, which looked more like a prop from an Indiana Jones film, placed into a body bag in an effort to try and keep as much of it as possible in one piece, we then transported it to the coroner's mortuary in King's Cross for the investigative scrutinising to begin.

Feeling quite deflated, Adam and I were somewhat disappointed after all the build-up to the suspected 'badly decomposed body'. That said, we were also quite relieved that our stomach contents could continue their journey through our digestive systems, on this occasion. There would be plenty of other opportunities to experience the wonders of nature's decomposing process – of that we had no doubt. But little did we know how soon that time would come, or how common an occurrence it would become.

Decomposition *(Not for the Squeamish)*

When any living organism dies, nature has developed it in such a way that it will revert back to its simplest molecular structure in order for it to be recycled. That which exists cannot cease to exist but merely changes its form, in this day and age, is probably a statement that no longer holds true. And although I'm fairly certain that our species is probably more than capable of totally obliterating something into nonexistence, including ourselves, that's not generally the way nature likes to do things.

In accordance with the laws of nature, after death, the once friendly bacteria in the body turn hostile and kick-start the process of cellular breakdown by producing destructive acids and chemicals. As the process progresses, each stage of decomposition becomes even more disgusting than the previous stage. Somewhere between three to five days the body starts to bloat, bringing with it the formation of foul-smelling gases. It then goes through several artistic colour changes including a wide variety of impressive greens and purples before finally turning black. The skin becomes unstable and fragile and can easily be damaged, sometimes coming away in sheets like a snake shedding its skin, leaving the underlying raw tissues exposed. Giant blisters are formed, hair and nails loosen and the body's internal organs begin to liquefy as they are broken down into simpler molecular structures, oozing from the body's orifices as a viscous reddish-brown liquid.

Bodies decompose at varying rates depending on internal influences such as age, size, illness, and condition before death. Environmental surroundings can also play a huge part in the rate of decomposition; these include temperature, moisture, and exposure to the elements. Nature also sends along an array of efficient little helpers in various guises to assist in the breaking-down process – our bodies supplying food for them and their young.

All the gory and unpleasant stories that the lads had told Adam and me were far from exaggerated. Something we eventually found out for ourselves. The stench of a rotting corpse is definitely by far the worst thing I have ever smelt. Sometimes it was so bad that we could smell it as we pulled up outside the premises in the van; usually after the neighbours had finally admitted something wasn't right and alerted the authorities. How it took people so long to react, when the smell was clearly so bad, was unbelievable. If you've ever smelt a body in the advance stages of decomposition, animal or human, you'll know exactly what I mean.

Handling a body in even the early stages of decomposition can be quite challenging and is not the most pleasant of experiences. Skin slip can occur quite early on in the breakdown process and fragile veins close to the skin's surface can rupture as your fingers sink into the soft dead flesh. Subsequently, when a body is in the more advanced stages of decomposition, one wrong move and it can become a very messy affair indeed. When faced with this type of situation, it's best to devise a battle plan and then get on with it as quickly and efficiently as possible (always maintaining a caring and respectful manner, of course, and trying to avoid creating any unnecessary complications for yourself, or your fellow work colleagues).

Simon Snorkel

There were very few changes of staff during my time at Mortimer and Sons. From time to time the occasional new face would appear at the yard and various branches due to the natural process of staff moving on, retirement, and of course, death. Ken, who was Eddie's elder brother and Joe's uncle, was one such new face. A particularly interesting feature of Ken's face was that it was partially covered by an expanse of facial hair in the form of a rather impressive full beard. Mr Dickinson no doubt felt quite disheartened with the addition of Ken and his beard to our ranks at the yard, and his lifelong ambition of only fresh-faced, clean-shaven staff on the front line at Mortimer and Sons.

Before joining Mortimer and Sons, Ken had his own business and worked in the building trade. Now he was of a more mature age, he wanted a nine-to-five job with less hassle and stress that running your own business invariably involves, but most importantly, more time to spend with his family. Ken and Eddie were both what I would describe as deep thinkers. They both had a good sense of humour, but Ken was definitely the more serious of the two. Possibly because he was the eldest and felt it was his duty to be – especially around his younger brother. Both men had clearly gained their education from the 'University of Hard Knocks', and as such, their advice and words of wisdom were often sought on a variety of matters by those of us that were less experienced in life due to our younger years, and it was always freely given. It's fair to say, that the yard would have been a far drearier place to work without Ken's and Eddie's contributions of anecdotal jocular quips, but Eddie's melodic tones resonating around the rafters of the garage, as he serenaded us with his extensive repertoire of classic crooner songs while cleaning his limousine, were priceless in times of low morale and melancholy thoughts.

One very memorable night, Ali, Ken and I, were sent to Kilburn on a removal for the St Pancras coroner. If I remember rightly, it was about midnight when we actually got the call. Usually, it would have been my night off, as it wasn't my turn to be on call, but on this particular night I was covering for Joe, because he had a 'hot date'. Ali and Ken were the other two thirds of Joe's duty squad.

Thirty minutes after being contacted by Mr Dickinson, the out-of-hours duty manager that week, Ali, Ken and I were suited and booted and, having checked all the kit we needed for the removal was on board the van, we were on our way to Kilburn. It wasn't an area of London we ventured into often, and although we found the housing estate easy enough the actual address where our presence was required eluded us for some time. Until we spotted the police car outside the premises, that is.

As we entered the building and began walking up the stairs, we were met by the most awful, foul stench, and while this should have given us a good indication of what we were going to be up against, it in no way prepared us for what followed. According to the police, the deceased was a man in his mid-thirties, quite big, and somewhat decomposed. On entering the bedroom, we became very aware that the term 'quite big' was probably the understatement of the year. The man was absolutely huge! And the term, 'somewhat decomposed', was not the most accurate description of the man's current biological status either.

Lying face down on the bed, his unclothed body was only partially covered by the bedding. At first glance we thought the gentleman was black, but a closer examination revealed this was not the case. He was, in fact, at quite an advanced stage of decomposition and exuding a rather unpalatable smell that was quite overpowering – even to our experienced nasal passages.

Taking a closer look, I could have sworn I saw him breathing. Seeking clarification from my trusted colleagues, I pointed out my observation. I have to say, I felt a bit of a wally when Ali brought to my attention that the breathing movement of the deceased was actually being caused by the vast mass of feasting maggots wriggling closely under the thin layer of loose, blackened skin. It was clear to see that it wasn't going to be an easy task to transfer the man from the bed to the stretcher without things getting very messy and extremely unpleasant indeed.

Cause of death would, of course, have to be determined following a post-mortem, if that information was still available at such a late stage of decomposition. Although, in this day and age, with the wonders of modern science, I'm sure that it would be. And looking at the weight he was carrying, I'd be very surprised if it wasn't something to do with his heart that played a key part in his demise.

As we stood deliberating over our battle plan, a number of problems presented themselves that we had not previously considered. The first problem was the question of whether or not our stretcher was up to taking on the mammoth task in hand. The answer to that – was it had to be! The reality being, that it was all we had available, and that none of the other stretchers at the yard was any more capable of carrying a larger load than the one already in our possession.

The second problem was, even if we could manage with the stretcher we had, how on earth were we going to get the deceased down the short but narrow flight of stairs without doing ourselves a variety of very serious injuries? To give you some idea of the size of the gentleman that was presenting us with these dilemmas, when stood upright he would have taken up the entirety of the doorways which divided each of the rooms in the small flat. Even allowing for the extreme bloating and a build-up of gases, this was an extremely large man. It must have been quite a tight squeeze for him to actually get from one room to another when he was alive. Given the enormity of the task ahead, we decided to contact head office and ask for a fourth man to be drafted in to assist with the operation. Preferably, one of the more robust and stronger members of the staff. No offence, chaps!

After a great deal of thought on how to overcome the various obstacles that were presenting themselves, and weighing up our options – some of which were more sensible than others – Ken, with his infinite wisdom and many years of experience in the building trade, came up with the most sensible and most viable option. His suggestion was to extract the deceased from the premises via the bedroom window – or to be more precise – through the space that would be available if the bedroom window and window frame were completely removed. And as it happened, we knew just the man for the job.

The police contacted the fire brigade explaining the situation and requested assistance. Ken suggested that the council should be contacted to gain permission to remove the window and window frame. Subsequently, after numerous diverted telephone calls, permission was eventually given to go ahead with the necessary structural changes to the property; albeit from a somewhat reluctant and rather sleepy council representative from the maintenance department, who probably just wanted to get back to his bed. Even without his permission, I think it was obvious to all involved that it really was the only course of action available that would allow us to succeed in our endeavours.

Having been enlisted as fourth man, a beaming-faced Adam arrived on the scene and seemed quite keen to see what all the fuss was about. It didn't take him long to realise we hadn't requested a fourth man to make up the numbers for an all-night salsa class.

As we waited for the fire brigade to arrive, Ali decided to take a look around the man's flat, and much to his delight he discovered that they had something in common. They both appeared to be avid sci-fi fans. The man's living room, lounge, or sitting room, or whatever you like to call it depending on your upbringing, was absolutely packed full of sci-fi videos; most impressively, according to Ali, the complete collection of the *Star Trek* saga from the very first episode to the present day. I think it's fair to say that Ali was in his element, as he had a passion for all things sci-fi. He'd even had the small bedroom in his house converted to a sci-fi shrine after his daughter had got married and moved out, Ali's pride and joy being his collection of robots spanning decades of sci-fi history. Ali's other passion in life was tropical fish – and we would get regular updates on the trials and tribulations of the management of a tropical fish aquarium. Unfortunately, the life expectancy of many of Ali's fish seemed rather short – even for a fish! In an effort to reverse this trend he would often share his latest strategies and ideas with us, on what he could do to enhance their life expectancy, before trialling them out. Daily reports often followed any implementation of a new strategy, including updates on their progress and the final outcome – which I'm sad to say, was rarely a tale with a happy outcome for the fish.

Ali was a friendly, hardworking man, though his Mediterranean temper would often get the better of him. It was a stark contrast to us stiff-upper-lip Brits, who generally (although rarely to our advantage), just put up with things.

Ali was busy educating us and the police officers about the various captains of the Starship Enterprise over the timespan of the *Star Trek* series, when we heard the rumblings of a heavy vehicle and the loud hiss of its air brakes as it pulled up outside. Looking out of the window like a group of excited school boys, we were in awe at the sight of a very impressive bit of kit in the form of a bright-red Simon Snorkel fire truck, complete with hydraulic lifting platform – just the job!

The cavalry had arrived, and what a fine, keen bunch of lads they were – until they got a whiff of the deceased, that is. Then, for some reason, their keenness diminished ever so slightly. Fortunately we had a good supply of face masks which were dished out promptly to our rescuing heroes. Although, to be honest, the masks we used really didn't make a great deal of difference when the smell was as pungent as it was on this particular occasion. The main reason we wore them was for protection from any harmful bacteria that might be floating around the environment we were working in. They were also very useful at keeping out more visible forms of floating – or should I say, flying – life forms that could easily be swallowed if you weren't careful.

Insects aside, in an effort to appease the newcomers' nostrils, Ali suggested the firemen might like to apply some camphor vapour rub on the inside of the mask, to help dull the overpowering smell of the decomposing body (and it just so happened that Ali always kept some handy on his person, for just such an occasion). With the firefighters keen to follow Ali's suggestion, the vapour rub was dished out and applied liberally to the inside of the firefighters' face masks. I'd tried the vapour rub on the inside of the mask technique at Ali's suggestion once myself when I first started with the company. It made my eyes water so much I couldn't see where on earth I was going, and I nearly broke my neck when I misjudged my footing as we were carrying the body down a rather steep staircase. It seemed to be having a similar effect on most of the fire crew, too, judging by the tears in their eyes.

While the operation to remove the bedroom window and window frame was being carried out, using the combination of Ken's know-how and the fire crew's brute force and technical equipment, Ali, Adam and I, were trying to work out the logistics of how to get our rather large customer onto the inadequately sized removal stretcher. As well as the size of our extinguished Trekkie presenting quite a logistical challenge, there was the added problem of the effects of decomposition. Experience of dealing with badly decomposed bodies teaches you, if nothing else, that the movement of them will invariably result in at least one of a number of unpleasant outcomes. Including, the untimely release of its feasting visitors, their lively offspring, and copious amounts of potentially hazardous biological substances.

The plan in these circumstances is always to minimise direct physical contact with the body itself as much as possible, and not to waste time faffing about unnecessarily. Avoid the grabbing of arms and legs and steer clear of putting pressure of any sort on any part of the main torso – especially if it looks like it's ready to explode. The use of clothing, bedding, or anything else that may come to hand that is either on or around the body, can be a wise move in many ways and completely justified. Covering the body with a sheet and gently but swiftly rolling it into an open body bag, then sealing it promptly, will greatly reduce the amount of exposure to the aforementioned unsavoury scenarios.

Having previously pondered the suitability of the removal equipment in our possession (i.e., the fold-up stretcher and the job required of it), it was no revelation to discover that it was far from up to the job. Time for plan B! Unfortunately, we didn't have a plan B! After much deliberation and some rather ridiculous suggestions that might have seemed like good ideas at the time, but were not, one of the firemen shared a flash of inspiration and came up with the idea of using two twelve-foot ladders strapped together. Fortunately, they happened to have two on board the Simon Snorkel. Don't you just love it when a plan comes together!

The ladders were gathered and tethered together with rope – also provided by our firefighting heroes. The end result was a more than adequate makeshift stretcher for its proposed passenger, in length, width, and most importantly, strength.

Kitted out in full protective clothing from top to toe, including ice-rink simulator blue overshoes for added excitement, Ali, Ken, Adam and I readied ourselves for the big push – or pull – depending on your positioning during the proceedings.

All geared up and ready to go, a closer inspection of the man on the bed revealed that we may have only solved one of our problems with the use of the ladders. The underside of the deceased was in meltdown, and in its new, more viscous form had oozed through the bedding into the mattress, effectively adhering itself to its surroundings.

Adding to our list of obstacles to overcome, the largest of the body bags in our possession was going to be about as much use as an inflatable dartboard, with regard to the containment of wee beasties and noxious substances shortly to be unleashed by the relocation of our currently resting client. We were going to have to rely on the trusty white plastic sheeting for that job, by wrapping as much of it as possible around the man's generous frame and then rolling him onto an open body bag in the hope that we might at least be able to limit the inevitable and undesirable effects of movement. To our surprise, that part of our plan worked out fairly well – except for one little mishap when Adam slipped on an unknown gooey substance next to the bed and nearly fell out of the gaping hole where the window and window frame had once resided.

Once the deceased was securely strapped to the makeshift stretcher, it took all four of us, most of the fire crew and a large amount of huffing and puffing from all involved, to manhandle the heavily laden makeshift stretcher from the bed, out of the gap where the window frame had once been and then onto the hydraulic platform of the Simon Snorkel, in order to be lowered to ground level. Unable to close the back doors of the van due to the length of the ladders acting as a stretcher, the fire crew came up trumps yet again, supplying a huge piece of blue tarpaulin from the fire-truck version of Mary Poppins' handbag, which we used to cover the body. The fire crew also followed us to the coroner's mortuary, as closely and as safely as they could, in order to obstruct the view of the contents of the van. Not that there were many people about at that time in the morning. As well as being a thoughtful gesture, they would obviously need their ladders, rope, and tarpaulin back.

At the mortuary, transferring our guest onto the largest mortuary fridge-tray available was slightly easier than the removal itself. Although, it was a bit of a squeeze and still required a great deal of brute force and assistance from several of the fire crew. Thankfully, with the help of the magnificent men from the fire department, we managed to accomplish what seemed at times to be an impossible task.

It was definitely a night to remember, and a captivating tale to tell whilst enjoying a quick cup of tea in the tearoom at the yard the following day.

Smash and Grab

One of the strangest things that ever happened on a removal that I was part of, was when Oliver, Eddie and I, were sent to a flat on the seventh floor of a tower block in Kentish Town. The police were already on scene, a young female police officer, and it was a fairly straightforward removal, except for being on the seventh floor of the tower block, that is. At least the lift was working – which was always a bonus.

The deceased was only a little chap – seventy-two years young, according to the information on the pink card – and he was lying in the middle of his living room floor. Great for us, as there was plenty of room to manoeuvre and minimal obstructions impeding our access to the body. Allocated to the head end of the deceased, I placed my hands under the man's shoulders and Oliver took hold of the man's ankles. Eddie, in his supporting role, was positioned at the man's midsection with a hand either side of the man's waist. On the count of three, authoritatively relayed by Oliver, we lifted the man from the floor. In mid-lift, there was an almighty crash behind us, as one of the large windowpanes of the seventh-floor flat exploded outwards as though something had been thrown through it with tremendous force.

"What the hell was that?" Oliver exclaimed, as we all looked towards the shattered window.

It was all very dramatic, and the timing of the window's demise seemed uncannily coincidental to the movement of the deceased – almost as if the man's spirit was in a great hurry to leave the premises and had chosen the most viable exit route.

Interestingly, in some cultures, windows are left open after a death has occurred, in order to allow the spirit to be set free. A tradition that after the exploding window incident in the tower block, I believe may well have good foundation for belief. It also makes sense for other reasons, of course.

Not One from the Colour Chart

Another rather strange removal, involving a rather curious artistic mural, which I think it's fair to say, had my colleagues and I a little perplexed, was a removal from a ground-floor flat in Gospel Oak. A less than delicate and somewhat familiar aroma greeted us as we entered the flat and almost immediately we could tell that this was not going to be the most pleasant removal of the day. The information on the pink card told us that the body now lying before us, star-shaped and naked on a double bed in the middle of the sparsely furnished room, was the body of a fifty-year-old man. However, although the furniture may have been in short supply, when it came to the décor, the room was far from plain.

From floor to ceiling, all four walls were covered in some sort of Rolf Harris-styled mural. To digress for just a moment, while I realise many household names once used in conversation are now tainted, I really can't think of a better comparison to describe the artistic style used. Apologies if this comparison causes offence. The mural was clearly an interpretation of the London skyline. Many of the pictorial images were easily recognisable, such as St Paul's Cathedral, Big Ben, the Tower of London, and London Bridge.

It didn't take my colleagues and I long to work out why there was such a strong aroma of excrement when we had first entered the flat. Intriguingly, the mural's artist, who we presumed was the man on the bed, hadn't chosen any of the more traditional materials that most artists work with, such as paints, pastels and chalks, etc. No sir… this mural's innovative creator had opted for a slightly more primitive, and I expect, more readily available material – faeces! Aroma conundrum solved! Whether it was his own faeces plastered all over the walls, I can't say. I suspect it may well have been, if only for ease of supply.

"Can ya see what it is yet?"

"Yes; it's sh#t!"

What some people will do for their art!

All Doped Up and Nowhere to Go

Seeing the conditions that some people live in, often as a result of alcohol and drug abuse, really opened my eyes to the depths that some people can find themselves when embroiled in some of the darker and less desirable parts of society. I was always thankful that my exploration of those shadowy depths came only as a consequence of my job. It definitely wasn't a world that I wanted to spend any more time in than absolutely necessary. Sadly, there were many such removals, and one particular incident really sticks in my mind that took place on a rather notorious estate in King's Cross, that we were very familiar with; an estate that we generally visited in connection with murders, suicides and drug or alcohol-related deaths.

The police escorted us up to the first-floor flat and into the room where the body of a young man was lying. Scattered around the room were hypodermic needles and other drug-administering equipment, accompanied by a mountain of empty bottles and cans of booze. The police had apparently forgotten to mention that the dead man's friends were still sitting around him in the room where he had died. Needless to say, it was a bit of a surprise when we were suddenly confronted by the spaced-out group that seemed completely oblivious to the fact that something was awry. Still laughing and joking – despite the body of their so-called friend lying unresponsive, face down in a pile of vomit, in the middle of the room. Their delusion all the more incredible as the man's contorted features would seem to indicate that he must have been in a great deal of pain before he had died. I can remember looking to one police officer for some sort of support or guidance on how we should proceed and the feeling of disbelief as he just shrugged his shoulders and said, "What do you expect me to do?" It was all quite bizarre.

Is That Legal?

Although only a very small percentage of deaths occur during or as a consequence of the act of sexual activity, it does occur. Sex can be quite physically challenging, and as a consequence, lead to distinct changes in blood pressure, heart and respiratory rate, that may lead to vital complications. Not that I'm trying to put anyone off. The chances of such complications can, of course, be increased by the added link of prescription or use of recreational drugs during such activities. So, people, let's be careful out there!

For me, the implications of those facts tend to speak for themselves and generally reflect how we all need to look after our bodies and stay fit and healthy. Particularly as we get older, and not just to cope with a bit of hanky-panky in the bedroom – or wherever else you may enjoy having a bit of hanky-panky – but also for a healthier and better quality of life in general.

Some of the things that go on behind closed doors would definitely raise an eyebrow or two, even in the broadest-minded of circles. As an undertaker, it was often my experience that being more adventurous than your body might be able to cope with was definitely a recipe for disaster. 'Sticks and stones may break my bones, but whips and chains excite me' is not quite how I remember the rhyme that Mum used to recite when the other children called me names.

I suppose I've led quite a sheltered life sexually. Some of the things I've seen in some people's houses used for so-called pleasure don't look very pleasurable at all. Hanging over my bed by chains, on a frame made from scaffolding, with an orange in my mouth and a dildo up my bottom, is certainly not something I would contemplate to achieve sexual gratification, or the way I would want to leave this mortal coil or be remembered by my loved ones, thank you very much. Which by the way, was exactly how one unfortunate individual was discovered, and not just an image that came to mind out of nowhere. That would definitely be a little disconcerting. Call me old-fashioned if you like, but I think I'll stick to the old tried and tested methods of enjoying intimate relations, that don't have to come with a health warning, or could even be fatal.

Certain areas of King's Cross were rather infamous for promiscuous goings-on, and in our professional capacity as undertakers we visited many of them ourselves on numerous occasions while trying very hard not to get arrested for curb crawling as we searched for the address we'd been called to. (That's our story and we're sticking to it.) More often than not, the removal would be on behalf of the coroner to collect a deceased male from a seedy, back-street hotel, after overexerting himself during activities with rather dubious persons of the night. These were the removals where invariably a call would be made to the emergency services, but only the deceased would be found in the room. Still, at least the other party had bothered to make the call before they left.

A Bit of an Eyeful

One of the most embarrassing moments that I recall during my time at Mortimer and Sons, has to be the time that I was sent on a house removal in Hampstead with Joe and Frank. It was a tricky removal, involving a fair amount of complex manoeuvres in order to negotiate our way around the quaint, crooked house, made particularly awkward by one of the narrowest winding staircases I have ever had to negotiate in my entire life. Further hindrance, came from the deceased gentleman residing on board the stretcher. Though very aged and ill, he had obviously not lost his appetite during the latter period of his life – which really didn't help the situation.

Once the deceased had been removed from the house and was safely loaded into the van, I ventured back into the house to speak to his widow who had some questions about what she was required to do next, with regard to registering the death and organising the funeral. As I had become more experienced, I was allowed more responsibility and had progressed from carrying the stretcher and being the designated driver on removals, to now being trusted to be involved in communicating with the public, as well as various officials. Recovering from their strenuous ordeal, Joe and Frank waited in the van. Frank was tucking into a packet of Bombay mix. Frank liked his food, and he was never without a snack of some kind about his person. It was as though he lived in fear of wasting away. Which to be honest, far from being underweight to start with, would have taken a little more than him just missing a few meals.

On re-entering the quaint old house, I was directed into the front room and offered a seat in one of those flowery, Miss Marple-type, design armchairs, which I graciously accepted. Sinking into its remarkably low, flowery depths, when I finally reached sitting position, my knees were almost level with my chest. It crossed my mind that this was probably not the most practical piece of furniture for the elderly. Especially, for those whose level of mobility may not quite be what it once was. I even doubted my own ability to vacate the chair after the completion of our conversation, without it being a bit of a struggle and requiring some assistance.

The old lady was understandably very upset and became more and more distressed and agitated as we spoke, despite my efforts to try and ease her worries as best I could. What did seem a little strange at the time was that she didn't seem able to look me in the eye, and averted her gaze everywhere in the room, except in my direction. I took this action to be related to her present grief. Excusing herself to obtain a tissue, she left the room. As she did, I began to wonder if I may have upset her or even offended her in some way.

As I played back our recent conversation in my mind, a cool breeze wafted in from the open window opposite me and instantly alerted me to a possible reason for her discomfort. It was then that my own level of discomfort began to increase somewhat, too. For the past few months, I'd been asking head office for a new pair of trousers. I only had the one pair, and I wore them continuously – every day in fact, except for days off, of course. It was no wonder they were wearing a bit thin in places. And when I say wearing thin, there was in actual fact, quite a large hole flourishing in the crotch. Previously, as long as I was standing up, it was fairly well hidden. Even sitting, with a bit of good strategic positioning, I could just about get away without exposing flesh. However, I think the problem had been exacerbated during the removal, and had inadvertently enlarged the hole in my trousers without my knowledge. Looking down at my crotch during the old lady's absence, I realised that I had been showing her a little more than empathy during our conversation. If only I'd been wearing the more traditional style of men's underwear that I usually wear, things might not have been quite as revealing. Unfortunately, on this particular occasion I was wearing quite loose-fitting boxer shorts. Boxer shorts are definitely inferior when it comes to efficient containment of one's body parts – as this incident proved, unequivocally. No wonder the poor woman was so distressed!

For me, it was a most regrettable incident, and I cannot apologise enough for the distress I may have caused the poor woman. I can only hope, that through time or illness that affects the memory, the incident is now but a distant shadow – or even better – has been totally erased from the poor woman's mind. If the lady is no longer with us, as even when her husband passed away she was no spring chicken, I hope her spirit is finally at peace, and she forgives me my unknowing state of overexposure.

SUICIDE

'Suicide is painless, it brings on many changes...' according to the theme song from the hit film and popular TV series in the seventies *M*A*S*H*, about an army medical unit in South Korea, during the Korean War, a brilliant satirical comedy that Mum and I used to love and watch religiously when it was on TV in the seventies and eighties. The series is rerun every now and again, like many classic TV shows, and is still one of the best from that era, in my book. The music for the song was written by Jonny Mandel and the lyrics by Michael Altman.

The lyrics refer to suicide being painless, and although I'm not totally convinced about the painless bit, I am fairly sure it would bring on many changes. Death is surely the biggest change that can occur in anyone's life, and the lives of those they leave behind.

At the time of writing, according to statistics, every year an estimated one million people around the world take their own life. That's roughly one person every forty seconds. Suicide is one of the leading causes of death in people between the ages of fifteen and forty-four years of age, although, typically, a higher percentage of suicides are older individuals. Globally the suicide rate for men is twice as high as for women, and in some countries that ratio is even higher. Having said that, apparently women have higher rates of suicidal thinking and are three times more likely to attempt suicide, but the methods that men generally choose to end their life are usually more violent, and consequently more successful than the methods women tend to choose. Attempted suicides for both sexes, are twenty times more frequent than successful suicides. Sad statistics indeed!

During my time as an undertaker at Mortimer and Sons, I attended many suicides of the young and the old. More than I care to remember, and many that are hard to forget. The first suicide I ever attended, in my first week at Mortimer and Sons, was the lady who'd written 'Do not resuscitate' on her chest. Sadly, it was the first of many suicides that I would attend over the next few years.

The first suicide by hanging that I attended, was that of a young girl in Kentish Town. This particular suicide etched in my brain, not just because it was my first experience of seeing someone that had hung themselves, but because of certain aspects in the way it was carried out. The deceased was in her early-twenties – a very pretty girl. The flat that she was found in belonged to some friends of hers, which she was minding while they were away on holiday.

In the middle of the sitting room, her petite frame hanging by her neck from the light fitting was a sorrowful sight. The chair she had used to stand on lay on its side, and a book entitled, *Know Your Knots*, was sitting on a small coffee table next to an armchair. Clearly, she did not want anything to go wrong in the process of ending her life. What really struck me was how considerate she had been when preparing the setting for her exit from life. Even in the depths of such deep despair her thoughts were of how her actions would affect others, placing a tray beneath the spot where she hung herself to prevent soiling the carpet. It's not really how you expect someone to be thinking when they are about to end their own life. I felt the world would greatly miss this gentle soul, who would surely have made it a much better place.

Mistaken Identity

Another suicide by hanging that is very memorable but for very different reasons, was strangely just a few doors down from where we had picked up the young girl only six months earlier. Though for reasons I will divulge shortly, perhaps this one shouldn't technically have been classed as a hanging, at all.

Aside from the unfortunate and sad fate of the deceased, there is a slightly more light-hearted aspect to this tale which I feel compelled to share – mainly because, to this day, it still amuses me when I think of it.

In his mid-twenties, my colleague Graham was one of life's truly, genuinely nice blokes. A kind-hearted man who never had a bad word to say about anybody. You might imagine that someone with such an obliging disposition could easily fall victim to others' more predatory nature, but there was a strength in his gentleness that emanated confidence in who he was. To some, he may have appeared slightly boring, so it's fair to say that we were all very surprised when he decided to go for his motorcycle licence, and then buy himself a motorcycle. Oliver and I were particularly impressed, as you can imagine, being keen motorcycle enthusiasts ourselves. Suddenly, Graham was living on the wild side of life. Well, maybe not wild, but his latest chosen mode of transport had certainly unleashed something within him that was definitely a little less tame.

On this particular removal, Graham had been nominated as the pink card holder, and was therefore responsible for official acts of communication. And with his gentle manner and calm, kind tone he was well suited for the task. So, after all necessary intercourse with the representative of the local constabulary upon our arrival had been completed, Graham eagerly trundled off ahead of us and went up the stairs to the first-floor flat, where the gentleman we were to transport to the coroner's mortuary was presently tethered. Joe and I followed, in our more menial roles, a flight behind.

As we ascended the stairs, we could hear Graham introducing himself to someone as frontman of our little team from Mortimer and Sons. This perplexed not only Joe and I, but also the police officer accompanying us who had previously informed us that there was nobody upstairs – apart from the body of the deceased, of course. Standing on the second-floor landing behind Graham, now halfway up the third flight of stairs, the three of us watched in amazement as he carried on his rather one-way conversation with the silhouette of a tall man standing on the third-floor landing; or perhaps I should say, the man who appeared to be standing on the third-floor landing. As you might have gathered by now, the silhouette was, of course, the hanging, or rather, suspended body of the deceased. Admittedly, due to the light behind him from the open door of the flat, and with his feet appearing to be supporting his weight in the usual way when someone is standing, it did look remarkably like someone actually standing at the top of the stairs. So, we could say it was an honest mistake on Graham's part, that anyone could have made. Even so, it amazed us how long it took Graham to realise that he was actually talking to the deceased. Graham was going to have to live a very long time indeed to live this one down.

The man, who according to our information was forty-four years of age, had attached one end of a piece of rope securely around a sturdy beam in the attic, then placed the other end, the noose, around his neck. So far so good, in terms of a suicide attempt, that is. Presumably, thinking these were the only details he needed to give any consideration, he then jumped through the open hatch of the attic. Now, this is where it looks like things may have gone slightly wrong for the poor chap, and raised a few questions as to how much thought he'd actually put into the event, prior to carrying it out. Assuming his aim was – with the action of jumping from that height with a noose around his neck – to break his neck, thus ending his life as quickly and painlessly as possible, there seemed to be a serious lack of certain calculations which would have resulted in his success.

For example: taking into account the length of the rope, his height, and the distance to the ground from the beam in the attic. The man had obviously not heard of the concept of the 7 Ps, or any of its many variations, depending on how polite you want to be, when it came to making a good job of something. My personal preference is, 'Proper prior planning, prevents piss-poor performance'. Although, there are as I say, quite a few variations on the theme. The poor man had failed to realise that the rope around his neck, which was connected securely around the beam in the attic, was far too long if he had planned to break his neck in order to achieve a quick and as painless an end as possible. It was, however, precisely the correct length to allow his feet to make contact with the floor, but only just, thus tightening the rope around his neck, strangling him slowly.

Admittedly, his primary objective had been achieved, as his lifeless body bore witness, though I have my doubts that it was anywhere as near painless or as quick as he might have envisaged prior to carrying out the act. Of course, on the other hand, I may be totally wrong in my hypothesis and he had in fact, with great precision and accuracy, calculated all the necessary measurements to achieve exactly the accomplished outcome. Nothing would surprise me when it comes to this crazy species of ours.

For forensic purposes, when cutting down a body, it's important to cut the rope that is suspending them above the knot, and leave the rope around the deceased's neck for forensic examination. Nothing is assumed or taken for granted, just because it looks like a suicide.

The Vanishing Corpse

It was a cold, crisp New Year's Eve, and my compadres Oliver and Eddie and I, had been called out to a hanging in Chalk Farm, at a tastefully decorated studio-flat tucked away in one of the back streets. We were met, as was the norm in the case of a coroner's removal, by members of Her Majesty's law enforcement department who informed us that the body inside the flat was awaiting our professional expertise to facilitate its removal from the premises – or words to that effect.

It was, even as studio flats go, extremely compact. So compact, that you'd imagine a body hanging in it would have been fairly obvious, if not quite an obstruction. But alas, a hanging body was nowhere to be seen. We checked in all the usual places people usually hang themselves, several times, but to no avail. Reluctantly, after a short discussion about how stupid we were going to appear, we decided there was no other option than for one of us to return to the law enforcement representatives outside, and question the actual whereabouts of the body.

Oliver drew the short straw for this important and high-profile mission, with no evidence of cheating or sleight-of-hand whatsoever (not that could be proven in the time he had available anyway). Oliver ventured outside, and Eddie and I awaited his return with great anticipation. A short while later, Oliver returned with one of the police officers close behind who was wearing a rather smarmy and superior knowing grin on his face. On entering the flat, the officer momentarily revelled in our confusion and sarcastically questioned our credentials as undertakers, before closing the front door behind him to reveal our hide and seek quarry, who was nonchalantly hanging by his neck via his belt on the coat hook on the back of the door. Without wanting to appear callous, I could tell the deceased had obviously shared my views on the superior qualities of belts over braces. Even beyond their designated duties.

Overland Expeditions

Hampstead Heath was quite a popular venue for those that had an urge to end it all by hanging themselves, and it was usually late at night when we got called out to such deaths. It was always an interesting drive over Hampstead Heath in the middle of the night. Not least because of the challenging terrain for a two-wheel drive, Ford transit van, but also due to the almost comical array of surprised faces lit up by the headlights of the van, of people caught committing lewd acts among the foliage. Each one popping up like a scared rabbit. In fact, it wasn't unknown for us to be called out to collect some of those lit-up faces, who after being a little too adventurous with all kinds of stimulating substances that their hearts couldn't cope with during their lewd activities, ended up in the back of an undertaker's van destined for a cold tray in the coroner's mortuary.

Never a pleasant task, it always seemed to be a fresh-faced, young police officer who was left to watch over the dangling body, in the eerie darkness of the heath. All part of the training, I presume.

I have to admit, that hanging myself to end it all would not be high on my list of suicidal techniques. Just the thought of struggling for breath is unpleasant enough, without the neck-breaking thing; and that isn't always as easy to achieve successfully as you might think. It's rarely a pretty sight either, and not really the way I'd like to be remembered.

Geronimo!

Tower blocks, of which there are many in the fair city of London, present ideal platforms for those that desire to end their life by leaping from a great height. Although, from information received, I believe it's ultimately not the height that does the damage, but the ground on impact.

The first jumper (as we called them) that I attended, was from a tower block in Swiss Cottage. Looking up from the ground to the top of the block was enough to give me a heart attack – it must have been horrendous at the top looking down. The top diving-board at the swimming pool looks nothing from down below, but once you're up there standing on the edge of it looking down, it's terrifying – and that promises a far softer landing into water. Presuming you get your entry right, that is. Always an important factor in many aspects of life.

Looking over the man, it amazed me that there was so little damage to him externally, considering the unavoidable impact that would have been experienced by falling from such a great height. There was hardly a scratch on him and very little blood. When we went to pick him up, however, it was a different story, and it felt like every bone in his body had been shattered. This made lifting him into the body bag very awkward, and in the end we had to use his clothing to move him in the same way we would have done with a badly decomposed body.

On another occasion, another chap, who'd chosen a rather precarious spot for his long descent to the ground, was not quite so intact. He managed to sever his head and both feet on some railings in the process of implementing his self-inflicted demise. That gave Marcus the embalmer quite a challenge to sort out before the family could view him, but as usual, he worked his magic and did an amazing job.

Going off on a slight tangent, thinking of people that leap from great heights, it raises the question in my mind as to why people often shout 'Geronimo!' when leaping from a height. It was something my friends and I always did as we leapt from various structures during our youthful exploits, but I've no idea why. I don't remember receiving any formal training to do so, it just seemed the done thing. We knew that 'Geronimo' was a famous Apache Indian chief from the Wild West, having been educated by the many western films that appeared on our TV screens on a regular basis, but why his name seemed almost compulsory to shout out during such an act, never really crossed our minds.

In later life, my 'Geronimo!' shouting moments have been far less than in my youth, and I wish I'd taken the opportunity to shout it instead of shouting F*************k, when I did my 200ft bungie jump over the Thames. Unfortunately, my brain wasn't quite up to being that whimsical as I stood on the edge of the crane's cage, pre-jump – it was more preoccupied with thoughts of how I was going to be able to avoid having a heart attack.

I always assumed that the reason people shouted 'Geronimo!' must be because it was something the great chief had once done himself in a heroic gesture of defiance to the new rulers of the land of the free – as one of those that had once been free in that land. On researching the matter, there seems to be a few stories flying around as to the birth of the tradition. The one I tend to favour, is the version that tells of a group of trainee paratroopers from the 82nd Airborne, of the United States Army, who had seen a film about 'Geronimo' at a local cinema the weekend before their first jump. Supposedly, one of the men, for some strange reason, decided to shout Geronimo at the top of his voice as he jumped from the plane. The rest of his comrades, obviously thinking this was a great idea, followed suit and repeated his vocal gesture, giving birth to a tradition that reputedly still lives on to this day.

Not all jumpers jump from heights of course, some decide to leap from lower levels and throw themselves in front of things – usually quite large, fast-moving things. Trains were generally the most popular choice, but again, not always as quick and efficient as you might think as a method for ending life.

The London Underground and extensive rail network gives good opportunity for those people who decide to use the 'jumping in front of a large moving object' technique. As with those that choose the 'jumping from a height' option, some would amazingly have only a few scratches, but fatal internal injuries. Others, however, would be in several pieces and warrant a search party to locate any missing limbs or other body parts that might have gone astray. Walking up and down a railway track at 3 a.m. on a cold winter's morning looking for missing body parts, is not high on my list of activities to do at that ungodly hour, but it's something I've had to do on numerous occasions.

Not all jumpers are suicides, of course, there are quite a few fatal accidents that involve falling in either a horizontal or vertical manner. These accidents, in my experience, are often induced by the consumption of various substances that find their way into the human system, impairing its judgement and causing confusion between a person's ability to understand the difference between the meanings of the terms 'mortal', and 'immortal'. One of several examples of such a scenario, that comes to mind, was the night we were called out by the coroner to collect a young lad who had apparently been trying to impress his girlfriend with his Tarzan impression. Performing acrobatics at a considerable height from one window ledge to another, he lost his grip and fell to his death. His girlfriend, by all accounts, was not impressed, and a beautiful romance came to a rather abrupt and extremely permanent end.

Something's a Foot

It was a blustery, autumn Friday afternoon, and after a rather hectic day, Oliver, Eddie and I were sat in the tearoom at the yard enjoying a refreshing and well-deserved brew. With just fifteen minutes until home time, typically, a call came through from head office concerning a coroner's removal. Someone had apparently thrown themselves in front of a train at King's Cross Railway Station. How inconsiderate!

As we were the duty squad that week, we were duly despatched with all the necessary equipment that we were likely to require, and given the pink card containing all the relevant information – which on this occasion was 'Unknown Male' (the title given to a body if the identity is unknown). An ID tag with that information was attached via a paper clip to the pink card. Obviously, it could say 'Unknown Female' if the deceased was known to be female.

We were told to report to the office of the Transport Police situated inside the station, and after an extensive tour of a bustling King's Cross Station at the beginning of rush hour, with our trusty wheelie stretcher, we eventually located the office of the Transport Police. It turned out that we couldn't have parked further away from our destination if we'd tried, and I would have had severe words with the driver of the vehicle, if it wasn't for the fact, that it was me. Oliver and Eddie, however, had plenty to say on the matter.

Inside the rather small reception area of the Transport Police, we were met by an aged, dark-wood counter. Dividing the room in two, it was an imposing piece of furniture which had all the characteristics of the Victorian era. The lack of artistic embellishment did not detract from the grandeur and enormity of the solid wooden barrier that separated the two sides of the room. The public's side of the counter provided a modest amount of floor space to initiate an inquiry, and on the officers of the law of transport's side, although slightly smaller, it was more than adequate to receive those enquiries and relay information back to the enquirer. Screwed rather crudely to the top of the grand counter, obviously to gain attention if an enquirer found themselves unattended – as we did – was a small plastic black and white doorbell. Not exactly in keeping with the tone of the room, it was disappointing that it wasn't one of those old-fashioned brass ones that are hard to resist pinging (even if you don't actually want any attention), or one of those small, ornate hand-held bells, that someone who is ill might use to attract their carer's attention.

Oliver took the initiative and rang the bell. A short time passed before we were joined by an exceptionally tall police officer appearing from the door directly behind the counter. As broad as he was tall, in a depth of tone that matched his large frame perfectly, he asked if he could be of assistance. Oliver informed the officer that we were from Mortimer and Sons Funeral Directors, and that we had been sent on behalf of the coroner to collect the body of an unknown male that they currently had in their possession. The officer appeared amused by this statement. At that moment, another officer appeared from the door behind the counter, and was duly informed by the first officer of our objective. Looking us up and down, the second officer appeared even more amused than the first by the information we had just imparted, and without comment he disappeared back through the door behind the counter. Assuming he had gone to find out where we needed to be, we were surprised when he reappeared so quickly and presented us with a black bin bag.

"There you are, gentlemen, the remains of one… unknown… male."

Confused, we looked at the bag and at each other. Reading the label attached to the bag, we could see why the officers were so amused that three undertakers with a wheelie stretcher had turned up. In quite shaky writing, it read, 'Right foot of unknown male'. I remember wondering why the writing on the tag might have been so shaky – some things that came to mind were quite amusing, some were quite bizarre, so I kept them to myself. The fact that we hadn't been given all the relevant information about our pick-up, did make us look, and feel, a little foolish.

Oliver opened the bin bag to check the contents. True to the information provided, severed just above the ankle, was one right foot. It was unmistakably a man's foot – broad and very hairy. And although I must admit to having seen a few women's feet that were a little hairy, I would have been quite concerned if my girlfriend's or wife's foot had been as hairy as the foot in question (no disrespect to women with very hairy feet intended).

There was no point in applying our ID bracelet around the ankle, for obvious reasons, and placing the bag on the stretcher, containing the abandoned body part, we covered it over and set off on the epic return journey back to the van. The commuter mayhem of King's Cross Train Station now in full swing, it was survival of the fittest as we battled against the torrent of bodies racing to catch their trains home after a hard day's work.

On handing over the foot to Duncan, the mortician at the coroner's mortuary, he checked the label attached to the black bag, entered the details into the mortuary book, and placed the solitary foot on a tray in one of the fridges, until such time, presumably, that it could be reunited with its former owner. Apparently, as Duncan informed us, earlier that day a man's body had been located on the same stretch of railway line just north of London, and coincidentally was missing a right foot. Two and two being put together, it was fairly certain that the two discoveries were related.

A Watery Grave

Watery options for ending one's life seemed a less popular choice, but we had our fair share over the years. Not all were suicides of course, but usually after an investigation into the circumstances of the death, most were found to be related to the deceased's desire to end their own life. A trip to Poplar Mortuary in East London was a fairly sure bet that someone had been fished out of the Thames. Camden Lock was another watery venue where bodies were frequently discovered. Although often these were discovered not to be suicides, but the disposal of murder victims. Frequently, bodies from the lock would be in several pieces, obviously for ease of transportation and the act of disposal. I remember one time it got quite confusing because the police were finding body parts that turned out to belong to two different bodies.

The stench of a body that has been submerged at the bottom of a river or lake for some time, is quite unique and truly disgusting. The sludge and silt from the riverbed infused with the decaying flesh is so strong, that it gets right into the back of your throat and invades your nasal passages like a dose of smelling salts. It really is the most abhorrent smell. In fact, there are no words within my vocabulary or contained in my handy thesaurus that truly allow me to fully describe how awful it actually is. The stomach-churning aroma would escape even if the body was double bagged – which was usually the case with our underwater collections. No matter what the weather, on the journey back to the yard all the windows of the van would be fully open to try and combat the vile stench and nauseous urges. Deep breaths of the highly polluted London air eagerly gulped into our lungs as we drove along, was like heaven in comparison to what lingered inside.

A Cutting Remark

Although I attended many suicides during my time as an undertaker at Mortimer and Sons, I was never called out on a removal where a person had ended their own life by cutting their wrists. I have no recollection of any of my colleagues ever referring to any such cases either. Perhaps this type of suicide attempt is less successful because their attempts are more likely to be thwarted. Perhaps it's not as common as people assume it is.

Unhappy Hour

As previously mentioned, women are generally less likely to choose the more violent methods of suicide, and cocktails of pills usually combined with an alcoholic beverage is definitely a popular choice for ladies wishing to depart this earthly realm by their own hand. I can remember one lady in particular who had added a rather unique spin to the method; wrapping cling-film repeatedly around her head, covering her mouth and nose. If she'd had a change of heart the volume of cling-film used and the efficiency of its application would have made it extremely hard to remove, and I imagine the unusual embellishment would have hastened her demise quite considerably.

Over the years I have seen such a tragic waste of life through suicide, in both the young and the old. Sometimes the reasoning behind their actions would seem so futile and unworthy of their obvious despair and desire to depart this mortal earth. Bad exam results, lost love, betrayal, school or work-related problems, illness, and loneliness, to name but a few. But in truth, what seems trivial to some, is enough to tip others over the edge, and of course, may not be the whole picture to those looking in from the outside.

The mind can be a fragile thing, as can the spirit, and who knows what a person may have had to endure before they reached breaking point: Fear of situations, despair that there is no way out, despondency that there is no one to lean on or to help, and sorrow that no one will ever understand how they feel; the often self-imposed isolation and weariness of riding an emotional rollercoaster, persistently pushing to the surface such overpowering emotions, that leave them believing that their only option is to disembark. A tragedy that brings tremendous heartache to all those left behind.

The sad irony is that there is always someone who cares and that wants to help. There is no problem, be it large or small, that is new to our species or that can be made better by keeping it to ourselves. People are far less judgemental than you think and there's very little that can be said that hasn't been heard before. After all, nobody has a perfect life which is problem free. I know it's not always as simple as just having someone that will listen and wave a magic wand to make everything all right, but speaking to someone about how we feel is an important first step. Sometimes things can be more complicated, but when someone is struggling and desperate, getting the right support at the right time, whatever that might be, is vital.

It was during those difficult removals that I would promise myself never to put any children of my own under pressure to either perform or to achieve – their happiness would be paramount. I would never want them to feel life wasn't worth living whatever the circumstances. I would encourage them to see that there are always options and answers to problems, and that I would be there for them to help in any way that I could. No matter what, and for as long as I was able. Above all else, they would know how much I loved them.

Reflecting back, I realise that life is a funny old thing, and you never really know what's lurking around the next corner. It may not always be what we want or wish for, and it may not all be good, but it's not likely to be all bad either. Surely, it's the uncertainty of it all that makes life such an adventure. Life is a bit of a ying and yang sort of journey.

At the birth of each new day, as the darkness gives way to the light, new opportunities will present themselves, new adventures will unfold, new friends, and even new love, can all be waiting for us on the next horizon.

MURDER

Murder: the unlawful killing of a human being, by another human, with malice aforethought. (Premeditated)

According to statistics (and what would we do without all these wonderful statistics?), one in every 100,000 of us in the UK is likely to be murdered. With the population sitting somewhere around 63.5 million at present, that's an average of about 635 murders a year. Apparently, females are more likely to be murdered by a current or ex-partner, whereas males are more likely to be murdered by a friend or acquaintance, and under sixteens are more likely to be murdered by a parent or step-parent. Not the most comforting list of statistics for any of us really, but let's not get too paranoid here. We're talking about an extremely small percentage of the population that will sadly go on to become part of those statistics. However, with those statistics in mind, perhaps we should all work on our relationships a little more, be a bit choosier with who we hang around with, and look out for those tell-tale signs that might tell us that something isn't quite right.

The most common weapon used in this country when carrying out the act of murder comes in the form of a sharp instrument. Presumably, that's not a reference to musical instruments, although, I would imagine a penny whistle could do some serious damage in the wrong hands. And not just to your ear drums.

For me, one of the most shocking murders that I ever attended, where the victim had been stabbed to death, was that of an old lady who had been stabbed by her grandson seventy times. It seems he needed money to fund his drug addiction. After the frenzied attack, he managed to get a few pounds from her purse and then left her blood-covered body to be discovered by a neighbour on the hallway floor. A very sad affair indeed.

Last Man Standing

One morning, I arrived at work to find that the duty squad had picked up the grandad of a friend of mine. In a sad turn of events, he'd been stabbed in a pub in Kentish Town. By all accounts, the incident was triggered by him not standing up when a certain Irish song was being played at the end of the evening: or perhaps it was because he did stand up, I can't quite remember. Either way, it just goes to show how some people's minds work, or don't, as the case may be.

Such events can't be solely blamed on the influence of alcohol or drugs, of course; there are a lot of rather unsavoury characters out there who it seems are always looking to cause trouble and need little or no excuse to do so. But when added to the equation, especially in excess and in certain environments, alcohol and drugs certainly don't help. The weekend being party time for most people and a time of recreational excess – as well as the usual late-night call-outs – the duty squad could almost guarantee a few murders, suicides and other drink or drug-related deaths. However, all that aside, referring back to the statistics, it's clear that murder is often much closer to home.

Adam, Ali and I were once sent to West End Lane Police Station in West Hampstead, to collect the body of a woman. From what the police told us, it appeared that a man and his wife had been having a heated debate while they were driving southbound along the Finchley Road towards Swiss Cottage. Somewhere along the way, the man, obviously reaching a point in the discussion where he had no more to say and had heard enough of what his wife had to say, pulled over to the curb and proceeded to strangle her with his bare hands. At least those were the details that were shared with us at the time. (I'm not going to comment on the man's actions for a number of reasons that might be detrimental to my own health or marital status.) He then drove to West End Lane Police Station, with his wife's body in the car and gave himself up. Whether it was due to remorse or the realisation that it was going to be a difficult thing to deny, having carried out the deed in such a public place,your guess is as good as mine.

Often, when I've attended a murder scene or where a violent death has occurred, I get a strange feeling (and no, it's not my irritable bowel playing up – not all the time, anyway); it's a real feeling of dread. A heavy, ominous feeling. A darkness. A sense that something very bad, even evil, has taken place. I'm not sure if it's just knowing what has happened that makes me feel that way, or if it's something more than that. Either way, it's very strange.

Late one night in 1994, I was sent on a coroner's removal with Ali and Arthur. A fire had broken out at a small private cinema in the East End, which incidentally, showed films of dubious content. There, one of the patrons who on that night had been refused entry, had taken it upon himself to show that he was not a man to be trifled with. Deciding to teach them a lesson they would not forget, he visited a local petrol station and purchased some petrol. He then returned to the private cinema and subsequently set the place ablaze with all its occupants trapped inside. A tragedy in itself which was made worse by the fact that, for whatever reason, the building's contingency plans to be initiated in the event of a fire were far from adequate.

With the smell of the smoke still heavy in the air, and a darkness surrounding the burnt-out building that was far more sinister than the darkness of the night, we watched as the firemen lowered the bodies one by one from the smouldering building using the hydraulic platform on the fire truck. Sadly, eight people died that night. Three others were hospitalised with serious injuries, but their reprise from death was short-lived, as each one died in the days that followed.

The first burnt body I ever saw was at a flat in Swiss Cottage, where a man had fallen asleep in his bed with a cigarette still burning. The badly charred body was twisted and deformed, and the smell of the crisp black flesh was absolutely revolting. It was not a sight or smell I was in a hurry to experience again. When they say 'Smoking kills', you don't often think about it happening in that way, and it certainly put me off barbeques for a while. And smoking in bed, of course!

As I mentioned previously, Camden Lock was a popular place for the dumping of bodies and body parts. As undertakers, we would often find ourselves wandering up and down the towpath of the Regents Canal, collecting them for the local coroner, once they had been efficiently wrapped in plastic by the forensic team to preserve any evidence that may still be present.

In 2002 body parts in black bin bags started turning up in wheelie bins around Camden. Coincidently, some were found just around the corner from head office. I would just like to point out that these were nothing to do with us, and were, in fact, the unsuspecting victims of a local chap by the name of Anthony Hardy, but thanks to the inventiveness of the media was probably best known as the 'Camden Ripper'. He was found to be responsible for the murders of a number of young women in the area who turned out to be known prostitutes. In an effort to cover up his crimes, he had distributed their dismembered remains in the canal and local refuse bins.

At 3 a.m. on New Year's Day 2003, Mr Henry Mortimer and I – due to the duty squad already being out on a removal – went to collect the head of one of Hardy's last victims, that had been found in a communal bin. However, the true extent of Hardy's macabre goings-on only came to light a few days later, when Eddie, Joe and I were called to Hardy's ground-floor flat in Royal College Street, to collect the limbless torso of a woman. Never have I felt so close to real evil as I did in that flat that day.

A Friend in Need

Wading through the blood and guts of humanity's violence towards itself and its despair can take its toll on even the strongest of us. As undertakers, we were not spared those feelings of despair and there was no counselling available for us – unless you count the 'If you can't cope get another job' advice we were often given after a challenging removal. To be fair, it wasn't bad advice, just a little insensitive at times.

To survive the job, we became our own counsellors. Good colleagues, good humour, and a few beers after work helped us through the darker moments. Without which, we might otherwise have been dragged screaming into the dark abyss.

Take Me Home, Country Road...

Following a particularly unpleasant coroner's removal late one night with Ken and Frank, as we made our way back to the yard, I noticed that Ken was a little more subdued than usual. Knowing how much he liked his country and western music, I decided to try and cheer him up. Banishing the rather repetitive and fairly predictable choice of music that was already playing on the van's prerequisite radio station, I searched out the country and western channel. Succeeding in my quest, luckily the song playing at the time on the country and western music station was a jolly little tune. I say 'lucky' because a lot of country and western songs can be quite melancholy. However, as my ears tuned into the song, I realised it had some quite interesting and rather unusual lyrics. The singer, in a traditional country and western twang, was singing with such vigour and emotion, about his desire to set his chickens free. A sentiment I'm definitely in favour of, if the process is properly thought out and if future support for the survival of the birds is taken into account. That said, the urge to join in with the uplifting chorus was just too much for us all to resist, and a very cherished and memorable moment was had by all. With our spirits lifted, and my objective achieved, we all returned home to our beds to try and get a couple of hours' sleep before our day's work began. In the hope that we weren't called out again, before it did.

MORTUARIES

Mortuaries are without a doubt, among some of the creepiest and least desirable places to be. A place most people wouldn't want to venture in during the day, let alone in the middle of the night, when they take on a whole new dimension. Especially, when you're on your own because your colleagues have deserted you after delivering the body and left you with the job of locking up the premises. That's when your mind really loves to play tricks on you and have a little fun. Or maybe it's not just the mind playing tricks!

Like the bodies that reside within them, hospital and public mortuaries come in many shapes and sizes and vary vastly between the old and the new. From the antiquated Victorian type of mortuary often associated with Jack the Ripper-type films, to the more clinical, stainless-steel-clad examination rooms of modern day.

The older mortuary buildings, unsurprisingly, tended to be the most eerie, possibly due to their morbid history. They were also often the most aromatically revolting, which was most likely down to the efficiency of the aged drainage systems. Although, in some cases, it may well have had as much to do with the way they were cleaned and maintained as anything else. That said, the coroner's mortuaries would be more likely to have decomposed bodies housed within their walls. A hospital mortuary would be far less likely to contain bodies in that category.

As in any profession, the morticians that my colleagues and I met were a varied bunch and came from all backgrounds. Most were quite ordinary and really nice people, just doing a job. There were one or two whose sanity was slightly questionable, but they probably thought the same about us.

When I first started working at Mortimer and Sons, being called out in the middle of the night for a coroner's removal often meant that we would have to wait for the on-call mortician to arrive at the mortuary so that they could book the body in and check through all the details. As you can imagine, unless they lived close by or stayed on the premises overnight, this was a very inconvenient process which could make a simple and potentially quick removal last well into the night. Particularly, if we had to wait for a mortician on a clapped-out moped to travel from South London to North London in the middle of the night. Which was often the case at one particular mortuary we regularly frequented.

Eventually, most of the local coroners granted us the knowledge of the security code so we could access the mortuary buildings ourselves. Presumably to save money by not having to pay the mortician for being on call, but it was also a far more practical and less time-consuming process for us.

EMBALMING

For thousands of years ancient civilisations have developed and used numerous techniques to try and slow down the natural decaying processes of the human body once cessation of life has occurred. Historically, as well as for practical reasons, embalming was used as a way to venerate the dead and fulfil religious ceremonies and beliefs. The Egyptians, for example, believed that the soul would return after its journey in the afterlife and re-inhabit the body.

There are many misconceptions and some very strange ideas about what the process of embalming actually entails, or why it is even necessary at all. Modern-day embalming, sanitising, or hygienic treatment – to use more modern terms – is a far cry from the ancient methods once used. Now, the process of embalming is more about cleansing and sanitising the body and the presentation, rather than to be preserved for a returning spirit. It protects those that may come into contact with it from potentially harmful bacteria. It neutralises and slows down the process of decomposition and allows the body to be preserved in the best and most presentable state that it can be, for the comfort of loved ones and friends who choose to view the body before saying their last goodbyes.

Viewing a loved one can be very distressing. However, for many it's an experience that can give comfort at a very difficult time. Seeing someone you love at peace and looking more like their old self, can help when coming to terms with their passing, and for some it can be an essential part of the grieving process. Especially, if the last time the deceased was seen they were in a lot of pain, were very ill, or had died in traumatic circumstances. That said, embalming is not compulsory – though it's definitely advisable if the person is being viewed or going home for any period of time for a wake or for the purpose of a religious ceremony, as is the custom of some cultures. If the deceased is going into church or a religious building overnight, it's also advisable to have them embalmed.

Many people don't like the idea of embalming and some even think it's disrespectful to treat the remains of a loved one in such a way. While I can completely empathise why some people feel that way, if you want to view or be with your loved one for any length of time after they have died, it's likely to be a great deal more distressing and also rather unpleasant, if they've not been embalmed. Not everyone looks like they're just sleeping peacefully when they're dead, and the odour of death can be rather potent and is very hard to cover up after only a short time, even if the deceased is in a sealed coffin, let alone in an open coffin in a chapel of rest, at home, or in church.

As much as I feel embalming is about respect for the deceased, by presenting them in the best possible way, the process of embalming is also for the living. It enables family and friends to have time with the deceased which they may need. Time to be with them for just a few moments more, to say what they may not have had a chance to say before the person died, to say their goodbyes. I have seen the difference that this precious time can mean to so many. It can be a difficult concept to grasp for some, until they've experienced the comfort it can bring.

The Embalming Process

The order that specific embalming procedures need to be carried out, are not set in stone, some things can be performed at various stages in the process. This is often down to an individual embalmer's personal preferences – although at times it can be dictated by the condition of the body. That said, there are some specific procedures that will generally need to be done in a particular order because of the way the embalming process works.

As a rule, the body should be washed thoroughly before embalming. The limbs, if needs be, can be flexed and manipulated to gently work out any rigor mortis (the rigidity caused by a chemical reaction in the muscle tissue after death). This manipulation of the body not only makes it more manageable, it also precipitates a better flow of fluids during drainage. The body's own circulatory system, with its extensive network of arteries, veins and capillaries that spread around its entirety, is ideal for draining the unwanted body fluids, and also very useful when introducing the embalming solution comprising of sanitising and preservative chemicals.

Draining the unwanted body fluids is done by accessing the preferred, or most appropriate artery, and inserting a small arterial tube into it. An arterial tube resembles a small, thick needle that is hollow along its length like a straw, which allows the fluid to flow through it. It is important to remove as much of the existing body fluids as possible, not only to allow the embalming solution to flow around the body effectively, but also because of its influence upon the decomposing process as it deteriorates. The preserving action of the embalming solution comes from a chemical reaction that happens when combined with the proteins of the cells, literally changing their molecular structure and thereby inhibiting the process of decomposition. It was once described to me as a procedure that almost plasticises the tissues of the body in order to protect them from the biological processes of decomposition.

There are some situations when the circulatory system may be very poor due to illness, old age, or possibly from damage sustained from injury. In these cases, it may be necessary to access specific areas via individual arteries or by directly injecting into the actual tissue. This is also the case with a body that has undergone a full post-mortem, as the circulatory system will no longer be intact. A body that has had a full post-mortem will also have had its internal organs removed for examination. These are usually placed back into the thoracic cavity afterwards. During the embalming process, the organs are soaked in a strong embalming solution.

Once the main embalming process has been carried out, the orifices are cleansed and sealed, using cotton wool or wadding.

This helps to prevent any unpleasant leakages and deter unwelcome visitors. And I'm not referring to double-glazing salesmen, as much as any steps to avoid their intrusions would be well worth the effort!

Next, the ears, nose, mouth and eyes must be cleaned and the facial features set. Eye caps resembling contact lenses can be placed on the eyes if they have become dehydrated and deep set into the eye sockets, giving a much more natural appearance. If the person wore dentures, they would be used, but if not available, for whatever reason, a mouth guard rather like a thin transparent gumshield can be placed in the mouth instead. This fills out the face and cheeks giving a more natural look rather than a horrifying gaunt expression – particularly if the person is very old or has lost a lot of weight. The mouth is then carefully set in the closed position.

The facial features need to be correct before the embalming solution sets to a thicker viscosity, and the stronger certain chemical elements are in the solution, the sooner that will be. Therefore, great care must be taken to try and obtain as natural an appearance as possible, in as short a space of time as possible. That doesn't mean the process should be rushed in any way, but just being mindful of the science behind the embalming process. It's very easy to change someone's natural facial expression by any of the procedures if not done cautiously and with great care.

Lastly, the hair should be washed again, before drying and styling it. The correct hairstyle is paramount. The wrong hairstyle can totally change someone's appearance and be quite distressing to family and friends. For all of these reasons, the most helpful thing for any embalmer is to have a recent photo of the deceased. This provides them with vital and important visual information such as shade of skin, and amount of makeup usually used by the deceased. Having the deceased's own makeup is ideal for this purpose. It's those little things that matter, and make all the difference.

Of course, not all relatives want their loved one embalmed, and occasionally, if a family did want to view the deceased but really didn't want them embalmed, a facial tidy-up might be carried out. This, however, is not advisable in a time frame where there are long periods of waiting before the funeral, due to reasons I have already mentioned about nature's very efficient biological process of decomposition. In all fairness, the tidy-up is really just a quick fix for a very short time, in order to prevent what could be quite an unpleasant and distressing experience.

Mortimer and Sons embalmer Marcus, was a very talented and highly skilled embalmer, a true alchemist of the flesh. His expertise in the art of embalming was second to none and testimony to his pursuit of perfection. He was also a man who appreciated real craftsmanship, and in his spare time enjoyed the challenge of fixing things and restoring them to their former glory – particularly things that were originally created by real craftsmen, or that were a little out of the ordinary.

During my time at Mortimer and Sons, within the field of embalming, I'd seen Marcus do some incredible reconstructive work on those who had sustained severe head injuries. This would enable the family and friends to view their recently departed loved one without it being quite the traumatic experience it might have been. I can remember walking into the embalming room on one occasion, being greeted by a head sitting on Marcus's embalming table. A strange sight indeed, and more than just a tidy-up required for viewing.

The head belonged to a man who had been decapitated after falling on some railings when he jumped from the top of a tower block. Once the man's head and body had been embalmed, which was quite an intricate job from what I gather, they were placed in their more natural positions for viewing in the coffin. Marcus seemed to be able to work miracles. Sadly, not the miracle the family would have liked, but miracles that hopefully helped them in their time of grief.

Due to the stressful nature of the job and an often hefty workload, Marcus's occasional early or extended lunch breaks were respectfully ignored by the hierarchy, who were obviously keen to keep such a skilled and dedicated embalmer in their employment. And although the rest of us would often take the mickey by tapping our watches and asking him what time he thought it was, as he strolled down the cobbled mews back to the mortuary – knowing what he had to deal with day in and day out – we in no way begrudged him one minute of that extra bit of time away from it all.

The Trainee Embalmer

My first encounter with the dissected remains of a human being that had undergone a post-mortem on Marcus's embalming table, was without a doubt the most bizarre and disgusting thing I had ever seen. However, that natural morbid fascination that we as a species seem to possess soon got the better of me and curiosity took over. The first opportunity I got to watch the embalming process from start to finish, although I was even more disgusted by the sight, I was equally more fascinated. I hope that doesn't make me sound like some kind of weirdo.

It was captivating watching Marcus work his magic. Totally transforming the often sorry-looking human remains before him, back into a proud mum, a knowing nan, a loving wife, a caring sister, and a beautiful daughter. A doting dad, a comical grandad, a loyal brother, and a handsome son. A truly amazing thing to be able to do, and something that I wanted to be able to do for people.

With Eamon's blessing, who was also a fully qualified embalmer himself, visits to the embalming room during the quieter periods at Mortimer and Sons became more frequent. I gradually learnt more about the magical art of human alchemy, and eventually began assisting with some of the less-skilled parts of the process.

The human body is an incredible piece of biological engineering. It's an astounding intricacy of networks and systems, so simple in design and basic in nature, yet incredibly mysterious within its unseen complexity. And just as I am with all nature in its entirety, on this amazing living sphere that we inhabit – spinning within an even more unimaginable and mysterious expanse of the cosmos – I was truly amazed and intrigued.

Eamon's responsibilities as foreman had to take priority over his embalming duties, which often meant that Marcus was at the end of his tether trying to cope with a heavy workload. With this in mind, I decided to approach Kenneth Mortimer about the possibility of becoming a trainee embalmer. After deep consideration, and taking into account the fact that Eamon would also be retiring in a few years, Mr Mortimer decided it wouldn't be such a bad idea and agreed to finance the official course. His only proviso was that my funeral, workshop and removal duties, would have to come first.

The theoretical side of my training was supported by an official tutor, Mr David Burns, and assignments were submitted via our trusty postal network. This left Marcus and Eamon to teach me the practical skills of embalming. I admired Marcus's embalming skills immensely, but on the occasions when I was assisting Eamon, I learnt a great deal more. Eamon seemed more than happy to pass on his knowledge and even seemed quite excited to have been given the opportunity to do so. Marcus, however, was exactly the opposite and always seemed to be holding back. It was almost as if he didn't want me to know quite as much as he did, even though he was always complaining about being overworked and needing more help.

Embalming was never something I would have ever thought myself capable of doing, and it wasn't the most pleasant job at the best of times. It was interesting though, and often quite challenging. Although it wasn't until I was actually the one carrying out the embalming procedure and had to overcome the difficulties myself using my own initiative, that I realised how challenging it could be. Saying that, it was very rewarding, especially when a call came from one of the branches informing us how pleased the family were with how the deceased looked, and how much it meant to them to be able to see their loved one looking so peaceful.

Unfortunately, with my other responsibilities at the yard, it became more and more difficult to find the time to practise the practical side of the embalming. Trying to study at home after work when I was tired was very difficult, and not being very academically-minded didn't help matters. I also wanted to be spending time with my family at the end of the day and felt I was neglecting them if I didn't. After a while, I had to re-evaluate whether it was what I really wanted to do with my life, and if it was worth all the effort and time away from the family. Decision made, I gave up the embalming and returned to my role as a menial bearer – with the occasional limousine or hearse drive.

Dressing

Once a body has been prepared, if they are to be viewed, they will usually be dressed in either their own clothes or one of the more luxurious selection of shrouds. Shrouds normally come in three pieces; two sleeves and the main piece. They are available in various colours, though generally white or ivory are used unless otherwise specified. More basic, plain shrouds, are usually used for non-viewers. If the deceased is not in a particularly good condition and difficult to handle, or in a body bag, the shroud is generally just placed on top in such a way as to appear that the deceased is wearing it. This is not done to be deceitful in any way, and although it obviously makes things easier for the undertaker, it's really done more out of respect for the deceased. Shrouds are generally quite easy to put on, with only the odd exception on some of the larger clients, but once on, they can transform even the most unlikely candidate into quite an angelic vision.

My main concern with the shrouds, which some might think is a little foolish, but nevertheless was and is still something I think about to this day, is… in the afterlife (assuming there is one), will we be wearing the clothing we were laid to rest in? Because if we are, the afterlife is going to be home to some very embarrassed spirits who will either need to avoid standing up or get used to a constant level of chilly exposure from behind. Unless eternity is to be spent lying in a coffin, and depending on how 'hot' or 'cold' it may be, of course.

Hopefully, if things have been properly thought out by the omnipotent deity or whoever might be in charge of such things in the afterlife, those poor souls in the disintegrating shrouds will be issued with something a little more suitable and practical for eternal life. If not, I imagine a great many undertakers will have a few complaints to deal with from a large number of previous customers, if they were ever to meet up in the afterlife. Personally, if I were the one being viewed by my family and friends – which one day I'm very likely to be – I would much rather be wearing my own clothes than a shroud. Not only because I think it's much better to see a person dressed in the clothes that we were familiar seeing them in, and that they liked to wear themselves, but because I really don't fancy my derriere being on display for all of eternity.

When it comes to dressing a body, it can be a great deal more challenging than you might think. While they're not likely to complain if you're a little heavy-handed, they can be quite uncooperative when it comes to things like keeping fingers together to slip arms easily through sleeves, or angling feet correctly to slide into trouser legs. Frequently, the clothing supplied by the family would not make things any easier either; clothing the deceased hadn't worn for years and that was often several sizes too small. Tight-fitting clothes can be a bit of a nightmare, but fortunately a small snip or two in the right place can easily solve the problem. More creative alterations would always have to be agreed by the family first.

Dressing was always complicated by the fact that the bodies, after being removed from the coolness of the refrigerator, were often clammy. Anyone who has tried to get dressed after swimming or showering without drying properly knows how obstinate clothing can be in those circumstances. It was always a relief when the clothing was too big, as this was a problem we could cope with. It's far easier to dress a body in larger clothes, and once tucked in strategically around the body, they can be made to appear to be a perfect fit.

Clothing-wise, you name it we'd probably dressed someone in it during my time as an undertaker. Smart, casual, and clothing from many different cultures. In fact, Joe and I were once asked to dress an Indian lady in a sari. Extremely surprised that the female members of her family were not going to be doing this themselves, we just looked at the expanse of flowing silk without a clue about where to start. Luckily, the cavalry arrived in the nick of time in the form of Marcus, who knew exactly what to do and how to do it. Joe and I watched in awe, assisting when required, as Marcus expertly and with the greatest of care, wrapped the beautiful flowing material of the uniquely intricate garment around the lady's body.

I still think Joe's idea about being dressed in a scuba-diver's outfit to make it as hard as possible for the undertakers, is the best suggestion I've heard to date. But I'm very glad that I've never actually had to dress a body in one.

It's fair to say that even some of the more common items of clothing presented their own challenges, too, and like many of my colleagues, I found it very difficult to put a tie on someone else. It's far easier to tie it on yourself first and then put it on the person afterwards. I eventually mastered the art of doing a Windsor knot – although, it was never quite in the same league as Joe's Windsor knots, of course.

Then there were feet. Feet are funny things! Not in the funny, comical sense of the word or in their practical design and ability to do what they've been assigned to do, but in a dressing and footwear application sense. Tights, stockings and socks, particularly on a cold, clammy body, can keep you occupied for far longer than you might imagine. Applying socks and other forms of footwear to one's own feet can be quite problematic, even for an adult. Especially that last struggle to get the heel properly bedded into a shoe or boot. Fortunately, this is a problem that our species has even developed a tool for, 'the shoehorn'. A simple but ingenious little device that can come in very handy. However, if someone has been ill for a long time, confined to bed, or possibly only worn bed socks or soft stretchy footwear like slippers for a while, the feet can spread. Medications can also cause swelling and shoes that may have once slipped on with ease and fit perfectly, could often give us a great deal of resistance when we were trying to put them on the deceased. I definitely think flip flops should be compulsory coffin footwear – or at least those wide-fitting, Velcro-fastening type shoes. Either would solve a lot of problems and make life a lot less stressful for the poor undertaker.

On some occasions the deceased was to wear gloves. Gloves can be quite cantankerous items to get on a cooperative hand, let alone on an uncooperative clammy hand. Particularly those long lacy ones that occasionally accompanied a wedding dress. Trying to get hands that were sometimes like shovels into probably the daintiest design of glove ever created, was no simple task.

Also, have you ever wondered why ladies' clothes fasten on the opposite side to men's clothes.' This particular question was raised one afternoon during the dressing of multiple deceased persons. During my subsequent investigations, I discovered something quite interesting. Allegedly, the practice goes back to a time when ladies needed assistance to dress and undress because of the vast number of fastenings on their garments, and had servants to help them. Right over left, by all accounts, being easier for someone else to do when standing in front of you, than left over right.

Some dressing challenges were more difficult on an emotional level. Dealing with youngsters, in all aspects of the funeral business, was always a poignant and thought-provoking experience, particularly for those staff with their own children. Dressing a child in their favourite football club's kit, or their Snow White dressing-up outfit, was a heart-rending experience. So tragic and so unfair that their young life was over before it had even begun.

I can remember on one occasion where I had to dress a stillborn baby that was due to be taken to the Tufnell Park branch for the parents to view and spend time with before the funeral. The poor little thing was in a terrible state of quite advanced decomposition. I contacted Rose at the branch and relayed my concerns about how distressing I thought this might be for the parents. Rose informed me that the parents already knew the condition their baby was in, but it was still their little girl, and they wanted to spend some time with her to say their last goodbyes. I dressed the tiny baby in the items of clothing her parents had chosen for her and placed her in the tiny white coffin. Next to her I placed a small white teddy that was almost as big as she was.

Later that day Rose contacted me to pass on the family's thanks. She said they were so pleased to have been given the opportunity to spend those last precious moments with their baby girl. For me, I wouldn't have felt right if I hadn't aired my concerns that day, but it just goes to show that ultimately people have to do what feels right for them, and make their own decisions about such things. We can only guide and advise with the knowledge and experience we have, and support people as best we can in their time of grief.

Viewing

The decision on whether or not to view someone can be a difficult one. Some will wish they had if they hadn't, and some will wish they hadn't if they had. I will say, generally, it was my experience that most people who decided to view a loved one did not regret it. To tell the truth, many said it was a very important thing for them to have done, in many ways. Saying that, we didn't view Mum after she died. As a family we felt no need. We decided we would rather remember her how she used to be. We didn't view Dad either, for the same reasons. I did however dress Dad in his best suit and tie and placed him in his coffin myself. I was really pleased that I found the strength to do it – it made me feel better. Which for me, is as good a reason as any for doing it.

If the deceased is to be viewed, viewing usually takes place in the funeral company's chapel of rest. Occasionally, the deceased is viewed in an open coffin in church or an equivalent religious establishment, but this is usually on the day before, or on the actual day of the funeral. There is, of course, also the option for the deceased to be taken home in order to hold a wake. Wakes where the deceased is present were far more common in this country years ago than they are today, but for some cultures it's still a large part of the time of mourning, and time to carry out essential religious ceremonies before the funeral itself.

Personally, I quite like the idea of having that time with a loved one at home one last time before the funeral. A time to chat, play music, read a favourite passage from a book or a piece of poetry, etc. Some might find this choice a little strange, preferring to view in a chapel of rest or a place of worship. However, when it comes to paying our last respects, nothing is particularly right or wrong, it's more about personal preference and the family's and deceased's wishes and beliefs.

I've been told by a number of people that the term 'wake', and having the coffin open for a period of time, was originally a way of making sure that someone who had passed from this earthly realm, was actually dead. Hence the term, a-wake! Other sources disagree with this, and suggest it has always been more to do with ceremonial practices. Whatever the reason, medical methods of deducing death being somewhat questionable in days gone by, it seems sensible to have a coffin open during such times, just in case!

Throughout history, many generations of people have feared that they might be buried or cremated alive. The Victorians were particularly terrified of this happening, and maybe with good cause. A number of coffins have been dug up for various reasons, showing clear evidence on the underside of the coffin lid, that the person inside had obviously not been dead when buried and had tried to claw their way out. Numerous systems were designed incorporating various devices, but the most popular seems to have been the use of a bell above ground, connected to a cord that would enable an occupant of a coffin that had been buried slightly prematurely, to try and alert passers-by that they were, in fact, not dead. How effective those systems were, your guess is as good as mine! But apparently, very often no thought of providing a method of supplying air to the person in the coffin was considered. Which seems to be quite a crucial element of the life-saving strategy.

As I've mentioned previously, removing a body on a stretcher from most residential settings usually involved negotiating some very awkward environments and nearly always required some precarious acrobatic skills, with endurance in fitness and strength a bonus. When it came to manhandling a finished coffin containing the body of the deceased, all neatly presented and ready to view, into those same environments, those skills were required tenfold.

Over the years, on many occasions, it was often necessary to enter a building via a window or to have to remove a door or two in order to allow access. We would always try to avoid having to strike the coffin or casket upright, but at times it was unavoidable. If we did have to, it was essential to have a few moments before revealing the deceased to family and friends, to make sure they had not been disturbed too much by the coffin's ballet-like movements.

One Size Does Not Fit All

The accurate measuring of bodies is paramount in avoiding many problems that can become an undertaker's worst nightmare. However, it's not always the easiest of procedures to carry out. Late one afternoon, Joe and I were sent to a hospital in South London to collect a body. We'd been instructed by Mr Carter, the office manager at head office, to let him know the size of coffin required as soon as possible, so one could be immediately fitted with the appropriate furnishings. The family wanted to view before the funeral which was in the afternoon the following day, and Marcus was staying on late to prepare the body for viewing in the morning.

We had just left the hospital and were heading back to North London, when we realised in our rush to get back to the yard, we had forgotten to measure the body. There was only one thing for it. Immediate action was required post-haste and a suitable secluded spot to stop and measure the body would have to be sought out. After several route diversions, we eventually managed to find a nice little spot in a quiet side road. A row of garages, set back slightly from the road, seemed an ideal place to carry out our important tactical manoeuvres. So, reversing up to one of the garage doors as close as we could, leaving just enough room to open the back doors of the vehicle to access the body, we set about the task in hand. The first problem with our cunning plan was the absence of a tape measurer. Not perturbed by this minor setback, we considered our options and after some deep contemplation of our predicament, we found the solution to our dilemma. We opted to use a variation of what we like to call, 'The Fisherman's Technique'. Now, admittedly it's not the most accurate of measuring techniques, but it seemed the best idea at the time. Actually, it was the only idea we had at the time.

'The Fisherman's Technique' involves the use of both hands to judge the size of something from memory, and then greatly exaggerate it to impress, fiction often playing quite a large part in the proceedings. Obviously, on this occasion, we were not out to impress or include any fictional embellishment, we simply required a measurement as near to the correct measurement as possible. The last phase in the fisherman's technique could therefore be omitted.

Estimating the height, or length, of the body was child's play. The deceased was well under six feet judging by the gap at the foot end of the stretcher, so a six-foot coffin would be a fairly safe bet. The tricky bit, was getting the correct shoulder width – a problem, even when we were equipped with one of Eamon's so-called foolproof measuring devices. Comical chaos ensued, as we took it in turns to crawl into the back of the van and use our variation of 'The Fisherman's Technique' to try and judge the width of the body. 'Chuckle Brothers' undertakers at work. In theory the idea seemed simple and quite viable, in practice it was a shambles and totally inaccurate.

The plan to measure the width of the body by placing a hand on each shoulder was easily achieved. It was the act of wriggling out of the van without using our hands, while trying to keep them fixed apart at the same distance as they were when either side of the body's shoulders, where the technique fell apart. It was no good, we had no other option but to err on the side of caution and overestimate the width of the body, hoping it was not too excessive. Some fictional embellishment, in other words. Some readers may be asking the question, why didn't we use the sliding side door on the side of the van to gain access to the body to get the required measurements? The answer to that, of course, is because it would have defeated the object of carrying out the operation in question as low key as possible.

The call was made to Mr Carter and the relevant information passed on – a 6' x 22" coffin would be perfect. It was now in the hands of the gods, and assistance from any deity not too busy to come to our rescue, would be greatly appreciated. On our return to the yard, we nervously measured the body with one of Eamon's foolproof measuring devices. The gods had been kind to us, forgiving us our stupidity and granting us continued employment at Mortimer and Sons Funeral Directors – for the time being, at least.

A large, synchronised sigh of relief echoed in the coldness of the mortuary, as the fridge door was shut and the whole nerve-racking episode put to rest.

ROAD RUNS

Road runs involved the transportation of bodies to, or from, various points of call around the country. They were a welcome distraction from the everyday, often hectic routine of removals, funerals, fitting up coffins, and cleaning vehicles. They were an opportunity to sit back and hit the open highways of this green and pleasant land. A chance to breathe in some fresh air and to escape the rat race for a few hours – roadworks, diversions and volume of traffic permitting, that is. They were usually carried out in the black Ford Granada estate or its replacement the black Ford Mondeo estate, after the Granada was finally put out to stud – an event that was long overdue even when I started with the company.

When it was time to say goodbye to the aging Granada, Marcus, the embalmer, purchased it from the company for what he claimed was a bargain price. That said, he refused to disclose exactly what the bargain price was, which led my colleagues and I to think it may not have been such a bargain after all. Either way, he was pleased with the deal, which is all that really mattered, and in no time at all he was proudly displaying his 'Granada Owners Club' badge, on its aged windscreen.

The vans were sometimes used for road runs, but were rather rattly when travelling at over fifty miles per hour, which as you can imagine would become quite irritating after a while, the elusive bangs, thuds and rattles, pushing you across that fine line between sanity and insanity as you trundled towards your destination; if you were one of the luckier members of staff that was still balancing precariously along that very fine line, of course. Although, which side of that fine line is preferable in this crazy world of ours, is definitely up for debate. Luckily, the vans were usually needed more in town for the high volume of local removals and the transportation of bodies between the branches.

One of the biggest problems with the estate cars was the safety aspect, or rather, the lack of it. They weren't long enough or properly adapted in any way for the job they were being used for. It was just a matter of lowering the back seat down, angling the wheelie stretcher or coffin diagonally towards the front passenger's seat and pushing the passenger seat as far forward as possible without incapacitating the passenger in the process. Then, as they say, Bob's your uncle, Fanny's your aunt, and you were all set to go off on your merry – if not ever so slightly unnerving – way.

Sharp breaking was, needless to say, to be avoided at all costs for both the comfort and safety of the person occupying the front passenger seat. The consequences of an emergency stop for the person sitting in the front passenger seat, did not bear thinking about. Which is probably why most of us preferred the role of driver on road runs.

Another drawback with the estate cars, that affected both passenger and driver, was the fact that you were in very close proximity to the body for what could often be quite a few hours on a long journey. If they were a bit odoriferous, it could feel like an even longer journey. Fortunately for us, most of the road runs were fairly recent deaths – usually from either a hospital or another undertakers. The deceased would generally not have been absent of life for very long. Another positive with the bodies that were being collected from – or delivered to – another undertakers, was that they would usually be in a finished coffin, quite often embalmed, and thus far less likely to be emitting any unpleasant odours.

Aside from gaining a nice little break from our normal, quite hectic routine, the best thing about being on a road run was the monetary float supplied for food and refreshments. The first stop on any journey, lengthy or not, was nearly always for the 'compulsory' full English Olympic-size breakfast with all the extras. Except for

Morris that is, who preferred to go all continental, with croissants and a fruit juice. By far the healthier option, but a great deal less enjoyable or as satisfying.

If not out on a funeral, Morris could nearly always be found in his overalls, tinkering around underneath the bonnet or another part of his hearse. God only knows what was left on the vehicle that needed tinkering with. And even if it was a genuine issue of maintenance or repair, you could be sure Morris would milk it for as long as humanly possible, to avoid being sent out on removals or any other funeral-related business that he didn't want to be involved in. You had to be careful what you said in front of Morris, especially if you were having a bit of a moan about anything to do with Mortimer and Sons. It was bound to get back to ears you'd rather it didn't get back to.

A road run to the seaside was always a welcome distraction and an opportunity to purchase the traditional stick of rock for loved ones to prove the location of our macabre adventure. Besides the seaside (see what I did there?), Wales was also a popular destination for many of our road runs. So popular, that at one point I began to wonder if the Welsh were trying to knock off the English one by one. Most of the time our trips to Wales were to collect ill-fated climbers that had come a cropper on the unforgiving mountainous terrain so readily available in the west of our beautiful isle. Did they fall, or were they pushed?

Survival Instincts

I can remember one gloomy day when Oliver and I were sent out on an excursion to Wales. Driving through the dense fog which so often inhabits the Welsh mountains, we could hardly see the end of the car's bonnet in front of us. I remember thinking what a shame it was to be missing out on all that beautiful scenery. Having stopped for a coffee at a service station just prior to entering the fog, I decided to use my initiative (something I have been encouraged to do on numerous occasions over my lifespan by various individuals), and save my lovely hot coffee in case we got stranded. My clever plan meant I would have a hot drink to keep me nice and warm, as well as giving me the chance to assist my colleague with his survival too, by sharing the beverage. I felt quite confident in my clever little plan – until I mentioned it to Oliver. Oliver, with his public-school education, immediately spotted a slight flaw in my 'not' so clever plan. Once he had stopped laughing, he smugly pointed out that if we did get stranded, the coffee would probably be stone cold by the time we would actually need it, thus rendering its warming-up capabilities void and null. 'Smart arse!' It's worth mentioning at this point, that on many occasions where I have endeavoured to use my initiative, I have subsequently been advised that I shouldn't have done. Sometimes you just can't win!

Bates Motel

On another occasion, Adam and I were sent to collect a body from an undertaker in a small village in Cumbria. When we arrived, we were very surprised to find that the actual premises of the undertakers was nothing more than an old cottage. The garage attached to the cottage had been cleverly converted for the business side of things, including a chapel of rest, and a single fridge unit that contained three trays. The cottage was used for the office side of things, such as interviewing the bereaved and arranging the funerals. More interestingly, the cottage itself was full, from top to bottom, of stuffed animals in various poses, from all manner of species. Rather unnervingly, it gave the place a very 'Norman Bates' sort of feel (star of the original Alfred Hitchcock psychological horror film, *Psycho* – for those of you wondering where you might have heard the name before).

As it turned out, the undertaker who resided in the cottage spent his spare time practising the art of taxidermy – the art of preparing, stuffing, and mounting animals for display. Clearly, he enjoyed the aesthetic nature of his hobby, as he even made all the foliage and the contents of the diorama that the animals were set in. It was actually quite amazing and he was obviously very skilled, even if I found the finished article to be quite eerie. How the undertaker's clients felt when arranging funerals for their loved ones, surrounded by dead animals, goodness knows. Personally, I prefer to observe wildlife running around freely in its own habitat, rather than seeing it as a stuffed example staring intently at me from the mantelpiece.

The road runs were done on a rota basis, which gave everyone at the yard a chance to escape the daily routine and enjoy one of the adventurous little excursions with a fellow colleague. It was all working well until Mortimer and Sons decided they were being too extravagant sending two members of staff, when they could potentially just send one. We pleaded our case and gave many good reasons why this was not a good or practical idea, but our pleas unfortunately fell on deaf ears. I think we might have stood a better chance with our negotiations if a certain person who shall remain nameless (in his blue overalls), hadn't said he would be quite happy to do all the road runs on his own. So much for solidarity! Well, there's always one, as they say. It just so happened that for us, it was always the same one. Over the following weeks and months, most of us opted to come off the road run list because of it – leaving a certain person to the pleasure of his own company.

Airport runs supporting exports and imports of human remains were usually carried out by the duty squad, as they often ran into the after-hours time frame. In the case of exporting human remains, we would usually have to make our journey via the relevant embassy to collect paperwork, and when required, get an official seal applied to the coffin. Not quite foreign travel, but the closest most of us got to it in our job.

THE WORKSHOP
AND GARAGE AREA

As menial bearers, when not out on funerals or removals or transporting bodies to and from branches, Adam and I were expected to fulfil our duties in the workshop. Primarily, this meant fitting up the coffins and engraving the nameplates for the coffins, wooden plaques, urns and crosses. With responsibility came great expectation, and just as it was for the other menials, Joe, Frank, Graham, Howard and Reg, we bore the burden of checking what was required, and making sure it was done, when it was required. Fortunately, Eamon's various lists, systems and boards with bits of coded paper clipped to them with the relevant information we needed, assisted us to do this quite effectively and efficiently. Well, most of the time they did! Suffice to say, any time we weren't performing any other work-related duties, we could usually be found in the workshop, or very occasionally, the tearoom.

Adam and I soon became experts in the art of fitting up coffins. Although, when I say experts, what I really mean is, more accomplished. Eventually, just like Old Des, we could have performed the task in our sleep. Which, after being out all night on removals when on call, could come in quite handy – and definitely not dangerous in any way, shape or form, with the various power tools and sharp objects that were at our disposal. The precision creases we were now capable of producing with the white plastic sheeting that lined the coffins, put us at least at black belt status in the art of origami. The need for rulers became unnecessary and therefore obsolete, as our eyes developed the judgement of distance and alignment that we once could only dream about.

During my time at Mortimer and Sons, various adaptations were made to the internal aesthetics of the coffin. For example, when I first started in the workshop, the pillows were built into the coffin using the ever versatile white plastic sheeting that lined the inside, and was stapled in place using shredded paper as padding. Later, we started using properly styled coffin pillow-cases made out of the same material as the inside sets. This made fine adjustments to the positioning of the head and body much easier and meant the height and angle of the head could be simply adjusted by adding, or extracting, the desired amount of shredded paper. Something that was extremely difficult to do with the built-in pillows.

The height of the head is always a priority when placing a body in a coffin. Too high, and the clearance between the nose and the lid could be compromised – the importance of which I have covered in a previous section of the book – and especially important when trying to avoid the Tyson sparring-partner look. The angle of the head is also a major consideration when it comes to coffin pillows, as it is with normal pillows, I suppose, but for different reasons. If the head is not positioned in a natural position, the deceased will just look uncomfortable and certainly not at peace. Even worse, staring up a loved one's nostrils as you say your final goodbyes, is not really the last vision of them you want to be left with.

Coffins

Over the years, I've seen many types of coffins, ranging from the most basic and very plain, to the most elaborate. The huge American-style metal caskets, like the one I saw on my first day and suggested would make a good sidecar – a statement made in jest, but was taken a little more seriously than intended – really are like the stretched limo equivalent of a coffin, fitted with the most luxurious padding and flamboyant inside sets you're ever likely to see. Then there are the solid wood caskets with intricate carvings of biblical scenes such as the 'Last Supper', as well as non-religious subjects like fields of sunflowers, etc.

However, for me, I've always preferred the much simpler designs. I was quite impressed with the wooden flat-pack ones which we started to use for some of the eco woodland burials. They were put together using wooden dowels. A smidgen of glue was also used on the dowel, just to be on the safe side. An eco-friendly glue, of course! In keeping with the theme, the handles were made of rope instead of plastic or metal, which actually looked quite effective in a rustic sort of way.

While I do like the idea of coffins being eco-friendly, my colleagues and I did get a little concerned when the rep from a company who made cardboard coffins tried to sell the idea to Mortimer and Sons. The theory behind them is great, as they are both eco-friendly and more economical – although they aren't as cheap as you might think. Logistically, our main concern was that if we got caught carrying the coffin in the rain, we would end up looking like we'd been in an argument with a load of papier mâché, and lost, our biggest fear being that after the unplanned disintegration of the cardboard coffin, the once contained occupant would end up balanced on our shoulders for all to see. It didn't bear thinking about, and we definitely weren't convinced – even after the rep did his best to reassure us that they were far more robust than they looked. I'm not sure whether Mortimer and Sons actually offered the cardboard option when people were arranging funerals. If they did, I was never on a funeral that used one, and I don't recall ever seeing one on the premises again.

Occasionally, families would want the coffin to be personalised in some way. Something that told you a bit about the person or their life, or just something the deceased would have liked themselves. A becoming tribute rather than just a box to be buried or cremated in. This enabled the family and friends to feel more involved, and do something a little more special for that final goodbye. One family had an artist friend come to the yard and paint a wonderful country meadow scene over the entirety of the coffin, complete with blue skies, fluffy white clouds and fields of bright yellows surrounded by rolling green hills. A few strategically placed sheep also enjoyed the idyllic scene. It was beautifully done and a real work of art.

Capable of creating our own beautiful designs when we needed to, Oliver once used multicoloured strips of material to completely cover a coffin and create the colours of the rainbow, to represent the gay flag. It took him quite a while to complete, but it was very effective and looked amazing.

The most unusual coffin we ever had, which was supplied by the family, was made of wicker and shaped like a giant pair of hands clasped together as if in prayer, or possibly a representation of the hands of God holding the deceased. Either way, there was a very spiritual feel about it.

Nowadays there are companies that can supply some amazingly creative, weird and wonderful coffins, on literally any theme you desire, if you choose to stray away from the traditionally built coffin. There are also all sorts of materials available, too, including wicker, willow, bamboo, seagrass, banana leaves, hemp, and cork, to name but a few. Some choices may be less available in certain countries, of course.

I absolutely love the idea of personalised coffins, although it's probably worth enquiring if the crematorium or cemetery have any regulations or restrictions as to size or type of coffin, before getting all creative. Saying that, as much as I think the idea of something more personal and a little different is a great idea, there's certainly nothing wrong with the more traditional.

Engraved On Our Hearts Forever

In many countries it's a legal requirement – for identification purposes – for a coffin to have a nameplate containing, at least, the name of the deceased. In some countries, the date of birth and date of death is also required. The nameplate, or plaque as they are otherwise known, may also contain an inscription of some kind, a simple phrase or verse dedicated to their memory.

The engraving of the plaques was not always a simple task, and the engraving machines in the Mortimer and Sons workshop continued to test every ounce of patience a person possessed – edging most of us that used them, ever closer towards that fine line of mental stability. In the corner of the workshop where the two engravers resided, new words of cursing were born due to the vast overuse of old ones that no longer fully expressed the true feelings of the desperately frustrated operative. Angry jigs were performed, that would definitely have got you thrown off any dance floor – except at a wedding perhaps – and tempers were frequently frayed.

On the other hand, the euphoria and experience of completing an engraved plate without any problems or mishaps – any that were noticeable, that is – were emotions without comparison. Except perhaps, those that overwhelm you when you witness your own child being born, or discover your mum has rewarded you and put pickle in your cheese sandwiches without telling you. Much more tantalising than the taste of cheese on its own!

Eventually, Mortimer and Sons moved into the twenty-first century and progressed to a computerised engraver. Although 'the powers that be' obviously didn't think that we at the yard were capable of grasping the advanced technology and didn't want us damaging their rather costly prize piece of equipment, so it was kept at head office and operated by management only.

The upgrade was a sad occasion in many ways. As cantankerous and demonic as the two antiquated engraving machines could be, oddly, we missed them. Not only because it was a good little number for getting the occasional bit of overtime, but also because, just like having a senile old grandparent, we had grown accustomed to their abuse, mockery and strange little idiosyncratic ways. In actual fact, we shared a strange fondness for the cantankerous old things. Technology may be a wonderful thing in the right hands, and the left of course – if left-handed – or in both if ambidextrous. Inevitably though, as with all technology, it is destined to fail you at a crucial moment.

Fortunately, Eamon was no fool and had taken precautionary measures for just such an occasion. So, when the prized computerised engraver at head office decided to have a breakdown, Eamon was ready for action, and the lesser antiquated of the two engravers was brought out of exile, dusted down, and put to work once more. As if grateful for this new lease of life, its antagonistic nature seemed much more forgiving than before its departure – for a short time, at least. Eventually, frustration returned as the machine had obviously had enough of being amiable, and the language in the far corner of the workshop resumed its colourful nature with a blueish tint.

Nostalgia is a sentimental thing which can trick us into remembering times gone by as better times, when actually, in many ways they probably weren't better times at all. *Vive le progress!*

Sanctuary Much

Having mastered the various skills required in the workshop, time spent there became quite a therapeutic part of the job. Our little sanctuary behind the scenes, an oasis in a desert of woe. A place where we could let go, relax and not be so serious, if only for a short while. It was a welcome break from the sadness of the funerals, a chance to take time off from wrestling with decomposed bodies, and a place away from the constant scrutiny of the public eye. Maintaining a perpetual funeral face for hours on end must surely have detrimental effects on a person's positive equilibrium – as well as the facial muscles. And if I remember correctly, should the wind change, your face would be destined to stay like that forever. Being in the workshop gave us time to regain those laughter lines, and maybe even add a few more, whilst still getting the work done.

Looking back on it now, I can see how important it was to have that time, and that it played such a huge part in helping us to cling on to some level of sanity, in this mad and sometimes very cruel and unfair world. Although, how sane any of us were before becoming undertakers, is debatable.

As important as our time in our sanctuary was, enabling us to share some slightly less serious moments scattered through the day, by the time you'd fitted up your eighth coffin, been tormented by the antiquated engraving machines (before we were computerised), and spent half an hour unblocking the jammed-up teeth on the paper shredder, you'd be praying for Eamon's office phone to ring with orders from head office, to go out on a nice gruesome coroner's removal.

A Time to Weep, and a Time to Laugh
A Time to Work, and a Time to Play

On those rare occasions when times were quiet at the yard, when all the coffins required were finished, all the bodies for viewing or for funerals were dressed and boxed up, all deliveries and collections completed, when all the black beasts had been watered and groomed, and Eamon's office phone fell silent – a small window of opportunity for various distractions from the day's toil and seriousness was briefly permitted, or at least, unofficially tolerated.

With trestles and any other obstacles removed, the workshop's smooth, hard flooring, was the ideal venue for an improvised game of ice hockey. Mysteriously, some hockey sticks had appeared in the coffin stores that nobody seemed to know anything about. One of the black plastic washers from under a screw that secures the lid to an unfinished coffin, in order to protect the lid, although slightly small, was an ideal stand-in ice-hockey puck.

As an alternative, there was always the opportunity to enjoy a game of football using a ball made out of elastic bands. The elastic bands had been commandeered during the elastic band war truce – a war that had quickly got out of hand and produced some very nasty bruises, and caused a few nervous twitches to develop. The elastic band ball was fine for a makeshift game of course, but a proper football when available, was a whole different 'ballgame'.

For those days when energy levels were running low, a game of darts could be enjoyed. The dartboard, rescued from a skip, was mounted on the back of the coffin stores door and paved the way for a variety of very entertaining games. A particular favourite with the old arrows, rather appropriately named, was a game called Killer.

There are no restrictions on the number of players that can participate, in fact, the more the merrier. The rules of 'Killer' are as follows.

Initially all darts must be thrown using the opposite hand to the one you naturally use. This is a particularly amusing part of the game as it can take a few shots to actually hit the board, and as an observer you need to be very careful where you stand. Once you have hit the playing area of the board, whatever number the dart lands in, is your allocated target number for the rest of the game. Each player is given five lives. These are chalked up on a blackboard, represented by five lines. Reverting back to your natural throwing hand, each player must get the double of their own number before they can start their game. From that point on, the objective of the game is to take away the lives of the other players by getting your darts in their number. If you land in their number on the board, one of their lives is gone. Land in a double, you take two of their lives, and a treble takes three. It's a game of elimination, and one which can frequently lead you to question who your real friends are and make some people quite paranoid – especially if it appears everyone else seems to be going for your number. It's also possible to eliminate yourself if you hit your own number – which can be quite infuriating but very amusing to the other players. As with many games, it can start out to be a harmless bit of fun, but all too often, it can end in tears.

Send in the Clowns

Pranks and practical jokes were also very much a sanity saver in our line of work. Some of our favourites included: stapling a colleague's tie, while they were wearing it, to various wooden objects in the vicinity; throwing someone into the large storage box of shredded paper; ripping out the plastic sheeting from a coffin after someone has spent a great deal of effort getting each crease razor sharp and geometrically perfect; having a staple-gun gunfight, and elastic band battles.

To some, these activities and pranks may seem rather immature, and some even a little dangerous. Although, as I have mentioned, the elastic band battles were stopped before they got seriously out of hand. However, I honestly believe that those light-hearted moments were essential self-therapy sessions, that helped us to cope with the death and grief that engulfed our everyday lives. And although those moments were generally very few and far between, they were a very welcome distraction when time allowed.

For me, humour is one of the ultimate weapons to have in the battle to survive the trials and tribulations of both life, and death. If I see an opportunity to make someone laugh, I find it very hard to resist. Just to see their face light up and hear the sound of laughter, is quite magical. A good example of this was when we were issued with canvas aprons to help keep our suits clean while carrying out our duties in the workshop. With all the times we were in and out of the yard during the day, it was a bit of a pain to keep getting changed into our civvies, so the aprons were a very practical and welcome addition to our work attire.

It was quite soon after being issued the aprons, that whilst removing remnants of sawdust from one before putting it on, it came to my attention that the sound the canvas aprons made when flapped vigorously was uncannily similar to what I imagined the sound of the huge sails of a galleon ship would make, as they bellowed in the wind on the high seas. This created an opportunity for me to entertain my colleagues, which I could not resist. In an attempt to transport them, through the power of suggestion, I took them one by one on a virtual tour of a high-seas adventure. Encouraging my willing participant to close their eyes, I would stand to their right – or to use the correct nautical term, 'starboard' – and flap my canvas apron. Not only was the auditory effect very convincing, the wind created by the flapping added an additional sensory element to the atmosphere. Trying to enhance the realism of the historical naval experience further, I added some traditional sailing cries.

"Hoista da main sail," I exclaimed.

Although, why the words came out in a Spanish accent, I have no idea. I can only surmise that my inner psyche wanted this to be a Spanish galleon experience.

Always striving for perfection, a completely new dimension to the theme was developed when Joe became involved and added some special effects of his own. By blowing into the face of the high-seas-experience candidate and simultaneously flicking water at them from a cup – to represent the ocean spray – thanks to Joe, a new and more true to life feature was added. Honestly, you really had to be there to fully appreciate the effort that went into creating this amazingly realistic experience, and how ridiculous we must have looked doing it.

As the song written by soul artist Seal and Guy Sigsworth says, *'We're never going to survive, unless we get a little crazy'*, something I wholeheartedly agree with, and think we managed quite successfully to achieve in this particular instance.

One Lump or Two?

The tearoom was also a place where, if we were lucky, we not only found time for the occasional 'quick cup of tea' or coffee, and a bite to eat, we could relax and unwind away from the solemnity of the public domain, and engage in inane drivel and playful banter. Some intellectual exchanges may have wormed their way into the conversation every now and again, but rarely lasted for more than a couple of sentences before being swiftly banished from whence they came.

Card games were also a popular pastime in the tearoom, in particular, one called kalooki, which is apparently a Jamaican version of rummy. It's fair to say that these games could get very lively and were sometimes quite disruptive to any kind of conversation.

The Garage

Each vehicle in the garage had its own allocated spot where it lived when not in use – marked out by faded white painted lines on the dark concrete floor. The three Daimler hearses sat side by side in the far left corner diagonally opposite the entrance to the garage. The Ford hearse, ostracised for its lack of breeding, sat almost hidden behind one of the vans in the corner next to the entrance. The Ford had been acquired along with the old Granada estate, when

Mortimer and Sons had taken over another undertakers, which was now the Holloway branch. It was always deemed as inferior to its much bigger and more regal four-wheeled rivals, yet in many ways it was a much more practical vehicle, nicer to drive, and probably a great deal cheaper to run than its Daimler counterparts. I suppose it didn't quite have the same swagger and command of respect that the larger, more charismatic Daimlers had, and it was eventually sold off to a rural undertakers at a bargain price, where I'm sure it was much happier and more appreciated. The three Daimler limousines resided in the remaining spaces in the garage, two next to one of the huge concertina doors, and one next to the pedestrian entrance to the workshop.

The vehicles would need to be cleaned before, during, and after each use, to try and keep them as pristine as possible. This was often a soul-destroying task, especially in winter with all the mud, rain, and occasional snow on the roads.

A Home From Home

Not only was the garage home for the vehicles, it was also another place where we were not under constant scrutiny or in the public eye, unless the huge black concertina gates were fully open revealing us to the world, that is. The corner of the garage behind the three hearses was known as 'the comfy-corner'; a home from home that consisted of a saggy three-seater sofa, a threadbare armchair, and a badly scratched mahogany coffee table sitting on a moth-eaten old rug. All were unwanted items of furniture salvaged either from skips or donated by some of the yard's staff. The 'comfy-corner' was officially Dean and Oliver's territory, but a weary colleague searching for solace would rarely be turned away. It was also a handy place to crash out if you'd been called out in the middle of the night and it wasn't worth you going back home again. Mind you, it could be a wee bit nippy during the colder months – in which case the back seat of a limousine was far cosier to catch up on a bit of shut-eye, if the need arose. For the shorter ones of us, at least.

During the hotter summer months, any excuse to splash a bit of water around in the garage was taken full advantage of, and if you'd just spent the last hour or so waxing and polishing a vehicle for its next public appearance, a bit of playful fun could soon turn into a full-scale war.

Artistic Tendencies

During one of the occasional lulls in our workload, Oliver had an urge to repaint the nearly extinct white lines on the garage floor, a job he had apparently been putting off for years. His vision for the new artwork was illuminating and involved a bright luminous yellow paint with the viscosity of molasses that would harden to an indestructible compound and probably last for at least the next four generations of the Mortimer dynasty.

Watching Oliver from my position in the 'comfy-corner' armchair, I noticed that the thickness of the paint seemed to be presenting him with some problems during its application. Trying to be helpful, I suggested that he place the spray-can into a bucket of warm water for a while, to allow it to thin out a bit. Truth be known, Oliver was far more experienced and knowledgeable about the properties of paint and its application than I was. He'd done a lovely job of spray-painting the motorcycle that he bought off me and rebuilt. The fact that it was bright orange instead of the fire engine red he wanted it to be, due to him being colour blind, was neither here nor there.

Having placed the spray-can into some hot water, we retired to the tearoom to partake in a brew. Sitting in the tearoom, during the consumption of our refreshments there was an almighty bang from the vicinity of the garage. Time seemed to stand still for a brief moment as we looked at each other's shocked expressions. Realisation dawning, we rushed out of the tearoom dodging the various profanities that echoed around its magnolia eggshell paintwork, to see what the origins of such an unexpected noise could be.

Thankfully, we had not been the victims of an undertaker turf war. The explosion was a result of our own innocent, yet foolish attempt to overcome a simple viscous problem. The hearse and van next to the bucket of water where the spray-can of luminous paint once bathed, were now sporting a new look. If Crinkly Bottom's Mr Blobby was ever looking to go into the funeral business, we had just the vehicles for him. After a moment or two of panic, the white spirit emerged and vigorous arm movements not seen since our teenage years were employed to try and rectify our predicament. Judging by the amount of hysterical laughter emanating from various parts of the yard, our work colleagues were clearly tickled by the eruptive incident. Two hours later and copious amounts of sweat lighter, all but a few stubborn molecules of the thick luminous paint had been removed from the bodywork of each vehicle. Nobody would be any the wiser – as long as they didn't look too closely that is.

Oliver learnt two valuable lessons that day. Firstly, not to leave an aerosol paint-can in hot water for longer than necessary, or preferably, not at all. And secondly, not to take any notice of any advice I might pass his way in the future. Especially, if it involved paint preparation and its application.

FUNERALS

The Final Journey

Whether it's a solitary hearse going direct to the cemetery or crematorium and meeting a handful of mourners at the venue (or no mourners at all in some cases), or a mile-long procession of flora-covered vehicles and 100,000 mourners, the sentiment of the journey is ultimately the same. A life is over – it's time to pay your respects and say a last goodbye.

Visually, the conductor is generally the most prominent member of the funeral team and throughout modern history has been governed by fairly specific funeral protocol and etiquette. The visible presence of the conductor is often quite theatrical, with the use of their props – top hat and cane – they set the tone for the sombre occasion and is the image most associated with funerals. However, this is not always the case; some funeral directors prefer to take a less formal approach, and do this successfully without compromising the dignity of the occasion.

During my time as an undertaker there was quite a high percentage of women in organisational roles within the funeral business, yet there were very few who took on the role of a conductor. In recent years the balance has changed and more women have stepped into the role. A truly positive step, not just for equality, but also because in my experience the feminine touch often encourages a more empathic feel. Saying that, over recent years, many men now feel more confident in showing an emotional response when dealing with the bereaved in a sensitive and respectful way. This evolution has made the role of a conductor, whether they are male or female, a more sensitive and compassionate role to the one it once was. Even though many funerals are becoming more and more personalised and varied in many ways, the role of the conductor, whether male or female, remains the same – to support the family and keep things running smoothly.

The traditional black hearse is the most common way of transporting a coffin on the funeral, both in this and many other countries. Variations of makes and models used by different undertakers range from vintage to the very latest top of the range models. There are slightly more options these days, as people steer away from the traditional black, in favour of something more unique and personal – particularly for youngsters' funerals. Two-tone livery, silver, white, and even pink hearses are now a more common site. Other modes of modern transport have also become more commonplace and I've seen the likes of lorries, specially adapted motorcycle and sidecar hearses, trikes with trailers, and purpose-built trike hearses, used on various occasions. And nowadays there seems to be a plethora of interesting alternative forms of funeral vehicles evolving, as people want to do something a little more special or out of the ordinary for their loved one's last journey.

The horse-drawn carriage, previously the only option for obvious reasons (apart from a human-propelled cart, that is) has also again become a popular and more elegant choice to transport the deceased to their final resting place. The carriages are usually original ornate Victorian carriages, complimented by impressive Belgian Black horses with highly polished bridles and elegant black ostrich plumes. An impressive sight indeed.

The Flowers

The number of floral tributes on a funeral can vary greatly, from none to hundreds – even thousands. Sometimes a separate vehicle may even be required on the day of the funeral to cope with the volume of flowers. Often being a hearse, due to its practical design for displaying quite a large amount of flowers, the floral hearse, as it's called, usually leads the funeral procession and contains only floral tributes. The remaining tributes would typically be distributed between the main hearse and the limousines. On occasions where there are more flowers than can be catered for, the mourners in their private cars may be asked to assist in transporting them to the funeral venue. I've even been on a few funerals where open-back lorries have been used because of the sheer volume of flowers. However, the volume of flowers is not always the only reason for the use of a lorry, it can often be because the deceased was involved in the haulage industry in some way or they had a particular interest in such vehicles.

One of the most memorable floral tributes I can recall – although possibly not the most spectacular – was handed to me in the car park of the West Chapel at Golders Green Crematorium. It was an empty lager tin (of a particular Australian brand), and protruding from the open can was a magnificent long-stemmed sunflower in full bloom. At the time I was quite shocked, thanking the person who had handed it to me and then realising what it was. It was rather odd and far from the usual funeral flower arrangement. Obviously a personal connection going on there, which meant something special between the deceased and the mourner. Brilliant!

The more traditional tributes come in all shapes and sizes, and some are real works of art. You name it, I'm fairly sure I've seen it created using flora. Animals, vehicles, alcoholic beverages, various sporting equipment, such as snooker tables – complete with balls and cues, football club emblems, etc., etc. Thousands of pounds can easily be spent on floral tributes for just one funeral, yet as spectacular as they may be visually, even the most amazing of floral creations will soon wither and die. And while a beautiful addition to any funeral, these days it's becoming more and more common to only have flowers from the immediate family or in some instances, to have none at all. When this is the case, the mourners are often given the option of either making a donation to a charity of the family's choice, one the deceased may have supported, or an organisation that may have been involved in the deceased's care in some way during their illness. Donation to a charity always seems like a nice idea and quite appropriate.

The Procession

Keeping the vehicles spick and span for their funeral duties could be quite an arduous task. Continuous from the start of the day to the very end, maintaining the high level of cleanliness as you worked over from one funeral to the next was no mean feat. Often with only a few spare minutes to pull over and give the car a quick once-over – if you were lucky – with this country's usual weather system, the task often fell well into the 'fighting a losing battle' context. During the winter months it was an absolute nightmare. As a driver, you could easily spend every waking hour washing, waxing, polishing, shedding blood, sweat and tears to keep the black beasts presentable. Which is great if you're the Karate Kid (for those who remember the 'wax on, wax off' scene), but it can become a bit tedious and quite soul-destroying, day in and day out.

My first official limousine drive, after being with Mortimer and Sons for a few months, was driving Arthur's limousine when he rang in sick one morning. Luckily, he'd given it a good clean the previous evening and it just needed a bit of a dust-over and the windows cleaned to remove a mass of grubby fingerprints from the previous days pawing.

As a driver, it's fairly important to know your way around. Fortunately, having had numerous driving jobs before becoming an undertaker, my knowledge of London was fair to middling – although there was still plenty of room for improvement. On the two limousine drives I was doing that day, thankfully I was the second car on both funerals, and Eddie was first car. That meant that I was following him on both jobs, which took the pressure off and made things a great deal easier for me.

Of course, on any journey, knowing where you are going is one thing, but when driving in a funeral cortège, you have to be quite cunning and diplomatically assertive with other road users – particularly when you're somewhere like London. It really is a rat race out there, and many drivers are far less courteous than any rats might be, cutting in between the limousines and the hearse, blasting their horns, and cursing you for slowing down their fast-paced, busy lives.

As a driver, keeping the cortège as close together as you can is a prime concern, but not an easy task through the busy streets of London whilst trying to drive in the correct manner for a funeral and not a Formula One race. Discreet communication with the other vehicles in the cortège is key to keeping everyone together, wherever the vehicle you were driving is positioned in the cortège, pulling over and signalling to the other vehicles in front or behind you – by flashing the headlights or by giving a quick hoot of the horn – to let them know what's going on. The old Daimlers were not the most manoeuvrable of vehicles at the best of times – particularly around the narrower back roads. It only takes one badly parked car on a tight corner to create a challenge that even 'The Stig' would struggle to navigate.

Occasionally, it was nice to have a change and drive on some of the funerals, rather than just take a back seat as a menial bearer. Although, if I'm honest, being the driver could be a lot more stressful, and there was no financial incentive at all except maybe the prospect of a bit more overtime. This was probably why being a full-time driver didn't really appeal to me and why I never accepted the role whenever a vacancy came up.

When driving a limousine, if the family didn't want the partition window up, it could be quite interesting and often very entertaining listening to family stories about the deceased, especially the more jovial stories that they recalled and shared. It was also a good opportunity to meet many of the local ministers from various churches, as well as those representing other religions and non-religious organisations. Some interesting conversations were exchanged on many a journey to a crematorium or cemetery, or when picking them up and dropping them off at various points of call. If they could manage to stay awake on the slow, hypnotic, bouncy ride, that is.

Some ministers were quite cunning on the actual funeral, and would disguise their sneaky little nap in the car by making it look as though they were contemplating sections of their religious manuscripts, prayer book or notes, as it sat open-paged on their lap in front of them. Which would have been totally convincing – had they not been snoring! Staying awake could also be a huge problem if you were a menial bearer sat in the back of the hearse or in the front of the limousine – particularly if you'd been up most of the night on removals. Fighting the soothing, rocking motion and the soft lullaby of the Daimler's purring motor, was futile.

On one occasion, sat behind Mr Kenneth Mortimer in the hearse, I came very close to assaulting my employer during one of my nodding dog impersonations. The previous night had been very busy for my colleagues and me call-out wise, and having had very little sleep I was really struggling to stay awake. Luckily for me, one of the more violent nods shook me up enough to prevent all-out slumber. Joe, sat on the opposite back seat, for his entertainment on the journey, had been watching me, waiting for me to make contact with the back of Mr Mortimer's head. The wee rascal! Or words to that effect!

Howard seemed to have got the technique of sleeping, without looking like he was sleeping, down to a fine art. It was absolutely amazing how he could sit so rigid in what seemed like an almost comatose state, in the back of a hearse or in the front of a limousine. It was as though his spine had been fused together from his head to his lumber region. That, or he had a metal pole shoved up his jacket for support. Honestly, if it wasn't for his eyes being shut, you would never have known he was enjoying his forty winks.

A Dead End

My first ever hearse drive was on a funeral from the North Finchley branch with Mr Barker as the conductor. Once the coffin was on board the hearse, we headed to the house accompanied by the two limousines to pick up the family. On leaving the house, several private cars joined us, following the main cortège. I'd decided to play it safe and take a route to the cemetery which we regularly used and was one I was familiar with. Simple and scenic, the set route should get us to our destination, Southgate Cemetery, at the appropriate time. Barring any unexpected delays along the way.

As the hearse driver it's important to dictate the speed of the funeral cortège in a suitable manner that befits the occasion, and aim to arrive at the funeral venue just before the allotted time. This gives the conductor enough time to deal with any preparations for the service such as the service sheets and music, etc. It also gives the minister or person presiding over the service time to get ready, and of course, allows the mourners to park up and make their way over to the church or equivalent place of worship, crematorium chapel, or wherever the service is being held. If running early, a slight detour to lose some time might be necessary – you don't want to arrive before the previous funeral has finished. That's considered poor funeral etiquette. Although sometimes it couldn't be helped, especially if the previous funeral was running late. Being late wasn't quite as bad as being too early, but was to be avoided if possible.

With Mr Barker sat in the hearse beside me, I was happily driving along the familiar route to the cemetery (not looking happy of course, I was in full funeral-face mode), when suddenly we came across a new mini roundabout that had not existed on our last journey along that route. The unfamiliarity of the road layout disorientated me somewhat and I inadvertently took the wrong exit, which instead of taking us towards our destination, led us into the construction site of a new housing estate. The entire funeral cortège, including all the private cars, followed me like ducklings trustingly following their mother. With limited turning space a U-turn was out of the question. So, in order to get us back on track, I had to get out of the hearse, apologise profusely to each limousine driver and all the occupants of the private cars, and get the whole cortège to reverse back onto the main road. It's fair to say, I did feel a bit of a 'silly Billy'. Mr Barker, however, with his laid-back manner, was so calm, that any panic I felt welling up inside me seemed to be quite unnecessary. All's well that ends well, as they say, and we arrived at the cemetery in perfect time with no harm done, except maybe to my pride. A quirky story for the family, that will no doubt be told for many years to come. The tale of Aunty Maud's funeral procession detour.

Every Rose has its Thorn

Another time when I was driving the hearse – leading the funeral cortège along Camden High Street – I noticed one of the borough's more eccentric characters walking in the middle of the road ahead of us. I'd seen him before on a number of occasions strutting around Camden. And to be honest, it was hard not to notice him.

He was a black chap in his mid-ish-twenties. Whenever I'd seen him previously, he would nearly always be dressed like a ballet dancer, in tight leggings and a sweatshirt, his footwear on those occasions not unlike actual ballet shoes. His posture and the way he moved was very elegant and exaggerated – exactly what you'd expect from someone who performed ballet. His facial expression however, said different, and was generally one of disgust. Disgust with everything and everybody around him. There was also an unrest in his demeanour that was slightly unnerving. He appeared permanently poised to either spring into an intricate ballet movement, or shout at someone aggressively. Possibly both, simultaneously. On this particular day, he'd really excelled himself in the eccentricity department and strayed into the 'completely lost it' departure lounge.

As we drove closer to him in the hearse, my passengers and I (Mr Dickinson, Frank and Howard), could not help but notice something slightly odd about the young man's attire. He had cut a circular hole about the size of a small tea plate in the back of his grey leggings, and protruding from his pert black bottom cheeks that were clearly visible through the hole and glistening in the midday sun, was a long-stemmed yellow rose. Ouch! I kid you not.

We passed him slowly, trying to maintain our funeral faces and contain our amusement. No mean feat with such an unexpected vision of 'bot-anical' art on display. The funeral cortège passing him didn't seem to faze him in the slightest, or distract him from his rather erotic human vase impersonation. Looking in the rear-view mirror, I watched to see if the two limousine drivers and mourners had noticed the gluteus maximus floral display – as if they could miss it. There was definitely a slight disturbance in the vehicles behind, which indicated the event had not gone unnoticed. It was quite a sight and an interesting talking point in the tearoom later that day, and probably at the reception after the funeral. Only in Camden!

Whether the yellow rose so originally displayed was from Texas or not, I can't say for sure. And for those of you who might be a little confused about that last remark, it refers to a famous American folk song that dates back to the 1850s. Not that I remember the original, of course, but Elvis Presley did quite a nice rendition of it that he sang in the film *Viva Las Vegas*, in the wonderful year of 1964.

The Blind Leading the Blind

Another incident which involved someone walking in the middle of the road on one of my hearse drives, was slightly more disconcerting. An old lady was being guided by her guide dog along the white lines in the middle of a very busy road in Kentish Town. My first thoughts at the time were that the dog must have been fairly new at its important supporting role and not quite got the hang of things yet. That, or he, or she, was not happy about something the old lady had done and was on a mission of revenge. Concerned for the safety of both the lady and her dog, I was just about to stop the hearse and get out to try and help – even though we had a coffin on board and two limousines following – when thankfully a pedestrian went to the lady's rescue.

I've always been a great admirer of the 'Guide Dogs Association' and the amazing work they do to help the blind become more independent, but on this occasion, I couldn't help thinking that this particular little canine helper might need to go on a bit of a refresher course.

Following the Instructions to the Letter

On some occasions the family may ask for the funeral procession to pass or stop at a specific spot along the funeral route. Popular venues being the deceased's local pub, their home, their local football team's stadium, or just a favourite place they used to frequent. One particular funeral where this was the case, Joe was driving the Ford hearse and I, as his passenger, had been given the responsible job of reading out the three pages of instructions detailing the route the family wanted us to take to the church, where the service and burial were to take place. It was an area of a North London suburb that we were unacquainted with, therefore the written instructions were most advantageous. Mr Best, who was conducting the funeral, was meeting us at the church – hence my responsible navigational role.

Joe followed the instructions I read out to the letter as the immediate family followed behind us in the limousine driven by Old Burt, and the private cars shadowed our every turn. All seemed to be going well. As instructed, we had paused outside the King's Head public house where the deceased had been a regular for the last thirty or so years, the pub's locals raising their glasses to the deceased as we paused. We passed by the house where the deceased had lived most of his adult life, pausing once again for a moment of reflection. It was the next part of the instructions however, that had me slightly perplexed.

With a puzzled expression, I looked over at Joe.

"What?" he asked.

"It says here," I stopped briefly to take a breath, "as we go past the golf course, we're to pause and sigh."

"Pause and sigh?" Joe repeated, reflecting my puzzled expression.

"As we go past the golf course, 'pause and sigh'," I reiterated, carefully reading the instructions to make sure I had not misread it.

We ventured forth in silence for the next mile or so along the quiet country road, contemplating, with a certain amount of confusion, the instruction I had just read from the paper in front of me. Undertakers get used to odd requests. Little things that might only be significant to the family and the deceased. But if it was important to them, we would always do our very best to oblige.

Seeing the sign ahead, informing us of our pending arrival at the entrance to the golf course on our right, Joe slowly brought the hearse to a halt opposite the entrance. We looked at each other, still a little unsure whether our actions truly demonstrated the request of the written instructions – but there it was in black and white and at that moment there seemed no doubt. So, simultaneously, shrugging our shoulders and breathing in deeply, we exhaled and gave a heartfelt sigh. It was hard not to be slightly amused by the strange request, but it was what the family wanted and it was obviously very important for them that the instructions were followed to the letter. We had done our duty.

As we drove away from the golf course a little voice inside my head encouraged me to reread the instructions we had just carried out.

"What a plonka!" I exclaimed, sounding more like Del Boy having a go at Rodney, from *Only Fools and Horses*, than myself with my Gloucestershire twang.

"Who?" asked Joe.

"Me! It doesn't say pause and sigh at all. It says… pause at sign. The n looks like an h."

Feeling a little foolish, our amusement was no longer containable and I am ashamed to say a certain amount of subdued chuckling managed to escape from our well-meaning bodies. The family were of course, oblivious to our misinterpretation of the written instructions. In fact, the next day we were informed of how pleased they were that it had all gone so well. Which at the end of the day, was all that really mattered.

Top Gear Challenge

It was common practice, particularly during the busier periods, for Mortimer and Sons to hire in extra vehicles and drivers. Some would be from hire firms and some would be individuals with their own limousine (and occasionally hearse), like Old Burt. All in all, they were generally a good bunch, although some were more helpful than others. One particular hired driver that the company used, who we will call Dave, because that was his name, had quite a reputation regarding his reversing skills – or rather the lack of them. He openly admitted himself that it was not his strongest attribute as a driver, and had developed quite a phobia about it. Apart from that, he always endeavoured to do his best and was a really nice chap. I'd been on many funerals with Dave and never observed any untoward incidents involving his reversing to back up the rumours, until that is, the day he accompanied us on a funeral in Hampstead.

The hearse and the three limousines left the family's house and headed to the church in Hampstead. Dave was tasked with driving the third limousine, with me sat next to him in the passenger seat. Three rather large African ladies, all in colourful traditional dress, were cosily squeezed together on the back seat. On our arrival at the church, all of the vehicles were required to reverse through an extremely narrow gateway in order to position themselves correctly in the somewhat restricted space provided for the funeral vehicles. Correct positioning would also facilitate an easier and more dignified exit after the service. The church was on a very busy main road and it soon became clear that some very skilful driving would be required in order to manoeuvre the vehicles through the narrow gateway.

Dave and I watched intently as the hearse and the other two limousines carried out a nail-biting exhibition of their reversing skills. A bead of sweat ran down the side of Dave's face. It may have been a tear. I sensed there was a very worried man sat beside me. It really was quite a tricky manoeuvre and with the added pressure of being watched by all the traffic that had been stopped by Mr Dickinson, which had already built up to epic proportions. The mourners waiting outside the church were also at this point scrutinising our every move. Dave was looking very pale and decidedly unwell.

Taking his turn, the smoothness and precision with which Dave carried out each phase of the manoeuvre to get his vehicle in position and then reverse through the narrow gap was impeccable and absolutely faultless. I was very impressed, as were the other drivers who were now watching from inside the church car park. It would have brought a tear to any Advanced Driving Instructor's eye to witness such control of a motorised vehicle. Dave drove that limousine like it was an extension of his own being. It was faultless. Right up to the point where it all went horribly wrong.

Continuing to reverse towards the church, and to a point where you would normally expect to feel the smooth application of the braking system bringing you to a gentle halt, unfortunately, we didn't. Dave's opportunity to expel the myths about his lack of reversing skills, forever, were about to fade into oblivion. His right leg, for some inexplicable reason, rather than releasing the accelerator pedal and applying force to the brake pedal (as is the usual technique in most vehicles to facilitate the cessation of motion), decided to surprise us all – particularly Dave himself – and do exactly the opposite by remaining on the accelerator pedal and pressing it to the floor. As mentioned in a previous chapter, 'Ye cannae change the laws of physics', and the reaction to Dave's action, was that instead of the gently purring 4.2 Jaguar engine gliding to a halt, the limousine suddenly woke with a start and roared into life like a dozing lion being thrown a piece of raw meat.

To cut a long story short – although perhaps it's already a bit late for that – the influx of fuel now being delivered to the 245bhp lump under the long black bonnet of the Daimler, suddenly produced a surge of power which instantly found its way via the drive shaft to the back wheels and subsequently propelled the black beast with great force in a backwards direction. It was only Dave's lightning reactions, like that of a mongoose attacking a rattlesnake, that saved the day – his brain, presumably realising the error of his right leg's ways, rapidly and forcefully flying into action sending his right foot from the accelerator to the brake pedal. Again, due to those intriguing and unchanging laws of physics, the provoked rolling chassis driven by the 4.2 beast of a motor was dramatically brought to an extremely abrupt halt. The three large African ladies that once cosily occupied the rear seat of the DS420, also responding to the same laws of physics, were now occupying a more forward position on the floor of the vehicle. The laughter emanating from the three ladies in the back of the car, compared to various scenarios which could have followed, was a great relief. One lady remarked that she hadn't felt the earth move like that for a very long time – sending the other two women into hysterical laughter.

I include this story, not to mock or embarrass, but to celebrate the ability of some of our species to laugh in the face of adversity and to rise above disaster. Without such occasions and the ability to see the funny side of things, I fear life with all its struggles and woes would drag us into the abyss of despair. Laughter is a magical thing that can lift the spirit, heal the body, and lighten the troubles of the mind. There is of course, a time and a place for such behaviour. Although, explaining that to our sense of humour can be a little difficult at times.

The Venue

The venue for the funeral and the type of service performed is usually determined by the faith or beliefs of the deceased, or the faith or beliefs of the family. Sometimes the matter might be discussed beforehand, and personal preferences or dying wishes taken into consideration.

Most cemeteries have their own chapel where a service can be held before the burial, if a service is not held at another venue prior to the burial, that is. If the cemetery does not have a chapel of its own but is connected to a crematorium, the crematorium's chapel is often used to hold the service. The venues used for funerals vary in grandeur greatly, and I have been in some of the grandest and some of the humblest places of worship over the years: elaborately decorated chapels of kings and queens, and cathedrals bursting with priceless antiquities and treasures, the cold stone corridors still holding on to the echoes of whispered plots, tangled webs of deceit, intrigue and treachery. Places where wars were declared and peace bargained for, all surrounded by the graves and ghosts of the most famous – and most infamous – who have shaped and sculpted this country and the world we live in today. And as impressive as some of the grandest were, at times they seemed quite obscene. The small, terraced house, converted into a Methodist church, in its humble simplicity, often felt far godlier and more spiritual. As did a woodland burial set within nature's own beauty, surrounded by birdsong and the rustling leaves in the trees. But that's just my personal opinion – for what it's worth.

The Carry In

While the technique used to carry, lift, and lower a coffin on a funeral can vary quite a bit between different undertakers, one of the most important things is that all the bearers match in height as well as possible. Bearers varying in height can be fine, as long as they are well matched in their opposing positions. Extremes in height difference can cause all kinds of chaos. For example, if the bearers at the front are four-foot nothing and the bearers at the back are six-foot five, it's going to look ridiculous – and doubly ridiculous the other way round.

Bearers that are badly matched or wrongly positioned will not only look unprofessional but the carry will, without a doubt, be clumsy or even farcical. It can also be quite hazardous to one's health. If the weight of the coffin is not evenly distributed between the bearers, some will be taking all of the weight and others hardly any. I've already mentioned how some bearers can be quite cunning in the way they position themselves under the coffin to lighten their own burdens. In contrast, it can also be an act of kindness to assist one's colleagues who may be suffering, by shifting some of the weight from their shoulders onto your own. A heavy coffin digging into your shoulder can be excruciating. Not unlike the heel of a stiletto shoe, apparently. And while I did question the colleague who made that comparison, no further information was volunteered as to how that interesting analogy was discovered.

Not only could the weight and size of a coffin cause us problems but some carries were also like a marathon endurance test – up and down vast amounts of steps, along winding corridors, and down church aisles that resembled an airport runway. Some of the older and less fit of my colleagues – the older ones in particular – could get quite out of breath. With all the huffing and puffing, it would sound like a steam train was coming up the aisle. Quite appropriate if the deceased had been a locomotive enthusiast, I suppose. It always amazed me that none of the older blokes ever had a heart attack during some of the more strenuous carries, given some of the medical conditions a few of them had.

When I first started working at Mortimer and Sons, I remember Sally walking into the bathroom when I was having a bath one time, and she noticed some marks on my shoulder that looked like love bites. Protesting my innocence, I couldn't understand where on earth I'd got them from. Then I realised it must have been bruising from carrying the coffins. I could tell by the look on Sally's face that she wasn't entirely convinced by my explanation.

Curiouser and Curiouser

Eddie and I were once sent on a funeral out in the sticks in Oxfordshire. I was driving the hearse, Eddie was driving the limousine and Mr Best was conducting the funeral. At the time, we were extremely busy, so Mortimer and Sons had arranged for two bearers from a local undertakers to make up the four-man bearer party – a fairly common practice in the funeral business. When the two bearers arrived at the tiny country church, Eddie and I could hardly believe our eyes. Not only did they look like twins, they were also quite a bit shorter than the both of us – each standing no more than five-foot tall at the most. Eddie and I felt like giants. It was like looking at Tweedledee and Tweedledum from Lewis Carroll's *Through the Looking Glass*.

The height situation posed somewhat of a dilemma for Eddie and me. Neither of us had ever carried at the head end of a coffin before, which now as the taller bearers, we would be. We'd always been the ones at the front on the foot, being among Mortimer and Sons' shorter bearers. The position you are in under the coffin, gives you certain responsibilities. Suddenly, Eddie and I were no longer going to be the ones dictating the speed and timing of the proceedings, instead, we were going to be following the lead of Mr Dee and Mr Dum. We had no idea of the techniques they employed to carry, lift or lower, etc. A problem only exacerbated by the fact that when the two gentlemen had arrived, the vicar and Mr Best were already poised and waiting for us to carry the coffin into the church. We had no time to question our guest bearers to confirm such details.

With experience, you get used to how things feel, and can often anticipate the other bearers' movements – to a degree. Particularly, if you work with them frequently. However, in the absence of prior knowledge on this occasion, the whole thing went surprisingly smoothly, given our initial concerns about our unexpected repositioning under the coffin. A strange experience indeed, it certainly gave Eddie and me a whole new perspective on things.

Touchy Feely

Things didn't always go quite as smoothly when working with unfamiliar bearers, especially when they made moves that you weren't expecting them to. When Joe and I were on the 'Pause and Sigh' funeral, we were working with hired bearers. Carrying the coffin, we were both taken by surprise when they linked arms with us. It was somewhat unnerving and a great deal more intimate than we were used to being with our regular carrying companions. Uncomfortably so! It wouldn't have been appropriate for us to start wrestling with them to break free while carrying the coffin, which meant we had to endure the unwelcome closeness until we reached the grave.

Keeping a Level Head

Occasionally, members of the deceased's family or friends wanted to be involved in carrying the coffin, either with us or on their own. The carry wasn't always as smoothly executed as when it was just us, but we would always be close by to assist or take over if any of the mourners became too emotional, or got into difficulty.

On the subject of well-matched bearers, I'm reminded about one particular funeral where the six sons of the deceased wanted to carry the coffin. Already having the perfect number of bearers, it only remained to assemble them in the correct positions height wise at the back of the hearse and give advice on technique. Positioning them was an easy task, as they were all almost exactly the same height. Being dwarfs, or people of short stature, none of them could have been much more than four-foot tall. I can honestly say, I've never seen a coffin carried at such a perfect level, and rarely as smoothly, except by my colleagues and me, of course.

Some people aren't aware that they can be involved in carrying the coffin if they would like to be. When I've helped to carry the coffin on my own family or friends' funerals, either with the undertakers or with other members of my family or friends, not only does it feel a very natural thing to do, I feel privileged to do so, and I know other family members and friends generally feel the same. For some cultures it's traditional for family and friends to carry the coffin. Mind you, the Hindu funerals can get a bit chaotic when you've got twenty people or so, scrambling underneath one coffin all trying to do their bit.

Timing and coordination between bearers is of the essence when it comes to the handling and manoeuvring of the coffin. Smooth, controlled footwork correctly carried out, can make or break the visual aesthetics of the entire performance.

Certain venues insist on funeral directors using a trolley instead of the coffin being carried. There doesn't always seem to be any particular reason why, and although it can be easier in some respects, it can sometimes cause problems that are less likely to occur when carrying the coffin. Generally, I think it seems far less reverent to have the coffin on a trolley. That said, there would be no complaints from us if the coffin was very heavy and the venue preferred the undertakers to use a trolley.

Music Maestro Please

During the entry of the coffin into the church, chapel, etc., verses from a book of worship, prayers, or similar may be read aloud by the representing minister or the person leading the funeral. A hymn or a favourite piece of music may be played. While hymns can be very uplifting and quite stirring, they're not everyone's cup of tea – particularly if the majority of the mourners are not religious – and if only a few people are singing, it can sound pretty dire.

Music plays a very large part in most people's lives – whether it's rock, pop, rap, rave, country, reggae, classical, opera, or a little bit of everything – and funerals are no exception. Music and songs can be a very powerful medium at emotional times, helping to express feelings when it can be difficult to find the right words yourself. A firm funeral favourite during my years as an undertaker was Frank Sinatra's, 'I Did It My Way', although Whitney Houston's, 'I Will Always Love You', and Rod Stewart's 'Sailing', were also very popular tunes. It may be favourite songs of the deceased that are chosen, or songs where the words seem appropriate to them.

I think I've probably heard most types of music played at a funeral, including a fair amount of humorous ones, Monty Python's, 'Always Look on the Bright Side of Life', definitely being one of the most popular in that category, although 'Come on Baby Light my Fire' by The Doors, at the crematorium would always raise a few eyebrows. Doctor and The Medics' 'Spirit in the Sky' was another popular tune – and the list goes on. With some of the catchier tunes, you have to be careful when carrying the coffin that you don't get too carried away with the rhythm. The slightest swagger or rhythmic motion will show in the movement of the coffin, and the momentum will start to cause the coffin to zigzag up the aisle as though you're dodging sniper fire.

There's also live music, of course, and not just the obvious church organ. Following a jazz band through a South London cemetery has to be one of the best examples of live music on a funeral that I can remember. It was all very reminiscent of a particular scene in the James Bond film, *Live and Let Die*. But without the murderous dramatics.

We once had a very out-of-tune piano at a Baptist funeral service. Either that, or the woman playing it had studied at the Les Dawson School of Music. (His comical renditions of piano playing were so funny – playing the wrong notes on purpose while staying so straight-faced.) Perhaps she even taught him. It was extremely difficult to keep a straight face. Bless her!

Personally, I don't think you can beat the bagpipes. Dad, being Scottish, loved the pipes so at his funeral we had a piper walk the hearse from the crematorium gates to the chapel – which was quite a walk. The piper also played as we left the chapel after the service. It was a perfect send-off, for a very special man. At Mum's funeral we had her favourite Barry White tune played as her coffin entered the crematorium chapel, and Abba's, 'Dancing Queen' during the service. Which again, with her love of dancing, was absolutely perfect for her.

Euston, We Have Touchdown

Once the coffin is placed safely onto the trestles, or the catafalque, in the case of crematoriums, the bearers will usually take one pace backwards and bow. Synchronisation with your colleagues is extremely important. You don't want a bowing action resembling a cranial Mexican wave. Neither should the bow be a half-hearted nod. There needs to be an indication of a slight forward movement of the upper body. Not a full-blown bow like you're bowing to an audience; the appearance of reverence and solemnity is paramount.

When you're working with the same people day in, day out, you get to know each other's body language. This helps greatly in getting the timing of various movements as near to simultaneous as is humanly possible – without the aid of telepathy. It's generally when new staff are introduced to the team, hired-in bearers are being used, or if you're carrying with some of the family members who have never carried a coffin before, that things can sometimes become a little disorderly.

After the bow, flowers might be placed around the coffin. Other finishing touches, such as a pall being placed over the coffin, religious icons, or occasionally a photo of the deceased may be displayed. The bearers will then take their leave in the appropriate manner via the most convenient exit, depending on the venue's architectural layout.

Going Commando

I owned two pairs of black shoes that I used for work. You really needed at least two pairs, particularly in the winter when they would regularly get wet through and plastered in mud. One pair was my trusty old Doc Martens, the other pair were of unknown origin but not as comfortable as the Docs, so I only really used those as a last resort.

After I'd been with Mortimer and Sons for a few years and covered a fair bit of mileage in both pairs of shoes, the unnamed pair's soles (in tyre-tread terms) were far from legal and downright dangerous on smooth flooring. Instead of buying a new pair of shoes, Eddie said he knew of a good shoe menders in Kentish Town, where I could get them resoled.

"Cobblers," I said.

"No," he replied, "they're actually very good." Ah, the old jokes are the best.

Eddie and I were off to the Royal Free Hospital that morning, so Eddie suggested we pop into the cobblers on the way and see what they could do for me. The cobbler was most helpful, and after browsing through the selection of new soles on display that would be suitable, I decided to opt for the ruggedly named, 'Commandos'. I have never seen such an impressive-looking sole. They had a tread on them like a tractor tyre. Ideal for our off-road escapades on the heath and overland expeditions through the undergrowth of Highgate Cemetery. Receipt in hand, I entrusted the cobbler with my formula-one slicks of the shoe world to undergo their transformation into a pair of elite all-terrain footwear.

A few days later I went back to pick them up. They looked amazing and I couldn't wait to put them on. In fact, I didn't wait, I put them on as soon as I got back to the van. Never have I worn a pair of shoes that made me feel so invincible. I was ready to take on the world with these assault course, crushing beauties and felt six feet tall. They probably only elevated my stature to five-foot seven, instead of my normal five-foot six and a half, but the illusion was well worth the £12 that was extracted from my wallet for their purchase.

My enthusiasm for the new commando-soled footwear, however, was to be short-lived. As we carried the coffin down the long centre aisle of the first church I wore them in, you could hardly hear the priest over the high shrieking noise my commando soles were making on the highly polished tiled flooring. Any commando wearing such shoes would surely not have returned from their first mission, having been shot as soon as they took their first step into the building they were storming. Unless it had a nice deep shag-pile carpet fitted. But that's not really something you can gauge a highly important military mission's success on really, is it?

My withdrawal after placing the coffin onto the trestles at the altar, as silence fell for prayer, was equally as embarrassing. Suffice to say, the commando soles were kept for external duties only, and the trusty Doc Martens for creeping around churches and other hard-floored venues. Purely for work related purposes – not in a creepy-stalker sort of way.

The Waiting Game

On average, the length of a standard funeral service can vary from twenty to forty-five minutes. Occasionally they can be longer, depending on various contributory factors such as the type of service, the amount of people attending, and the venue's timetable, etc. If the service was being held at a church or place of worship and then going on to a cemetery or crematorium, we would have time to ponder life's little mysteries until summoned back to carry the coffin out again. This may take place in a specific waiting area, a convenient hideaway, on a nearby bench (weather permitting), sat in the hearse, or in the back of one of the limousines. A hot or cold beverage may be sought out, or even some nutritional sustenance, if time and geographical logistics allowed.

Breast is Best

On one occasion when we were waiting for the service to finish, I was sitting in the waiting room at Enfield Cemetery, looking through a magazine about memorial plaques. Not the most riveting read I'll grant you, but it was passing the time and the only reading material in the room. The other lads had gone out for a smoke.

A woman, one of the mourners, came in and asked me if I minded if she breastfed her baby. Having recently become a father myself I was fully aware of the importance of regular nutritional input for the correct development of the young, and was very used to this activity going on around me.

"Of course I don't mind," I said, and continued to read my magazine.

There was a cough from the other side of the waiting room where the lady had sat down with her baby. It was clearly one of those attention-seeking coughs, rather than an irritation of the throat or a medical condition. My attention caught, I glimpsed over the top of my magazine to see the woman staring intently in my direction. I was confused at first by her slightly agitated body language, but then the penny dropped and I realised that she was uncomfortable with my presence in the room during the proceedings of the breast-feeding process. Apologising for my slow, and what might have appeared, somewhat ignorant response, getting up to leave the room I tried to explain, but the lady was clearly not impressed.

A Healing Hug

It was a balmy summer afternoon at Southgate Cemetery. My colleagues and I had just carried the coffin into the chapel for the funeral service and were waiting to be called back in to take the coffin to the grave. Standing in the shade of the mighty conifers that overlooked the chapel, I was telling the lads about a programme I'd been watching on television which explained the scientific theory behind the therapeutic benefits of hugging trees. I was winding my colleagues up, of course – telling them that I did it all the time and what an amazing, calming effect it seemed to have on me. I hadn't ever really hugged a tree before, except perhaps because I was in danger of falling out of it when I was a child. Though I don't think that's quite the same as giving it an actual hug.

Trying to sound convincing and demonstrating the hugging technique on one of the magnificent towering conifers that stretched high above us, I explained that it's all about the vibrations of nature and the connectivity among all living things within creation. My arms barely reached a quarter of the way around its large, heavily gnarled trunk. During the demonstration, I have to admit to some stirrings and to a pleasant, peaceful feeling that came over me. It was actually quite a nice experience. Perhaps there really is something in it, after all. Within moments, all six of us were hugging the large, majestic conifer trees. Unfortunately, engrossed in our embrace with nature, we were all unaware that the funeral service had finished early. The bizarre site that Martin, the chapel attendant, was greeted with when he opened the chapel doors was not something we were going to be able to explain easily or live down for a very long time. Thankfully, none of the mourners was witness to what would obviously have appeared a rather perplexing scene.

I would like to say, joviality aside, that my colleagues and I all agreed that the experience of hugging trees had definitely brought us all a little closer to nature. Adding to that, we would like to offer our sincerest apologies to any squirrels to which we may have caused any unnecessary distress or concerns regarding the safety of their nuts.

The Service

During the main service, most funerals will include some hymns and/or some music. There may be a reading or two from religious or non-religious writings, a short sermon or address and a time of prayer or contemplative reflection. A brief, or sometimes not so brief, eulogy about the person's life is a traditional part of most funeral services, and at the end of the service there is the committal – a final few words or prayer before either the burial or the cremation. Nothing is set in stone, particularly these days, but this is quite a typical funeral service.

The Quaker funerals we attended were quite intriguing, in so far as there was no particular order of service at all. The congregation would sit in silence until someone felt moved enough by the spirit to speak, possibly read a passage from the Bible, or to share something with the other members of the congregation. Not the most ideal way to do things when you have a tight schedule to keep, although, it usually worked out in the end. I suppose even though God may work in mysterious ways, he understands that we often have to work within a certain time frame, down here.

It's interesting to see how different cultures carry out funerals, and the variations of religious and non-religious beliefs. Generally, the sentiments and objectives of the funeral are fairly similar whatever the belief structure. It does make you wonder, though. Surely only one faith can be the right one, which if true, would make a lot of people all over the world, wrong. Perhaps they're all wrong. I suppose one day we'll all find out for sure, one way or the other. Or not!

The Eulogy

When I first joined Mortimer and Sons, where we had to wait to carry the coffin out after the service, I would usually join my colleagues and wait outside. On a few occasions where we had to sit at the back of the church during the service, I found it really interesting and quite humbling listening to the stories about people's lives: their ambitions, their achievements, their struggles and sacrifices. Ordinary people to whom we would not have given a second thought had we passed them in the street when they were alive. People whose blood, sweat and tears had fuelled the progress and survival of humanity. The kings and queens, and rulers of the world may be making the decisions – but where would they be without the so-called 'ordinary' people. Sounds a bit seditious, that – I'd better take care I don't get mistaken for a revolutionary subversive.

It was one particular eulogy which really got me hooked. When we placed the frail, almost skeletal remains of the old lady into her coffin, we had no idea about the trials and tribulations of her life. How could we if we hadn't known her during her lifetime? An hour later I was sat at the back of the church listening to her incredible story. She'd had a rough start in life, by all accounts. Orphaned at a very young age, she managed to work her way up the social ladder and became a school teacher. In her early twenties, during the Second World War, she travelled to France and joined the French Resistance. At the end of the war, obviously not having had enough excitement for one lifetime, she became a missionary in Africa. Returning to England after a number of years, she eventually became headmistress at the school in North London where she had started out all those years previously. And that's just the very brief version of the eulogy.

I felt so humbled when listening to her story. It really made me think about my own life and what I had achieved so far – or not, as the case may be. Her courage and strength were an inspiration, and it made me realise that it's not what life throws at us that makes us who we are, it's what we throw back at it that matters, and shapes the world we live in for both ourselves and others.

The Truth, the Whole Truth, and Nothing but the Truth

Being so familiar with the 'He was a good man or woman' type of eulogy, it was quite a shock to hear an alternative spin on the theme from one widow about her husband. Standing in front of the congregation she appeared to be speaking more to him, than about him, saying how he had promised her so much when they had first met, but that he had let her and the children down in every way; how he'd made their lives a misery, a living hell; how he had stolen the best years of her life, and that she would never forgive him. She went on to say that he had gambled away their possessions and been abusive to her and the children, when drunk. Which by all accounts, was most of the time.

It was extremely sad, yet refreshing to hear such honesty in a world that usually seems to struggle with the truth. A world where we often say what we feel we're expected to say, so we don't upset anybody or create waves. Not speaking ill of the dead isn't a bad philosophy, but making them out to be angels when they clearly were not, is probably just as bad. Saying that, we all have our faults, but it's nice to think we might be remembered for what we got right, rather than our downfalls and mistakes.

It's for Yooooouuuu!

During my earlier days at Mortimer and Sons, when we were on call-out duty we were issued with pagers. With technological advancements the pagers were soon replaced by mobile phones, which we carried at all times during the working day – not just when on call, out of hours. This enabled us to keep in touch with head office, the various branches and the yard, at the touch of a button – as well as them with us, of course. It took us a while to get used to putting them on silent when required, and then to remember to take them off silent again afterwards. This meant we often missed a call or the phone would ring at rather inopportune moments when you really didn't want it to.

I can remember one time when we were waiting for a funeral service to end, poised for action at the back of the impressive old church in Brompton, and all was still and quiet as the final prayers were in progress. Suddenly, the solemnity of the occasion was abruptly broken by the melody of 'Amazing Grace' (the hymn, that is, not someone called Grace who was amazing starting to sing). It was the ring tone of a mobile phone – my mobile phone, to be more precise. The acoustics of the colossal church were incredible, which on another occasion might well have been appreciated a great deal more. Thinking quickly on my feet and trying to draw the accusing looks away from myself, I pretended to look around in disgust for the perpetrator. Raising my hands, shrugging my shoulders and shaking my head in dismay, I think I just about managed to get away with it.

On the plus side, at least the ring tone was a hymn. Slightly more appropriate than some of the ring tones I could have selected, that might have been far more embarrassing and got me into a lot more trouble.

The Carry Out

The carry out, after the funeral service, is basically the reverse of the carry in. Music might be played, there may be religious or non-religious readings, or a mixture of both.

As the service draws to a close, using the shadows along the outer edges of the building to obscure our movements, we would edge our way slowly and as quietly as possible towards the coffin. If such manoeuvres were not an option, we would stay at the back of the building waiting for a nod from the minister or equivalent official, walking up the centre aisle and into position when signalled to do so. With all the nodding and signalling gestures on funerals, it's like being at an auction; something I did once participate in and nearly came away with a few items I had no idea I had bid for, due to my habit of pointing. I can remember on one occasion the minister officiating on the funeral had a nervous twitch. It was very confusing, until we realised it was actually a twitch and that he wasn't giving us subtle signals to carry out our duties.

Once the coffin is back in the hearse, after a short period of mingling, the mourners would be gently encouraged into the limousines and any private vehicles to travel to the cemetery, burial site, or the crematorium. In the larger cemeteries, it might be necessary to drive to the gravesite after a service in the cemetery chapel. If the gravesite was fairly close, the coffin might be carried, or in some cases, taken on a trolley.

The only time we didn't have to carry a coffin back out after a service was if the entire service had been performed in the crematorium chapel and was a cremation.

Cremations

Cremations have become much more popular these days. Partly, I imagine, due to changing ideas, and partly due to cost and convenience. The whole service and committal can be carried out in one venue – religious or non-religious. You can have a traditional organist playing hymns, or music of your choice on a decent and generally reliable sound system. Many of the churches we went to, we had to provide a portable machine – the quality of the sound lacking somewhat and the reliability of the machine literally in the hands of the gods.

If the second part of the funeral is at a crematorium, after the main service at another venue there will usually be another short ceremony of committal. The family can choose whether the coffin remains in place until they have left the chapel, or if they want to watch it slowly depart from view through the small portal at the end of the catafalque. In some chapels the coffin may not move, but a curtain will slowly surround the coffin until it can no longer be seen. Music is often played at this point, or possibly a reading or some poignant words.

The ashes of the deceased can be kept in an urn, scattered in the gardens of remembrance at the crematorium, or somewhere that meant something special to the deceased or their family. They can even be placed into a family grave at a cemetery. Crematoriums also have memorial buildings called a Columbarium where the urns can be stored or put on display if so desired.

Some faiths totally forbid cremation, for others it is essential. Some have re-evaluated the benefits, and now allow cremation when previously they did not. There are also variations within different faiths as to what is acceptable or allowed in respect of what may be done with the ashes.

Although most of the older crematoriums are more interesting architecturally, and through design resemble more of a church-type building, modern crematoriums can be quite pleasant and well designed for their purpose. Each is suited to any type of funeral service, and although I used to think that some of the more modern crematoriums seemed a little clinical, the less formal layout and light and airy surroundings can be quite agreeable, and have definitely grown on me.

Golders Green Crematorium, being close to many of the branches of Mortimer and Sons, was somewhere we spent a great deal of our time. It's one of London's oldest crematoriums, built in 1902, in the style of Italian Lombardic architecture. The grounds, as with most crematoriums I have frequented in my professional capacity as an undertaker, and on a more personal level, are well looked after and quite picturesque, although, at certain times of the year, the gardens at Golders Green Crematorium are particularly beautiful. If ever a moment presented itself, in between funerals, my colleagues and I would always make the most of any time that could be spent enjoying their beauty; a tranquil break away from the usual hustle and bustle of our working day, as well as partaking in a quick cup of tea, or coffee, and some of Fran and Edith's culinary delights in the tearoom, of course.

Many famous people have been cremated at Golders Green, and have memorials in their name: Bram Stoker, creator of *Dracula*, the actor, Peter Sellers, probably best known for his portrayal of the bumbling Inspector Clouseau, in the *Pink Panther* films; Enid Blyton, well-known children's author; singer, Matt Monro; comedy actor and *Carry-On* star, Sid James; Marc Bolan, singer songwriter, and front man of T-Rex, seventies glam rock band – to name but a few.

Singer, songwriter and actor, Ian Dury's funeral was held at Golders Green Crematorium. He had a horse-drawn carriage and the pallbearers that carried his coffin into the chapel were the gents from the band Madness. A Mortimer and Sons funeral.

A Blushing Pair

Joe and I were walking through the car park of Golders Green Crematorium one day, after having carried a coffin into the West Chapel. I was telling him about a problem I had with my knee and was saying how I would have to ask Oliver if I could borrow his large black strap-on. I was of course referring to the large black neoprene knee support that Oliver had been kind enough to lend me once before. Not that the two women we passed as I said it would have had any knowledge of that specific and vital piece of information of the conversation's transcript. Which just goes to show you, if you don't get all the information, things can be seriously misinterpreted.

To be Frank

Another rather embarrassing moment occurred after we had just carried the coffin into Kensal Green Crematorium, in North West London. After laying out the flowers in the cloisters, I made an executive decision to use the crematorium's toilet facilities before we embarked on our journey back to the yard (just in case we got caught in traffic). The stirrings in my bladder clearly indicated that such a need would be necessary in the not too distant future. On entry to the toilet, I noticed Frank had had the same idea.

"Hello, big boy," I said jokingly. Only to discover that it wasn't Frank at all. It was a mourner from the previous funeral.

The man, still in mid pee, looked over his left shoulder and gave me a rather nervous look. In my embarrassment, I quickly apologised.

"Sorry, I thought you were someone else," I said, trying to smooth things over and avoid a tabloid scandal.

On reflection, that probably didn't make the poor man feel any more at ease, and he left hastily, mid zip-up, giving me the widest berth possible that he was able within the confines of the spatially limited toilet facilities. As far as I know, there was never any official complaint made. Thank goodness!

Burials

Burials are a little more involved than cremations. If the funeral service had been held in a church and the burial was in the church's own graveyard, we would, of course, carry the coffin from the church to the grave. However, in these circumstances access to the graveside was not always straightforward. Most churchyards are rather overcrowded and the graves usually have very little space between them, let alone enough room for another grave to be wedged in amongst them. Which is why most new graves in a graveyard are invariably situated around the edges and outer boundaries. This, as you would expect, meant we often had to negotiate a barricade of existing gravestones and memorials to reach the new grave. As you can imagine, it can be quite difficult to retain poise when carrying a coffin under such conditions and often a fair amount of manhandling of the coffin would be required to reach the deceased's final resting place.

On some occasions an existing family grave would be reopened, and while this may help matters when it came to more room around the grave, it could still be a major trek through an assault course of existing graves to reach it. These days, in the less congested and more modern cemeteries with row upon row of graves regimentally evenly spaced, covering acres of land, most of the graves are dug using a mini digger. However, for most of the older, more crowded cemeteries and graveyards, it's back to basics with a trusty old spade, other hand-held implements, and a great deal of hard work.

Many of the public cemeteries we regularly used were so vast that often, if the funeral service was held in the cemetery's own chapel, a further journey in the hearse would invariably be required afterwards to take the coffin to the grave. Occasionally, you might be lucky and get a plot positioned near the chapel, but that's quite rare. If the grave was a fair distance away but not far enough to warrant the mourners getting into their vehicles, they would be given the option to walk behind the hearse to the grave.

Highgate Cemetery was by far one of the most challenging environments to carry out a burial, particularly the old section on the west side, which had opened in the 1830s. With its elaborate memorials and gothic gravestones, it's a favourite haunt on Halloween for ghostly shenanigans.

A long, steep and arduous journey from hearse to grave was usually the norm at Highgate Cemetery. Working our way through the overgrown jungle-like terrain, it wouldn't have surprised us to see a half-naked man in a loin cloth swinging through the vines yodelling. Well, it was London, you get all sorts of funny folk there! The gravediggers at Highgate were always very helpful – real stars – unlike some in a few of the other cemeteries, who would just stand back and watch us struggle.

Sally and I once went on the official tour of Highgate Cemetery. It was fascinating to hear about the history of the place, and stories about some of the many famous and not so famous people buried there. The catacombs there are by far one of the eeriest places I have ever set foot in, each of the fifty-five vaults able to accommodate at least twelve coffins. The overgrown vegetation almost completely blocking out the light along the narrow pathways without a doubt helps to create a very creepy atmosphere. That, and the thought of all the dead lying behind each ancient-looking door. There's definitely the feeling you are being watched by someone, or by some… thing!

A Hole Lot of Trouble

The boards that are placed around the top of a grave to stand on can vary tremendously in stability, with some being a positive addition to aid stability, and some being positively lethal. Only through our agility, acrobatic skills, and often sheer luck, did we manage to avoid many a nasty tumble. Preventing the coffin taking a nasty tumble at the graveside was down to the condition of the webbing used to lower it into the grave, and can make a vast amount of difference to the handling ability and control of the coffin's descent. If wet and muddy or dry and rough, they can be quite problematic – particularly for an inexperienced bearer.

Another challenging aspect of burials is graves becoming unwanted water features. Our wonderful British climate is definitely a major cause, but this can also be due to the cemetery being close to an underground water source. In either case, the whole affair can feel more like a burial at sea. Water pumps are often drafted in, when available, but not always successful. Attempts to disguise the water content in the grave by using foliage and flower petals, as clever and effective as this can be visually, the splash when the coffin is lowered into the grave tends to be a bit of a giveaway as to its watery secret. There is also the danger that a grave may collapse due to weather conditions, soil type, or both. When there is a chance this might happen, shoring systems may be required to support the sides of the grave. These metallic scaffolding-like structures, however, can create quite an obstacle when lowering a coffin into the grave, making it difficult to maintain a dignified descent.

Different faiths have various beliefs and traditions involving the placing of food and other objects into the grave. Often, these are said to assist the spirit on their journey and gives them supplies for the afterlife. Sometimes the flowers on the top of the coffin will stay on and go into the grave. If removed, they will usually be placed on top of the grave with the other floral tributes, after it has been filled in. Occasionally, some or all of the flowers might be taken to a nursing home, hospice, church, or other venue, at the request of the deceased's family.

For some cultures it's traditional for the family and friends to fill in the grave, or at least partially fill it. The gravediggers will then complete the task. Like many of the things I have mentioned where mourners get more involved, it seems a very natural thing to do, possibly going back to a time when it would only have been family or friends that carried out the funeral themselves.

A newly dug grave must be left to settle before a heavy gravestone or memorial can be placed upon it. Usually about six months to a year, depending on the type of soil.

I've seen some incredible memorials over the years. Some quite imposing in size, stunning in complexity and impressively ornate. Yet, as with many aspects of the funeral concept, sometimes it's the simplest of things that come from the heart, which say all that needs to be said.

The Hitchcock Effect

Doves, for many cultures over thousands of years, have come to symbolise love, peace, grace, divinity, ascension, and free spirit. Releasing them to represent those various subjects above, including at funerals, can be quite effective visually at evoking the emotions and feelings that the bird is said to symbolise. The first funeral that I was on where I witnessed the releasing of doves, however, didn't entirely go to plan.

The smartly dressed young lady in her mourning attire, was standing slightly to our right at the graveside. Held at her left side was a nicely crafted, mahogany wood-effect cage with a pair of beautiful white doves pleasantly cooing inside. At the appropriate moment, after we had lowered the coffin and moved away from the grave, the smartly dressed young lady opened the door to the cage to release the doves. Once released, the doves were meant to fly straight up, pause briefly while they got their bearings, and then fly off gracefully in a spiritually metaphoric manner. Unfortunately, that's not quite what happened. As soon as the cage door was opened, the two doves inside shot out like bats out of you know where, flying only inches above the mourners' heads. The unauthorised maverick fly-by caused the mourners to hit the deck in fear of being attacked by the psychotic, avian endothermic vertebrates. What is it they say about working with animals?

The doves were apparently homing doves and in theory should fly straight back to base once released. This got the old cogs working and I started to think that there might be an opportunity to expand on the idea, perhaps having the favourite animal of the deceased by the graveside during the burial; cats, dogs, rabbits, horses, penguins, elephants, etc. It didn't take long to realise some of the impracticalities of the idea though, or some of the problems one might run into, or have to run away from. Hence, the idea never really got past the drawing-board stage. In fact, it never even made it to the drawing board. Although, it could be a way of creating some extra revenue for the struggling zoos and wildlife parks.

Brass Monkeys

Any job involving being outside in the elements is bound to be less pleasant in winter, though, I once heard the saying, 'There's no such thing as bad weather, just the wrong clothing'. I'm not sure I would completely agree with that, even if there is a certain amount of sense lurking within the statement.

For the more traditional British weather, we were issued with rain macs. These were okay in the warmer months, but they weren't waterproof, and if you got soaked on the first funeral, you were stuck in a wet mac all day. In the winter, when wet, you'd probably have double pneumonia by home time. Even on a dry day, being fairly thin they were of little use or comfort when standing at the graveside during the winter months in the snow and bitter cold wind. Mel used to wear a jumper under his jacket, but officially any non-Mortimer and Sons attire was forbidden. Mel being Mel didn't care – if he was cold and Mortimer and Sons didn't supply clothing that kept him warm, he would supply his own. Which seemed fair enough.

After numerous years of moaning, we were eventually measured up for some lovely thick grey winter coats, that resembled something the Russian military would wear. Perhaps Mortimer and Sons had got a good deal on some army surplus. When the coats arrived, even though I'd been measured in what seemed a fairly accurate manner by someone who appeared to know what they were doing, I was absolutely swamped by my new winter coat. It almost reached my ankles, and was as wide as I was tall with its glam rock type shoulder pads that even Mr Bowie would have thought a little extreme. At first I thought there had been some sort of mix-up. Perhaps it wasn't my coat after all. Names on attached labels were checked and double checked, but no discrepancies discovered. Everyone else's coat seemed to fit perfectly – it was only mine that made me look like a vertically challenged bouncer from the Moscow State Circus.

It reminded me of the first parka that Mum bought me when I was at primary school. She had obviously bought it a few sizes too big, with the intention of it lasting me a few years – which it did. The entirety of my primary school education, in fact. Although, by the time I had grown into it, it had seen a great deal of action and was in quite a sorry state. The fur around the hood was almost non-existent which made it look like it had a bad case of the mange, the zip had ceased to function back in year three, and I had lost many a decent conker and fruit salad chew from the holes in each pocket – as well as most of my marbles. Which explains a great deal.

Alas, we weren't permitted to wear hats in the winter at Mortimer and Sons. Evidently it wouldn't suit the image. It was a shame really – in the cold winter months one of those Russian military hats would have matched our coats perfectly, and kept our heads and ears lovely and warm. Likewise, our suggestion of pinstriped shorts and sandals in the summer to help keep us nice and cool, was ignored with equal contempt.

Mary, Mary, Quite Contrary...

Seemingly, it's easier to get permission to bury someone in your garden than it is to put up a conservatory or have an extension built. There are certain regulations, of course. By all accounts, the burial site has to be more than ten metres away from standing water and at least fifty metres away from a drinking source. I presume they're referring to an underground water source rather than a public house. The grave should also be deep enough to prevent wildlife or pets from digging up the deceased. That really would put a dampener on the family barbecue on a sunny Sunday afternoon, wouldn't it?

"Look, Mummy, Fido's dug Nanny up again."

The first garden burial I was involved in was in the back garden of a house in Hampstead – just around the corner from where Mum and I used to live when she looked after Bibi and Ninka. It was all quite surreal – like attending a garden party with a burial thrown in. Not literally, of course; they were placed in gently and in a dignified manner befitting the occasion, as always.

I'm not so sure it would help the resale value of a property, and if you moved house, you'd probably have to have the body exhumed and take your late departed relative or whoever it was with you. You'd then have to have them buried at your new address – unless it didn't have a garden, in which case you'd need a large window box, or have to make alternative arrangements.

Funerals of the Young

Funerals for the young are by far the saddest and hardest to come to terms with. Regrettably, due to the amount of specialist children's hospitals in the area we covered, funerals for the young were a great deal more frequent than we would have preferred.

The size of a youngster's coffin would determine the number of staff required on the funeral. A coffin over three feet would usually warrant at least two staff to carry on the funeral, and a conductor. Anything smaller than three feet, it would generally only be the one member of staff attending who would conduct the funeral and carry the coffin.

I remember one particular funeral of a two-year-old very well. It was a lovely service and the parents' strength in their Christian faith, even in the depths of such grief, was quite overwhelming.

Their little boy had been ill from birth and was never expected to live a long life. They thanked God for such a precious gift and were so grateful for the wonderful time that they had been able to have together, as short as it may have been. They talked of how they had made the most of every precious day and thanked God for the angel that had changed their lives forever, and for the cherished memories that would keep them close until the time that they would all be together again.

Even when you don't have your own children, it's hard not to get emotional at such times. If you do have children, particularly if the deceased child was around the same age as your own, it makes you realise how fragile life is and that we should never take anything, or anyone, for granted.

On a baby's funeral, there would be no conductor – a member of staff from the yard would usually be required to officiate. We didn't use a hearse for baby funerals as the tiny coffin would have been completely lost in such a large vehicle. The estate car was far more suitable. We would usually have to pick up the parents in the estate car, with the baby's coffin in the back of the vehicle. Green matting, the same as that used around the graves on the burials, would be placed under and around the coffin which, I suppose, made it look a little less like it was in the boot space of an estate car. I know it doesn't sound very professional, but it worked quite well in terms of the scale of things and it was a little less formal in ways that suited the occasion.

I would always ask the parents if they would prefer the coffin to be placed next to them on the back seat, to be closer. With this in mind, I would also ask if they would like to carry the coffin at any point during the funeral. This was their time, and it seemed only right to give them the opportunity to do as much or as little as they wanted, or however much they felt able to. I would always be close by to support them or take over if need be. As would one of my colleagues if they were conducting the funeral.

When Mortimer and Sons got the contract with a number of local hospitals to carry out funerals for NVFs (non-viable-foetus) it would, as with a baby's funeral, often only be myself or one of my colleagues present. On some occasions one or both of the parents might attend, and possibly a minister. Some hospitals have ministers of various faiths that may attend if no mourners were expected, but this was rare. If it was only me or a colleague attending, a service would, of course, not be carried out. I would always say a prayer for them, though. I didn't think it mattered what faith they or the parents might have been, it just seemed the right thing to do. If there was no minister and no parents present, at least someone had said something and given some thought for their passing.

EXHUMATIONS

An exhumation is when a body that has been buried needs to be raised from the grave for some reason. For instance, if the body required re-examining for further forensic tests due to some new findings or evidence regarding the death. Another reason may be for relocation of the remains to another place of rest.

We were once involved in the exhumation of a Native American Indian who was part of Buffalo Bill's Circus that was touring England in the 1800s. His death was due to an injury sustained during a performance of one of the Wild-West shows, and for convenience he was buried in Brompton Cemetery. His remains were being flown back to America to be placed in the burial grounds of his ancestors, where he belonged. What a sad and tragic end to a magnificent and proud people; to end up a circus sideshow.

There's a great deal of legal red tape involved in the process of exhuming human remains. The exhumations we were involved in were usually carried out in the early hours of the morning and often resembled a crime scene, the white gazebo overhead and people milling around in their protective white over-suits. Exhumations could be quite interesting though, and made a change from the daily routine. A trip to the Highgate Cemetery catacombs once, to replace a coffin that had been damaged during a Halloween prank, was certainly a change from the normal routine. The aged human remains and the broken coffin were placed into a new, solid oak coffin, before being left to rest in peace.

ROSIE

When Rosie was a year old, due to the discovery made by the heart specialist that was visiting the Whittington Hospital when Rosie was taken ill at four months old, and finding a slight irregularity with her heartbeat, we received a letter from the Royal Brompton Hospital with an appointment for Rosie to have her heart checked out. Quite confident that they would find nothing wrong with our very energetic, non-afternoon napping, mini dynamo, we went along for the appointment at the allocated time. The news we were given after the various tests were completed hit us like a sledgehammer. Rosie had a hole in her heart that was interfering with its correct functioning and efficiency. How could this be? She was unstoppable. She never seemed to get worn out and it was almost impossible to get her to take an afternoon nap. She seemed fine in every way.

It was explained to us that sometimes these holes can heal themselves but if they don't it's best to operate when the child is between three and four years of age. We were told not to worry but to watch out for certain signs that may indicate the condition was affecting Rosie's health.

Rosie, none the wiser to her condition, remained the lively, unstoppable rascal she always had been, and life for Rosie and Jack returned to its normal everyday routine. Sally and I, on the other hand, shocked and numb, had a little more on our minds about what the future may have in store for us and Rosie.

Ferrying Jack to and from his various ventures to discover his hidden talents – first karate, then football, and finally ice hockey – Sally, Rosie and I would cheer him on relentlessly. He was only a little chap for his age and with all the protective equipment required to avoid serious injury during the high-contact sport of ice hockey, he was wider than he was tall and moved like a musclebound bodybuilder across the ice. Jack was rather accident prone and trips to the local, and some not so local hospital A & E departments on the away games, became quite a regular occurrence. That boy would probably have needed protective padding and goggles to play tiddlywinks. Never daunted by his injuries, however, he would soldier on regardless, padded, bandaged, and ready for action. One of his proudest moments on the ice was not when he scored his first goal, but as one of the smallest and less intimidating of the team, getting sent to the sin-bin for being too rough.

Rosie attended the Royal Brompton Hospital periodically, to keep a check on the hole in her heart. Having been told that these things can sometimes sort themselves out as the child grows, we were hopeful that this would be the case. Unfortunately, as time went by, there was no sign of Rosie's heart condition improving on its own; an operation would be necessary to correct it. It was just a matter of waiting for the hospital to set the date.

The Dreaded Call

In the December of '98, Sally got a call from the Royal Brompton with a date for Rosie's operation. It was for the following week. Sally rang me on my work mobile, as the hospital wanted an answer as soon as possible. I was on my way back from a funeral in the back of the hearse at the time. My heart sank and my head went into a spin. I had been dreading this moment. I knew I had to say yes but part of me really didn't want it to be happening at all.

After saying we would go ahead with the operation, we had just come to terms with the idea, then on the day before Rosie was due to go into hospital, we got a call to say there had been an unforeseen emergency and Rosie's operation would have to be cancelled. Overwhelmed with mixed emotions, we didn't know whether to laugh or cry.

About two weeks later, on a Thursday if I remember correctly, we got another call from the hospital. Rosie could have her operation on the following Monday if we agreed. It was all systems go, once again. We were to take her in on the Sunday to get her settled in and to have her pre-op checks. The operation would be first thing on the Monday morning. We were told that a child psychologist would see Rosie prior to the operation to help her understand what was going on, in a way that we might not be able to.

The Friday before Rosie's op, Eddie and I were sent to a local children's hospital to collect the body of a young girl. She was the same age as Rosie and had just had a similar operation to the one Rosie was about to undergo. The little girl was still on the bed in the intensive care unit with her family around her when we arrived. The distraught parents desperately pleaded with us and the hospital staff not to take their little girl away. Sadly, it had become a coroner's case and was out of our hands. In the end the police had to be called to allow us to carry out our duties. It was an awful situation, and certainly didn't help to reduce any fears I might have already had about Rosie's pending operation.

Sally and I were told we could stay at the hospital in a room a few floors up from the ward where Rosie would be. One of us would be able to be with her at all times on the ward, even at night. Work was very supportive and allowed me to take some of my holiday time to cover the week Rosie would be in hospital. I had faith in the medical profession but my fears regarding the fragility and cruelty of life were hard to ignore. As much as I wanted to believe that a loving God existed and would help us in our time of need, there were times when you just couldn't help but wonder. Especially, when faced with scenes like that of the little girl and her grieving parents, only a few days prior to Rosie's operation.

We arrived as instructed on the Sunday and parked in the small car park at the front of the hospital. It was free of charge because of the circumstances and we were allowed to leave the car there as long as we needed to during Rosie's stay. Sally stayed with Rosie the night before the operation on the ward and I tried to get some sleep in the little room we had been given a few floors up. Needless to say, I couldn't. My mind raced and my heart pounded as I stared into the darkness.

Rosie was familiar with the hospital and I think it was all a bit of an adventure for her. Which I suppose was a good thing. On the Monday morning she was her usual lively, playful self. We were told again that the child psychologist would speak to Rosie before the operation, but by the time the pre-op meds had to be given, there was still no sign of them. We had to explain to Rosie that the doctors had found a little hole in her heart and were going to fix it while she was asleep. When she woke up, it would all be mended. She cuddled her favourite teddy and smiled.

She was so brave as they gave her the pre-meds. When she started to get drowsy, I was asked if I wanted to carry her down to the operating theatre. I was really shocked at this – I expected them to be taking her on the bed or a trolley. Taking the opportunity to give my baby girl one last cuddle before her operation and escorted by two of the medical staff, I carried a very drowsy Rosie along the corridor to the lift in my arms. As we stood waiting for the lift, Sally and I exchanged a nervous smile, simultaneously looking down at Rosie. The ding of the lift broke the silence, we got in and went down to the operating theatre. I felt so emotional, fighting back the tears that were welling up in my eyes. The green-gowned person outside the theatre indicated for me to place Rosie onto the awaiting trolley. Sally and I kissed her little forehead, the tears no longer barricaded by embarrassment running down our cheeks, as Rosie was wheeled away.

We walked to the small chapel in the hospital where we prayed for our little girl like we had never prayed before, hoping with all our hearts that God would hear us among all the other prayers that must have been being said at that exact same moment all around the world.

The operation would take about five or six hours, so Sally and I decided to get a change of scenery and some fresh air. Well, maybe not fresh, but at least cooler. The warmth of the hospital had become quite stifling. We went for a walk along the Kings Road a short distance from the hospital. We didn't want to be too far away but we needed to do something and we had done all we could at the hospital for the time being. We had reached the point where we just had to have faith and trust the doctors to do their bit.

As Sally and I walked silently along hand in hand, the rat race was already in full swing and unfolding around us, people going about their hectic daily routines oblivious to the anxious man and woman in their midst. We had a coffee but I can't remember where. Our nerves were getting the better of us. We didn't stay out for long, and when we got back to the hospital we went to the little room we'd been given to stay in during Rosie's time in hospital. Silently lying on the bed staring at the ceiling, still hand in hand, our every thought was focused on our little girl in the operating theatre downstairs. I tried not to think about the little girl that Eddie and I had picked up only days before, but it was impossible not to.

The operation took the longest five and a half hours I've ever experienced. However, our wait wasn't over and we had to wait until Rosie was settled into the intensive care unit before we were able see her. All had gone well, thank God. Which we did.

I don't know what I was expecting as we walked in to see our little girl, but when I first saw Rosie on the ventilator and all the tubes and wires in her helpless little body, I became so emotional that I had to walk out. Knowing I had to be strong for Rosie and Sally, I took a deep breath and composed myself before going back in. Thick transparent tubes were inserted into her abdomen, draining excess fluid into large glass containers at the side of the bed. There were wires going into both her tiny neck and chest, and a dressing was placed over the centre of her chest where they had removed the sternum (part of the ribcage), to get to her heart. As we watched our little girl, she started to become restless and suddenly appeared to panic in her semi-anaesthetised state, trying to pull the ventilator from her mouth. It was very distressing to watch but the doctor and the nurses reassured us and said it was a good sign. She was taken off the ventilator and soon settled down to sleep. Over the next few days, the tubes and wires were gradually removed. Our participation in distracting Rosie during such procedures, with some of her favourite story books, was an important factor in their success.

Rosie's bed in the ICU ward overlooked the church that was used in the *101 Dalmatians* film where Pongo and Perdy were married. This excited Rosie immensely. As well as us reading her favourite stories, she watched Disney videos on a small portable telly the hospital had provided.

On the Wednesday, now void of most of the restrictive tubes and wires, Rosie was returned to the main ward. To our joy – and horror – the same afternoon she was out of bed pushing another little girl along the corridor in a pedal car at full speed. We couldn't believe she was up so soon and being so boisterous after what she had just gone through. While it was incredible, we were also terrified that she would fall and do herself some damage. After the operation, we'd been told that her breast bone was being held together with wire while it knitted together, and that new bone would eventually grow over it, information that didn't exactly ease our concerns but was obviously important to know. The doctors and nurses, on the other hand, seemed quite unperturbed by her risk taking and were exceptionally pleased with Rosie's progress and enthusiasm to play.

The rest of the week mainly consisted of the medical team monitoring Rosie's progress and me entertaining her in the ward's playroom with the puppet theatre provided. The other children also seemed to quite enjoy the puppet performances, my audience growing as word travelled the ward of the unscheduled entertainment. Visits from relatives to see our brave girl during her recovery in hospital ensued, and the acquisition of a variety of new cuddly toys, to her already extensive collection, inevitably began. Friday afternoon, incredibly, we were sat back in our little flat in Islington. It had been the longest and most emotionally draining week of our lives. Sally and I were absolutely exhausted. Rosie was ready for pizza!

The recovery of the few remaining wounds from Rosie's time in hospital became our responsibility. We were given instructions on how to care for Rosie's wounds and further instructions on how to remove the stitches that were left scattered around her little body;

tiny reminders of where the various tubes and wires had once been inserted – as well as the ones in the main wound which tracked the soon-to-be scar from the top of her chest to a point just above her belly button.

WHAT??? Sally and I couldn't believe the responsibility that we were being given and that we were expected – even considered eligible – to undertake such delicate medical procedures. But we were. Over the next few weeks, the remaining stitches were removed by torch light using tweezers and scissors with the stealth of an SAS medic team – if such a thing exists. It was like that board game 'Operation', where you have to remove certain internal body parts without touching the sides and waking the patient up. If you did, the patient's nose would light up and a loud buzzing noise would cause you to jump out of your skin. I have a sneaking suspicion Rosie would have done a lot more than buzz loudly and have a glowing nose if she had woken during any of the procedures of our surreptitious night-time activities.

A GOOD MOVE

Sally and I had been trying, for what seemed an eternity, to get into a larger council property since Rosie came on the scene, but with no luck. The cosy one-bedroomed flat seemed smaller than ever with the four of us sharing its various nooks and crannies. Jack and Rosie both occupied the flat's one and only bedroom. They had a captain's cabin bed each, located on either side of the room to maximise the limited space. This wasn't ideal, as Jack was now eleven years old and really needed his own space. Sally and I were still going oriental in the front room. Bed-wise that is, on the Futon.

Along our road there were plenty of vacant properties that seemed to have been empty for ages. We even offered to do the repair work that most of the ones we had seen so desperately needed, only to be told, 'that's not the way the system works', and we would just have to wait. Eventually, we were offered a three-bedroom flat on a new estate on Essex Road. The flat itself was fine but there was no way we were going to be able to afford the rent, so we had to turn it down. We seemed to be stuck in a catch-22 situation.

Then out of the blue, Mortimer and Sons came up with an interesting proposal for us. One of the three flats above head office was going to be vacant in a few months as its current occupants, Jeremy Wainwright and his partner, were going to be moving out. The flat would be rent free, on the understanding that we would share the out-of-hours duties with the other two flats occupants, the Dickinsons and the Carters. This meant that every third week we would have to cover the phones out of hours, deal with the chapel viewings and do the cleaning for that week. I was already on call- out duty once every four weeks, which I would still have to do, but with the prospect of a bedroom each for Jack, Rosie and ourselves, a newly fitted kitchen and huge living room, the offer was just too good to turn down.

It was a great deal noisier than we were used to, being on a main road, but it's amazing what you can get used to after a while. Even the clatter of the trains at the rear of the flat in Islington became a comforting occurrence. The eternal emergency sirens and people shouting until the early hours outside the flat above head office weren't quite so comforting but we got used to it after a while, and having all that space was absolute heaven. The area itself wasn't an area that I would have chosen to live, especially with children. There were quite a lot of drugs and alcohol-related problems, which I often got to see the end result of as one of the local undertakers. It also seemed to have more than its fair share of people with mental health issues – possibly due to the amount of supported living places in the area. It certainly wasn't an uneventful place to live, that's for sure.

With safety in mind, we always had to be on the alert for hypodermics in the car park around the back of head office where the drug addicts would often go, in case Rosie, Jack, or anyone else picked them up. At the local primary school – where Rosie eventually went – they had to search the playground daily for discarded hypodermics before the children could go out and play. It was a significant problem and a considerable worry. Stepping over the passed-out alcoholics and the minefields of vomit, was far from the environment Sally and I would have chosen to bring our children up in, but as I said, at the time, we didn't really have much choice.

Don't get me wrong, most of the local people were the salt of the earth, and like us were just trying to make the best of what they had. It can often be the individuals we least expect who become our towers of strength and our heroes. Fortunately, we had a good network of friends, particularly through the local church, and through small acts of compassion and a little thought, we helped each other through. Restoring faith in humanity for each other on a regular basis was high on the agenda.

Once Rosie was at nursery, and then primary school, Sally started doing some part-time work for Mortimer and Sons, covering the branches when managers were out on funerals, house calls, or on leave, etc. She really enjoyed the work and helping families through a very difficult time.

The duty week could be a bit hectic, covering head office, and sometimes the phones wouldn't stop ringing all night. It was even more hectic when I was on call-out on the same week. Our new responsibilities made family life quite difficult at times, but there are plenty of other jobs that do that, and with most of those you don't get a nice three-bedroom flat thrown into the bargain.

When Jack was between jobs, in his late teens, he helped out at Mortimer and Sons for a while. It was great having him on the team and although he fitted in well and enjoyed the work, it wasn't quite the career he had in mind for himself. When I asked him recently about his time at Mortimer and Sons, his stories and memories were very similar to my own. Sharing some of our stories, he reminded me of the time that Eddie had taken his dog's medication by accident, mistaking it for his own, and the canine-related jokes that followed Eddie throughout the day and the following weeks. A fond memory that makes us laugh as much now as it did then.

OUT OF THE ORDINARY

Over the years, Mortimer and Sons performed many high-profile funerals of the nobility, the famed, the prominent and the renowned from all walks of life – as well as many that were a little more discreet. And while logistics may have partly contributed to that, I do believe that it's also partly because they were, and still are, one of the best funeral directors around. Naturally, I may be a little biased.

I've never believed one person to be more important than another, whether they are famous, more intelligent, richer, or even royalty. However, dealing with the more well known, definitely made the job a great deal more varied and interesting in many ways, taking us to places we would probably never have ventured had it not been in our professional capacity.

The best photographic evidence of my time at Mortimer and Sons, was a close-up of myself and my colleagues carrying the coffin of Enoch Powell in 1998, the Conservative MP who got himself into a bit of trouble with his 'Rivers of Blood' speech, back in 1968. The photograph that appeared in the *Independent* newspaper was taken after the funeral service at St Margaret's Church in the grounds of Westminster Abbey, as we carried the coffin back to the hearse. St Margaret's is actually the parish church for the House of Commons and where Enoch Powell MBE, had once been the churchwarden for a period of ten years. He was also one of the very few people to join the army as a private and reach the rank of brigadier, which he accomplished during the Second World War. Despite the now infamous speech that he made back in 1968 that marred his career, he was by all accounts quite a remarkable man and was involved in many important social reforms.

CHANGES

Eventually, the old DS420 Daimlers were put out to stud and replaced by newer, sleeker models. When we eventually got the new vehicles, the drivers were told by the company that supplied them that due to the way funeral vehicles are driven, the new Daimlers would need a good blast up and down the motorway at least once a month to blow the cobwebs out. This news was greeted with a few large grins and an exuberant 'YES' from the back of the garage – the vocalisation coming from Oliver who had a glint in his eye that needed no translation. The new Daimlers were extremely plush and although the manoeuvrability was still fairly abysmal, the air conditioning in the summer was pure heaven.

The cars weren't the only changes; there were a few structural alterations around the yard, too. Oliver and I lost the makeshift motorcycle workshop area in the garage to new changing rooms. By that time though, we were both spending less time dabbling with the bikes anyway, what with family commitments, i.e. the pitter-patter of tiny feet. To be fair, a decent changing room was desperately needed and well overdue – if only to keep the peace.

Over the years there were the natural changes to the staffing line-up too, due to some people leaving, some being promoted, and some retiring. Frank and Bradley Masters left for pastures new, and when Lucy and her partner Gary left the Holloway branch, Mel became the manager. Mild-mannered Graham became part of the managerial team based at head office. Mum eventually retired after thirteen loyal years' service – going into full-time charity-shop mode. When

Eamon retired, Dean took over as foreman and Oliver became under-foreman. I have to admit they did a fairly good job between them, but they weren't nearly as entertaining as Eamon. Unfortunately, in addition to the natural movement of staff, there were also a few deaths, and sadly we said our last farewells to Arthur, Howard, Old Burt and Reg.

And as it always is, 'out with the old', brings with it 'in with the new', and an interesting and diverse bunch of characters were waiting in the wings to join us, including Eddie's other two sons, Dan and John. We used to joke that Mortimer and Sons would have to change the company name to Cook and Sons, Cook being Eddie's family surname. The trials and tribulations of the staff of Mortimer and Sons, without a doubt, created as much intrigue and surprise as any television soap opera. However, their stories are theirs to tell, not for me to gossip about.

As for myself, in 2002, after breaking my leg, I returned to work with my fetching leg brace and took up light duties in the workshop. As my bones healed, I started going out on the easier removals, mainly hospitals or nursing homes where a wheelie stretcher was used. Funeral wise, I was put on most of the baby and children's funerals.

I think that's when things started to get to me a bit. Having to do youngsters' funerals now and then is one thing, but having to do them day in and day out can be rather hard-going emotionally. A couple of times, struggling with those emotions and feeling very down, my lunch break became a liquid lunch in the pub around the corner. Dean, then foreman, and Joe, would come to the rescue. They were both very supportive and helped me get through some difficult days. In fact, I would gladly have given Dean all of my sandwiches, without a second thought!

It was at that point in my career as an undertaker, that I felt I'd had enough of death and it was time for a change. Sally and I had been talking about a move out of London for a while – somewhere a little more rural with a slower pace of life. She and the children enjoyed our little excursions to Cheltenham when we went to visit Dad, so we decided to look in that direction. After a few reconnaissance missions to find somewhere to live, check out schools and find work, everything seemed to just fall into place. And so it was, in the September of 2003, we made the move to my home town Cheltenham, in the glorious county of Gloucestershire.

But that's a whole other story!

DEATH

(The Final Word)

If I'm ever asked whether I fear death or not, my answer, without hesitation, is always 'no, I don't'. Not my own death, at least, and it's never been a subject that I've ever dwelled on at any point in my life – even as an undertaker. I'm not particularly relishing the process of death itself, and I'd prefer it not to be too painful and unpleasant, or drag on. However, death is inevitable, the natural way of things, and the one and only certainty in life – whether we like it or not.

My only fear of death, as I'm sure it must be for many of us, is when it involves the loss of those I cherish and love, and the sadness and pain that inevitably comes with such loss. Saying that, I don't believe for one minute that this is all we are, that life as we know it is all there is, or that death is the end of us. I believe that it's merely the end of one chapter in readiness for the next. What comes next, who can say for certain, though I have been adequately convinced during my lifetime to expect something, rather than nothing. I have also been adequately convinced that we will meet those close to us in this life, wherever, and whatever, that next chapter might be.

There is, of course, a great deal I will miss about being alive. The nicer things. Simple things. At the very top of my list, as I'm sure it is for most of us, are those treasured moments that we share with our family and friends. Moments that enrich our lives and make it all worthwhile. Parenthood might not be everyone's cup of tea, but personally, the joys have far outweighed the inevitable worries and woes. It's an experience I feel privileged to have had and I wouldn't have missed for the world.

Among those simpler things I will miss, are the loving touch of a tender hand, the tight embrace of a caring hug, the laughter of others, the warmth of the sun on my face, the caress of a gentle breeze, the beauty and wonder of nature, and the heart-warming companionship of animals. Not to mention the bewitching sound of a Harley Davidson big v-twin, once you've ditched the factory-fitted exhaust pipes for something a little less baffled and a lot more throaty. But who knows, maybe we also get what we enjoyed in this life, in the afterlife, too. I hope so!

As I venture through life, people never cease to amaze me. Some in good ways, some not so good, but generally speaking I have been pleasantly surprised and often quite humbled. And it reminds me, rather importantly, 'that we should never judge a book by its cover'.

At the time of writing, I'm not really sure where I stand as far as God goes – by whatever name, shape, or form – though I find it hard to believe that within the complexity of all that we know and understand about the intricate workings of Creation and the science behind it, however small that may be with all there is yet to learn, that it all just coincidentally happens to work quite well. (At least, it did until we came along and mucked it all up!) And how could there be an afterlife if there isn't a spiritual aspect to Creation? There are certainly far more questions about life and death than there are answers, that's for sure.

If I have learnt anything at all about life, surrounded by death, it's that it may be shorter than you think. With that thought in mind – as our solar system orbits the centre of the Milky Way galaxy once every 230 million years as it spins like a Frisbee at 540,000mph heading in a straight line at 1.3 million mph away from the big bang – which happened fourteen billion years ago – in an expanding universe that contains billions of other galaxies which each in themselves contain billions of stars (exact data varies between sources) – among all that matter, it's the little things that we do for each other in the here and now on this wee speck we call Earth... that really matter.

THE END?

Acknowledgements

I would like to thank all those near and far who have endured the long wait and repeated tales and quotes that dwell within these pages, sharing this journey actively or in a supporting role, your encouragement has been greatly appreciated. Special thanks goes to those that have played a part in my story, without whom there would, of course, be no story to tell. Extra special thanks, goes to all that have helped with constructive criticism, in the writing and in the editing process of the book. Sally my wife and Rosie my daughter. Debbie Bartlett, for her patience and fastidious above and beyond editing skills that have made such a difference to the finished work. Also, Tim Drywood, Jane Neale, Lucy Grant and Sean Craemer for their valuable contributions. A huge thank you must also go to Andrew for his unexpected but much appreciated guidance.

Last but not least, I would like to thank all at Book Guild Publishing for their friendly and professional assistance, in making my ambitions come true.